taste of home®

BEST LOVED
HEALTHY
Recipes

taste of home
BOOKS

REIMAN MEDIA GROUP, LLC • GREENDALE, WI

taste of home   Reader's Digest

Best Loved Healthy Recipes

A TASTE OF HOME/READER'S DIGEST BOOK

EDITORIAL

Editor-in-Chief: Catherine Cassidy

Executive Editor, Print and Digital Books: Stephen C. George
Creative Director: Howard Greenberg
Editorial Services Manager: Kerri Balliet

Senior Editor, Print and Digital Books: Mark Hagen
Editors: Amy Glander, Krista Lanphier, Michelle Rozumalski
Associate Creative Director: Edwin Robles Jr.
Art Directors: Gretchen Trautman, Jessie Sharon
Food Editor: Peggy Woodward, RD
Content Production Manager: Julie Wagner
Copy Chief: Deb Warlaumont Mulvey
Copy Editors: Mary C. Hanson, Alysse Gear
Contributing Proofreader: Valerie Phillips
Recipe Editor: Mary King
Recipe Content Manager: Colleen King
Recipe Testing: Taste of Home Test Kitchen
Food Photography: Taste of Home Photo Studio
Executive Assistant: Marie Brannon
Editorial Assistant: Marilyn Iczkowski

BUSINESS

Vice President, Publisher: Jan Studin, jan_studin@rd.com
Regional Account Director: Donna Lindskog,
donna_lindskog@rd.com
Eastern Account Director: Joanne Carrara
Eastern Account Manager: Kari Nestor
Account Manager: Gina Minerbi
Midwest & Western Account Director: Jackie Fallon
Midwest Account Manager: Lorna Phillips
Michigan Sales Representative: Linda C. Donaldson
Southwestern Account Representative: Summer Nilsson

Corporate Digital and Integrated Sales Director, N.A.: Steve Sottile
Associate Marketing Director, Integrated Solutions:
Katie Gaon Wilson
Digital Sales Planner: Tim Baarda

General Manager, Taste of Home Cooking Schools: Erin Puariea

Direct Response Advertising: Katherine Zito,
David Geller Associates

Senior Marketing Manager: Vanessa Bailey
Associate Marketing Manager: Betsy Connors

Vice President, Magazine Marketing: Dave Fiegel

READER'S DIGEST NORTH AMERICA

Vice President, Business Development: Jonathan Bigham
President, Books and Home Entertaining: Harold Clarke
Chief Financial Officer: Howard Halligan
VP, General Manager, Reader's Digest Media: Marilynn Jacobs
Chief Marketing Officer: Renee Jordan
Vice President, Chief Sales Officer: Mark Josephson
General Manager, Milwaukee: Frank Quigley
Vice President, Chief Content Officer: Liz Vaccariello

THE READER'S DIGEST ASSOCIATION, INC.
President and Chief Executive Officer: Robert E. Guth

For other Taste of Home books and products,
visit us at **tasteofhome.com**.

For more Reader's Digest products and information,
visit **rd.com** (in the United States)
or see **rd.ca** (in Canada).

International Standard Book Number: 978-1-61765-199-1
Library of Congress Control Number: 2012949699

Pictured on front cover (from left to right):
Turkey Meatballs and Sauce, page 298
Makeover Frozen Grasshopper Torte, page 559
Savory Turkey Potpies, page 300

Pictured on spine:
Barbecued Turkey Sandwiches, page 297

Pictured on back cover (from top to bottom):
Grilled Beef Tenderloins, page 461
Chicken Tacos with Avocado Salsa, page 280
Savory Turkey Potpies, page 300

Printed in USA.
13 5 7 9 10 8 6 4 2

Contents

From no-fuss nibbles to decadent desserts, you'll find everything you need with *Taste of Home Best Loved Healthy Recipes*. Consider these 17 chapters when you need a satisfying dish that contributes to a heart-smart lifestyle.

Family Favorites

With *Taste of Home Best Loved Healthy Recipes*, it's a cinch to lighten up the foods your family craves! Here, home cooks share simple snacks, weeknight dinners and delicious desserts that pare down calories but punch up flavor!

What do you think of when you hear the words "comfort food"? Satisfying stews and piping-hot casseroles? What about chocolate cakes? A few words you probably don't think of are "light" and "low-calorie." That's why I'm happy to bring you *Taste of Home Best Loved Healthy Recipes*!

Inside you'll find more than 1,000 family-favorite dishes that pare down calories, fat and sodium without sacrificing flavor. That means you'll feel good about serving stick-to-your-ribs meals because they won't pack on pounds. With all of these options, your family won't even notice that they're eating lighter!

Feel like Italian tonight? Check out Makeover Traditional Lasagna on page 240. It offers fewer calories than its full-fat counterpart, and it even contains 35% less sodium! Consider adding Artichoke Arugula Salad (p. 52) or Parmesan Herb Loaf (p. 428) to the lineup and a tasty yet health-minded dinner is ready.

In a rush? Enjoy a comforting bite without hitting the fast-food drive-thru. See the chapter "Ready in 30" where you'll find quick dinner ideas that are so yummy, they keep unhealthy cravings in check. When the clock is ticking, consider Mom's Sloppy Tacos (p. 201), Pork 'n' Potato Skillet (p. 197) or Chicken Sausage Gyros (p. 208). These specialties are ready in half an hour, and they keep fat and calories at bay!

If you crave sweets, you can still indulge with the fantastic treats found here. Consider Toffee Cheesecake Bars (p. 522) and Raspberry Baked Alaska Pie (p. 529). Not only will they satiate a sweet tooth, but each dessert provides a complete set of Nutrition Facts.

In fact, every item in *Best Loved Healthy Recipes* offers Nutrition Facts and many include Diabetic Exchanges. It's so easy to calculate points for various weight-loss programs, plan calorie-conscious menus and stick to low-sodium or low-carb meal plans with this information.

And because we know your time is valuable, we continue to include special-diet icons to help you find those dishes that may be of particular interest to you. Just see the key on the opposite page to easily understand what the four indicators stand for.

I know your gang will adore these trimmed-down takes on classic foods, because most of them come from home cooks just like you and me! They know how to feed their families hearty meals without much fat yet keep flavor to a maximum—and they're happy to share those secrets.

In additon, we tested all the recipes in the Taste of Home Test Kitchen, so you can rest assured that everything will turn out great whether it's the first time you make it or the fiftieth! And if your family is like mine, you'll be happily making these guilt-free comfort foods time and again!

Peggy Woodward, RD

Nutrition Fact Nuggets

Nutritional Guidelines

All of the recipes in *Best Loved Healthy Recipes* cookbook fit the lifestyle of a health-conscious cook and his or her family. The recipes represent a variety of foods that will fit into any meal plan that is within the standards of the USDA's "MyPlate Plan" for moderately active adults (see box below).

Facts

- Whenever a choice of ingredients is given in a recipe (such as 1/3 cup of sour cream or plain yogurt), the first ingredient listed is always the one calculated in the Nutrition Facts.
- When a range is given for an ingredient (such as 2 to 3 teaspoons), we calculate the first amount given.
- Only the amount of marinade absorbed during preparation is calculated.
- Garnishes listed in recipes are generally included in our calculations.

Diabetic Exchanges

All recipes in *Best Loved Healthy Recipes* have been reviewed by a registered dietitian. Diabetic Exchanges are assigned to recipes in accordance with guidelines from the American Diabetes Association and the Academy of Nutrition and Dietetics.

The majority of recipes in this cookbook are suitable for diabetics, but please check the Diabetic Exchanges to make sure the recipe is in accordance with your doctor's instructions and fits your particular dietary guidelines.

Special Diet Indicators

To help those on restricted diets easily find dishes to suit their needs, we clearly indicate recipes that are particularly low in fat, sodium or carbohydrates as well as those that contain no meat. You will find these colored special diet indicators directly after the recipe title where appropriate:

F One serving contains 3 grams or less of fat

S One serving contains 140 milligrams or less of sodium

C One serving contains 15 grams or less of carbohydrates

M Appetizers, salads, soups, side dishes and entrees that contain no meat

---

A Word About Meat-Free Recipes

Enjoying meatless menus is a lifestyle choice that many people make. Others, however, prepare meat-free entrees only occasionally in order to cut back fat and calories or to simply mix up their supper-time routines. Regardless of how often you prepare meatless recipes, you can easily find such dishes identified with the meatless icon.

When flipping through this edition of *Best Loved Healthy Recipes*, please note that the icon highlights items that are meatless and not lacto-ovo vegetarian. As such, recipes containing eggs and cheese are marked as meat-free options.

Dishes that contain meat products such as marshmallows, marshmallow creme, gelatin and Worcestershire sauce are not labeled with a meatless icon.

Some dishes call for "reduced-sodium chicken broth or vegetable broth." While the Nutrition Facts for these recipes are published using the chicken broth as an ingredient, these dishes may offer the meatless icon since vegetarian broth is an option in the ingredient list.

So whether you depend on meatless meals for your family or simply want to try something new, look for the meatless icon to help you get the dinner bell ringing in no time!

DAILY NUTRITION GUIDE

	Women 25–50	Women over 50	Men 50–65
CALORIES	2,000	1,800	2,400
FAT	67 g or less	60 g or less	80 g or less
SATURATED FAT	22 g or less	20 g or less	27 g or less
CHOLESTEROL	300 mg or less	300 mg or less	300 mg or less
SODIUM	2,300 mg or less	1,500 mg or less	1,500 mg or less
CARBOHYDRATES	300 g	270 g	360 g
FIBER	20–30 g	20–30 g	30–40 g
PROTEIN	50 g	45 g	60 g

This chart is only a guide. Requirements vary, depending on age, weight, height and amount of activity.
Children's dietary needs vary as they grow.

GLUTEN-FREE CHOCOLATE SNACK MIX

ORANGE & COFFEE MARTINI

TZATZIKI SHRIMP
CUCUMBER ROUNDS

Starters & Snacks

Let's party! After all, watching what you eat doesn't mean avoiding favorite party fare. You can enjoy dips, snack mixes and all sorts of appetizers when you turn to this chapter's selection of munchies and beverages.

Orange & Coffee Martini **F** **S** **C**

PREP/TOTAL TIME: 5 min. YIELD: 1 serving

HEALTHY COOKING TEST KITCHEN

With its pretty jeweled appearance and complementary orange-coffee flavor, this impressive martini lends an elegant, upscale feel to any get-together.

Ice cubes
- 2 oz. strong brewed coffee, cooled
- 1 oz. vodka
- 1/2 oz. orange liqueur
- 1/2 oz. hazelnut liqueur

1. Fill a mixing glass or tumbler three-fourths full with ice cubes. Add remaining ingredients; stir until condensation forms on outside of glass. Strain into a chilled cocktail glass. Serve immediately.

Nutrition Facts: 1/2 cup equals 172 calories, trace fat (trace saturated fat), 0 cholesterol, 2 mg sodium, 13 g carbohydrate, 0 fiber, trace protein.

Lo-Cal Cheese Dip **F** **C**

PREP: 5 min. + chilling YIELD: 1-3/4 cups

JOYCE MONTAGUE • WICHITA, KANSAS

Working in a local deli and retail outlet that sells herbs and spices gives me a chance to create many recipes. Cottage cheese is a heart-smart main ingredient in this savory dip that's terrific with crackers or veggies.

- 2 cups (16 oz.) 2% cottage cheese
- 1 Tbsp. reduced-sodium beef bouillon granules
- 1 Tbsp. dried minced onion
- 2 tsp. lemon juice
Raw vegetables or crackers

1. In a blender, combine cottage cheese, bouillon, onion and lemon juice; cover and process until smooth. Cover and chill for at least 1 hour. Serve with vegetables or crackers.

Nutrition Facts: One serving (1/4 cup dip) equals 68 calories, 2 g fat (1 g saturated fat), 6 mg cholesterol, 291 mg sodium, 3 g carbohydrate, trace fiber, 9 g protein. **Diabetic Exchange:** 1 lean meat.

Tzatziki Shrimp Cucumber Rounds **F** **S** **C**

PREP: 25 min. COOK: 10 min./batch
YIELD: 24 appetizers

SHANNON ROSE FLAHERTY • HAMPTON BAYS, NEW YORK

I created this appetizer with what I had on hand one night, and now it's one of my husband's favorites! The bacon-wrapped shrimp, garlicky sauce and burst of cool cuke flavor make this a surefire crowd-pleaser.

- 1/4 cup reduced-fat plain yogurt
- 2 Tbsp. finely chopped peeled cucumber
- 1/8 tsp. garlic salt
- 1/8 tsp. dill weed
- 6 bacon strips
- 24 peeled and deveined cooked medium shrimp, tails removed
- 2 medium cucumbers, cut into 1/4-in. slices

1. In a small bowl, combine the yogurt, chopped cucumber, garlic salt and dill; set aside.

2. Cut each bacon strip in half widthwise and then lengthwise. Wrap a piece of bacon around each shrimp. Secure with toothpicks.

3. In a large nonstick skillet coated with cooking spray, cook shrimp in batches over medium heat for 3-4 minutes on each side or until bacon is crisp.

4. Spoon a rounded 1/2 tsp. yogurt sauce onto each cucumber slice; top with shrimp.

Nutrition Facts: 1 appetizer equals 27 calories, 1 g fat (trace saturated fat), 18 mg cholesterol, 63 mg sodium, 1 g carbohydrate, trace fiber, 3 g protein.

Here's a great way to keep **cucumbers fresh** longer. Purchase a plastic lettuce keeper and place up to six cucumbers in it. They don't get soft spots and stay fresh and crisp for almost 2 weeks. This should work with just about any veggie.

Italian-Style Snack Mix F C M

PREP/TOTAL TIME: 15 min. YIELD: 1-1/2 qt.

KATIE GOLWITZER • WILMINGTON, ILLINOIS

A touch of heat comes through in this tasty, toasty blend of cereals, pretzels and bagel chips. Parmesan, garlic and Italian seasonings boost the flavor of this fun energy mix.

1-1/2	cups	Corn Chex
1-1/2	cups	Rice Chex
1-1/2	cups	Wheat Chex
1/2	cup	garlic bagel chips
1/2	cup	miniature pretzels
3	Tbsp.	butter, melted
1/2	tsp.	garlic salt
1/2	tsp.	dried basil
1/2	tsp.	dried oregano
1/2	tsp.	crushed red pepper flakes
1/4	tsp.	onion powder
2	Tbsp.	grated Parmesan cheese

1. In a large microwave-safe bowl, combine the first five ingredients. In a small bowl, combine the butter, garlic salt, basil, oregano, pepper flakes and onion powder; pour over cereal mixture and toss to coat.

2. Microwave, uncovered, on high for 2 minutes, stirring once. Stir in cheese. Cook 4 minutes longer, stirring twice. Spread onto waxed paper to cool. Store in an airtight container.

Editor's Note: This recipe was tested in a 1,100-watt microwave.

Nutrition Facts: 1/2 cup equals 80 calories, 3 g fat (2 g saturated fat), 8 mg cholesterol, 235 mg sodium, 11 g carbohydrate, 1 g fiber, 2 g protein. **Diabetic Exchanges:** 1 starch, 1/2 fat.

Ginger-Peach Milk Shakes F S

PREP/TOTAL TIME: 5 min. YIELD: 3 servings

HEALTHY COOKING TEST KITCHEN

Is our milk shake better than yours? Give this treat from our Test Kitchen a try and see for yourself!

1	cup	fat-free milk
1	cup	reduced-fat vanilla ice cream
1	cup	frozen unsweetened sliced peaches
1/4	tsp.	ground ginger

Unsweetened chopped peaches

1. In a blender, combine all ingredients; cover and process until smooth. Pour into chilled glasses; garnish with chopped peaches. Serve immediately.

Nutrition Facts: 3/4 cup (calculated without garnish) equals 121 calories, 2 g fat (1 g saturated fat), 14 mg cholesterol, 67 mg sodium, 20 g carbohydrate, 1 g fiber, 5 g protein. **Diabetic Exchanges:** 1 starch, 1/2 fat.

Blooming Onions F C M

PREP: 20 min. BAKE: 40 min. YIELD: 8 servings

KENDRA DOSS • KANSAS CITY, MISSOURI

Instead of being battered and deep-fried, this onion is brushed with melted butter and mustard, sprinkled with bread crumbs and seasonings, and baked. It's an impressive-looking appetizer, and the dip can be used for veggies and crackers, too.

2		large sweet onions
1	Tbsp.	butter, melted
2	tsp.	Dijon mustard
3	Tbsp.	dry bread crumbs
1/4	tsp.	salt
1/4	tsp.	pepper

SAUCE:

1/4	cup	fat-free sour cream

ITALIAN-STYLE SNACK MIX

GINGER-PEACH MILK SHAKES

1/4   cup fat-free mayonnaise
1-1/2 tsp. dried minced onion
1/4   tsp. garlic powder
1/4   tsp. dill weed

1. With a sharp knife, slice 1/2 in. off the top of the onions; peel onions. Cut each into 16 wedges to within 1/2 in. of root end.

2. Place each onion on a double thickness of heavy-duty foil (about 12 in. square). Fold foil around onions and seal tightly. Place in an ungreased 11-in. x 7-in. baking dish. Bake, uncovered, at 425° for 20 minutes.

3. In a small bowl, combine butter and mustard. Open foil; fold foil around onions. Brush butter mixture over onions; sprinkle with bread crumbs, salt and pepper.

4. Bake 18-22 minutes longer or until crisp-tender. Meanwhile, in a small bowl, combine sauce ingredients. Serve with onions.

Nutrition Facts: 1/4 onion with 1 Tbsp. sauce equals 65 calories, 2 g fat (1 g saturated fat), 6 mg cholesterol, 205 mg sodium, 11 g carbohydrate, 1 g fiber, 2 g protein. **Diabetic Exchanges:** 1 vegetable, 1/2 starch.

Chunky Salsa F S C M

PREP: 45 min. **PROCESS:** 15 min. **YIELD:** 7 pints

DANA HAYES • CANTON, OHIO

My fresh-tasting salsa is wonderfully chunky. If you like it hotter, add more habanero peppers; if you prefer a mild salsa, simply add fewer.

5 lbs. tomatoes
4 large green peppers, chopped
3 large onions, chopped
2 large sweet red peppers, chopped
2 habanero peppers, seeded and finely chopped
1 cup white vinegar
1 can (6 oz.) tomato paste
3 tsp. salt

1. Fill a Dutch oven two-thirds with water; bring to a boil. Score an "X" on the bottom of each tomato. Using a slotted spoon, place tomatoes, one at a time, in boiling water for 30-60 seconds. Remove tomatoes and immediately plunge in ice water. Discard peel; chop tomatoes.

2. In a stockpot, combine the remaining ingredients. Stir in tomatoes. Bring to a boil over medium-high heat. Reduce heat; simmer, uncovered, for 15-20 minutes or until desired thickness.

3. Carefully ladle hot mixture into seven hot 1-pint jars, leaving 1/2-in. headspace. Remove air bubbles; wipe rims and adjust lids. Process for 15 minutes in a boiling-water canner.

Editor's Note: We recommend wearing disposable gloves when cutting hot peppers. Avoid touching your face. The processing time listed is for altitudes of 1,000 feet or less. For altitudes up to 3,000 feet, add 5 minutes; 6,000 feet, add 10 minutes; 8,000 feet, add 15 minutes; 10,000 feet, add 20 minutes.

Nutrition Facts: 1/4 cup equals 18 calories, trace fat (trace saturated fat), 0 cholesterol, 131 mg sodium, 4 g carbohydrate, 1 g fiber, 1 g protein. **Diabetic Exchange:** Free food.

SPICED CHIPS AND
ROASTED TOMATILLO SALSA

Spiced Chips and
Roasted Tomatillo Salsa Ⓜ

PREP: 25 min. **BAKE:** 15 min. + cooling
YIELD: 10 servings

MARY RELYEA • CANASTOTA, NEW YORK

My food processor does most of the work for me where this green salsa is concerned. Studded with mango and splashed with lime, it's yummy with no-fuss homemade chips.

   10   flour tortillas (6 in.)
Cooking spray
    3   tsp. chili powder
    1   tsp. ground cumin
1/2   tsp. salt
SALSA:
3/4   lb. tomatillos, husks removed, quartered
    1   small onion, cut into wedges
    1   jalapeno pepper, halved and seeded
    2   garlic cloves
    3   Tbsp. fresh cilantro leaves

1-1/2 tsp. lime juice
  1/2 tsp. salt
    1 medium mango, peeled and diced

1. Cut each tortilla into six wedges; place on ungreased baking sheets. Spritz with cooking spray. Combine the chili powder, cumin and salt; sprinkle over wedges. Bake at 425° for 5-8 minutes or just until edges begin to brown.

2. For salsa, place the tomatillos, onion, jalapeno and garlic in a single layer in a 15-in. x 10-in. x 1-in. baking pan coated with cooking spray. Broil 4-6 in. from the heat for 14-17 minutes or until tender and lightly browned, stirring once. Cool to room temperature.

3. Transfer to a food processor; add the cilantro, lime juice and salt. Cover and process until coarsely chopped. Stir in mango. Refrigerate until serving. Serve with chips.

Editor's Note: Wear disposable gloves when cutting hot peppers; the oils can burn skin. Avoid touching your face.

Nutrition Facts: 6 chips with 1/4 cup salsa equals 127 calories, 4 g fat (trace saturated fat), 0 cholesterol, 470 mg sodium, 20 g carbohydrate, 2 g fiber, 4 g protein.

Spiced Coffee F S C

PREP/TOTAL TIME: 20 min. YIELD: 2 servings

JILL GARN • CHARLOTTE, MICHIGAN

Here's a quick and easy coffee made with instant granules. What's not to love about this autumnal beverage?

- 2 cups water
- 5 tsp. instant coffee granules
- 1/2 cinnamon stick (3 in.)
- 4 whole cloves
- 5 tsp. sugar

Whipped topping, optional

1. In a small saucepan, combine the water, coffee granules, cinnamon stick and cloves. Bring to a boil. Remove from the heat; cover and let stand for 5-8 minutes. Strain and discard spices. Stir in sugar until dissolved. Ladle into mugs. Serve with whipped topping if desired.

Nutrition Facts: 1 cup (calculated without whipped topping) equals 46 calories, trace fat (trace saturated fat), 0 cholesterol, 1 mg sodium, 11 g carbohydrate, 0 fiber, trace protein. **Diabetic Exchange:** 1/2 starch.

Greek Sandwich Bites C M

PREP/TOTAL TIME: 25 min. YIELD: 16 appetizers

LYNN SCULLY • RANCHO SANTA FE, CALIFORNIA

My appetizer tastes just like traditional spanakopita, but it's much less work to prepare.

- 1 medium onion, finely chopped
- 1 Tbsp. olive oil
- 2 garlic cloves, minced
- 1 lb. fresh baby spinach
- 1 cup (4 oz.) crumbled feta cheese
- 1/4 cup pine nuts, toasted
- 1/4 tsp. salt
- 1/4 tsp. pepper
- 1/8 tsp. ground nutmeg
- 8 slices Italian bread (1/2 in. thick)
- 4 tsp. butter, softened

1. In a large nonstick skillet, saute onion in oil until tender. Add garlic; cook 1 minute longer. Stir in the spinach; cook and stir until wilted. Drain. Stir in the feta, pine nuts, salt, pepper and nutmeg.

2. Spread over four bread slices; top with remaining bread. Spread outsides of sandwiches with butter. Grill, uncovered, over medium heat for 3-4 minutes or until bread is browned and cheese is melted, turning once. Cut each sandwich into quarters.

Nutrition Facts: 1 appetizer equals 87 calories, 5 g fat (2 g saturated fat), 6 mg cholesterol, 200 mg sodium, 8 g carbohydrate, 1 g fiber, 4 g protein. **Diabetic Exchanges:** 1 fat, 1/2 starch.

Greek Sandwich Bites make for a hearty appetizer so be sure to serve them with plates and napkins nearby. You may also wish to **dress them up** with frilly toothpicks or skewer each appetizer with a cherry tomato or olive garnish that sits nicely on top of each sandwich quarter.

SPICED COFFEE

GREEK SANDWICH BITES

Iced Melon Moroccan Mint Tea F S

PREP/TOTAL TIME: 20 min. YIELD: 5 servings

SARAH BATT THRONE • EL CERRITO, CALIFORNIA

I grow mint on my balcony, and this refreshing beverage is a wonderful way to use it. It combines two of my favorite drinks—Moroccan Mint Tea and Honeydew Agua Fresca. For extra flair, add some ginger ale.

     2   cups water
    12   fresh mint leaves
     4   individual green tea bags
    1/3 cup sugar
    2-1/2 cups diced honeydew
    1-1/2 cups ice cubes
Additional ice cubes

1. In a large saucepan, bring water to a boil. Remove from the heat; add mint leaves and tea bags. Cover and steep for 3-5 minutes. Discard the mint and tea bags. Stir in the sugar.

2. In a blender, process honeydew until blended. Add 1-1/2 cups ice and tea; process until blended. Serve over additional ice.

Nutrition Facts: 1 cup equals 81 calories, trace fat (trace saturated fat), 0 cholesterol, 9 mg sodium, 21 g carbohydrate, 1 g fiber, trace protein. **Diabetic Exchange:** 1 starch.

ICED MELON MOROCCAN MINT TEA

Baked Veggie Chips C M

PREP/TOTAL TIME: 30 min. YIELD: 7 servings

CHRISTINE SCHENHER • SAN CLEMENTE, CALIFORNIA

Colorful roasted root vegetables are a fun, festive snack or casual side dish. These perfectly seasoned chips are so tasty they don't even need dip!

    1/2 lb. fresh beets (about 2 medium)
     1   medium potato
     1   medium sweet potato
     1   medium parsnip
     2   Tbsp. canola oil
     2   Tbsp. grated Parmesan cheese
    1/2 tsp. salt
    1/2 tsp. garlic powder
    1/2 tsp. dried oregano
Dash pepper

1. Peel vegetables and cut into 1/8-in. slices. Place in a large bowl. Drizzle with oil. Combine the remaining ingredients; sprinkle over vegetables and toss to coat.

2. Arrange in a single layer on racks in two ungreased 15-in. x 10-in. x 1-in. baking pans. Bake at 375° for 15-20 minutes or until golden brown, turning once.

Nutrition Facts: 1/2 cup equals 108 calories, 5 g fat (1 g saturated fat), 1 mg cholesterol, 220 mg sodium, 15 g carbohydrate, 2 g fiber, 2 g protein.

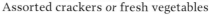

Make-Ahead Crab Dip F C

PREP/TOTAL TIME: 10 min. YIELD: 2 cups

MARY DIAMOND • NEW PORT RICHEY, FLORIDA

Busy hostesses love the make-ahead convenience of this elegant dip with a lick of lemon and horseradish. Serve it with crackers or fresh veggies.

    3/4 cup fat-free mayonnaise
    1/4 cup chili sauce
     1   Tbsp. lemon juice
     1   tsp. horseradish
    1/2 tsp. garlic powder
    1/4 tsp. pepper
     2   cans (6 oz. *each*) lump crabmeat, drained
Assorted crackers or fresh vegetables

MAKE-AHEAD CRAB DIP

CHIPOTLE PEA SPREAD

1. In a small bowl, combine the first six ingredients; fold in crab. Chill until serving. Serve with crackers.

Nutrition Facts: 3 Tbsp. (calculated without crackers or vegetables) equals 54 calories, 1 g fat (trace saturated fat), 32 mg cholesterol, 349 mg sodium, 4 g carbohydrate, trace fiber, 7 g protein. **Diabetic Exchange:** 1 lean meat.

Chipotle Pea Spread C

PREP/TOTAL TIME: 20 min. **YIELD:** 1-1/2 cups

FRANCES "KAY" BOUMA • TRAIL, BRITISH COLUMBIA

I love hummus and bacon, but I needed to make something green for a Healthy Cooking contest. It took a few tries to come up with a recipe everyone loves. I hope you do, too!

 2 cups frozen peas
1/3 cup grated Parmesan cheese
 3 cooked bacon strips, chopped
1/4 cup reduced-fat sour cream
 2 Tbsp. olive oil
 1 Tbsp. lime juice
 2 garlic cloves
 1 to 2 tsp. minced chipotle pepper in adobo sauce
1/4 tsp. pepper
Assorted fresh vegetables or crackers

1. In a small saucepan, bring 4 cups water to a boil. Add peas; cover and cook for 1 minute. Drain and immediately place peas in ice water. Drain and pat dry.

2. Place peas in a food processor; add the cheese, bacon, sour cream, oil, lime juice, garlic, chipotle pepper and pepper. Cover and process until smooth. Serve with vegetables or crackers.

Nutrition Facts: 1/4 cup (calculated without vegetables) equals 129 calories, 8 g fat (2 g saturated fat), 11 mg cholesterol, 207 mg sodium, 8 g carbohydrate, 2 g fiber, 6 g protein. **Diabetic Exchanges:** 1-1/2 fat, 1/2 starch.

Curried Chicken And Rice Tartlets F S C

PREP: 30 min. BAKE: 10 min. YIELD: 24 appetizers

HEALTHY COOKING TEST KITCHEN

These simple starters feature a yummy curried chicken filling that guests will love. A cute little phyllo dough cup makes the appetizers seem extra special.

1/2	cup reduced-sodium chicken broth
1/4	cup uncooked long grain rice
3/4	cup cubed cooked chicken breast
1/2	cup frozen peas and carrots, thawed and drained
3	Tbsp. reduced-fat mayonnaise
1	green onion, chopped
1/2	tsp. salt
1/4	tsp. pepper
1/4	tsp. curry powder
1/8	tsp. garlic powder
1/8	tsp. ground turmeric
1/8	tsp. ground coriander

8   sheets phyllo dough (14 in. x 9 in.)

Butter-flavored cooking spray

Minced chives, optional

1. In a small saucepan, bring broth and rice to a boil. Reduce heat; cover and simmer for 15-18 minutes or until liquid is absorbed and rice is tender. In a large bowl, combine the rice, chicken, peas and carrots, mayonnaise, green onion and seasonings.

2. Place one sheet of phyllo dough on a work surface; spritz with butter-flavored spray. Top with another sheet of phyllo; spritz with spray. (Keep remaining phyllo covered with plastic wrap and a damp towel to prevent it from drying out.) Cut into 12 squares. Repeat three times, making 48 squares.

3. Stack two squares of layered phyllo in each of 24 muffin cups coated with cooking spray, rotating squares so corners do not overlap. Spoon 1 tablespoon rice mixture into each cup. Bake at 375° for 8-10 minutes or until golden brown. Garnish with chives if desired. Serve warm.

Nutrition Facts: 1 tartlet equals 35 calories, 1 g fat (trace saturated fat), 4 mg cholesterol, 96 mg sodium, 4 g carbohydrate, trace fiber, 2 g protein.

Family-Favorite Taco Dip C

PREP/TOTAL TIME: 10 min. **YIELD:** 3 cups

LAURIE ELLSWORTH • TULLY, NEW YORK

I've tasted many different dips, but this is my favorite. Not only does it feature a cream cheese base, but the tomato, olives and jalapeno pepper add a fun burst of color and flavor. Best of all, it comes together in just a few minutes!

- 2 pkg. (8 oz. *each*) fat-free cream cheese
- 2 Tbsp. reduced-sodium taco seasoning
- 1 Tbsp. fat-free milk
- 1 cup (4 oz.) shredded cheddar cheese
- 1 medium tomato, diced
- 1/4 cup sliced ripe olives, drained
- 1/4 cup pickled jalapeno pepper

Baked tortilla chips

1. In a small bowl, beat the cream cheese, taco seasoning and milk until blended. Spread mixture into a 9-in. pie plate. Sprinkle with cheese, tomato, olives and jalapenos. Serve with chips.

Nutrition Facts: 1/4 cup (calculated without chips) equals 81 calories, 4 g fat (2 g saturated fat), 13 mg cholesterol, 393 mg sodium, 5 g carbohydrate, trace fiber, 8 g protein.

Pineapple Salsa F S C

PREP/TOTAL TIME: 20 min. **YIELD:** 3-1/2 cups

SUZI LAPAR • WAHIAWA, HAWAII

This mouthwatering salsa features fresh pineapple and a handful of seasonings. Serve it with tortilla chips or grilled chicken or fish for a jazzed-up meal.

- 2 cups diced fresh pineapple
- 2 medium tomatoes, seeded and chopped
- 3/4 cup chopped sweet onion
- 1/4 cup minced fresh cilantro
- 1 jalapeno pepper, seeded and chopped
- 1 Tbsp. olive oil
- 1 tsp. ground coriander
- 3/4 tsp. ground cumin
- 1/2 tsp. salt
- 1/2 tsp. minced garlic

Tortilla chips

1. In a large bowl, combine the first 10 ingredients. Cover and refrigerate until serving. Serve with chips.

Editor's Note: Wear disposable gloves when cutting hot peppers; the oils can burn skin. Avoid touching your face.

Nutrition Facts: 1/4 cup (calculated without chips) equals 29 calories, 1 g fat (trace saturated fat), 0 cholesterol, 87 mg sodium, 5 g carbohydrate, 1 g fiber, trace protein. **Diabetic Exchange:** Free food.

To remove the seeds from a **tomato,** cut it in half horizontally and remove the stem. Holding a tomato half over a bowl or sink, scrape out seeds with a small spoon or squeeze the tomato to force out the seeds. Then slice or dice as directed in the recipe.

PINEAPPLE SALSA

FAMILY-FAVORITE TACO DIP

Basil Citrus Cocktail F S C

PREP/TOTAL TIME: 10 min. YIELD: 1 serving

HEALTHY COOKING TEST KITCHEN

Fruity, fantastic and lighter in calories, this refreshing beverage is perfect for adult parties.

    6   fresh basil leaves
1-1/2 to 2 cups ice cubes
    2   oz. white grapefruit juice
    2   oz. mandarin orange juice
  3/4 oz. gin
  1/2 oz. Domaine de Canton ginger liqueur

1. In a shaker, muddle the basil leaves.

2. Fill shaker three-fourths full with ice. Add the juices, gin and ginger liqueur; cover and shake for 10-15 seconds or until condensation forms on outside of shaker. Strain into a chilled cocktail glass.

Nutrition Facts: 1 serving equals 136 calories, trace fat (trace saturated fat), 0 cholesterol, trace sodium, 14 g carbohydrate, trace fiber, 1 g protein.

Mulled Merlot F S C

PREP: 10 min. COOK: 1 hour YIELD: 9 servings

HEALTHY COOKING TEST KITCHEN

Here's a traditional beverage that's sure to warm you up!

    4   cinnamon sticks (3 in.)
    4   whole cloves
    2   bottles (750 milliliters *each*) merlot
  1/2 cup sugar
  1/2 cup orange juice
  1/2 cup brandy
    1   medium orange, thinly sliced

1. Place cinnamon sticks and cloves on a double thickness of cheesecloth; bring up corners of cloth and tie with string to form a bag.

2. In a 3-qt. slow cooker, combine the wine, sugar, orange juice, brandy and orange slices. Add spice bag. Cover and cook on high for 1 hour or until heated through. Discard the spice bag and the orange slices. Serve warm.

Nutrition Facts: 1 serving (3/4 cup) equals 143 calories, trace fat (trace saturated fat), 0 cholesterol, 4 mg sodium, 15 g carbohydrate, trace fiber, trace protein.

Parmesan Sesame Crackers F S C M

PREP: 25 min. BAKE: 15 min. + cooling YIELD: 4 dozen

ELENA IORGA • HELENA, MONTANA

I love these snacks! The rustic-looking crackers are crispy, crunchy and topped with cheese and plenty of seeds. Perfect for parties, they are only missing the preservatives and additives of store-bought alternatives.

    2   cups all-purpose flour
  1/3 cup sesame seeds
  1/3 cup shredded Parmesan cheese
    2   Tbsp. poppy seeds
    1   tsp. baking powder
  1/2 tsp. salt
  2/3 cup plus 2 Tbsp. warm water, *divided*
  1/3 cup canola oil
    1   egg white

TOPPING:
    2   Tbsp. shredded Parmesan cheese
    1   Tbsp. sesame seeds
    1   Tbsp. poppy seeds

1. In a small bowl, combine the first six ingredients. Gradually add 2/3 cup water and oil, tossing with a fork until dough forms a ball. Turn onto a lightly floured surface; knead 8-10 times.

2. Divide dough in half. Roll each ball directly on a baking sheet coated with cooking spray into a 12-in. x 9-in. rectangle. Pierce dough with a fork.

BASIL CITRUS COCKTAIL

MULLED MERLOT

PARMESAN SESAME CRACKERS
NUTTY BLUE CHEESE SPREAD

3. Whisk together egg white and remaining water; brush over dough. Combine topping ingredients; sprinkle over tops.

4. Score dough in each pan into 24 pieces. Bake at 400° for 15-18 minutes or until golden brown. Immediately cut along the scored lines; cool in pans on wire racks. Store in an airtight container.

Nutrition Facts: 1 cracker equals 44 calories, 3 g fat (trace saturated fat), 1 mg cholesterol, 47 mg sodium, 4 g carbohydrate, trace fiber, 1 g protein.

Nutty Blue Cheese Spread C M

PREP: 15 min. + chilling **YIELD:** 1-1/2 cups

SHERRY HULSMAN • ELKTON, FLORIDA

With great blue cheese flavor and nice texture from the pecans, this super simple spread has a company-special feel. It's just perfect for formal and casual parties alike.

> 1 pkg. (8 oz.) reduced-fat cream cheese
> 1-1/4 tsp. sugar
> 1/8 tsp. salt
> 1/4 cup crumbled blue cheese
> 3 Tbsp. finely chopped pecans, toasted
> Assorted crackers

1. In a large bowl, beat the cream cheese, sugar and salt until blended. Stir in blue cheese. Refrigerate for at least 1 hour. Just before serving, stir in pecans. Serve with crackers.

Nutrition Facts: 2 Tbsp. (calculated without crackers) equals 71 calories, 6 g fat (3 g saturated fat), 15 mg cholesterol, 144 mg sodium, 1 g carbohydrate, trace fiber, 3 g protein.

CHUTNEY CHEESE BALL

Chutney Cheese Ball C M

PREP/TOTAL TIME: 15 min. YIELD: 2-1/2 cups

PATRICIA SCHNEIDER • ROLLINSFORD, NEW HAMPSHIRE

This party starter goes great with crackers, bread cubes or fruit. Best of all, no one suspects it's light!

- 1 pkg. (8 oz.) reduced-fat cream cheese
- 1 pkg. (8 oz.) fat-free cream cheese
- 1 cup (4 oz.) shredded reduced-fat Colby-Monterey Jack cheese
- 1/2 cup mango chutney
- 2 green onions, finely chopped
- 1 garlic clove, minced
- 1/4 tsp. salt
- 1/4 tsp. pepper
- 1/2 cup finely chopped walnuts
- 2 Tbsp. minced fresh parsley

Crackers, bread cubes and apple slices

1. In a small bowl, combine the first eight ingredients. Shape into a ball and roll in walnuts. Press parsley into ball; cover and chill until serving. Serve with crackers, bread cubes and apple slices.

Nutrition Facts: 2 Tbsp. (calculated without crackers) equals 99 calories, 5 g fat (3 g saturated fat), 12 mg cholesterol, 254 mg sodium, 7 g carbohydrate, trace fiber, 5 g protein. **Diabetic Exchanges:** 1 fat, 1/2 starch.

Citrusy Fruit Kabobs F S M

PREP/TOTAL TIME: 20 min. YIELD: 8 kabobs

MARY RELYEA • CANASTOTA, NEW YORK

Fresh, fruity—and lower in sodium and fat—these grilled kabobs are great picks for health-minded hostesses.

- 1/3 cup orange juice
- 2 Tbsp. lemon juice
- 4-1/2 tsp. honey
- 2 tsp. cornstarch

1-1/2 tsp. grated lemon peel

1/4 tsp. ground allspice

24 fresh strawberries

16 cubes fresh pineapple

2 small bananas, cut into 1-in. pieces

2 tsp. minced fresh mint

1. In a small saucepan, combine the first six ingredients. Bring to a boil; cook and stir for 2 minutes or until thickened. Remove from the heat; cool to room temperature.

2. Alternately thread an eighth of the fruit onto one metal or soaked wooden skewer. Repeat seven times. Brush with half of glaze. Moisten a paper towel with cooking oil; using long-handled tongs, lightly coat the grill rack.

3. Grill, covered, over medium heat for 5-7 minutes or until lightly browned, turning occasionally and basting frequently with remaining glaze. Just before serving, sprinkle with mint. Serve warm.

Nutrition Facts: 1 kabob equals 83 calories, trace fat (trace saturated fat), 0 cholesterol, 2 mg sodium, 21 g carbohydrate, 2 g fiber, 1 g protein. **Diabetic Exchange:** 1 fruit.

Champagne Punch

PREP: 5 min. + chilling YIELD: 16 servings

AMY SHORT • BARBOURSVILLE, WEST VIRGINIA

A blend of four fruit juices pairs well with bubbly Champagne in my party-pleasing punch. I like to add a strawberry garnish for a festive touch.

4 cups orange juice

1 cup ruby red grapefruit juice

1/2 cup lemon juice

1/2 cup lime juice

2 bottles (750 milliliters *each*) Champagne, chilled

1. In a 3-qt. pitcher, combine the juices. Refrigerate until chilled. Just before serving, stir in Champagne. Serve in Champagne glasses.

Nutrition Facts: 3/4 cup equals 101 calories, trace fat (0 saturated fat), 0 cholesterol, trace sodium, 11 g carbohydrate, trace fiber, trace protein.

Raspberry Merry F S C

PREP/TOTAL TIME: 5 min. YIELD: 1 serving

HEALTHY COOKING TEST KITCHEN

Here's a lighter cocktail with a festive, merry flavor and plenty of holiday flair!

5 fresh raspberries

1/4 cup crushed ice

1 navel orange wedge

1 oz. pomegranate-flavored vodka

1-1/2 oz. Prosecco

GARNISH:
Pomegranate seeds

1. In a shaker, muddle raspberries. Add ice. Squeeze the juice from the orange wedge into the shaker; add orange wedge and vodka. Cover and shake for 10-15 seconds or until condensation forms on outside of the shaker.

2. Strain into a chilled cocktail glass. Stir in Prosecco. Garnish with pomegranate seeds.

Nutrition Facts: 1 serving equals 112 calories, trace fat (trace saturated fat), 0 cholesterol, trace sodium, 5 g carbohydrate, 1 g fiber, trace protein.

CHAMPAGNE PUNCH

RASPBERRY MERRY

BBQ Chicken Pizza Roll-Up F C

PREP: 15 min. **BAKE:** 15 min. + cooling
YIELD: 24 servings

TRACEY BIRCH • QUEEN CREEK, ARIZONA

Warm slices of my hearty appetizer make a fab, filling snack with loads of sweet and tangy flavor.

1	tube (13.8 oz.) refrigerated pizza crust
1/4	cup honey barbecue sauce
1-1/2	cups (6 oz.) shredded part-skim mozzarella cheese
1-1/2	cups shredded cooked chicken breast
1	small red onion, finely chopped
1/4	cup minced fresh cilantro
1	tsp. Italian seasoning, optional
1	egg white
1	Tbsp. water
1/4	tsp. garlic powder

1. On a lightly floured surface, roll crust into a 12-in. x 9-in. rectangle; brush with barbecue sauce. Layer with cheese, chicken, onion, cilantro and Italian seasoning if desired.

2. Roll up jelly-roll style, starting with a long side; pinch seams to seal. Place seam side down on a baking sheet coated with cooking spray.

3. Beat the egg white and water; brush over top. Sprinkle with garlic powder. Bake at 400° for 15-20 minutes or until lightly browned. Cool for 10 minutes before slicing.

Nutrition Facts: 1 slice equals 81 calories, 2 g fat (1 g saturated fat), 11 mg cholesterol, 177 mg sodium, 9 g carbohydrate, trace fiber, 6 g protein. **Diabetic Exchanges:** 1 lean meat, 1/2 starch.

Spicy Tomato Juice F

PREP: 45 min. + chilling **COOK:** 20 min.
YIELD: 15 servings

MARTHA PHILBECK • LA FONTAINE, INDIANA

This zesty juice is good hot or cold. People love the spicy taste all year-round.

12	lbs. tomatoes
9	dried ancho chilies
3	medium onions, chopped
1	celery rib, chopped
1/4	cup chopped seeded jalapeno pepper
1/2	cup sugar
1	Tbsp. Worcestershire sauce
2	tsp. salt
1/4	tsp. pepper

1. Fill a Dutch oven two-thirds with water; bring to a boil. Score an "X" on the bottom of each tomato. Using a slotted spoon, place tomatoes, one at a time, in boiling water for 30-60 seconds. Remove tomatoes and immediately plunge in ice water. Discard peel; chop and place in a stockpot.

2. Add the chilies, onions, celery and jalapenos. Bring to a boil. Reduce heat; simmer, uncovered, for 20-25 minutes or until vegetables are tender. Cool slightly. In a food processor, process juice in batches until blended. Strain and discard seeds and pulp. Return puree to a large saucepan.

3. Stir in the remaining ingredients; heat through. Cool. To serve, refrigerate until chilled or transfer to storage containers. May be refrigerated for up to 3 days or frozen for up to 3 months.

Editor's Note: Wear disposable gloves when cutting hot peppers; the oils can burn skin. Avoid touching your face.

Nutrition Facts: 1 cup equals 134 calories, 2 g fat (trace saturated fat), 0 cholesterol, 351 mg sodium, 29 g carbohydrate, 7 g fiber, 5 g protein. **Diabetic Exchange:** 2 starch.

BBQ CHICKEN PIZZA ROLL-UP

SPICY TOMATO JUICE

Triple Berry Salsa `F` `S` `C` `M`

PREP/TOTAL TIME: 20 min. **YIELD:** 22 servings

RAYMONDE BOURGEOIS • SWASTIKA, ONTARIO

Blueberries are nutritious, low in calories and packed with vitamin C, fiber and disease-fighting antioxidants. My chunky salsa is a fresh, flavorful blend of berries and veggies that is great scooped up with chips or served over grilled chicken.

1-1/2 cups fresh blueberries
3/4 cup chopped fresh strawberries
3/4 cup fresh raspberries
1 medium tomato, seeded and chopped
1 small sweet yellow pepper, chopped
1/4 cup finely chopped red onion
1/4 cup minced fresh cilantro
1 jalapeno pepper, seeded and minced
2 green onions, chopped

1 Tbsp. cider vinegar
1 Tbsp. olive oil
2 tsp. lime juice
2 tsp. orange juice
1 tsp. honey
1/4 tsp. salt
Baked tortilla chip scoops

1. In a large bowl, combine the first nine ingredients. In a small bowl, whisk the remaining ingredients. Drizzle over salsa; toss to coat. Chill until serving. Serve with chips.

Editor's Note: Wear disposable gloves when cutting hot peppers; the oils can burn skin. Avoid touching your face.

Nutrition Facts: 1/4 cup (calculated without chips) equals 20 calories, 1 g fat (trace saturated fat), 0 cholesterol, 28 mg sodium, 3 g carbohydrate, 1 g fiber, trace protein. **Diabetic Exchange:** Free food.

Couscous Caps F S C M

PREP: 30 min. BAKE: 10 min. YIELD: 20 appetizers

KENDRA DOSS • KANSAS CITY, MISSOURI

Couscous makes a pleasant change from bread crumbs in these savory appetizers—and provides nice texture as well.

20	large fresh mushrooms
4	green onions, chopped
1	cup reduced-sodium chicken broth, *divided*
1/3	cup uncooked whole wheat couscous
1/4	cup grated Parmesan cheese, *divided*
4	tsp. reduced-fat mayonnaise
1	tsp. dried basil
1/2	tsp. dried tarragon
1/2	tsp. paprika

1. Remove stems from mushrooms and finely chop stems; set caps aside. In a large nonstick skillet coated with cooking spray, saute onions and chopped mushrooms until crisp-tender. Add 1/2 cup broth; cook and stir until liquid is evaporated and vegetables are tender, about 10 minutes.

2. Meanwhile, in a small saucepan, bring remaining broth to a boil. Stir in couscous. Remove from the heat; cover and let stand for 5-10 minutes or until broth is absorbed. Fluff with a fork. Add to onion mixture. Stir in 2 Tbsp. cheese, mayonnaise, basil and tarragon. Stuff into mushroom caps.

3. Place on a foil-lined baking sheet. Sprinkle with remaining cheese. Bake at 375° for 10-15 minutes or until mushrooms are tender. Just before serving, sprinkle with paprika.

Nutrition Facts: 1 stuffed mushroom equals 26 calories, 1 g fat (trace saturated fat), 1 mg cholesterol, 49 mg sodium, 4 g carbohydrate, 1 g fiber, 2 g protein.

Granola-To-Go Bars ⓈⓂ

PREP: 30 min. BAKE: 15 min. + cooling YIELD: 3 dozen

SALLY HAEN • MENOMONEE FALLS, WISCONSIN

This grab-and-go goodie makes a portable breakfast or a hearty snack for a long day out. Chewy and sweet, these fruity oat bars really satisfy!

3-1/2 cups quick-cooking oats
    1 cup chopped almonds
    1 egg, lightly beaten
  2/3 cup butter, melted
  1/2 cup honey
    1 tsp. vanilla extract
  1/2 cup sunflower kernels
  1/2 cup flaked coconut
  1/2 cup chopped dried apples
  1/2 cup dried cranberries
  1/2 cup packed brown sugar
  1/2 tsp. ground cinnamon

1. Combine the oats and the almonds in a 15-in. x 10-in. x 1-in. baking pan that has been coated with cooking spray. Bake at 350° for 15 minutes or until toasted, stirring occasionally.

2. In a large bowl, combine the egg, butter, honey and vanilla. Stir in the sunflower kernels, coconut, apples, cranberries, brown sugar and cinnamon. Stir in oat mixture.

3. Press into a 15-in. x 10-in. x 1-in. baking pan coated with cooking spray. Bake at 350° for 13-18 minutes or until set and edges are lightly browned. Cool on a wire rack. Carefully cut into bars. Store in an airtight container.

Nutrition Facts: 1 bar equals 130 calories, 7 g fat (3 g saturated fat), 15 mg cholesterol, 40 mg sodium, 16 g carbohydrate, 2 g fiber, 2 g protein.

Peanut Caramel Corn Ⓜ

PREP: 20 min. BAKE: 45 min. YIELD: 2 qt.

LOIS WARD • PUSLIN, ONTARIO

I found this reduced-fat recipe a few years ago and always give it away in small packages at Christmas.

    8 cups air-popped popcorn
  1/2 cup salted peanuts
  1/2 cup packed brown sugar
    3 Tbsp. light corn syrup
4-1/2 tsp. molasses
    1 Tbsp. butter
  1/4 tsp. salt
  1/2 tsp. vanilla extract
  1/8 tsp. baking soda

1. Place popcorn and peanuts in a large bowl coated with cooking spray; set aside.

2. In a large heavy saucepan, combine the brown sugar, corn syrup, molasses, butter and salt. Bring to a boil over medium heat, stirring constantly. Boil for 2-3 minutes without stirring.

3. Remove from the heat; stir in vanilla and baking soda (mixture will foam). Quickly pour over popcorn and mix well.

4. Transfer to a 15-in. x 10-in. x 1-in. baking pan coated with cooking spray. Bake at 250° for 45 minutes, stirring every 15 minutes. Remove from pan and place on waxed paper to cool. Store in an airtight container.

Nutrition Facts: 1 cup equals 181 calories, 6 g fat (2 g saturated fat), 4 mg cholesterol, 155 mg sodium, 30 g carbohydrate, 2 g fiber, 3 g protein. **Diabetic Exchanges:** 2 starch, 1 fat.

PEANUT CARAMEL CORN

GRANOLA-TO-GO BARS

California Wassail F S

PREP/TOTAL TIME: 30 min. YIELD: 16 servings

PATRICIA NIEH • PORTOLA VALLEY, CALIFORNIA

Here's a healthy and delicious family-friendly punch that's a cozy way to welcome family and friends in from the cold or just celebrate the holiday season. Serve it in small cups, as it tastes best when piping hot!

- 24 whole cloves
- 1 large navel orange, cut into six wedges
- 4 cups orange juice
- 4 cups unsweetened apple juice
- 4 cups cranberry juice
- 16 maraschino cherries
- 4 cinnamon sticks (3 in.)

1. Insert four cloves into each orange wedge. In a Dutch oven, combine the orange juice, apple juice and cranberry juice. Add orange wedges, cherries and cinnamon sticks.

2. Bring to a boil. Reduce heat; simmer, uncovered, for 15-20 minutes or until flavors are blended. Discard cinnamon sticks. Serve warm.

Nutrition Facts: 3/4 cup equals 101 calories, trace fat (trace saturated fat), 0 cholesterol, 3 mg sodium, 26 g carbohydrate, trace fiber, 1 g protein. **Diabetic Exchange:** 1-1/2 fruit.

When buying oranges, select those that are heavy for their size and feel firm. Avoid any with mold or spongy spots. Buying a **big bag of oranges** may be a bargain, but keep in mind that you can't see all areas on each orange. One pound equals about 3 medium oranges.

CALIFORNIA WASSAIL

Gluten-Free Chocolate Snack Mix M

PREP/TOTAL TIME: 25 min. YIELD: 3 qt.

ANGELA BUCHANAN • LONGMONT, COLORADO

Being gluten-intolerant, I experiment with a lot of recipes. This sweet snack is fun for kids and adults alike!

- 5 cups Chocolate Chex
- 4 cups Cinnamon Chex
- 1 cup salted cashews
- 1 cup dried banana chips
- 6 Tbsp. butter, cubed
- 1 cup flaked coconut
- 1/4 cup honey
- 2 Tbsp. baking cocoa
- 1 tsp. coconut extract
- 1/2 tsp. ground cinnamon

1. In a large microwave-safe bowl, combine the cereals, cashews and banana chips. In a small microwave-safe bowl, melt butter. Add the coconut, honey, cocoa, extract and cinnamon; stir until blended. Pour over cereal mixture and toss to coat.

2. Microwave, uncovered, on high for 4 minutes, stirring every minute. Spread onto waxed paper to cool. Store in an airtight container.

Editor's Note: Read all ingredient labels for possible gluten content prior to use. Ingredient formulas can change, and production facilities vary among brands. If you're concerned that your brand may contain gluten, contact the company. This recipe was tested in a 1,100-watt microwave.

Nutrition Facts: 1/2 cup equals 182 calories, 10 g fat (5 g saturated fat), 8 mg cholesterol, 185 mg sodium, 23 g carbohydrate, 1 g fiber, 2 g protein.

Tuscan Bean And Olive Spread C M

PREP/TOTAL TIME: 20 min. YIELD: 1-1/2 cups

DIANE NEMITZ • LUDINGTON, MICHIGAN

The wonderful flavors of garlic, rosemary and basil blend in this hearty spread. Lucky enough to have leftovers? Serve it as a sandwich topper.

- 6 sun-dried tomato halves (not packed in oil), finely chopped
- 1/2 cup boiling water
- 1 can (15 oz.) white kidney *or* cannellini beans, rinsed and drained
- 2 Tbsp. water
- 1 Tbsp. olive oil
- 1-1/2 tsp. dried basil
- 1 garlic clove, halved
- 1/2 tsp. dried rosemary, crushed
- 1/4 tsp. pepper
- 1/8 tsp. crushed red pepper flakes
- 1/4 cup Greek olives, chopped

Bagel chips

1. In a small bowl, combine tomatoes and boiling water. Let stand for 5 minutes; drain and set aside.

SPARKLING
PARTY PUNCH

TUSCAN BEAN AND OLIVE SPREAD

GARLIC-HERB
MINI QUICHES

2. Place the beans, water, oil, basil, garlic, rosemary, pepper and pepper flakes in a food processor; cover and process until blended. Stir in tomatoes. Transfer to a serving bowl; sprinkle with olives. Serve with bagel chips.

Nutrition Facts: 1/4 cup (calculated without chips) equals 99 calories, 4 g fat (1 g saturated fat), 0 cholesterol, 231 mg sodium, 12 g carbohydrate, 3 g fiber, 3 g protein.

Sparkling Party Punch F S

PREP/TOTAL TIME: 5 min. YIELD: 17 servings

JAN WITTEVEEN • NORBORNE, MISSOURI

This has been my "signature" punch for years. When, after several years of using it for the family Christmas party, the punch was changed to a festive red punch recipe, everyone wondered what happened to Jan's punch...needless to say, the Sparkling (yellow) Party Punch has been served ever since!

  1 can (46 oz.) unsweetened pineapple juice, chilled
  3 cups apricot nectar *or* juice, chilled
  1 liter diet lemon-lime soda, chilled
Pineapple sherbet, optional

1. In a punch bowl, combine the pineapple juice, apricot nectar and soda. Top with scoops of sherbet if desired. Serve immediately.

Nutrition Facts: 3/4 cup (calculated without sherbet) equals 66 calories, trace fat (trace saturated fat), 0 cholesterol, 9 mg sodium, 16 g carbohydrate, trace fiber, trace protein. **Diabetic Exchange:** 1 fruit.

Garlic-Herb Mini Quiches F S C M

PREP/TOTAL TIME: 25 min. YIELD: 45 appetizers

JOSEPHINE PIRO • EASTON, PENNSYLVANIA

Looking for a wonderful way to ring in the New Year or celebrate an extra-special occasion? You've got it—and you need only five ingredients to make these tasty apps!

  1 carton (6-1/2 oz.) reduced-fat spreadable garlic and herb cream cheese
1/4 cup fat-free milk
  2 eggs
  3 pkg. (1.9 oz. *each*) frozen miniature phyllo tart shells
  2 Tbsp. minced fresh parsley
Minced chives, optional

1. In a small bowl, beat the cream cheese, milk and eggs. Place tart shells on an ungreased baking sheet; fill each with 2 tsp. mixture. Sprinkle with parsley.

2. Bake at 350° for 10-12 minutes or until filling is set and shells are lightly browned. Sprinkle with chives if desired. Serve warm.

Nutrition Facts: 1 mini quiche equals 31 calories, 2 g fat (trace saturated fat), 12 mg cholesterol, 32 mg sodium, 2 g carbohydrate, trace fiber, 1 g protein.

Healthy Snack Mix M

PREP: 15 min. **BAKE:** 1 hour + cooling
YIELD: 3-1/2 qt.

MELISSA HANSEN • ROCHESTER, MINNESOTA

Party mix has always been a tradition in our home. I lightened my mom's recipe, replacing margarine with heart-healthy olive oil. No one even noticed.

3	cups Corn Chex
3	cups Rice Chex
3	cups Wheat Chex
3	cups Multi Grain Cheerios
1	cup salted peanuts
1-1/2	cups pretzel sticks
1/3	cup olive oil
4	tsp. Worcestershire sauce
1	tsp. seasoned salt
1/8	tsp. garlic powder

1. In a large bowl, combine the cereals, peanuts and pretzels. In a small bowl, combine the remaining ingredients; pour over the cereal mixture and toss to coat.

2. Transfer to two 15-in. x 10-in. x 1-in. baking pans coated with cooking spray. Bake at 250° for 1 hour, stirring every 15 minutes. Cool completely on wire racks. Store in an airtight container.

Nutrition Facts: 3/4 cup equals 150 calories, 8 g fat (1 g saturated fat), 0 cholesterol, 310 mg sodium, 19 g carbohydrate, 2 g fiber, 4 g protein. **Diabetic Exchanges:** 1-1/2 starch, 1-1/2 fat.

Apricot-Ricotta Stuffed Celery F S C M

PREP/TOTAL TIME: 15 min. YIELD: about 2 dozen

DOROTHY REINHOLD • MALIBU, CALIFORNIA

This healthful protein filling can double as a dip for sliced apples. I often make it ahead, so kids can help themselves to an after-school snack.

- 3 dried apricots
- 1/2 cup part-skim ricotta cheese
- 2 tsp. brown sugar
- 1/4 tsp. grated orange peel
- 1/8 tsp. salt
- 5 celery ribs, cut into 1-1/2-in. pieces

1. Place apricots in a food processor. Cover and process until finely chopped. Add the ricotta cheese, brown sugar, orange peel and salt; cover and process until blended. Stuff or pipe into celery. Chill until serving.

Nutrition Facts: 1 piece equals 12 calories, trace fat (trace saturated fat), 2 mg cholesterol, 25 mg sodium, 1 g carbohydrate, trace fiber, 1 g protein. **Diabetic Exchange:** Free food.

Veggie Pinwheel Appetizers F S C M

PREP TIME: 20 min. + chilling YIELD: 32 appetizers

BEVERLY JONES • CAMBRIDGE, MARYLAND

My son, Tyler, loves these and even asked me to make them for his school party instead of cupcakes! Now his classmates love them, too, and I make them for every party.

- 1 pkg. (8 oz.) reduced-fat cream cheese
- 2 Tbsp. Vidalia onion salad dressing
- 1/2 cup finely chopped fresh broccoli
- 1/4 cup grated carrot
- 1/4 cup finely chopped red onion
- 1/2 tsp. dill weed
- 4 whole wheat tortillas (8 in.)

1. In a small bowl, beat cream cheese and salad dressing until blended. Stir in the broccoli, carrot, onion and dill weed. Spread over tortillas. Roll up tightly; wrap in plastic wrap. Refrigerate for at least 2 hours. Unwrap and cut each into eight slices.

Nutrition Facts: 1 piece equals 40 calories, 2 g fat (1 g saturated fat), 5 mg cholesterol, 56 mg sodium, 4 g carbohydrate, trace fiber, 1 g protein.

APRICOT-RICOTTA STUFFED CELERY

Have leftover tortillas? Let tortillas dry on racks until brittle, then **crumble into pieces** to use in soups or salads in place of crackers and croutons.

VEGGIE PINWHEEL APPETIZERS

Creamy Radish Dip F C M

PREP/TOTAL TIME: 10 min. YIELD: 1-1/2 cups

TERRI CHATFIELD • HAMILTON, OHIO

This Scandinavian dish is one of our favorite spring appetizers. We use homegrown onions and radishes. The best part is that the dip only calls for four ingredients! I can whip it up in no time, which is great when unexpected company drops by.

- 1 cup chopped radishes
- 1/2 cup reduced-fat sour cream
- 4 green onions, sliced
- 1/2 tsp. salt

Rye crackers

1. In a small bowl, combine the radishes, sour cream, onions and salt. Serve on crackers.

Nutrition Facts: 1/4 cup (calculated without crackers) equals 33 calories, 2 g fat (1 g saturated fat), 7 mg cholesterol, 219 mg sodium, 3 g carbohydrate, 1 g fiber, 2 g protein.

Chilly-Day Hot Cocoa Mix F S

PREP/TOTAL TIME: 15 min.
YIELD: 10 servings (2-1/2 cups hot chocolate mix)

MARIE WIERSMA • ST. JOHNS, MICHIGAN

Here's a great way to chase the chills when winter winds blow. Not only does it taste great, but the easy-to-assemble mix is a perfect gift for teachers, friends, neighbors and anyone you'd like to surprise with a gift during the holidays.

- 2 cups nonfat dry milk powder
- 6 Tbsp. baking cocoa
- 5 Tbsp. confectioners' sugar
- 5 Tbsp. sugar

EACH SERVING:
- 1/2 cup hot fat-free milk
- 1/2 cup hot water

1. In a small airtight container, combine the milk powder, cocoa, confectioners' sugar and sugar. Store in a cool dry place for up to 2 months. For each serving, place 1/4 cup mix in a mug; stir in hot milk and water until blended.

Nutrition Facts: 1 cup equals 137 calories, trace fat (trace saturated fat), 5 mg cholesterol, 127 mg sodium, 25 g carbohydrate, 1 g fiber, 10 g protein. **Diabetic Exchanges:** 1 fat-free milk, 1/2 starch.

CREAMY RADISH DIP

CHILLY-DAY HOT COCOA MIX

CRUNCHY VANILLA WALNUTS

Crunchy Vanilla Walnuts
S C M

PREP: 10 min. **BAKE:** 35 min. **YIELD:** 4-1/3 cups

GABRIELE OSBORN • RANCHO SANTA FE, CALIFORNIA

A source of omega-3s and B vitamins, walnuts are always a hit at my house. Featuring coriander, cinnamon, nutmeg and allspice, this change-of-pace version is oh-so delicious.

1/3	cup sugar
1/4	tsp. salt
1/4	tsp. ground coriander
1/4	tsp. ground cinnamon
1/4	tsp. ground nutmeg
1/4	tsp. ground allspice
1/8	tsp. pepper
4	cups walnut halves
2	Tbsp. canola oil
1	tsp. vanilla extract

1. In a small bowl, combine the first seven ingredients; set aside. In a large bowl, combine the walnuts, oil and vanilla. Add sugar mixture; toss to coat.

2. Transfer walnuts to a 15-in. x 10-in. x 1-in. foil-lined baking pan coated with cooking spray. Bake at 325° for 35 minutes, stirring occasionally. Cool completely. Store in an airtight container.

Nutrition Facts: 1/3 cup equals 243 calories, 22 g fat (2 g saturated fat), 0 cholesterol, 46 mg sodium, 10 g carbohydrate, 2 g fiber, 5 g protein.

Makeover Nutty Monkey Malts **F**

PREP/TOTAL TIME: 5 min. **YIELD:** 5 servings

HEALTHY COOKING TEST KITCHEN

Say goodbye to guilt with this no-fuss take on an all-time favorite. You can get all the flavor of a classic diner milk shake with only a fraction of the calories and fat if you follow this recipe. Flavored with peanut butter and bananas, it's one treat that kids of all ages will go crazy for!

1/4	cup fat-free milk
1	small banana, cut into chunks
1/4	cup chocolate malted milk powder
2	Tbsp. reduced-fat creamy peanut butter
2	cups fat-free frozen chocolate yogurt

Whipped cream, optional

1. In a blender, combine the milk, banana, malted milk powder and peanut butter. Cover and process for 10 seconds or until smooth. Add frozen yogurt. Cover and process 10 seconds longer or until blended. Stir if necessary. Pour into chilled glasses; garnish with whipped cream if desired. Serve immediately.

Nutrition Facts: 1/2 cup (calculated without whipped cream) equals 203 calories, 3 g fat (1 g saturated fat), 1 mg cholesterol, 190 mg sodium, 39 g carbohydrate, 3 g fiber, 8 g protein.

Chocolate Cheesecakes [S] [C]

PREP: 15 min. **BAKE:** 10 min. + chilling **YIELD:** 2 dozen

SHARON VALENTA • WESTCHESTER, ILLINOIS

Try this bite-sized chocolaty treat that's rich, creamy and guaranteed to satisfy any sweet tooth.

24	miniature vanilla wafers *or* gingersnap cookies
1	pkg. (8 oz.) reduced-fat cream cheese

Sugar substitute equivalent to 1/2 cup sugar

1/2	cup semisweet chocolate chips, melted and cooled
1	tsp. vanilla extract
1	egg, lightly beaten
1/3	cup heavy whipping cream
4	tsp. confectioners' sugar

Chocolate curls, optional

1. Place wafers flat side down in paper-lined miniature muffin cups; set aside.

2. In a small bowl, beat cream cheese and sugar substitute until smooth. Add chocolate chips and vanilla; mix well. Add egg; beat on low speed just until combined. Spoon about 1 Tbsp. into each cup.

3. Bake at 350° for 10-12 minutes or just until set. Cool completely on a wire rack. Cover and refrigerate for 1 hour.

4. In a small bowl, beat cream until it begins to thicken. Add confectioners' sugar; beat until stiff peaks form. Top cheesecakes with whipped cream mixture; garnish with chocolate curls if desired.

Nutrition Facts: 1 cheesecake (calculated without chocolate curls) equals 65 calories, 5 g fat (3 g saturated fat), 20 mg cholesterol, 50 mg sodium, 5 g carbohydrate, trace fiber, 2 g protein. **Diabetic Exchange:** 1 fat.

Buttermilk Dill Dip F C M

PREP/TOTAL TIME: 15 min. **YIELD:** 1 cup

BETSY KING • DULUTH, MINNESOTA

This light, flavorful dip provides protein and perks up fresh sliced veggies in a hurry.

- 1/2 cup buttermilk
- 4 oz. fat-free cream cheese
- 3 green onions, finely chopped
- 1/4 cup finely chopped green pepper
- 3 Tbsp. snipped fresh dill *or* 1 Tbsp. dill weed
- 4-1/2 tsp. horseradish sauce
- 1/8 tsp. garlic powder
- Assorted fresh vegetables

1. In a small bowl, beat buttermilk and cream cheese until blended. Stir in the onions, pepper, dill, horseradish sauce and garlic powder. Chill until serving. Serve with vegetables.

Nutrition Facts: 1/4 cup (calculated without vegetables) equals 68 calories, 2 g fat (trace saturated fat), 9 mg cholesterol, 228 mg sodium, 6 g carbohydrate, trace fiber, 5 g protein. **Diabetic Exchanges:** 1/2 starch, 1/2 fat.

Party Shrimp F S C

PREP: 15 min. + marinating **BROIL:** 10 min.
YIELD: 2-1/2 dozen

KENDRA DOSS • KANSAS CITY, MISSOURI

This is such a flavorful appetizer, you won't need a dipping sauce. Even those who claim they don't like shellfish rave about these shrimp. It's such an easy recipe, and I enjoy serving it at all sorts of parties and get-togethers.

- 1 Tbsp. olive oil
- 1-1/2 tsp. brown sugar
- 1-1/2 tsp. lemon juice
- 1 garlic clove, thinly sliced
- 1/2 tsp. paprika
- 1/2 tsp. Italian seasoning
- 1/2 tsp. dried basil
- 1/4 tsp. pepper
- 1 lb. uncooked large shrimp, peeled and deveined

1. In a large resealable plastic bag, combine the first eight ingredients. Add the shrimp; seal bag and turn to coat. Refrigerate for 2 hours. Drain and discard marinade.

2. Place shrimp on an ungreased baking sheet. Broil 4 in. from the heat for 6-8 minutes or until shrimp turn pink, turning once.

Nutrition Facts: 1 shrimp equals 14 calories, trace fat (trace saturated fat), 18 mg cholesterol, 18 mg sodium, trace carbohydrate, trace fiber, 2 g protein. **Diabetic Exchange:** Free food.

> Uncooked shrimp will have shells that range in color from gray to pink. Fresh shrimp should have a **firm texture** with a mild aroma.

PARTY SHRIMP

BUTTERMILK DILL DIP

Cinnamon Granola Bars ⓢ

PREP: 15 min. BAKE: 15 min. + cooling YIELD: 1 dozen

JESSICA VANLANINGHAM • COCKEYSVILLE, MARYLAND

I make these at least once a week for my husband, David. He takes one in his lunch every week and never gets tired of them. I love providing him with something so healthy to munch on that doesn't taste low-fat.

- 1/4 cup butter, softened
- 1 cup packed brown sugar
- 1 egg
- 2 Tbsp. ground flaxseed
- 2 Tbsp. honey
- 2 cups old-fashioned oats
- 1 cup all-purpose flour
- 1 tsp. ground cinnamon
- 1/2 tsp. baking soda
- 1/2 cup raisins

1. In a large bowl, beat butter and brown sugar until crumbly, about 2 minutes. Add egg; beat well. Stir in flax and honey. In a small bowl, combine the oats, flour, cinnamon and baking soda; stir into creamed mixture just until blended. Gently stir in raisins.

2. Press into an 11-in. x 7-in. baking dish coated with cooking spray. Bake at 350° for 14-18 minutes or until set and edges are lightly browned. Cool on a wire rack. Cut into bars.

Nutrition Facts: 1 bar equals 231 calories, 6 g fat (3 g saturated fat), 28 mg cholesterol, 94 mg sodium, 43 g carbohydrate, 2 g fiber, 4 g protein.

CINNAMON GRANOLA BARS

Frappe Mocha

PREP: 5 min. + freezing YIELD: 2 servings

BEVERLY COYDE • GASPORT, NEW YORK

Using coffee ice cubes adds body to this refreshing drink. What a treat!

- 1 tsp. instant coffee granules
- 1/4 cup boiling water
- 1 cup milk
- 4-1/2 tsp. chocolate syrup
- 1/2 cup crushed ice

Whipped topping and additional chocolate syrup, optional

1. In a small bowl, dissolve coffee granules in water. Pour into an ice cube tray; freeze.

2. In a blender, combine the milk, chocolate syrup and coffee ice cubes. Cover and process until smooth. Add crushed ice; blend. Pour into chilled glasses; serve immediately. Garnish with whipped topping and additional chocolate syrup if desired.

Nutrition Facts: 1 cup (calculated without garnishes) equals 114 calories, 4 g fat (3 g saturated fat), 17 mg cholesterol, 67 mg sodium, 15 g carbohydrate, trace fiber, 4 g protein.

Orange Fruit Cups Ⓕ Ⓢ Ⓜ

PREP/TOTAL TIME: 20 min. YIELD: 4 servings

SUSAN WIENER • SPRING HILL, FLORIDA

This is always a favorite with children who come to visit. It's a wonderful snack that is healthy, fast and easy to make.

- 2 medium navel oranges, halved
- 1 small apple, chopped
- 1 small banana, sliced
- 1/4 cup plain yogurt
- 1/4 tsp. ground cinnamon

Additional ground cinnamon, optional

ORANGE FRUIT CUPS

1. Using a paring or grapefruit knife and spoon, scoop out pulp from oranges, leaving a shell. Separate orange sections and chop; transfer to a small bowl.

2. Add the apple, banana, yogurt and cinnamon. Fill orange shells with fruit mixture. Sprinkle with additional cinnamon if desired. Serve immediately.

Nutrition Facts: 1/2 cup fruit equals 80 calories, 1 g fat (trace saturated fat), 2 mg cholesterol, 8 mg sodium, 19 g carbohydrate, 3 g fiber, 2 g protein. **Diabetic Exchange:** 1 fruit.

Parmesan Popcorn F C M

PREP/TOTAL TIME: 10 min. YIELD: 2 qts.

BETSY KING • DULUTH, MINNESOTA

Give popcorn a new twist with this fun and tasty recipe. It's great for watching movies or as an on-the-go snack. Kids and adults alike are sure to gobble it up.

    8 cups air-popped popcorn
    2 Tbsp. reduced-fat butter, melted
    2 Tbsp. grated Parmesan cheese

    1/4 tsp. salt
    1/4 tsp. dried oregano
    1/8 tsp. garlic salt

1. Place popcorn in a large bowl. Drizzle with butter. Combine the remaining ingredients; sprinkle over popcorn and toss to coat.

Nutrition Facts: 1 cup equals 49 calories, 2 g fat (1 g saturated fat), 5 mg cholesterol, 146 mg sodium, 7 g carbohydrate, 1 g fiber, 2 g protein. **Diabetic Exchange:** 1/2 starch.

When making a popcorn treat, remember that 1 cup of unpopped kernels equals about 8 cups of popped popcorn. Don't **pre-salt the kernels** before popping as this can toughen the popcorn.

STARTERS & SNACKS   33

SPINACH CHEESE TRIANGLES

Spinach Cheese Triangles F S C M

PREP: 40 min. BAKE: 10 min. YIELD: 4 dozen

SHERRI MELOTIK • OAK CREEK, WISCONSIN

Filled with three kinds of cheese and lots of spinach, these light little bites pack a delectable punch. Friends and family will think you fussed, but these starters come together quickly, making them perfect for hurried holidays.

1/3	cup finely chopped onion
1	Tbsp. butter
1	pkg. (10 oz.) frozen chopped spinach, thawed and squeezed dry
1	cup grated Parmesan cheese
3/4	cup shredded part-skim mozzarella cheese
3	Tbsp. crumbled feta cheese
2	eggs, lightly beaten
2	Tbsp. soft bread crumbs
1/4	tsp. salt
1/4	tsp. pepper
12	sheets phyllo dough (14 in. x 9 in.)

Butter-flavored cooking spray

1. In a large skillet, saute onion in butter until tender. Stir in spinach; cook over medium-low heat just until spinach is wilted. Transfer to a large bowl; add the cheeses, eggs, bread crumbs, salt and pepper. Set aside.

2. Place one sheet of phyllo dough on a work surface with a long side facing you. (Keep remaining phyllo covered with plastic wrap to prevent it from drying out.) Spray sheet with butter-flavored spray; cut into four 9-in. x 3-1/2-in. strips.

3. Place 1 Tbsp. filling on lower corner of each strip. Fold dough over filling, forming a triangle. Fold triangle up, then fold triangle over, forming another triangle. Continue folding, like a flag, until you come to the end of the strip.

4. Spritz end of dough with cooking spray and press onto triangle to seal. Turn triangle and spritz top with spray. Repeat with remaining phyllo and filling.

5. Place triangles on baking sheets coated with cooking spray. Bake at 375° for 10-12 minutes or until golden brown.

Nutrition Facts: 1 appetizer equals 30 calories, 2 g fat (1 g saturated fat), 12 mg cholesterol, 71 mg sodium, 2 g carbohydrate, trace fiber, 2 g protein.

Cucumber Punch F S C

PREP: 10 min. + chilling
YIELD: 25 servings (4-3/4 qt.)

RENEE OLSON • KENDRICK, IDAHO

I first tasted this at a ladies' luncheon, and it was the most unique and refreshing drink I'd ever had. I've served it numerous times since and always get requests for the recipe.

- 2 medium cucumbers
- 3 cups water
- 1 can (12 oz.) frozen lemonade concentrate, thawed
- 2 liters diet ginger ale, chilled
- 4-1/2 cups diet grapefruit *or* citrus soda, chilled

1. With a zester or fork, score cucumbers lengthwise; cut widthwise into thin slices. In a large pitcher, combine water and lemonade concentrate; add cucumbers. Cover and refrigerate overnight.

2. Just before serving, transfer cucumber mixture to a punch bowl; stir in ginger ale and grapefruit soda.

Nutrition Facts: 3/4 cup equals 29 calories, trace fat (trace saturated fat), 0 cholesterol, 15 mg sodium, 7 g carbohydrate, trace fiber, trace protein. **Diabetic Exchange:** 1/2 starch.

Broccoli Fritters C M

PREP: 20 min. **COOK:** 10 min./batch **YIELD:** 6 servings

TRACY EUBANKS • EWING, KENTUCKY

These cute cakes offer a fun and kid-friendly way to use up broccoli. They're tasty as a side dish paired with any meat, or you can serve them with salsa and a dollop of fat-free sour cream for a festive appetizer.

- 1 bunch broccoli, cut into florets
- 2 eggs, lightly beaten
- 2 egg whites, lightly beaten
- 1/3 cup grated Parmesan cheese
- 2 Tbsp. all-purpose flour
- 1/2 tsp. salt
- 1/2 tsp. garlic powder
- 1/2 tsp. pepper
- 2 Tbsp. canola oil

Salsa, optional

1. Place broccoli in a steamer basket; place in a small saucepan over 1 in. of water. Bring to a boil; cover and steam for 3-4 minutes or until crisp-tender. Coarsely chop broccoli and set aside.

2. In a large bowl, combine the eggs, egg whites, cheese, flour, salt, garlic powder and pepper. Stir in the broccoli.

3. Heat 1 Tbsp. oil in a large nonstick skillet over medium heat. Drop batter by 2 heaping tablespoonfuls into oil; press lightly to flatten. Cook in batches for 3-4 minutes on each side or until golden brown, using remaining oil as needed. Drain on paper towels. Serve with salsa if desired.

Nutrition Facts: 2 fritters (calculated without salsa) equal 129 calories, 8 g fat (2 g saturated fat), 74 mg cholesterol, 334 mg sodium, 8 g carbohydrate, 3 g fiber, 8 g protein. **Diabetic Exchanges:** 1 medium-fat meat, 1 vegetable, 1 fat.

CUCUMBER PUNCH

BROCCOLI FRITTERS

Antipasto Kabobs F C

PREP: 30 min. + marinating YIELD: 12 kabobs

KENDRA DOSS • KANSAS CITY, MISSOURI

This is one elegant, easy recipe people really seem to like at every party. I found a marinade recipe that wasn't so heavy on olive oil and modified it to my taste. The kabobs are a snap to assemble. You don't even need to turn on the oven.

- 1 cup refrigerated cheese tortellini
- 1/2 cup balsamic vinegar
- 1/4 cup grated Parmesan cheese
- 1/4 cup minced fresh basil
- 2 Tbsp. Dijon mustard
- 1 Tbsp. olive oil
- 2 tsp. honey
- 1/4 tsp. pepper
- 1 can (14 oz.) water-packed artichoke hearts, rinsed and drained
- 1 large green pepper, cut into 1-in. pieces
- 1 cup grape tomatoes
- 1 cup pitted ripe olives
- 1/4 lb. thinly sliced deli ham, cut into 1-in. strips
- 12 wooden skewers (6 in.)

1. Cook tortellini according to package directions.

2. Meanwhile, in a large resealable plastic bag, combine the vinegar, cheese, basil, mustard, oil, honey and pepper. Add the artichokes, green pepper, tomatoes, olives and ham. Drain and rinse tortellini in cold water; add to bag. Seal bag and turn to coat. Refrigerate for 4 hours or overnight.

3. Drain and discard marinade. For each kabob, thread tortellini, artichokes, green pepper, tomatoes, olives and folded ham onto a skewer.

Nutrition Facts: 1 kabob equals 90 calories, 3 g fat (1 g saturated fat), 9 mg cholesterol, 356 mg sodium, 11 g carbohydrate, 1 g fiber, 5 g protein.

Presto Chocolate Dessert Dip F S

PREP/TOTAL TIME: 10 min. YIELD: 1/2 cup

KAREN OWEN • RISING SUN, INDIANA

This fun and fancy dessert dip is ideal for special occasions and doubles nicely for get-togethers with friends. But it tastes so wonderful, you'll have a hard time sharing it at all!

- 1/4 cup reduced-fat sour cream
- 2 Tbsp. honey
- 2 Tbsp. baking cocoa
- 1/4 tsp. vanilla extract

Assorted fresh fruit *and/or* cubed angel food cake

1. In a small bowl, combine the sour cream, honey, cocoa and vanilla. Cover and refrigerate until serving. Serve with fruit and/or cake.

Nutrition Facts: 1/4 cup (calculated without fruit and cake) equals 121 calories, 3 g fat (2 g saturated fat), 10 mg cholesterol, 21 mg sodium, 22 g carbohydrate, 1 g fiber, 3 g protein. **Diabetic Exchanges:** 1-1/2 starch, 1/2 fat.

ANTIPASTO KABOBS

PRESTO CHOCOLATE DESSERT DIP

IRRESISTIBLE GRILLED SHRIMP WITH FRUIT SALSA

Irresistible Grilled Shrimp with Fruit Salsa F C

PREP: 20 min. + marinating GRILL: 5 min.
YIELD: 8 servings (1-1/4 cups salsa)

AGNES WARD • STRATFORD, ONTARIO

These skewers are super lean and scrumptious—especially when dipped in the fresh fruit salsa. My guests rave about the salsa's sweet heat and the shrimp's party-pretty look.

3 Tbsp. reduced-sodium soy sauce
2 Tbsp. brown sugar
2 Tbsp. lime juice
1 Tbsp. olive oil
1 Tbsp. ketchup
2 garlic cloves, minced
1 tsp. ground coriander
1/2 tsp. ground cumin
1 lb. uncooked large shrimp, peeled and deveined

FRUIT SALSA:
1 medium tart apple, peeled and cut into wedges
3/4 cup orange segments

2 Tbsp. lime juice
2 green onions, cut into 2-in. pieces
1 Tbsp. minced fresh mint *or* 1 tsp. dried mint
1 tsp. sugar
1/2 tsp. crushed red pepper flakes

1. In a large resealable plastic bag, combine the first eight ingredients. Add the shrimp; seal bag and turn to coat. Refrigerate for 30 minutes.

2. Meanwhile, place salsa ingredients in a food processor; cover and process until finely chopped. Transfer to a small bowl. Chill until serving.

3. Drain and discard marinade. Using long-handled tongs, moisten a paper towel with cooking oil and lightly coat the grill rack. Thread shrimp onto three metal or soaked wooden skewers. Grill shrimp, covered, over medium heat or broil 4 in. from the heat for 5-8 minutes or until shrimp turn pink, turning once. Serve with salsa.

Nutrition Facts: 3 shrimp with about 2 Tbsp. salsa equals 78 calories, 1 g fat (trace saturated fat), 69 mg cholesterol, 150 mg sodium, 7 g carbohydrate, 1 g fiber, 10 g protein. **Diabetic Exchanges:** 1 lean meat, 1/2 starch.

CRISPY CARIBBEAN VEGGIE WRAPS

Crispy Caribbean Veggie Wraps F C M

PREP: 40 min. **BAKE:** 15 min. **YIELD:** 22 appetizers

MARY BETH HARRIS-MURPHREE • TYLER, TEXAS

Filled with a sweet potato mixture, these delicious wraps are great for vegetarians, and they're relatively high in fiber, too. Served with salsa, they are sure to disappear from appetizer trays fast.

1	medium sweet potato
1/2	cup canned black beans, rinsed and drained
1/4	cup chopped red onion
2	Tbsp. minced fresh cilantro
1	Tbsp. lime juice
1	tsp. salt
1	tsp. ground cumin
1	tsp. chopped jalapeno pepper
1	garlic clove, minced
22	wonton wrappers

Cooking spray

1-1/2 cups salsa

1. Scrub and pierce sweet potato; place on a microwave-safe plate. Microwave, uncovered, on high for 12-14 minutes or until tender, turning once. When cool enough to handle, cut the potato in half. Scoop out the pulp discarding shell; place pulp in a small bowl and mash. Stir in the beans, onion, cilantro, lime juice, salt, cumin, jalapeno and garlic.

2. Lightly brush water over all four edges of one wonton wrapper. (Keep remaining wrappers covered with a damp paper towel until ready to use.) Spread 1 Tbsp. filling along one edge of wrapper; roll up tightly. Repeat with remaining wrappers and filling.

3. Place seam side down on a baking sheet coated with cooking spray. Lightly spritz wraps with cooking spray. Bake at 375° for 15 minutes or until golden brown. Serve warm with salsa.

Editor's Note: This recipe was tested in a 1,100-watt microwave. When cutting hot peppers, disposable gloves are recommended. Avoid touching your face.

Nutrition Facts: 1 wrap with about 1 Tbsp. salsa equals 42 calories, trace fat (trace saturated fat), 1 mg cholesterol, 230 mg sodium, 8 g carbohydrate, 1 g fiber, 1 g protein. **Diabetic Exchange:** 1/2 starch.

Chocolate Zucchini Snack Cake

PREP: 20 min. **BAKE:** 30 min. + cooling
YIELD: 18 servings

MARGO SEEGRIST • SHELTON, WASHINGTON

I like to make this when the zucchini in my garden gets ahead of me. It's a great way to get children to eat their veggies because, after all, who doesn't like a bite of decadent chocolate cake? The next time you give some zucchini to a friend, considering handing them this recipe, too!

1/3	cup butter, softened
1-1/4	cups sugar
2	eggs
1/2	cup buttermilk
1/3	cup unsweetened applesauce
2	oz. semisweet chocolate, melted
1	tsp. vanilla extract
2-1/4	cups all-purpose flour
1-1/2	tsp. baking powder
1	tsp. salt
1/4	tsp. baking soda
2	cups shredded zucchini
2	tsp. confectioners' sugar

1. In a large bowl, beat butter and sugar until crumbly, about 2 minutes. Add eggs; mix well. Beat in the buttermilk, applesauce, chocolate and vanilla. Combine the flour, baking powder, salt and baking soda; beat into butter mixture just until moistened. Stir in zucchini.

2. Transfer to a 13-in. x 9-in. baking dish coated with cooking spray. Bake at 350° for 30-35 minutes or until a toothpick inserted near the center comes out clean. Cool on a wire rack. Sprinkle with confectioners' sugar.

Nutrition Facts: 1 piece equals 172 calories, 5 g fat (3 g saturated fat), 33 mg cholesterol, 223 mg sodium, 29 g carbohydrate, 1 g fiber, 3 g protein. **Diabetic Exchanges:** 2 starch, 1 fat.

Makeover Hot Pizza Dip

PREP/TOTAL TIME: 25 min. **YIELD:** about 4 cups

TRISHA KRUSE • EAGLE, IDAHO

This standout makeover from the Healthy Cooking Test Kitchen has less than half the saturated fat and way fewer calories than the original recipe. It's hard to believe it's light. I promise it will be a hit at your next gathering!

1	pkg. (8 oz.) fat-free cream cheese
1-1/2	tsp. Italian seasoning
1	cup (4 oz.) shredded part-skim mozzarella cheese, *divided*
1/2	cup grated Parmigiano-Reggiano cheese, *divided*
1	small sweet red pepper, chopped
1/4	cup chopped sweet onion
1	tsp. olive oil
1	garlic clove, minced
1	can (8 oz.) pizza sauce
4	oz. sliced turkey pepperoni, chopped
1	can (2-1/4 oz.) sliced ripe olives, drained
1	French bread baguette (10-1/2 oz.), cut into 1/4-in. slices, toasted

1. In a small bowl, beat cream cheese and Italian seasoning until smooth; spread into a 9-in. microwave-safe pie plate. Sprinkle with 1/2 cup mozzarella cheese and 1/4 cup Parmigiano-Reggiano cheese.

2. In a small nonstick skillet, saute pepper and onion in oil until tender. Add garlic; cook 1 minute longer. Spoon over cheeses. Spread pizza sauce over pepper mixture. Sprinkle with remaining cheeses, pepperoni and olives.

3. Microwave, uncovered, at 70% power for 5-7 minutes or until cheese is melted. Serve with toasted baguette slices.

Editor's Note: This recipe was tested in a 1,100-watt microwave.

Nutrition Facts: 1/4 cup dip with 4 baguette slices equals 154 calories, 6 g fat (2 g saturated fat), 16 mg cholesterol, 466 mg sodium, 17 g carbohydrate, 2 g fiber, 9 g protein.

> If you don't have any **Italian seasoning** on hand, simply blend together 1/4 teaspoon each of dried basil, thyme, rosemary and oregano for every teaspoon of Italian seasoning called for in a recipe.

MAKEOVER HOT PIZZA DIP

Phyllo Fruit Tart M

PREP: 15 min. **BAKE:** 5 min. + cooling **YIELD:** 8 servings

HEALTHY COOKING TEST KITCHEN

Always impressive on a buffet table, this elegant treat tastes as fantastic as it looks. Try it for a bridal shower or ladies' lunch. You can also try it with a wonderful topping of mixed berries.

- 1 Tbsp. butter, melted
- 1 Tbsp. canola oil
- 8 sheets phyllo dough (14 in. x 9 in.)
- 1 pkg. (8 oz.) fat-free cream cheese
- 3 Tbsp. confectioners' sugar
- 1 cup reduced-fat whipped topping
- 1 can (11 oz.) mandarin oranges, drained
- 4 kiwifruit, peeled and sliced
- 1-1/2 cups sliced fresh strawberries
- 1 oz. white baking chocolate, melted

1. In a small bowl, combine butter and oil. Place one sheet of phyllo dough on a work surface; brush evenly with butter-oil mixture. Repeat with seven more sheets of phyllo, brushing each layer and stacking on previous sheet. (Keep remaining phyllo dough covered with waxed paper to prevent it from drying out.)

2. Place phyllo dough on a baking sheet. Bake at 400° for 5-7 minutes or until golden. Cool on a wire rack.

3. In a small bowl, beat cream cheese and confectioners' sugar until smooth; fold in whipped topping. Gently spread over cooled crust. Arrange fruits over cream cheese layer; drizzle with chocolate.

Nutrition Facts: 1 piece equals 183 calories, 6 g fat (3 g saturated fat), 7 mg cholesterol, 222 mg sodium, 26 g carbohydrate, 3 g fiber, 6 g protein. **Diabetic Exchanges:** 1 starch, 1 fat, 1/2 fruit.

Spicy Chunky Salsa F S C M

PREP: 1-1/2 hours **PROCESS:** 15 min./batch
YIELD: 8 pints

DONNA GOUTERMONT • JUNEAU, ALASKA

Here's a delectable way to use up a summer bounty of garden-fresh tomatoes, onions, peppers and cilantro. Vinegar adds delightful tang to this sweet salsa. You'll love its flavor, but for more heat, leave in some of the hot pepper seeds.

- 6 lbs. tomatoes
- 3 large green peppers, chopped
- 3 large onions, chopped
- 2 cups white vinegar
- 1 large sweet red pepper, chopped
- 1 can (12 oz.) tomato paste
- 4 jalapeno peppers, seeded and chopped
- 2 serrano peppers, seeded and chopped
- 1/2 cup sugar
- 1/2 cup minced fresh cilantro
- 1/2 cup bottled lemon juice
- 3 garlic cloves, minced
- 4 tsp. ground cumin
- 3 tsp. salt
- 2 tsp. dried oregano
- 1 tsp. hot pepper sauce

1. In a large saucepan, bring 8 cups water to a boil. Using a slotted spoon, place tomatoes, a few at a time, in boiling water for 30-60 seconds. Remove each tomato and immediately plunge into ice water. Drain and pat dry. Peel and finely chop tomatoes to measure 9 cups. In a stockpot, combine the tomatoes and remaining ingredients. Bring to a boil. Reduce heat; simmer, uncovered, for 30 minutes or until slightly thickened.

2. Carefully ladle hot mixture into hot 1-pint jars, leaving 1/2-in. headspace. Remove air bubbles; wipe rims and adjust lids. Process for 15 minutes in a boiling-water canner.

Editor's Note: When cutting hot peppers, disposable gloves are recommended. Avoid touching your face. The processing time listed is for altitudes of 1,000 feet or less. For altitudes up to 3,000 feet, add 5 minutes; 6,000 feet, add 10 minutes; 8,000 feet, add 15 minutes; 10,000 feet, add 20 minutes.

Nutrition Facts: 1/4 cup equals 25 calories, trace fat (trace saturated fat), 0 cholesterol, 117 mg sodium, 6 g carbohydrate, 1 g fiber, 1 g protein. **Diabetic Exchange:** 1/2 starch.

PHYLLO FRUIT TART

Roasted Vegetable Dip F S C M

PREP: 15 min. **BAKE:** 25 min. + cooling
YIELD: 2-1/2 cups

SARAH VASQUES • MILFORD, NEW HAMPSHIRE

Roasting brings out the best flavor in red pepper, onion and zucchini, making this appetizer a great way to use your garden bounty. Blended with cream cheese, the vegetables make a delicious dip perfect on crackers. You can even try it as a spread on lean turkey sandwiches.

- 2 large sweet red peppers, cut into 1-in. pieces
- 1 large zucchini, cut into 1-in. pieces
- 1 medium onion, cut into 1-in. pieces
- 1 Tbsp. olive oil
- 1/2 tsp. salt
- 1/4 tsp. pepper
- 1 pkg. (8 oz.) reduced-fat cream cheese
  Assorted crackers

1. Place the red peppers, zucchini and onion in a 15-in. x 10-in. x 1-in. baking pan coated with cooking spray. Combine the olive oil, salt and pepper; drizzle over vegetables and toss to coat. Bake, uncovered, at 425° for 25-30 minutes or until tender, stirring occasionally. Cool to room temperature.

2. Place cream cheese and vegetables in a food processor; cover and process until blended. Chill until serving. Serve with crackers.

Nutrition Facts: 2 Tbsp. (calculated without crackers) equals 44 calories, 3 g fat (2 g saturated fat), 8 mg cholesterol, 110 mg sodium, 3 g carbohydrate, 1 g fiber, 2 g protein.

Maple-Glazed Snack Mix M

PREP: 10 min. **BAKE:** 45 min. + cooling
YIELD: 7-1/2 cups

CYNTHIA NORRIS • WINNETKA, CALIFORNIA

I haven't met a kid who doesn't love this mix! My three children especially enjoy it for snacks during the school year.

- 2 cups Corn Chex
- 2 cups Rice Chex
- 2 cups Honey-Nut Cheerios
- 1 cup miniature pretzels
- 1/2 cup pecan halves, coarsely chopped
- 1/3 cup maple syrup
- 1 Tbsp. butter
- 1 tsp. vanilla extract

1. In a large bowl, combine the cereals, pretzels and pecans. In a small microwave-safe dish, combine maple syrup and butter. Cover and microwave on high for 45 seconds or until butter is melted. Stir in vanilla. Pour over cereal mixture and toss to coat.

2. Transfer to a 15-in. x 10-in. x 1-in. baking pan coated with cooking spray. Bake at 250° for 45 minutes, stirring every 15 minutes. Cool on a wire rack. Store in an airtight container.

Editor's Note: This recipe was tested in a 1,100-watt microwave.

Nutrition Facts: 1/2 cup equals 104 calories, 4 g fat (1 g saturated fat), 2 mg cholesterol, 141 mg sodium, 17 g carbohydrate, 1 g fiber, 2 g protein. **Diabetic Exchanges:** 1 starch, 1/2 fat.

ON-THE-GO SNACK MIX

On-the-Go Snack Mix S M

PREP/TOTAL TIME: 10 min. YIELD: 7 cups

LEAH FIRESTONE • SCOTTDALE, PENNSYLVANIA

Since there's no baking required, this savory snack mix is really a simple treat to make. Plus, it's also healthy and tasty. If you want a snack that delivers protein and a few vitamins and minerals, this will do it.

3	cups Wheat Chex
1/2	cup blanched almonds
1/2	cup unsalted peanuts
1/2	cup lightly salted cashews
1/2	cup chopped pecans
1/2	cup fat-free miniature pretzels
1/2	cup raisins
1/2	cup milk chocolate M&M's
1/4	cup dried banana chips
1/4	cup dried cranberries

1. In a large bowl, combine all ingredients. Store in an airtight container.

Nutrition Facts: 1/2 cup equals 217 calories, 13 g fat (3 g saturated fat), 1 mg cholesterol, 93 mg sodium, 23 g carbohydrate, 3 g fiber, 5 g protein.

Garlic Artichoke Dip F C M

PREP: 25 min. + chilling YIELD: 2-1/2 cups

LISA VARNER • CHARLESTON, SOUTH CAROLINA

This chilled dip is quite delicious, lower in fat and offers almost effortless and time-saving preparation.

1	large onion, chopped
1/2	tsp. dried oregano
1/2	tsp. dried thyme
2	Tbsp. olive oil
5	garlic cloves, minced
1	can (15 oz.) white kidney *or* cannellini beans, rinsed and drained
1	can (14 oz.) water-packed artichoke hearts, rinsed and drained
1	Tbsp. lemon juice
1/2	tsp. salt
1/8	tsp. cayenne pepper

Assorted fresh vegetables *and/or* baked pita chips

1. In a small nonstick skillet, saute the onion, oregano and thyme in oil until onion is tender. Add garlic; cook 1 minute longer. Remove from the heat; cool slightly.

2. In a food processor, combine the beans, artichokes, lemon juice, salt, cayenne and onion mixture; cover and process until pureed.

3. Transfer to a small bowl. Cover and refrigerate at least 2 hours before serving. Serve with vegetables and/or pita chips.

Nutrition Facts: 1/4 cup (calculated without vegetables and chips) equals 81 calories, 3 g fat (trace saturated fat), 0 cholesterol, 271 mg sodium, 11 g carbohydrate, 2 g fiber, 3 g protein. **Diabetic Exchanges:** 1 vegetable, 1/2 starch, 1/2 fat.

Smoked Salmon Cucumber Canapes F S C

PREP: 25 min. + chilling YIELD: about 3-1/2 dozen

JUDY GREBETZ • RACINE, WISCONSIN

This is one appetizer I'm always asked to bring to parties. It's make-ahead convenient, pretty and a winner.

    2 medium cucumbers, peeled
    4 oz. smoked salmon, flaked
    2 Tbsp. lemon juice
    1 Tbsp. finely chopped onion
    1 Tbsp. capers, drained
    1 Tbsp. minced fresh parsley
  1/2 tsp. Dijon mustard
  1/8 tsp. pepper

1. Cut cucumbers in half lengthwise; remove and discard seeds. In a small bowl, combine the remaining ingredients. Spoon into cucumber halves.

2. Wrap in plastic wrap. Refrigerate for 3-4 hours or until filling is firm. Cut into 1/2-in. slices.

Nutrition Facts: 1 canape equals 6 calories, trace fat (trace saturated fat), 1 mg cholesterol, 27 mg sodium, 1 g carbohydrate, trace fiber, 1 g protein. **Diabetic Exchange:** Free food.

Lime Cilantro Hummus C M

PREP/TOTAL TIME: 20 min. YIELD: 3 cups

KIMBERLY GRUSENDORF • MEDINA, OHIO

Enjoy this fun dip with crackers or veggies or on your favorite sandwich or burger. To make it smoother, add a bit more olive oil. If you prefer a more rustic texture, decrease the oil a little.

      2 cans (15 oz.) garbanzo beans or chickpeas, rinsed and drained
      1 cup coarsely chopped cilantro leaves
    1/2 cup lime juice
    1/4 cup water
      3 Tbsp. olive oil
      4 garlic cloves, halved
  1-1/2 tsp. grated lime peel
      1 tsp. garlic salt
    1/2 tsp. cayenne pepper
Assorted fresh vegetables *or* crackers

1. In a food processor, combine garbanzo beans, cilantro, lime juice, water, oil, garlic, lime peel, garlic salt and cayenne; cover and process until blended. Serve with vegetables or crackers.

Nutrition Facts: 1/4 cup (calculated without vegetables or crackers) equals 100 calories, 5 g fat (trace saturated fat), 0 cholesterol, 244 mg sodium, 12 g carbohydrate, 3 g fiber, 3 g protein. **Diabetic Exchanges:** 1 starch, 1 fat.

LIME CILANTRO HUMMUS

SMOKED SALMON CUCUMBER CANAPES

MEXICAN CHICKEN MEATBALLS

Mexican Chicken Meatballs
F S C

PREP: 20 min. BAKE: 15 min. YIELD: 5 dozen

KATRINA LOPES • LYMAN, SOUTH CAROLINA

These low-fat meatballs taste fabulous on their own, but if you want to kick things up a notch, serve with a dip of melted Velveeta cheese and salsa. You could also sub in ground white turkey for chicken.

1/2	cup egg substitute
1	can (4 oz.) chopped green chilies
1	cup crushed cornflakes
1	cup (4 oz.) shredded reduced-fat Mexican cheese blend
1/2	tsp. seasoned salt
1/4	tsp. cayenne pepper
1	pkg. (1 lb.) ground chicken

Salsa, optional

1. In a large bowl, combine the first six ingredients. Crumble chicken over mixture and mix well. Shape into 1-in. balls. Place on baking sheets coated with cooking spray.

2. Bake at 375° for 12-15 minutes or until golden brown, turning occasionally. Serve with salsa if desired.

Nutrition Facts: 1 meatball (calculated without salsa) equals 21 calories, 1 g fat (trace saturated fat), 6 mg cholesterol, 49 mg sodium, 1 g carbohydrate, trace fiber, 2 g protein.

Trail Mix **S M**

PREP/TOTAL TIME: 10 min. YIELD: 4 cups

MICHAEL VYSKOCIL • GLEN ROCK, PENNSYLVANIA

This recipe is so fast and fun that the kids can help you put it together! It makes a great little present for teachers, coaches and even scout leaders.

1/2	cup unblanched whole almonds
1/2	cup coarsely chopped walnuts
1/2	cup golden raisins
1/2	cup chopped dates
1/2	cup dried apple slices, chopped
1/2	cup dried apricots, chopped
1/2	cup semisweet chocolate chips
1/2	cup Honey Nut Cheerios

1. In a large bowl, combine all ingredients. Store in an airtight container.

Nutrition Facts: 1/3 cup equals 169 calories, 8 g fat (2 g saturated fat), 0 cholesterol, 15 mg sodium, 24 g carbohydrate, 3 g fiber, 4 g protein.

Yummy S'more Snack Cake

PREP: 20 min. **BAKE:** 20 min. + cooling
YIELD: 20 servings

DEBORAH WILLIAMS • PEORIA, ARIZONA

My delicious snack cake is a close second to yummy s'mores enjoyed by the campfire.

2-1/2 cups reduced-fat graham cracker crumbs (about 15 whole crackers)
  1/2 cup sugar
  1/3 cup cake flour
  1/3 cup whole wheat flour
    2 tsp. baking powder
  1/4 tsp. salt
    3 egg whites
    1 cup light soy milk
  1/4 cup unsweetened applesauce
  1/4 cup canola oil
    2 cups miniature marshmallows
    1 cup (6 oz.) semisweet chocolate chips

1. In a large bowl, combine the first six ingredients. In a small bowl, whisk the egg whites, soy milk, applesauce and oil. Stir into dry ingredients just until moistened. Transfer to a 13-in. x 9-in. baking pan coated with cooking spray.

2. Bake at 350° for 12-15 minutes or until a toothpick inserted near the center comes out clean. Sprinkle with marshmallows. Bake 4-6 minutes longer or until marshmallows are softened. Cool cake on a wire rack for 10 minutes.

3. In a microwave, melt chocolate chips; stir until smooth. Drizzle over cake. Cool cake completely on a wire rack.

YUMMY S'MORE SNACK CAKE

Nutrition Facts: 1 piece equals 168 calories, 6 g fat (2 g saturated fat), 0 cholesterol, 159 mg sodium, 28 g carbohydrate, 2 g fiber, 3 g protein. **Diabetic Exchanges:** 2 starch, 1 fat.

Creamy Dill Dip ⒻⒸⓂ

PREP/TOTAL TIME: 10 min. + chilling **YIELD:** 1-1/3 cup

CORKY HUFFSMITH • INDIO, CALIFORNIA

Beau Monde seasoning is the secret ingredient that adds a little special zing to this low-fat, classic dill dip. It gets better after a couple of days in the fridge, so I double the recipe to be sure there's plenty left over to enjoy.

  2/3 cup fat-free mayonnaise
  2/3 cup reduced-fat sour cream
    1 Tbsp. chopped green onions
    1 Tbsp. dried parsley flakes
    2 tsp. Beau Monde seasoning
    2 tsp. dill weed
Assorted fresh vegetables

1. In a small bowl, combine the first six ingredients. Cover and refrigerate overnight. Serve with assorted fresh vegetables.

Nutrition Facts: 3 Tbsp. (calculated without vegetables) equals 49 calories, 3 g fat (1 g saturated fat), 10 mg cholesterol, 371 mg sodium, 5 g carbohydrate, 1 g fiber, 2 g protein.

"Beau Monde" is French for **"beautiful world,"** and just as its name implies, the seasoning blend is a delightful balance of onion, celery and salt. Feel free to use it with any savory dish you may be preparing.

CREAMY DILL DIP

Spiced Apple Tea F S C

PREP/TOTAL TIME: 25 min.   YIELD: 5 servings

SHARON DELANEY-CHRONIS • SOUTH MILWAUKEE, WISCONSIN

I love to try new recipes for my husband and our friends. This spiced tea is one of our favorites. I enjoy it warm, and I refrigerate and serve it cold, too.

- 2 cups unsweetened apple juice
- 6 whole cloves
- 1 cinnamon stick (3 in.)
- 3 cups water
- 5 individual tea bags

Additional cinnamon sticks (3 in.), optional

1. In a small saucepan, combine the apple juice, cloves and cinnamon stick. Bring to a boil. Reduce heat; simmer, uncovered, for 10-15 minutes.

2. Meanwhile, in a large saucepan, bring water to a boil. Remove from the heat; add tea bags. Cover and steep for 5 minutes. Discard tea bags. Strain juice mixture, discarding cloves and cinnamon. Stir into tea. Serve warm with additional cinnamon sticks for garnish if desired.

Nutrition Facts: 1 cup equals 47 calories, trace fat (trace saturated fat), 0 cholesterol, 3 mg sodium, 12 g carbohydrate, trace fiber, trace protein. **Diabetic Exchange:** 1 fruit.

Crunchy Spiced Nuts

PREP: 20 min.   BAKE: 45 min. + cooling   YIELD: 3 cups

SUZANNE WOOD • HOUSTON, TEXAS

These flavor-packed nuts provide vitamin E and omega-3 fatty acids. You'll love 'em!

- 2 egg whites
- 2 Tbsp. water
- 2 cups confectioners' sugar
- 3 Tbsp. ground cinnamon
- 2 Tbsp. ground ginger
- 1 Tbsp. ground cloves
- 2 tsp. salt
- 1 tsp. ground nutmeg
- 1 cup unblanched almonds
- 1/2 cup pecan halves
- 1/2 cup walnut halves

1. In a shallow bowl, whisk egg whites and water. Sift together the confectioners' sugar, cinnamon, ginger, cloves, salt and nutmeg; place sugar mixture in another shallow bowl. Coat nuts in egg mixture, then dip in sugar mixture.

2. Transfer to a baking sheet coated with cooking spray. Bake at 250° for 45 minutes, stirring nuts occasionally. Cool completely. Store nuts in an airtight container.

Nutrition Facts: 1/4 cup equals 182 calories, 12 g fat (1 g saturated fat), 0 cholesterol, 243 mg sodium, 17 g carbohydrate, 3 g fiber, 4 g protein.

SPICED APPLE TEA

SHRIMP WITH ORANGE PINEAPPLE SAUCE

Shrimp with Orange Pineapple Sauce F S C

PREP/TOTAL TIME: 15 min.
YIELD: about 2-1/2 dozen (2/3 cup sauce)

RADELLE KNAPPENBERGER • OVIEDO, FLORIDA

This is a light appetizer that's easy to make. I've been asked for the recipe many times. In fact, my husband even likes it as a main dish!

- 1/4 cup pineapple preserves
- 1/4 cup orange marmalade
- 1/4 cup lemon juice
- 1 Tbsp. water
- 1 tsp. cornstarch
- 1 lb. cooked medium shrimp, peeled and deveined

1. In a small saucepan, combine the first five ingredients. Bring to a boil; cook and stir for 2 minutes or until thickened. Chill until serving. Serve with shrimp.

Nutrition Facts: 1 shrimp with 1 tsp. sauce equals 29 calories, trace fat (trace saturated fat), 22 mg cholesterol, 23 mg sodium, 4 g carbohydrate, trace fiber, 3 g protein.

Easy Buffalo Chicken Dip S C

PREP/TOTAL TIME: 30 min. **YIELD:** 4 cups

JANICE FOLTZ • HERSHEY, PENNSYLVANIA

Guys of all ages will simply devour this savory and delicious dip. The spicy kick makes it perfect football-watching food. It always brings raves. Serve it with crackers or even celery sticks.

- 1 pkg. (8 oz.) reduced-fat cream cheese
- 1 cup (8 oz.) reduced-fat sour cream
- 1/2 cup Louisiana-style hot sauce
- 3 cups shredded cooked chicken breast
Assorted crackers

1. In a large bowl, beat the cream cheese, sour cream and hot sauce until smooth; stir in chicken.

2. Transfer to an 8-in. square baking dish coated with cooking spray. Cover and bake at 350° for 18-22 minutes or until heated through. Serve dip warm with crackers.

Nutrition Facts: 3 Tbsp. (calculated without crackers) equals 77 calories, 4 g fat (2 g saturated fat), 28 mg cholesterol, 71 mg sodium, 1 g carbohydrate, trace fiber.

MAKEOVER CREAMY COLESLAW

PEAR COTTAGE CHEESE SALAD

OLIVE ORANGE SALAD

Salads

Whether you prefer crispy greens, creamy pasta or refreshing fruit salads, this chapter's assortment of healthy specialties will keep you happy! Turn here for great meal starters, side salads or even meatless main dishes.

Pear Cottage Cheese Salad C

PREP/TOTAL TIME: 10 min. YIELD: 6 servings

JEANNIE THOMAS • DRY RIDGE, KENTUCKY

This quick-to-fix snack is perfect any time of day. It makes a great pack-along lunch, too.

- 2 cups (16 oz.) 2% cottage cheese
- 2 medium pears, chopped
- 2 celery ribs, chopped
- 1/3 cup chopped pecans
- 1/2 tsp. ground ginger

1. In a large bowl, combine all ingredients. Chill until serving.

Nutrition Facts: 2/3 cup equals 135 calories, 6 g fat (1 g saturated fat), 9 mg cholesterol, 255 mg sodium, 14 g carbohydrate, 3 g fiber, 8 g protein. **Diabetic Exchanges:** 1 lean meat, 1 fat, 1/2 fruit.

Makeover Creamy Coleslaw F

PREP: 10 min. + chilling YIELD: 8 servings

RENEE ENDRESS • GALVA, ILLINOIS

Here's a lightened-up take on my family's favorite coleslaw recipe. The flavor is very much the same as our full-fat version, but for the sake of making it healthier, the slight change is definitely worth it.

- 2 pkg. (14 oz. *each*) coleslaw mix
- 3/4 cup fat-free mayonnaise
- 1/3 cup reduced-fat sour cream
- 1/4 cup sugar
- 3/4 tsp. seasoned salt
- 1/2 tsp. ground mustard
- 1/4 tsp. celery seed

1. Place coleslaw mix in a large bowl. In a small bowl, combine the remaining ingredients. Pour over coleslaw mix and toss to coat. Refrigerate for at least 2 hours before serving.

Nutrition Facts: 3/4 cup equals 85 calories, 2 g fat (1 g saturated fat), 6 mg cholesterol, 358 mg sodium, 16 g carbohydrate, 3 g fiber, 2 g protein. **Diabetic Exchange:** 1 starch.

Olive Orange Salad M

PREP/TOTAL TIME: 20 min. YIELD: 6 servings

CAROL GAUS • ELK GROVE VILLAGE, ILLINOIS

This easy side salad is fancy enough to serve to dinner guests, but quick enough to make during the week. It pairs well with spicy meals, such as blackened fish or pasta with zesty sausage.

- 6 medium navel oranges
- 6 lettuce leaves
- 6 thin slices red onion, separated into rings
- 6 Tbsp. sliced ripe olives
- 6 Tbsp. Italian salad dressing

1. Peel and cut each orange widthwise into three slices. Place lettuce leaves on individual salad plates. Top with orange slices and onion. Sprinkle with olives; drizzle with dressing.

Nutrition Facts: 1 serving equals 138 calories, 7 g fat (1 g saturated fat), 0 cholesterol, 330 mg sodium, 20 g carbohydrate, 4 g fiber, 2 g protein. **Diabetic Exchanges:** 1 fruit, 1 fat.

Honey Fruit Salad F S

PREP/TOTAL TIME: 10 min. YIELD: 4 servings

DOROTHY DINNEAN • HARRISON, ARKANSAS

What's not to love about this refreshing assortment of berries and fruit? The delightful medley is even treated to a no-fuss dressing of honey, lemon juice and poppy seeds!

- 1 medium banana, chopped
- 1 cup fresh blueberries
- 1 cup fresh raspberries
- 1 cup sliced fresh strawberries
- 2 Tbsp. honey
- 1/2 tsp. lemon juice
- 1/4 tsp. poppy seeds

1. In a small bowl, combine banana and berries. In another small bowl, combine the honey, lemon juice and poppy seeds. Pour over fruit; toss to coat.

Nutrition Facts: 3/4 cup equals 109 calories, 1 g fat (trace saturated fat), 0 cholesterol, 2 mg sodium, 28 g carbohydrate, 5 g fiber, 1 g protein. **Diabetic Exchanges:** 1 fruit, 1/2 starch.

Portobello Spinach Salad [S] [C] [M]

PREP: 15 min. + marinating **GRILL:** 10 min.
YIELD: 6 servings

THOMAS MCCLEARY • KANSAS CITY, KANSAS

Grilled portobellos add a healthy heartiness to this meatless main-dish salad.

- 1 cup orange juice
- 1/4 cup olive oil
- 4 tsp. grated orange peel
- 1 tsp. fennel seed
- 1/2 tsp. pepper
- 1/4 tsp. salt
- 1/2 lb. sliced baby portobello mushrooms
- 1 pkg. (6 oz.) fresh baby spinach
- 1 can (11 oz.) mandarin oranges, drained
- 1/2 medium red onion, thinly sliced
- 1/4 cup slivered almonds

1. In a small bowl, combine the first six ingredients. Pour 1/2 cup marinade into a large resealable plastic bag. Add the mushrooms; seal bag and turn to coat. Refrigerate for 15 minutes. Cover and refrigerate remaining marinade.

2. Drain mushrooms and discard marinade. Transfer mushrooms to a grill wok or basket. Grill, uncovered, over medium heat for 8-12 minutes or until tender, stirring frequently. Cool slightly.

3. Meanwhile, in a large bowl, combine the spinach, oranges, onion, almonds and grilled mushrooms.

4. Drizzle with reserved marinade; toss to coat. Serve immediately.

Editor's Note: If you do not have a grill wok or basket, use a disposable foil pan. Poke holes in the bottom of the pan with a meat fork to allow liquid to drain.

Nutrition Facts: 1 cup equals 129 calories, 8 g fat (1 g saturated fat), 0 cholesterol, 90 mg sodium, 12 g carbohydrate, 2 g fiber, 3 g protein. **Diabetic Exchanges:** 1-1/2 fat, 1 vegetable, 1/2 starch.

Hawaiian Spinach Salad [F]

PREP/TOTAL TIME: 25 min. **YIELD:** 4 servings

ANITA ASHE • SHERBROOKE, NOVA SCOTIA

Toss together fresh spinach, veggies, pineapple and ham for this light, lovely entree salad.

- 4 cups fresh baby spinach
- 2 cups grape tomatoes
- 2/3 cup seeded chopped cucumber
- 1/2 cup sliced fresh mushrooms
- 8 slices red onion, halved
- 1 can (20 oz.) unsweetened pineapple chunks, drained
- 8 oz. sliced deli ham, julienned
- 1/3 cup fat-free poppy seed salad dressing

HAWAIIAN SPINACH SALAD

PORTOBELLO SPINACH SALAD

1. Divide spinach among four plates. Top with tomatoes, cucumber, mushrooms and onion. Arrange pineapple and ham over mushrooms. Drizzle with dressing.

Nutrition Facts: 2 cups equals 184 calories, 2 g fat (trace saturated fat), 29 mg cholesterol, 615 mg sodium, 31 g carbohydrate, 3 g fiber, 13 g protein. **Diabetic Exchanges:** 2 lean meat, 2 vegetable, 1/2 starch, 1/2 fruit.

Taco Salad with a Twist M

PREP/TOTAL TIME: 25 min. **YIELD:** 4 servings

HEATHER CARROLL • COLORADO SPRINGS, COLORADO

You won't even miss the meat in this satisfying salad chock-full of beans, veggies and mouthwatering Southwest flavor.

- 1 pkg. (5 oz.) spring mix salad greens
- 1 large tomato, seeded and chopped
- 1 large red onion, chopped
- 1 medium ripe avocado, peeled and chopped
- 1 cup canned black beans, rinsed and drained
- 4 green onions, chopped
- 1/2 cup shredded reduced-fat cheddar cheese
- 1/2 cup minced fresh cilantro

DRESSING:
- 1/2 cup green chili salsa
- 1/2 cup fat-free plain Greek yogurt
- 2 Tbsp. minced fresh cilantro
- 1 Tbsp. thinly sliced green onion
- 1 Tbsp. lemon juice
- 1 Tbsp. white wine vinegar
- 1 Tbsp. olive oil
- 1-1/2 tsp. honey
- 1/8 tsp. pepper

1. In a large bowl, combine the first eight ingredients. In a small bowl, whisk the remaining ingredients. Pour over salad mixture; toss to coat.

Nutrition Facts: 2 cups salad equals 277 calories, 14 g fat (3 g saturated fat), 10 mg cholesterol, 439 mg sodium, 29 g carbohydrate, 10 g fiber, 14 g protein. **Diabetic Exchanges:** 2 lean meat, 2 vegetable, 1-1/2 fat, 1 starch.

Artichoke Arugula Salad M

PREP/TOTAL TIME: 25 min. **YIELD:** 10 servings

BARBARA BEGLEY • FAIRFIELD, OHIO

Packed with artichokes, dried cranberries and lots of fresh flavors, this salad is sure to be a favorite.

- 8 cups fresh arugula *or* baby spinach
- 1 can (14 oz.) water-packed artichoke hearts, rinsed, drained and chopped
- 1 cup dried cranberries
- 3/4 cup chopped pecans, toasted
- 4 green onions, chopped
- 1/2 cup reduced-fat raspberry vinaigrette
- 3/4 cup crumbled feta cheese

1. In a large bowl, combine the arugula, artichokes, cranberries, pecans and green onions. Drizzle with vinaigrette; toss to coat. Sprinkle with cheese.

Nutrition Facts: 1 cup equals 158 calories, 9 g fat (2 g saturated fat), 5 mg cholesterol, 314 mg sodium, 16 g carbohydrate, 2 g fiber, 4 g protein. **Diabetic Exchanges:** 1-1/2 fat, 1 starch.

Beet Spinach Salad M

PREP: 10 min. **COOK:** 30 min. + cooling
YIELD: 4 servings

DARLENE BRENDEN • SALEM, OREGON

Here's a colorful combination: beets, spinach, orange and apples. Tossing everything with a vinaigrette keeps it healthy.

- 6 small fresh beets (about 1-1/2 lb.)
- 4 cups fresh baby spinach
- 2 medium tart apples, peeled and sliced
- 1 medium orange, sectioned
- 3 Tbsp. raspberry hazelnut vinaigrette
- 2 Tbsp. chopped hazelnuts, toasted

1. Scrub beets and trim tops to 1 in. Place in a Dutch oven and cover with water. Bring to a boil. Reduce heat; cover and simmer for 30-60 minutes or until the beets are tender. Remove beets from the water; cool. Peel beets and cut into 1-in. wedges.

2. Divide spinach among four plates. Top with apples, orange and beets. Drizzle with vinaigrette; sprinkle with hazelnuts.

Nutrition Facts: 1 serving equals 175 calories, 5 g fat (1 g saturated fat), 0 cholesterol, 252 mg sodium, 32 g carbohydrate, 5 g fiber, 4 g protein. **Diabetic Exchanges:** 2 starch, 1 fat.

Feta Romaine Salad C M

PREP/TOTAL TIME: 15 min. **YIELD:** 6 servings

MICHAEL VOLPATT • SAN FRANCISCO, CALIFORNIA

Feta cheese and Greek olives add a taste of the Mediterranean to this quick and easy dish.

- 1 bunch romaine, chopped
- 3 plum tomatoes, seeded and chopped
- 1 cup (4 oz.) crumbled feta cheese
- 1 cup chopped seeded cucumber
- 1/2 cup Greek olives, chopped
- 2 Tbsp. minced fresh parsley
- 2 Tbsp. minced fresh cilantro
- 3 Tbsp. lemon juice
- 2 Tbsp. olive oil
- 1/4 tsp. pepper

1. In a large bowl, combine the first seven ingredients. In a small bowl, whisk the remaining ingredients. Drizzle over salad; toss to coat. Serve immediately.

Nutrition Facts: 1-1/3 cups equals 139 calories, 11 g fat (3 g saturated fat), 10 mg cholesterol, 375 mg sodium, 6 g carbohydrate, 3 g fiber, 5 g protein. **Diabetic Exchanges:** 2 fat, 1 vegetable.

Light Green Goddess Salad Dressing C

PREP/TOTAL TIME: 10 min. **YIELD:** 2 cups

PAGE ALEXANDER • BALDWIN CITY, KANSAS

Try my do-it-yourself version of a popular salad dressing that's lower in calories and fat but keeps all the flavor.

- 1 cup reduced-fat mayonnaise
- 1/2 cup reduced-fat sour cream
- 1/4 cup chopped green pepper
- 1/4 cup packed fresh parsley sprigs
- 3 anchovy fillets
- 2 Tbsp. lemon juice
- 2 green onion tops, coarsely chopped
- 1 garlic clove, peeled
- 1/4 tsp. pepper
- 1/8 tsp. Worcestershire sauce

1. Place all ingredients in a blender; cover and process until smooth. Transfer to a bowl or jar; cover and store in the refrigerator.

Nutrition Facts: 2 Tbsp. equals 64 calories, 6 g fat (1 g saturated fat), 8 mg cholesterol, 153 mg sodium, 2 g carbohydrate, trace fiber, 1 g protein. **Diabetic Exchange:** 1 fat.

FETA ROMAINE SALAD

LIGHT GREEN GODDESS SALAD DRESSING

Broccoli Tomato Salad F C M

PREP: 10 min. + chilling **YIELD:** 6 servings

HELEN MEADOWS • TROUT CREEK, MONTANA

I found this recipe more than 25 years ago. I made a few changes to it, and our family has enjoyed it ever since. The colorful combo is perfect for the holidays, but it's equally delightful at summer picnics.

5	cups broccoli florets
1	Tbsp. water
1	pint cherry tomatoes, cut in half
2	Tbsp. chopped green onion
1/4	cup fat-free mayonnaise
1/4	cup reduced-fat sour cream
1	Tbsp. lemon juice
1/2	tsp. salt
1/4	tsp. pepper

It takes longer to cook food when the **microwave's power** (wattage) is lower. We suggest that you start with a cooking time that is one-third longer than what is called for in the recipe.

BROCCOLI TOMATO SALAD

1. Place broccoli and water in a 2-qt. microwave-safe bowl. Cover and microwave on high for 1-1/2 to 2-1/2 minutes or until crisp-tender, stirring once; drain. Cool completely.

2. Place broccoli in a serving bowl; gently stir in tomatoes and onion. In a small bowl, combine the mayonnaise, sour cream, lemon juice, salt and pepper; pour over vegetables and stir gently. Cover and refrigerate for 1 hour.

Editor's Note: This recipe was tested in a 1,100-watt microwave.

Nutrition Facts: 3/4 cup equals 49 calories, 1 g fat (1 g saturated fat), 4 mg cholesterol, 304 mg sodium, 8 g carbohydrate, 3 g fiber, 3 g protein. **Diabetic Exchange:** 1 vegetable.

Pepperoncini Arugula Salad F C M

PREP/TOTAL TIME: 5 min. **YIELD:** 4 servings

TABITHA FREEMAN • MERIDEN, CONNECTICUT

This fantastic salad is short on time but not on taste. In about 5 minutes you can have a salad that goes well with just about any beef or pork dish.

2	cups fresh arugula *or* baby spinach
2	cups torn romaine
1/4	cup chopped red onion
2	pepperoncini, sliced
1	medium tomato, sliced
1/4	cup balsamic vinaigrette

1. In a large salad bowl, combine the arugula, romaine, onion and tomato. Drizzle with vinaigrette; gently toss to coat.

Editor's Note: Look for pepperoncinis (pickled peppers) in the pickle and olive section of your grocery store.

Nutrition Facts: 1-1/4 cups equals 50 calories, 3 g fat (trace saturated fat), 0 cholesterol, 197 mg sodium, 6 g carbohydrate, 1 g fiber, 1 g protein. **Diabetic Exchanges:** 1 vegetable, 1/2 fat.

Citrus-Marmalade Vinaigrette S C

PREP/TOTAL TIME: 10 min. **YIELD:** 3/4 cup

SARAH VASQUES • MILFORD, NEW HAMPSHIRE

Add this fresh-tasting splash of citrus to a wide variety of salad mixings.

1/3	cup olive oil
3	Tbsp. lemon juice
2	Tbsp. orange marmalade
4	tsp. minced fresh thyme
1	Tbsp. Dijon mustard
2	tsp. grated lemon peel
1/8	tsp. salt

1. In a small bowl whisk all ingredients. Chill until serving.

Nutrition Facts: 2 Tbsp. equals 128 calories, 12 g fat (2 g saturated fat), 0 cholesterol, 113 mg sodium, 6 g carbohydrate, trace fiber, trace protein. **Diabetic Exchanges:** 2 fat, 1/2 starch.

Makeover Italian Pasta Salad C M

PREP: 25 min. + chilling **YIELD:** 8 servings

HEALTHY COOKING TEST KITCHEN

Here's the perfect side dish for summer picnics or fall potlucks—and no one would ever guess that it's been slimmed down.

- 1   cup uncooked whole wheat spiral pasta
- 1-1/2   cups halved cherry tomatoes
- 1   cup sliced fresh mushrooms
- 1/2   cup fat-free Italian salad dressing
- 1/4   cup chopped sweet red pepper
- 1/4   cup chopped green pepper
- 3   Tbsp. thinly sliced green onions
- 1/2   cup fat-free mayonnaise
- 1/3   cup grated Parmesan cheese
- 1/3   cup cubed provolone cheese
- 1   can (2-1/4 oz.) sliced ripe olives, drained

1. Cook pasta according to package directions; rinse with cold water and drain. Place in a large bowl; add the tomatoes, mushrooms, salad dressing, peppers and onions. Cover and refrigerate for at least 4 hours or overnight.

2. In a small bowl, combine mayonnaise and Parmesan cheese; stir in provolone cheese and olives. Gently fold into the pasta mixture. Chill until serving.

Nutrition Facts: 3/4 cup equals 101 calories, 4 g fat (2 g saturated fat), 9 mg cholesterol, 507 mg sodium, 12 g carbohydrate, 2 g fiber, 5 g protein. **Diabetic Exchanges:** 1 starch, 1/2 fat.

SPICY FRUIT SALAD

Spicy Fruit Salad F S

PREP/TOTAL TIME: 15 min. **YIELD:** 10 servings

REBECCA STURROCK • LONGVIEW, TEXAS

Definitely not your mother's fruit salad, this one balances cool fruit and hot spices to perfection.

> 2 medium apples, halved and sliced
> 2 medium pears, halved and sliced
> 2 medium mangoes, peeled, halved and sliced
> 1 lb. fresh strawberries, sliced

VINAIGRETTE:
> 1/4 cup lime juice
> 1/4 cup orange juice
> 1/4 cup minced fresh cilantro
> 2 Tbsp. Champagne vinegar
> 1-1/2 tsp. grated lime peel
> 1/4 tsp. sriracha Asian hot chili sauce *or* 1/8 tsp. hot pepper sauce

1. In a large bowl, combine the apples, pears, mangoes and strawberries. In a small bowl, whisk the juices, cilantro, vinegar, lime peel and hot chili sauce. Drizzle over fruit mixture; toss to coat.

Nutrition Facts: 3/4 cup equals 81 calories, trace fat (trace saturated fat), 0 cholesterol, 6 mg sodium, 21 g carbohydrate, 3 g fiber, 1 g protein. **Diabetic Exchange:** 1-1/2 fruit.

Tangy Four-Bean Salad M

PREP: 20 min. + chilling **YIELD:** 12 servings

SHARON CAIN • REVELSTOKE, BRITISH COLUMBIA

This colorful salad is easy to fix, and a no-fuss dressing lends sweet-sour flair. Green pepper and mushrooms help it stand out from other bean medleys.

> 1 can (16 oz.) kidney beans, rinsed and drained
> 1 can (15 oz.) garbanzo beans or chickpeas, rinsed and drained
> 1 can (14-1/2 oz.) cut green beans, drained
> 1 can (14-1/2 oz.) cut wax beans, drained
> 1 cup sliced fresh mushrooms
> 1 cup chopped green pepper
> 1 cup chopped onion

DRESSING:
> 1/2 cup cider vinegar
> 1/3 cup sugar
> 1/4 cup canola oil

1 tsp. celery seed
1/2 tsp. pepper
1/4 tsp. salt
1/8 tsp. dried basil
1/8 tsp. dried oregano

1. In a large bowl, combine the beans, mushrooms, green pepper and onion. In a small bowl, whisk the dressing ingredients.

2. Pour dressing over bean mixture and stir to coat. Cover and refrigerate for at least 4 hours. Serve with a slotted spoon.

Nutrition Facts: 3/4 cup equals 162 calories, 6 g fat (trace saturated fat), 0 cholesterol, 366 mg sodium, 24 g carbohydrate, 5 g fiber, 5 g protein. **Diabetic Exchanges:** 1 starch, 1 vegetable, 1 fat.

Mediterranean Tabbouleh

PREP: 25 min. + standing **BAKE:** 15 min.
YIELD: 8 servings

KEITH DREITLEIN • CRANSTON, RHODE ISLAND
Fresh, filling and packed with flavor, this is a great make-ahead idea for a snack or mini-meal you can enjoy all weekend!

1 cup bulgur
2 cups boiling water
5 garlic cloves, unpeeled
5 Tbsp. olive oil, *divided*
1/2 lb. peeled and deveined cooked medium shrimp, chopped
3 medium tomatoes, seeded and chopped
1 medium cucumber, chopped
1 cup chopped sweet onion
2 green onions, thinly sliced
1/2 cup minced fresh parsley
2 Tbsp. minced fresh cilantro
3 Tbsp. lemon juice

1/2 tsp. salt
1/4 tsp. pepper

1. Place bulgur in a large bowl. Stir in boiling water. Cover and let stand for 30 minutes or until most of the liquid is absorbed.

2. Meanwhile, place garlic on a double thickness of heavy-duty foil. Drizzle with 1/2 tsp. oil. Wrap foil around garlic. Bake at 425° for 15-20 minutes. Cool for 10-15 minutes.

3. Drain bulgur well; transfer to a large serving bowl. Stir in the shrimp, tomatoes, cucumber, onion, green onions, parsley and cilantro. Squeeze softened garlic into a small bowl and mash. Whisk in the lemon juice, salt, pepper and remaining oil; drizzle over salad. Toss to coat. Chill until serving.

Nutrition Facts: 3/4 cup equals 195 calories, 9 g fat (1 g saturated fat), 43 mg cholesterol, 199 mg sodium, 20 g carbohydrate, 5 g fiber, 9 g protein. **Diabetic Exchanges:** 1-1/2 fat, 1 starch, 1 lean meat, 1 vegetable.

To keep fresh parsley in the refrigerator for several weeks, wash the entire **bunch of parsley** in warm water, shake off all excess moisture, wrap in a paper towel and seal in a plastic bag. If you need a longer storage time, remove paper towel and place the sealed bag in the freezer.

MEDITERRANEAN TABBOULEH

TANGY FOUR-BEAN SALAD

Gingered Green Bean Salad S C M

PREP/TOTAL TIME: 30 min. **YIELD:** 8 servings

TRISHA KRUSE • EAGLE, IDAHO

This crisp summer salad keeps well in the refrigerator—if it lasts that long. The tangy sweetness and toasty flavor in the sesame dressing are almost addictive!

    2 lb. fresh green beans, trimmed
    1 cup thinly sliced red onion, separated into
       rings
    1 cup canned bean sprouts, rinsed and drained

VINAIGRETTE:
    1/4 cup rice vinegar
    2 Tbsp. sesame oil
    1 Tbsp. minced fresh gingerroot
    1 Tbsp. reduced-sodium soy sauce
    2 tsp. sesame seeds, toasted
    1 tsp. honey
    1/2 tsp. minced garlic

1. Place green beans in a large saucepan and cover with water. Bring to a boil. Cook, uncovered, for 4-7 minutes or until crisp-tender. Drain and immediately place in ice water; drain and pat dry.

2. In a large salad bowl, combine the beans, onion and bean sprouts. In a small bowl, whisk the

vinaigrette ingredients. Pour over bean mixture and toss to coat.

Nutrition Facts: 1 cup equals 88 calories, 4 g fat (1 g saturated fat), 0 cholesterol, 93 mg sodium, 12 g carbohydrate, 4 g fiber, 3 g protein. **Diabetic Exchanges:** 2 vegetable, 1 fat.

Tortellini Chicken Salad

PREP: 25 min. **COOK:** 15 min. + chilling
YIELD: 6 servings

EDIE DESPAIN • LOGAN, UTAH

If you love pesto, you'll love it even more mixed with fresh veggies and chicken in this good-for-you summer salad.

    1 pkg. (9 oz.) refrigerated cheese tortellini
    1 cup frozen peas
    5 cups torn romaine
    1-1/2 cups shredded carrots
    2 cups cubed cooked chicken breast
    1/2 cup julienned sweet red pepper
    1/2 cup fat-free mayonnaise
    1 jar (3 oz.) prepared pesto
    1/4 cup buttermilk
    2 Tbsp. minced fresh parsley

1. Cook tortellini according to package directions, adding the peas during the last 4-5 minutes of cooking. Drain and rinse in cold water.

2. In a large salad bowl, layer the romaine, carrots, chicken, tortellini and peas, and red pepper. In a small bowl, combine the mayonnaise, pesto and buttermilk. Spread over top. Sprinkle with parsley. Refrigerate until chilled.

Nutrition Facts: 1-1/2 cups salad equals 337 calories, 13 g fat (4 g saturated fat), 62 mg cholesterol, 525 mg sodium, 32 g carbohydrate, 5 g fiber, 25 g protein. **Diabetic Exchanges:** 3 lean meat, 2 starch, 1 fat.

GINGERED GREEN BEAN SALAD

TORTELLINI CHICKEN SALAD

ROASTED BEET-ORANGE SALAD

Roasted Beet-Orange Salad F S C M

PREP: 20 min. + chilling **BAKE:** 40 min.
YIELD: 6 servings

KATHY RAIRIGH • MILFORD, INDIANA

Tender beets and tangy vinaigrette are the stars of this fresh, colorful salad.

5	whole fresh beets
4	green onions, thinly sliced
1/4	cup cider vinegar
2	Tbsp. olive oil
1	Tbsp. canola oil
2	Tbsp. sugar
1/2	tsp. salt
1/2	tsp. curry powder
1/4	tsp. white pepper
6	lettuce leaves
2	medium oranges, peeled and sectioned

1. Place beets in an 11-in. x 7-in. baking dish; add 1 in. of water. Cover and bake at 400° for 40-45 minutes or until tender. Cool; peel, slice and quarter beets. In a large bowl, combine beets and green onions. In a small bowl, whisk the vinegar, oils, sugar, salt, curry and white pepper. Pour over beets; toss to coat. Cover and refrigerate for 2 hours.

2. Divide lettuce among six plates. Using a slotted spoon, top with beet mixture. Arrange orange sections over salad.

Nutrition Facts: 1 serving equals 59 calories, 2 g fat (trace saturated fat), 0 cholesterol, 96 mg sodium, 9 g carbohydrate, 1 g fiber, 1 g protein. **Diabetic Exchange:** 1/2 starch.

Olive oil can be stored tightly capped at room temperature or in the refrigerator for up to 1 year. When chilled, the oil turns cloudy and thick. Chilled **olive oil** will return to its original consistency when left at room temperature for a short period of time.

Strawberry Spinach Salad

PREP: 25 min. **COOK:** 10 min. **YIELD:** 8 servings

MARY BUFORD SHAW • MT. PLEASANT, SOUTH CAROLINA

Here's a colorful salad packed full of flavor. Toasted walnuts add texture and crunch.

- 3 bacon strips, chopped
- 3 Tbsp. rice vinegar
- 2 Tbsp. honey
- 5 tsp. olive oil
- 1 tsp. Dijon mustard
- 1/2 tsp. pepper
- 1/4 tsp. salt
- 1 pkg. (6 oz.) fresh baby spinach
- 2 medium navel oranges, peeled and chopped
- 12 fresh strawberries, quartered
- 1 cup thinly sliced cucumber
- 1/2 cup thinly sliced red onion
- 1 medium carrot, shredded
- 1/2 cup chopped walnuts, toasted

1. In a small skillet, cook bacon over medium heat until crisp. Remove to paper towels with a slotted spoon; drain.

2. In a small bowl, whisk the vinegar, honey, oil, mustard, pepper and salt. In a large bowl, combine the spinach, oranges, strawberries, cucumber, onion and carrot. Pour dressing over salad; toss to coat. Sprinkle with walnuts and bacon. Serve immediately.

Nutrition Facts: 1 cup equals 142 calories, 9 g fat (1 g saturated fat), 3 mg cholesterol, 168 mg sodium, 15 g carbohydrate, 3 g fiber, 3 g protein. **Diabetic Exchanges:** 1-1/2 fat, 1 starch.

Chicken Curry Fruit Salad

PREP: 20 min. + chilling **YIELD:** 6 servings

PJ ANDERSON • SALT LAKE CITY, UTAH

Perfect for a special spring luncheon, this refreshing combo blends chicken, apple, celery and grapes with a splash of lime and the crunch of nuts and chow mein noodles. Yum!

- 4 cups cubed cooked chicken breasts
- 2 celery ribs, diced
- 1 cup seedless red grapes, halved

- 1 medium apple, peeled and diced
- 1 small red onion, diced
- 1 cup fat-free mayonnaise
- 1 Tbsp. orange marmalade
- 2 tsp. lime juice
- 1 tsp. curry powder
- 1/2 cup lightly salted cashews
- 1/2 cup chow mein noodles

1. In a large bowl, combine the first five ingredients. In a small bowl, combine the mayonnaise, marmalade, lime juice and curry. Pour over chicken mixture and toss to coat. Cover and refrigerate for at least 1 hour.

2. Just before serving, sprinkle with cashews and chow mein noodles.

Nutrition Facts: 1-1/3 cups salad equals 305 calories, 11 g fat (2 g saturated fat), 76 mg cholesterol, 431 mg sodium, 22 g carbohydrate, 3 g fiber, 30 g protein. **Diabetic Exchanges:** 4 lean meat, 1 starch, 1 fat, 1/2 fruit.

Makeover Loaded Baked Potato Salad

PREP: 20 min. **BAKE:** 30 min. + cooling
YIELD: 12 servings (3/4 cup each)

HEALTHY COOKING TEST KITCHEN

Crispy bacon, crunchy pickle, cheddar cheese and a creamy dressing are guaranteed to make this salad a family favorite.

- 2-1/2 lb. small unpeeled red potatoes, cubed
- 1/2 tsp. salt
- 1/4 tsp. pepper
- 2 hard-cooked eggs, chopped
- 4 bacon strips, cooked and crumbled
- 1/2 cup shredded reduced-fat cheddar cheese
- 1 cup chopped sweet onion
- 1 dill pickle, chopped
- 1/2 cup reduced-fat sour cream
- 1/2 cup fat-free mayonnaise
- 1 tsp. prepared mustard

1. Place potatoes in a 15-in. x 10-in. x 1-in. baking pan coated with cooking spray; sprinkle with salt and pepper. Bake, uncovered, at 425° for 30-35 minutes or until tender. Cool on a wire rack.

2. In a large bowl, combine the potatoes, eggs, bacon, cheese, onion and pickle. In a small bowl, combine the sour cream, mayonnaise and mustard; pour over the potato mixture and toss to coat.

Nutrition Facts: 3/4 cup equals 133 calories, 4 g fat (2 g saturated fat), 45 mg cholesterol, 340 mg sodium, 19 g carbohydrate, 2 g fiber, 6 g protein. **Diabetic Exchanges:** 1 starch, 1 medium-fat meat.

> Reduced-fat cheese products refer to products that contain at least **25% less fat** than the original version. These products can be used in most recipes that are heated or melted. Fat-free cheese must contain less than 0.5 g fat per serving.

MAKEOVER LOADED BAKED POTATO SALAD

CHICKEN CURRY FRUIT SALAD

Cannellini Bean Salad M

PREP/TOTAL TIME: 30 min. YIELD: 5 servings

ALDEN THORNTON • WARRENTON, OREGON

I've had this recipe quite a long time, although I have changed it somewhat from the original. It has always been popular, particularly when served at picnics and potlucks.

1	large sweet red pepper
2	cans (15 oz. *each*) white kidney *or* cannellini beans, rinsed and drained
1	medium red onion, sliced and separated into rings
1/4	cup minced fresh basil
3	Tbsp. red wine vinegar
2	Tbsp. olive oil
1/4	tsp. salt
1/4	tsp. pepper

1. Cut red pepper in half; remove seeds. Broil pepper cut side down 4 in. from the heat until skin is blistered and charred, about 8 minutes. Immediately place pepper in a small bowl; cover and let stand for 15-20 minutes.

2. Peel off and discard charred skin. Cut pepper into strips; place in a large bowl. Add the beans, onion and basil. In a jar with a tight-fitting lid, combine the vinegar, oil, salt and pepper; shake well. Pour over bean mixture; toss to coat.

Nutrition Facts: 3/4 cup equals 190 calories, 6 g fat (1 g saturated fat), 0 cholesterol, 472 mg sodium, 26 g carbohydrate, 7 g fiber, 7 g protein. **Diabetic Exchanges:** 1-1/2 starch, 1 lean meat, 1 fat.

Makeover Fluffy Lime Salad S

PREP: 15 min. + chilling YIELD: 8 servings

HEALTHY COOKING TEST KITCHEN

Loaded with crunchy walnuts, tangy pineapple and lip-smacking lime flavor, this refreshing salad could even double as dessert!

1	can (8 oz.) unsweetened crushed pineapple, undrained
1	pkg. (0.3 oz.) sugar-free lime gelatin
3	Tbsp. water
6	oz. reduced-fat cream cheese
1	cup miniature marshmallows
1/2	cup chopped walnuts
1	carton (8 oz.) frozen reduced-fat whipped topping, thawed

1. Drain pineapple, reserving juice; set pineapple aside. In a small saucepan, combine the gelatin, water and reserved juice. Cook and stir over low heat until gelatin is dissolved. Refrigerate until syrupy, about 30 minutes.

2. In a small bowl, beat cream cheese until fluffy. Stir in gelatin mixture, marshmallows, walnuts and pineapple. Fold in whipped topping.

3. Transfer to a serving bowl. Cover and refrigerate for 2 hours or until set.

Nutrition Facts: 3/4 cup equals 206 calories, 12 g fat (7 g saturated fat), 15 mg cholesterol, 125 mg sodium, 21 g carbohydrate, 1 g fiber, 4 g protein.

Frosted Fruit Salad F S

PREP/TOTAL TIME: 10 min. YIELD: 6 servings

ANN FOX • AUSTIN, TEXAS

I came up with this breakfast recipe that's easy, light, delicious and uses up the bananas and apples I always have on hand.

CANNELLINI BEAN SALAD

MAKEOVER FLUFFY LIME SALAD

STRAWBERRY SALAD WITH MOJITO VINAIGRETTE

2 large apples, cut into 3/4-in. cubes
2 medium firm bananas, sliced
2 tsp. lemon juice
1 carton (6 oz.) fat-free sugar-free raspberry yogurt
1/4 cup raisins
1 Tbsp. sunflower kernels

1. In a large bowl, combine apples and bananas. Sprinkle with lemon juice; toss to coat. Stir in the yogurt, raisins and sunflower kernels.

Nutrition Facts: 3/4 cup equals 124 calories, 1 g fat (trace saturated fat), 1 mg cholesterol, 31 mg sodium, 28 g carbohydrate, 3 g fiber, 3 g protein. **Diabetic Exchange:** 2 fruit.

Strawberry Salad With Mojito Vinaigrette M

PREP/TOTAL TIME: 20 min. **YIELD:** 5 servings

DONNA MARIE RYAN • TOPSFIELD, MASSACHUSETTS

Mojitos are a fun summery drink and the inspiration behind this refreshing side salad. No rum was used in my recipe, but it certainly could be added to the vinaigrette.

1/4 cup white wine vinegar
4 fresh strawberries, hulled

2 Tbsp. water
2 Tbsp. lime juice
2 Tbsp. coarsely chopped fresh mint
2 Tbsp. honey
1/4 tsp. salt
Dash pepper
2 Tbsp. olive oil

SALAD:
1 pkg. (5 oz.) spring mix salad greens
2 cups fresh strawberries, hulled and sliced
1 small red onion, thinly sliced
3 oz. fresh goat cheese, crumbled
1/4 cup chopped walnuts

1. In a blender, combine the first eight ingredients. While processing, gradually add oil in a steady stream. Set aside.

2. Divide salad greens among five salad plates; top with strawberries, onion, cheese and walnuts. Drizzle with vinaigrette.

Nutrition Facts: 1-1/2 cups salad with 2 Tbsp. vinaigrette equals 178 calories, 11 g fat (3 g saturated fat), 11 mg cholesterol, 195 mg sodium, 17 g carbohydrate, 3 g fiber, 4 g protein. **Diabetic Exchanges:** 2 fat, 1 vegetable, 1/2 starch, 1/2 fruit.

CONFETTI COUSCOUS SALAD

Confetti Couscous Salad

PREP/TOTAL TIME: 30 min. **YIELD:** 6 servings

SUZANNE KESEL • COHOCTON, NEW YORK

Bursting with color and flavor, this delightful side dish will take any entree up a notch.

- 1 cup reduced-sodium chicken broth
- 1 cup uncooked couscous
- 1 can (15 oz.) black beans, rinsed and drained
- 3/4 cup frozen corn, thawed
- 1 medium sweet red pepper, chopped
- 6 green onions, chopped
- 1/4 cup minced fresh cilantro

DRESSING:
- 2 Tbsp. plus 1 tsp. olive oil
- 2 Tbsp. lime juice
- 1-1/2 tsp. red wine vinegar
- 1/2 tsp. ground cumin
- 1/4 tsp. salt
- 1/4 tsp. pepper

Pine nuts, optional

1. In a large saucepan, bring broth to a boil. Stir in couscous. Remove from the heat; cover and let stand for 5-10 minutes or until broth is absorbed.

2. Fluff with a fork. Stir in the beans, corn, red pepper, onions and cilantro. In a small bowl, whisk the oil, lime juice, vinegar, cumin, salt and pepper. Drizzle over salad and toss to coat. Sprinkle with the pine nuts if desired.

Nutrition Facts: 3/4 cup (calculated without pine nuts) equals 245 calories, 6 g fat (1 g saturated fat), 0 cholesterol, 335 mg sodium, 41 g carbohydrate, 5 g fiber, 9 g protein.

Apple Salad with Maple-Mustard Vinaigrette F S C M

PREP/TOTAL TIME: 15 min.
YIELD: 16 servings (3/4 cup each)

BETH DAUENHAUER • PUEBLO, COLORADO

This seasonal salad will be a hit at any large gathering. It's also easy for family dinners; just halve the recipe.

- 9 cups torn mixed salad greens
- 2 large tart apples, chopped
- 1 small red onion, thinly sliced
- 1/3 cup chopped walnuts, toasted

DRESSING:
- 1/4 cup thawed frozen apple juice concentrate
- 2 Tbsp. cider vinegar
- 2 Tbsp. canola oil
- 2 Tbsp. maple syrup
- 2 Tbsp. spicy brown mustard
- 1/4 tsp. salt
- 1/8 tsp. pepper

1. In a large bowl, combine the salad greens, apples, onion and walnuts. In a small bowl, whisk the dressing ingredients. Drizzle over salad; toss to coat.

Nutrition Facts: 3/4 cup equals 68 calories, 3 g fat (trace saturated fat), 0 cholesterol, 71 mg sodium, 9 g carbohydrate, 2 g fiber, 1 g protein. **Diabetic Exchanges:** 1/2 starch, 1/2 fat.

Peachy Chicken Salad

PREP/TOTAL TIME: 10 min. **YIELD:** 4 servings

RADELLE KNAPPENBERGER • OVIEDO, FLORIDA

This is a very healthy and simple salad to make; even my non-cooking husband can whip it together in minutes. We've served this to friends over the years, and they always ask us to share the recipe.

- 2 cups cubed cooked chicken breast
- 2 medium peaches, coarsely chopped
- 1/2 cup chopped walnuts
- 1/2 cup fat-free mayonnaise
- 1/4 cup raisins
- 1 tsp. curry powder
- 1 pkg. (5 oz.) spring mix salad greens

1. In a small bowl, combine the first six ingredients. Divide salad greens among four plates; top each with 1/2 cup chicken salad.

Nutrition Facts: 1/2 cup chicken salad with 2 cups salad greens equals 277 calories, 12 g fat (1 g saturated fat), 57 mg cholesterol, 295 mg sodium, 19 g carbohydrate, 3 g fiber, 26 g protein. **Diabetic Exchanges:** 3 lean meat, 1-1/2 fat, 1 starch.

PEACHY CHICKEN SALAD

APPLE SALAD WITH MAPLE-MUSTARD VINAIGRETTE

Crunchy Broccoli Salad C

PREP/TOTAL TIME: 20 min. **YIELD:** 10 servings

JESSICA CONREY • CEDAR RAPIDS, IOWA

Growing up, I never cared for broccoli. But after one taste of this light, sweet salad, I was officially hooked. The homemade dressing and toppings give the vegetable a whole new flavor.

8	cups fresh broccoli florets
1	bunch green onions, thinly sliced
1/2	cup dried cranberries
3	Tbsp. canola oil
3	Tbsp. seasoned rice vinegar
2	Tbsp. sugar
1/4	cup sunflower kernels
3	bacon strips, cooked and crumbled

1. In a large bowl, combine the broccoli, onions and cranberries. In a small bowl, whisk the oil, vinegar and sugar; drizzle over broccoli and toss to coat. Chill until serving. Sprinkle with sunflower kernels and bacon.

Nutrition Facts: 1 serving (3/4 cup) equals 121 calories, 7 g fat (1 g saturated fat), 2 mg cholesterol, 233 mg sodium, 14 g carbohydrate, 3 g fiber, 3 g protein. **Diabetic Exchanges:** 1 vegetable, 1 fat, 1/2 starch.

Quinoa Wilted Spinach Salad S M

PREP/TOTAL TIME: 30 min. **YIELD:** 10 servings

SHARON RICCI • MENDON, NEW YORK

Get all the nutritious benefits of quinoa, spinach and cranberries paired with the crunchy texture of nuts in this easy and scrumptious salad. A light, flavorful dressing splashed with citrus tops off everything!

1	cup quinoa, rinsed
2	cups water
1	pkg. (6 oz.) fresh baby spinach, torn
1/2	cup dried cranberries

DRESSING:
- 3 Tbsp. olive oil
- 2 Tbsp. orange juice
- 1 Tbsp. red wine vinegar
- 1 Tbsp. maple syrup
- 1 garlic clove, minced
- 1/2 tsp. salt
- 1/8 tsp. pepper
- 1 green onion, finely chopped
- 1/2 cup chopped pecans, toasted

1. In a small saucepan, bring quinoa and water to a boil. Reduce heat; cover and simmer for 12-15 minutes or until water is absorbed. Remove from the heat; fluff with a fork. Cover and let stand for 10 minutes.

2. In a large bowl, combine the warm quinoa, spinach and cranberries. For dressing, in a small bowl, whisk the oil, orange juice, vinegar, maple syrup, garlic, salt and pepper. Stir in onion. Pour over quinoa mixture; toss to coat. Sprinkle with pecans.

Editor's Note: Look for quinoa in the cereal, rice or organic food aisle.

Nutrition Facts: 3/4 cup equals 171 calories, 9 g fat (1 g saturated fat), 0 cholesterol, 136 mg sodium, 20 g carbohydrate, 2 g fiber, 3 g protein.

Spinach Orzo Salad

PREP/TOTAL TIME: 30 min. **YIELD:** 10 servings

DONNA BARDOCZ • HOWELL, MICHIGAN

This incredibly tasty salad couldn't be any simpler to put together, and since it feeds a bunch, you won't have to double the recipe for potlucks or picnics. Chill it for about an hour to bring out all the fresh flavors.

- 1 pkg. (16 oz.) orzo pasta
- 1 pkg. (6 oz.) fresh baby spinach, finely chopped
- 3/4 cup crumbled feta cheese
- 3/4 cup finely chopped red onion
- 3/4 cup reduced-fat balsamic vinaigrette
- 1/2 tsp. dried basil
- 1/4 tsp. white pepper
- 1/4 cup pine nuts, toasted

1. Cook orzo according to package directions. Drain and rinse in cold water.

2. In a large bowl, combine the spinach, cheese, onion and orzo. In a small bowl, combine the vinaigrette, basil and pepper. Pour over orzo; toss to coat. Chill until serving. Just before serving, stir in pine nuts.

Nutrition Facts: 3/4 cup equals 249 calories, 7 g fat (2 g saturated fat), 5 mg cholesterol, 235 mg sodium, 38 g carbohydrate, 2 g fiber, 9 g protein.

It may look like rice, but **orzo**, which is Italian for "barley," is actually a form of macaroni. It works well in most any soup or salad that calls for noodles, but also makes a tasty side dish on its own.

SPINACH ORZO SALAD

QUINOA WILTED SPINACH SALAD

Roasted Pear Salad M

PREP: 15 min. BAKE: 15 min. + cooling YIELD: 4 servings

HEALTHY COOKING TEST KITCHEN

Oven-roasted pears are tossed with crispy greens, dried cranberries and nuts. Sweetened with a touch of honey, the creamy dressing adds even more pear flavor.

- 2 medium pears, halved and cored
- 4 tsp. olive oil, *divided*
- 2 Tbsp. cider vinegar
- 1 tsp. water
- 1 tsp. honey
- 1/4 tsp. salt
- 1/8 tsp. white pepper
- 1 pkg. (10 oz.) mixed baby salad greens
- 1 cup watercress sprigs
- 1/4 cup chopped hazelnuts, toasted
- 1/4 cup dried cranberries

1. In a small bowl, toss pears with 1 tsp. oil. Place in a 15-in. x 10-in. x 1-in. baking pan coated with cooking spray. Bake at 400° for 10 minutes. Turn pears over; bake 5-7 minutes longer or until golden and tender.

2. When cool enough to handle, peel pears. Thinly slice two pear halves lengthwise and set aside. Place remaining pear halves in a blender. Add the vinegar, water, honey, salt and white pepper; cover and process until smooth. While processing, gradually add the remaining oil in a steady stream.

3. In a large bowl, toss the salad greens, watercress, hazelnuts and cranberries. Arrange reserved pear slices on top; drizzle with dressing.

Nutrition Facts: 1 serving equals 174 calories, 9 g fat (1 g saturated fat), 0 cholesterol, 178 mg sodium, 24 g carbohydrate, 5 g fiber, 3 g protein.

Makeover Cleo's Potato Salad

PREP: 30 min. COOK: 20 min.
YIELD: 16 servings (3/4 cup each)

JOAN HALLFORD • NORTH RICHLAND HILLS, TEXAS

This recipe is perfect for large gatherings, and now with this healthy version, I can enjoy it all summer long.

- 6 large potatoes
- 6 bacon strips, diced
- 1/4 cup sugar
- 1 Tbsp. all-purpose flour
- 1/2 cup water
- 1 egg, lightly beaten
- 2 cups fat-free Miracle Whip
- 3 Tbsp. cider vinegar
- 1/2 cup heavy whipping cream, whipped
- 2 medium celery ribs, sliced
- 2 hard-cooked eggs, chopped
- 1 Tbsp. grated onion
- 1 tsp. celery seed
- 1/2 tsp. salt

1. Scrub and cube potatoes; place in a Dutch oven and cover with water. Bring to a boil. Reduce heat; cover and cook for 15-20 minutes or until tender. Drain and cool to room temperature.

2. Meanwhile, in a small saucepan, cook bacon over medium heat until crisp. Using a slotted spoon, remove to paper towels; drain, reserving 1 Tbsp. drippings. Add sugar and flour to the pan; stir in water until blended. Cook and stir over medium-high heat until thickened and bubbly.

MAKEOVER CLEO'S POTATO SALAD

ROASTED PEAR SALAD

SPINACH SALAD WITH PENNE

3. Remove from the heat. Stir a small amount of hot mixture into egg; return all to the pan, stirring constantly. Bring to a gentle boil; cook and stir for 2 minutes. Remove from the heat and cool completely. Stir in Miracle Whip and vinegar. Fold in cream.

4. In a large bowl, combine the potatoes, celery, eggs, onion, celery seed and salt. Add dressing and bacon; stir until blended. Chill until serving.

Nutrition Facts: 3/4 cup equals 215 calories, 6 g fat (3 g saturated fat), 53 mg cholesterol, 407 mg sodium, 33 g carbohydrate, 2 g fiber, 5 g protein. **Diabetic Exchanges:** 2 starch, 1 fat.

Spinach Salad with Penne C M

PREP/TOTAL TIME: 25 min. YIELD: 9 servings

LYNNELL LOWNEY • WAUNAKEE, WISCONSIN

Loaded with fresh greens, this delightful pasta salad fits the season perfectly.

    1 cup uncooked whole wheat penne pasta
    1 pkg. (6 oz.) fresh baby spinach
  3/4 cup grated Parmesan cheese
  3/4 cup reduced-fat balsamic vinaigrette
  1/3 cup pine nuts, toasted
    8 fresh basil leaves, thinly sliced

1. Cook pasta according to package directions; drain and rinse in cold water.

2. In a large bowl, combine the spinach, cheese, vinaigrette, pine nuts, basil and the pasta. Serve the salad immediately.

Nutrition Facts: 3/4 cup equals 144 calories, 8 g fat (2 g saturated fat), 6 mg cholesterol, 269 mg sodium, 13 g carbohydrate, 2 g fiber, 7 g protein. **Diabetic Exchanges:** 1 vegetable, 1 fat, 1/2 starch.

Small, elongated and ivory-colored, pine nuts have a soft texture and buttery flavor. Frequently used in salads, sauces and Italian entrees, **pine nuts** are often toasted to enhance their delightfully earthy flavor.

GREEN SALAD WITH TANGY BASIL VINAIGRETTE

Green Salad with Tangy Basil Vinaigrette C M

PREP/TOTAL TIME: 15 min. YIELD: 4 servings

KRISTIN RIMKUS • SNOHOMISH, WASHINGTON

My tart and tangy dressing turns a basic salad into something special. It works for weeknight dining but is good enough for company and pairs perfectly with just about anything.

3	Tbsp. white wine vinegar
4-1/2	tsp. minced fresh basil
4-1/2	tsp. olive oil
1-1/2	tsp. honey
1/4	tsp. salt
1/8	tsp. pepper
6	cups torn mixed salad greens
1	cup cherry tomatoes, halved
2	Tbsp. shredded Parmesan cheese

1. In a small bowl, whisk the first six ingredients until blended. In a large bowl, combine salad greens and tomatoes. Drizzle with vinaigrette; toss to coat. Sprinkle with cheese.

Nutrition Facts: 1 cup equals 89 calories, 6 g fat (1 g saturated fat), 2 mg cholesterol, 214 mg sodium, 7 g carbohydrate, 2 g fiber, 3 g protein. **Diabetic Exchanges:** 1 vegetable, 1 fat.

Cilantro Blue Cheese Slaw F C

PREP/TOTAL TIME: 25 min. YIELD: 8 servings

CHRISTI DALTON • HARTSVILLE, TENNESSEE

A zesty dressing, crisp cabbage, fresh cilantro and a jalapeno pepper make this recipe a runaway hit! Serve the slaw as a side dish to any meal, or use it to top your favorite fish taco recipe instead of lettuce and the usual toppings.

8	cups shredded cabbage
1	small red onion, halved and thinly sliced
1/3	cup minced fresh cilantro
1	jalapeno pepper, seeded and minced
1/4	cup crumbled blue cheese
1/4	cup fat-free mayonnaise
1/4	cup reduced-fat sour cream
2	Tbsp. rice vinegar
2	Tbsp. lime juice
1	garlic clove, minced
1	tsp. sugar
1	tsp. grated lime peel
3/4	tsp. salt
1/2	tsp. coarsely ground pepper

1. In a large bowl, combine the cabbage, onion, cilantro and jalapeno. In a small bowl, combine the remaining ingredients; pour over salad and toss to coat.

Editor's Note: When cutting hot peppers, disposable gloves are recommended. Avoid touching your face.

Nutrition Facts: 3/4 cup equals 63 calories, 2 g fat (1 g saturated fat), 6 mg cholesterol, 362 mg sodium, 9 g carbohydrate, 3 g fiber, 3 g protein. **Diabetic Exchanges:** 1 vegetable, 1/2 fat.

Flank Steak Salad C

PREP: 25 min. + marinating GRILL: 15 min. + standing
YIELD: 8 servings

JENNIFER HUNSAKER • ROY, UTAH

This beautiful salad combines perfectly marinated flank steak with a tasty homemade dressing for a satisfying meal that's sure to please.

- 2 Tbsp. lime juice
- 2 Tbsp. reduced-sodium soy sauce
- 3 garlic cloves, minced
- 2 tsp. minced fresh gingerroot
- 1 beef flank steak (2 lbs.)

VINAIGRETTE:
- 2 Tbsp. plus 2 tsp. white vinegar
- 1 Tbsp. reduced-sodium soy sauce
- 1 tsp. ketchup
- 3 Tbsp. chopped onion
- 1 Tbsp. sugar
- 1 small garlic clove, peeled and halved
- 1/2 tsp. minced fresh gingerroot
- 1/4 tsp. salt
- 1/4 tsp. pepper
- 3 Tbsp. canola oil
- 1 bunch romaine, torn
- 1 cup grape tomatoes

1. In a large resealable plastic bag, combine the lime juice, soy sauce, garlic and ginger; add the beef. Seal bag and turn to coat; refrigerate for 8 hours or overnight.

2. Drain beef and discard marinade. Using long-handled tongs, moisten a paper towel with cooking oil and lightly coat the grill rack. Grill beef, covered, over medium heat or broil 4 in. from the heat for 6-8 minutes on each side or until meat reaches desired doneness (for medium-rare, a thermometer should read 145°; medium, 160°; well-done, 170°). Let stand for 10 minutes. To serve, thinly slice across the grain.

3. Meanwhile, in a blender, combine the vinegar, soy sauce, ketchup, onion, sugar, garlic, ginger, salt and pepper; cover and process until pureed. While processing, gradually add oil in a steady stream.

4. Place romaine and tomatoes in a large bowl. Drizzle with vinaigrette; toss to coat. Divide among eight plates; top with steak.

Nutrition Facts: 1 cup salad with 3 oz. cooked beef equals 237 calories, 14 g fat (4 g saturated fat), 54 mg cholesterol, 270 mg sodium, 5 g carbohydrate, 1 g fiber, 23 g protein. **Diabetic Exchanges:** 3 lean meat, 1 vegetable, 1 fat.

Balsamic-Salmon Spinach Salad C

PREP/TOTAL TIME: 20 min. YIELD: 2 servings

KAREN1969 • TASTE OF HOME ONLINE COMMUNITY

This main-dish salad is really healthy, and it's a cinch to make after a hard day at work.

- 1 salmon fillet (6 oz.)
- 2 Tbsp. reduced-fat balsamic vinaigrette, *divided*
- 3 cups fresh baby spinach
- 1/4 cup cubed avocado
- 1 Tbsp. chopped walnuts, toasted
- 1 Tbsp. sunflower kernels, toasted
- 1 Tbsp. dried cranberries

1. Drizzle salmon with 1 Tbsp. vinaigrette. Place on a broiler pan coated with cooking spray. Broil 3-4 in. from the heat for 10-15 minutes or until fish flakes easily with a fork. Cut salmon into two pieces.

2. Meanwhile, in a large bowl, toss spinach with remaining vinaigrette. Divide between two plates. Top each with half of the salmon, avocado, walnuts, sunflower kernels and cranberries.

Nutrition Facts: 1 serving equals 283 calories, 19 g fat (3 g saturated fat), 50 mg cholesterol, 219 mg sodium, 9 g carbohydrate, 3 g fiber, 21 g protein. **Diabetic Exchanges:** 2 medium-fat meat, 2 fat, 1 vegetable.

BALSAMIC-SALMON SPINACH SALAD

Pecan Sweet Potato Salad Ⓜ

PREP: 40 min. + chilling YIELD: 12 servings

PATRICIA SWART • GALLOWAY, NEW JERSEY

A new twist on an old favorite, my tasty, easy-to-make sweet potato salad is sure to be the talk of your next party.

- 6 to 7 large sweet potatoes (about 5 lbs.), peeled and cut into 1-in. cubes
- 4 celery ribs, chopped
- 2 green onions, thinly sliced
- 1 cup fat-free mayonnaise
- 1/2 cup reduced-fat sour cream
- 2/3 cup chopped pecans, toasted

1. Place sweet potatoes in a Dutch oven and cover with water. Bring to a boil. Reduce heat; cover and cook for 10-15 minutes or just until tender. Drain. Transfer to a large bowl; cool to room temperature. Stir in celery and green onions.

2. In a small bowl, combine mayonnaise and sour cream. Gently stir into potato mixture. Cover and refrigerate for several hours or overnight. Just before serving, sprinkle with pecans.

Nutrition Facts: 3/4 cup equals 184 calories, 6 g fat (1 g saturated fat), 5 mg cholesterol, 188 mg sodium, 30 g carbohydrate, 4 g fiber, 3 g protein. **Diabetic Exchanges:** 2 starch, 1 fat.

Minty-Watermelon Cucumber Salad Ⓕ Ⓢ Ⓒ Ⓜ

PREP/TOTAL TIME: 20 min.
YIELD: 16 servings (3/4 cup each)

ROBLYNN HUNNISETT • GUELPH, ONTARIO

Capturing the fantastic flavors of summer, this refreshing, beautiful salad truly shines at picnics and potlucks.

- 8 cups cubed seedless watermelon
- 2 medium English cucumbers, halved lengthwise and sliced
- 6 green onions, chopped
- 1/4 cup minced fresh mint
- 1/4 cup olive oil
- 1/4 cup balsamic vinegar
- 1/2 tsp. salt
- 1/2 tsp. pepper

1. In a large bowl, combine the watermelon, cucumbers, onions and mint. In a small bowl, whisk the oil, vinegar, salt and pepper. Pour over watermelon mixture; toss to coat. Serve immediately or cover and refrigerate for up to 2 hours.

Nutrition Facts: 3/4 cup equals 60 calories, 3 g fat (trace saturated fat), 0 cholesterol, 78 mg sodium, 9 g carbohydrate, 1 g fiber, 1 g protein. **Diabetic Exchanges:** 1/2 fruit, 1/2 fat.

Four-Fruit Salad Ⓕ Ⓢ Ⓒ

PREP: 15 min. + chilling
YIELD: 12 servings (3/4 cup each)

KRISTIN RIMKUS • SNOHOMISH, WASHINGTON

With a honey glaze and a hint of mint, this fresh fruit medley captures the mouthwatering flavors folks crave.

FOUR-FRUIT SALAD

PECAN SWEET POTATO SALAD

4 cups fresh raspberries
4 medium plums, coarsely chopped
4 medium apricots, coarsely chopped
2 medium peaches, coarsely chopped
2 Tbsp. minced fresh mint
2 Tbsp. honey

1. In a large bowl, combine the first five ingredients. Drizzle with honey and toss to coat. Refrigerate the mixture until chilled.

Nutrition Facts: 3/4 cup equals 55 calories, trace fat (trace saturated fat), 0 cholesterol, trace sodium, 13 g carbohydrate, 4 g fiber, 1 g protein. **Diabetic Exchange:** 1 fruit.

Seafood & Shells Salad [F]

PREP/TOTAL TIME: 30 min. **YIELD:** 13 servings

ROSALEE RAY • LANSING, MICHIGAN

My family asks for this salad often during the summer months. Packed with garden-fresh vegetables and succulent seafood, it has become a favorite.

2 cups uncooked small pasta shells
3 pkg. (8 oz. *each*) imitation crabmeat

1 lb. cooked small shrimp, peeled and deveined
1/4 cup finely chopped sweet onion
1/4 cup finely chopped celery
3 Tbsp. *each* finely chopped green, sweet red and yellow pepper
3 Tbsp. minced fresh parsley
2 Tbsp. snipped fresh dill *or* 2 tsp. dill weed
1-1/2 cups fat-free mayonnaise
2 Tbsp. lemon juice
1/4 tsp. salt
1/4 tsp. pepper

1. Cook pasta according to package directions; drain and rinse in cold water.

2. In a large bowl, combine the crab, shrimp, onion, celery, peppers, parsley and dill. Stir in pasta. In a small bowl, combine the mayonnaise, lemon juice, salt and pepper. Pour over salad and toss to coat. Chill until serving.

Nutrition Facts: 3/4 cup equals 164 calories, 2 g fat (trace saturated fat), 62 mg cholesterol, 612 mg sodium, 22 g carbohydrate, 1 g fiber, 14 g protein. **Diabetic Exchanges:** 2 lean meat, 1-1/2 starch.

WILD RICE SALAD

Wild Rice Salad

PREP: 15 min. **COOK:** 55 min. + chilling
YIELD: 15 servings (2/3 cup each)

BARBARA SCHULTE • PAYSON, ARIZONA

Nutty, fruity and packed with flavor, this make-ahead dish is a wholesome side for a variety of entrees.

3	cups water
2	cups uncooked wild rice
2	cups finely chopped dried apricots
2	cups dried cherries
1	cup chopped walnuts
1/2	cup olive oil
1/3	cup lemon juice
2	Tbsp. maple syrup
1-1/2	tsp. salt

1. In a large saucepan, bring water and rice to a boil. Reduce heat; cover and simmer for 45-50 minutes or until rice is tender. Drain if necessary. Transfer to a large bowl; cool completely.

2. Meanwhile, place apricots in a small bowl; cover with boiling water. Let stand for 5 minutes; drain.

Stir the apricots, cherries and walnuts into rice. In a small bowl, whisk the oil, lemon juice, maple syrup and salt. Pour over rice mixture and mix well. Refrigerate for at least 30 minutes.

Nutrition Facts: 2/3 cup equals 293 calories, 12 g fat (1 g saturated fat), 0 cholesterol, 234 mg sodium, 44 g carbohydrate, 3 g fiber, 5 g protein.

Makeover Creamy Cranberry Salad

PREP: 15 min. + chilling
YIELD: 12 servings (2/3 cup each)

ALEXANDRA LYPECKY • DEARBORN, MICHIGAN

This luscious makeover takes a longtime family favorite and makes it even better. With just a fourth of the original's saturated fat but all of the creamy flavor, it will be enjoyed by everyone.

3	cups fresh or frozen cranberries, thawed and coarsely chopped
1	can (20 oz.) unsweetened crushed pineapple, drained
2	cups miniature marshmallows
1	medium apple, chopped

Sugar substitute equivalent to 1/2 cup sugar

  1/8 tsp. salt
   1 carton (8 oz.) frozen reduced-fat whipped
      topping, thawed
  1/4 cup chopped walnuts

1. In a large bowl, combine the cranberries, pineapple, marshmallows, apple, sugar substitute and salt. Cover and refrigerate overnight.

2. Just before serving, fold in whipped topping and walnuts.

Editor's Note: This recipe was tested with Splenda no-calorie sweetener.

Nutrition Facts: 2/3 cup equals 133 calories, 4 g fat (2 g saturated fat), 0 cholesterol, 29 mg sodium, 24 g carbohydrate, 2 g fiber, 1 g protein. **Diabetic Exchanges:** 1 starch, 1/2 fruit, 1/2 fat.

Bulgur Greek Salad

PREP: 20 min. + standing **YIELD:** 12 servings

JENNIFER ANDRZJEWSKI • GRIZZLY FLATS, CALIFORNIA

I've tried to start eating healthier, and this recipe is wonderful and so versatile. The ingredients are easy to find...and to have on hand at all times.

1-1/2 cups bulgur
   3 cups boiling water
  1/4 cup plus 2 Tbsp. lemon juice, *divided*
   1 tsp. salt, *divided*
1-1/4 cups cubed cooked chicken breast
1-1/4 cups chopped cucumber
  1/2 cup cherry tomatoes, halved

  1/3 cup Greek olives
  1/4 cup minced fresh parsley
  1/4 cup roasted sweet red peppers, drained and
      chopped
  1/4 cup chopped red onion
   3 Tbsp. minced fresh basil
   3 Tbsp. olive oil
  1/4 tsp. dried oregano
  1/4 tsp. pepper
  1/8 tsp. cayenne pepper
  1/4 cup crumbled feta cheese

1. Place bulgur in a small bowl. Stir in the water, 1/4 cup lemon juice and 1/2 tsp. salt. Cover and let stand for 30 minutes or until most of the liquid is absorbed. Drain well.

2. In a large bowl, combine the chicken, cucumber, tomatoes, olives, parsley, red peppers, onion and basil. Stir in bulgur.

3. In a small bowl, whisk the oil, oregano, pepper, cayenne and remaining lemon juice and salt. Pour over bulgur mixture; toss to coat. Sprinkle with cheese.

Nutrition Facts: 2/3 cup equals 137 calories, 5 g fat (1 g saturated fat), 12 mg cholesterol, 313 mg sodium, 16 g carbohydrate, 4 g fiber, 7 g protein. **Diabetic Exchanges:** 1 starch, 1 lean meat, 1/2 fat.

BULGUR GREEK SALAD

MAKEOVER CREAMY CRANBERRY SALAD

Apricot Orange Vinaigrette S C

PREP/TOTAL TIME: 5 min. YIELD: about 3/4 cup

DIANA RIOS • LYTLE, TEXAS

This sweet and tangy citrus dressing perks up any salad, lending appeal to even a simple blend of mixed greens.

- 1/4 cup apricot preserves
- 2 Tbsp. orange juice
- 2 Tbsp. rice vinegar
- 2 Tbsp. canola oil
- 1 Tbsp. water
- 1/8 tsp. salt

Dash pepper

1. Place all ingredients in a jar with a tight-fitting lid; shake well. Cover and refrigerate until serving.

Nutrition Facts: 2 Tbsp. equals 78 calories, 5 g fat (trace saturated fat), 0 cholesterol, 55 mg sodium, 10 g carbohydrate, trace fiber, trace protein. **Diabetic Exchanges:** 1 fat, 1/2 starch.

Homemade Ranch Dressing Mix C

PREP/TOTAL TIME: 5 min.
YIELD: 4 batches (about 3/4 cup)

HEALTHY COOKING TEST KITCHEN

Used as both a mix for a dip and a salad dressing, this tongue-tingling ranch mix is both tasty and versatile.

- 1/3 cup buttermilk blend powder
- 1/4 cup dried parsley flakes
- 2 Tbsp. dried minced onion
- 2 tsp. salt
- 2 tsp. garlic powder

ADDITIONAL INGREDIENTS FOR SALAD DRESSING:
- 1 cup reduced-fat mayonnaise
- 1 cup plus 6 Tbsp. buttermilk

ADDITIONAL INGREDIENTS FOR DIP:
- 2 cups (16 oz.) reduced-fat sour cream

1. Combine the first five ingredients. Store in an airtight container in a cool dry place for up to 1 year.

For salad dressing: In a small bowl, whisk the mayonnaise, buttermilk and 3 Tbsp. mix. Refrigerate for at least 1 hour. Yield: about 2 cups.

For dip: In a small bowl, combine sour cream and 3 Tbsp. mix. Refrigerate for at least 2 hours. Serve with assorted crackers and fresh vegetables. Yield: about 2 cups.

Nutrition Facts–Ranch Salad Dressing: 2 Tbsp. equals 62 calories, 5 g fat (1 g saturated fat), 7 mg cholesterol, 219 mg sodium, 3 g carbohydrate, trace fiber, 1 g protein.

Nutrition Facts–Ranch Dip: 2 Tbsp. equals 42 calories, 3 g fat (2 g saturated fat), 10 mg cholesterol, 73 mg sodium, 2 g carbohydrate, trace fiber, 2 g protein.

Zucchini "Linguine" Salad C M

PREP: 30 min. + chilling YIELD: 6 servings

LILY JULOW • GAINESVILLE, FLORIDA

This idea came to me from a recipe I saw for zucchini cut into noodle-like strips and dressed with a creamy sauce.

- 5 medium zucchini
- 3/4 tsp. salt, *divided*

APRICOT ORANGE VINAIGRETTE

ZUCCHINI "LINGUINE" SALAD

1   large sweet red pepper, julienned
1   large tomato, seeded and cut into thin strips
1/2   cup thinly sliced sweet onion
3   Tbsp. olive oil
2   Tbsp. cider vinegar
1/4   cup minced fresh parsley
1-1/2   tsp. minced fresh oregano *or* 1/2 tsp. dried oregano
1/4   tsp. pepper
Shredded Parmesan cheese, optional

1. Cut the ends off each zucchini. Using a cheese slicer or vegetable peeler, cut zucchini into thin lengthwise strips. Cut zucchini on all sides, as if peeling a carrot, until the seeds become visible. Discard seeded portion or save for another use. Cut zucchini strips into 1/4-in. widths.

2. Place in a strainer; sprinkle with 1/2 tsp. salt and gently toss to coat. Let stand for 15 minutes. Gently shake strainer. Drain zucchini on paper towels and pat dry.

3. Transfer to a large bowl; add the red pepper, tomato and onion. In a small bowl, whisk the oil, vinegar, parsley, oregano, pepper and remaining salt. Pour over zucchini mixture and toss to coat. Cover and refrigerate for at least 30 minutes before serving. Sprinkle with cheese if desired.

Nutrition Facts: 3/4 cup equals 100 calories, 7 g fat (1 g saturated fat), 0 cholesterol, 254 mg sodium, 9 g carbohydrate, 3 g fiber, 2 g protein. **Diabetic Exchanges:** 1 vegetable, 1 fat.

Mediterranean Tuna Salad

PREP/TOTAL TIME: 25 min. **YIELD:** 4 servings

RENEE NASH • SNOQUALMIE, WASHINGTON

In spite of a long list of ingredients, this salad is very quick to prepare. You'll love the fresh flavors.

1   can (15 oz.) garbanzo beans *or* chickpeas, rinsed and drained
3   celery ribs, chopped
1   small sweet red pepper, chopped
4   green onions, chopped
2   Tbsp. olive oil
2   Tbsp. balsamic vinegar
2   Tbsp. spicy brown mustard
1/2   tsp. dried basil
1/4   tsp. salt
1/4   tsp. pepper
2   cans (5 oz. *each*) white water-packed tuna
4   cups shredded lettuce
1/2   cup crumbled feta *or* blue cheese, optional

1. In a large bowl, combine the beans, celery, red pepper and onions. In a small bowl, whisk the oil, vinegar, mustard, basil, salt and pepper. Pour over bean mixture; toss to coat. Gently stir in tuna. Serve over lettuce. Sprinkle with cheese if desired.

Nutrition Facts: 1-1/2 cups tuna salad with 1 cup shredded lettuce (calculated without cheese) equals 282 calories, 11 g fat (2 g saturated fat), 30 mg cholesterol, 682 mg sodium, 23 g carbohydrate, 6 g fiber, 23 g protein. **Diabetic Exchanges:** 3 lean meat, 1 starch, 1 vegetable, 1 fat.

BLT-AND-MORE SALAD

BLT-and-More Salad ⓒ

PREP/TOTAL TIME: 20 min. YIELD: 4 servings

PAULA MARCHESI • LENHARTSVILLE, PENNSYLVANIA

I created this when my husband and I were looking for something quick, yet different. The blend of flavors is wonderful, and I make it often. It's simply the best!

1-1/2 cups yellow cherry tomatoes, halved
1-1/2 cups cherry tomatoes, halved
   1/3 cup cubed avocado
     2 bacon strips, cooked and crumbled
     2 Tbsp. fat-free sour cream
     2 Tbsp. fat-free mayonnaise
     2 Tbsp. fat-free milk
     1 garlic clove, minced
   1/2 tsp. dill weed
Dash *each* salt and pepper
   1/3 cup crumbled goat cheese
     2 Tbsp. pine nuts
     4 Bibb lettuce leaves

1. In a small bowl, combine the tomatoes, avocado and bacon. In another small bowl, whisk the sour cream, mayonnaise, milk, garlic, dill, salt and pepper; pour over salad. Gently toss to coat. Sprinkle with cheese and pine nuts. Serve immediately in lettuce leaves.

Nutrition Facts: 3/4 cup equals 129 calories, 8 g fat (3 g saturated fat), 17 mg cholesterol, 236 mg sodium, 10 g carbohydrate, 3 g fiber, 6 g protein. **Diabetic Exchanges:** 1 high-fat meat, 1 vegetable.

Berry Chicken Salad ⓒ

PREP/TOTAL TIME: 20 min. YIELD: 4 servings

WENDY BALL • BATTLE CREEK, MICHIGAN

Bright berries and creamy goat cheese make this colorful salad a new twist on an all-time classic. No matter how you look at it, it's a true winner! Ideal on its own, the salad could also work as a sandwich filling on whole wheat bread.

     4 boneless skinless chicken breast halves
        (4 oz. *each*)
   1/4 tsp. salt
   1/4 tsp. pepper
     1 pkg. (6 oz.) fresh baby spinach
     1 cup fresh raspberries
     1 cup halved fresh strawberries
   2/3 cup crumbled goat cheese
     3 Tbsp. chopped pecans, toasted
   1/4 cup prepared fat-free raspberry vinaigrette

1. Sprinkle chicken with salt and pepper. Grill chicken, covered, over medium heat or broil 4 in. from the heat for 4-7 minutes on each side or until juices run clear.

2. In a large bowl, combine the spinach, raspberries, strawberries, cheese and pecans. Divide among four serving plates. Slice chicken and arrange over spinach mixture; drizzle with vinaigrette.

Nutrition Facts: 1-1/2 cups salad with 1 chicken breast half and 1 Tbsp. dressing equals 268 calories, 12 g fat (4 g saturated fat), 86 mg cholesterol, 391 mg sodium, 15 g carbohydrate, 5 g fiber, 28 g protein. **Diabetic Exchanges:** 4 lean meat, 1 vegetable, 1 fat, 1/2 fruit.

Teriyaki Chicken Salad with Poppy Seed Dressing

PREP: 30 min. + marinating GRILL: 10 min.
YIELD: 6 servings

CATHLEEN LEONARD • WOODBRIDGE, CALIFORNIA

I've made this salad so often and shared it with many people. It's originally from my good friend's daughter, and we always receive compliments on how wonderfully the light fruit flavors come alive with the poppy seed dressing.

- 1 cup honey teriyaki marinade
- 1 lb. boneless skinless chicken breasts
- 6 cups torn romaine
- 3 medium kiwifruit, peeled and sliced
- 1 can (20 oz.) unsweetened pineapple chunks, drained
- 1 can (11 oz.) mandarin oranges, drained
- 2 celery ribs, chopped
- 1 medium sweet red pepper, chopped
- 1 medium green pepper, chopped
- 1 cup fresh raspberries
- 1 cup sliced fresh strawberries
- 3 green onions, chopped
- 1/2 cup salted cashews
- 1/3 cup reduced-fat poppy seed salad dressing

1. Place marinade in a large resealable plastic bag; add the chicken. Seal bag and turn to coat; refrigerate for 8 hours or overnight. Drain and discard marinade.

2. Grill chicken, covered, over medium heat for 5-7 minutes on each side or until a thermometer reads 170°.

3. Slice chicken. Divide the romaine, kiwi, pineapple, oranges, celery, peppers, raspberries and strawberries among six plates; top with chicken. Sprinkle with green onions and cashews. Drizzle with salad dressing.

Nutrition Facts: 1 serving equals 361 calories, 11 g fat (2 g saturated fat), 42 mg cholesterol, 761 mg sodium, 49 g carbohydrate, 7 g fiber, 20 g protein. **Diabetic Exchanges:** 2 lean meat, 1-1/2 starch, 1-1/2 fat, 1 vegetable, 1 fruit.

Shrimp Spinach Salad C

PREP/TOTAL TIME: 20 min. YIELD: 4 servings

JAMIE LARSON • DODGE CENTER, MINNESOTA

Shrimp and garlic are sauteed in butter, then set atop a bed of spinach in this no-fuss salad. Almonds, tomatoes and a squeeze of lemon finish off this beauty.

- 2 Tbsp. butter
- 1 lb. uncooked medium shrimp, peeled and deveined
- 3 garlic cloves, minced
- 2 Tbsp. minced fresh parsley
- 4 cups fresh baby spinach
- 3/4 cup cherry tomatoes, halved
- 1/4 cup sliced almonds, toasted
- 1 medium lemon
- 1/4 tsp. salt
- 1/4 tsp. pepper

1. In a large nonstick skillet over medium heat, melt butter. Add the shrimp. Cook and stir for 3-4 minutes or until shrimp turn pink. Add garlic and parsley; cook 1 minute longer. Remove from the heat.

2. Place spinach in a salad bowl. Top with tomatoes, almonds and shrimp mixture. Squeeze the juice from the lemon; drizzle over the salad. Sprinkle with the salt and pepper.

Nutrition Facts: 1 cup equals 201 calories, 10 g fat (4 g saturated fat), 153 mg cholesterol, 350 mg sodium, 6 g carbohydrate, 2 g fiber, 21 g protein. **Diabetic Exchanges:** 3 lean meat, 1-1/2 fat, 1 vegetable.

TERIYAKI CHICKEN SALAD WITH POPPY SEED DRESSING

SHRIMP SPINACH SALAD

Balsamic Green Bean Salad S C M

PREP: 30 min. + chilling **YIELD:** 16 servings

MEGAN SPENCER • FARMINGTON HILLS, MICHIGAN

Serve up those green beans in a whole new way! The tangy flavors and crunch of this eye-appealing side complement any special meal or holiday potluck.

2	lbs. fresh green beans, trimmed and cut into 1-1/2-in. pieces
1/4	cup olive oil
3	Tbsp. lemon juice
3	Tbsp. balsamic vinegar
1/4	tsp. salt
1/4	tsp. garlic powder
1/4	tsp. ground mustard
1/8	tsp. pepper
1	large red onion, chopped
4	cups cherry tomatoes, halved
1	cup (4 oz.) crumbled feta cheese

1. Place beans in a Dutch oven and cover with water. Bring to a boil. Cover and cook for 8-10 minutes or until crisp-tender. Drain and immediately place beans in ice water. Drain and pat dry.

2. In a small bowl, whisk the oil, lemon juice, vinegar, salt, garlic powder, mustard and pepper. Drizzle over beans. Add the onion; toss to coat. Cover and refrigerate for at least 1 hour. Just before serving, stir in tomatoes and cheese.

Nutrition Facts: 3/4 cup equals 77 calories, 5 g fat (1 g saturated fat), 4 mg cholesterol, 112 mg sodium, 7 g carbohydrate, 3 g fiber, 3 g protein. **Diabetic Exchanges:** 1 vegetable, 1 fat.

Blue Cheese Waldorf Salad M

PREP: 20 min. + chilling **YIELD:** 12 servings

DEBORAH WILLIAMS • PEORIA, ARIZONA

Blue cheese perks up this version of a traditional Waldorf salad. Serve over lettuce leaves for a great lunch.

4	large apples, chopped
2	cups green grapes, halved
1-1/3	cups chopped celery
1/2	cup raisins
1	Tbsp. lemon juice
2/3	cup fat-free mayonnaise
2/3	cup buttermilk
1/3	cup crumbled blue cheese
1	Tbsp. sugar
1/4	cup chopped walnuts, toasted

1. In a large bowl, combine the apples, grapes, celery, raisins and lemon juice.

2. In a small bowl, combine the mayonnaise, buttermilk, blue cheese and sugar. Pour over apple mixture and toss to coat. Cover and refrigerate for at least 1 hour.

3. Just before serving, sprinkle with walnuts.

Nutrition Facts: 3/4 cup equals 126 calories, 4 g fat (1 g saturated fat), 5 mg cholesterol, 192 mg sodium, 24 g carbohydrate, 3 g fiber, 3 g protein. **Diabetic Exchanges:** 1 fruit, 1/2 starch, 1/2 fat.

Grecian Garden Salad C M

PREP: 20 min. + chilling **YIELD:** 6 servings

MELISSA SIPHERD • SALT LAKE CITY, UTAH

My mom often makes this for guests. Colorful and healthy, it doesn't taste light because of the generous amount of cheese.

1-1/2	cups cut fresh asparagus (1-in. pieces)
3	medium tomatoes, seeded and chopped
2	Tbsp. balsamic vinegar
4-1/2	tsp. minced fresh basil or 1-1/2 tsp. dried basil
1	Tbsp. olive oil
1	tsp. salt
1/2	tsp. pepper
1	cup (4 oz.) crumbled feta cheese

BLUE CHEESE WALDORF SALAD

BALSAMIC GREEN BEAN SALAD

1. In a large saucepan, bring 3 cups water to a boil. Add asparagus; cover and boil for 3 minutes. Drain and immediately place asparagus in ice water. Drain and pat dry. Transfer to a serving bowl. Stir in the tomatoes.

2. In a small bowl, whisk the vinegar, basil, oil, salt and pepper. Drizzle over vegetables; toss to coat. Cover and refrigerate for at least 1 hour. Just before serving, stir in cheese.

Nutrition Facts: 2/3 cup equals 92 calories, 5 g fat (2 g saturated fat), 10 mg cholesterol, 579 mg sodium, 6 g carbohydrate, 2 g fiber, 5 g protein. **Diabetic Exchanges:** 1 vegetable, 1 fat.

Southwest Crunch Chicken Salad c

PREP/TOTAL TIME: 30 min. **YIELD:** 13 servings

SALLY SIBTHORPE • SHELBY TOWNSHIP, MICHIGAN

It's hard to believe that this party-perfect chicken salad with cashews and turkey bacon is low in carbs, high in protein and only contains 3 g of saturated fat per serving! Enjoy it as is, on a bed of lettuce or wrapped in a tortilla.

1-1/3 cups fat-free mayonnaise
  1/2 cup minced fresh cilantro
  1/4 cup lime juice
  1/4 cup orange juice
    2 garlic cloves, minced
1-3/4 tsp. ground cumin
  3/4 tsp. grated orange peel
  1/2 tsp. salt
    9 cups cubed cooked chicken breast
1-3/4 cups julienned peeled jicama
1-3/4 cups chopped celery
1-3/4 cups chopped sweet red peppers
    1 cup chopped cashews
  1/2 lb. turkey bacon strips, diced and cooked

1. In a small bowl, combine the first eight ingredients. In a large bowl, combine the remaining ingredients. Add mayonnaise mixture; toss to coat. Chill until serving.

Nutrition Facts: 1 cup equals 286 calories, 12 g fat (3 g saturated fat), 95 mg cholesterol, 653 mg sodium, 11 g carbohydrate, 3 g fiber, 33 g protein. **Diabetic Exchanges:** 4 very lean meat, 1-1/2 fat, 1 starch.

Thai Pasta Side Salad M

PREP/TOTAL TIME: 25 min. **YIELD:** 10 servings

LAURIE DAVISON • CLEARWATER, FLORIDA

A tasty peanut dressing lightly coats pasta and cabbage in this easy-to-make side dish that's perfect for potlucks or outdoor events.

2	cups uncooked bow tie pasta
4	cups chopped red cabbage
1	medium green pepper, chopped
1	medium sweet red pepper, chopped
4	green onions, thinly sliced
1/4	cup rice vinegar
1/4	cup reduced-fat creamy peanut butter
4-1/2	tsp. reduced-sodium soy sauce
1	Tbsp. honey
1-1/2	tsp. olive oil
1/2	cup dry roasted peanuts

1. Cook pasta according to package directions. Meanwhile, in a large bowl, combine the cabbage, peppers and onions. In a small bowl, whisk the vinegar, peanut butter, soy sauce, honey and oil.

2. Drain pasta and rinse in cold water; add to cabbage mixture. Pour dressing over salad; toss to coat. Just before serving, sprinkle with peanuts.

Nutrition Facts: 3/4 cup equals 161 calories, 7 g fat (1 g saturated fat), 0 cholesterol, 194 mg sodium, 21 g carbohydrate, 3 g fiber, 6 g protein. **Diabetic Exchanges:** 1-1/2 starch, 1 fat.

Layered Salad with Curry Dressing F C M

PREP/TOTAL TIME: 20 min. **YIELD:** 16 servings

KERRI PELZ • HENDERSONVILLE, NORTH CAROLINA

Light mayonnaise and yogurt cut calories and fat in this lighter version of seven-layer salad. Curry powder adds a unique twist and complements the other ingredients.

1	pkg. (10 oz.) ready-to-serve salad greens
2	celery ribs, chopped
1/2	cup chopped green pepper
1/2	cup chopped cauliflower
2	green onions, thinly sliced
1	pkg. (10 oz.) frozen peas, thawed
3/4	cup fat-free mayonnaise
3/4	cup (6 oz.) reduced-fat plain yogurt
1	Tbsp. lemon juice
1	tsp. curry powder
3/4	cup shredded reduced-fat cheddar cheese
1/2	cup sliced almonds

1. In a 3-qt. glass bowl, layer the salad greens, celery, pepper, cauliflower, green onions and peas. In a small bowl, whisk the mayonnaise, yogurt, lemon juice and curry; carefully spread over salad. Sprinkle with cheese. Chill until serving. Just before serving, sprinkle with almonds.

Nutrition Facts: 3/4 cup equals 67 calories, 3 g fat (1 g saturated fat), 6 mg cholesterol, 161 mg sodium, 7 g carbohydrate, 2 g fiber, 4 g protein.

Crunchy Apple Salad [F] [S]

PREP: 15 min. + chilling **YIELD:** 5 servings

KATHLEEN LAW • BELLINGHAM, WASHINGTON

With fiber-rich fruit, light dressing and crunchy walnuts, this is a great snack. Try it with low-fat granola.

- 6 Tbsp. fat-free sugar-free vanilla yogurt
- 6 Tbsp. reduced-fat whipped topping
- 1/4 tsp. plus 1/8 tsp. ground cinnamon, *divided*
- 2 medium red apples, chopped
- 1 large Granny Smith apple, chopped
- 1/4 cup dried cranberries
- 2 Tbsp. chopped walnuts

1. In a large bowl, combine the yogurt, whipped topping and 1/4 tsp. cinnamon. Add apples and cranberries; toss to coat. Refrigerate until serving. Sprinkle with walnuts and remaining cinnamon before serving.

Nutrition Facts: 3/4 cup equals 109 calories, 3 g fat (1 g saturated fat), trace cholesterol, 12 mg sodium, 22 g carbohydrate, 3 g fiber, 2 g protein. **Diabetic Exchanges:** 1 fruit, 1/2 starch, 1/2 fat.

Fruit & Cream Layered Salad [S]

PREP/TOTAL TIME: 25 min. **YIELD:** 13 servings

APRIL LANE • GREENEVILLE, TENNESSEE

I love salads, especially fruit salads, and try to cook light meals. I found a similar recipe to this one a few years ago and have revised it to make it a lot healthier.

- 3 oz. reduced-fat cream cheese
- 1 Tbsp. sugar
- 2 tsp. lemon juice
- 1/4 tsp. almond extract
- 1 carton (6 oz.) strawberry yogurt
- 2 cups reduced-fat whipped topping
- 3 medium peaches, peeled and sliced
- 2 cups halved fresh strawberries
- 2 cups fresh blueberries
- 2 cups green grapes
- 1 can (11 oz.) mandarin oranges, drained
- 1/4 cup sliced almonds, toasted

Fresh strawberries, optional

1. In a small bowl, beat the cream cheese, sugar, lemon juice and extract until smooth. Add yogurt; beat until blended. Fold in whipped topping.

2. In a 3-qt. trifle bowl, layer the peaches, strawberries and blueberries. Top with half of the whipped topping mixture. Layer with grapes, oranges and remaining whipped topping mixture. Refrigerate until serving. Sprinkle with almonds just before serving. Garnish with strawberries if desired.

Nutrition Facts: 3/4 cup (calculated without optional strawberries) equals 124 calories, 4 g fat (2 g saturated fat), 5 mg cholesterol, 37 mg sodium, 22 g carbohydrate, 2 g fiber, 2 g protein. **Diabetic Exchanges:** 1 fruit, 1/2 starch, 1/2 fat.

> Over the past years, blueberries have received notice in the press for being a **power food.** And for good reason: The berries are loaded with vitamins, minerals and fiber.

CRUNCHY APPLE SALAD

FRUIT & CREAM LAYERED SALAD

CURRY CHICKEN SOUP

TURKEY CHILI WITH PENNE

CURRIED CHICKEN PANINIS

Soups & Sandwiches

Just because you're watching your weight doesn't mean you have to turn down a classic soup-and-sandwich pairing. Turn here when you need a savory soup and piled-high sandwich that keep fat and calories at bay!

Curried Chicken Paninis

PREP/TOTAL TIME: 20 min. YIELD: 4 servings

MICHAELA ROSENTHAL • WOODLAND HILLS, CALIFORNIA

Serve the leftover chutney with chicken or pork tenderloin or with fat-free cream cheese as a fast cracker spread.

- 2 cups cubed cooked chicken breast
- 1/4 cup chopped celery
- 1/4 cup fat-free mayonnaise
- 3/4 tsp. curry powder
- 1/4 tsp. grated lemon peel
- 8 slices whole wheat bread
- 1/3 cup mango chutney
- 1 cup watercress *or* fresh arugula
- 2 Tbsp. butter, softened

1. In a small bowl, combine the first five ingredients.

2. Spread four bread slices with chutney. Layer each with 1/2 cup chicken salad and 1/4 cup watercress; top with remaining bread. Spread outsides of sandwiches with butter.

3. Cook on a panini maker or indoor grill for 3-4 minutes or until bread is browned.

Nutrition Facts: 1 sandwich equals 389 calories, 10 g fat (5 g saturated fat), 71 mg cholesterol, 705 mg sodium, 44 g carbohydrate, 4 g fiber, 28 g protein. **Diabetic Exchanges:** 3 starch, 3 lean meat, 1-1/2 fat.

Makeover Tuna Melt Bites

PREP/TOTAL TIME: 25 min. YIELD: 4 servings

HEALTHY COOKING TEST KITCHEN

For a healthier take on this diner special, our Test Kitchen updated to tinier "tuna melt bites," pumped up nutrition with whole wheat buns, slashed fat by substituting fat-free mayo and reduced-fat cheese, and added tomato and spinach on top. Give these a try!

- 2 cans (5 oz. *each*) light water-packed tuna, drained and flaked
- 1 celery rib, finely chopped
- 1/2 cup fat-free mayonnaise
- 1/4 cup shredded carrot
- 1 Tbsp. lemon juice

- 1/4 tsp. pepper
- 4 whole wheat hot dog buns, split
- 2 plum tomatoes, sliced
- 3 slices reduced-fat cheddar cheese, quartered
- 1/2 cup fresh baby spinach

1. In a small bowl, combine the first six ingredients; set aside. Place hot dog buns cut side up on an ungreased baking sheet. Broil 4-6 in. from the heat for 2-3 minutes or until golden brown.

2. Spoon tuna mixture over bottom halves; top with tomato and cheese slices. Broil 1-2 minutes longer or until cheese is melted. Top with spinach. Replace bun tops. Secure with toothpicks; cut each of the sandwiches into thirds.

Nutrition Facts: 3 mini sandwiches equals 274 calories, 6 g fat (3 g saturated fat), 34 mg cholesterol, 806 mg sodium, 29 g carbohydrate, 5 g fiber, 27 g protein.

Berry Turkey Sandwich

PREP/TOTAL TIME: 5 min. YIELD: 2 servings

EDWARD MEYER • ARNOLD, MISSOURI

Sliced fresh strawberries, Swiss cheese and a nutty cream cheese spread make this turkey sandwich different. Try it on whole wheat, oatmeal or sunflower seed bread. It's tasty and simple to put together.

- 4 slices whole wheat bread
- 2 lettuce leaves
- 2 slices reduced-fat Swiss cheese
- 1/4 lb. thinly sliced deli turkey breast
- 4 fresh strawberries, sliced
- 2 Tbsp. reduced-fat spreadable cream cheese
- 2 tsp. finely chopped pecans

1. On two slices of bread, layer with lettuce, cheese, turkey and strawberries. Combine cream cheese and pecans; spread over remaining bread. Place over the strawberry slices.

Nutrition Facts: One sandwich equals 356 calories, 10 g fat (3 g saturated fat), 39 mg cholesterol, 932 mg sodium, 39 g carbohydrate, 5 g fiber, 28 g protein.

Open-Faced Ham and Apple Melts F

PREP/TOTAL TIME: 15 min. **YIELD:** 4 servings

SALLY MALONEY • DALLAS, GEORGIA

As a homework snack or light lunch, these yummy melts combine the crunch of sweet apple with the tangy flavor of ham and Dijon mustard!

- 2   whole wheat English muffins, split
- 2   tsp. Dijon mustard
- 4   slices deli ham
- 1/2   medium apple, thinly sliced
- 2   slices reduced-fat Swiss cheese, halved

1. Place English muffin halves cut side up on a baking sheet. Broil 4-6 in. from the heat for 2-3 minutes or until golden brown.

2. Spread with mustard. Top with ham, apple slices and cheese. Broil 3-4 minutes longer or until cheese is melted.

Nutrition Facts: 1 muffin half equals 130 calories, 3 g fat (1 g saturated fat), 14 mg cholesterol, 429 mg sodium, 17 g carbohydrate, 3 g fiber, 10 g protein.

Black Bean-Pumpkin Soup M

PREP: 30 min. **COOK:** 30 min. **YIELD:** 8 servings (2 qt.)

JENNIFER FISHER • AUSTIN, TEXAS

This is such a healthy recipe, packed with protein from the beans and vitamins from the pumpkin.

- 2 cans (15 oz. *each*) black beans, rinsed and drained
- 1 can (14-1/2 oz.) diced tomatoes, drained
- 2 medium onions, finely chopped
- 1 tsp. olive oil
- 3 garlic cloves, minced
- 1 tsp. ground cumin
- 3 cups vegetable broth
- 1 can (15 oz.) solid-pack pumpkin
- 2 Tbsp. cider vinegar
- 1/2 tsp. pepper
- 2 Tbsp. bourbon, optional
- 1/2 cup reduced-fat sour cream
- 1/2 cup thinly sliced green onions
- 1/2 cup roasted salted pumpkin seeds

1. Place beans and tomatoes in a food processor; cover and process until blended. Set aside.

2. In a Dutch oven, saute onions in oil until tender. Add garlic and cumin; saute 1 minute longer. Stir in the broth, pumpkin, vinegar, pepper and bean mixture. Bring to a boil. Reduce heat; cover and simmer for 20 minutes.

3. Stir in bourbon if desired. Garnish each serving with sour cream, green onions and pumpkin seeds.

Nutrition Facts: 1 cup (calculated without bourbon) equals 238 calories, 8 g fat (2 g saturated fat), 5 mg cholesterol, 716 mg sodium, 30 g carbohydrate, 9 g fiber, 13 g protein. **Diabetic Exchanges:** 1-1/2 starch, 1-1/2 fat, 1 lean meat, 1 vegetable.

Turkey Avocado Sandwiches

PREP/TOTAL TIME: 10 min. **YIELD:** 2 servings

DAVE BREMSON • PLANTATION, FLORIDA

Hearty and delicious, these satisfying sandwiches have just the right amount of heat!

- 3 oz. fat-free cream cheese
- 2 tsp. taco sauce
- 4 drops hot pepper sauce
- 4 slices whole wheat bread
- 4 oz. sliced cooked turkey
- 1/2 medium ripe avocado, peeled and sliced
- 1 medium tomato, sliced
- 2 to 4 Tbsp. minced fresh cilantro
- 2 lettuce leaves

1. In a large bowl, beat cream cheese until smooth. Beat in taco sauce and pepper sauce; spread over bread.

2. Layer the turkey, avocado and tomato on two bread slices; sprinkle with cilantro. Top with lettuce and remaining bread.

Nutrition Facts: 1 sandwich equals 399 calories, 11 g fat (2 g saturated fat), 52 mg cholesterol, 617 mg sodium, 40 g carbohydrate, 7 g fiber, 33 g protein. **Diabetic Exchanges:** 3 lean meat, 2 starch, 1 vegetable, 1 fat.

BLACK BEAN-PUMPKIN SOUP

Makeover Beef & Potato Soup

PREP: 30 min. **COOK:** 6-1/2 hours
YIELD: 10 servings (3 qt.)

SHEILA HOLDERMAN • BERTHOLD, NORTH DAKOTA

Slow cooker ease makes this healthy version of our favorite soups a Christmas Eve tradition after church services.

1-1/2	lbs. lean ground beef (90% lean)
3/4	cup chopped onion
1/2	cup all-purpose flour
2	cans (14-1/2 oz. *each*) reduced-sodium chicken broth, *divided*
5	medium potatoes, peeled and cubed
5	medium carrots, chopped
3	celery ribs, chopped
3	tsp. dried basil
2	tsp. dried parsley flakes
1	tsp. garlic powder
1/2	tsp. pepper
12	oz. reduced-fat process cheese (Velveeta), cubed
1-1/2	cups 2% milk
1/2	cup reduced-fat sour cream

1. In a large skillet, cook beef and onion over medium heat until meat is no longer pink; drain. Combine flour and 1 can broth until smooth. Add to beef mixture. Bring to a boil; cook and stir for 2 minutes or until thickened.

2. Transfer to a 5-qt. slow cooker. Stir in the potatoes, carrots, celery, seasonings and remaining broth. Cover and cook on low for 6-7 hours or until vegetables are tender.

3. Stir in cheese and milk. Cover and cook 30 minutes longer or until cheese is melted. Just before serving, stir in sour cream.

Nutrition Facts: 1-1/4 cups equals 327 calories, 11 g fat (5 g saturated fat), 61 mg cholesterol, 832 mg sodium, 32 g carbohydrate, 3 g fiber, 25 g protein.

Seafood Salad Pitas [F]

PREP: 20 min. + chilling **YIELD:** 8 servings

LINDA EVANCOE-COBLE • LEOLA, PENNSYLVANIA

You can make this lovely, interesting sandwich as a refreshing light lunch...or pair it with a hearty soup for a change-of-pace supper.

2	cups chopped imitation crabmeat (about 10 oz.)
1/2	lb. cooked medium shrimp, peeled, deveined and chopped (about 1 cup)
2	celery ribs, chopped
1/2	cup thinly sliced green onions
3/4	cup fat-free mayonnaise
3/4	tsp. seafood seasoning
1/4	tsp. salt
1/8	tsp. pepper
8	whole wheat pita pocket halves

1. In a large bowl, combine the crab, shrimp, celery and onions. In a small bowl, combine the mayonnaise, seafood seasoning, salt and pepper. Pour over crab mixture; toss to coat. Cover and refrigerate for at least 2 hours. Spoon into pita halves.

Nutrition Facts: 1 filled pita half equals 162 calories, 2 g fat (trace saturated fat), 27 mg cholesterol, 755 mg sodium, 28 g carbohydrate, 3 g fiber, 10 g protein. **Diabetic Exchanges:** 2 starch, 1 lean meat.

MAKEOVER BEEF & POTATO SOUP

SEAFOOD SALAD PITAS

Roasted Garlic Butternut Soup

PREP: 35 min. **COOK:** 20 min.
YIELD: 9 servings (2-1/4 qt.)

ROBIN HAAS • CRANSTON, RHODE ISLAND

This lower-fat soup is creamy, really intense in flavor and offers 545 mg of potassium.

1	whole garlic bulb
1	tsp. olive oil
1	medium butternut squash (3 lb.), peeled and cubed
1	medium sweet potato, peeled and cubed
1	large onion, chopped
2	Tbsp. butter
3-1/4	cups water
1	can (14-1/2 oz.) reduced-sodium chicken broth
1	tsp. paprika
1/2	tsp. pepper
1/4	tsp. salt
9	Tbsp. crumbled blue cheese

1. Remove papery outer skin from garlic (do not peel or separate cloves). Cut top off of garlic bulb. Brush with oil; wrap in heavy-duty foil. Bake at 425° for 30-35 minutes or until softened. Cool for 10-15 minutes.

2. Meanwhile, in a Dutch oven, saute the squash, sweet potato and onion in butter until crisp-tender. Add the water, broth, paprika, pepper and salt; squeeze softened garlic into pan. Bring to a boil. Reduce heat; cover and simmer for 20-25 minutes or until vegetables are tender. Cool slightly.

3. In a food processor, process soup in batches until smooth. Return all to pan and heat through. Ladle into bowls; top with blue cheese.

Nutrition Facts: 1 cup soup with 1 Tbsp. blue cheese equals 144 calories, 6 g fat (3 g saturated fat), 13 mg cholesterol, 340 mg sodium, 21 g carbohydrate, 5 g fiber, 4 g protein.
Diabetic Exchanges: 1 starch, 1 fat.

Easy Minestrone

PREP: 25 min. **COOK:** 40 min.
YIELD: 11 servings (2-3/4 qt.)

LAUREN BRENNAN • HOOD RIVER, OREGON

This recipe is special to me because it's one of the few dinners my entire family loves. And I can feel good about serving it because it's nutritious and low in fat.

   2 large carrots, diced
   2 celery ribs, chopped
   1 medium onion, chopped
   1 Tbsp. olive oil
   1 Tbsp. butter
   2 garlic cloves, minced
   2 cans (14-1/2 oz. *each*) reduced-sodium chicken broth
   2 cans (8 oz. *each*) no-salt-added tomato sauce
   1 can (16 oz.) kidney beans, rinsed and drained
   1 can (15 oz.) garbanzo beans or chickpeas, rinsed and drained
   1 can (14-1/2 oz.) diced tomatoes, undrained

1-1/2 cups shredded cabbage
   1 Tbsp. dried basil
1-1/2 tsp. dried parsley flakes
   1 tsp. dried oregano
  1/2 tsp. pepper
   1 cup uncooked whole wheat elbow macaroni
  11 tsp. grated Parmesan cheese

1. In a large saucepan, saute the carrots, celery and onion in oil and butter until tender. Add garlic; cook 1 minute longer.

2. Stir in the broth, tomato sauce, beans, tomatoes, cabbage, basil, parsley, oregano and pepper. Bring to a boil. Reduce heat; cover and simmer for 20 minutes. Meanwhile, cook pasta according to package directions; drain.

3. Return soup to a boil. Stir in pasta; heat through. Ladle into bowls. Sprinkle with cheese.

Nutrition Facts: 1 cup equals 180 calories, 4 g fat (1 g saturated fat), 4 mg cholesterol, 443 mg sodium, 29 g carbohydrate, 7 g fiber, 8 g protein. **Diabetic Exchanges:** 2 starch, 1 lean meat.

Saucy Portobello Pitas

PREP: 25 min. COOK: 10 min. YIELD: 4 servings

LISA HUNDLEY • ABERDEEN, NORTH CAROLINA

Portobello mushrooms replace spicy lamb in this healthier version of a gyro. The sandwich is served with the refreshing cucumber-mint yogurt sauce of the Greek classic.

CUCUMBER SAUCE:

    1   cup (8 oz.) reduced-fat plain yogurt
  1/2   cup chopped peeled cucumber
  1/4   to 1/3 cup minced fresh mint
    1   Tbsp. grated lemon peel
    1   Tbsp. lemon juice
    1   tsp. garlic powder

PITAS:

    4   large portobello mushrooms, stems removed
  1/2   tsp. pepper
  1/4   tsp. onion powder
  1/4   tsp. garlic powder
  1/4   tsp. Greek seasoning
    2   Tbsp. canola oil
    8   pita pocket halves, warmed
    8   thin slices red onion, separated
        into rings
    8   slices tomato

1. In a small bowl, combine the cucumber sauce ingredients. Cover and refrigerate until serving.

2. Sprinkle mushrooms with pepper, onion powder, garlic powder and Greek seasoning. In a large skillet, cook mushrooms in oil for 3-5 minutes on each side or until tender.

3. Cut pita breads in half; line each with a slice of onion and tomato. Cut mushrooms in half; place in pitas. Serve with cucumber sauce.

Nutrition Facts: 2 filled pita halves with 1/3 cup sauce equals 303 calories, 9 g fat (1 g saturated fat), 3 mg cholesterol, 411 mg sodium, 45 g carbohydrate, 4 g fiber, 11 g protein. **Diabetic Exchanges:** 3 starch, 1 fat.

So Easy Gazpacho C M

PREP: 10 min. + chilling YIELD: 5 servings

LORNA SIRTOLI • CORTLAND, NEW YORK

My daughter got this lovely salad recipe from a college friend and shared it with me. Now I serve it often as an appetizer. It certainly is the talk of the party.

    2   cups tomato juice
    4   medium tomatoes, peeled and finely chopped
  1/2   cup chopped seeded peeled cucumber
  1/3   cup finely chopped onion
  1/4   cup olive oil
  1/4   cup cider vinegar
    1   tsp. sugar
    1   garlic clove, minced
  1/4   tsp. salt
  1/4   tsp. pepper

1. In a large bowl, combine all ingredients. Cover and refrigerate for at least 4 hours or until chilled.

Nutrition Facts: 1 cup equals 146 calories, 11 g fat (2 g saturated fat), 0 cholesterol, 387 mg sodium, 11 g carbohydrate, 2 g fiber, 2 g protein.

SO EASY GAZPACHO

SAUCY PORTOBELLO PITAS

Shrimp 'n' Mushroom Lettuce Wraps C

PREP: 40 min. COOK: 10 min. YIELD: 4 servings

MARY BETH VULTEE • OCEAN BEACH, NORTH CAROLINA

Here's a nutritious but special option for a luncheon. To add some hands-on fun, serve the filling on a platter with the lettuce leaves on the side, and let your guests wrap their own.

- 1 Tbsp. water
- 1 Tbsp. lime juice
- 1 Tbsp. cider vinegar
- 1 Tbsp. reduced-sodium soy sauce
- 1/4 cup reduced-fat creamy peanut butter
- 1 Tbsp. chopped jalapeno pepper
- 3/4 tsp. minced fresh gingerroot
- 1 garlic clove, peeled
- 3/4 tsp. sesame oil
- 3/4 tsp. honey
- 1 lb. uncooked medium shrimp, peeled, deveined and coarsely chopped
- 1/4 tsp. salt
- 1/4 tsp. pepper
- 2 tsp. canola oil, *divided*
- 1 pkg. (6 oz.) portobello mushrooms, coarsely chopped
- 1/2 cup chopped red onion
- 1 cup canned bean sprouts
- 1/4 cup minced fresh cilantro
- 2 Tbsp. minced fresh basil
- 4 green onions, sliced
- 2 Tbsp. chopped salted peanuts
- 8 Bibb or Boston lettuce leaves

1. For sauce, in a blender, combine the first 10 ingredients; cover and process until smooth. Set aside.

2. Sprinkle shrimp with salt and pepper. In a large nonstick skillet, saute shrimp in 1 tsp. canola oil for 4-6 minutes or until shrimp turn pink; remove and keep warm.

3. In the same skillet, saute mushrooms and red onion in remaining oil for 5-8 minutes or until tender. Return shrimp to the pan. Add bean sprouts, cilantro and basil; cook and stir for 1 minute or until heated through.

4. Remove from the heat; stir in green onions and peanuts. Divide among lettuce leaves; drizzle each with 1 Tbsp. sauce. Fold lettuce over filling.

Editor's Note: Wear disposable gloves when cutting hot peppers; the oils can burn skin. Avoid touching your face.

Nutrition Facts: 2 wraps with 2 Tbsp. sauce equals 268 calories, 12 g fat (2 g saturated fat), 168 mg cholesterol, 619 mg sodium, 15 g carbohydrate, 4 g fiber, 26 g protein. **Diabetic Exchanges:** 3 lean meat, 2 fat, 1 vegetable, 1/2 starch.

Mediterranean Chicken Sandwiches

PREP: 20 min. + chilling YIELD: 6 servings

MARCIA FULLER • SHERIDAN, MONTANA

Here's a refreshing lunch flavored with oregano and mint.

- 1-1/4 lbs. boneless skinless chicken breasts, cut into 1-in. strips
- 2 medium tomatoes, seeded and chopped
- 1/2 cup sliced, quartered seeded cucumber
- 1/2 cup sliced sweet onion
- 2 Tbsp. cider vinegar
- 1 Tbsp. olive oil
- 1 Tbsp. minced fresh oregano or 1 tsp. dried oregano
- 1 to 2 tsp. minced fresh mint or 1/2 tsp. dried mint
- 1/4 tsp. salt
- 6 whole wheat pita pocket halves, warmed
- 6 lettuce leaves

1. In a large nonstick skillet coated with cooking spray, cook chicken for 5 minutes or until no longer pink. Remove from the skillet; cool slightly.

2. In a large bowl, combine the chicken, tomatoes, cucumber and onion. In a small bowl, whisk the vinegar, oil, oregano, mint and salt. Pour over chicken mixture; toss gently.

3. Cover and refrigerate for at least 1 hour. Line pita halves with lettuce; fill with chicken mixture, using a slotted spoon.

Nutrition Facts: 1 sandwich equals 227 calories, 4 g fat (1 g saturated fat), 55 mg cholesterol, 335 mg sodium, 22 g carbohydrate, 3 g fiber, 26 g protein. **Diabetic Exchanges:** 3 lean meat, 1 starch, 1 vegetable.

SHRIMP 'N' MUSHROOM LETTUCE WRAPS

TURKEY-SWEET POTATO SOUP

Turkey-Sweet Potato Soup F

PREP: 20 min. COOK: 30 min. YIELD: 4 servings

RADINE KELLOGG • FAIRVIEW, ILLINOIS

This yummy soup brings the flavors and aroma of Thanksgiving to my table all year long.

2	cups water
2	tsp. sodium-free chicken bouillon granules
2	medium sweet potatoes, cubed
1	can (14-3/4 oz.) cream-style corn
1	Tbsp. minced fresh sage
1/4	tsp. pepper
1	Tbsp. cornstarch
1	cup 2% milk
2	cups cubed cooked turkey breast

1. In a large saucepan, bring water and bouillon to a boil. Add sweet potatoes. Reduce heat; cover and cook for 10-15 minutes or until potatoes are tender. Stir in the corn, sage and pepper; heat through. Combine cornstarch and milk until smooth. Stir into pan. Bring to a boil; cook and stir for 2 minutes or until thickened. Stir in turkey; heat through.

Nutrition Facts: 1-1/2 cups equals 275 calories, 3 g fat (1 g saturated fat), 65 mg cholesterol, 374 mg sodium, 39 g carbohydrate, 3 g fiber, 26 g protein. **Diabetic Exchanges:** 3 lean meat, 2-1/2 starch.

Greek Sloppy Joes

PREP/TOTAL TIME: 25 min. YIELD: 6 servings

SONYA LABBE • LOS ANGELES, CALIFORNIA

Here's a tasty take on an all-time family classic. For a great meal, add a green salad dotted with olives and feta cheese.

1	lb. lean ground beef (90% lean)
1	small red onion, chopped
1	can (15 oz.) tomato sauce
1	tsp. dried oregano
2	cups chopped romaine
6	kaiser rolls, split and toasted
1/2	cup crumbled feta cheese

1. In a large skillet, cook beef and onion over medium heat until meat is no longer pink; drain. Stir in tomato sauce and oregano. Bring to a boil. Reduce heat; simmer, uncovered, for 8-10 minutes or until sauce thickens slightly, stirring occasionally.

2. Place romaine on roll bottoms. Top each with 1/2 cup meat mixture and sprinkle with feta. Replace roll tops.

Nutrition Facts: 1 sandwich equals 335 calories, 10 g fat (4 g saturated fat), 52 mg cholesterol, 767 mg sodium, 36 g carbohydrate, 3 g fiber, 23 g protein. **Diabetic Exchanges:** 3 lean meat, 2 starch, 1 vegetable.

CUBAN-STYLE PORK SANDWICHES

Cuban-Style Pork Sandwiches

PREP: 20 min. **COOK:** 6 hours + standing
YIELD: 10 servings

ROBIN HAAS • CRANSTON, RHODE ISLAND

Loaded with tangy flavor, this is a slow-cooked version of a favorite restaurant-style sandwich. If you don't have a panini maker, tuck the sandwiches under the broiler until the bread is browned and the cheese is melted.

- 1 large onion, cut into wedges
- 3/4 cup reduced-sodium chicken broth
- 1 cup minced fresh parsley
- 7 garlic cloves, minced, *divided*
- 2 Tbsp. cider vinegar
- 1 Tbsp. plus 1-1/2 tsp. lemon juice, *divided*
- 2 tsp. ground cumin
- 1 tsp. ground mustard
- 1 tsp. dried oregano
- 1/2 tsp. salt
- 1/2 tsp. pepper
- 1 boneless pork shoulder butt roast (3 to 4 lb.)
- 1-1/4 cups fat-free mayonnaise
- 2 Tbsp. Dijon mustard
- 10 whole wheat hamburger buns, split
- 1-1/4 cups (5 oz.) shredded reduced-fat Swiss cheese
- 1 medium onion, thinly sliced and separated into rings
- 2 whole dill pickles, sliced

1. Place onion wedges and broth in a 5-qt. slow cooker. In a small bowl, combine the parsley, 5 garlic cloves, vinegar, 1 Tbsp. lemon juice, cumin, mustard, oregano, salt and pepper; rub over pork. Add to slow cooker. Cover and cook on low for 6-8 hours or until meat is tender.

2. Remove meat; let stand for 10 minutes before slicing. In another small bowl, combine the mayonnaise, mustard and remaining garlic and lemon juice; spread over buns. Layer bun bottoms with pork, cheese, sliced onion and pickles; replace tops.

3. Cook on a panini maker or indoor grill for 2-3 minutes or until buns are browned and cheese is melted.

Nutrition Facts: 1 sandwich equals 415 calories, 18 g fat (6 g saturated fat), 90 mg cholesterol, 943 mg sodium, 32 g carbohydrate, 5 g fiber, 33 g protein.

Italian Sausage Bean Soup

PREP: 20 min. **COOK:** 1-1/2 hours
YIELD: 8 servings (3 qt.)

GLENNA REIMER • GIG HARBOR, WASHINGTON

In the cold months, I like to put on a big pot of this comforting soup. It cooks away while I do other things, such as baking bread, crafting or even cleaning the house.

> 1 lb. bulk Italian sausage
> 1 medium onion, finely chopped
> 3 garlic cloves, sliced
> 4 cans (14-1/2 oz. *each*) reduced-sodium chicken broth
> 2 cans (15 oz. *each*) pinto beans, rinsed and drained
> 1 can (14-1/2 oz.) diced tomatoes, undrained
> 1 cup medium pearl barley
> 1 large carrot, sliced
> 1 celery rib, sliced
> 1 tsp. minced fresh sage
> 1/2 tsp. minced fresh rosemary *or* 1/8 tsp. dried rosemary, crushed
> 6 cups chopped fresh kale

1. In a Dutch oven, cook sausage and onion over medium heat until meat is no longer pink. Add garlic; cook 1 minute longer. Drain.

2. Stir in the broth, beans, tomatoes, barley, carrot, celery, sage and rosemary. Bring to a boil. Reduce heat; cover and simmer for 45 minutes.

3. Stir in kale; return to a boil. Reduce heat; cover and simmer for 25-30 minutes or until vegetables are tender and kale is wilted.

Nutrition Facts: 1-1/2 cups equals 339 calories, 9 g fat (3 g saturated fat), 23 mg cholesterol, 1,100 mg sodium, 48 g carbohydrate, 11 g fiber, 19 g protein.

Creamy Turnip Soup

PREP: 20 min. **COOK:** 20 min.
YIELD: 9 servings (2-1/4 qt.)

LIZ WHEELER • WILMINGTON, VERMONT

Nearby Wardsboro, Vermont, hosts a fall festival where one of the entrees is this delicious soup. It reheats wonderfully in a slow cooker.

> 1 medium onion, chopped
> 2 Tbsp. butter
> 3 garlic cloves, minced

> 1/2 cup white wine *or* reduced-sodium chicken broth
> 3 lb. turnips, peeled and cut into 1-in. cubes
> 1 carton (32 oz.) reduced-sodium chicken broth
> 1 medium potato, peeled and cubed
> 1 cup half-and-half cream
> 1/2 tsp. salt
> 1/2 tsp. ground nutmeg
> 3 cups fresh baby spinach
> 1/2 tsp. olive oil

1. In a Dutch oven, saute onion in butter until tender. Add garlic; cook 1 minute longer. Stir in wine. Bring to a boil; cook until liquid is reduced by half.

2. Add the turnips, broth and potato. Bring to a boil. Reduce heat; simmer, uncovered, for 20-25 minutes or until vegetables are tender. Cool slightly.

3. In a food processor, process soup in batches until smooth. Return all to pan. Stir in the cream, salt and nutmeg; heat through. Meanwhile, in a large nonstick skillet, saute spinach in oil until tender. Garnish soup with spinach.

Nutrition Facts: 1 cup equals 138 calories, 6 g fat (3 g saturated fat), 20 mg cholesterol, 526 mg sodium, 17 g carbohydrate, 4 g fiber, 4 g protein. **Diabetic Exchanges:** 1 starch, 1 fat.

Found in grocery stores in bulk or in cellophane bags, baby spinach can be eaten cooked or uncooked. It is a tender variety of spinach that has a **small, flat leaf.** The bagged variety is usually pre-washed.

CREAMY TURNIP SOUP

Easy Tortellini Soup

PREP/TOTAL TIME: 30 min. YIELD: 6 servings

GAYE THOMPSON • ST. CHARLES, MISSOURI

Quick, simple and colorful, this soup makes a cozy cup or even a light lunch on blustery days. Veggies add nutrition, and cheese tortellini makes it hearty and delicious.

- 1 medium onion, chopped
- 1 tsp. olive oil
- 1 garlic clove, minced
- 2 cans (14-1/2 oz. *each*) reduced-sodium chicken broth
- 1 can (14-1/2 oz.) diced tomatoes, undrained
- 1 pkg. (9 oz.) refrigerated cheese tortellini *or* tortellini of your choice
- 3 cups chopped fresh spinach
- 1 Tbsp. balsamic vinegar
- 1/4 tsp. pepper

Shredded Parmesan cheese, optional

1. In a Dutch oven, saute onion in oil until tender. Add garlic; cook 1 minute longer. Stir in broth and tomatoes. Bring to a boil. Reduce heat; simmer, uncovered, for 10 minutes, stirring occasionally.

2. Add tortellini; cook for 7-9 minutes or until tender. Stir in the spinach, vinegar and pepper. Cook and stir until heated through and spinach is wilted. Sprinkle with cheese.

Nutrition Facts: 1 cup (calculated without cheese) equals 178 calories, 4 g fat (2 g saturated fat), 18 mg cholesterol, 652 mg sodium, 27 g carbohydrate, 3 g fiber, 9 g protein. **Diabetic Exchanges:** 1 starch, 1 lean meat, 1 vegetable.

Veggie Chicken Pitas

PREP/TOTAL TIME: 30 min. YIELD: 5 servings

BILL PARKIS • WILMINGTON, NORTH CAROLINA

These delicious pita pockets are literally stuffed with veggies, chicken and cheese. They make for great on-the-go dinners. (But bring a napkin!)

- 1 medium red onion, sliced
- 1 cup julienned carrots
- 1 cup chopped fresh broccoli
- 1 cup fresh snow peas
- 2 Tbsp. olive oil
- 1/2 tsp. minced garlic
- 1 cup cubed cooked chicken
- 1 jar (7 oz.) roasted sweet red peppers, drained and chopped
- 1/4 cup white wine *or* chicken broth
- 1/2 tsp. dried oregano
- 1/2 tsp. cayenne pepper
- 10 pita pocket halves
- 1/3 cup shredded part-skim mozzarella cheese
- 1/3 cup shredded cheddar cheese

1. In a large skillet, saute the onion, carrots, broccoli and peas in oil for 4-5 minutes or until tender. Add garlic; cook 1 minute longer.

2. Stir in the chicken, red peppers, wine, oregano and cayenne. Bring to a boil. Reduce heat; simmer, uncovered, for 5-6 minutes or until heated through. Spoon mixture into pita breads; sprinkle with cheeses.

Nutrition Facts: 2 stuffed pita halves equals 373 calories, 12 g fat (4 g saturated fat), 37 mg cholesterol, 595 mg sodium, 43 g carbohydrate, 4 g fiber, 19 g protein. **Diabetic Exchanges:** 2 starch, 2 lean meat, 2 vegetable, 1 fat.

EASY TORTELLINI SOUP

VEGGIE CHICKEN PITAS

CALYPSO BURRITOS

Calypso Burritos M

PREP/TOTAL TIME: 30 min. YIELD: 8 servings

DARLENE DEEG • VERNON, BRITISH COLUMBIA

Because these burritos are packed with a bounty of beans, veggies, cheese and salsa, my husband doesn't notice he's not getting meat. Set out toppings such as sour cream, chopped tomatoes and avocado.

   2 small zucchini, shredded
   2 medium carrots, shredded
   1 medium onion, finely chopped
   1 Tbsp. canola oil
   1 can (16 oz.) kidney beans, rinsed and drained
   1 can (15 oz.) black beans, rinsed and drained
1-1/2 cups frozen corn, thawed
  3/4 cup salsa
   2 Tbsp. reduced-sodium taco seasoning
   2 tsp. ground cumin
   1 cup (4 oz.) shredded part-skim mozzarella cheese
  1/4 cup minced fresh cilantro
   8 flour tortillas (8 in.), warmed

1. In a large skillet over medium heat, cook and stir the zucchini, carrots and onion in oil for 3-5 minutes or until tender. Stir in the beans, corn, salsa, taco seasoning and cumin. Cook and stir for 5-7 minutes or until vegetables are tender.

2. Remove from the heat. Stir in cheese and cilantro. Spoon about 2/3 cupful filling off center on each tortilla. Fold sides and ends over filling and roll up.

Nutrition Facts: 1 burrito equals 349 calories, 7 g fat (2 g saturated fat), 8 mg cholesterol, 744 mg sodium, 55 g carbohydrate, 8 g fiber, 16 g protein.

Zesty Dill Tuna Sandwiches

PREP/TOTAL TIME: 15 min. **YIELD:** 2 servings

JENNY DUBINSKY • INWOOD, WEST VIRGINIA

I absolutely love tuna salad. With this recipe, I brought together all of my favorite things to make the best tuna salad sandwich ever!

1	can (5 oz.) light water-packed tuna, drained
1/4	cup reduced-fat mayonnaise
1	Tbsp. grated Parmesan cheese
1	Tbsp. sweet pickle relish
1	Tbsp. minced fresh parsley
1	tsp. spicy brown mustard
1/4	tsp. dill weed
1/8	tsp. onion powder
1/8	tsp. curry powder
1/8	tsp. garlic powder
4	slices whole wheat bread

1. In a small bowl, combine the first 10 ingredients. Spread over two slices of bread. Top with the remaining bread.

Nutrition Facts: 1 sandwich equals 346 calories, 13 g fat (3 g saturated fat), 34 mg cholesterol, 877 mg sodium, 29 g carbohydrate, 4 g fiber, 27 g protein. **Diabetic Exchanges:** 3 lean meat, 2 starch, 1-1/2 fat.

Italian Pulled Pork Sandwiches

PREP: 20 min. **COOK:** 8 hours **YIELD:** 12 servings

LIA DELLARIO • MIDDLEPORT, NEW YORK

Enjoy all the flavors of Italian sausage sandwiches with this healthier alternative.

1	Tbsp. fennel seed, crushed
1	Tbsp. steak seasoning
1	tsp. cayenne pepper, optional
1	boneless pork shoulder butt roast (3 lbs.)
1	Tbsp. olive oil

2 medium green *or* sweet red peppers, thinly sliced

2 medium onions, thinly sliced

1 can (14-1/2 oz.) diced tomatoes, undrained

12 whole wheat hamburger buns, split

1. In a small bowl, combine the fennel seed, steak seasoning and cayenne if desired. Rub over pork. In a large skillet, brown roast in oil on all sides. Place in a 4- or 5-qt. slow cooker. Add the peppers, onions and tomatoes; cover and cook on low for 8-10 hours or until meat is tender.

2. Remove roast; cool slightly. Skim fat from cooking juices. Shred pork with two forks and return to slow cooker; heat through. Using a slotted spoon, place 1/2 cup meat mixture on each bun.

Editor's Note: This recipe was tested with McCormick's Montreal Steak Seasoning. Look for it in the spice aisle.

Nutrition Facts: 1 sandwich equals 288 calories, 8 g fat (2 g saturated fat), 56 mg cholesterol, 454 mg sodium, 27 g carbohydrate, 5 g fiber, 26 g protein. **Diabetic Exchanges:** 3 lean meat, 2 starch.

Hearty Split Pea Soup

PREP: 30 min. **COOK:** 7 hours
YIELD: 6 servings (2-1/4 qt.)

DEBRA KEIL • OWASSO, OKLAHOMA

We started a 39-day Soup Challenge to eat healthier after the holidays, figuring if "Survivor" contestants could last 39 days on little food, surely we could survive on soup! This was a family favorite—chunky, hearty and smooth.

1 large onion, chopped

1 cup chopped celery

1 cup chopped fresh carrots

1 tsp. dried thyme

2 Tbsp. olive oil

1 pkg. (16 oz.) dried green split peas, rinsed

4 cups vegetable broth

2 cups water

6 oz. Canadian bacon, chopped

1/4 tsp. pepper

1. In a large skillet, saute the onion, celery, carrots and thyme in oil until tender.

2. Transfer to a 5-qt. slow cooker. Add the peas, broth and water. Cover and cook on low for 7-8 hours or until peas are tender.

3. Cool slightly. In a blender, process half of the soup until smooth. Return all to the slow cooker. Add bacon and pepper; heat through.

Nutrition Facts: 1-1/2 cups equals 363 calories, 7 g fat (1 g saturated fat), 10 mg cholesterol, 945 mg sodium, 53 g carbohydrate, 21 g fiber, 24 g protein.

Southwest Chicken Soup ▣

PREP: 15 min. **COOK:** 25 min. **YIELD:** 5 servings

WILL SMITH • BEEBE, ARKANSAS

Simmer up a big pot of this hearty soup on Sunday. Then, reheat and ladle it up for lunches during the week! Serve the change-of-pace dish with corn bread and baked tortilla chips.

1/2 lb. boneless skinless chicken breast, cut into 3/4-in. pieces

2 tsp. canola oil

1 small sweet red pepper, finely chopped

1 medium onion, chopped

1 garlic clove, minced

2 cans (14-1/2 oz. *each*) reduced-sodium chicken broth

1 can (15 oz.) black beans, rinsed and drained

1 cup frozen corn

1 medium lime, peeled, seeded and finely chopped

1 jalapeno pepper, seeded and chopped

1/4 tsp. pepper

1/8 to 1/4 tsp. cayenne pepper

1 small tomato, peeled, seeded and chopped

2 green onions, sliced

1. In a large nonstick saucepan, saute chicken in oil until no longer pink. Remove and keep warm.

2. In the same pan, saute red pepper and onion until tender. Add the garlic; cook 1 minute longer. Add the broth, beans, corn, lime, jalapeno, black pepper and cayenne; bring to a boil. Reduce heat; cover and simmer for 10 minutes.

3. Stir in the tomato, green onions and chicken; heat through.

Editor's Note: Wear disposable gloves when cutting hot peppers; the oils can burn skin. Avoid touching your face.

Nutrition Facts: 1-1/2 cups equals 199 calories, 3 g fat (trace saturated fat), 25 mg cholesterol, 621 mg sodium, 26 g carbohydrate, 6 g fiber, 17 g protein. **Diabetic Exchanges:** 2 lean meat, 1-1/2 starch, 1 vegetable.

SOUTHWEST CHICKEN SOUP

Butternut Turkey Soup F

PREP: 30 min. **COOK:** 35 min. **YIELD:** 6 servings (2 qt.)

DENISE LAROCHE • HUDSON, NEW HAMPSHIRE

Although hearty with lots of nutritious vegetables and turkey, this soup is also light and luscious.

3	shallots, thinly sliced
1	tsp. olive oil
3	cups reduced-sodium chicken broth
3	cups cubed peeled butternut squash (3/4-in. cubes)
2	medium red potatoes, cut into 1/2-in. cubes
1-1/2	cups water
2	tsp. minced fresh thyme
1/2	tsp. pepper
2	whole cloves
3	cups cubed cooked turkey breast

1. In a large saucepan coated with cooking spray, cook shallots in oil over medium heat until tender. Stir in the broth, squash, potatoes, water, thyme and pepper.

2. Place cloves on a double thickness of cheesecloth; bring up corners of cloth and tie with string to form a bag. Stir into soup. Bring to a boil. Reduce heat; cover and simmer for 10-15 minutes or until vegetables are tender. Stir in turkey; heat through. Discard spice bag.

BUTTERNUT TURKEY SOUP

Nutrition Facts: 1-1/3 cups equals 192 calories, 2 g fat (trace saturated fat), 60 mg cholesterol, 332 mg sodium, 20 g carbohydrate, 3 g fiber, 25 g protein. **Diabetic Exchanges:** 3 lean meat, 1 starch.

Veggie Tortellini Soup M

PREP: 15 min. **COOK:** 20 min. **YIELD:** 7 servings

PRISCILLA GILBERT • INDIAN HARBOUR BEACH, FLORIDA

Italian cuisine has more to offer than spaghetti and pizza. Just check out this healthy, mouthwatering soup. I've served it to company with rave reviews along with requests for the recipe.

3	medium carrots, chopped
1	large onion, chopped
1	Tbsp. olive oil
4	garlic cloves, minced
2	cans (14-1/2 oz. *each*) vegetable broth
2	medium zucchini, chopped
4	plum tomatoes, chopped
2	cups refrigerated cheese tortellini
1/3	cup chopped fresh spinach
1	tsp. minced fresh rosemary *or* 1/4 tsp. dried rosemary, crushed
1/4	tsp. pepper
1	Tbsp. red wine vinegar

1. In a Dutch oven, saute the carrots and onion in oil until the onion is tender. Add the garlic; cook 1 minute longer.

2. Stir in the broth, zucchini, tomatoes, tortellini, spinach, rosemary and pepper. Bring to a boil. Reduce heat; cover and simmer for 8-10 minutes or until the tortellini are tender. Just before serving, stir in the vinegar.

Nutrition Facts: 1 cup equals 155 calories, 5 g fat (2 g saturated fat), 13 mg cholesterol, 693 mg sodium, 24 g carbohydrate, 3 g fiber, 6 g protein. **Diabetic Exchanges:** 1 starch, 1 vegetable, 1/2 fat.

VEGGIE TORTELLINI SOUP

PEANUTTY ASIAN LETTUCE WRAPS

Peanutty Asian Lettuce Wraps

PREP/TOTAL TIME: 30 min. **YIELD:** 6 servings

MANDY RIVERS • LEXINGTON, SOUTH CAROLINA

This recipe packs so much flavor into a beautiful, healthy presentation. I love to serve it as an hors d'oeuvre or as the main dish when I have folks over. It's always a hit! I usually offer it with a little extra hoisin on the side.

1-1/2 lbs. lean ground turkey
1/2 cup shredded carrot
2 Tbsp. minced fresh gingerroot
4 garlic cloves, minced
1 can (8 oz.) whole water chestnuts, drained and chopped
4 green onions, chopped
1/2 cup chopped fresh snow peas
1/3 cup reduced-sodium teriyaki sauce
1/4 cup hoisin sauce
3 Tbsp. creamy peanut butter
1 Tbsp. rice vinegar
1 Tbsp. sesame oil
12 Bibb lettuce leaves
Additional hoisin sauce, optional

1. In a large skillet, cook turkey and carrot over medium heat until meat is no longer pink and carrot is tender; drain. Add ginger and garlic; cook 1 minute longer.

2. Stir in the chestnuts, onions, snow peas, teriyaki sauce, hoisin sauce, peanut butter, vinegar and oil; heat through. Divide among lettuce leaves; drizzle with additional hoisin sauce if desired. Fold lettuce over filling.

Nutrition Facts: 2 lettuce wraps (calculated without additional hoisin sauce) equals 313 calories, 16 g fat (4 g saturated fat), 90 mg cholesterol, 613 mg sodium, 18 g carbohydrate, 3 g fiber, 24 g protein. **Diabetic Exchanges:** 3 lean meat, 2 vegetable, 2 fat, 1/2 starch.

HEARTY LEEK AND POTATO SOUP

Hearty Leek and Potato Soup M

PREP: 20 min. COOK: 30 min. YIELD: 8 servings (2 qt.)

RACHEL TAYLOR • SPRINGFIELD, TENNESSEE

This thick, flavorful soup is a winner in our home and makes a nice starter dish. The leeks and green pepper offer a fantastic addition to traditional potato soup.

- 3 celery ribs, chopped
- 2 medium onions, chopped
- 3 medium leeks (white portion only), chopped
- 1 medium green pepper, chopped
- 2 jalapeno peppers, seeded and chopped
- 6 garlic cloves, minced
- 2 Tbsp. olive oil
- 4 medium potatoes, peeled and cubed
- 2 cans (14-1/2 oz. *each*) vegetable broth
- 1 cup water
- 1/2 tsp. pepper
- 1/4 tsp. salt
- 3 Tbsp. all-purpose flour
- 1/4 cup fat-free milk
- 1/2 cup reduced-fat sour cream
- 2 green onions, chopped

1. In a nonstick Dutch oven, saute the celery, onions, leeks, green pepper, jalapenos and garlic in oil until tender. Add the potatoes, broth, water, pepper and salt. Bring to a boil. Reduce heat; cover and simmer for 10-15 minutes or until potatoes are tender, stirring occasionally.

2. Combine flour and milk until smooth; stir into soup. Cook and stir for 2 minutes or until thickened and bubbly. Reduce heat to low. Stir in sour cream and green onions until blended; heat through (do not boil).

Editor's Note: Wear disposable gloves when cutting hot peppers; the oils can burn skin. Avoid touching your face.

Nutrition Facts: 1 cup equals 180 calories, 5 g fat (1 g saturated fat), 5 mg cholesterol, 598 mg sodium, 30 g carbohydrate, 3 g fiber, 4 g protein. **Diabetic Exchanges:** 1-1/2 starch, 1 vegetable, 1 fat.

Cashew Turkey Salad Sandwiches

PREP/TOTAL TIME: 15 min. **YIELD:** 4 servings

MARY WILHELM • SPARTA, WISCONSIN

One bite and you're sure to be hooked on this sweet and savory sandwich. It's protein-packed, so you can feel good about it while you munch.

1-1/2 cups cubed cooked turkey breast
1/4 cup thinly sliced celery
2 Tbsp. chopped dried apricots
2 Tbsp. chopped unsalted cashews
1 green onion, chopped
1/4 cup reduced-fat mayonnaise
2 Tbsp. reduced-fat plain yogurt
1/4 tsp. salt
1/4 tsp. pepper
4 lettuce leaves
8 slices pumpernickel bread

1. In a small bowl, combine the turkey, celery, apricots, cashews and onion. In another bowl, combine the mayonnaise, yogurt, salt and pepper; add to turkey mixture and stir to coat.

2. Place a lettuce leaf on half of the bread slices; top each with 1/2 cup turkey salad and remaining bread.

Nutrition Facts: 1 sandwich equals 298 calories, 9 g fat (2 g saturated fat), 51 mg cholesterol, 664 mg sodium, 32 g carbohydrate, 4 g fiber, 22 g protein. **Diabetic Exchanges:** 2 starch, 2 lean meat, 1-1/2 fat.

Mexican Lettuce Wraps

PREP/TOTAL TIME: 20 min. **YIELD:** 6 servings

JUNE BARRUS • SPRINGVILLE, UTAH

This recipe proved to be a winner, not only when wrapped in lettuce, but also when served as a dip with tortilla chips. It is so easy to make ahead, chill and take for a picnic or potluck.

3 cups cubed cooked chicken breast
1 can (15 oz.) black beans, rinsed and drained
1 medium tomato, seeded and finely chopped
1 can (4 oz.) chopped green chilies

1/2 cup salsa
1/4 cup finely chopped onion
1/4 cup finely chopped sweet red pepper
1 Tbsp. lime juice
1/2 tsp. ground cumin
1/2 tsp. seasoned salt
1/4 tsp. garlic powder
1 medium ripe avocado, peeled and finely chopped
12 Bibb or Boston lettuce leaves
1/2 cup reduced-fat sour cream

1. In a large bowl, combine the first 11 ingredients. Refrigerate until serving.

2. Just before serving, stir in avocado. Place 1/2 cup chicken mixture on each lettuce leaf; top each with 2 tsp. sour cream. Fold lettuce over filling.

Nutrition Facts: 2 wraps equals 259 calories, 8 g fat (2 g saturated fat), 61 mg cholesterol, 478 mg sodium, 19 g carbohydrate, 6 g fiber, 26 g protein. **Diabetic Exchanges:** 3 lean meat, 1 starch, 1 vegetable, 1 fat.

To keep lettuce crisp and fresh, wash it in cold water and drain very well. Use a salad spinner or pat dry with paper towels. Store **washed lettuce** in a resealable plastic bag or an airtight container with a dry paper towel in the bottom to absorb leftover moisture.

MEXICAN LETTUCE WRAPS

Skinny Turkey-Vegetable Soup [F]

PREP: 30 min. **COOK:** 35 min.
YIELD: 6 servings (2-1/4 qt.)

CHARLOTTE WELCH • UTICA, NEW YORK

The blend of flavors and colors in this hearty soup will bring everyone at the table back for more.

- 2 medium onions, chopped
- 2 medium carrots, halved and thinly sliced
- 2 celery ribs, chopped
- 1/2 cup chopped sweet red pepper
- 1 Tbsp. olive oil
- 3 garlic cloves, minced
- 4 cups water
- 1 can (10 oz.) diced tomatoes and green chilies, undrained
- 1/2 cup frozen peas
- 1 bay leaf
- 4 tsp. sodium-free chicken bouillon granules
- 1/2 tsp. dried basil
- 1/2 tsp. dried thyme
- 1/4 tsp. ground cumin
- 1/4 tsp. pepper
- 1/4 to 1/2 tsp. hot pepper sauce, optional
- 1/2 cup uncooked whole wheat orzo pasta
- 2 cups cubed cooked turkey breast
- 1 Tbsp. minced fresh cilantro

1. In a large saucepan, saute the onions, carrots, celery and red pepper in oil until tender. Add garlic; cook 2 minutes longer. Stir in the water, tomatoes, peas, bay leaf, bouillon, basil, thyme, cumin, pepper and pepper sauce if desired. Bring to a boil. Reduce heat; simmer, uncovered, for 15 minutes.

2. Meanwhile, cook orzo according to package directions; drain. Stir orzo and turkey into soup; heat through. Discard bay leaf. Sprinkle with cilantro.

Nutrition Facts: 1-1/2 cups equals 191 calories, 3 g fat (1 g saturated fat), 40 mg cholesterol, 257 mg sodium, 22 g carbohydrate, 5 g fiber, 18 g protein. **Diabetic Exchanges:** 2 lean meat, 1 starch, 1 vegetable, 1/2 fat.

> Because of orzo's similar shape and mild flavor, this pasta can be substituted for rice in many recipes. Nutritionally speaking, the two are alike as well. Ounce for ounce, **rice and orzo** contain a similar amount of fat, sugar, carbohydrates and even sodium.

SKINNY TURKEY-VEGETABLE SOUP

Bistro Tuna Sandwiches

PREP: 25 min. **GRILL:** 10 min. **YIELD:** 4 servings

SONYA LABBE • LOS ANGELES, CALIFORNIA

Your family and friends will love this fun French take on a grilled tuna sandwich. Tucked into a crusty baguette, it's fast, easy and packed with veggies and fresh flavor.

- 2 Tbsp. Greek olives
- 1 Tbsp. capers, drained
- 1 Tbsp. lemon juice
- 1 tsp. grated lemon peel
- 1 garlic clove, peeled
- 1 Tbsp. plus 2 tsp. olive oil, *divided*
- 2 tuna steaks (6 oz. *each*)
- 1/4 tsp. pepper
- 1 French bread baguette (10-1/2 oz.)
- 1/3 cup reduced-fat mayonnaise
- 2 Tbsp. Dijon mustard
- 1/4 cup roasted sweet red peppers, drained and cut into strips
- 4 slices red onion
- 4 Boston lettuce leaves

1. Place the olives, capers, lemon juice, peel, garlic and 1 Tbsp. oil in a food processor; cover and process until finely chopped. Set aside.

2. Brush tuna with remaining oil; sprinkle with pepper. Using long-handled tongs, moisten a paper towel with cooking oil and lightly coat the grill rack. For medium-rare, grill tuna, covered, over high heat or broil 3-4 in. from the heat for 3-4 minutes on each side or until slightly pink in the center.

3. Cut baguette in half horizontally. Grill bread cut side down, uncovered, for 1-2 minutes or until toasted. Slice tuna into 1/2-in. thick slices. Combine mayonnaise and mustard until smooth; spread over baguette bottoms. Layer with peppers, onion, tuna, olive mixture and lettuce; replace tops. Cut into slices.

SPICY BLACK BEAN SOUP

Nutrition Facts: 1 sandwich equals 456 calories, 16 g fat (2 g saturated fat), 45 mg cholesterol, 1,044 mg sodium, 48 g carbohydrate, 2 g fiber, 29 g protein.

Spicy Black Bean Soup F M

PREP: 25 min. **COOK:** 40 min. **YIELD:** 12 servings

TIA MUSSER • HUDSON, INDIANA

A splash of sherry enhances this filling, easy-to-make soup. For a milder flavor, remove the ribs and seeds from the jalapeno before dicing.

1	large red onion, chopped
1	medium sweet red pepper, chopped
1	jalapeno pepper, seeded and minced
2	Tbsp. olive oil
3	garlic cloves, minced
3	cans (15 oz. *each*) black beans, rinsed and drained
3-1/2	cups vegetable broth
1	can (14-1/2 oz.) diced tomatoes with mild green chilies, undrained
1	can (4 oz.) chopped green chilies
1/3	cup sherry *or* additional vegetable broth
2	Tbsp. minced fresh cilantro
1/2	cup fat-free sour cream
1/4	cup shredded cheddar cheese

1. In a Dutch oven, saute onion and peppers in oil until tender. Add garlic; cook 1 minute longer.

2. Stir in the beans, broth, tomatoes and chopped green chilies. Bring to a boil. Reduce heat; simmer, uncovered, for 25 minutes. Add sherry and cilantro; cook 5 minutes longer.

3. Remove from the heat; cool slightly. Place half of soup in a blender; cover and process until pureed. Return to the pan and heat through. Top each serving with 2 tsp. sour cream and 1 tsp. cheese.

Editor's Note: Wear disposable gloves when cutting hot peppers; the oils can burn skin. Avoid touching your face.

Nutrition Facts: 3/4 cup equals 150 calories, 3 g fat (1 g saturated fat), 4 mg cholesterol, 667 mg sodium, 23 g carbohydrate, 5 g fiber, 7 g protein.

Taco Salad Wraps

PREP/TOTAL TIME: 25 min. YIELD: 2 servings

MARLENE ROBERTS • MOORE, OKLAHOMA

These change-of-pace Southwestern wraps will be a hit the next time you need a quick lunch or dinner.

- 1/4 lb. lean ground beef (90% lean)
- 1/3 cup plus 2 Tbsp. salsa, *divided*
- 1/4 cup chili beans, drained
- 1-1/2 tsp. Worcestershire sauce
- 1 tsp. onion powder
- 1 tsp. chili powder
- 1/8 tsp. garlic powder
- Pepper to taste
- 2 flour tortillas (8 in.), warmed
- 1/3 cup shredded lettuce
- 1 plum tomato, chopped
- 2 Tbsp. shredded cheddar cheese
- 6 baked tortilla chip scoops, coarsely crushed

1. In a small nonstick skillet, cook beef over medium heat until no longer pink; drain. Stir in 1/3 cup salsa, beans, Worcestershire sauce, onion powder, chili powder, garlic powder and pepper. Bring to a boil; reduce heat and simmer, uncovered, for 5 minutes.

2. Spoon meat mixture onto each tortilla. Layer with lettuce, tomato, cheese, crushed tortilla chips and remaining salsa; roll up.

Nutrition Facts: 1 wrap equals 345 calories, 10 g fat (4 g saturated fat), 35 mg cholesterol, 764 mg sodium, 42 g carbohydrate, 5 g fiber, 20 g protein.

Butternut Squash & Pear Soup

PREP: 1-1/4 hours COOK: 45 min. YIELD: 9 servings

SARAH VASQUES • MILFORD, NEW HAMPSHIRE

Pears give this harvest soup a pleasant sweetness and lovely velvety finish, while curry and ginger provide delightful flavor.

- 1 medium butternut squash (about 3 lbs.)
- 1 medium onion, chopped
- 2 Tbsp. canola oil
- 1 Tbsp. curry powder
- 2 garlic cloves, minced
- 2 tsp. minced fresh gingerroot
- 1 tsp. salt
- 4 cups reduced-sodium chicken broth
- 4 medium pears, peeled and chopped
- 1/2 cup heavy whipping cream
- Balsamic vinegar and snipped chives, optional

1. Cut squash in half; discard seeds. Place squash cut side down in a 15-in. x 10-in. x 1-in. baking pan coated with cooking spray. Bake at 400° for 40-50 minutes or until tender. Cool slightly; scoop out pulp and set aside.

2. In a Dutch oven, saute onion in oil until tender. Add the curry, garlic, ginger and salt; cook 1 minute longer. Stir in the broth, pears and squash. Bring to a boil. Reduce heat; simmer, uncovered, for 30 minutes. Cool slightly.

3. In a blender, process soup in batches until smooth. Return all to the pan; add cream and heat through. Top with balsamic vinegar and chives if desired.

Nutrition Facts: 3/4 cup equals 190 calories, 8 g fat (3 g saturated fat), 18 mg cholesterol, 527 mg sodium, 29 g carbohydrate, 7 g fiber, 4 g protein. **Diabetic Exchanges:** 2 starch, 1 fat.

TACO SALAD WRAPS

BUTTERNUT SQUASH & PEAR SOUP

CHICKEN BARLEY SOUP

Chicken Barley Soup

PREP: 20 min. **COOK:** 45 min. **YIELD:** 6 servings

PATRICIA RANDALL • NEWTON, KANSAS

With chicken, barley and a host of delicious veggies, this is a yummy way to beat winter's chill. The leeks add an unexpected twist to the soup.

1 lb. boneless skinless chicken breasts, cut into 3/4-in. pieces

2 Tbsp. canola oil, *divided*

2 cups chopped leeks (white portion only)

1 celery rib, thinly sliced

1 carrot, thinly sliced

2 cups sliced fresh mushrooms

1 garlic clove, minced

2 cans (14-1/2 oz. *each*) reduced-sodium chicken broth

2-1/4 cups water

1 bay leaf

1/2 tsp. dried thyme

1/4 tsp. salt

1/4 tsp. pepper

1/2 cup quick-cooking barley

1. In a Dutch oven, brown chicken in 1 Tbsp. oil. Remove and set aside.

2. In the same pan, saute the leeks, celery and carrot in remaining oil for 4 minutes. Add mushrooms and garlic; cook 2 minutes longer. Stir in the broth, water, bay leaf, seasonings and chicken. Bring to a boil. Reduce heat; cover and simmer for 15 minutes.

3. Stir in barley and return to a boil. Reduce heat; cover and simmer for 10-12 minutes or until barley and vegetables are tender. Discard bay leaf.

Nutrition Facts: 1 cup equals 218 calories, 7 g fat (1 g saturated fat), 42 mg cholesterol, 550 mg sodium, 19 g carbohydrate, 4 g fiber, 21 g protein. **Diabetic Exchanges:** 2 lean meat, 1 starch, 1 vegetable, 1 fat.

Turkey-White Bean Soup F

PREP: 20 min. **COOK:** 40 min. **YIELD:** 6 servings (2 qt.)

MARY RELYEA • CANASTOTA, NEW YORK

Packed with veggies, turkey and nutrition, this hearty soup will warm 'em up right down to their toes. For an extra-special touch, top the soup with shredded Parmesan cheese.

- 2 garlic cloves, minced
- 2 tsp. olive oil
- 1/2 tsp. dried rosemary, crushed
- 1/4 tsp. crushed red pepper flakes
- 1 can (28 oz.) whole tomatoes in puree, cut up
- 1 can (14-1/2 oz.) reduced-sodium chicken broth
- 1 pkg. (6 oz.) fresh baby spinach, cut into thin strips
- 2 cups shredded carrots
- 2 cans (15 oz. *each*) white kidney *or* cannellini beans, rinsed and drained
- 1-1/2 cups cubed cooked turkey breast

Shredded Parmesan cheese, optional

1. In a large saucepan over medium heat, cook garlic in oil for 1 minute. Add rosemary and pepper flakes; cook 1 minute longer.

2. Stir in the tomatoes, broth, spinach and carrots. Bring to a boil. Reduce heat; cover and simmer for 15 minutes. Stir in beans and turkey; return to a boil. Reduce heat; cover and simmer 10 minutes longer. Serve with cheese if desired.

Nutrition Facts: 1-1/3 cups (calculated without cheese) equals 233 calories, 3 g fat (trace saturated fat), 30 mg cholesterol, 893 mg sodium, 32 g carbohydrate, 9 g fiber, 20 g protein.

Potluck Sloppy Joes

PREP: 30 min. **COOK:** 15 min. **YIELD:** 12 servings

RICK BOLTE • MONTCLAIR, CALIFORNIA

For a change of pace, I suggest swapping out the green pepper in these comforting sloppy joes for an Anaheim pepper if available. Anaheim peppers are longer and lighter in color than green bell peppers, and they add a tiny bite, which is just perfect for those who like a little kick in their food.

- 3 lbs. lean ground turkey
- 3 celery ribs, chopped
- 2 medium onions, chopped
- 1 large green pepper, chopped
- 1-3/4 cups ketchup
- 1 can (8 oz.) no-salt-added tomato sauce
- 3 Tbsp. all-purpose flour
- 3 Tbsp. sugar
- 3 Tbsp. cider vinegar
- 1 Tbsp. prepared mustard
- 12 whole wheat hamburger buns, split and toasted

1. In a large nonstick skillet, cook the turkey, celery, onions and pepper over medium heat until meat is no longer pink; drain.

2. Stir in the ketchup, tomato sauce, flour, sugar, vinegar and mustard. Bring to a boil. Reduce heat; cover and simmer for 10-15 minutes or until heated through. Spoon 2/3 cup turkey mixture onto each bun.

Nutrition Facts: 1 sandwich equals 360 calories, 11 g fat (3 g saturated fat), 90 mg cholesterol, 785 mg sodium, 41 g carbohydrate, 4 g fiber, 24 g protein. **Diabetic Exchanges:** 3 lean meat, 2-1/2 starch.

Open-Faced Meatball Sandwiches

PREP: 30 min. COOK: 10 min. YIELD: 8 servings

KAREN BARTHEL • NORTH CANTON, OHIO

My husband and I love classic meatball subs, but I wanted to create a version that's fast to fix after a long day. This recipe always comes together in a snap, and the meatballs are very freezer-friendly as well.

- 1/4 cup egg substitute
- 1/2 cup soft bread crumbs
- 1/4 cup finely chopped onion
- 2 garlic cloves, minced
- 1/2 tsp. onion powder
- 1/2 tsp. dried oregano
- 1/2 tsp. dried basil
- 1/4 tsp. pepper

Dash salt

- 1-1/4 lbs. lean ground beef (90% lean)
- 2 cups garden-style pasta sauce
- 4 hoagie buns, split
- 2 Tbsp. shredded part-skim mozzarella cheese

Shredded Parmesan cheese, optional

1. In a large bowl, combine the first nine ingredients. Crumble beef over mixture and mix well. Shape into 40 meatballs. In a large skillet coated with cooking spray, brown meatballs in batches; drain.

2. Place meatballs in a large saucepan. Add pasta sauce; bring to a boil. Reduce heat; cover and simmer for 10-15 minutes or until meat is no longer pink. Spoon meatballs and sauce onto bun halves; sprinkle with mozzarella and Parmesan cheese if desired.

Nutrition Facts: 1 sandwich (calculated without Parmesan cheese) equals 277 calories, 10 g fat (4 g saturated fat), 47 mg cholesterol, 506 mg sodium, 28 g carbohydrate, 3 g fiber, 20 g protein.

Asian Chicken Salad Wraps

PREP/TOTAL TIME: 25 min. YIELD: 6 servings

JASON BRANNON • CONWAY, ARKANSAS

Loaded with chicken, cabbage and carrots, these wraps feature a fantastic homemade dressing. They'll be a yummy, nutritious lunch or dinner any time of year.

- 3 cups shredded cooked chicken breasts
- 4 green onions, finely chopped
- 1 cup finely shredded cabbage
- 1/2 cup shredded carrot

DRESSING:

- 3 Tbsp. seasoned rice vinegar
- 3 Tbsp. canola oil
- 2 Tbsp. honey
- 1 Tbsp. water
- 1 garlic clove, halved
- 3/4 tsp. minced fresh gingerroot
- 1/4 tsp. coarsely ground pepper
- 1 cup fresh cilantro leaves
- 6 lettuce leaves
- 6 whole wheat tortillas (8 in.), room temperature

1. In a large bowl, combine the chicken, green onions, cabbage and carrot. For dressing, in a small food processor, combine the vinegar, oil, honey, water, garlic, ginger and pepper. Cover and process until blended. Add cilantro; cover and process until chopped. Pour over chicken mixture; toss to coat.

2. Place a lettuce leaf on each tortilla; top with chicken mixture. Roll up tightly.

Nutrition Facts: 1 wrap equals 370 calories, 13 g fat (1 g saturated fat), 60 mg cholesterol, 503 mg sodium, 34 g carbohydrate, 3 g fiber, 26 g protein.

ASIAN CHICKEN SALAD WRAPS

OPEN-FACED MEATBALL SANDWICHES

Italian Lentil Soup F M

PREP: 15 min. **COOK:** 40 min. **YIELD:** 6 servings (2 qt.)

MARYBETH GESSELE • GASTON, OREGON

Lentils, like beans, are part of the legume family and add cholesterol-reducing fiber to this no-fuss soup.

1	medium onion, chopped
1	Tbsp. olive oil
2	garlic cloves, minced
3-1/4	cups water
1	can (14-1/2 oz.) vegetable broth
1	cup dried lentils, rinsed
1	medium carrot, shredded
1	small green pepper, finely chopped
1	tsp. dried oregano
1/2	tsp. dried basil
1/4	tsp. crushed red pepper flakes, optional
1	can (14-1/2 oz.) no-salt-added diced tomatoes
1	can (6 oz.) tomato paste
1	Tbsp. lemon juice
2	cups cooked brown rice

1. In a Dutch oven, saute onion in oil until tender. Add garlic; cook 1 minute longer. Add the water, broth, lentils, carrot, green pepper, oregano, basil and pepper flakes if desired. Bring to a boil. Reduce heat; cover and simmer for 20-25 minutes or until lentils are almost tender.

2. Stir in the tomatoes, tomato paste and lemon juice. Bring to a boil. Reduce heat; cover and simmer 10 minutes longer or until lentils are tender. Serve with the rice.

Nutrition Facts: 1-1/3 cups with 1/3 cup rice equals 269 calories, 3 g fat (trace saturated fat), 0 cholesterol, 383 mg sodium, 48 g carbohydrate, 14 g fiber, 13 g protein.

Turkey Chili with Penne

PREP: 25 min. **COOK:** 1 hour **YIELD:** 12 servings

PATRICIA BURK • NORTH CANTON, OHIO

This recipe easily turns into a vegetarian dish by leaving out the meat or replacing it with soy crumbles. A topping of goat cheese makes this hearty chili stand out from others.

1-1/2	lbs. extra-lean ground turkey
1	tsp. olive oil
3	celery ribs, chopped
3	large carrots, sliced
1	medium onion, chopped
1	poblano pepper, seeded and finely chopped
1/2	cup marsala wine *or* reduced-sodium chicken broth
1	can (28 oz.) diced tomatoes, undrained
2	cans (one 15 oz., one 8 oz.) tomato sauce
1	can (4 oz.) chopped green chilies
1	Tbsp. chili powder
1	Tbsp. honey
3-1/2	cups uncooked whole wheat penne pasta
2	cans (15 oz. *each*) black beans, rinsed and drained
8	oz. fresh goat cheese, cut into 12 slices

1. In a Dutch oven, cook turkey in oil over medium heat until no longer pink. Stir in the celery, carrots, onion, pepper and wine; cook until the vegetables are tender.

2. Stir in the tomatoes, tomato sauce, chilies, chili powder and honey. Bring to a boil. Reduce heat; simmer, uncovered, for 1 hour or until thickened.

3. Meanwhile, cook pasta according to package directions. Stir beans into chili; heat through. Drain pasta; spoon 1/2 cup into each serving bowl. Spoon chili over pasta; top with cheese.

Nutrition Facts: 1 cup chili with 1/2 cup pasta and 2/3 oz. cheese equals 343 calories, 4 g fat (2 g saturated fat), 35 mg cholesterol, 642 mg sodium, 48 g carbohydrate, 9 g fiber, 27 g protein.

ITALIAN LENTIL SOUP

TURKEY CHILI WITH PENNE

New Orleans-Style Subs

PREP: 30 min. **BROIL:** 5 min. **YIELD:** 12 servings

SHANNON LEE DENNEY • MILWAUKEE, WISCONSIN

This satisfying muffuletta-style sandwich contains loads of meat and cheese. The chopped olive spread makes it a true New Orleans classic.

1-1/3 cups giardiniera
  2/3 cup chopped pitted green olives
  2/3 cup pitted ripe olives
    2 loaves (1 lb. *each*) unsliced French bread
  1/4 cup fat-free Italian salad dressing
  1/2 lb. thinly sliced deli ham
  1/2 lb. thinly sliced deli turkey
  1/2 lb. sliced reduced-fat provolone cheese
  1/2 lb. thinly sliced deli roast beef
  1/2 lb. sliced reduced-fat Colby-Monterey Jack cheese
    2 medium tomatoes, sliced
    2 cups shredded lettuce
    1 large red onion, thinly sliced and separated into rings

1. Place giardiniera and olives in a food processor; cover and process until coarsely chopped. Set aside.

2. Cut bread in half lengthwise; carefully hollow out top and bottom of loaves, leaving 1/2-in. shells (discard removed bread or save for another use). Place on two large baking sheets. Broil 4-6 in. from the heat for 3-4 minutes or until toasted. Brush bottom halves with dressing; layer with ham, turkey and provolone cheese. Spread top halves with olive mixture; layer with roast beef and Colby-Monterey Jack cheese.

3. Broil 2-3 minutes longer or until cheese is melted. Layer bottom halves with tomatoes, lettuce and onion; replace tops. Cut each loaf into six slices.

Nutrition Facts: 1 slice equals 336 calories, 11 g fat (5 g saturated fat), 46 mg cholesterol, 1,368 mg sodium, 32 g carbohydrate, 2 g fiber, 27 g protein.

Italian Turkey Sloppy Joes

PREP: 15 min. **COOK:** 45 min. **YIELD:** 8 servings

CHARLENE CHAMBERS • ORMOND BEACH, FLORIDA

Everyone seems to love my take on sloppy joes. For a change, I often fix them with ground chicken instead of ground turkey and use fresh parsley and oregano.

1	pkg. (19-1/2 oz.) hot Italian turkey sausage links, casings removed
1	lb. extra-lean ground turkey
1	medium green pepper, chopped
1	small onion, chopped
4	garlic cloves, minced
2	cans (8 oz. *each*) no-salt-added tomato sauce
2	Tbsp. no-salt-added tomato paste
1	Tbsp. chili powder
2	tsp. dried parsley flakes
1	tsp. dried oregano
8	whole wheat hamburger buns, split
3/4	cup shredded part-skim mozzarella cheese
1/4	cup shredded Parmesan cheese

1. In a Dutch oven, cook the sausage, turkey, pepper and onion over medium heat until meat is no longer pink. Add garlic; cook 1 minute longer. Drain. Stir in the tomato sauce, tomato paste and seasonings. Bring to a boil. Reduce the heat; cover and simmer meat mixture for 30 minutes.

2. Spoon 3/4 cup turkey mixture onto each bun; sprinkle with cheeses.

Nutrition Facts: 1 sandwich equals 348 calories, 12 g fat (3 g saturated fat), 72 mg cholesterol, 775 mg sodium, 30 g carbohydrate, 5 g fiber, 33 g protein. **Diabetic Exchanges:** 4 medium-fat meat, 2 starch, 1 vegetable.

Spicy Chicken Tomato Pitas

PREP/TOTAL TIME: 30 min. **YIELD:** 4 servings

CORI COOPER • BOISE, IDAHO

This is a terrific recipe. It cooks up quickly, too, which is always a big bonus. A sizzling blend of Southwest tastes with a bright splash of lemon, this one's a crowd-pleaser!

TOMATO RELISH:

4	medium tomatoes, seeded and chopped
1	small onion, chopped
1/4	cup minced fresh parsley
1/4	cup lemon juice
1	Tbsp. olive oil
1	tsp. ground coriander
1	tsp. ground cumin
1/4	tsp. crushed red pepper flakes

CHICKEN PITAS:

1	Tbsp. ground cumin
1	Tbsp. paprika
1-1/2	tsp. dried oregano
1-1/2	tsp. ground coriander
1/2	tsp. crushed red pepper flakes
1/4	tsp. salt
4	boneless skinless chicken breast halves (4 oz. *each*)
8	whole wheat pita pocket halves

1. Combine the relish ingredients; chill until serving.

2. Combine the cumin, paprika, oregano, coriander, pepper flakes and salt; rub over both sides of chicken. Grill chicken, covered, over medium heat or broil 4 in. from the heat for 4-7 minutes on each side or until juices run clear.

3. Slice chicken. Fill each pita half with chicken and tomato relish.

Nutrition Facts: 2 filled pita halves equals 383 calories, 9 g fat (2 g saturated fat), 63 mg cholesterol, 558 mg sodium, 47 g carbohydrate, 9 g fiber, 32 g protein.

Pea Soup with Mushroom Cream Sauce

PREP: 25 min. **COOK:** 15 min. **YIELD:** 6 servings

SALLY SIBTHORPE • SHELBY TOWNSHIP, MICHIGAN

Fresh garden peas combine with a hint of basil for a delightfully light spring soup. A unique mushroom drizzle adds extra depth to this beautiful dish.

- 1/2 lb. sliced baby portobello mushrooms, *divided*
- 1 Tbsp. butter
- 1/4 cup chopped onion
- 1 garlic clove, minced
- 1/2 cup half-and-half cream
- 3 Tbsp. sherry *or* reduced-sodium chicken broth
- 1 Tbsp. minced fresh thyme *or* 1 tsp. dried thyme
- 3/4 tsp. salt, *divided*
- 5 cups fresh *or* frozen peas, *divided*
- 3 cups reduced-sodium chicken broth
- 2 Tbsp. lemon juice
- 4-1/2 tsp. minced fresh basil *or* 1-1/2 tsp. dried basil

1. Set aside 3 Tbsp. mushrooms for garnish. In a large skillet, saute remaining mushrooms in butter until tender.

2. Add onion and garlic to skillet; saute until tender. Stir in the cream, sherry, thyme and 1/4 tsp. salt. Bring to a boil. Reduce heat; simmer, uncovered, for 2 minutes. Cool slightly. Transfer to a blender; process until smooth. Set aside.

3. In a Dutch oven, combine 4-1/2 cups peas, chicken broth and remaining salt. Bring to a boil. Reduce heat; simmer, uncovered, for 4 minutes or until peas are tender. Stir in lemon juice and basil; heat through. Transfer to a blender; process in batches until blended.

4. Ladle soup into serving bowls; top with mushroom cream sauce. Garnish with reserved mushrooms and remaining peas.

Nutrition Facts: 3/4 cup soup with 2 Tbsp. sauce equals 169 calories, 5 g fat (3 g saturated fat), 15 mg cholesterol, 612 mg sodium, 22 g carbohydrate, 7 g fiber, 10 g protein. **Diabetic Exchanges:** 1-1/2 starch, 1 fat.

Day After Easter Soup

PREP: 25 min. **COOK:** 45 min.
YIELD: 9 servings (2-1/4 qt.)

SUSAN WILSON • MILWAUKEE, WISCONSIN

Every spring I wait impatiently for the asparagus crop to arrive so I can make my cream of asparagus soup. One year I added the leftovers from Easter, and it turned into this hit that has since become a spring tradition.

- 2 medium leeks (white portion only), chopped
- 2 Tbsp. butter
- 2 Tbsp. all-purpose flour
- 1 carton (32 oz.) vegetable broth
- 1 cup water
- 1 Tbsp. minced fresh parsley
- 1 tsp. herbes de Provence
- 1 tsp. minced chives
- 1/2 tsp. celery seed
- 1/4 tsp. ground nutmeg
- 1 lb. fresh asparagus, trimmed
- 5 medium red potatoes, peeled and cut into 1/2-in. cubes
- 1-1/2 cups cubed fully cooked lean ham
- 1-1/4 cups half-and-half cream
- 3 Tbsp. shredded Gruyere *or* Swiss cheese

1. In a large saucepan, saute leeks in butter until tender. Stir in flour until blended. Gradually add the broth, water, parsley, herbes de Provence, chives, celery seed and nutmeg. Bring to a boil; cook and stir for 2 minutes or until thickened.

2. Cut tips off asparagus and set aside. Cut stalks into 1/2-in. pieces; add to pan. Reduce heat; cover and simmer for 10-15 minutes or until asparagus is tender. Cool slightly.

3. In a blender, process soup in batches until smooth. Return all to pan. Stir in potatoes. Bring to a boil. Reduce heat; cover and simmer for 10 minutes. Stir in asparagus tips; cover and simmer 5-8 minutes longer or until vegetables are tender. Stir in ham and cream; heat through. Sprinkle with cheese.

Editor's Note: Look for herbes de Provence in the spice aisle.

Nutrition Facts: 1 cup equals 207 calories, 8 g fat (5 g saturated fat), 35 mg cholesterol, 824 mg sodium, 24 g carbohydrate, 2 g fiber, 9 g protein.

DAY AFTER EASTER SOUP

Open-Faced Chicken Salad Sandwiches

PREP/TOTAL TIME: 25 min. YIELD: 6 servings

CHRISTINA BALDWIN • COVINGTON, LOUISIANA

These uniquely flavored chicken sandwiches, with their sweet-tangy-tart combo of ingredients, are absolutely delectable. Enjoy this recipe as it is or, even better, use a panini press and fix it as a normal sandwich—it works fabulously.

- 3 cups cubed cooked chicken breast
- 3 celery ribs, finely chopped
- 1 cup fat-free mayonnaise
- 1 small onion, finely chopped
- 1/2 cup dried cranberries
- 1/4 cup chopped pecans
- 2 Tbsp. white wine vinegar
- 2 Tbsp. Creole mustard
- 1 Tbsp. lemon juice
- 1/4 tsp. pepper
- 6 slices sourdough bread

Butter-flavored cooking spray

- 3/4 cup sugar-free apricot preserves
- 6 slices Brie cheese (1/2 oz. *each*)

1. In a large bowl, gently combine the first 10 ingredients. Place bread slices on a baking sheet; spritz with butter-flavored cooking spray. Broil 4 in. from the heat for 2-3 minutes or until golden brown.

2. Spread preserves over untoasted sides of bread slices. Top each with 2/3 cup chicken salad and a slice of cheese. Broil 2-3 minutes longer or until the cheese is melted.

Nutrition Facts: 1 sandwich equals 381 calories, 12 g fat (4 g saturated fat), 72 mg cholesterol, 780 mg sodium, 46 g carbohydrate, 3 g fiber, 28 g protein.

Sweet Potato & Black Bean Chili M

PREP: 25 min. COOK: 35 min. YIELD: 8 servings (2 qt.)

JOY PENDLEY • ORTONVILLE, MICHIGAN

My whole family enjoys this chili, but my daughter especially loves it. I like to make it because it's so easy and very flavorful.

- 3 large sweet potatoes, peeled and cut into 1/2-in. cubes
- 1 large onion, chopped
- 1 Tbsp. olive oil
- 2 Tbsp. chili powder
- 3 garlic cloves, minced
- 1 tsp. ground cumin
- 1/4 tsp. cayenne pepper
- 2 cans (15 oz. *each*) black beans, rinsed and drained
- 1 can (28 oz.) diced tomatoes, undrained
- 1/4 cup brewed coffee
- 2 Tbsp. honey
- 1/2 tsp. salt
- 1/4 tsp. pepper
- 1/2 cup shredded reduced-fat Monterey Jack cheese *or* reduced-fat Mexican cheese blend

1. In a nonstick Dutch oven coated with cooking spray, saute sweet potatoes and onion in oil until crisp-tender. Add the chili powder, garlic, cumin and cayenne; cook 1 minute longer. Stir in the beans, tomatoes, coffee, honey, salt and pepper.

2. Bring to a boil. Reduce heat; cover and simmer for 30-35 minutes or until sweet potatoes are tender. Sprinkle with cheese.

Nutrition Facts: 1 cup chili with 1 Tbsp. cheese equals 252 calories, 4 g fat (1 g saturated fat), 5 mg cholesterol, 554 mg sodium, 47 g carbohydrate, 9 g fiber, 10 g protein.

OPEN-FACED CHICKEN SALAD SANDWICHES

Garbanzo Bean Burgers M

PREP: 25 min. COOK: 10 min. YIELD: 6 servings

BEREA RIDER • EAST POINT, KENTUCKY

These meatless burgers are totally awesome. I think I'd rather have one than any cheeseburger at a restaurant. They really rock! Need I say more?

- 1 can (15 oz.) garbanzo beans *or* chickpeas, rinsed and drained
- 3 Tbsp. water
- 1 tsp. lemon juice
- 1 cup dry bread crumbs
- 1 egg
- 1 tsp. Italian seasoning
- 1/2 tsp. garlic powder
- 1/2 tsp. onion powder

Dash crushed red pepper flakes

- 2 Tbsp. canola oil
- 6 whole wheat hamburger buns, split and toasted
- 6 slices reduced-fat process American cheese product

Dill pickle slices, fat-free mayonnaise and ketchup, optional

1. Place the beans, water and lemon juice in a food processor; cover and process until blended. Transfer to a large bowl. Add the bread crumbs, egg and seasonings and mix well. Shape into six patties.

2. In a large skillet, cook patties in oil in batches for 3-4 minutes on each side or until lightly browned. Serve on buns with cheese. Top with pickle slices, mayonnaise and ketchup if desired.

Nutrition Facts: 1 burger (calculated without optional ingredients) equals 346 calories, 11 g fat (2 g saturated fat), 40 mg cholesterol, 641 mg sodium, 48 g carbohydrate, 7 g fiber, 15 g protein.

Curry Chicken Soup

PREP: 20 min. **COOK:** 15 min. **YIELD:** 4 servings

JANE HACKER • MILWAUKEE, WISCONSIN

Despite the longer ingredient list, this yummy soup is simple and fast. What a fantastic way to get your veggies!

1/2	lb. boneless skinless chicken breast, cut into 1/2-in. cubes
3	tsp. canola oil, *divided*
3/4	cup chopped onion
1/2	cup chopped carrot
1/2	cup chopped celery
1/2	cup chopped green pepper
1	cup chopped peeled apple

2	Tbsp. all-purpose flour
1/4	tsp. salt
2	cans (14-1/2 oz. *each*) reduced-sodium chicken broth
1/4	cup tomato paste
2 to 3	tsp. curry powder
1	tsp. ground ginger
1/4 to 1/2	tsp. crushed red pepper flakes
2	Tbsp. minced fresh parsley

1. In a large saucepan coated with cooking spray, cook chicken in 1 tsp. oil for 4-5 minutes or until no longer pink. Remove chicken and set aside.

2. In the same saucepan, saute the onion, carrot, celery and green pepper in remaining oil for 4 minutes. Add apple; cook 2 minutes longer. Combine flour and salt. Sprinkle over vegetable mixture; cook and stir for 1 minute. Gradually stir in broth and tomato paste. Bring to a boil; cook and stir 1-2 minutes longer or until slightly thickened.

3. Stir in the curry, ginger and pepper flakes. Return chicken to saucepan and bring to a boil. Reduce heat; simmer, uncovered, for 8-10 minutes or until the vegetables are tender. Sprinkle with parsley.

Nutrition Facts: 1-1/2 cups equals 183 calories, 5 g fat (1 g saturated fat), 31 mg cholesterol, 752 mg sodium, 19 g carbohydrate, 4 g fiber, 16 g protein. **Diabetic Exchanges:** 2 lean meat, 2 vegetable, 1/2 starch, 1/2 fat.

Cajun Catfish Sandwiches

PREP/TOTAL TIME: 25 min. **YIELD:** 4 servings

SHAUNIECE FRAZIER • LOS ANGELES, CALIFORNIA

This spicy bistro-style sandwich makes such an effortless summertime supper. Serve it alongside your favorite vegetable side dish and enjoy.

- 3/4 tsp. seasoned pepper
- 1/2 tsp. chili powder
- 1/2 tsp. cayenne pepper
- 1/4 tsp. seasoned salt
- 4 catfish fillets (4 oz. *each*)
- 2 tsp. olive oil, *divided*
- 2 green onions, chopped
- 3 garlic cloves, minced
- 1/2 cup fat-free mayonnaise
- 4 French *or* kaiser rolls, split and toasted
- 4 romaine leaves

1. Combine the seasoned pepper, chili powder, cayenne and seasoned salt; sprinkle over fillets. In a large skillet, cook fillets in 1 tsp. oil for 4-6 minutes on each side or until fish flakes easily with a fork. Remove and keep warm.

2. In the same skillet, saute onions and garlic in remaining oil until tender. Remove from the heat; stir in mayonnaise. Spread over rolls; top each with a romaine leaf and fillet. Replace tops.

Nutrition Facts: 1 sandwich equals 373 calories, 14 g fat (3 g saturated fat), 56 mg cholesterol, 710 mg sodium, 37 g carbohydrate, 3 g fiber, 24 g protein.

Sausage Pizza Soup

PREP: 10 min. **COOK:** 25 min. **YIELD:** 4 servings

BETH SHERER • MILWAUKEE, WISCONSIN

Here's a healthy take on ooey-gooey sausage pizza. You won't believe something so comforting could be so light.

- 1/2 lb. Italian turkey sausage links, casings removed
- 1 medium zucchini, sliced
- 1 cup sliced fresh mushrooms
- 1 small onion, chopped
- 1 can (14-1/2 oz.) no-salt-added diced tomatoes
- 1 cup water
- 1 cup reduced-sodium chicken broth
- 1 tsp. dried basil
- 1/4 tsp. pepper

Minced fresh basil and crushed red pepper flakes, optional

1. In a large saucepan, cook the sausage, zucchini, mushrooms and onion over medium heat until meat is no longer pink; drain. Add the tomatoes, water, broth, dried basil and pepper. Bring to a boil. Reduce heat; simmer, uncovered, for 15 minutes. Sprinkle with fresh basil and pepper flakes if desired.

Nutrition Facts: 1 cup equals 128 calories, 5 g fat (1 g saturated fat), 34 mg cholesterol, 528 mg sodium, 9 g carbohydrate, 3 g fiber, 12 g protein. **Diabetic Exchanges:** 2 vegetable, 1 medium-fat meat.

Lightened-Up Pasta Fagioli Soup

PREP: 20 min. COOK: 40 min.
YIELD: 6 servings (2-1/4 qt.)

CINDIE KITCHIN • GRANTS PASS, OREGON

After trying pasta fagioli at a popular restaurant, I was determined to make it at home, only healthier. It turns out mine was a big hit! Loaded with veggies, it is such a simple way to boost nutrition and fiber at mealtime.

- 1 lb. lean ground turkey
- 1 large onion, chopped
- 2 celery ribs, chopped
- 2 medium carrots, sliced
- 1 garlic clove, minced
- 3 cups water
- 1 can (16 oz.) kidney beans, rinsed and drained
- 2 cans (8 oz. *each*) no-salt-added tomato sauce
- 1 can (14-1/2 oz.) no-salt-added diced tomatoes, undrained
- 1 Tbsp. dried parsley flakes
- 2 tsp. reduced-sodium beef bouillon granules
- 1/2 tsp. dried oregano
- 1/2 tsp. dried basil
- 1/4 tsp. pepper
- 2 cups shredded cabbage
- 1 cup fresh *or* frozen cut green beans (1-in. pieces)
- 1/2 cup uncooked elbow macaroni

1. In a Dutch oven coated with cooking spray, cook the turkey, onion, celery and carrots over medium heat until meat is no longer pink. Add garlic; cook 1 minute longer. Add the water, beans, tomato sauce, tomatoes, parsley, bouillon, oregano, basil and pepper. Bring to a boil. Reduce heat; cover and simmer for 20 minutes.

2. Add the cabbage, green beans and macaroni; cover and simmer 8-10 minutes longer or until the vegetables and macaroni are tender.

Nutrition Facts: 1-1/2 cups equals 276 calories, 7 g fat (2 g saturated fat), 60 mg cholesterol, 379 mg sodium, 33 g carbohydrate, 8 g fiber, 21 g protein. **Diabetic Exchanges:** 2 starch, 2 lean meat.

Mango Shrimp Pitas

PREP: 15 min. + marinating GRILL: 10 min.
YIELD: 4 servings

BEVERLY OFERRALL • LINKWOOD, MARYLAND

Mango, ginger and curry combine with a splash of lime juice to coat this juicy, grilled shrimp. Stuffed in pitas, the shrimp combo makes for an easy-to-hold, fabulous entree! You could also serve it on a bed of rice.

- 1/2 cup mango chutney
- 3 Tbsp. lime juice
- 1 tsp. grated fresh gingerroot
- 1/2 tsp. curry powder
- 1 lb. uncooked large shrimp, peeled and deveined
- 2 pita breads (6 in.), halved
- 8 Bibb *or* Boston lettuce leaves
- 1 large tomato, thinly sliced

1. In a small bowl, combine the chutney, lime juice, ginger and curry. Pour 1/2 cup marinade into a large resealable plastic bag; add the shrimp. Seal bag and turn to coat; refrigerate for at least 15 minutes. Cover and refrigerate remaining marinade.

2. Drain and discard marinade. Thread shrimp onto four metal or soaked wooden skewers. Using long-handled tongs, moisten a paper towel with cooking oil and lightly coat the grill rack. Grill shrimp, covered, over medium heat or broil 4 in. from the heat for 6-8 minutes or until shrimp turn pink, turning frequently.

3. Fill pita halves with lettuce, tomato and shrimp; spoon reserved chutney mixture over filling.

Nutrition Facts: 1 filled pita half equals 230 calories, 2 g fat (trace saturated fat), 138 mg cholesterol, 410 mg sodium, 29 g carbohydrate, 1 g fiber, 22 g protein. **Diabetic Exchanges:** 3 lean meat, 2 starch.

MANGO SHRIMP PITAS

LIGHTENED-UP PASTA FAGIOLI SOUP

Curried Parsnip Soup **F**

PREP: 15 min. COOK: 35 min. YIELD: 6 servings

JULIE MATHIESON • BRISTOL, TENNESSEE

My mum used to make this recipe at home in England, where parsnips are more widely used than here. It's very aromatic and has a nice bite from the curry and pepper.

- 1 large onion, chopped
- 1 large carrot, chopped
- 1 Tbsp. butter
- 1 lb. parsnips, peeled and chopped
- 2 cans (14-1/2 oz. *each*) reduced-sodium chicken broth
- 1 tsp. curry powder
- 1/4 tsp. salt
- 1/4 tsp. pepper
- 1 cup fat-free milk

1. In a large saucepan, saute onion and carrot in butter until onion is tender. Add parsnips; cook 2 minutes longer. Stir in broth and seasonings. Bring to a boil. Reduce heat; cover and simmer for 12-15 minutes or until parsnips are tender.

2. Cool slightly. In a blender, process soup in batches until smooth. Return all to the pan; stir in milk and heat through.

Nutrition Facts: 1 cup equals 113 calories, 2 g fat (1 g saturated fat), 6 mg cholesterol, 513 mg sodium, 20 g carbohydrate, 5 g fiber, 5 g protein. **Diabetic Exchanges:** 1 starch, 1/2 fat.

Turkey Wraps with Maple Mustard Dressing

PREP/TOTAL TIME: 30 min. YIELD: 4 servings

MICHELLE FRATI • MANORVILLE, NEW YORK

These came about when I needed to make a meal with the few ingredients I had in my fridge. Now they're a favorite.

- 8 fresh asparagus spears
- 4 tsp. stone-ground mustard
- 1 Tbsp. fat-free mayonnaise
- 1 Tbsp. maple syrup
- 4 whole wheat tortillas (8 in.), warmed
- 1/2 lb. sliced deli turkey
- 1/2 medium ripe avocado, peeled and sliced
- 2 turkey bacon strips, diced and cooked
- 1 cup shredded lettuce
- 1/8 tsp. pepper

1. In a large skillet, bring 3 cups water to a boil. Add asparagus; cover and cook for 2-4 minutes. Drain and immediately place asparagus in ice water. Drain and pat dry.

2. Combine the mustard, mayonnaise and syrup; spread over each tortilla. Layer with turkey, avocado, bacon, lettuce and asparagus. Sprinkle with pepper. Roll up and secure with toothpicks.

Nutrition Facts: 1 wrap equals 288 calories, 9 g fat (1 g saturated fat), 28 mg cholesterol, 894 mg sodium, 32 g carbohydrate, 5 g fiber, 18 g protein.

Italian Tortellini Soup

PREP: 15 min. COOK: 25 min. YIELD: 8 servings (2 qt.)

GILDA LESTER • MILLSBORO, DELAWARE

You can pick up everything for this hearty soup at the supermarket on the way home, then put it together in minutes. To save more time, purchase sliced mushrooms. Serve with crusty bread and salad greens.

CURRIED PARSNIP SOUP

TURKEY WRAPS WITH MAPLE MUSTARD DRESSING

1/2 lb. sliced fresh mushrooms
  2 tsp. olive oil
4-1/2 cups water
  1 can (14-1/2 oz.) no-salt-added diced tomatoes, undrained
  3 Tbsp. grated Romano cheese
  5 tsp. sodium-free chicken bouillon granules
  1 Tbsp. prepared pesto
  1 jar (7 oz.) roasted sweet red peppers, drained
  1 pkg. (9 oz.) refrigerated cheese tortellini

GARNISH:
  8 thin slices prosciutto *or* deli ham
  8 tsp. grated Romano cheese

1. In a Dutch oven, saute mushrooms in oil until tender. Add the water, tomatoes, cheese, bouillon and prepared pesto.

2. Place peppers in a food processor; cover and process until blended. Add to mushroom mixture and bring to a boil. Reduce the heat; cover and simmer for 10 minutes.

3. Stir in the tortellini; return to a boil. Cook for 7-9 minutes or until tender, stirring occasionally. Cut the prosciutto into thin strips; garnish each individual serving with 1 slice prosciutto and 1 tsp. cheese. Serve immediately.

Nutrition Facts: 1 cup equals 201 calories, 8 g fat (3 g saturated fat), 32 mg cholesterol, 609 mg sodium, 20 g carbohydrate, 2 g fiber, 12 g protein. **Diabetic Exchanges:** 1 starch, 1 medium-fat meat, 1 vegetable.

Plum Chicken Wraps

PREP/TOTAL TIME: 20 min. YIELD: 4 servings

JENNIFER MICHALICEK • PHOENIX, ARIZONA

Dinner's a wrap with this easy, nutritious recipe that's loaded with the fruity flavors of pineapple and plum. It makes a sweet-and-sour chicken handheld specialty that is hard to beat any time of the year.

  1 can (8 oz.) unsweetened crushed pineapple, drained
1/3 cup plum sauce
  1 Tbsp. rice vinegar
1/2 tsp. sesame oil
  2 cups cubed cooked chicken breast
1/2 cup chopped green onions
1/4 cup salted cashews
  2 medium fresh plums, sliced
 12 Boston *or* Bibb lettuce leaves

1. In a large saucepan, combine the pineapple, plum sauce, vinegar and oil. Cook and stir over medium heat for 5 minutes.

2. Stir in the chicken, green onions and cashews; heat through. Remove from the heat; stir in plums. Place 1/3 cup chicken mixture on each lettuce leaf. Fold lettuce over filling.

Nutrition Facts: 3 filled wraps equals 298 calories, 8 g fat (2 g saturated fat), 54 mg cholesterol, 237 mg sodium, 32 g carbohydrate, 2 g fiber, 23 g protein. **Diabetic Exchanges:** 3 lean meat, 1-1/2 fruit, 1 fat, 1/2 starch.

Pretty Autumn Soup **F** **M**

PREP: 15 min. **COOK:** 20 min. **YIELD:** 6 servings

MARGARET ALLEN • ABINGDON, VIRGINIA

Carrots, squash and sweet potato combine to make a healthy and colorful fall soup. This one's loaded with vitamin A!

2-1/2	cups cubed peeled butternut squash
1	large sweet potato, peeled and cubed
3	medium carrots, sliced
1/4	cup orange juice concentrate
3	cups fat-free milk
1/4	tsp. salt
1/4	tsp. pepper
3	Tbsp. reduced-fat sour cream
2	Tbsp. minced chives
1	Tbsp. sesame seeds, toasted

1. Place the squash, sweet potato and carrots in a steamer basket; place in a large saucepan over 1 in. of water. Bring to a boil; cover and steam for 12-16 minutes or until tender. Cool slightly. Transfer to a food processor; add juice concentrate. Cover and process until smooth.

2. Transfer to a large saucepan; stir in the milk, salt and pepper. Cook and stir over low heat until heated through (do not boil). Top each serving with 1-1/2 tsp. sour cream, 1 tsp. chives and 1/2 tsp. sesame seeds.

Nutrition Facts: 1 cup equals 166 calories, 1 g fat (1 g saturated fat), 5 mg cholesterol, 190 mg sodium, 33 g carbohydrate, 6 g fiber, 7 g protein. **Diabetic Exchanges:** 1-1/2 starch, 1 vegetable, 1/2 fat-free milk.

Italian Beef Sandwiches

PREP: 20 min. **COOK:** 8 hours **YIELD:** 12 servings

CHER SCHWARTZ • ELLISVILLE, MISSOURI

These sandwiches are fork-tender, mouthwatering good, and so easy to fix. They always get rave reviews!

1	beef rump roast or bottom round roast (3 lbs.)
3	cups reduced-sodium beef broth
1	envelope Italian salad dressing mix
1	tsp. garlic powder
1	tsp. onion powder
1	tsp. dried parsley flakes
1	tsp. dried basil
1	tsp. dried oregano
1	tsp. pepper
1	large onion, julienned
1	large green pepper, julienned
4-1/2	tsp. olive oil
12	hamburger buns, split
12	slices reduced-fat provolone cheese

1. Cut roast in half; place in a 4-qt. slow cooker. Combine the broth, dressing mix and seasonings; pour over meat. Cover and cook on low for 8 hours or until tender.

2. Remove roast; cool slightly. Skim fat from cooking juices; reserve 1 cup juices. Shred beef and return to slow cooker. Stir in reserved cooking juices; heat through.

3. Meanwhile, in a large skillet, saute onion and green pepper in oil until tender.

4. Using a slotted spoon, place beef on bun bottoms; layer with cheese and vegetables. Replace bun tops.

Nutrition Facts: 1 sandwich equals 346 calories, 12 g fat (5 g saturated fat), 79 mg cholesterol, 707 mg sodium, 25 g carbohydrate, 2 g fiber, 32 g protein. **Diabetic Exchanges:** 4 lean meat, 1-1/2 starch, 1 fat.

Herbed Turkey Stock **F** **S** **C**

PREP: 1-1/4 hours **COOK:** 1-1/2 hours
YIELD: 14 servings (3-1/2 qt.)

HEALTHY COOKING TEST KITCHEN

Spending a little extra time in the kitchen can yield big flavor, plus you'll be saving about 850 mg of sodium per cup versus store-bought chicken broth.

1	leftover turkey carcass (from a 12- to 14-lb. turkey)
2	medium onions, cut into wedges
2	celery ribs, cut into 1-in. pieces
2	medium carrots, cut into 1-in. pieces
6	garlic cloves, peeled
4	qt. plus 1 cup water, divided
1/2	cup packed fresh parsley sprigs
1/3	cup fresh sage leaves
1/4	cup fresh thyme sprigs
4	bay leaves
1	Tbsp. whole peppercorns

1. Place the turkey carcass, onions, celery, carrots and garlic in a shallow roasting pan coated with cooking spray. Bake, uncovered, at 400° for 1 hour, turning once.

2. Transfer the turkey carcass and vegetables to a stockpot; add 4 qt. water. Pour remaining water into the roasting pan, stirring to loosen browned bits; add to stockpot. Place the parsley, sage, thyme, bay leaves and peppercorns on a double thickness of cheesecloth; bring up corners of cloth and tie with string to form a bag; add to stockpot. Slowly bring to a boil over low heat; cover and simmer for 1-1/2 hours.

PRETTY AUTUMN SOUP

BUTTERNUT SOUP WITH PARMESAN CROUTONS

3. Discard the carcass and herb bag. Strain broth through a cheesecloth-lined colander. If using immediately, skim fat. Or cool, then refrigerate for 8 hours or overnight; remove fat from surface before using. Broth may be refrigerated for up to 3 days or frozen for 4-6 months.

Nutrition Facts: 1 cup equals 33 calories, 1 g fat (trace saturated fat), 1 mg cholesterol, 89 mg sodium, 6 g carbohydrate, 1 g fiber, 2 g protein.

Butternut Soup With Parmesan Croutons

PREP: 50 min. **COOK:** 25 min. **YIELD:** 8 servings

JEN LEHNER • SEATTLE, WASHINGTON

Roasting creates a rich, caramelized flavor, but you can cook the squash cubes directly in the broth if you're short on time. They should pierce easily with a fork when they're done.

- 1 medium butternut squash (about 3 lbs.), peeled, seeded and cut into 1-in. cubes
- 2 Tbsp. olive oil, divided
- 1/4 tsp. pepper
- 1 large onion, chopped
- 3 celery ribs, chopped
- 2 Tbsp. minced fresh sage or 2 tsp. rubbed sage
- 3 cans (14-1/2 oz. each) reduced-sodium chicken broth

CROUTONS:
- 2 Tbsp. grated Parmesan cheese
- 2 Tbsp. olive oil
- 1 Tbsp. minced fresh sage or 1 tsp. rubbed sage
- 2 garlic cloves, minced
- 2 cups cubed French bread (1/2-in. cubes)

Cooking spray

Additional grated Parmesan cheese, optional

1. Place squash in a 15-in. x 10-in. x 1-in. baking pan lightly coated with cooking spray. Drizzle with 1 Tbsp. oil; sprinkle with pepper. Toss to coat. Bake, uncovered, at 425° for 30-35 minutes or until tender, stirring every 15 minutes. Set aside.

2. In a Dutch oven, saute the onion, celery and sage in remaining oil until tender. Stir in broth and reserved squash. Bring to a boil. Reduce heat; cover and simmer for 15-20 minutes or until heated through. Cool slightly.

3. In a blender, puree soup in batches until smooth. Return to the pan; heat through.

4. For croutons, in a small bowl, combine the cheese, oil, sage and garlic. Add bread cubes and spritz with cooking spray; toss to coat. Place on a baking sheet coated with cooking spray. Bake at 425° for 5-8 minutes or until golden brown, stirring occasionally. Serve with soup and sprinkle with additional Parmesan cheese if desired.

Nutrition Facts: 1 cup soup with 1/4 cup croutons equals 179 calories, 8 g fat (1 g saturated fat), 1 mg cholesterol, 541 mg sodium, 25 g carbohydrate, 6 g fiber, 5 g protein. **Diabetic Exchanges:** 1-1/2 starch, 1 fat.

Artichoke Chicken Pockets

PREP: 20 min. **BAKE:** 15 min. **YIELD:** 6 servings

BEVERLY O'FERRALL • LINKWOOD, MARYLAND

You'll have a hard time believing these hefty, pizza-crust pockets are light! Packed full of cheese, artichokes, chicken, spinach and fabulous flavor, they're great even without the sauce and sure to become a family favorite.

2	cups shredded cooked chicken breast
2	cups thinly sliced fresh spinach
1-1/4	cups shredded provolone cheese
3/4	cup water-packed artichoke hearts, rinsed, drained and chopped
1	garlic clove, minced
1/4	tsp. pepper
1	tube (13.8 oz.) refrigerated pizza crust
2	tsp. cornmeal

Marinara sauce, optional

1. In a large bowl, combine the first six ingredients. Unroll pizza dough; cut into six 4-1/2-in. squares. Spoon 1 cup chicken mixture onto the center of each square; brush edges of dough with water. Fold one corner of each square over filling to the opposite corner, forming a triangle. Using a fork, crimp edges to seal.

2. Sprinkle cornmeal over a 15-in. x 10-in. x 1-in. baking pan coated with cooking spray. Place pockets in pan; prick tops with a fork. Bake at 425° for 12-15 minutes or until golden brown. Serve with marinara sauce if desired.

Nutrition Facts: 1 pocket (calculated without marinara sauce) equals 355 calories, 11 g fat (5 g saturated fat), 55 mg cholesterol, 776 mg sodium, 34 g carbohydrate, 1 g fiber, 27 g protein. **Diabetic Exchanges:** 3 lean meat, 2 starch, 1 fat.

Spicy Chicken Chili

PREP: 30 min. **COOK:** 30 min. **YIELD:** 12 servings (4 qt.)

NATALIE HUGHES • YUKON, OKLAHOMA

My recipe was inspired by the fact that I've been on a low-calorie, low-fat, high-fiber diet. I entered this in a chili cookoff and had several people say that it was the best chili they'd ever had!

1	small onion, chopped
1	small green pepper, chopped
1	small sweet red pepper, chopped
2	jalapeno peppers, seeded and chopped
1	serrano pepper, seeded and chopped
3	garlic cloves, minced
1	Tbsp. olive oil

1 can (28 oz.) crushed tomatoes
1 can (14-1/2 oz.) stewed tomatoes, cut up
1 can (14-1/2 oz.) diced tomatoes with mild green chilies
1 can (16 oz.) kidney beans, rinsed and drained
1 can (15 oz.) black beans, rinsed and drained
1 carton (32 oz.) reduced-sodium chicken broth
3 Tbsp. chili powder
1 Tbsp. ground cumin
1 to 2 tsp. crushed red pepper flakes
2 to 4 Tbsp. Louisiana-style hot sauce
2-1/2 cups cubed cooked chicken breast
2 cups frozen corn
3/4 cup reduced-fat sour cream
3/4 cup shredded reduced-fat cheddar cheese

1. In a Dutch oven, saute the first six ingredients in oil until tender; add the tomatoes, beans, broth, seasonings and hot sauce. Bring to a boil. Reduce heat; simmer, uncovered, for 15 minutes. Stir in chicken and corn; heat through. Garnish each serving with 1 Tbsp. each of sour cream and cheese.

Editor's Note: When cutting hot peppers, disposable gloves are recommended. Avoid touching your face.

Nutrition Facts: 1-1/3 cups equals 242 calories, 6 g fat (2 g saturated fat), 32 mg cholesterol, 694 mg sodium, 31 g carbohydrate, 7 g fiber, 19 g protein. **Diabetic Exchanges:** 2 very lean meat, 2 vegetable, 1 starch, 1 fat.

Turkey Meatball Soup

PREP: 30 min. **COOK:** 40 min. **YIELD:** 6 servings

CHRISTIE LADD • MECHANICSBURG, PENNSYLVANIA

Every Italian-American family I know seems to have their own take on meatball soup. This recipe is based on my family's classic version.

2 egg whites, beaten
1/2 cup seasoned bread crumbs
1 Tbsp. grated Parmesan cheese
4 tsp. Italian seasoning, divided
1 lb. lean ground turkey
3 medium carrots, sliced
3 celery ribs, finely chopped
4 garlic cloves, minced
1 Tbsp. olive oil
3 cans (14-1/2 oz. each) reduced-sodium chicken broth
1/4 tsp. pepper
1/2 cup ditalini or other small pasta

1. In a small bowl, combine the egg whites, bread crumbs, cheese and 2 tsp. Italian seasoning. Crumble turkey over mixture and mix well. Shape into 3/4-in. balls. Place in a 15-in. x 10-in. x 1-in. baking pan coated with cooking spray. Bake, uncovered, at 350° for 10-15 minutes or until no longer pink.

2. Meanwhile, in a Dutch oven, saute the carrots, celery and garlic in oil until tender. Add the broth, pepper and remaining Italian seasoning. Bring to a boil. Reduce heat; cover and simmer for 20 minutes. Stir in pasta; cook 10-12 minutes longer or until

vegetables and pasta are tender. Stir in meatballs; heat through.

Nutrition Facts: 1 cup equals 258 calories, 10 g fat (2 g saturated fat), 60 mg cholesterol, 783 mg sodium, 21 g carbohydrate, 2 g fiber, 21 g protein. **Diabetic Exchanges:** 2 lean meat, 1-1/2 starch, 1/2 fat.

Super-Duper Tuna Sandwiches

PREP/TOTAL TIME: 15 min. **YIELD:** 4 servings

NAE BARTOLOMEO • INDIANOLA, IOWA

You can also try serving this fantastic tuna salad on tortillas for wraps or with crackers as an appetizer.

2 cans (6 oz. each) light water-packed tuna, drained and flaked
1/3 cup shredded apple
1/3 cup finely shredded cabbage
1/3 cup finely shredded carrot
3 Tbsp. finely chopped celery
3 Tbsp. finely chopped onion
3 Tbsp. sweet pickle relish
2 Tbsp. reduced-fat mayonnaise
8 slices whole wheat bread

1. In a large bowl, combine first eight ingredients. Spread 1/2 cup tuna mixture over four slices of bread; top with remaining bread slices.

Nutrition Facts: 1 sandwich equals 291 calories, 5 g fat (1 g saturated fat), 28 mg cholesterol, 717 mg sodium, 31 g carbohydrate, 5 g fiber, 29 g protein. **Diabetic Exchanges:** 3 very lean meat, 2 starch, 1/2 fat.

SUPER-DUPER TUNA SANDWICHES

MAKEOVER SAUSAGE & SPINACH PIE

EGGS BENEDICT

MAKEOVER BLUEBERRY FRENCH TOAST

Good Mornings

Get your day off to a healthy start with the eye-opening breakfast items found here. Whether you need something quick before work or a contribution to a friendly brunch, these rise-and-shine delights can't be beat!

Makeover Blueberry French Toast M

PREP: 30 min. + chilling **BAKE:** 55 min.
YIELD: 8 servings (1-1/2 cups sauce)

JOAN HALLFORD • NORTH RICHLAND HILLS, TEXAS

With this luscious makeover from the Healthy Cooking Test Kitchen, I can enjoy all the richness and flavor of my original recipe but with fewer calories and less fat and cholesterol.

  6 whole wheat hamburger buns
  1 pkg. (8 oz.) reduced-fat cream cheese
  1 cup fresh *or* frozen blueberries
  6 eggs
  1 cup egg substitute
  2 cups fat-free milk
1/3 cup maple syrup or honey

SAUCE:
1/2 cup sugar
  2 Tbsp. cornstarch
  1 cup grape juice
  1 cup fresh *or* frozen blueberries

1. Cut buns into 1-in. cubes; place half in a 13-in. x 9-in. baking dish coated with cooking spray. Cut cream cheese into 1-in. cubes; place over buns. Top with blueberries and remaining bun cubes.

2. In a large bowl, beat eggs and egg substitute. Add milk and syrup; mix well. Pour over bun mixture. Cover and refrigerate for 8 hours or overnight.

3. Remove from the refrigerator 30 minutes before baking. Cover and bake at 350° for 30 minutes. Uncover; bake 25-30 minutes longer or until golden brown and center is set.

4. Meanwhile, in a small saucepan, combine sugar and cornstarch; stir in juice until smooth. Bring to a boil over medium heat; cook and stir for 2 minutes. Stir in blueberries. Reduce heat; simmer, uncovered, for 8-10 minutes or until berries burst, stirring occasionally. Serve with French toast.

Nutrition Facts: 1 slice with 3 Tbsp. sauce equals 375 calories, 11 g fat (6 g saturated fat), 180 mg cholesterol, 418 mg sodium, 54 g carbohydrate, 3 g fiber, 16 g protein.

Makeover Sausage & Spinach Pie

PREP: 20 min. **BAKE:** 40 min. + standing
YIELD: 6 servings

CAROL HANEMAN • ST. LOUIS, MISSOURI

Thanks to its flaky crust and savory filling, this sausage and spinach pie is a showstopping entree fit for any time of day. Now that it's lightened up, it's just as delicious as it is good for you!

  1 frozen deep-dish pie shell
1/2 lb. Italian turkey sausage links, casings removed
  1 cup egg substitute
  1 pkg. (10 oz.) frozen chopped spinach, thawed and squeezed dry
  1 cup (4 oz.) shredded part-skim mozzarella cheese
2/3 cup reduced-fat ricotta cheese
1/8 tsp. pepper

1. Line unpricked pastry shell with a double thickness of heavy-duty foil. Bake at 400° for 4 minutes. Remove foil; bake 4 minutes longer. Remove from the oven; reduce heat to 375°.

2. Meanwhile, in a large nonstick skillet, cook sausage over medium heat until no longer pink; drain. In a large bowl, whisk the egg substitute, spinach, cheeses, pepper and cooked sausage. Pour into crust. Place pie on a baking sheet. Cover the edges loosely with foil.

3. Bake for 40-45 minutes or until a knife inserted near the center comes out clean. Let stand for 10 minutes before cutting.

Nutrition Facts: 1 piece equals 282 calories, 14 g fat (5 g saturated fat), 40 mg cholesterol, 563 mg sodium, 19 g carbohydrate, 1 g fiber, 19 g protein.

> You can substitute **2 fresh eggs** for 1/2 cup of egg substitute in your recipes. There might be a slight change in texture, but the results are still great!

Makeover Hash Brown Casserole

PREP: 15 min. **BAKE:** 40 min. **YIELD:** 8 servings

KELLY KIRBY • WESTVILLE, NOVA SCOTIA

This new, revised and lightened-up recipe is just as tasty as the original full-fat version!

- 1 pkg. (30 oz.) frozen shredded hash brown potatoes, thawed
- 1 can (10-3/4 oz.) reduced-fat reduced-sodium condensed cream of chicken soup, undiluted
- 1 cup (4 oz.) shredded reduced-fat sharp cheddar cheese
- 2/3 cup reduced-fat sour cream
- 1 small onion, chopped
- 1/2 tsp. salt
- 1/2 tsp. pepper
- 1/4 cup crushed cornflakes
- 1 Tbsp. butter, melted

1. In a large bowl, combine the first seven ingredients. Transfer to a 13-in. x 9-in. baking dish coated with cooking spray. Combine cornflakes and butter; sprinkle over top. Bake at 350° for 40-45 minutes or until golden brown.

Nutrition Facts: 1-1/4 cups equals 203 calories, 7 g fat (4 g saturated fat), 24 mg cholesterol, 443 mg sodium, 27 g carbohydrate, 2 g fiber, 9 g protein. **Diabetic Exchanges:** 2 starch, 1 medium-fat meat.

Honey Cinnamon Milk F S

PREP/TOTAL TIME: 10 min. **YIELD:** 1 serving

LEONY SANTOSO • WINTER, VIRGINIA

I know you'll enjoy this warm, soothing beverage on a bleak wintry day. It's a nice alternative to hot cocoa or tea.

- 1 cup fat-free milk
- 1 cinnamon stick (3 in.)
- Dash ground nutmeg
- Dash ground allspice
- 1-1/2 tsp. honey

1. In a small saucepan, combine the milk, cinnamon stick, nutmeg and allspice. Cook and stir over medium heat until heated through; whisk in honey. Serve warm in a mug; garnish with cinnamon stick.

Nutrition Facts: 1 cup equals 117 calories, trace fat (trace saturated fat), 5 mg cholesterol, 103 mg sodium, 21 g carbohydrate, trace fiber, 8 g protein. **Diabetic Exchanges:** 1 fat-free milk, 1/2 starch.

Hearty Pepper Strata M

PREP: 15 min. + chilling **BAKE:** 50 min. + standing
YIELD: 8 servings

HEALTHY COOKING TEST KITCHEN

Here's a hearty make-ahead strata that's as satisfying and delicious for dinner as it is for breakfast. You'll want to give this eye-opening recipe a try!

- 9 slices whole wheat bread, cubed
- 1 pkg. (14 oz.) frozen pepper strips
- 1 cup sliced fresh mushrooms
- 1 medium onion, chopped
- 1 Tbsp. canola oil
- 8 eggs
- 8 egg whites
- 2-1/2 cups fat-free milk
- 1 cup (4 oz.) shredded cheddar cheese
- 1/2 tsp. salt
- 1/2 tsp. pepper

1. Place bread cubes in a 13-in. x 9-in. baking dish coated with cooking spray; set aside.

2. In a large skillet, saute the peppers, mushrooms and onion in oil until tender. In a large bowl, combine the eggs, egg whites, milk, cheese, salt, pepper and vegetable mixture; pour over the top. Cover and refrigerate overnight.

3. Remove from the refrigerator 30 minutes before baking. Bake, uncovered, at 350° for 50-60 minutes or until a knife inserted near the center comes out clean. Let stand for 10 minutes before cutting.

Nutrition Facts: 1 piece equals 283 calories, 12 g fat (5 g saturated fat), 228 mg cholesterol, 546 mg sodium, 22 g carbohydrate, 3 g fiber, 21 g protein. **Diabetic Exchanges:** 2 medium-fat meat, 1 starch, 1 vegetable, 1/2 fat.

HEARTY PEPPER STRATA

Zucchini Swiss Frittata C M

PREP: 20 min. BAKE: 20 min. YIELD: 4 servings

MICHELLE SANDOVAL • ESCALON, CALIFORNIA

Surprisingly hearty, with a fresh veggie flavor as big as its serving size, this cheesy frittata also qualifies as a nice lunch option or late-night supper.

1	large onion, chopped
2	medium zucchini, halved and thinly sliced
1	cup thinly sliced fresh mushrooms
4-1/2	tsp. butter
3	eggs
1/3	cup fat-free milk
1	tsp. Dijon mustard
1/2	tsp. ground mustard
1/4	tsp. salt
1/4	tsp. pepper
1	cup (4 oz.) shredded reduced-fat Swiss cheese
2	Tbsp. dry bread crumbs

1. In a large skillet, saute the onion, zucchini and mushrooms in butter until tender; drain. Transfer to an 8-in. square baking dish coated with cooking spray.

2. In a large bowl, whisk the eggs, milk, mustards, salt and pepper; pour over vegetable mixture. Sprinkle with cheese and bread crumbs. Bake, uncovered, at 375° for 18-22 minutes or until set. Let stand for 5 minutes.

Nutrition Facts: 1 piece equals 209 calories, 10 g fat (5 g saturated fat), 182 mg cholesterol, 391 mg sodium, 13 g carbohydrate, 2 g fiber, 17 g protein. **Diabetic Exchanges:** 2 medium-fat meat, 1 vegetable, 1 fat.

ZUCCHINI SWISS FRITTATA

Makeover Noodle Kugel M

PREP: 15 min. BAKE: 45 min. + standing
YIELD: 15 servings

CATHY TANG • REDMOND, WASHINGTON

I can finally feel good serving this fabulous brunch dish, particularly now that it's lower in saturated fat and cholesterol than my original recipe.

1	pkg. (12 oz.) yolk-free noodles
2	Tbsp. butter, melted
2	cups (16 oz.) 1% cottage cheese
1-1/2	cups sugar
4	eggs
1	cup egg substitute
1	cup (8 oz.) reduced-fat sour cream
1	cup reduced-fat ricotta cheese

TOPPING:

1/2	cup cinnamon graham cracker crumbs (about 3 whole crackers)
1	Tbsp. butter, melted

1. Cook noodles according to package directions; drain. Toss with butter; set aside.

2. In a large bowl, beat the cottage cheese, sugar, eggs, egg substitute, sour cream and ricotta cheese until well blended. Stir in noodles.

3. Transfer to a 13-in. x 9-in. baking dish coated with cooking spray. Combine cracker crumbs and butter; sprinkle over top.

4. Bake, uncovered, at 350° for 45-50 minutes or until a thermometer reads 160°. Let stand for 10 minutes before cutting.

Nutrition Facts: 1 piece equals 271 calories, 6 g fat (3 g saturated fat), 73 mg cholesterol, 235 mg sodium, 41 g carbohydrate, 1 g fiber, 13 g protein. **Diabetic Exchanges:** 2-1/2 starch, 1 lean meat, 1/2 fat.

Mustard Ham Strata C

PREP: 15 min. + chilling BAKE: 45 min.
YIELD: 12 servings

DOLORES ZORNOW • POYNETTE, WISCONSIN

I had this at a bed-and-breakfast years ago. They were kind enough to share the recipe, and I've made it many times since.

12	slices day-old bread, crusts removed and cubed
1-1/2	cups cubed fully cooked ham
1	cup chopped green pepper
3/4	cup shredded cheddar cheese
3/4	cup shredded Monterey Jack cheese
1/3	cup chopped onion
7	eggs
3	cups whole milk
3	tsp. ground mustard
1	tsp. salt

1. In a 13-in. x 9-in. baking dish coated with cooking spray, layer the bread cubes, ham, green pepper, cheeses and onion. In a large bowl, combine the eggs, milk, mustard and salt. Pour over top. Cover and refrigerate overnight.

GOOD MORNING FRITTATA

2. Remove from the refrigerator 30 minutes before baking. Bake, uncovered, at 325° for 45-50 minutes or until a knife inserted near the center comes out clean. Let stand for 5 minutes before cutting.

Nutrition Facts: 1 piece equals 198 calories, 11 g fat (5 g saturated fat), 153 mg cholesterol, 648 mg sodium, 11 g carbohydrate, 1 g fiber, 13 g protein. **Diabetic Exchanges:** 2 medium-fat meat, 1 starch.

Good Morning Frittata [C]

PREP/TOTAL TIME: 20 min. **YIELD:** 2 servings

MARY RELYEA • CANASTOTA, NEW YORK

Start the day bright with this light, fluffy, fast-fixing dish. Orange peppers add sunshiny sweetness.

  1 cup egg substitute
1/4 cup fat-free milk
1/8 tsp. pepper
Dash salt
1/4 cup chopped sweet orange pepper
  2 green onions, thinly sliced
1/2 tsp. canola oil
1/3 cup cubed fully cooked ham
1/4 cup shredded reduced-fat cheddar cheese

1. In a small bowl, whisk the egg substitute, milk, pepper and salt; set aside. In an 8-in. ovenproof skillet, saute orange pepper and onions in oil until tender. Add ham; heat through. Reduce heat; top with egg mixture. Cover and cook for 4-6 minutes or until nearly set.

2. Uncover skillet; sprinkle with cheese. Broil 3-4 in. from the heat for 2-3 minutes or until eggs are completely set. Let stand for 5 minutes. Cut into wedges.

Nutrition Facts: 1 slice equals 169 calories, 6 g fat (3 g saturated fat), 23 mg cholesterol, 727 mg sodium, 7 g carbohydrate, 1 g fiber, 21 g protein. **Diabetic Exchanges:** 3 lean meat, 1/2 starch.

Fluffy Pumpkin Pancakes M

PREP: 15 min. COOK: 10 min./batch YIELD: 4 pancakes

MINDY BAUKNECHT • TWO RIVERS, WISCONSIN

These pancakes are also delicious served with butter or whipped topping and a sprinkle of pumpkin pie spice. Freeze any extras in a single layer on a cookie sheet, then store in a freezer bag. They're great fresh out of the toaster!

- 1/3 cup all-purpose flour
- 1/3 cup whole wheat flour
- 2 Tbsp. sugar
- 1/2 tsp. baking powder
- 1/2 tsp. baking soda
- 1/4 tsp. pumpkin pie spice
- 1/8 tsp. ground cinnamon

Dash salt

- 1/2 cup fat-free milk
- 1/3 cup vanilla yogurt
- 1/3 cup canned pumpkin
- 1 egg, lightly beaten
- 1 Tbsp. canola oil
- 1/8 tsp. vanilla extract

Maple syrup

1. In a large bowl, combine the first eight ingredients. In another bowl, whisk the milk, yogurt, pumpkin, egg, oil and vanilla; stir into dry ingredients just until moistened.

2. Pour batter by 1/2 cupfuls onto a hot griddle coated with cooking spray; turn when bubbles form on top. Cook until the second side is golden brown. Serve with syrup.

Nutrition Facts: 2 pancakes (calculated without syrup) equals 360 calories, 11 g fat (2 g saturated fat), 109 mg cholesterol, 579 mg sodium, 55 g carbohydrate, 5 g fiber, 13 g protein.

Berry & Yogurt Phyllo Nests F S C

PREP: 25 min. + cooling YIELD: 6 servings

HEALTHY COOKING TEST KITCHEN

These elegant cups add a special touch to any breakfast. Add variety by using your favorite combination of flavored yogurt and fresh fruit.

6	sheets phyllo dough (14 inches x 9 inches)

Butter-flavored cooking spray

2-1/2	tsp. sugar, divided
1/3	cup vanilla yogurt
1	tsp. grated orange peel
1	tsp. orange juice
1/2	cup halved fresh strawberries
1/2	cup fresh raspberries
1/2	cup fresh blueberries

Fresh mint leaves, optional

1. Place one sheet of phyllo dough on a work surface; spritz with butter-flavored spray. Top with another sheet of phyllo; spritz with spray. Cut into six squares. (Keep the remaining phyllo covered with plastic wrap to avoid drying out.) Repeat with the remaining phyllo.

2. Stack three squares of layered phyllo in each of six muffin cups coated with cooking spray, rotating squares so corners do not overlap. Sprinkle 1/4 tsp. sugar into each cup. Spritz with cooking spray. Bake at 375° for 6-8 minutes or until golden brown. Cool on a wire rack.

3. Meanwhile, in a small bowl, whisk the yogurt, orange peel and juice, and remaining sugar. Spoon yogurt mixture into cups; top with berries. Garnish with mint if desired.

Nutrition Facts: 1 serving equals 72 calories, 1 g fat (trace saturated fat),1 mg cholesterol, 54 mg sodium, 14 g carbohydrate, 2 g fiber, 2 g protein. **Diabetic Exchange:** 1 starch.

Waffle Sandwich

PREP/TOTAL TIME: 20 min. YIELD: 1 serving

MICHELE MCHENRY • BELLINGHAM, WASHINGTON

Keep 'em going right through to lunchtime with this quick and hefty breakfast sandwich idea!

1	slice Canadian bacon
1	egg
1	green onion, chopped
2	frozen low-fat multigrain waffles
1	Tbsp. shredded reduced-fat cheddar cheese

1. In a small nonstick skillet coated with cooking spray, cook bacon for 1-2 minutes on each side or until lightly browned. Remove and keep warm.

2. Whisk egg and green onion. In the same skillet, add egg mixture. Cook and stir until completely set.

3. Meanwhile, prepare waffles according to package directions. Place one waffle on a plate. Layer with bacon, egg mixture, cheese and remaining waffle.

Nutrition Facts: 1 sandwich equals 261 calories, 10 g fat (3 g saturated fat), 223 mg cholesterol, 733 mg sodium, 30 g carbohydrate, 3 g fiber, 16 g protein. **Diabetic Exchanges:** 2 starch, 2 medium-fat meat.

Makeover Overnight French Toast M

PREP: 15 min. + chilling BAKE: 25 min. YIELD: 8 servings

SONYA LABBE • LOS ANGELES, CALIFORNIA

We tried this lighter version recently, and the whole family really loved it! You can bet this dish is going to become a brand-new family favorite.

4	eggs
1	cup egg substitute
3	cups fat-free milk
1/4	cup sugar
2	tsp. vanilla extract
1/4	tsp. salt
16	slices French bread (1 in. thick)

BERRY SAUCE:

| 2 | pkg. (12 oz. *each*) frozen unsweetened mixed berries, thawed |
| 1/4 | cup sugar |

1. In a large bowl, combine the eggs, egg substitute, milk, sugar, vanilla and salt. Place bread slices in two ungreased 13-in. x 9-in. baking dishes; pour egg mixture over top. Cover and refrigerate overnight.

2. Coat two 15-in. x 10-in. x 1-in. baking pans with butter-flavored cooking spray. Carefully transfer bread to prepared pans. Bake, uncovered, at 400° for 15 minutes. Carefully turn slices over. Bake 10-15 minutes longer or until golden and slightly puffed.

3. Meanwhile, combine berries and sugar. Serve with French toast.

Nutrition Facts: 2 slices French toast with 1/3 cup sauce equals 294 calories, 4 g fat (1 g saturated fat), 108 mg cholesterol, 486 mg sodium, 50 g carbohydrate, 3 g fiber, 13 g protein.

MAKEOVER OVERNIGHT FRENCH TOAST

Makeover Farm Girl Breakfast Casserole C M

PREP: 15 min. BAKE: 35 min. YIELD: 8 servings

NANCY ZIMMERMAN • CAPE MAY COURT HOUSE, NEW JERSEY

I served this lightened-up makeover casserole to my husband, Ken. He said it was fluffy and very good!

4	eggs
1-1/2 cups	egg substitute
1/2 cup	all-purpose flour
1 tsp.	baking powder
2 cups (16 oz.)	1% cottage cheese
2 cups (8 oz.)	shredded reduced-fat Monterey Jack cheese *or* reduced-fat Mexican cheese blend, *divided*
1 can (4 oz.)	chopped green chilies

1. In a large bowl, beat eggs and egg substitute on medium-high speed for 3 minutes or until light and lemon-colored. Combine flour and baking powder; gradually add to egg mixture and mix well. Stir in the cottage cheese, 1-1/2 cups shredded cheese and chilies.

2. Pour into a 13-in. x 9-in. baking dish coated with cooking spray. Bake, uncovered, at 350° for 35-40 minutes or until a knife inserted near the center comes out clean. Sprinkle with remaining cheese. Let stand for 5 minutes before serving.

Nutrition Facts: 1 piece equals 210 calories, 9 g fat (4 g saturated fat), 128 mg cholesterol, 665 mg sodium, 10 g carbohydrate, trace fiber, 24 g protein.

MAKEOVER FARM GIRL BREAKFAST CASSEROLE

Southwestern Eggs Benedict

PREP: 35 min. COOK: 10 min. YIELD: 4 servings

CATHY HALL • PHOENIX, ARIZONA

This colorful dish makes a beautiful, hearty, rise-and-shine breakfast. The potatoes and pepper are tender, the poached eggs are perfect and the flavor combination is wonderful.

4	medium red potatoes, cubed
3 Tbsp.	water
1	small sweet red pepper, sliced
1/2 cup	sliced sweet onion
2 tsp.	olive oil
4	turkey bacon strips, chopped and cooked
1/4 tsp.	salt
1/4 tsp.	pepper

SAUCE:
1-1/2 tsp.	butter
1 Tbsp.	all-purpose flour
1/8 tsp.	salt
1/8 tsp.	pepper
3/4 cup	fat-free milk
1/4 cup	shredded reduced-fat Colby-Monterey Jack cheese
1 Tbsp.	chopped green chilies

EGGS:
1 Tbsp.	white vinegar
4	eggs

Chopped plum tomatoes and minced fresh cilantro, optional

1. Place potatoes and water in a microwave-safe dish. Cover and microwave on high for 4-5 minutes or until tender; drain. In a large skillet, saute pepper and onion in oil until onion is tender. Add the potatoes, bacon, salt and pepper; saute 8-10 minutes longer or until potatoes are lightly browned.

2. In a small saucepan, melt butter. Stir in the flour, salt and pepper until smooth. Gradually add milk. Bring to a boil; cook and stir for 1 minute or until thickened. Stir in cheese and chilies; cook and stir until cheese is melted.

3. Meanwhile, place 2-3 in. of water in a large skillet with high sides; add vinegar. Bring to a boil; reduce heat and simmer gently. Break cold eggs, one at a time, into a custard cup or saucer; holding the cup close to the surface of the water, slip each egg into water.

4. Cook, uncovered, until whites are completely set and yolks are still soft, about 4 minutes. Divide potato mixture among four plates. Using a slotted spoon, lift eggs out of water and place on potato mixture. Top with sauce; sprinkle with tomatoes and cilantro if desired.

Nutrition Facts: 1 cup potato mixture with 1 poached egg and 2 Tbsp. sauce (calculated without optional ingredients) equals 277 calories, 13 g fat (5 g saturated fat), 235 mg cholesterol, 585 mg sodium, 26 g carbohydrate, 3 g fiber, 14 g protein. **Diabetic Exchanges:** 2 medium-fat meat, 1 starch, 1 fat.

Yogurt Pancakes

PREP: 15 min. **COOK:** 5 min./batch **YIELD:** 12 pancakes

CHERYLL BABER • HOMEDALE, IDAHO

Get your day off to a great start. Short on time? Make a batch on the weekend.

2	cups all-purpose flour
2	Tbsp. sugar
2	tsp. baking powder
1	tsp. baking soda
2	eggs
2	cups (16 oz.) plain yogurt
1/4	cup water

Semisweet chocolate chips, dried cranberries, sliced ripe bananas and coarsely chopped pecans, optional

1. In a small bowl, combine the flour, sugar, baking powder and baking soda. In another bowl, whisk the eggs, yogurt and water. Stir into dry ingredients just until moistened.

2. Pour batter by 1/4 cupfuls onto a hot griddle coated with cooking spray. Sprinkle with optional ingredients if desired. Turn when bubbles form on top; cook until the second side is golden brown.

3. To freeze, arrange cooled pancakes in a single layer on sheet pans. Freeze overnight or until frozen. Transfer to a resealable plastic freezer bag. May be frozen for up to 2 months.

To use frozen pancakes: Place pancake on a microwave-safe plate; microwave on high for 40-50 seconds or until heated through.

Nutrition Facts: 2 pancakes (calculated without optional ingredients) equals 242 calories, 5 g fat (2 g saturated fat), 81 mg cholesterol, 403 mg sodium, 40 g carbohydrate, 1 g fiber, 9 g protein. **Diabetic Exchange:** 3 starch.

DELIGHTFUL APPLE-PINEAPPLE DRINK

Delightful Apple-Pineapple Drink F S

PREP: 5 min. COOK: 30 min. YIELD: 8 servings

NANCY JOHNSON • LAVERNE, OKLAHOMA

Chase winter doldrums and chills with this warm and tangy fruit drink that will appeal to both kids and adults. Not overly sweet, it has a nice touch of nutmeg and cinnamon.

- 4 cups unsweetened apple juice
- 4 cups unsweetened pineapple juice
- 2 Tbsp. lemon juice
- 2 Tbsp. honey
- 4 cinnamon sticks (3 in.)
- 1/8 tsp. ground nutmeg

Additional cinnamon sticks (3 in.), optional

1. In a large saucepan, combine the juices, honey, cinnamon sticks and nutmeg. Bring to a boil. Reduce heat; simmer, uncovered, for 25-30 minutes or until flavors are blended. Discard cinnamon. Serve warm in mugs with additional cinnamon sticks if desired.

Nutrition Facts: 1 cup equals 142 calories, trace fat (trace saturated fat), 0 cholesterol, 6 mg sodium, 35 g carbohydrate, trace fiber, 1 g protein.

Prosciutto Egg Panini

PREP/TOTAL TIME: 30 min. YIELD: 8 servings

ERIN RENOUF MYLROIE • SANTA CLARA, UTAH

Try a yummy new twist on the usual bacon and egg sandwich. It's a breakfast worth waking up for!

- 3 eggs
- 2 egg whites
- 6 Tbsp. fat-free milk
- 1 green onion, thinly sliced
- 1 Tbsp. Dijon mustard
- 1 Tbsp. maple syrup
- 8 slices sourdough bread
- 8 thin slices prosciutto *or* deli ham
- 1/2 cup shredded sharp cheddar cheese
- 8 tsp. butter

1. In a small bowl, whisk the eggs, egg whites, milk and onion. Coat a large skillet with cooking spray and place over medium heat. Add egg mixture; cook and stir over medium heat until completely set.

2. Combine mustard and syrup; spread over four bread slices. Layer with scrambled eggs, prosciutto and cheese; top with remaining bread. Butter outsides of sandwiches.

3. Cook on a panini maker or indoor grill for 3-4 minutes or until bread is browned and cheese is melted. Cut each panini in half to serve.

Nutrition Facts: 1/2 sandwich equals 228 calories, 10 g fat (5 g saturated fat), 111 mg cholesterol, 640 mg sodium, 21 g carbohydrate, 1 g fiber, 13 g protein. **Diabetic Exchanges:** 1-1/2 starch, 1-1/2 fat, 1 lean meat.

Mini Ham 'n' Cheese Frittatas C

PREP: 15 min. BAKE: 25 min. YIELD: 8 servings

SUSAN WATT • BASKING RIDGE, NEW JERSEY

Portion control is easy with these healthful mini frittatas—and so is breakfast!

- 1/4 lb. cubed fully cooked ham
- 1 cup (4 oz.) shredded fat-free cheddar cheese
- 6 eggs
- 4 egg whites
- 3 Tbsp. minced chives
- 2 Tbsp. fat-free milk
- 1/4 tsp. salt
- 1/4 tsp. pepper

1. Divide ham among eight muffin cups coated with cooking spray; top with cheese. In a large bowl, beat eggs and whites. Beat in the chives, milk, salt and pepper. Pour over cheese, filling each muffin cup three-fourths full.

2. Bake at 375° for 22-25 minutes or until a knife inserted near the center comes out clean. Carefully run a knife around edges to loosen; remove from pan. Serve warm.

Nutrition Facts: 1 frittata equals 106 calories, 4 g fat (1 g saturated fat), 167 mg cholesterol, 428 mg sodium, 2 g carbohydrate, trace fiber, 14 g protein. **Diabetic Exchange:** 2 medium-fat meat.

PROSCIUTTO EGG PANINI

MINI HAM 'N' CHEESE FRITTATAS

Gluten-Free Banana Pancakes

PREP: 15 min. **COOK:** 5 min./batch **YIELD:** 12 pancakes

SHAREN GUSTAFSON • SOUTH LYON, MICHIGAN

When one of my sons and I had to change to a gluten-free diet, I searched for recipes that tasted great. These pancakes are low-cal as well. I cook extras and freeze them. Then, when I'm short on time, I toss a couple in the toaster. You'll love the chocolate flavor and fluffy texture.

- 1 cup gluten-free all-purpose baking flour
- 3 tsp. baking powder
- 1/2 tsp. salt
- 2/3 cup gluten-free rice milk
- 1/4 cup unsweetened applesauce
- 2 Tbsp. olive oil
- 3 tsp. vanilla extract
- 1-1/3 cups mashed ripe bananas (3 medium)
- 1/2 cup semisweet chocolate chips, optional

Maple syrup

1. In a large bowl, combine the flour, baking powder and salt. In another bowl, whisk the rice milk, applesauce, oil and vanilla; stir into dry ingredients just until moistened. Stir in bananas and chocolate chips if desired.

2. Pour batter by 1/4 cupfuls onto a hot griddle coated with cooking spray; turn when bubbles form on top. Cook until the second side is golden brown. Serve with syrup.

GLUTEN-FREE BANANA PANCAKES

Editor's Note: Read all ingredient labels for possible gluten content prior to use. Ingredient formulas can change, and production facilities vary among brands. If you're concerned that your brand may contain gluten, contact the company.

Nutrition Facts: 2 pancakes (calculated without chocolate chips and syrup) equals 173 calories, 6 g fat (1 g saturated fat), 0 cholesterol, 407 mg sodium, 30 g carbohydrate, 3 g fiber, 3 g protein. **Diabetic Exchanges:** 2 starch, 1 fat.

Good Mornin' Pancake Mix

PREP: 15 min. **COOK:** 5 min./batch
YIELD: 10 pancakes per batch

SHARON SUTTON • LINDSEY, OHIO

I love these moist, fluffy pancakes on a wintry day. They make a perfect gift for family and friends. Just put the mix in two plastic bags tied with ribbons and include the prep directions.

- 2 cups all-purpose flour
- 1-1/4 cups whole wheat flour
- 1 cup buttermilk blend powder
- 1 cup old-fashioned oats
- 1/3 cup sugar
- 3 Tbsp. baking powder
- 3 tsp. baking soda
- 1 tsp. dried orange peel
- 1/2 tsp. ground cinnamon
- 1 cup golden raisins
- 1 cup sliced almonds, toasted

ADDITIONAL INGREDIENTS (FOR EACH BATCH):
- 1 egg
- 3/4 cup water
- 2 Tbsp. canola oil

1. Place the first nine ingredients in a food processor; cover and process until oats are ground. Place 1 cup in each of four resealable plastic bags. In each of four separate resealable plastic bags, place 1/4 cup raisins and 1/4 cup almonds. Store for up to 6 months. **Yield:** 4 batches (6 cups mix).

2. To prepare pancakes, in a large bowl, combine the contents of one pancake mix bag and one fruit-nut bag. In a small bowl, whisk the egg, water and oil. Stir into dry ingredients just until moistened.

3. Pour batter by 1/4 cupfuls onto a hot griddle coated with cooking spray. Turn when bubbles form on top; cook until second side is golden brown.

Nutrition Facts: 2 pancakes equals 236 calories, 10 g fat (1 g saturated fat), 46 mg cholesterol, 416 mg sodium, 31 g carbohydrate, 3 g fiber, 8 g protein. **Diabetic Exchanges:** 2 starch, 1 fat.

Delectable Granola

PREP: 20 min. **BAKE:** 30 min. + cooling **YIELD:** 11 cups

LORI STEVENS • RIVERTON, UTAH

Here's a great make-ahead recipe! Be sure to remove the granola from the cookie sheets within 20 minutes after baking to prevent sticking.

- 8 cups old-fashioned oats
- 1 cup finely chopped almonds
- 1 cup finely chopped pecans

1/2 cup flaked coconut
1/2 cup packed brown sugar
1/2 cup canola oil
1/2 cup honey
1/4 cup maple syrup
2 tsp. ground cinnamon
1-1/2 tsp. salt
2 tsp. vanilla extract
Plain yogurt, optional

1. In a large bowl, combine the oats, almonds, pecans and coconut. In a small saucepan, combine the brown sugar, oil, honey, maple syrup, cinnamon and salt. Heat for 3-4 minutes over medium heat until sugar is dissolved. Remove from the heat; stir in vanilla. Pour over the oat mixture; stir to coat.

2. Transfer to two 15-in. x 10-in. x 1-in. baking pans coated with cooking spray. Bake at 350° for 30-35 minutes or until crisp, stirring every 10 minutes.

Cool completely on wire racks. Store in an airtight container. Serve with yogurt if desired.

Nutrition Facts: 1/2 cup (calculated without yogurt) equals 288 calories, 15 g fat (2 g saturated fat), 0 cholesterol, 170 mg sodium, 36 g carbohydrate, 4 g fiber, 6 g protein. **Diabetic Exchanges:** 2-1/2 starch, 2 fat.

To soften brown sugar, place a slice of bread or an apple wedge with it in a covered container for a few days. If you're in a hurry, microwave the **brown sugar** on high for 20-30 seconds. Repeat if necessary, watching it carefully, because the sugar will begin to melt. Always store brown sugar in an airtight container.

Makeover Waffles M

PREP/TOTAL TIME: 25 min. YIELD: 10 waffles

CAROL BURGER • PHILLIPS, WISCONSIN

These waffles taste just as terrific as the original recipe—with only half the fat. In other words, dust off that waffle iron because these breakfast sensations are a wonderful way to start your day!

1-3/4 cups all-purpose flour
   3 tsp. baking powder
 1/2 tsp. salt
   2 egg yolks
1-3/4 cups fat-free milk
 1/4 cup canola oil
 1/4 cup unsweetened applesauce
   2 egg whites

1. In a large bowl, combine the flour, baking powder and salt. In a small bowl, whisk the egg yolks, milk, oil and applesauce. Stir into the dry ingredients just until moistened.

2. In another small bowl, beat egg whites until stiff peaks form. Fold into batter. Bake in a preheated waffle iron according to manufacturer's directions until golden brown.

Nutrition Facts: 2 waffles equals 321 calories, 13 g fat (2 g saturated fat), 84 mg cholesterol, 538 mg sodium, 39 g carbohydrate, 1 g fiber, 10 g protein.

Roasted Red Pepper Omelets C M

PREP/TOTAL TIME: 20 min. YIELD: 2 servings

HEALTHY COOKING TEST KITCHEN

Roasted red peppers, Muenster cheese and green onions give this breakfast favorite vibrant color and flavor.

   3 eggs
   3 Tbsp. water
 1/4 tsp. salt
 1/8 tsp. pepper
 1/2 cup chopped roasted sweet red peppers
 1/4 cup shredded Muenster cheese
   2 green onions, chopped

1. Coat an 8-in. nonstick skillet with cooking spray and place over medium heat. In a small bowl, whisk the eggs, water, salt and pepper. Add half of egg mixture to skillet (mixture should set immediately at the edges).

2. As eggs set, push cooked edges toward the center, letting uncooked portion flow underneath. When the eggs are set, add half of the red peppers, cheese and onions on one side; fold other side over filling. Slide omelet onto a plate. Repeat.

Nutrition Facts: 1 omelet equals 185 calories, 12 g fat (5 g saturated fat), 331 mg cholesterol, 714 mg sodium, 4 g carbohydrate, trace fiber, 13 g protein.

Makeover Apple Coffee Cake

PREP: 20 min. BAKE: 40 min. + cooling
YIELD: 12 servings

DENISE SNYDER • LEMOYNE, OHIO

This sugary-topped apple coffee cake is a delicious way to get your family out of bed in the morning. The pros at Healthy Cooking lightened up the original, but this makeover version is still scrumptious to the core!

 1/3 cup butter, softened
 2/3 cup sugar
   2 eggs
   1 tsp. vanilla extract
   2 cups all-purpose flour
   1 tsp. baking soda
   1 cup (8 oz.) reduced-fat sour cream

MAKEOVER WAFFLES

ROASTED RED PEPPER OMELETS

TOPPING:

1/3 cup chopped walnuts

1/3 cup packed brown sugar

2 Tbsp. sugar

1 tsp. ground cinnamon

2 medium tart apples, peeled and thinly sliced

1. In a large bowl, beat butter and sugar until crumbly, about 2 minutes. Add eggs, one at a time, beating well after each addition. Beat in vanilla. Combine flour and baking soda; add to creamed mixture alternately with sour cream, beating well after each addition (batter will be sticky).

2. In a small bowl, combine the walnuts, sugars and cinnamon. Spread half of the batter into an 11-in. x 7-in. baking dish coated with cooking spray. Top with apples; sprinkle with half of the topping. Gently top with remaining batter and topping.

3. Bake at 350° for 40-45 minutes or until a toothpick inserted near the center comes out clean. Cool on a wire rack.

Nutrition Facts: 1 piece equals 266 calories, 10 g fat (5 g saturated fat), 55 mg cholesterol, 169 mg sodium, 40 g carbohydrate, 1 g fiber, 5 g protein.

Eggs Benedict

PREP: 25 min. COOK: 15 min. YIELD: 8 servings

REBECCA BAIRD • SALT LAKE CITY, UTAH

This mock hollandaise sauce is smooth and creamy—and much healthier than the regular version.

8 slices Canadian bacon

8 eggs

HOLLANDAISE SAUCE:

2 Tbsp. all-purpose flour

1/4 tsp. salt

1/4 tsp. ground mustard

1/8 tsp. cayenne pepper

1/2 cup fat-free milk

1/2 cup fat-free evaporated milk

1 egg yolk, lightly beaten

1 Tbsp. butter-flavored sprinkles

1 Tbsp. lemon juice

4 whole wheat English muffins, split and toasted

1. In a nonstick skillet coated with cooking spray, brown bacon on both sides; remove and keep warm.

2. Place 2-3 in. of water in a large skillet with high sides. Bring to a boil; reduce heat and simmer gently. Break cold eggs, one at a time, into a custard cup or saucer; holding the cup close to the surface of the water, slip each egg into water. Cook, uncovered, until whites are completely set and yolks begin to thicken but are not hard, about 4 minutes.

3. Meanwhile, in a small saucepan, combine the flour, salt, mustard and cayenne. Gradually stir in milk and evaporated milk until smooth. Bring to a boil; cook and stir for 1-2 minutes or until thickened. Remove from the heat.

4. Stir a small amount of sauce into egg yolk; return all to the pan, stirring constantly. Bring to a gentle boil; cook and stir for 2 minutes. Remove from the heat; stir in butter-flavored sprinkles and lemon juice.

5. With a slotted spoon, lift each egg out of the water. Top each muffin half with a slice of bacon, an egg and 2 Tbsp. sauce. Serve immediately.

Editor's Note: This recipe was tested with Molly McButter. Look for it in the spice aisle.

Nutrition Facts: 1 serving equals 216 calories, 8 g fat (3 g saturated fat), 252 mg cholesterol, 752 mg sodium, 19 g carbohydrate, 2 g fiber, 17 g protein. **Diabetic Exchanges:** 2 medium-fat meat, 1 starch.

Whole Wheat Pancakes M

PREP/TOTAL TIME: 25 min. YIELD: 20 pancakes

LINE WALTER • WAYNE, PENNSYLVANIA

These light, fluffy pancakes seem like a treat. Whole wheat flour and toasted wheat germ make them so filling.

- 2 cups whole wheat flour
- 1/2 cup toasted wheat germ
- 1 tsp. baking soda
- 1/2 tsp. salt
- 2 eggs, lightly beaten
- 3 cups buttermilk
- 1 Tbsp. canola oil

1. In a large bowl, combine the flour, wheat germ, baking soda and salt. In another bowl, whisk the eggs, buttermilk and oil. Stir into dry ingredients just until blended.

2. Pour batter by 1/4 cupfuls onto a hot griddle coated with cooking spray; turn when bubbles form on top. Cook until the second side is golden brown.

Nutrition Facts: 2 pancakes equals 157 calories, 4 g fat (1 g saturated fat), 45 mg cholesterol, 335 mg sodium, 24 g carbohydrate, 4 g fiber, 9 g protein. **Diabetic Exchanges:** 1-1/2 starch, 1 fat.

Makeover Hearty Egg Casserole C

PREP: 20 min. BAKE: 35 min. YIELD: 12 servings

KRISTINE OCIEPA • MILWAUKEE, WISCONSIN

Here's a down-home breakfast bake that's true to its name. Packed with sausage, veggies, eggs and cheese, this dish will get you going and keep you feeling satisfied.

- 1 lb. bulk pork sausage
- 3/4 cup sliced fresh mushrooms
- 1 small onion, chopped

- 1 pkg. (10 oz.) frozen chopped spinach, thawed and well drained
- 3/4 cup shredded sharp cheddar cheese, *divided*
- 6 eggs
- 1-1/2 cups egg substitute
- 1 cup half-and-half cream
- 1 cup fat-free milk
- 1/4 tsp. ground nutmeg

1. In a large nonstick skillet, cook the sausage, mushrooms and onion over medium heat until meat is no longer pink; drain. Remove from the heat; stir in spinach and 1/2 cup cheese. Transfer to a 13-in. x 9-in. baking dish coated with cooking spray.

2. In a large bowl, beat the eggs, egg substitute, cream, milk and nutmeg. Pour over sausage mixture. Bake, uncovered, at 350° for 35-40 minutes or until a knife inserted near the center comes out clean. Sprinkle with remaining cheese. Let stand for 5 minutes before cutting.

Nutrition Facts: 1 piece equals 195 calories, 14 g fat (6 g saturated fat), 137 mg cholesterol, 332 mg sodium, 5 g carbohydrate, 1 g fiber, 13 g protein.

Cinnamon Mocha Coffee F S

PREP/TOTAL TIME: 20 min. YIELD: 6 servings

BERNICE MORRIS • MARSHFIELD, MISSOURI

One snowy day, my neighbor called and invited me over to try a new beverage she'd made. It was delicious! This spiced coffee is a lovely treat any time of year.

- 1/2 cup ground dark roast coffee
- 1 Tbsp. ground cinnamon
- 1/4 tsp. ground nutmeg
- 5 cups water
- 1 cup milk
- 1/3 cup chocolate syrup

1/4 cup packed brown sugar
1 tsp. vanilla extract
Whipped cream, optional

1. In a small bowl, combine the coffee grounds, cinnamon and nutmeg; pour into a coffee filter of a drip coffeemaker. Add water; brew according to manufacturer's directions.

2. In a large saucepan, combine the milk, chocolate syrup and brown sugar. Cook over low heat until sugar is dissolved, stirring occasionally. Stir in the vanilla and brewed coffee. Ladle into mugs; garnish with whipped cream if desired.

Nutrition Facts: 1 cup equals 126 calories, 2 g fat (1 g saturated fat), 6 mg cholesterol, 34 mg sodium, 25 g carbohydrate, 1 g fiber, 3 g protein.

Maple Nut Bagel Spread S C M

PREP/TOTAL TIME: 10 min. **YIELD:** 1-1/4 cups

HEALTHY COOKING TEST KITCHEN

You won't believe how easy it is to whip up this creamy, four-ingredient bagel spread. It's also wonderful on toast or English muffins.

1 carton (8 oz.) reduced-fat spreadable cream cheese
3 Tbsp. maple syrup
1/8 tsp. ground cinnamon
1/4 cup finely chopped walnuts, toasted
Bagels, split

1. In a large bowl, beat the cream cheese, syrup and cinnamon until smooth; stir in walnuts. Chill until serving. Serve with bagels.

Nutrition Facts: 2 Tbsp. equals 84 calories, 5 g fat (3 g saturated fat), 11 mg cholesterol, 107 mg sodium, 6 g carbohydrate, trace fiber, 3 g protein. **Diabetic Exchanges:** 1 fat, 1/2 starch.

Baked Eggs with Cheddar and Bacon C

PREP/TOTAL TIME: 25 min. **YIELD:** 4 servings

CATHERINE WILKINSON • DEWEY, ARIZONA

These little treats are super-easy to make and perfect for a special breakfast. They're also very nice for a casual dinner. The smoky cheese and bacon elevate eggs to a new level!

4 eggs
4 Tbsp. fat-free milk, *divided*
2 Tbsp. shredded smoked cheddar cheese
2 tsp. minced fresh parsley
1/4 tsp. salt
1/8 tsp. pepper
2 bacon strips

1. Coat four 4-oz. ramekins with cooking spray; break an egg into each dish. Spoon 1 Tbsp. milk over each egg. Combine the cheese, parsley, salt and pepper; sprinkle over tops.

2. Bake, uncovered, at 325° for 12-15 minutes or until whites are completely set and yolks begin to thicken but are not firm.

3. Meanwhile, in a small skillet, cook bacon over medium heat until crisp. Remove to paper towels to drain. Crumble bacon and sprinkle over eggs.

Nutrition Facts: 1 serving equals 107 calories, 7 g fat (3 g saturated fat), 219 mg cholesterol, 319 mg sodium, 1 g carbohydrate, trace fiber, 9 g protein. **Diabetic Exchange:** 1 medium-fat meat.

MAPLE NUT BAGEL SPREAD

BAKED EGGS WITH CHEDDAR AND BACON

Ultimate Fruity Granola [S]

PREP: 15 min. **BAKE:** 20 min. + cooling **YIELD:** 9 cups

SARAH VASQUES • MILFORD, NEW HAMPSHIRE

Honey, maple syrup and vanilla coat this wonderfully crunchy treat that's fantastic no matter how you serve it—alone, with cold milk or in a yogurt parfait.

- 5 cups old-fashioned oats
- 1 cup sliced almonds
- 1/2 cup sunflower kernels
- 1/2 cup ground flaxseed
- 1/2 cup packed brown sugar
- 1/4 cup maple syrup
- 1/4 cup honey
- 2 Tbsp. canola oil
- 1/2 tsp. salt
- 1/2 tsp. ground cinnamon
- 1 tsp. vanilla extract
- 1/2 cup dried cranberries
- 1/2 cup dried banana chips
- 1/2 cup dried apricots, halved

1. In a large bowl, combine the oats, almonds, sunflower kernels and flax. In a small saucepan, combine the brown sugar, maple syrup, honey, oil, salt and cinnamon. Cook and stir over medium heat for 2-3 minutes or until brown sugar is dissolved and mixture is heated through. Remove from the heat; stir in vanilla. Pour over oat mixture and toss to coat.

2. Transfer to a 15-in. x 10-in. x 1-in. baking pan coated with cooking spray. Bake at 350° for 20-25 minutes or until golden brown, stirring every 8 minutes. Cool completely on a wire rack. Stir in dried fruits. Store in an airtight container.

Nutrition Facts: 1/2 cup equals 253 calories, 10 g fat (2 g saturated fat), 0 cholesterol, 86 mg sodium, 38 g carbohydrate, 5 g fiber, 6 g protein. **Diabetic Exchanges:** 2-1/2 starch, 1 fat.

Fruit Smoothies [F] [S]

PREP/TOTAL TIME: 5 min. **YIELD:** 3 servings

BRYCE SICKICH • NEW PORT RICHEY, FLORIDA

With its combination of fruits, this delicious, quick-to-fix smoothie is a powerhouse of nutrition.

- 3/4 cup fat-free milk
- 1/2 cup orange juice
- 1/2 cup unsweetened applesauce
- 1 small ripe banana, halved
- 1/2 cup frozen unsweetened raspberries
- 7 to 10 ice cubes

1. In a blender, combine all ingredients; cover and process until smooth. Pour into chilled glasses; serve immediately.

Nutrition Facts: 1 cup equals 97 calories, trace fat (trace saturated fat), 1 mg cholesterol, 33 mg sodium, 22 g carbohydrate, 2 g fiber, 3 g protein. **Diabetic Exchange:** 1-1/2 fruit.

ULTIMATE FRUITY GRANOLA

FRUIT SMOOTHIES

COLORFUL CHEESE OMELET

Colorful Cheese Omelet C M

PREP/TOTAL TIME: 20 min. YIELD: 1 serving

LYNDA O'DELL LYNCH • PORT HURON, MICHIGAN

When I start my day with this omelet, I'm able to go nonstop and know I'm getting valuable nutrients besides.

- 1 egg
- 2 egg whites
- 2 Tbsp. chopped fresh baby spinach
- 1/8 tsp. hot pepper sauce
- 2 Tbsp. chopped sweet red pepper
- 1 green onion, chopped
- 2 Tbsp. shredded cheddar cheese

1. In a small bowl, whisk the egg, egg whites, spinach and pepper sauce; set aside. In a small nonstick skillet coated with cooking spray, saute red pepper and onion until tender. Reduce heat to medium.

2. Add egg mixture to skillet (mixture should set immediately at edges). As eggs set, push cooked edges toward the center, letting uncooked portion flow underneath. When the eggs are set, sprinkle with cheese; fold other side over filling. Carefully slide omelet onto a plate.

Nutrition Facts: 1 omelet equals 167 calories, 9 g fat (5 g saturated fat), 227 mg cholesterol, 276 mg sodium, 4 g carbohydrate, 1 g fiber, 17 g protein. **Diabetic Exchange:** 2 medium-fat meat.

Tropical Yogurt F S

PREP/TOTAL TIME: 5 min. YIELD: 4 servings

HEALTHY COOKING TEST KITCHEN

Plain yogurt becomes a flavorful sensation with help from coconut extract, pineapple and a hint of lime. It's great with granola in the morning or as a low-fat snack during the day.

- 2 cups (16 oz.) reduced-fat plain yogurt
- 1 can (8 oz.) unsweetened crushed pineapple, drained
- 2 tsp. sugar
- 1/4 tsp. coconut extract
- 1/4 tsp. grated lime peel

1. In a small bowl, combine all ingredients. Chill mixture until serving.

Nutrition Facts: 1/2 cup equals 121 calories, 2 g fat (1 g saturated fat), 7 mg cholesterol, 86 mg sodium, 20 g carbohydrate, trace fiber, 7 g protein. **Diabetic Exchanges:** 1 fat-free milk, 1/2 fruit.

VEGETARIAN EGG STRATA

Vegetarian Egg Strata M

PREP: 25 min. + chilling **BAKE:** 45 min. + standing
YIELD: 12 servings

DANNA ROGERS • WESTPORT, CONNECTICUT

I used to make this with turkey or chicken sausage but adapted it for a vegetarian friend, and it was a huge hit. I serve it with fresh breads or bagels and a big mixed salad featuring arugula, apples and walnuts for brunch. It also works well for lunch, served with tomato bisque.

    1   medium zucchini, finely chopped
    1   medium sweet red pepper, finely chopped
    1   cup sliced baby portobello mushrooms
    1   medium red onion, finely chopped
    2   tsp. olive oil
    3   garlic cloves, minced
    2   tsp. minced fresh thyme *or* 1/2 tsp. dried thyme
  1/2   tsp. salt
  1/4   tsp. pepper
    1   loaf (1 lb.) day-old French bread, cubed
    2   pkg. (5.3 oz. *each*) fresh goat cheese, crumbled
1-3/4   cups grated Parmesan cheese
    6   eggs
    2   cups fat-free milk
  1/4   tsp. ground nutmeg

1. In a large skillet, saute the zucchini, red pepper, mushrooms and onion in oil until tender. Add the garlic, thyme, salt and pepper; saute 2 minutes longer.

2. In a 13-in. x 9-in. baking dish coated with cooking spray, layer half of the bread cubes, zucchini mixture, goat cheese and Parmesan cheese. Repeat layers.

3. In a small bowl, whisk the eggs, milk and nutmeg. Pour over top. Cover and refrigerate overnight.

4. Remove from the refrigerator 30 minutes before baking. Bake, uncovered, at 350° for 45-50 minutes or until a knife inserted near the center comes out clean. Let stand for 10 minutes before cutting.

Nutrition Facts: 1 piece equals 281 calories, 12 g fat (6 g saturated fat), 140 mg cholesterol, 667 mg sodium, 27 g carbohydrate, 2 g fiber, 17 g protein.

Homemade Granola S

PREP: 15 min. **BAKE:** 20 min. + cooling **YIELD:** 5 cups

NANCY JOHNSON • LAVERNE, OKLAHOMA

If you ask me, this crunchy treat is absolutely fantastic! And with 7 g of protein and 4 g of fiber, the sweet mixture helps fill you up deliciously.

4-1/2   cups old-fashioned oats
  1/3   cup sliced almonds
  1/4   cup unsweetened apple juice
  1/4   cup maple syrup
    1   Tbsp. canola oil
    2   tsp. ground cinnamon
  1/2   tsp. salt
  1/2   cup flaked coconut, toasted
  1/2   cup raisins
Fat-free milk, optional

1. In a large bowl, combine oats and almonds. In a small saucepan, combine the apple juice, syrup, oil, cinnamon and salt. Cook and stir for 3-4 minutes over medium heat until heated through. Remove from the heat. Pour over oat mixture; stir to coat.

2. Transfer to a 15-in. x 10-in. x 1-in. baking pan coated with cooking spray. Bake at 350° for 20-25 minutes or until crisp, stirring every 10 minutes. Cool completely on a wire rack. Stir in coconut and raisins. Store in an airtight container. Serve granola with milk if desired.

Nutrition Facts: 1/2 cup (calculated without milk) equals 234 calories, 7 g fat (2 g saturated fat), 0 cholesterol, 133 mg sodium, 39 g carbohydrate, 4 g fiber, 7 g protein. **Diabetic Exchanges:** 2-1/2 starch, 1 fat.

Spiced Apple-Grape Juice F S

PREP: 10 min. **COOK:** 1 hour **YIELD:** 8 servings

CLAIRE BEATTIE • TORONTO, ONTARIO

Round out any brunch with this warming apple drink. Spiced with cinnamon, cloves and allspice, it will wrap your guests in a tempting aroma as it simmers.

- 4 cups white grape juice
- 3 cups unsweetened apple juice
- 1 cup water
- 2 cinnamon sticks (3 in.)
- 12 whole cloves
- 8 whole allspice

1. In a large saucepan, combine the grape juice, apple juice and water. Place the cinnamon, cloves and allspice on a double thickness of cheesecloth; bring up corners of cloth and tie with string to form a bag. Add to the pan.

2. Bring to a boil. Reduce heat; simmer, uncovered, for 1 to 1-1/2 hours or until flavors are blended. Discard spice bag. Serve warm in mugs.

Nutrition Facts: 3/4 cup equals 121 calories, trace fat (trace saturated fat), 0 cholesterol, 10 mg sodium, 29 g carbohydrate, trace fiber, 1 g protein.

Isaiah's Gingerbread Pancakes with Apple Slaw M

PREP: 25 min. **COOK:** 5 min./batch
YIELD: 10 servings (3 cups slaw)

SILVANA NARDONE • BROOKLYN, NEW YORK

Perfect for weekend mornings, these gluten-free pancakes are served with a sweet slaw. I suggest using decaf coffee for kids, and swapping pears for apples to change things up.

- 2 cups gluten-free pancake mix
- 2 Tbsp. brown sugar
- 1 Tbsp. baking cocoa
- 1-1/2 tsp. ground ginger
- 1 tsp. pumpkin pie spice
- 1/2 tsp. baking soda
- 2 eggs, *separated*
- 1 cup rice milk
- 1/2 cup plus 1 Tbsp. brewed coffee, room temperature
- 2 Tbsp. canola oil
- 1 Tbsp. molasses

SLAW:
- 3 medium apples, grated
- 1/2 cup chopped pecans, toasted
- 1/4 cup golden raisins
- 2 Tbsp. lemon juice
- 1 Tbsp. honey

Maple syrup, warmed

1. In a large bowl, combine the first six ingredients. Combine the egg yolks, rice milk, coffee, oil and molasses; add to dry ingredients just until moistened. In a small bowl, beat egg whites on medium speed until stiff peaks form. Fold into batter.

2. Pour batter by scant 1/4 cupfuls onto a hot griddle coated with cooking spray; turn when bubbles form on top. Cook until the second side is golden brown.

3. Meanwhile, in a small bowl, combine the apples, pecans, raisins, lemon juice and honey. Serve with pancakes and syrup.

Editor's Note: Read all ingredient labels for possible gluten content prior to use. Ingredient formulas can change, and production facilities vary among brands. If you're concerned that your brand may contain gluten, contact the company.

Nutrition Facts: 2 pancakes with 1/4 cup slaw (calculated without syrup) equals 225 calories, 8 g fat (1 g saturated fat), 42 mg cholesterol, 231 mg sodium, 36 g carbohydrate, 2 g fiber, 3 g protein. **Diabetic Exchanges:** 1-1/2 starch, 1-1/2 fat, 1/2 fruit.

SPICED APPLE-GRAPE JUICE

ISAIAH'S GINGERBREAD PANCAKES WITH APPLE SLAW

Gluten-Free Breakfast Blintzes Ⓜ

PREP: 30 min. + chilling **BAKE:** 10 min. **YIELD:** 9 servings

LAURA FALL-SUTTON • BUHL, IDAHO

These cheese-filled, berry-topped blintzes taste just as mouthwatering and special as they look. Enjoy!

- 1-1/2 cups fat-free milk
- 3 eggs
- 2 Tbsp. butter, melted
- 2/3 cup gluten-free all-purpose baking flour
- 1/2 tsp. salt

FILLING:
- 1 cup (8 oz.) 2% cottage cheese
- 3 oz. reduced-fat cream cheese
- 2 Tbsp. sugar
- 1/4 tsp. almond extract
- 2-1/4 cups *each* fresh blueberries and raspberries
- Confectioners' sugar, optional

1. In a small bowl, combine the milk, eggs and butter. Combine the flour and salt; add to milk mixture and mix well. Cover and refrigerate for 1 hour.

2. Coat an 8-in. nonstick skillet with cooking spray; heat over medium heat. Stir crepe batter; pour 2 Tbsp. into center of skillet. Lift and tilt pan to coat bottom evenly. Cook until top appears dry; turn and cook 15-20 seconds longer. Remove to a wire rack. Repeat with remaining batter, coating skillet with cooking spray as needed. When cool, stack crepes with waxed paper or paper towels in between.

3. In a blender, cover and process cheeses until smooth. Add sugar and extract; pulse until combined. Spread a scant 1 tablespoonful onto each crepe. Fold opposite sides of crepe over filling, forming a bundle.

4. Place seam side down in a 15-in. x 10-in. x 1-in. baking pan coated with cooking spray. Bake, uncovered, at 350° for 10-12 minutes or until heated through. Serve topped with berries and dust with confectioners' sugar if desired.

Editor's Note: Read all ingredient labels for possible gluten content prior to use. Ingredient formulas can change, and production facilities vary among brands. If you're concerned that your brand may contain gluten, contact the company.

Nutrition Facts: 2 blintzes with 1/2 cup fruit (calculated without confectioners' sugar) equals 180 calories, 7 g fat (4 g saturated fat), 88 mg cholesterol, 319 mg sodium, 22 g carbohydrate, 4 g fiber, 9 g protein. **Diabetic Exchanges:** 1 starch, 1 lean meat, 1/2 fruit, 1/2 fat.

Scrambled Egg Poppers

PREP: 15 min. **BAKE:** 25 min. **YIELD:** 8 servings

KATIE WILLIAMS • BLACK CREEK, WISCONSIN

These handy grab-and-go breakfast treats are ideal for busy mornings and sure to be a favorite with kids of all ages.

- 2 loaves (1 lb. *each*) frozen whole wheat bread dough, thawed
- 8 eggs
- 1/2 cup fat-free milk
- 1/4 tsp. salt
- 1/4 tsp. pepper
- 1/2 cup bacon bits, *divided*
- 1/2 cup shredded cheddar cheese

1. Divide each loaf into eight pieces. Roll into balls. Place in muffin cups coated with cooking spray. Bake at 350° for 20-25 minutes or until golden brown.

2. Meanwhile, in a large bowl, whisk the eggs, milk, salt and pepper; stir in 1/4 cup bacon bits. Coat a large nonstick skillet with cooking spray and place over medium heat. Add egg mixture to skillet (mixture should set immediately at edges).

3. As eggs set, push cooked edges toward the center, letting uncooked portion flow underneath. When the eggs are set, remove from the heat.

GLUTEN-FREE BREAKFAST BLINTZES

SCRAMBLED EGG POPPERS

OMELET TORTILLA WRAP

4. Using a melon baller, scoop out the center of each roll, leaving a 1/4-in. shell (discard removed bread or save for another use). Spoon 3 Tbsp. cooked egg mixture into each roll. Top with remaining bacon bits and sprinkle with cheese. Bake 2-3 minutes longer or until cheese is melted.

Nutrition Facts: 2 poppers equals 252 calories, 10 g fat (4 g saturated fat), 224 mg cholesterol, 637 mg sodium, 25 g carbohydrate, 3 g fiber, 17 g protein.

Omelet Tortilla Wrap

PREP/TOTAL TIME: 25 min. YIELD: 1 serving

INGRID PARKER • HATTIESBURG, MISSISSIPPI

Here's a hearty, better-for-you breakfast that can be eaten right out of hand. Kids just love it.

1	egg
2	egg whites
2	Tbsp. finely chopped fully cooked lean ham
1	green onion, thinly sliced
1	Tbsp. chopped sweet red pepper
1	Tbsp. fat-free milk
2	tsp. chopped seeded jalapeno pepper
1/8	tsp. pepper

Dash hot pepper sauce, optional

2 Tbsp. shredded reduced-fat Monterey Jack cheese *or* Mexican cheese blend

1 whole wheat tortilla (8 in.), warmed

1. In a small bowl, whisk the egg, egg whites, ham, onion, red pepper, milk, jalapeno, pepper and pepper sauce if desired. Coat a small nonstick skillet with cooking spray and place over medium heat. Add egg mixture to skillet (mixture should set immediately at edges).

2. As eggs set, push cooked edges toward the center, letting uncooked portion flow underneath. When the eggs are set, remove from the heat; sprinkle with cheese. Slide omelet onto tortilla; roll up tightly.

Editor's Note: When cutting hot peppers, disposable gloves are recommended. Avoid touching your face.

Nutrition Facts: 1 wrap equals 322 calories, 12 g fat (4 g saturated fat), 229 mg cholesterol, 701 mg sodium, 26 g carbohydrate, 3 g fiber, 25 g protein.

Test egg dishes containing beaten eggs–like quiche, strata or custard—**for doneness** by inserting a knife near the center of the dish. If the knife comes out clean, the eggs are cooked.

QUICK OATMEAL RAISIN PANCAKES

Quick Oatmeal Raisin Pancakes M

PREP: 15 min. **COOK:** 10 min./batch **YIELD:** 12 pancakes

KAREL HURT • CORTEZ, COLORADO

I found this recipe in a newspaper nearly 50 years ago and have used it regularly ever since.

2	cups quick-cooking oats
2	cups buttermilk
1/2	cup egg substitute
2	Tbsp. canola oil
1/2	cup all-purpose flour
2	Tbsp. sugar
1	tsp. baking powder
1	tsp. baking soda
1	tsp. ground cinnamon
1/4	tsp. salt
1/2	cup raisins

1. In a small bowl, combine oats and buttermilk; let stand for 5 minutes. Stir in egg substitute and oil; set aside.

2. In a large bowl, combine the flour, sugar, baking powder, baking soda, cinnamon and salt. Stir in the wet ingredients just until moistened; add raisins.

3. Pour batter by heaping 1/4 cupfuls onto a hot griddle coated with cooking spray; turn when bubbles form on top. Cook until second side is golden brown.

Nutrition Facts: 2 pancakes equals 274 calories, 7 g fat (1 g saturated fat), 3 mg cholesterol, 505 mg sodium, 44 g carbohydrate, 3 g fiber, 10 g protein. **Diabetic Exchanges:** 2 starch, 1 fruit, 1 fat.

Cinnamon Bagels With Crunchy Topping F

PREP: 40 min. + rising **BAKE:** 15 min. **YIELD:** 1 dozen

KRISTEN STREEPEY • GENEVA, ILLINOIS

Once you get the hang of it, you won't believe how simple it is to make these bakery-quality bagels right in your kitchen.

- 2 Tbsp. active dry yeast
- 1-1/2 cups warm water (110° to 115°)
- 1/4 cup packed brown sugar, *divided*
- 3 tsp. ground cinnamon
- 1-1/2 tsp. salt
- 2-3/4 to 3-1/4 cups all-purpose flour

TOPPING:
- 1/4 cup sugar
- 1/4 cup packed brown sugar
- 3 tsp. ground cinnamon

1. In a large bowl, dissolve yeast in warm water. Add 3 Tbsp. brown sugar, cinnamon and salt; mix well. Stir in enough flour to form a soft dough.

2. Turn onto a lightly floured surface; knead until smooth and elastic, about 6-8 minutes. Place in a bowl coated with cooking spray, turning once to coat the top. Cover and let rise in a warm place until doubled, about 1 hour.

3. Punch dough down. Shape into 12 balls. Push thumb through centers to form a 1-1/2-in. hole. Stretch and shape dough to form an even ring. Place on a floured surface. Cover and let rest for 10 minutes.

4. Fill a Dutch oven two-thirds full with water and remaining brown sugar; bring to a boil. Drop bagels, two at a time, into boiling water. Cook for 45 seconds; turn and cook 45 seconds longer. Remove with a slotted spoon; drain well on paper towels.

5. Combine topping ingredients; sprinkle over bagels. Place 2 in. apart on baking sheets coated with cooking spray. Bake at 400° for 15-20 minutes or until golden brown. Remove to wire racks to cool.

Nutrition Facts: 1 bagel equals 164 calories, trace fat (trace saturated fat), 0 cholesterol, 300 mg sodium, 37 g carbohydrate, 2 g fiber, 4 g protein.

Makeover Hash and Eggs

PREP/TOTAL TIME: 30 min. **YIELD:** 4 servings

HEALTHY COOKING TEST KITCHEN

Loaded with red potatoes and deli corned beef, our lightened up version of corned beef hash delivers fresh flavors and a dose of fiber. It's so spot on, you'll swear you're in a diner!

- 1 large onion, chopped
- 1 Tbsp. canola oil
- 6 medium red potatoes (about 1-1/2 lbs.), cut into 1/2-in. cubes
- 1/4 cup water
- 3 pkg. (2 oz. *each*) thinly sliced deli corned beef, coarsely chopped
- 1/4 tsp. pepper
- 4 eggs

1. In a large nonstick skillet, saute onion in oil until tender. Stir in potatoes and water. Bring to a boil. Reduce heat; cover and simmer for 15-20 minutes or until potatoes are tender. Stir in corned beef and pepper; heat through.

2. Meanwhile, in a large nonstick skillet coated with cooking spray, fry eggs as desired. Serve with corned beef hash.

Nutrition Facts: 1 cup corned beef hash with 1 egg equals 301 calories, 12 g fat (3 g saturated fat), 239 mg cholesterol, 652 mg sodium, 31 g carbohydrate, 4 g fiber, 18 g protein.

MAKEOVER HASH AND EGGS

CINNAMON BAGELS WITH CRUNCHY TOPPING

Hearty Confetti Breakfast M

PREP: 35 min. **BROIL:** 5 min. **YIELD:** 4 servings

LORI MERRICK • DANVERS, ILLINOIS

Start your day the right way with a glass of orange juice and this all-in-one potato-and-egg skillet. Or, serve it with iced tea as an easy weeknight dinner.

1	large sweet potato, peeled and cut into 1/2-in. cubes
1	large Yukon Gold potato, cut into 1/2-in. cubes
1	medium red potato, cut into 1/2-in. cubes
1	small onion, finely chopped
3/4	tsp. minced fresh rosemary or 1/4 tsp. dried rosemary, crushed
3/4	tsp. minced fresh thyme or 1/4 tsp. dried thyme
1/4	tsp. salt
1/4	tsp. pepper
2	tsp. butter
2	tsp. olive oil
4	eggs
1/4	cup shredded Asiago cheese

1. In a 10-in. ovenproof skillet, saute the potatoes, onion and seasonings in butter and oil until vegetables are golden brown and tender. With the back of a spoon, make four wells in the potato mixture; add an egg to each well. Remove from the heat; sprinkle with cheese.

2. Broil 3-4 in. from the heat for 3-4 minutes or until eggs are completely set.

Nutrition Facts: 1 serving equals 297 calories, 11 g fat (4 g saturated fat), 223 mg cholesterol, 262 mg sodium, 37 g carbohydrate, 4 g fiber, 12 g protein. **Diabetic Exchanges:** 2 starch, 1-1/2 fat, 1 medium-fat meat.

Blueberry Orange Blast F S

PREP/TOTAL TIME: 5 min. **YIELD:** 4 servings

DIANE NEIBLING • OVERLAND PARK, KANSAS

I developed this healthful, pretty smoothie after our annual blueberry-picking trip. As you may know, blueberries are loaded with antioxidants and flavor!

1	cup orange juice
1	cup (8 oz.) vanilla yogurt
1	medium banana, sliced and frozen
1	cup frozen unsweetened blueberries
1/2	cup silken firm tofu

1. In a blender, combine all of the ingredients; cover and process until smooth. Pour into chilled glasses; serve immediately.

Nutrition Facts: 3/4 cup equals 140 calories, 2 g fat (1 g saturated fat), 3 mg cholesterol, 49 mg sodium, 27 g carbohydrate, 2 g fiber, 5 g protein. **Diabetic Exchanges:** 1 fruit, 1/2 reduced-fat milk.

Sage Turkey Sausage Patties C

PREP/TOTAL TIME: 30 min. **YIELD:** 12 servings

SHARMAN SCHUBERT • SEATTLE, WASHINGTON

This is a very easy recipe that's full of flavor but cuts salt and saturated fat. The taste panel loved the aroma of this savory alternative to pork sausage.

1/4	cup grated Parmesan cheese
3	Tbsp. minced fresh parsley or 1 Tbsp. dried parsley flakes
2	Tbsp. fresh sage or 2 tsp. dried sage leaves
2	garlic cloves, minced
1	tsp. fennel seed, crushed
3/4	tsp. salt
1/2	tsp. pepper
1-1/2	lbs. lean ground turkey
1	Tbsp. olive oil

HEARTY CONFETTI BREAKFAST

SAGE TURKEY SAUSAGE PATTIES

SUNDAY BRUNCH STRATA

1. In a large bowl, combine the first seven ingredients. Crumble turkey over mixture and mix well. Shape into twelve 3-in. patties.

2. In a large skillet coated with cooking spray, cook patties in oil in batches over medium heat for 3-5 minutes on each side or until meat is no longer pink. Drain on paper towels if necessary.

Nutrition Facts: 1 patty equals 104 calories, 6 g fat (2 g saturated fat), 46 mg cholesterol, 227 mg sodium, trace carbohydrate, trace fiber, 11 g protein. **Diabetic Exchanges:** 1 lean meat, 1 fat.

Sunday Brunch Strata M

PREP: 25 min. + chilling **BAKE:** 50 min. + standing
YIELD: 8 servings

SONYA LABBE • SANTA MONICA, CALIFORNIA
Hearty and fresh-tasting, this classic strata makes a wonderful breakfast dish.

8	slices whole wheat bread, cubed
3	cups sliced fresh mushrooms
1	medium red onion, chopped
1	Tbsp. olive oil
2	garlic cloves, minced
8	eggs
8	egg whites
2	cups fat-free milk
1	pkg. (10 oz.) frozen chopped spinach, thawed and squeezed dry
2/3	cup shredded Swiss cheese
1/2	cup shredded sharp cheddar cheese
1	Tbsp. Dijon mustard
3/4	tsp. salt
1/2	tsp. ground nutmeg
1/2	tsp. pepper

1. Place bread cubes in a 13-in. x 9-in. baking dish coated with cooking spray; set aside.

2. In a large skillet, saute mushrooms and onion in oil until tender. Add garlic; cook 1 minute longer. In a large bowl, combine the eggs, egg whites, milk, spinach, cheeses, mustard, salt, nutmeg, pepper and mushroom mixture; pour over top. Cover and refrigerate overnight.

3. Remove from the refrigerator 30 minutes before baking. Bake, uncovered, at 350° for 50-60 minutes or until a knife inserted near the center comes out clean. Let stand for 10 minutes before cutting.

Nutrition Facts: 1 piece equals 277 calories, 12 g fat (5 g saturated fat), 228 mg cholesterol, 644 mg sodium, 20 g carbohydrate, 4 g fiber, 22 g protein.

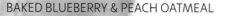

BAKED BLUEBERRY & PEACH OATMEAL

Baked Blueberry & Peach Oatmeal M

PREP: 20 min. BAKE: 35 min. YIELD: 9 servings

ROSEMARIE WELESKI • NATRONA HEIGHTS, PENNSYLVANIA

This oatmeal bake is a staple in our home. It's very easy to prepare the night before; just keep the dry and wet ingredients separate until ready to bake. I've tried a variety of fruits, but the blueberries and peaches are our favorite.

3	cups old-fashioned oats
1/2	cup packed brown sugar
2	tsp. baking powder
1/2	tsp. salt
2	egg whites
1	egg
1-1/4	cups fat-free milk
1/4	cup canola oil
1	tsp. vanilla extract

1	can (15 oz.) sliced peaches in juice, drained and chopped
1	cup fresh or frozen blueberries
1/3	cup chopped walnuts

Additional fat-free milk, optional

1. In a large bowl, combine the oats, brown sugar, baking powder and salt. Whisk the egg whites, egg, milk, oil and vanilla; add to dry ingredients and stir until blended. Let stand for 5 minutes. Stir in peaches and blueberries.

2. Transfer to an 11-in. x 7-in. baking dish coated with cooking spray. Sprinkle with walnuts. Bake, uncovered, at 350° for 35-40 minutes or until top is lightly browned and a thermometer reads 160°. Serve with additional milk if desired.

Nutrition Facts: 1 serving (calculated without additional milk) equals 277 calories, 11 g fat (1 g saturated fat), 24 mg cholesterol, 263 mg sodium, 38 g carbohydrate, 3 g fiber, 8 g protein. **Diabetic Exchanges:** 2 starch, 2 fat, 1/2 fruit.

Wake-Up Wonton Cups

PREP/TOTAL TIME: 20 min. YIELD: 10 wonton cups

GINA BERRY • CHANHASSEN, MINNESOTA

Dainty, delectable and delightfully different, these yummy breakfast bites add a fun touch to a healthy morning meal. Pepper sauce lends just a bit of heat...adjust to your liking.

- 10   wonton wrappers
- Cooking spray
- 4   eggs
- 1/2   tsp. garlic powder
- 1/4   tsp. salt
- 1   medium tomato, seeded and chopped
- 10   drops hot pepper sauce

1. Press wonton wrappers into miniature muffin cups coated with cooking spray. Spritz wrappers with cooking spray. Bake at 350° for 10-12 minutes or until lightly browned.

2. Meanwhile, in a small bowl, whisk the eggs, garlic powder and salt. Heat a small nonstick skillet coated with cooking spray until hot. Add the egg mixture; cook and stir over medium heat until the eggs are completely set.

3. Spoon eggs into cups. Top each with chopped tomato and a drop of pepper sauce.

Nutrition Facts: 2 wonton cups equals 110 calories, 4 g fat (1 g saturated fat), 171 mg cholesterol, 269 mg sodium, 11 g carbohydrate, 1 g fiber, 7 g protein. **Diabetic Exchanges:** 1 starch, 1 lean meat.

Spinach Swiss Quiche

PREP: 25 min. BAKE: 35 min. + standing
YIELD: 6 servings

APRIL MILNER • DEARBORN HEIGHTS, MICHIGAN

My family requests this dish year-round. You can saute the bacon mixture the night before to reduce prep time on busy or eventful mornings.

- 1   refrigerated pie pastry
- 4   turkey bacon strips, diced
- 1/4   cup chopped onion
- 1/4   cup chopped sweet red pepper
- 1   pkg. (10 oz.) frozen chopped spinach, thawed and squeezed dry
- 2   cups egg substitute
- 1/2   cup fat-free cottage cheese
- 1/4   cup shredded reduced-fat Swiss cheese
- 1/2   tsp. dried oregano
- 1/4   tsp. dried parsley flakes
- 1/4   tsp. each salt, pepper and paprika
- 6   Tbsp. fat-free sour cream

1. On a lightly floured surface, unroll pastry. Transfer to a 9-in. pie plate. Trim pastry to 1/2 in. beyond edge of plate; flute edges. Line unpricked pastry with a double thickness of heavy-duty foil. Bake at 450° for 8 minutes. Remove foil; bake 5 minutes longer. Cool on a wire rack. Reduce heat to 350°.

2. In a small skillet, cook the bacon, onion and red pepper until vegetables are tender; drain. Stir in spinach. Spoon spinach mixture into pastry. In a small bowl, combine the egg substitute, cottage cheese, Swiss cheese and seasonings; pour over spinach mixture.

3. Bake for 35-40 minutes or until a knife inserted near the center comes out clean. Let stand for 10 minutes before cutting. Serve with sour cream.

Nutrition Facts: 1 piece with 1 Tbsp. sour cream equals 278 calories, 12 g fat (5 g saturated fat), 22 mg cholesterol, 659 mg sodium, 26 g carbohydrate, 2 g fiber, 17 g protein. **Diabetic Exchanges:** 2 lean meat, 2 fat, 1-1/2 starch.

SPINACH SWISS QUICHE

WAKE-UP WONTON CUPS

Frittata Florentine C

PREP/TOTAL TIME: 30 min. YIELD: 4 servings

JENNY FLAKE • GILBERT, ARIZONA

This frittata is loaded with huge flavor and is good for you. Thanks to the eggs, cheese and spinach, you get a healthy dose of calcium and more.

- 6 egg whites
- 3 eggs
- 1/2 tsp. dried oregano
- 1/4 tsp. garlic powder
- 1/4 tsp. salt
- 1/4 tsp. pepper
- 1 small onion, finely chopped
- 1/4 cup finely chopped sweet red pepper
- 2 turkey bacon strips, chopped
- 1 Tbsp. olive oil
- 1 cup fresh baby spinach
- 3 Tbsp. thinly sliced fresh basil leaves
- 1/2 cup shredded part-skim mozzarella cheese

1. In a small bowl, whisk the first six ingredients; set aside. In an 8-in. ovenproof skillet, saute onion, red pepper and bacon in oil until tender. Reduce heat; top with spinach.

2. Pour reserved egg mixture over spinach. As eggs set, push cooked edges toward the center, letting uncooked portion flow underneath until eggs are nearly set. Sprinkle with basil and cheese.

3. Broil 3-4 in. from the heat for 2-3 minutes or until eggs are completely set. Let stand for 5 minutes. Cut into wedges.

Nutrition Facts: 1 wedge equals 176 calories, 11 g fat (4 g saturated fat), 174 mg cholesterol, 451 mg sodium, 4 g carbohydrate, 1 g fiber, 15 g protein.

Energizing Granola S

PREP: 25 min. BAKE: 25 min. + cooling YIELD: 6 cups

NINA WISEMAN • BATAVIA, OHIO

Not only is this munchable granola packed with vitamin E, but flaxseed offers omega-3 fatty acids as well.

- 2-1/2 cups old-fashioned oats
- 3/4 cup chopped walnuts
- 1/2 cup unsalted sunflower kernels
- 1/3 cup packed brown sugar
- 1/4 cup flaked coconut
- 1/4 cup toasted wheat germ
- 2 Tbsp. sesame seeds
- 2 Tbsp. ground flaxseed
- 1/3 cup water
- 2 Tbsp. honey
- 2 Tbsp. molasses
- 1 Tbsp. canola oil
- 3/4 tsp. vanilla extract
- 1/2 tsp. salt
- 1/2 tsp. ground cinnamon
- 1/3 cup dried cranberries
- 1/3 cup golden raisins
- 1/4 cup dried banana chips

1. In a large bowl, combine the first eight ingredients. In a small saucepan, combine water, honey, molasses and oil. Heat for 3-4 minutes over medium until heated through. Remove from heat; stir in vanilla, salt and cinnamon. Pour over the oat mixture; stir to coat.

2. Transfer to a 15-in. x 10-in. x 1-in. baking pan coated with cooking spray. Bake at 350° for 25-30 minutes or until lightly browned, stirring every 10 minutes. Cool completely on a wire rack. Stir in dried fruits. Store in an airtight container.

Nutrition Facts: 1/2 cup equals 260 calories, 12 g fat (2 g saturated fat), 0 cholesterol, 110 mg sodium, 35 g carbohydrate, 4 g fiber, 7 g protein. **Diabetic Exchanges:** 2-1/2 starch, 1-1/2 fat.

FRITTATA FLORENTINE

ENERGIZING GRANOLA

Banana Pancakes M

PREP/TOTAL TIME: 25 min. **YIELD:** 10 pancakes

PEGGY GWILLIM • STRASBOURG, SASKATCHEWAN

My daughter Karen created these pancakes, and they've become a favorite at our house. We love how the cardamom and brown sugar complement the flapjacks.

2	cups all-purpose flour
2	Tbsp. brown sugar
1	tsp. baking soda
1/2	tsp. salt
1/2	tsp. ground cardamom
2	eggs, lightly beaten
2	cups buttermilk
2	Tbsp. canola oil
1	tsp. vanilla extract
1	small firm banana, finely chopped

1. In a small bowl, combine the flour, brown sugar, baking soda, salt and cardamom. Combine the eggs, buttermilk, oil and vanilla; stir into dry ingredients just until moistened. Fold in banana.

2. Pour batter by 1/4 cupfuls onto a hot griddle coated with cooking spray. Turn when bubbles form on top; cook until second side is golden brown.

Nutrition Facts: 2 pancakes equals 342 calories, 9 g fat (2 g saturated fat), 89 mg cholesterol, 619 mg sodium, 53 g carbohydrate, 2 g fiber, 11 g protein.

Baked Oatmeal M

PREP: 15 min. **BAKE:** 30 min. **YIELD:** 4 servings

DIANE BELL • MANCHESTER, NEW HAMPSHIRE

You can top this oatmeal bake with vanilla yogurt, milk, applesauce or syrup, but it's also comforting on its own!

2	cups quick-cooking oats
1/3	cup packed brown sugar
1-1/2	tsp. baking powder
1/2	tsp. salt
1	cup fat-free milk
1/2	cup egg substitute
2	Tbsp. canola oil
1/4	tsp. ground cinnamon

Yogurt and fruit, optional

1. In a large bowl, combine the oats, brown sugar, baking powder and salt. Combine the milk, egg substitute and oil; add to the dry ingredients and stir until blended. Let stand for 5 minutes.

2. Transfer to an 8-in. square baking dish coated with cooking spray. Bake, uncovered, at 350° for 30-35 minutes or until a knife inserted near the center comes out clean. Sprinkle with cinnamon. Serve with yogurt and fruit if desired.

Nutrition Facts: 1 serving (calculated without yogurt and fruit) equals 316 calories, 10 g fat (1 g saturated fat), 1 mg cholesterol, 542 mg sodium, 49 g carbohydrate, 4 g fiber, 11 g protein.

Too-Yummy-To-Share Scramble C M

PREP/TOTAL TIME: 15 min. **YIELD:** 1 serving

VICKEY ABATE • GREEN ISLAND, NEW YORK

Pamper yourself some sunny morning with this scrumptious, single-serving egg dish...you're worth it! I've gotten many compliments on this recipe; basil gives it fresh flavor.

1/4	cup chopped sweet onion
1/4	cup chopped tomato
1/8	tsp. dried basil
Dash salt and pepper	
1	egg
1	Tbsp. water
2	Tbsp. shredded reduced-fat cheddar cheese

1. In a small nonstick skillet coated with cooking spray, cook and stir onion over medium heat until tender. Add the tomato, basil, salt and pepper; cook 1 minute longer.

2. In a small bowl, whisk egg and water. Add egg mixture to the pan; cook and stir until the egg is completely set. Remove from the heat. Sprinkle with cheese; cover and let stand until cheese is melted.

Nutrition Facts: 1 serving equals 136 calories, 8 g fat (4 g saturated fat), 222 mg cholesterol, 310 mg sodium, 7 g carbohydrate, 1 g fiber, 11 g protein.

Banana Blueberry Smoothies F S

PREP/TOTAL TIME: 10 min. **YIELD:** 6 servings

KRISTA FRANK • RHODODENDRON, OREGON

My sons love this smoothie, whether it's served frozen or with a straw. Either way, I feel good giving them this healthy treat.

1	cup fat-free milk
1	cup orange juice
1/2	tsp. vanilla extract
2	medium bananas, halved
1	cup unsweetened applesauce
1	cup frozen unsweetened blueberries

1. In a blender, combine all ingredients; cover and process for 30 seconds or until blended. Pour into chilled glasses; serve immediately.

Nutrition Facts: 3/4 cup equals 99 calories, trace fat (trace saturated fat), 1 mg cholesterol, 19 mg sodium, 23 g carbohydrate, 2 g fiber, 2 g protein. **Diabetic Exchange:** 1-1/2 fruit.

Makeover Breakfast Cake

PREP: 20 min. BAKE: 25 min. + cooling
YIELD: 20 servings

NANCY TAYLOR • SEDRO WOOLLEY, WASHINGTON

This yummy morning treat, a family favorite for years, was redone and now has about half the fat and a fourth fewer calories. That's something to crow about!

- 1 cup buttermilk
- 3/4 cup sugar
- 1/2 cup unsweetened applesauce
- 2 eggs
- 2 Tbsp. canola oil
- 1-1/2 cups whole wheat flour
- 1-1/4 cups all-purpose flour
- 1/2 cup oat bran
- 1/2 cup ground flaxseed
- 2 tsp. ground cinnamon
- 1-1/4 tsp. baking powder
- 1 tsp. salt
- 1/2 tsp. baking soda

TOPPING:
- 1 cup packed brown sugar
- 1/4 cup all-purpose flour
- 2 Tbsp. butter, melted

1. In a large bowl, beat the buttermilk, sugar, applesauce, eggs and oil until well blended. Combine the flours, oat bran, flax, cinnamon, baking powder, salt and baking soda; gradually beat into buttermilk mixture until blended.

2. Coat a 13-in. x 9-in. baking pan with cooking spray and sprinkle with flour; add batter. Combine topping ingredients; sprinkle over batter.

3. Bake at 350° for 25-30 minutes or until a toothpick inserted near the center comes out clean. Cool for 10 minutes on a wire rack. Serve warm.

Nutrition Facts: 1 piece equals 193 calories, 5 g fat (1 g saturated fat), 25 mg cholesterol, 209 mg sodium, 36 g carbohydrate, 3 g fiber, 4 g protein.

Start-Right Strata

PREP: 15 min. + chilling BAKE: 35 min. + standing
YIELD: 4 servings

CECILE BROWN • CHILLICOTHE, TEXAS

I reworked this recipe to fit my diet...and my tastes! It's ideal for overnight guests.

- 4 slices white bread, torn into pieces
- 4 breakfast turkey sausage links, casings removed, crumbled
- 1/3 cup chopped onion
- 1 cup fat-free milk
- 3/4 cup egg substitute
- 1/2 cup reduced-fat sour cream
- 1/4 cup shredded reduced-fat cheddar cheese
- 1/4 cup salsa

1. Place bread in an 8-in. square baking dish coated with cooking spray; set aside.

2. In a small nonstick skillet, cook the sausage and onion over medium heat until meat is no longer pink; drain. Spoon over bread. In a small bowl, combine milk, egg substitute and sour cream. Stir in cheese. Pour over the meat mixture. Cover baking dish and refrigerate overnight.

3. Remove from the refrigerator 30 minutes before baking. Bake, uncovered, at 325° for 35-40 minutes or until a knife inserted near the center comes out clean. Let stand for 10 minutes before cutting. Serve the strata with salsa.

Nutrition Facts: 1 piece with 1 Tbsp. salsa equals 247 calories, 10 g fat (4 g saturated fat), 39 mg cholesterol, 580 mg sodium, 21 g carbohydrate, 1 g fiber, 17 g protein. **Diabetic Exchanges:** 2 lean meat, 1-1/2 starch, 1 fat.

MAKEOVER BREAKFAST CAKE

START-RIGHT STRATA

Nutmeg Waffles F M

PREP/TOTAL TIME: 15 min. **YIELD:** 8 waffles

JAMES CHRISTENSEN • ST. ANTHONY, IDAHO

Bake an extra batch of these tender, golden waffles on the weekend. Eat one, then freeze the other in packages of two, to pop in the toaster and reheat on hurried mornings. Nutmeg adds to their warm, feel-good flavor!

1-1/4 cups all-purpose flour
    1 tsp. baking powder
    1 tsp. ground cinnamon
  1/2 tsp. salt
  1/2 tsp. ground nutmeg
  1/4 tsp. baking soda
    1 egg, lightly beaten
    1 cup fat-free milk
    1 tsp. canola oil
    1 tsp. vanilla extract
Butter and maple syrup, optional

1. In a small bowl, combine the flour, baking powder, cinnamon, salt, nutmeg and baking soda. In another bowl, combine the egg, milk, oil and vanilla; stir into dry ingredients until smooth.

2. Bake in a preheated waffle iron according to manufacturer's directions until golden brown. Serve with butter and syrup if desired.

Nutrition Facts: 2 waffles (calculated without butter and syrup) equal 196 calories, 3 g fat (1 g saturated fat), 54 mg cholesterol, 518 mg sodium, 34 g carbohydrate, 1 g fiber, 8 g protein. **Diabetic Exchanges:** 2 starch, 1 fat.

Spiced Bacon Twists C

PREP: 10 min. **BAKE:** 25 min. **YIELD:** 5 servings

GLENDA EVANS WITTNER • JOPLIN, MISSOURI

A sweet and savory rub makes these tasty twists of bacon deliciously different and worth the extra step to prepare. Cook a bit longer if you want them crispy.

  1/4 cup packed brown sugar
1-1/2 tsp. ground mustard
  1/8 tsp. ground cinnamon
  1/8 tsp. ground nutmeg
Dash cayenne pepper
  10 center-cut bacon strips

1. Combine the first five ingredients; rub over bacon on both sides. Twist bacon; place on a rack in a 15-in. x 10-in. x 1-in. baking pan.

2. Bake at 350° for 25-30 minutes or until firm; bake longer if desired.

Nutrition Facts: 2 bacon twists equals 75 calories, 4 g fat (1 g saturated fat), 15 mg cholesterol, 212 mg sodium, 6 g carbohydrate, trace fiber, 5 g protein. **Diabetic Exchanges:** 1 lean meat, 1/2 starch.

Potato Egg Bake M

PREP: 20 min. **BAKE:** 35 min. **YIELD:** 8 servings

RENA CHARBONEAU • GANSEVOORT, NEW YORK

No one will guess this mouthwatering breakfast bake is lighter than other morning casseroles.

2	lbs. Yukon Gold potatoes (about 6 medium), peeled and diced
1/2	cup water
1	cup frozen chopped broccoli, thawed
6	green onions, thinly sliced
1	small sweet red pepper, chopped
6	eggs
8	egg whites
1	cup (8 oz.) 1% cottage cheese
1	cup (4 oz.) shredded reduced-fat cheddar cheese
1/2	cup grated Parmesan cheese
1/2	cup fat-free milk
2	Tbsp. dried parsley flakes
1/2	tsp. salt
1/4	tsp. pepper

1. Place potatoes and water in a microwave-safe dish. Cover and microwave on high for 7 minutes or until tender; drain.

2. Spread potatoes in a 13-in. x 9-in. baking dish coated with cooking spray. Top with broccoli, onions and red pepper. In a large bowl, whisk the remaining ingredients until blended. Pour over vegetables. Bake, uncovered, at 350° for 35-40 minutes or until center is set.

Nutrition Facts: 1 piece equals 263 calories, 9 g fat (4 g saturated fat), 174 mg cholesterol, 558 mg sodium, 25 g carbohydrate, 2 g fiber, 21 g protein.

Cherry Yogurt F S

PREP: 10 min. + chilling **YIELD:** 3 cups

HEALTHY COOKING TEST KITCHEN

Serve wholesome granola over this thick, rich yogurt for a quick breakfast. Or layer it in parfait glasses with granola and fruit for something special. For a healthy touch, look for 100 percent cherry juice at the store; the cocktail blends have added sugar.

4	cups (32 oz.) reduced-fat plain yogurt
1	cup frozen pitted dark sweet cherries, thawed and quartered
1/2	cup cherry juice
3	Tbsp. confectioners' sugar
1-1/2	tsp. vanilla extract

1. Line a strainer with four layers of cheesecloth or one coffee filter and place over a bowl. Place yogurt in prepared strainer; cover yogurt with edges of cheesecloth. Refrigerate for 8 hours or overnight.

2. Remove yogurt from cheesecloth and discard liquid from bowl. Place the yogurt in a small bowl; stir in the remaining ingredients. Cover and refrigerate until serving.

Nutrition Facts: 1/2 cup equals 147 calories, 3 g fat (2 g saturated fat), 10 mg cholesterol, 115 mg sodium, 22 g carbohydrate, 1 g fiber, 9 g protein. **Diabetic Exchanges:** 1 reduced-fat milk, 1/2 fruit.

CHERRY YOGURT

POTATO EGG BAKE

SPICY PEPPER SLAW

PEAR APPLESAUCE

LEMON COUSCOUS WITH BROCCOLI

Side Dishes

Need a great veggie to complement your beef roast? How about a no-fuss pasta salad to serve alongside a turkey sub? The simple side dishes offered here are ideal ways to complete menus and maintain your healthy lifestyle.

Lemon Couscous With Broccoli F

PREP/TOTAL TIME: 25 min. YIELD: 6 servings

BETH DAUENHAUER • PUEBLO, COLORADO

A splash of lemon brightens this versatile side dish. It combines whole wheat couscous with fresh broccoli and a sprinkling of almonds on top.

- 4 cups fresh broccoli florets, cut into small pieces
- 1 Tbsp. olive oil
- 1 cup uncooked whole wheat couscous
- 2 garlic cloves, minced
- 1-1/4 cups reduced-sodium chicken broth
- 1 tsp. grated lemon peel
- 1 tsp. lemon juice
- 1/2 tsp. salt
- 1/2 tsp. dried basil
- 1/4 tsp. coarsely ground pepper
- 1 Tbsp. slivered almonds, toasted

1. In a large skillet, saute broccoli in oil until crisp-tender. Add couscous and garlic; saute 1-2 minutes longer.

2. Stir in the broth, lemon peel, lemon juice, salt, basil and pepper. Bring to a boil. Remove from the heat; cover and let stand for 5-10 minutes or until broth is absorbed. Fluff with a fork. Sprinkle with toasted almonds.

Nutrition Facts: 2/3 cup equals 115 calories, 3 g fat (trace saturated fat), 0 cholesterol, 328 mg sodium, 18 g carbohydrate, 4 g fiber, 5 g protein. **Diabetic Exchanges:** 1 starch, 1/2 fat.

Corn and Bean Medley M

PREP/TOTAL TIME: 25 min. YIELD: 6 servings

WENDY CAMPBELL • NEW WILMINGTON, PENNSYLVANIA

Frozen corn and edamame make this side dish a breeze to toss together. The black beans and green pepper add a nice touch, and the garlic salt and cayenne really pump up the flavor.

- 1 small green pepper, chopped
- 1/3 cup chopped onion
- 1-1/2 tsp. butter
- 1-1/2 tsp. olive oil
- 1-3/4 cups frozen corn, thawed
- 1-1/2 cups frozen shelled edamame, thawed
- 3/4 cup black beans, rinsed and drained
- 1/4 tsp. garlic salt
- 1/8 tsp. cayenne pepper

1. In a large nonstick skillet, saute green pepper and onion in butter and oil until tender. Add the remaining ingredients. Cook and stir over medium heat for 4-5 minutes or until heated through.

Nutrition Facts: 2/3 cup equals 137 calories, 4 g fat (1 g saturated fat), 3 mg cholesterol, 148 mg sodium, 19 g carbohydrate, 4 g fiber, 7 g protein. **Diabetic Exchanges:** 1-1/2 starch, 1/2 fat.

Pear Applesauce F S

PREP/TOTAL TIME: 30 min. YIELD: about 2 cups

JENNY COHEN • BALTIMORE, MARYLAND

Here's a great way to satisfy your sweet tooth. Best of all, it's fat-free and only 120 calories!

- 3 medium apples, peeled and coarsely chopped
- 2 medium pears, peeled and coarsely chopped
- 3/4 cup water
- 2 Tbsp. sugar
- 1/4 tsp. ground cinnamon
- 1/8 tsp. ground nutmeg

1. In a large saucepan, combine all ingredients. Bring to a boil. Reduce heat; cover and simmer for 15-20 minutes or until tender, stirring occasionally. Mash until sauce is desired consistency. Serve warm or cold.

Nutrition Facts: 1/2 cup equals 120 calories, trace fat (trace saturated fat), 0 cholesterol, 1 mg sodium, 31 g carbohydrate, 4 g fiber, trace protein. **Diabetic Exchanges:** 2 fruit, 1/2 starch.

Sunny Snow Peas F C M

PREP/TOTAL TIME: 25 min. YIELD: 6 servings

KATHLEEN BAILEY • CHESTER SPRINGS, PENNSYLVANIA

Turn crispy snow peas into something special by tossing them with this lovely honey-orange sauce. I enjoy serving fresh vegetables, especially when I can prepare a sauce that seems to add the bright warmth of the sun.

1/2	cup orange juice
2	Tbsp. honey
1	Tbsp. butter
1 to 2 tsp.	grated orange peel
1/2	tsp. salt
1/8	tsp. ground cardamom
1	lb. fresh snow peas *or* sugar snap peas

1. In a small saucepan, combine the orange juice, honey, butter, orange peel, salt and cardamom; bring to a boil. Reduce heat; simmer, uncovered, until mixture is reduced by half, about 15 minutes.

2. Meanwhile, in another saucepan, bring 1 in. of water to a boil. Add peas. Reduce heat; cover and simmer for 3-4 minutes or until crisp-tender. Drain and transfer to a serving bowl. Add orange juice mixture and toss to coat.

Nutrition Facts: 2/3 cup equals 80 calories, 2 g fat (1 g saturated fat), 5 mg cholesterol, 213 mg sodium, 14 g carbohydrate, 2 g fiber, 2 g protein. **Diabetic Exchanges:** 1 vegetable, 1/2 starch.

Cheese Smashed Potatoes M

PREP: 10 min. COOK: 25 min. YIELD: 4 servings

JANET HOMES • SURPRISE, ARIZONA

Try this delicious, versatile side dish with a variety of entrees. It's perfect for a summer barbecue or a winter feast!

1	lb. small red potatoes, quartered
1	cup fresh cauliflowerets
2/3	cup shredded reduced-fat cheddar cheese
1/4	cup reduced-fat sour cream
1/4	tsp. salt

1. Place potatoes in a large saucepan and cover with water. Bring to a boil. Reduce heat; cover and cook for 10 minutes. Add cauliflower; cook 10 minutes longer or until vegetables are tender.

2. Drain; mash with cheese, sour cream and salt.

Nutrition Facts: 3/4 cup equals 161 calories, 5 g fat (3 g saturated fat), 18 mg cholesterol, 292 mg sodium, 21 g carbohydrate, 3 g fiber, 8 g protein. **Diabetic Exchanges:** 1 starch, 1 medium-fat meat.

Herbed Twice-Baked Potatoes M

PREP: 1-1/4 hours BAKE: 15 min. YIELD: 4 servings

RUTH ANDREWSON • LEAVENWORTH, WASHINGTON

Light cream cheese, garlic powder and butter make these classic potatoes irresistible. You can replace the basil with parsley.

2	medium baking potatoes
1-1/2	oz. reduced-fat cream cheese, cubed
1	Tbsp. minced chives
1/4	tsp. salt
1/4	tsp. dried basil
Dash	cayenne pepper
3	Tbsp. fat-free milk
3	tsp. butter, melted, *divided*
Dash	garlic powder
Dash	paprika

SUNNY SNOW PEAS

HERBED TWICE-BAKED POTATOES

RIGATONI CHARD TOSS

1. Scrub and pierce potatoes. Bake at 375° for 1 hour or until tender. Cool for 10 minutes. Cut potatoes in half lengthwise. Scoop out pulp, leaving thin shells.

2. In a large bowl, mash pulp with cream cheese, chives, salt, basil and cayenne. Add milk and 1-1/2 tsp. butter; mash. Spoon into potato shells. Drizzle with remaining butter; sprinkle with garlic powder and paprika.

3. Place on an ungreased baking sheet. Bake for 15-20 minutes or until heated through.

Nutrition Facts: 1/2 stuffed potato equals 150 calories, 5 g fat (3 g saturated fat), 15 mg cholesterol, 234 mg sodium, 23 g carbohydrate, 2 g fiber, 4 g protein. **Diabetic Exchanges:** 1-1/2 starch, 1 fat.

Rigatoni Chard Toss M

PREP: 25 min. **COOK:** 20 min. **YIELD:** 11 servings

CAROLYN KUMPE • EL DORADO, CALIFORNIA

Fresh chard and tomatoes add fiber and vitamins to this hearty, colorful side dish.

  8 oz. uncooked rigatoni or large tube pasta
  1 bunch Swiss chard, coarsely chopped
  1 small onion, thinly sliced
  2 Tbsp. olive oil
  2 garlic cloves, minced
  3 medium tomatoes, chopped
  1 can (15 oz.) white kidney or cannellini beans, rinsed and drained
 1/2 tsp. salt

 1/8 tsp. crushed red pepper flakes
 1/8 tsp. fennel seed, crushed
 1/8 tsp. pepper
 1/4 cup minced fresh basil
 1/2 cup grated Parmesan cheese

1. Cook rigatoni according to package directions.

2. Meanwhile, in a large skillet, saute chard and onion in oil for 4 minutes. Add garlic; cook 2 minutes longer. Stir in the tomatoes, beans, salt, pepper flakes, fennel and pepper; cook 3-4 minutes longer or until chard is tender.

3. Drain pasta, reserving 1/4 cup cooking liquid. Stir basil, rigatoni and reserved liquid into skillet; heat through. Transfer to a serving bowl; sprinkle with Parmesan cheese.

Nutrition Facts: 3/4 cup equals 159 calories, 4 g fat (1 g saturated fat), 3 mg cholesterol, 291 mg sodium, 24 g carbohydrate, 3 g fiber, 7 g protein. **Diabetic Exchanges:** 1-1/2 starch, 1/2 fat.

Drain pasta thoroughly in a colander without rinsing when it is to be served with a sauce or combined in a baked dish. **Rinsing pasta** can wash away starch that may help to slightly thicken the pasta sauce. Pasta can be rinsed in a colander when it is to be served cold.

Sweet Onion Spoon Bread Ⓜ

PREP: 15 min. **BAKE:** 25 min. **YIELD:** 9 servings

HEATHER THOMAS • FREDERICKSBURG, VIRGINIA

This unique recipe has been a family secret for years. The layers of tangy cheese, sour cream and sweet onions in this moist corn bread taste so great together! Chopped green chilies could add some fun zip.

1-1/3 cups chopped sweet onions
   1 Tbsp. butter
   1 can (8-1/4 oz.) cream-style corn
   1 pkg. (8-1/2 oz.) corn bread/muffin mix
   2 egg whites, lightly beaten
   2 Tbsp. fat-free milk
1/2 cup reduced-fat sour cream
1/3 cup shredded sharp cheddar cheese

1. In a small nonstick skillet coated with cooking spray, saute onions in butter until tender; set aside.

2. Meanwhile, in a large bowl, combine the corn, muffin mix, egg whites and milk. Pour into a 9-in. square baking dish coated with cooking spray. Combine sour cream and onions; spread over batter. Sprinkle with cheese.

3. Bake, uncovered, at 350° for 25-30 minutes or until a toothpick inserted near the center comes out clean.

Nutrition Facts: 1 piece equals 191 calories, 6 g fat (3 g saturated fat), 18 mg cholesterol, 361 mg sodium, 29 g carbohydrate, 1 g fiber, 6 g protein. **Diabetic Exchanges:** 2 starch, 1/2 fat.

Lemon Risotto With Broccoli F

PREP: 25 min. COOK: 30 min. YIELD: 8 servings

JUDY GREBETZ • RACINE, WISCONSIN

Here's a creamy, rich party-special alternative to potatoes. It seems time-consuming, but it's really quite easy, and the results are sure to impress. Try it with a chicken entree, or add a handful of mushrooms and enjoy it as a light main course. A sprinkling of chopped green onion makes an easy garnish.

3	cans (14-1/2 oz. *each*) reduced-sodium chicken broth
1	small onion, finely chopped
1	Tbsp. olive oil
1-1/2	cups uncooked arborio rice
2	tsp. grated lemon peel
1/2	cup dry white wine *or* additional reduced-sodium chicken broth
3	cups chopped fresh broccoli
1/3	cup grated Parmesan cheese
1	Tbsp. lemon juice
2	tsp. minced fresh thyme

1. In a large saucepan, heat broth and keep warm. In a large nonstick skillet coated with cooking spray, saute onion in oil until tender. Add rice and lemon peel; cook and stir for 2-3 minutes.

2. Reduce heat; stir in wine. Cook and stir until all of the liquid is absorbed. Carefully stir in 1 cup warm broth; cook and stir until all of the liquid is absorbed. Stir in broccoli.

3. Add remaining broth, 1/2 cup at a time, stirring constantly. Allow liquid to absorb between additions. Cook until risotto is creamy and rice is almost tender. (Cooking time is about 20 minutes.)

4. Remove from the heat; stir in cheese and lemon juice. Sprinkle with thyme. Serve immediately.

Nutrition Facts: 2/3 cup equals 198 calories, 3 g fat (1 g saturated fat), 3 mg cholesterol, 447 mg sodium, 34 g carbohydrate, 1 g fiber, 7 g protein. **Diabetic Exchanges:** 2 starch, 1/2 fat.

Roasted Pepper Salad F C M

PREP: 15 min. BAKE: 25 min. YIELD: 6 servings

TRISHA KRUSE • EAGLE, IDAHO

Here's a pretty, quick-prep side that will go with a summer full of grilled entrees.

2	cups cherry tomatoes, halved
1/2	cup minced fresh basil
8	garlic cloves, minced
1	Tbsp. balsamic vinegar
1/2	tsp. salt
1/2	tsp. pepper
3	large sweet yellow peppers, halved and seeded
2	Tbsp. shredded Parmesan cheese

1. In a small bowl, combine the tomatoes, basil, garlic, vinegar, salt and pepper. Spoon 1/3 cup into each pepper half.

2. Transfer to a 13-in. x 9-in. baking dish coated with cooking spray. Cover and bake at 400° for 20 minutes. Uncover; sprinkle with cheese. Bake 5-10 minutes longer or until cheese is melted.

Nutrition Facts: 1 stuffed pepper half equals 51 calories, 1 g fat (trace saturated fat), 1 mg cholesterol, 233 mg sodium, 10 g carbohydrate, 2 g fiber, 2 g protein. **Diabetic Exchange:** 2 vegetable.

Lemon Roasted Potatoes F

PREP: 10 min. BAKE: 35 min. YIELD: 6 servings

MITZI SENTIFF • ANNAPOLIS, MARYLAND

Delicious with almost any meat or fish dinner, these crispy potatoes are really something special. Tangy lemon permeates the potatoes and adds marvelous flavor.

2	lbs. small red potatoes, quartered
1	medium lemon, halved and sliced
1	Tbsp. olive oil
2	tsp. minced fresh rosemary
1/2	tsp. salt
1/8	tsp. coarsely ground pepper

1. In a large bowl, combine all ingredients; toss to coat. Arrange in a single layer in a 15-in. x 10-in. x 1-in. baking pan coated with cooking spray. Bake at 425° for 35-40 minutes or until potatoes are golden and tender.

Nutrition Facts: 3/4 cup equals 132 calories, 2 g fat (trace saturated fat), 0 cholesterol, 207 mg sodium, 25 g carbohydrate, 3 g fiber, 3 g protein. **Diabetic Exchanges:** 1-1/2 starch, 1/2 fat.

LEMON ROASTED POTATOES

Hot and Zesty Quinoa M

PREP/TOTAL TIME: 25 min. **YIELD:** 4 servings

SANDRA LETIZIA • PROVIDENCE, RHODE ISLAND

I created this healthy whole grain side to serve my family instead of potatoes or rice. It's so easy and has a little kick. Quinoa's a nurturing grain and a complete protein.

1	cup water
1/2	cup quinoa, rinsed
1	small onion, finely chopped
1	tsp. olive oil
2	garlic cloves, minced
1	can (10 oz.) diced tomatoes and green chilies
2	Tbsp. chopped marinated quartered artichoke hearts
2	Tbsp. grated Parmesan cheese

1. In a small saucepan, bring water to a boil. Add quinoa. Reduce heat; cover and simmer for 12-15 minutes or until liquid is absorbed. Remove from the heat; fluff with a fork.

2. In a large skillet, saute onion in oil until tender. Add garlic; cook 1 minute longer. Add tomatoes and green chilies. Bring to a boil over medium heat. Reduce heat; simmer, uncovered, for 10 minutes. Stir in quinoa and artichoke; heat through. Sprinkle with the cheese.

Editor's Note: Look for quinoa in the cereal, rice or organic food aisle.

Nutrition Facts: 1/2 cup equals 135 calories, 5 g fat (1 g saturated fat), 2 mg cholesterol, 361 mg sodium, 20 g carbohydrate, 2 g fiber, 5 g protein. **Diabetic Exchanges:** 1 starch, 1 vegetable, 1 fat.

Spicy Pepper Slaw C M

PREP: 20 min. + chilling **YIELD:** 8 servings

CHERYL MCCLEARY • KANSAS CITY, KANSAS

I love coleslaw but wanted to jazz it up and make it just a little healthier. This recipe not only makes a good side dish, but it's also great as a relish on a chicken sandwich or burger. Jalapenos give it just the right kick.

3	cups shredded cabbage
2	celery ribs, chopped
1	medium green pepper, julienned
1	cup cut fresh green beans (1-in. pieces)
1	cup cut fresh asparagus (1-in. pieces)
1	bunch green onions, chopped
1	banana pepper, seeded and chopped
2	jalapeno peppers, seeded and chopped
2	serrano peppers, seeded and chopped
1/2	cup cider vinegar
3	Tbsp. olive oil
1	Tbsp. lime juice
1	Tbsp. minced fresh thyme
1	Tbsp. snipped fresh dill
1	Tbsp. minced fresh cilantro
1	tsp. salt
1	tsp. pepper

1. In a large bowl, combine the first nine ingredients. In a small bowl, whisk the remaining ingredients; pour over salad and toss to coat. Refrigerate for at least 1 hour before serving.

Editor's Note: Wear disposable gloves when cutting hot peppers; the oils can burn skin. Avoid touching your face.

Nutrition Facts: 1 cup equals 76 calories, 5 g fat (1 g saturated fat), 0 cholesterol, 314 mg sodium, 6 g carbohydrate, 3 g fiber, 2 g protein. **Diabetic Exchanges:** 1 vegetable, 1 fat.

HOT AND ZESTY QUINOA

SPICY PEPPER SLAW

Spinach and Rice F

PREP: 20 min. COOK: 40 min. YIELD: 8 servings

LAURA NURSE • LILBURN, GEORGIA

Dill and oregano do a nice job of dressing up this dish. It makes a pleasing side with savory lamb or pork chops.

    6   green onions, chopped
    1   Tbsp. olive oil
    1   cup uncooked brown rice
2-3/4 cups water
  1/3   cup snipped fresh dill
    2   Tbsp. minced fresh oregano
  3/4   tsp. salt
  1/4   tsp. pepper
    1   pkg. (6 oz.) fresh baby spinach

1. In a large saucepan, saute onions in oil until tender. Add rice; cook and stir for 3-4 minutes or until rice is lightly browned.

2. Stir in the water, dill, oregano, salt and pepper. Bring to a boil. Reduce heat; cover and simmer for 35-40 minutes or until rice is tender. Add spinach; heat through.

Nutrition Facts: 3/4 cup equals 110 calories, 3 g fat (trace saturated fat), 0 cholesterol, 242 mg sodium, 20 g carbohydrate, 2 g fiber, 3 g protein. **Diabetic Exchanges:** 1 starch, 1 vegetable.

Roasted Dijon Broccoli C M

PREP/TOTAL TIME: 20 min. YIELD: 4 servings

AMY WINGENTER • TUSCALOOSA, ALABAMA

A hint of red wine vinegar and Dijon mustard wonderfully flavor this quick, easy and very versatile side dish. If you'd like, feel free to add a little more garlic or even a dash of red pepper flakes for extra flair!

    1   bunch broccoli, cut into florets
    2   Tbsp. olive oil
    1   Tbsp. red wine vinegar
    1   tsp. Dijon mustard
    1   garlic clove, minced
  1/4   tsp. salt
  1/4   tsp. pepper

1. Place broccoli on a baking sheet. In a small bowl, whisk the remaining ingredients. Drizzle over broccoli; toss to coat.

2. Bake, uncovered, at 425° for 10-15 minutes or until tender.

Nutrition Facts: 1 cup equals 106 calories, 7 g fat (1 g saturated fat), 0 cholesterol, 219 mg sodium, 9 g carbohydrate, 5 g fiber, 5 g protein. **Diabetic Exchanges:** 2 vegetable, 1 fat.

Savory Green Beans F C M

PREP/TOTAL TIME: 30 min. **YIELD:** 6 servings

CAROL ANN HAYDEN • EVERSON, WASHINGTON

This was my mother's favorite way to fix green beans. She always grew savory in her garden, which is the key ingredient to this recipe's fresh flavor. Not only is this dish low in fat, but it goes well with just about any main course.

3/4	cup chopped sweet red pepper
1	Tbsp. canola oil
1	garlic clove, minced
1-1/2	lbs. fresh green beans, trimmed and cut into 2-in. pieces
1/2	cup water
2	Tbsp. minced fresh savory or 2 tsp. dried savory
1	Tbsp. minced chives
1/2	tsp. salt

1. In a large skillet, saute red pepper in oil for 2-3 minutes or until tender. Add garlic; cook 1 minute longer. Stir in the green beans, water, savory, chives and salt. Bring to a boil. Reduce heat; cover and simmer for 8-10 minutes or until beans are crisp-tender.

Nutrition Facts: 3/4 cup equals 59 calories, 3 g fat (trace saturated fat), 0 cholesterol, 203 mg sodium, 9 g carbohydrate, 4 g fiber, 2 g protein. **Diabetic Exchanges:** 2 vegetable, 1/2 fat.

Spanish Rice with Bacon

PREP: 5 min. **COOK:** 40 min. **YIELD:** 6 servings

DAVID BIAS • SILOAM SPRINGS, ARKANSAS

I add bacon to this zippy rice dish for a flavorful change of pace. Being big fans of Mexican food, my family loves this simple recipe.

6	bacon strips, diced
1	Tbsp. canola oil
1	medium onion, chopped
1	cup uncooked long grain rice
1-3/4	cups water
2	large tomatoes, chopped

1 medium green pepper, chopped
2 jalapeno peppers, seeded and chopped
1 to 1-1/2 tsp. chili powder
1/2 tsp. salt

1. In a large skillet, cook bacon over medium heat until crisp. Remove to paper towels. Add oil to the drippings; saute onion for 3 minutes. Add rice; stir until golden brown, about 5 minutes. Stir in the remaining ingredients. Bring to a boil.

2. Reduce heat; cover and simmer for 30 minutes or until rice is tender. Sprinkle with bacon.

Editor's Note: Wear disposable gloves when cutting hot peppers; the oils can burn skin. Avoid touching your face.

Nutrition Facts: 3/4 cup equals 287 calories, 12 g fat (4 g saturated fat), 16 mg cholesterol, 514 mg sodium, 34 g carbohydrate, 2 g fiber, 10 g protein. **Diabetic Exchanges:** 2 starch, 2 fat, 1 vegetable.

Creamy Grilled Potato Salad Ⓜ

PREP: 15 min. GRILL: 25 min. YIELD: 6 servings

GAYLE ROBINSON • CARROLLTON, GEORGIA

I grill just about everything in the summer to avoid turning on my oven—including this salad. Friends dubbed this "The Best Potato Salad You'll Ever Put in Your Mouth!"

8 medium red potatoes (about 2 lbs.), cut into 1-in. slices
2 Tbsp. olive oil
1/2 tsp. garlic salt
1/4 tsp. paprika
1/4 tsp. pepper
1 cup fat-free mayonnaise
2 hard-cooked eggs, chopped
1 dill pickle spear, chopped
3 Tbsp. dill pickle juice
1 Tbsp. spicy brown mustard

1. Place the first five ingredients in a large bowl; toss to coat. Moisten a paper towel with cooking oil; using long-handled tongs, lightly coat the grill rack. Grill potatoes, covered, over medium heat for 25-30 minutes or until tender, turning once. Cool. Cut into quarters and place in a large bowl.

2. In a small bowl, combine remaining ingredients. Pour over potatoes; toss to coat. Serve immediately. Refrigerate leftovers.

Nutrition Facts: 3/4 cup equals 209 calories, 8 g fat (1 g saturated fat), 75 mg cholesterol, 651 mg sodium, 30 g carbohydrate, 4 g fiber, 5 g protein. **Diabetic Exchanges:** 2 starch, 1 fat.

Makeover Spinach and Artichoke Casserole Ⓜ

PREP: 35 min. BAKE: 30 min. YIELD: 12 servings

JUDY ARMSTRONG • PRAIRIEVILLE, LOUISIANA

Spinach never tasted better than in this creamy, colorful dish that's now even healthier and more delicious!

5 celery ribs, finely chopped
2 medium sweet red peppers, chopped

2 medium onions, finely chopped
2 Tbsp. butter
1 Tbsp. canola oil
6 garlic cloves, minced
3 Tbsp. all-purpose flour
1 cup half-and-half cream
1 cup fat-free milk
3 cups (12 oz.) shredded reduced-fat Mexican cheese blend
4 pkg. (10 oz. *each*) frozen chopped spinach, thawed and squeezed dry
2 cans (14 oz. *each*) water-packed artichoke hearts, rinsed, drained and quartered
1 tsp. salt
1 tsp. cayenne pepper
1 tsp. pepper
1/2 tsp. crushed red pepper flakes
1 cup grated Parmesan cheese

1. In a Dutch oven, saute the celery, red peppers and onions in butter and oil until tender. Add garlic; cook 1 minute longer. Stir in flour until blended; gradually add cream and milk. Bring to a boil; cook and stir for 2 minutes or until thickened. Stir in shredded cheese until melted.

2. Add the spinach, artichokes, salt, cayenne, pepper and pepper flakes. Transfer to a 13-in. x 9-in. baking dish coated with cooking spray. Sprinkle with Parmesan cheese.

3. Bake, uncovered, at 350° for 30-35 minutes or until bubbly.

Nutrition Facts: 1 cup equals 245 calories, 13 g fat (7 g saturated fat), 41 mg cholesterol, 781 mg sodium, 17 g carbohydrate, 4 g fiber, 17 g protein.

MAKEOVER SPINACH AND ARTICHOKE CASSEROLE

Slow-Roasted Tomatoes C M

PREP: 20 min. BAKE: 3 hours + cooling
YIELD: 4 cups

JULIE TILNEY • DOWNEY, CALIFORNIA

I love tomatoes, and these are so versatile. You can also use them in sandwiches, omelets and to top broiled chicken.

20	plum tomatoes (about 5 lbs.)
1/4	cup olive oil
5	tsp. Italian seasoning
2-1/2	tsp. salt

1. Cut tomatoes into 1/2-in. slices. Brush with oil; sprinkle with Italian seasoning and salt.

2. Place on racks coated with cooking spray in foil-lined 15-in. x 10-in. x 1-in. baking pans. Bake, uncovered, at 325° for 3 to 3-1/2 hours or until tomatoes are deep brown around the edges and shriveled. Cool for 10-15 minutes. Serve warm or at room temperature.

3. Store in an airtight container in the refrigerator for up to 1 week or freeze for up to 3 months. Bring tomatoes to room temperature before using.

Nutrition Facts: 1/4 cup equals 45 calories, 4 g fat (trace saturated fat), 0 cholesterol, 373 mg sodium, 3 g carbohydrate, 1 g fiber, 1 g protein.

Snow Pea & Carrot Saute F M

PREP/TOTAL TIME: 20 min. YIELD: 5 servings

HEALTHY COOKING TEST KITCHEN

SNOW PEA & CARROT SAUTE

With bright carrot strips and green snow peas, this makes a colorful dish with any entree. Short on time? You can also buy matchstick carrots at the grocery store.

1	lb. fresh snow peas
1	Tbsp. butter
2	medium carrots, julienned
1	garlic clove, minced
3	Tbsp. honey
1/4	tsp. salt
1/8	tsp. pepper

1. In a large skillet, saute snow peas in butter for 3 minutes. Add carrots and garlic; saute 1-2 minutes longer or until vegetables are crisp-tender. Add remaining ingredients; heat through.

Nutrition Facts: 3/4 cup equals 108 calories, 3 g fat (1 g saturated fat), 6 mg cholesterol, 155 mg sodium, 20 g carbohydrate, 3 g fiber, 3 g protein. **Diabetic Exchanges:** 2 vegetable, 1/2 starch.

Grilled Summer Squash C M

PREP/TOTAL TIME: 25 min. YIELD: 4 servings

LISA FINNEGAN • FORKED RIVER, NEW JERSEY

Grilling food in foil packets creates steam, so it cooks in its own juices, which makes this summer squash flavorful and keeps it light. Best of all, there's no cleanup! Just remember to keep the packet small enough to easily take off the grill.

2	medium yellow summer squash, sliced
2	medium sweet red peppers, sliced
1	large sweet onion, halved and sliced
2	Tbsp. olive oil
2	garlic cloves, minced
1	tsp. sugar
1/4	tsp. salt
1/4	tsp. pepper

GRILLED SUMMER SQUASH

MAKEOVER PECAN CORN PUDDING

1. In a large bowl, combine all ingredients. Divide between two double thicknesses of heavy-duty foil (about 18 in. x 12 in.). Fold foil around vegetable mixture and seal tightly.

2. Grill, covered, over medium heat for 10-15 minutes or until vegetables are tender. Open foil carefully to allow steam to escape.

Nutrition Facts: 3/4 cup equals 124 calories, 7 g fat (1 g saturated fat), 0 cholesterol, 159 mg sodium, 15 g carbohydrate, 3 g fiber, 3 g protein. **Diabetic Exchanges:** 2 vegetable, 1-1/2 fat.

Makeover Pecan Corn Pudding M

PREP: 20 min. **BAKE:** 45 min. **YIELD:** 12 servings

SHARON BESHOAR • MONTROSE, COLORADO

Every bit as rich and creamy as my original recipe, this magical makeover has crunchy pecans, loads of cheese and a touch of jalapeno. It's destined to become a favorite!

    1 cup yellow cornmeal
  3/4 tsp. baking soda
    3 eggs
1-1/4 cups buttermilk
  3/4 cup reduced-fat butter, melted
    2 cans (one 14-3/4 oz., one 8-1/4 oz.) cream-style corn
    2 cups frozen corn
    2 medium onions, chopped

1-1/2 cups (6 oz.) shredded sharp reduced-fat cheddar cheese
    4 jalapeno peppers, seeded and chopped
  1/2 cup chopped pecans, toasted

1. In a large bowl, combine cornmeal and baking soda. In a small bowl, whisk the eggs, buttermilk and butter. Add cream-style corn, corn and onions. Stir into dry ingredients just until moistened.

2. Pour half the mixture into a 13-in. x 9-in. baking dish coated with cooking spray. Sprinkle with cheese and jalapenos. Top with remaining batter; sprinkle with pecans.

3. Bake, uncovered, at 350° for 45-50 minutes or until a thermometer reads 160°. Serve warm.

Editor's Note: This recipe was tested with Land O'Lakes light stick butter. We recommend wearing disposable gloves when cutting hot peppers. Avoid touching your face.

Nutrition Facts: 3/4 cup equals 269 calories, 15 g fat (6 g saturated fat), 79 mg cholesterol, 465 mg sodium, 31 g carbohydrate, 3 g fiber, 10 g protein.

> White cornmeal is more popular in the South and yellow cornmeal is preferred in the North. Blue cornmeal can be found in specialty stores. All three types can be used interchangeably in recipes.

Heirloom Tomato Tart M

PREP: 20 min. **BAKE:** 10 min. + cooling
YIELD: 6 servings

KATHRYN CONRAD • MILWAUKEE, WISCONSIN

What a great way to showcase a summer harvest of tomatoes! Refrigerated pie pastry makes this pretty side dish easy, while goat cheese and fresh basil lend Mediterranean flair.

- 2 tsp. cornmeal, *divided*
- 1 refrigerated pie pastry

Cooking spray

- 3 Tbsp. shredded Asiago cheese
- 3 large heirloom tomatoes, cut into 1/4-in. slices
- 3 small heirloom tomatoes, cut into 1/4-in. slices
- 1 Tbsp. extra-virgin olive oil
- 1/2 tsp. coarsely ground pepper
- 1/4 tsp. salt
- 1/4 cup crumbled goat or feta cheese

Fresh basil leaves, optional

1. Sprinkle a large baking sheet with 1 tsp. cornmeal.

2. On a lightly floured surface, roll pastry into a 12-in. circle; transfer to prepared pan. Spritz dough with cooking spray. Sprinkle with remaining cornmeal, pressing cornmeal gently into dough. Prick thoroughly with a fork. Sprinkle with Asiago cheese.

3. Bake at 450° for 10 minutes or until lightly browned. Cool on a wire rack.

4. Layer with tomatoes. Drizzle with olive oil; sprinkle with pepper and salt. Top with goat cheese; garnish with basil if desired. Serve immediately.

Nutrition Facts: 1 slice equals 236 calories, 14 g fat (6 g saturated fat), 16 mg cholesterol, 270 mg sodium, 24 g carbohydrate, 2 g fiber, 4 g protein.

Grilled Cherry Tomatoes S C M

PREP/TOTAL TIME: 20 min. **YIELD:** 6 servings

LUCY MEYRING • WALDEN, COLORADO

This tasty side dish is seasoned with herbs and butter. Just tuck the foil packet beside any meat you happen to be grilling and you'll have dinner in a flash. Just be sure to cut the foil large enough to fold the edges over twice to seal.

    2 pints cherry tomatoes, halved
    2 garlic cloves, minced
  1/2 tsp. dried oregano
    3 Tbsp. butter

1. Place tomatoes on a double thickness of heavy-duty foil (about 24 in. x 12 in.). In a small skillet, saute garlic and oregano in butter for 2 minutes. Pour over tomatoes. Fold foil around tomatoes and seal tightly.

2. Grill, covered, over medium heat for 4-5 minutes on each side or until tomatoes are heated through. Open foil carefully to allow steam to escape.

Nutrition Facts: 1/2 cup equals 73 calories, 6 g fat (4 g saturated fat), 15 mg cholesterol, 67 mg sodium, 5 g carbohydrate, 1 g fiber, 1 g protein. **Diabetic Exchanges:** 1 vegetable, 1 fat.

Italian Vegetable Medley C M

PREP/TOTAL TIME: 15 min. **YIELD:** 4 servings

MARGARET WILSON • SUN CITY, CALIFORNIA

Round out a variety of menus with this veggie side that lends a delicious pop of color. If you can, use leftover vegetables. People are always surprised at how easy this dish is because the flavors are so bold and the colors are so bright! Feel free to experiment with different vegetable blends if you'd like.

    1 pkg. (16 oz.) frozen broccoli stir-fry vegetable blend
    2 Tbsp. grated Parmesan cheese
    1 Tbsp. seasoned bread crumbs
  1/8 tsp. garlic powder
  1/8 tsp. seasoned salt
  1/8 tsp. pepper
    1 Tbsp. butter

1. Microwave vegetables according to package directions. Meanwhile, in a small bowl, combine the cheese, bread crumbs, garlic powder, seasoned salt and pepper.

2. Drain vegetables; stir in butter. Sprinkle with cheese mixture.

Nutrition Facts: 3/4 cup equals 79 calories, 4 g fat (2 g saturated fat), 10 mg cholesterol, 174 mg sodium, 7 g carbohydrate, 2 g fiber, 2 g protein. **Diabetic Exchanges:** 1 vegetable, 1/2 fat.

Grilled Potatoes F M

PREP: 10 min. **GRILL:** 30 min. **YIELD:** 4 servings

JENA COFFEY • ROCK HILL, MISSOURI

Need a simple sidekick to serve with steaks or chops? Try these bursting-with-flavor potatoes. I make the recipe for picnics and potlucks. The potatoes turn out tender and well-seasoned. Plus, there's one less pot to wash.

    1 Tbsp. olive oil
    2 garlic cloves, minced
  1/2 tsp. dried basil
  1/4 tsp. salt
  1/8 tsp. pepper
    3 medium baking potatoes, peeled and cut into 1-in. cubes

1. In a large bowl, combine the first five ingredients. Add potatoes; toss to coat. Spoon onto a greased double thickness of heavy-duty foil (about 18 in. square).

2. Fold foil around potato mixture and seal tightly. Grill, covered, over medium heat for 30-35 minutes or until potatoes are tender, turning once. Open foil carefully to allow steam to escape.

Nutrition Facts: 3/4 cup equals 126 calories, 3 g fat (trace saturated fat), 0 cholesterol, 151 mg sodium, 22 g carbohydrate, 2 g fiber, 2 g protein. **Diabetic Exchanges:** 1-1/2 starch, 1/2 fat.

> To make **seasoned bread crumbs,** simply break slices of dried bread into pieces and process in a blender or food processor until you have fine crumbs. Then season the crumbs to accommodate your family's tastes.

GRILLED POTATOES

Agave Roasted Parsnips S M

PREP: 20 min. BAKE: 20 min. YIELD: 6 servings

KATHLEEN THORSON • MENOMONEE FALLS, WISCONSIN

Deliciously sweet and aromatic, this dinner addition nicely spices up any traditional meal.

6	medium parsnips, peeled and sliced
2	medium carrots, sliced
1	medium leek (white portion only), sliced
3	garlic cloves, sliced
2	Tbsp. butter, melted
2	Tbsp. agave nectar *or* honey
1/8	tsp. ground cinnamon
1/8	tsp. ground nutmeg

1. Divide the parsnips, carrots, leek and garlic between two 15-in. x 10-in. x 1-in. baking pans coated with cooking spray. Combine the remaining ingredients; drizzle over vegetables and toss to coat.

2. Bake, uncovered, at 425° for 20-25 minutes or until tender, stirring occasionally.

Nutrition Facts: 3/4 cup equals 187 calories, 4 g fat (3 g saturated fat), 10 mg cholesterol, 60 mg sodium, 37 g carbohydrate, 7 g fiber, 3 g protein.

Makeover Streusel-Topped Sweet Potatoes S M

PREP: 25 min. BAKE: 20 min. YIELD: 12 servings

TAMRA DUNCAN • LINCOLN, ARKANSAS

People really do eat with their eyes, and no one ever misses the fat and calories in this dish when they see how yummy and attractive this lightened-up version is.

6	medium sweet potatoes
1/2	cup reduced-fat butter, melted
3	eggs, lightly beaten
1/4	cup unsweetened apple juice
1-1/2	tsp. vanilla extract

TOPPING:

3/4	cup packed brown sugar
1/2	cup flaked coconut
1/2	cup chopped pecans
1/4	cup reduced-fat butter, melted

1. Scrub and pierce sweet potatoes; place on a microwave-safe plate. Microwave, uncovered, on high for 15-18 minutes or until tender, turning once.

2. When cool enough to handle, cut each potato in half lengthwise. Scoop out the pulp, leaving thin shells. In a large bowl, mash the pulp with butter and eggs. Stir in juice and vanilla. Carefully spoon into potato shells.

3. Divide between two 13-in. x 9-in. baking dishes coated with cooking spray. Combine the topping ingredients; spoon over potatoes. Bake at 375° for 20-25 minutes or until a thermometer reads 160°.

Editor's Note: This recipe was tested with Land O'Lakes light stick butter in a 1,100-watt microwave.

Nutrition Facts: 1 stuffed potato half equals 260 calories, 12 g fat (5 g saturated fat), 68 mg cholesterol, 136 mg sodium, 37 g carbohydrate, 3 g fiber, 4 g protein.

AGAVE ROASTED PARSNIPS

MAKEOVER STREUSEL-TOPPED SWEET POTATOES

MAKEOVER SAUSAGE PECAN STUFFING

Lemon-Garlic Green Beans F S C M

PREP/TOTAL TIME: 20 min. **YIELD:** 4 servings

GAIL ORSILLO • LYNNWOOD, WASHINGTON

My brother made this light stovetop dish as his contribution to Christmas dinner one year. We liked it so much that it became a mainstay in our house.

- 1 lb. fresh green beans, trimmed and cut into 2-in. pieces
- 2 tsp. olive oil
- 2 garlic cloves, minced
- 1 Tbsp. lemon juice
- 1/4 tsp. coarsely ground pepper
- 1/8 tsp. salt

1. In a large nonstick skillet coated with cooking spray, cook and stir beans in oil over medium heat for 10-13 minutes or until crisp-tender.

2. Add garlic; cook 1 minute longer. Stir in the lemon juice, pepper and salt.

Nutrition Facts: 3/4 cup equals 54 calories, 2 g fat (trace saturated fat), 0 cholesterol, 80 mg sodium, 8 g carbohydrate, 3 g fiber, 2 g protein. **Diabetic Exchanges:** 1 vegetable, 1/2 fat.

Makeover Sausage Pecan Stuffing

PREP: 30 min. **BAKE:** 30 min. **YIELD:** 12 servings

HEALTHY COOKING TEST KITCHEN

Nothing about this moist, pecan-topped stuffing says "light." The fabulous flavors are sure to captivate friends and family.

- 1 lb. lean ground turkey
- 2 cups sliced fresh mushrooms
- 2 celery ribs, chopped
- 1 medium onion, chopped
- 1 tsp. fennel seed
- 1/4 tsp. cayenne pepper
- 1/8 tsp. ground nutmeg
- 3 garlic cloves, minced
- 1 loaf (16 oz.) day-old white bread, cubed
- 1 large tart apple, chopped
- 2 tsp. rubbed sage
- 1-1/2 tsp. salt
- 1-1/2 tsp. poultry seasoning
- 1/2 tsp. pepper
- 2 eggs
- 1 cup reduced-sodium chicken broth
- 1/2 cup chopped pecans

1. In a Dutch oven, cook the turkey, mushrooms, celery, onion, fennel seed, cayenne and nutmeg over medium heat until turkey is no longer pink. Add garlic; cook 1 minute longer. Drain.

2. Transfer to a large bowl. Add the bread, apple, sage, salt, poultry seasoning and pepper. Whisk eggs and broth; pour over bread mixture and toss to coat. Transfer to a 13-in. x 9-in. baking dish coated with cooking spray; sprinkle with pecans.

3. Bake, uncovered, at 350° for 30-35 minutes or until top is lightly browned and a thermometer reads 160°.

Nutrition Facts: 3/4 cup equals 226 calories, 9 g fat (2 g saturated fat), 65 mg cholesterol, 654 mg sodium, 25 g carbohydrate, 2 g fiber, 12 g protein. **Diabetic Exchanges:** 1-1/2 starch, 1 lean meat, 1 fat.

DUCHESS POTATOES

Duchess Potatoes M

PREP: 35 min. **BAKE:** 20 min. **YIELD:** 6 servings

HEALTHY COOKING TEST KITCHEN

Potatoes always make for cozy, comfort-food flavor. Here, they're also presented in an attractive package!

2	lbs. russet potatoes, peeled and quartered
3	egg yolks
3	Tbsp. fat-free milk
2	Tbsp. butter
1	tsp. salt
1/4	tsp. pepper
1/8	tsp. ground nutmeg
1	egg, lightly beaten

1. Place potatoes in a large saucepan and cover with water. Bring to a boil. Reduce heat; cover and simmer for 15-20 minutes or until tender. Drain.

2. Over very low heat, stir potatoes for 1-2 minutes or until steam has evaporated. Press through a potato ricer or strainer into a large bowl. Stir in the egg yolks, milk, butter, salt, pepper and nutmeg.

3. Using a pastry bag or heavy-duty resealable plastic bag and a large star tip, pipe potatoes into six mounds on a parchment paper-lined baking sheet. Brush with beaten egg. Bake at 400° for 20-25 minutes or until golden brown.

Nutrition Facts: 1 serving equals 158 calories, 7 g fat (3 g saturated fat), 134 mg cholesterol, 437 mg sodium, 21 g carbohydrate, 1 g fiber, 4 g protein.

Easy Baked Mushrooms S C M

PREP/TOTAL TIME: 30 min. **YIELD:** 4 servings

DENISE DIPACE • MEDFORD, NEW JERSEY

This savory side couldn't be much easier or more delicious. The mushrooms are wonderful alongside steaks and other beefy dishes as well as pork entrees.

1 lb. medium fresh mushrooms, halved
2 Tbsp. olive oil
1/4 cup seasoned bread crumbs
1/4 tsp. garlic powder
1/4 tsp. pepper
Fresh parsley, optional

1. Place mushrooms on a baking sheet. Drizzle with oil; toss to coat. In a bowl, combine the bread crumbs, garlic powder and pepper; sprinkle over mushrooms.

2. Bake, uncovered, at 425° for 18-20 minutes or until lightly browned. Garnish with parsley if desired.

Nutrition Facts: 3/4 cup equals 116 calories, 8 g fat (1 g saturated fat), 0 cholesterol, 112 mg sodium, 10 g carbohydrate, 2 g fiber, 4 g protein.

Rice with Chilies 'n' Veggies F M

PREP: 15 min. **COOK:** 30 min. **YIELD:** 8 servings

KATE SELNER • LINO LAKES, MINNESOTA

I turned to a particular dish when I wanted to use peppers I grew in my garden. I promptly rewrote the recipe to include several other fresh veggies, and this was the result. It's a perfect complement for just about anything.

1/3 cup fat-free milk
1/2 cup frozen corn, thawed
1 cup uncooked long grain rice
2 tsp. canola oil
1 large onion, chopped
1 medium zucchini, chopped
1 medium sweet red pepper, chopped
1/2 cup chopped carrot
1 can (4 oz.) chopped green chilies
1 garlic clove, minced
2 cups vegetable broth
1 bay leaf

1. Place milk and corn in a food processor. Cover and process until smooth; set aside. In a large skillet, saute rice in oil for 5-6 minutes or until lightly browned. Stir in the onion, zucchini, red pepper, carrot, chilies, garlic and corn mixture; cook for 1 minute.

2. Stir in broth and bay leaf; bring to a boil. Reduce heat; cover and simmer for 20 minutes or until rice is tender and liquid is absorbed. Discard bay leaf.

Nutrition Facts: 3/4 cup equals 134 calories, 2 g fat (trace saturated fat), trace cholesterol, 318 mg sodium, 27 g carbohydrate, 2 g fiber, 4 g protein. **Diabetic Exchanges:** 1 starch, 1 vegetable, 1/2 fat.

Garlic and Artichoke Roasted Potatoes M

PREP: 15 min. **BAKE:** 35 min. **YIELD:** 10 servings

MARIE RIZZIO • INTERLOCHEN, MICHIGAN

I like to put this simple dish into the oven to roast with the main course. The artichokes give it a gourmet appeal.

2-1/2 lbs. medium red potatoes, cut into 1-1/2-in. cubes
2 pkg. (8 oz. *each*) frozen artichoke hearts
8 garlic cloves, halved
3 Tbsp. olive oil
3/4 tsp. salt
1/4 tsp. pepper
1/4 cup lemon juice
2 Tbsp. minced fresh parsley
1 tsp. grated lemon peel

1. Place the potatoes, artichokes and garlic in a 15-in. x 10-in. x 1-in. baking pan coated with cooking spray. Combine the oil, salt and pepper; drizzle over vegetables and toss to coat.

2. Bake, uncovered, at 425° for 35-40 minutes or until tender, stirring occasionally. Transfer to a large bowl. Add lemon juice, parsley and lemon peel; toss to coat. Serve warm.

Nutrition Facts: 3/4 cup equals 143 calories, 4 g fat (1 g saturated fat), 0 cholesterol, 209 mg sodium, 24 g carbohydrate, 4 g fiber, 4 g protein. **Diabetic Exchanges:** 1 starch, 1 vegetable, 1 fat.

Need grated lemon peel? **Citrus peel** can be grated into fine shreds with a Microplane grater. For slightly thicker shreds, use the zester; for long, continuous strips, use a stripper. Remove only the colored portion of the peel.

GARLIC AND ARTICHOKE ROASTED POTATOES

Sweet Corn and Potato Gratin M

PREP: 30 min. **BAKE:** 45 min. + standing
YIELD: 8 servings

JENNIFER OLSON • PLEASANTON, CALIFORNIA

This tasty side combines the distinctive flavors of garlic and onion, and kids love the crispy topping, too!

- 1 medium onion, thinly sliced
- 2 Tbsp. butter
- 2 Tbsp. all-purpose flour
- 2 garlic cloves, minced
- 1 tsp. salt
- 1/2 tsp. pepper
- 1 cup whole milk
- 2 lbs. medium Yukon Gold potatoes, peeled and cut into 1/8-in. slices
- 2 cups fresh or frozen corn
- 1 can (8-1/4 oz.) cream-style corn
- 3/4 cup panko (Japanese) bread crumbs
- 1 Tbsp. butter, melted

1. In a large saucepan, saute onion in butter until tender. Stir in the flour, garlic, salt and pepper until blended; gradually add milk. Stir in potatoes. Bring to a boil. Reduce heat; cook and stir for 8-10 minutes or until potatoes are crisp-tender.

2. Stir in corn and cream-style corn. Transfer to an 8-in. square baking dish coated with cooking spray.

3. In a small bowl, combine bread crumbs and butter; sprinkle over potatoes. Bake at 350° for 45-50 minutes or until golden brown and potatoes are tender. Let stand for 10 minutes before serving.

Nutrition Facts: 3/4 cup equals 213 calories, 6 g fat (3 g saturated fat), 14 mg cholesterol, 452 mg sodium, 37 g carbohydrate, 3 g fiber, 5 g protein. **Diabetic Exchanges:** 2 starch, 1 fat.

Mustard Brussels Sprouts M

PREP/TOTAL TIME: 25 min. **YIELD:** 5 servings

LEAH-ANNE SCHNAPP • GROVE CITY, OHIO

Mustard boosts the green flavor of the sprouts in this versatile favorite. It's lovely served with chicken or pork chops.

- 1-1/2 lb. fresh brussels sprouts
- 1/3 cup chopped shallots
- 1 Tbsp. butter
- 1/3 cup half-and-half cream
- 4-1/2 tsp. Dijon mustard
- 1/4 tsp. salt
- 1/4 tsp. dried tarragon
- 1/8 tsp. pepper
- 2 Tbsp. grated Parmesan cheese

1. Cut an "X" in the core of each brussels sprout. In a Dutch oven, bring 1/2 in. of water to a boil. Add brussels sprouts; cover and cook for 8-12 minutes or until tender.

2. Meanwhile, in a small saucepan, saute shallots in butter until tender. Add the cream, mustard, salt, tarragon and pepper. Cook and stir over medium heat until thickened. Drain sprouts; add cream mixture and heat through. Sprinkle with cheese.

SWEET CORN AND POTATO GRATIN

MUSTARD BRUSSELS SPROUTS

ASIAN BROCCOLI AND MUSHROOMS

Nutrition Facts: 1 cup equals 121 calories, 5 g fat (3 g saturated fat), 16 mg cholesterol, 316 mg sodium, 16 g carbohydrate, 5 g fiber, 6 g protein. **Diabetic Exchanges:** 2 vegetable, 1 fat.

Garlic-Chive Baked Fries M

PREP: 15 min. **BAKE:** 20 min. **YIELD:** 4 servings

HEALTHY COOKING TEST KITCHEN

Yes, you do want fries with that—especially these crispy, golden-brown fries, full of garlic flavor and just a little bit of heat from pepper.

- 4 medium russet potatoes
- 1 Tbsp. olive oil
- 4 tsp. dried minced chives
- 1/2 tsp. salt
- 1/2 tsp. garlic powder
- 1/4 tsp. pepper

1. Cut potatoes into 1/4-in. julienned strips. Rinse well and pat dry. Drizzle with oil and sprinkle with chives, salt, garlic powder and pepper; toss to coat. Arrange in a single layer on two 15-in. x 10-in. x 1-in. baking pans coated with cooking spray.

2. Bake at 450° for 20-25 minutes or until lightly browned, turning once.

Nutrition Facts: 1 serving equals 200 calories, 4 g fat (1 g saturated fat), 0 cholesterol, 308 mg sodium, 39 g carbohydrate, 4 g fiber, 5 g protein.

Asian Broccoli And Mushrooms C M

PREP/TOTAL TIME: 20 min. **YIELD:** 4 servings

CARLA PEELE • MULLINS, SOUTH CAROLINA

What a great way to round out a meal! These vegetables are easily dressed up with sesame oil and ground chipotle pepper.

- 3 cups fresh broccoli florets
- 4 oz. sliced baby portobello mushrooms
- 1 Tbsp. olive oil
- 1 tsp. sesame oil
- 1 tsp. butter
- 3 garlic cloves, minced
- 1/2 tsp. seasoning blend
- 1/4 tsp. ground chipotle pepper

1. In a large nonstick skillet coated with cooking spray, saute broccoli and mushrooms in olive oil, sesame oil and butter until tender. Add the garlic, seasoning blend and ground chipotle pepper; cook 1 minute longer.

Editor's Note: This recipe was tested with Nature's Seasons seasoning blend by Morton. It can be found in the spice aisle of your grocery store.

Nutrition Facts: 3/4 cup equals 74 calories, 6 g fat (1 g saturated fat), 3 mg cholesterol, 214 mg sodium, 5 g carbohydrate, 2 g fiber, 3 g protein. **Diabetic Exchanges:** 1 vegetable, 1 fat.

Herb-Topped Stuffed Tomatoes M

PREP/TOTAL TIME: 25 min. YIELD: 4 servings

MARY RELYEA • CANASTOTA, NEW YORK

This simple treatment perfectly complements the fresh taste of tomatoes. Serve it as a side dish to any entree or as a fresh summer appetizer.

- 1 cup chopped onion
- 1 garlic clove, minced
- 1 Tbsp. plus 2 tsp. butter, *divided*
- 1/4 cup plus 1 Tbsp. seasoned bread crumbs
- 2 Tbsp. grated Parmesan cheese
- 4 large tomatoes, halved
- 1 Tbsp. chopped fresh basil
- 1 Tbsp. minced fresh parsley

1. In a small skillet, saute onion and garlic in 1 Tbsp. butter until tender. Melt remaining butter. In a small bowl, combine the onion mixture, bread crumbs, cheese and melted butter. Spoon 2 Tbsp. onto each tomato half.

2. Place on a baking sheet. Broil 8 in. from the heat for 4-5 minutes or until lightly browned. Sprinkle with basil and parsley. Serve immediately.

Nutrition Facts: 2 halves equals 143 calories, 7 g fat (4 g saturated fat), 15 mg cholesterol, 247 mg sodium, 19 g carbohydrate, 3 g fiber, 4 g protein.

Sweet & Sour Carrots F M

PREP/TOTAL TIME: 30 min. YIELD: 6 servings

DELORES ROMYN • STRATTON, ONTARIO

I wanted to try serving carrots differently, and everyone raved over these. You'll love the combination of flavors and colors.

- 1 lb. medium carrots, cut into 1-in. slices
- 1 medium green pepper, cut into 1-in. chunks
- 1 can (20 oz.) unsweetened pineapple chunks, undrained
- 1/4 cup sugar
- 1 Tbsp. cornstarch
- 1/2 tsp. salt
- 2 Tbsp. cider vinegar
- 2 Tbsp. reduced-sodium soy sauce

1. Place 1 in. of water and carrots in a large saucepan. Bring to a boil. Reduce heat; cover and simmer for 7-9 minutes or until crisp-tender. Add green pepper. Cover and cook 3 minutes longer or until tender. Drain and set aside.

2. Drain pineapple, reserving juice; add enough water to the juice to measure 3/4 cup. Set pineapple aside. In a large saucepan, combine the sugar, cornstarch and salt. Stir in the pineapple juice mixture, vinegar and soy sauce until smooth. Bring to a boil. Cook and stir for 2 minutes or until thickened and bubbly. Stir in the reserved carrots and pineapple; heat through.

Nutrition Facts: 2/3 cup equals 123 calories, trace fat (trace saturated fat), 0 cholesterol, 459 mg sodium, 30 g carbohydrate, 3 g fiber, 1 g protein. **Diabetic Exchanges:** 1 vegetable, 1 fruit, 1/2 starch.

Sesame Green Beans F C M

PREP/TOTAL TIME: 30 min. YIELD: 6 servings

NOELLE MYERS • GRAND FORKS, NORTH DAKOTA

With Asian-inspired flair, this treatment for green beans is simply wonderful with light dishes such as marinated and grilled salmon. The colors also make it nice for holiday menus, so it's one dish you'll turn to all year long.

- 1 lb. fresh green beans, trimmed
- 1 medium sweet red pepper, julienned
- 1 Tbsp. sesame seeds
- 1 Tbsp. rice vinegar
- 1 Tbsp. sesame oil
- 1 Tbsp. reduced-sodium soy sauce
- 1/4 tsp. salt
- 1/4 tsp. pepper

1. Place beans and red pepper in a 15-in. x 10-in. x 1-in. baking pan coated with cooking spray. Combine the remaining ingredients. Drizzle over vegetables; stir to coat.

2. Bake, uncovered, at 425° for 20-25 minutes or until beans are tender, stirring once.

Nutrition Facts: 2/3 cup equals 55 calories, 3 g fat (trace saturated fat), 0 cholesterol, 205 mg sodium, 7 g carbohydrate, 3 g fiber, 2 g protein. **Diabetic Exchanges:** 1 vegetable, 1/2 fat.

SESAME GREEN BEANS

Honey Mustard Carrots F M

PREP/TOTAL TIME: 20 min. YIELD: 10 servings

TRISHA KRUSE • EAGLE, IDAHO

Wonderful color and flavor make fresh carrots a standout side dish for almost any entree you serve to loved ones.

    4 pkg. (10 oz. *each*) julienned carrots
  1/2 cup honey
  1/4 cup honey mustard
    4 tsp. butter
  1/2 tsp. salt

1. Place 1 in. of water in a large saucepan; add carrots. Bring to a boil. Reduce heat; cover and simmer for 3-4 minutes or until crisp-tender. Drain and set aside.

2. In a small saucepan, combine the remaining ingredients. Bring to a boil; cook and stir for 2-3 minutes or until slightly thickened. Pour over carrots; heat through.

Nutrition Facts: 1/2 cup equals 125 calories, 2 g fat (1 g saturated fat), 4 mg cholesterol, 259 mg sodium, 28 g carbohydrate, 3 g fiber, 1 g protein. **Diabetic Exchanges:** 2 vegetable, 1 starch, 1/2 fat.

Spiced Rhubarb Sauce F C

PREP: 20 min. COOK: 50 min. YIELD: 2-1/2 cups

KARA HAWKE • POLK, PENNSYLVANIA

Served here with pork chops, this unique sauce adds bold flavor to just about any cut of pork. The sweet-savory relish-like sauce is also a perfect complement to any variety of roasted, baked or grilled poultry.

    4 cups chopped fresh or frozen rhubarb, thawed
    2 large onions, chopped

    1 medium green pepper, chopped
  3/4 cup packed brown sugar
  3/4 cup cider vinegar
  1/4 cup reduced-sodium soy sauce
    2 tsp. steak seasoning
    1 garlic clove, minced
  1/2 tsp. celery seed
  1/2 tsp. ground coriander
  1/2 tsp. ground cinnamon
  1/2 tsp. ground allspice

1. In a large saucepan, combine all ingredients. Bring to a boil. Reduce heat; simmer, uncovered, for 45-50 minutes or until thickened. Serve warm with chicken or pork. Refrigerate leftovers.

Editor's Note: If using frozen rhubarb, measure rhubarb while still frozen, then thaw completely. Drain in a colander, but do not press liquid out. This recipe was tested with McCormick's Montreal Steak Seasoning. Look for it in the spice aisle.

Nutrition Facts: 2 Tbsp. equals 48 calories, trace fat (trace saturated fat), 0 cholesterol, 195 mg sodium, 11 g carbohydrate, 1 g fiber, 1 g protein. **Diabetic Exchange:** 1 starch.

Quinoa Pilaf M

PREP/TOTAL TIME: 30 min. YIELD: 4 servings

SONYA FOX • PEYTON, COLORADO

I created this recipe after tasting quinoa at a local restaurant. I really enjoy rice pilaf, but I don't usually have time to make it. This quick-cooking side is a tasty alternative.

    1 medium onion, chopped
    1 medium carrot, finely chopped
    1 tsp. olive oil
    1 garlic clove, minced
    1 can (14-1/2 oz.) reduced-sodium chicken broth or vegetable broth
  1/4 cup water
  1/4 tsp. salt
    1 cup quinoa, rinsed

HONEY MUSTARD CARROTS

QUINOA PILAF

1. In a small nonstick saucepan coated with cooking spray, cook onion and carrot in oil for 2-3 minutes or until crisp-tender. Add garlic; cook 1 minute longer. Stir in the broth, water and salt; bring to a boil.

2. Stir in quinoa; return to a boil. Reduce heat; cover and simmer for 12-15 minutes or until liquid is absorbed. Remove from the heat; let stand for 5 minutes. Fluff with a fork.

Editor's Note: Look for quinoa in the cereal, rice or organic food aisle.

Nutrition Facts: 3/4 cup equals 198 calories, 4 g fat (trace saturated fat), 0 cholesterol, 434 mg sodium, 35 g carbohydrate, 4 g fiber, 8 g protein. **Diabetic Exchanges:** 2 starch, 1/2 fat.

Feta Zucchini Pancakes S C M

PREP/TOTAL TIME: 25 min. YIELD: 8 pancakes

DIANA JOHNSON • AUBURN, WASHINGTON

Fun and flavorful, these rustic veggie pancakes make a wonderfully versatile side dish. They're also a great solution for what to do with all your extra zucchini!

1	cup shredded zucchini
1/4	cup panko (Japanese) bread crumbs
2	green onions, chopped
1	egg
3	Tbsp. minced fresh parsley
1	Tbsp. snipped fresh dill
1	garlic clove, minced
1/4	cup crumbled feta cheese
3	tsp. olive oil, *divided*

1. In a sieve or colander, drain zucchini, squeezing to remove excess liquid. Pat dry. In a small bowl, combine the zucchini, bread crumbs, onions, egg, parsley, dill, garlic and cheese.

2. Heat 1-1/2 tsp. oil in a large nonstick skillet over medium-low heat. Drop the batter by heaping tablespoonfuls into oil; press lightly to flatten. Fry in batches until golden brown on both sides, using remaining oil as needed.

Nutrition Facts: 2 pancakes equals 91 calories, 6 g fat (2 g saturated fat), 57 mg cholesterol, 104 mg sodium, 5 g carbohydrate, 1 g fiber, 4 g protein. **Diabetic Exchanges:** 1 fat, 1/2 starch.

When a recipe calls for green onions, it can be easier and faster to cut them with a **kitchen scissors** than with a knife. If the recipe calls for quite a few, grab a bunch of onions at one time and snip away. This saves time washing a cutting board, too.

Herbed Fennel and Onion C

PREP/TOTAL TIME: 30 min. **YIELD:** 3 servings

MEGHANN MINTON • PORTLAND, OREGON

Wondering what to do with those fennel bulbs you brought home from the market? Try them in this aromatic and savory side dish that's so rich, no one will guess it's healthy. Vinegar adds a slight tang.

- 1 large sweet onion, halved and sliced
- 1 medium fennel bulb, halved and cut into 1/2-in. slices
- 1 Tbsp. olive oil
- 1 cup reduced-sodium chicken broth
- 1 Tbsp. minced fresh sage *or* 1 tsp. dried sage leaves
- 2 tsp. minced fresh rosemary *or* 1/2 tsp. dried rosemary, crushed
- 2 tsp. balsamic vinegar
- 1/4 tsp. salt
- 1/4 tsp. pepper

1. In a large skillet, saute onion and fennel in oil until crisp-tender. Add the broth, sage and rosemary. Bring to a boil; cook until broth is evaporated.

2. Remove from the heat; stir in the vinegar, salt and pepper.

Nutrition Facts: 1/2 cup equals 109 calories, 5 g fat (1 g saturated fat), 0 cholesterol, 437 mg sodium, 15 g carbohydrate, 3 g fiber, 3 g protein. **Diabetic Exchanges:** 2 vegetable, 1 fat.

Pear Cranberry Sauce F S

PREP: 10 min. **COOK:** 15 min. + chilling **YIELD:** 3 cups

DEB WILLIAMS • PEORIA, ARIZONA

Pears and ginger turn a classic side into something spectacular. Best of all, it calls for just a moment of hands-on work.

- 1 pkg. (12 oz.) fresh or frozen cranberries
- 2 medium pears, peeled and cubed
- 1 cup sugar
- 3/4 cup water
- 1 to 2 tsp. minced fresh gingerroot
- 1/4 tsp. ground cinnamon
- 1/8 tsp. salt

1. In a large saucepan, combine all ingredients. Cook over medium heat until berries pop, about 15 minutes. Transfer to a small bowl; refrigerate until chilled.

Nutrition Facts: 1/4 cup equals 94 calories, trace fat (trace saturated fat), 0 cholesterol, 25 mg sodium, 24 g carbohydrate, 2 g fiber, trace protein. **Diabetic Exchanges:** 1 starch, 1/2 fruit.

Parsnips & Turnips Au Gratin

PREP: 20 min. **BAKE:** 15 min. **YIELD:** 8 servings

PRISCILLA GILBERT • INDIAN HARBOUR BEACH, FLORIDA

This is a delicious variation on au gratin that features something besides potatoes. I sometimes substitute rutabaga for the turnips. It's a well-guarded recipe in my collection. Until now that is!

1-1/2 lbs. parsnips, peeled and sliced
1-1/4 lbs. turnips, peeled and sliced
1 can (10-3/4 oz.) reduced-fat reduced-sodium condensed cream of celery soup, undiluted
1 cup fat-free milk
1/2 tsp. pepper
1 cup (4 oz.) shredded sharp cheddar cheese
1/2 cup panko (Japanese) bread crumbs
1 Tbsp. butter, melted

1. Place parsnips and turnips in a large saucepan; cover with water. Bring to a boil. Reduce heat; simmer, uncovered, for 5-7 minutes or until crisp-tender.

2. Meanwhile, in a small saucepan, combine the soup, milk and pepper. Bring to a boil; remove from the heat. Stir in cheese until melted.

3. Drain vegetables; transfer to an 11-in. x 7-in. baking dish coated with cooking spray. Pour sauce over vegetables.

4. Combine the bread crumbs and butter; sprinkle over the top. Bake, uncovered, at 400° for 15-20 minutes or until vegetables are tender and crumbs are golden brown.

Nutrition Facts: 3/4 cup equals 189 calories, 7 g fat (4 g saturated fat), 21 mg cholesterol, 309 mg sodium, 27 g carbohydrate, 4 g fiber, 7 g protein. **Diabetic Exchanges:** 1 starch, 1 high-fat meat, 1 vegetable.

Lemon Beans With Prosciutto C

PREP/TOTAL TIME: 25 min. YIELD: 6 servings

LORI WIESE • HUMBOLDT, MINNESOTA

There's nothing ordinary about these green beans. Prosciutto and white wine make them decadent and special.

8 thin slices prosciutto *or* deli ham, julienned
2 tsp. olive oil
1/2 cup white wine *or* reduced-sodium chicken broth
1/4 cup lemon juice
2 Tbsp. butter
1-1/2 lbs. fresh green beans, trimmed

1. In a large nonstick skillet coated with cooking spray, cook prosciutto in oil over medium heat until crisp. Remove to paper towels with a slotted spoon; drain.

2. In the same skillet, combine the wine, lemon juice and butter. Bring to a boil. Reduce heat; simmer, uncovered, for 5-6 minutes or until sauce is reduced by half.

3. Meanwhile, place beans in a large saucepan and cover with water. Bring to a boil. Cover and cook for 4-7 minutes or until crisp-tender; drain. Add beans to skillet; toss to coat. Sprinkle with prosciutto just before serving.

Nutrition Facts: 3/4 cup equals 127 calories, 8 g fat (3 g saturated fat), 27 mg cholesterol, 397 mg sodium, 8 g carbohydrate, 3 g fiber, 7 g protein. **Diabetic Exchanges:** 1 lean meat, 1 vegetable, 1 fat.

Easy Sauteed Spinach F C M

PREP/TOTAL TIME: 20 min. YIELD: 4 servings

HEALTHY COOKING TEST KITCHEN

Here's a light, lively side to complement almost any entree you put on the table. A little Test Kitchen know-how helps to dress up everyday spinach with garlic, onion, a lick of sherry and a sprinkling of pine nuts.

1 small onion, finely chopped
1 garlic clove, minced
2 pkg. (6 oz. *each*) fresh baby spinach
3 Tbsp. sherry *or* reduced-sodium chicken broth
1/4 tsp. salt
1/8 tsp. pepper
1 Tbsp. pine nuts

1. In a large nonstick skillet coated with cooking spray, saute onion until tender. Add garlic; cook 1 minute longer. Stir in the spinach, sherry, salt and pepper; cook and stir for 4-5 minutes or until spinach is wilted. Sprinkle with pine nuts.

Nutrition Facts: 1/2 cup equals 47 calories, 1 g fat (trace saturated fat), 0 cholesterol, 216 mg sodium, 5 g carbohydrate, 2 g fiber, 3 g protein. **Diabetic Exchange:** 1 vegetable.

Minced garlic that you can buy, garlic that's been finely chopped by hand and garlic that's been put through a press can all be used **interchangeably in recipes.** Choose whichever is easiest and most convenient for you.

EASY SAUTEED SPINACH

Broccoli-Cauliflower Cheese Bake C M

PREP: 35 min. **BAKE:** 20 min. **YIELD:** 16 servings

JENN TIDWELL • FAIR OAKS, CALIFORNIA

Creamy mozzarella and Swiss cheeses create the base for these tasty veggies, while a hint of cayenne pepper gives them a kick guests will adore.

7	cups fresh cauliflowerets
6	cups fresh broccoli florets
3	Tbsp. butter
1/3	cup all-purpose flour
1-1/2	tsp. spicy brown mustard
3/4	tsp. salt
1/4	tsp. ground nutmeg
1/4	tsp. cayenne pepper
1/4	tsp. pepper
3-3/4	cups fat-free milk
1-1/2	cups (6 oz.) shredded part-skim mozzarella cheese, *divided*
1-1/2	cups (6 oz.) shredded Swiss cheese, *divided*

1. Place cauliflower and broccoli in a Dutch oven; add 1 in. of water. Bring to a boil. Reduce heat; cover and simmer for 3-5 minutes or until crisp-tender. Drain; transfer to a 13-in. x 9-in. baking dish coated with cooking spray.

2. In small saucepan, melt butter. Stir in the flour, mustard, salt, nutmeg, cayenne and pepper until smooth; gradually add milk. Bring to a boil; cook and stir for 1-2 minutes or until thickened.

3. Stir in 1-1/4 cups each mozzarella and Swiss cheeses until melted. Pour over vegetables. Bake, uncovered, at 400° for 15-20 minutes or until bubbly. Sprinkle with remaining cheeses. Bake 5 minutes longer or until golden brown.

Nutrition Facts: 3/4 cup equals 132 calories, 7 g fat (4 g saturated fat), 22 mg cholesterol, 252 mg sodium, 9 g carbohydrate, 2 g fiber, 9 g protein. **Diabetic Exchanges:** 1 high-fat meat, 1 vegetable.

BROCCOLI-CAULIFLOWER CHEESE BAKE

Moist Turkey Sausage Stuffing

PREP: 20 min. **COOK:** 20 min.
YIELD: 16 servings (2/3 cup each)

PRISCILLA GILBERT • INDIAN HARBOUR BEACH, FLORIDA

With tangy apricots and turkey sausage, this stuffing is a terrific mix of sweet and savory.

1	pkg. (19-1/2 oz.) Italian turkey sausage links, casings removed
4	celery ribs, chopped
1	large onion, chopped
1-1/2	cups chopped dried apricots
1/4	cup minced fresh parsley
1	Tbsp. minced fresh sage *or* 1 tsp. dried sage
1	tsp. poultry seasoning
1/4	tsp. pepper
3	tsp. sodium-free chicken bouillon granules
3-1/4	cups boiling water
1	pkg. (14 oz.) crushed corn bread stuffing
1	cup fresh *or* frozen cranberries, chopped

1. In a Dutch oven, cook the turkey sausage, celery and onion over medium heat until meat is no longer pink and vegetables are tender; drain. Stir in the apricots, parsley, sage, poultry seasoning and pepper; cook 3 minutes longer.

2. Dissolve bouillon in boiling water; stir into sausage mixture. Stir in corn bread stuffing; cook and stir until liquid is absorbed. Gently stir in cranberries; heat through.

Editor's Note: This recipe makes enough stuffing to stuff a 14-lb. turkey. Bake until a meat thermometer reads 180° for turkey and 165° for stuffing.

Nutrition Facts: 2/3 cup equals 205 calories, 5 g fat (1 g saturated fat), 21 mg cholesterol, 540 mg sodium, 32 g carbohydrate, 3 g fiber, 9 g protein. **Diabetic Exchanges:** 2 starch, 1 lean meat.

Cheddar Mashed Potatoes M

PREP: 35 min. **COOK:** 10 min.
YIELD: 12 servings (3/4 cup each)

CONNIE BOLL • CHILTON, WISCONSIN

A sweet potato added to the usual Yukon Golds gives these cheesy potatoes a slightly sweet flavor and nice rich color. No one will believe they're lighter.

3-3/4	lbs. Yukon Gold potatoes, peeled and cubed
1	large sweet potato, peeled and cubed
6	garlic cloves, halved
1	cup (8 oz.) reduced-fat sour cream
1	tsp. minced fresh thyme *or* 1/4 tsp. dried thyme
1-1/2	tsp. salt
1/2	tsp. pepper
2	cups (8 oz.) shredded reduced-fat cheddar cheese, *divided*

1. Place potatoes and garlic in a large saucepan and cover with water. Bring to a boil. Reduce heat; cover and cook for 10-15 minutes or until potatoes are tender. Drain.

GRILLED ITALIAN EGGPLANT SLICES

2. In a large bowl, mash potatoes. Stir in the sour cream, thyme, salt, pepper and 1 cup cheese. Transfer to a 3-qt. baking dish coated with cooking spray. Sprinkle with remaining cheese. Bake, uncovered, at 350° for 10-15 minutes or until heated through.

Nutrition Facts: 3/4 cup equals 179 calories, 6 g fat (4 g saturated fat), 19 mg cholesterol, 434 mg sodium, 25 g carbohydrate, 2 g fiber, 8 g protein. **Diabetic Exchanges:** 1-1/2 starch, 1 medium-fat meat.

Grilled Italian Eggplant Slices S C M

PREP/TOTAL TIME: 25 min. YIELD: 5 servings

THERESA LASALLE • MIDLOTHIAN, VIRGINIA

What a fabulous way to dress up eggplant! Piled high with herbs, cheese and fresh tomatoes, this fail-proof, grilled side nicely matches a variety of main dishes.

1/4	cup shredded Parmesan cheese
3	Tbsp. lemon juice
2	Tbsp. minced fresh basil
5	tsp. olive oil
3	garlic cloves, minced
1	tsp. minced fresh oregano
1	large eggplant, cut into 10 slices
10	slices tomato
1/2	cup shredded part-skim mozzarella cheese

1. In a small bowl, combine the first six ingredients.

2. Grill eggplant, covered, over medium heat for 3 minutes. Turn slices; spoon Parmesan mixture onto each. Top with tomato; sprinkle with mozzarella cheese. Grill, covered, 2-3 minutes longer or until cheese is melted.

Nutrition Facts: 2 eggplant slices equals 134 calories, 8 g fat (3 g saturated fat), 9 mg cholesterol, 129 mg sodium, 12 g carbohydrate, 4 g fiber, 6 g protein. **Diabetic Exchanges:** 2 vegetable, 1 medium-fat meat.

Makeover Scalloped Pineapple M

PREP: 10 min. BAKE: 50 min. YIELD: 12 servings

NANCY BROWN • DAHINDA, ILLINOIS

This sweet holiday side dish is buttery, sugary and big on pineapple flavor, but now it's not nearly as bad for you as the original. In fact, you might not want to wait on the holidays.

1/2	cup butter, softened
1-1/2	cups sugar
4	eggs
4	egg whites
2	cans (20 oz. *each*) unsweetened crushed pineapple, undrained
1/2	cup fat-free milk
8	cups cubed bread

1. In a large bowl, beat butter and sugar until crumbly, about 2 minutes. Add eggs and egg whites, one at a time, beating well after each addition. Stir in pineapple and milk; add bread cubes and toss to coat.

2. Transfer to a 13-in. x 9-in. baking dish coated with cooking spray. Bake, uncovered, at 350° for 50-55 minutes or until bread cubes are lightly browned. Serve warm. Refrigerate leftovers.

Nutrition Facts: 1 cup equals 316 calories, 10 g fat (5 g saturated fat), 91 mg cholesterol, 260 mg sodium, 52 g carbohydrate, 1 g fiber, 6 g protein.

Creamed Garden Potatoes and Peas M

PREP/TOTAL TIME: 25 min. YIELD: 12 servings

JANE UPHOFF • CUNNINGHAM, KANSAS

New potatoes and colorful peas are treated to a creamy sauce for this special side dish.

- 2 lbs. small red potatoes, quartered
- 3 cups fresh or frozen peas
- 1 cup water
- 2 Tbsp. chopped onion
- 2 Tbsp. butter
- 3 Tbsp. plus 1 tsp. all-purpose flour
- 1-1/2 tsp. salt
- 1/4 tsp. pepper
- 2 cups 2% milk
- 1 cup half-and-half cream

1. Place potatoes in a large saucepan and cover with water. Bring to a boil. Reduce heat; cover and simmer for 8-12 minutes or until tender. Drain.

2. Meanwhile, place peas and water in a small saucepan. Bring to a boil. Reduce heat; cover and simmer for 3-5 minutes or until tender. Drain.

3. In a large saucepan, saute onion in butter until tender. Stir in the flour, salt and pepper until blended; gradually add milk and cream. Bring to a boil; cook and stir for 2 minutes or until thickened. Stir in potatoes and peas; heat through.

Nutrition Facts: 2/3 cup equals 156 calories, 5 g fat (3 g saturated fat), 18 mg cholesterol, 345 mg sodium, 22 g carbohydrate, 3 g fiber, 6 g protein. **Diabetic Exchanges:** 1-1/2 starch, 1 fat.

Sesame Snap Peas S C M

PREP/TOTAL TIME: 15 min. YIELD: 8 servings

HEALTHY COOKING TEST KITCHEN

With their fresh taste, these colorful snap peas make an ideal partner for most any entree. Sweet red pepper adds a pop to this sesame-infused favorite.

- 1-1/2 lbs. fresh sugar snap peas
- 1 small sweet red pepper, chopped
- 2 Tbsp. butter
- 1 Tbsp. sesame seeds, toasted
- 1 Tbsp. reduced-sodium soy sauce
- 1/8 tsp. pepper

1. In a large nonstick skillet, saute peas and red pepper in butter until crisp-tender. Stir in the remaining ingredients; heat through.

Nutrition Facts: 3/4 cup equals 70 calories, 4 g fat (2 g saturated fat), 8 mg cholesterol, 105 mg sodium, 7 g carbohydrate, 3 g fiber, 3 g protein. **Diabetic Exchanges:** 1 vegetable, 1/2 fat.

Dijon Veggies With Couscous M

PREP: 20 min. BAKE: 20 min. YIELD: 6 servings

JULIANA DUMITRU • FAIRVIEW PARK, OHIO

Coated in a tangy Dijon sauce, these tasty veggies and fluffy couscous make for a delightful side.

- 1/2 lb. medium fresh mushrooms, quartered
- 1 medium zucchini, halved lengthwise and cut into 1/4-in. slices
- 1 medium sweet red pepper, cut into 1-in. pieces

1/4	cup dry red wine *or* reduced-sodium chicken broth
3	Tbsp. Dijon mustard
2	Tbsp. olive oil
2	garlic cloves, minced
1	tsp. prepared horseradish
1/2	tsp. salt
1/4	tsp. pepper
1	cup water
1	cup uncooked couscous

1. Place an 18-in. x 12-in. piece of heavy-duty foil on a large baking sheet; set aside.

2. In a large bowl, combine the mushrooms, zucchini and red pepper. Combine the wine, mustard, oil, garlic, horseradish, salt and pepper; drizzle over vegetables. Toss to coat; transfer to baking sheet. Top with a second large piece of foil. Bring edges of foil pieces together; crimp to seal, forming a large packet.

3. Bake at 350° for 20-25 minutes or until vegetables are tender.

4. Meanwhile, in a small saucepan, bring water to a boil. Stir in couscous. Remove from the heat; cover and let stand for 5-10 minutes or until water is absorbed. Fluff with a fork. Transfer couscous and vegetables to a large serving bowl; toss to combine.

Nutrition Facts: 1 cup equals 182 calories, 5 g fat (1 g saturated fat), 0 cholesterol, 388 mg sodium, 29 g carbohydrate, 3 g fiber, 6 g protein. **Diabetic Exchanges:** 1-1/2 starch, 1 vegetable, 1 fat.

Garden Risotto F

PREP: 20 min. COOK: 25 min. YIELD: 8 servings

KENDRA DOSS • KANSAS CITY, MISSOURI

With asparagus, spinach and peas, this simple dish adds spectacular flavor and lots of health benefits from green veggies. Add some Parmesan cheese, and you've got one delectable delight!

1/2	lb. fresh asparagus, trimmed and cut into 3/4-in. pieces
4-1/2	cups reduced-sodium chicken broth
1	medium onion, chopped
2	tsp. olive oil
1-1/2	cups uncooked arborio rice
1/2	cup dry white wine *or* additional reduced-sodium chicken broth
1/2	tsp. salt
1/4	tsp. pepper
3	cups fresh baby spinach
1	cup frozen peas
1/4	cup grated Parmesan cheese

1. Place asparagus in a steamer basket; place in a small saucepan over 1 in. of water. Bring to a boil; cover and steam for 2-3 minutes or until crisp-tender. Set aside.

2. Meanwhile, in a small saucepan, heat broth and keep warm. In a large nonstick skillet coated with cooking spray, saute onion in oil until tender. Add rice; cook and stir for 2-3 minutes. Reduce heat; stir in the wine, salt and pepper. Cook and stir until all of the liquid is absorbed.

3. Add heated broth, 1/2 cup at a time, stirring constantly. Allow the liquid to absorb between additions. Cook just until risotto is creamy and rice is almost tender. (Cooking time is about 20 minutes.)

4. Add the spinach, peas, cheese and reserved asparagus; cook and stir until heated through. Serve immediately.

Nutrition Facts: 3/4 cup equals 203 calories, 2 g fat (1 g saturated fat), 2 mg cholesterol, 539 mg sodium, 36 g carbohydrate, 2 g fiber, 7 g protein.

GARDEN RISOTTO

DIJON VEGGIES WITH COUSCOUS

Sweet Potato Delight F S M

PREP: 25 min. **BAKE:** 30 min. **YIELD:** 10 servings

MARLENE KROLL • CHICAGO, ILLINOIS

My family wouldn't dream of a Thanksgiving dinner without this side dish, but it's great anytime—I serve it once a month. The fluffy texture and subtle orange flavor make it a standout.

4	large sweet potatoes, peeled and quartered
1/2	cup orange marmalade
1/2	cup orange juice
1/4	cup packed brown sugar
1/2	tsp. almond extract
3	egg whites
1/4	cup slivered almonds

1. Place sweet potatoes in a Dutch oven; cover with water. Bring to a boil. Reduce heat; cover and cook for 15-20 minutes or just until tender. Drain potatoes; place in a large bowl and mash. Stir in the orange marmalade, orange juice, brown sugar and extract. Cool slightly.

2. In a small bowl, beat egg whites until stiff peaks form. Fold into sweet potato mixture. Transfer to a 2-1/2-qt. baking dish coated with cooking spray. Sprinkle with almonds. Bake, uncovered, at 350° for 30-35 minutes or until a thermometer reads 160°.

Nutrition Facts: 3/4 cup equals 174 calories, 1 g fat (trace saturated fat), 0 cholesterol, 36 mg sodium, 38 g carbohydrate, 3 g fiber, 3 g protein. **Diabetic Exchange:** 2 starch.

SWEET POTATO DELIGHT

Nutty Gingered Carrots C M

PREP/TOTAL TIME: 30 min. **YIELD:** 6 servings

JEANNE HOLT • SAINT PAUL, MINNESOTA

My mother makes a delicious carrot and onion side dish, but it calls for a whole stick of butter. My lighter version uses only 1 tablespoon and relies on some lively Asian flavors to make up the difference.

1	large onion, chopped
2	tsp. canola oil
1	tsp. minced fresh gingerroot
6	large carrots, sliced
2/3	cup orange juice
1	Tbsp. butter
2	tsp. honey
1	tsp. grated orange peel
1/4	tsp. salt
1/8	tsp. pepper
1/4	cup chopped walnuts, toasted
1	Tbsp. minced fresh parsley

1. In a large skillet, saute onion in oil until tender. Add ginger; cook 1 minute longer. Stir in the carrots, orange juice, butter, honey, orange peel, salt and pepper.

2. Bring to a boil. Reduce heat; cover and simmer for 12-15 minutes or until carrots are tender. Stir in walnuts and sprinkle with parsley.

Nutrition Facts: 2/3 cup equals 122 calories, 7 g fat (2 g saturated fat), 5 mg cholesterol, 163 mg sodium, 15 g carbohydrate, 3 g fiber, 2 g protein. **Diabetic Exchanges:** 2 vegetable, 1 fat.

Summer Squash Medley F C M

PREP/TOTAL TIME: 25 min. **YIELD:** 6 servings

JENNIFER LEIGHTY • WEST SALEM, OHIO

This dish is fantastic as a side, but you can also add some cooked turkey sausage and serve it over rice for a meal.

1	large sweet onion, chopped
1	medium yellow summer squash, chopped
1	large green pepper, chopped
1	Tbsp. olive oil
1	garlic clove, minced
2	large tomatoes, seeded and chopped
1-1/2	tsp. Italian seasoning
1	tsp. salt
1/2	tsp. pepper
1/8	tsp. crushed red pepper flakes, optional

1. In a large nonstick skillet, saute the onion, squash and green pepper in oil until crisp-tender. Add the garlic; cook 1 minute longer. Stir in the tomatoes, Italian seasoning, salt, pepper and pepper flakes if desired; heat through.

Nutrition Facts: 2/3 cup equals 61 calories, 3 g fat (trace saturated fat), 0 cholesterol, 403 mg sodium, 9 g carbohydrate, 2 g fiber, 2 g protein. **Diabetic Exchanges:** 2 vegetable, 1/2 fat.

Green Rice Pilaf

PREP: 35 min. **BAKE:** 15 min. **YIELD:** 6 servings

SHERRI MELOTIK • OAK CREEK, WISCONSIN

With its mild heat and full flavors, this side pairs well with a variety of entrees, especially Southwest or Mexican specialties.

1/4	cup finely chopped onion
1	Tbsp. canola oil
1	cup uncooked long grain rice
1	can (14-1/2 oz.) reduced-sodium chicken broth
1	can (4 oz.) chopped green chilies
1	jalapeno pepper, seeded and chopped
1/2	tsp. ground cumin
1/4	tsp. garlic powder
1/8	tsp. salt
1/2	cup shredded part-skim mozzarella cheese
1/2	cup minced fresh cilantro

1. In a large saucepan, saute onion in oil until tender. Add the rice; cook and stir for 2 minutes or until lightly browned.

2. Add broth, chilies, jalapeno, cumin, garlic powder and salt. Bring to a boil. Reduce heat; cover and simmer for 12-15 minutes or until liquid is absorbed.

3. Stir in cheese and cilantro. Transfer to a 1-1/2-qt. baking dish coated with cooking spray. Cover and bake at 375° for 14-16 minutes or until rice is tender.

Editor's Note: When cutting hot peppers, disposable gloves are recommended. Avoid touching your face.

Nutrition Facts: 2/3 cup equals 171 calories, 4 g fat (1 g saturated fat), 5 mg cholesterol, 368 mg sodium, 27 g carbohydrate, 1 g fiber, 6 g protein. **Diabetic Exchanges:** 1-1/2 starch, 1 fat.

Thai-Style Green Beans

PREP/TOTAL TIME: 20 min. **YIELD:** 2 servings

CANDACE MCMENAMIN • LEXINGTON, SOUTH CAROLINA

Two for Thai, anyone? Peanut butter and soy and hoisin sauces flavor this quick and fabulous treatment for green beans.

1	Tbsp. reduced-sodium soy sauce
1	Tbsp. hoisin sauce
1	Tbsp. creamy peanut butter
1/8	tsp. crushed red pepper flakes
1	Tbsp. chopped shallot
1	tsp. minced fresh gingerroot
1	Tbsp. canola oil
1/2	lb. fresh green beans, trimmed

Minced fresh cilantro and chopped dry roasted peanuts, optional

1. In a small bowl, combine the soy sauce, hoisin sauce, peanut butter and red pepper flakes; set aside.

2. In a small skillet, saute shallot and ginger in oil over medium heat for 2 minutes or until crisp-tender. Add green beans; cook and stir for 3 minutes or until crisp-tender. Add reserved sauce; toss to coat. Sprinkle with cilantro and peanuts if desired.

Nutrition Facts: 1 serving (calculated without peanuts) equals 168 calories, 12 g fat (1 g saturated fat), trace cholesterol, 476 mg sodium, 14 g carbohydrate, 4 g fiber, 5 g protein.

RICE AND BARLEY PILAF

Rice and Barley Pilaf

PREP: 20 min. COOK: 1 hour YIELD: 6 servings

BARB TEMPLIN • NORWOOD, MINNESOTA

*With a trio of whole grains, wild and brown rice and barley,
this is packed with nutrition. Add half-and-half and Parmesan
cheese, and you've got one satisfying pilaf!*

3	cups reduced-sodium chicken broth
1/4	cup uncooked wild rice
1/4	cup medium pearl barley
1/4	cup uncooked brown rice
1/2	lb. baby portobello mushrooms, chopped
1	small onion, chopped
1	celery rib, finely chopped
1	Tbsp. butter
1	Tbsp. olive oil
3	garlic cloves, minced
1/4	cup grated Parmesan cheese
1/4	cup half-and-half cream
1/8	tsp. pepper

1. In a large saucepan, combine broth and wild rice.
Bring to a boil. Reduce heat; cover and simmer for 10
minutes. Stir in barley and brown rice; cover and
simmer for 40-45 minutes or until grains are tender
and the liquid is absorbed.

2. Meanwhile, in a large nonstick skillet, saute the
mushrooms, onion and celery in butter and oil until
tender. Add garlic; cook 1 minute longer. Stir in the
rice mixture, cheese, cream and pepper; heat through.

Nutrition Facts: 1/2 cup equals 176 calories, 7 g fat (3 g
saturated fat), 13 mg cholesterol, 363 mg sodium, 23 g
carbohydrate, 3 g fiber, 7 g protein. **Diabetic Exchanges:**
1-1/2 fat, 1 starch, 1 vegetable.

Colorful Broccoli Rice

PREP/TOTAL TIME: 15 min. YIELD: 2 servings

GALE LALMOND • DEERING, NEW HAMPSHIRE

*I found this microwave-quick and simple recipe years ago. It's
a favorite with many meals. Its buttery flavor and color make it
a great side for all kinds of meats.*

2/3	cup water
2	tsp. butter
1	tsp. reduced-sodium chicken bouillon granules
1	cup coarsely chopped fresh broccoli
1/2	cup instant brown rice
2	Tbsp. chopped sweet red pepper

1. In a small microwave-safe bowl, combine the
water, butter and bouillon. Cover and microwave on
high for 1-2 minutes; stir until blended. Add the
broccoli, rice and red pepper. Cover and cook 6-7
minutes longer or until broccoli is crisp-tender.

2. Let stand for 5 minutes. Fluff with a fork.

Editor's Note: This recipe was tested in a 1,100-watt
microwave.

Nutrition Facts: 1/2 cup equals 136 calories, 5 g fat (2 g
saturated fat), 10 mg cholesterol, 197 mg sodium, 20 g
carbohydrate, 2 g fiber, 3 g protein. **Diabetic Exchanges:**
1 starch, 1 fat.

Green Beans Provencale F C M

PREP/TOTAL TIME: 30 min. YIELD: 5 servings

PAULA WHARTON • EL PASO, TEXAS

*Garlic, tomatoes and olive oil are wonderful ingredients often
found in Southern French cooking. In this dish, they
complement the green beans perfectly.*

- 1 lb. fresh green beans, trimmed and cut into 2-in. pieces
- 4 green onions, sliced
- 2 Tbsp. minced shallot
- 4 garlic cloves, minced
- 2 tsp. minced fresh rosemary *or* 1/2 tsp. dried rosemary, crushed
- 1 Tbsp. olive oil
- 1-1/2 cups grape tomatoes, halved
- 2 Tbsp. minced fresh *or* 2 tsp. dried basil
- 1/2 tsp. salt
- 1/4 tsp. pepper

1. Place beans in a steamer basket; place in a large saucepan over 1 in. of water. Bring to a boil; cover and steam for 4-5 minutes or until crisp-tender.

2. Meanwhile, in a large skillet, saute the onions, shallot, garlic and rosemary in oil until vegetables are tender. Add the green beans, tomatoes, basil, salt and pepper; saute 2-3 minutes longer or until heated through.

Nutrition Facts: 3/4 cup equals 70 calories, 3 g fat (trace saturated fat), 0 cholesterol, 248 mg sodium, 10 g carbohydrate, 4 g fiber, 2 g protein. **Diabetic Exchanges:** 2 vegetable, 1/2 fat.

Spinach and Mushrooms C

PREP/TOTAL TIME: 30 min. **YIELD:** 4 servings

JOYCE FREY • MACKSVILLE, KANSAS

Warm sauteed spinach and fresh, garlicky mushrooms make for a perfect combination that tastes terrific and looks impressive, too. Water chestnuts add a fun crunch.

- 1/2 lb. sliced fresh mushrooms
- 1 Tbsp. butter
- 1 Tbsp. olive oil
- 2 garlic cloves, minced
- 1/4 cup dry white wine *or* reduced-sodium chicken broth
- 3 Tbsp. Worcestershire sauce
- 1 tsp. minced fresh oregano *or* 1/2 tsp. dried oregano
- 3/4 tsp. minced fresh thyme *or* 1/4 tsp. dried thyme
- 1/4 tsp. salt
- 1/4 tsp. pepper
- 1 pkg. (6 oz.) fresh baby spinach
- 1 can (8 oz.) sliced water chestnuts, drained

1. In a large nonstick skillet, saute mushrooms in butter and oil until tender. Add garlic; cook 1 minute longer. Stir in the wine, Worcestershire sauce and seasonings. Bring to a boil. Reduce heat; simmer, uncovered, for 7-8 minutes or until liquid has evaporated.

2. Add spinach; cook and stir until wilted. Stir in water chestnuts; heat through.

Nutrition Facts: 3/4 cup equals 124 calories, 7 g fat (2 g saturated fat), 8 mg cholesterol, 334 mg sodium, 14 g carbohydrate, 3 g fiber, 4 g protein. **Diabetic Exchanges:** 2 vegetable, 1 fat.

Grilled-to-Perfection Potatoes F M

PREP: 15 min. **GRILL:** 40 min. **YIELD:** 8 servings

ROBIN JOHNSON • RATTAN, OKLAHOMA

This is a wonderful side for any grilled meat. If you don't want to do both with the grill, just place the potatoes in a dish, cover and bake in the oven.

- 8 medium potatoes, cut into 1-in. cubes
- 2 large onions, halved and sliced
- 2 Tbsp. butter, melted
- 2 garlic cloves, minced
- 1/2 tsp. garlic salt
- 1/2 tsp. pepper

Reduced-fat sour cream, optional

1. In a large bowl, combine the first six ingredients. Divide mixture between two double thicknesses of heavy-duty foil (about 18 in. square). Fold foil around mixture and seal tightly.

2. Grill, covered, over medium heat for 40-45 minutes or until potatoes are tender, turning once. Open foil carefully to allow steam to escape. Serve with sour cream if desired.

Nutrition Facts: 3/4 cup (calculated without sour cream) equals 210 calories, 3 g fat (2 g saturated fat), 8 mg cholesterol, 148 mg sodium, 42 g carbohydrate, 4 g fiber, 5 g protein.

GRILLED-TO-PERFECTION POTATOES

Makeover Crunchy Sweet Potato Casserole S M

PREP: 20 min. **BAKE:** 35 min. **YIELD:** 6 servings

SCOTT JONES • TULSA, OKLAHOMA

This makeover recipe keeps all the crunchy texture from toasty pecans and all the healthy sweet potatoes, but half of the saturated fat and cholesterol of the original.

1-3/4 lbs. sweet potatoes (about 3 large), peeled and cut into 2-in. pieces
1/3 cup fat-free milk
1/4 cup egg substitute
1 egg
2 Tbsp. butter, softened
1 tsp. lemon extract
1 tsp. vanilla extract

TOPPING:
2/3 cup packed brown sugar
1/4 cup all-purpose flour
1 Tbsp. cold butter
1/4 cup chopped pecans

1. Place sweet potatoes in a large saucepan and cover with water. Bring to a boil. Reduce heat; cover and cook for 15-20 minutes or until tender. Drain and place in a food processor. Add the milk, egg substitute, egg, butter and extracts; cover and process until smooth. Pour into a 1-1/2-qt. baking dish coated with cooking spray.

2. In a small bowl, combine brown sugar and flour. Cut in butter until crumbly. Sprinkle over sweet potato mixture; sprinkle with pecans. Bake, uncovered, at 350° for 35-40 minutes or until a thermometer reads 160°.

Nutrition Facts: 1/2 cup equals 306 calories, 10 g fat (4 g saturated fat), 51 mg cholesterol, 114 mg sodium, 49 g carbohydrate, 3 g fiber, 5 g protein.

Five-Fruit Compote F S C

PREP/TOTAL TIME: 20 min. **YIELD:** 6 cups

JEAN ECOS • HARTLAND, WISCONSIN

Bring out the best in your Easter ham or lamb with this fast fruit compote.

2 cans (15 oz. *each*) sliced peaches in juice, drained
1 can (20 oz.) unsweetened pineapple chunks, drained
1 can (20 oz.) reduced-sugar cherry pie filling
2/3 cup chopped dried apricots
2/3 cup chopped dates
1/2 tsp. ground cinnamon
Fully cooked lean ham

1. In a large saucepan, combine the first six ingredients. Bring to a boil. Reduce heat; simmer, uncovered, for 5 minutes, stirring frequently. Serve warm with ham.

Nutrition Facts: 1/4 cup (calculated without ham) equals 57 calories, trace fat (trace saturated fat), 0 cholesterol, 5 mg sodium, 14 g carbohydrate, 2 g fiber, 1 g protein. **Diabetic Exchange:** 1 starch.

Makeover Creamed Corn M

PREP/TOTAL TIME: 30 min. **YIELD:** 10 servings

TRISHA KRUSE • EAGLE, IDAHO

This scrumptious makeover has all the rich feel and flavor of my original, but it only has about half the calories and about a third of the saturated fat.

4 pkg. (10 oz. *each*) frozen corn, thawed
1 cup half-and-half cream
1/4 cup butter, cubed

MAKEOVER CRUNCHY SWEET POTATO CASSEROLE

MAKEOVER CREAMED CORN

BROCCOLI CHEESE BAKE

2 Tbsp. sugar
2 tsp. salt
1/2 tsp. pepper
1/3 cup all-purpose flour
2 cups fat-free milk
1/2 cup shredded sharp cheddar cheese

1. In a Dutch oven, combine the first six ingredients. Cook and stir over medium heat for 8-10 minutes or until heated through.

2. Combine flour and milk until smooth. Stir into pan. Bring to a boil; cook and stir for 2 minutes or until thickened. Remove from the heat; stir in cheese until melted.

Nutrition Facts: 3/4 cup equals 234 calories, 9 g fat (6 g saturated fat), 31 mg cholesterol, 574 mg sodium, 33 g carbohydrate, 3 g fiber, 8 g protein.

Broccoli Cheese Bake C M

PREP: 20 min. BAKE: 25 min. YIELD: 4 servings

DEBORAH PATRAUCHUK • SICAMOUS, BRITISH COLUMBIA

Here's a handy and versatile side that's creamy, colorful and bursting with flavor and nutrition. Pair it with almost any entree for a terrific meal.

1-3/4 cups fresh broccoli florets
1 Tbsp. cornstarch
1/8 tsp. salt
Dash pepper
2/3 cup fat-free milk
1 medium onion, chopped
1/2 cup shredded cheddar cheese
2 Tbsp. grated Parmesan cheese

1. Place 1 in. of water and broccoli in a small saucepan; bring to a boil. Reduce heat; cover and simmer for 3-5 minutes or until crisp-tender.

2. Meanwhile, in a small saucepan, combine the cornstarch, salt, pepper and milk until smooth. Bring to a boil; cook and stir for 1 minute or until thickened. Stir in onion and cheddar cheese until cheese is melted. Drain broccoli; stir into cheese sauce.

3. Transfer to a 1-qt. baking dish coated with cooking spray. Sprinkle with Parmesan cheese. Cover and bake at 350° for 25-30 minutes or until vegetables are tender.

Nutrition Facts: 3/4 cup equals 106 calories, 5 g fat (3 g saturated fat), 18 mg cholesterol, 224 mg sodium, 10 g carbohydrate, 2 g fiber, 7 g protein. **Diabetic Exchanges:** 1 high-fat meat, 1 vegetable.

MOM'S SLOPPY TACOS

PORK 'N' POTATO SKILLET

MEXICAN BEANS AND RICE

One of the hardest parts about maintaining a healthy diet is cooking light on busy nights. The next time the kitchen clock is ticking, turn to this chapter of quick family favorites. Each dish is ready in 30 minutes—or less!

Pork 'n' Potato Skillet

PREP/TOTAL TIME: 20 min. **YIELD:** 4 servings

MARY TALLMAN • ARBOR VITAE, WISCONSIN

This scrumptious skillet dinner makes the ideal hurry-up entree for a hungry family. Round out the meal with steamed vegetables or a rustic green salad.

    4 boneless pork loin chops (1 in. thick and
       4 oz. *each*)
1/4 tsp. pepper
    1 Tbsp. olive oil
    4 medium red potatoes, thinly sliced
    1 medium onion, sliced
    1 tsp. dried oregano
    1 cup chicken broth
1/2 cup diced roasted sweet red peppers

1. Sprinkle pork chops with pepper. In a large skillet, cook chops in oil over medium heat for 2-3 minutes on each side or until chops are lightly browned; drain. Remove and keep warm.

2. In the same skillet, saute the potatoes, onion and oregano for 6-8 minutes or until potatoes are almost tender. Stir in broth and red peppers; bring to a boil.

3. Top with pork chops. Reduce heat; cover and simmer for 4-6 minutes or until a thermometer reads 145°, stirring occasionally. Let stand 5 minutes before serving.

Nutrition Facts: 1 serving (prepared with reduced-sodium broth) equals 292 calories, 10 g fat (3 g saturated fat), 55 mg cholesterol, 297 mg sodium, 24 g carbohydrate, 3 g fiber, 26 g protein. **Diabetic Exchanges:** 3 lean meat, 1 starch, 1 vegetable.

Sweet Mustard Salmon C

PREP/TOTAL TIME: 25 min. **YIELD:** 4 servings

CORTNEY CLAESON • SPOKANE, WASHINGTON

Lemon juice, mustard and brown sugar add something special to this salmon dish.

    4 salmon fillets (6 oz. *each*)
    2 Tbsp. lemon juice
    3 Tbsp. yellow mustard
1/4 cup packed brown sugar

1. Place salmon on a 15-in. x 10-in. x 1-in. baking pan coated with cooking spray. Drizzle with lemon juice; brush with mustard. Sprinkle with brown sugar.

2. Bake, uncovered, at 375° for 12-15 minutes or until fish flakes easily with a fork.

Nutrition Facts: 1 fillet equals 326 calories, 16 g fat (3 g saturated fat), 85 mg cholesterol, 218 mg sodium, 15 g carbohydrate, trace fiber, 29 g protein. **Diabetic Exchanges:** 4 lean meat, 1-1/2 fat, 1 starch.

Mexican Beans and Rice M

PREP/TOTAL TIME: 30 min. **YIELD:** 4 servings

LORRAINE CALAND • THUNDER BAY, ONTARIO

This skillet supper is terrific for a cold or rainy day. It's easy, comforting and really fills the tummy. Sometimes I switch up pinto beans for kidney beans or white rice for brown.

       2 celery ribs, chopped
       1 medium green pepper, chopped
       1 medium onion, chopped
       1 Tbsp. canola oil
       1 can (28 oz.) diced tomatoes, undrained
       1 can (16 oz.) kidney beans, rinsed and drained
       2 cups cooked brown rice
       2 tsp. Worcestershire sauce
1-1/2 tsp. chili powder
   1/4 tsp. pepper
   1/4 cup shredded cheddar cheese
   1/4 cup reduced-fat sour cream
       2 green onions, chopped

1. In a large nonstick skillet, saute the celery, green pepper and onion in oil until tender.

2. Stir in the tomatoes, beans, rice, Worcestershire sauce, chili powder and pepper. Bring to a boil. Reduce heat; cover and simmer for 7-9 minutes or until heated through. Top with cheese, sour cream and green onions.

Nutrition Facts: 1-1/2 cups equals 354 calories, 8 g fat (3 g saturated fat), 13 mg cholesterol, 549 mg sodium, 58 g carbohydrate, 12 g fiber, 15 g protein.

Chicken Stir-Fry with Noodles

PREP/TOTAL TIME: 30 min. **YIELD:** 4 servings

BEVERLY NORRIS • EVANSTON, WYOMING

This nutritious meal is fast-fixing, filling and full of flavor and vitamins. Feel free to garnish individual servings with a sprinkling of chopped pecans or green onions. For extra crunch, try adding a handful of chow mein noodles right before serving.

- 8 oz. uncooked whole wheat spaghetti
- 1 head bok choy (16 oz.)
- 1 lb. boneless skinless chicken breasts, cubed
- 2 Tbsp. canola oil, *divided*
- 1 celery rib, sliced
- 1/2 cup chopped green pepper
- 1/2 cup chopped sweet red pepper
- 1/3 cup chopped onion
- 6 Tbsp. reduced-sodium teriyaki sauce

1. Cook the spaghetti according to package. directions; drain.

2. Meanwhile, cut off and discard root end of bok choy. Cut leaves from stalks; coarsely chop and set aside. Cut stalks into 1-in. pieces.

3. In a large skillet or wok, stir-fry chicken in 1 Tbsp. oil until no longer pink. Remove and keep warm.

4. Stir-fry the bok choy stalks, celery, peppers and onion in remaining oil for 4 minutes. Add bok choy leaves; stir-fry 2-4 minutes longer or until vegetables are crisp-tender. Stir in teriyaki sauce. Add chicken and spaghetti; heat through.

Nutrition Facts: 1-1/2 cups equals 434 calories, 11 g fat (1 g saturated fat), 63 mg cholesterol, 623 mg sodium, 53 g carbohydrate, 9 g fiber, 35 g protein.

Honey Chicken Stir-Fry

PREP/TOTAL TIME: 30 min. **YIELD:** 4 servings

CAROLINE SPERRY • ALLENTOWN, MICHIGAN

I'm a new mom, and my schedule is very dependent upon our young son. So I like meals that can be ready in as little time as possible. This all-in-one stir-fry with a hint of sweetness from honey is a big time-saver.

- 1 lb. boneless skinless chicken breasts, cut into 1-in. pieces
- 1 garlic clove, minced
- 3 tsp. olive oil, *divided*
- 3 Tbsp. honey
- 2 Tbsp. reduced-sodium soy sauce
- 1/8 tsp. salt
- 1/8 tsp. pepper
- 1 pkg. (16 oz.) frozen broccoli stir-fry vegetable blend
- 2 tsp. cornstarch
- 1 Tbsp. cold water

Hot cooked rice

1. In a large nonstick skillet, stir-fry chicken and garlic in 2 tsp. oil for 1 minute. Add the honey, soy sauce, salt and pepper. Cook and stir until chicken is lightly browned and no longer pink. Remove the chicken and keep warm.

2. In the same pan, stir-fry the vegetables in remaining oil for 4-5 minutes or until tender. Return chicken to the pan; stir to coat. Combine cornstarch and cold water until smooth; gradually stir into chicken mixture. Bring to a boil; cook and stir for 1 minute or until thickened. Serve with rice.

Nutrition Facts: 1 cup stir-fry mixture (calculated without rice) equals 243 calories, 5 g fat (1 g saturated fat), 66 mg cholesterol, 470 mg sodium, 19 g carbohydrate, 3 g fiber, 28 g protein. **Diabetic Exchanges:** 3 lean meat, 3 vegetable.

Shrimp Orzo with Feta

PREP/TOTAL TIME: 25 min. **YIELD:** 4 servings

SARAH HUMMEL • MOON TOWNSHIP, PENNSYLVANIA

Simple yet special, this refreshing pasta dish is one of my favorites. You can serve it as a main course or as a side.

- 1-1/4 cups uncooked whole wheat orzo pasta
- 2 garlic cloves, minced
- 2 Tbsp. olive oil
- 2 medium tomatoes, chopped
- 2 Tbsp. lemon juice
- 1-1/4 lbs. uncooked large shrimp, peeled and deveined
- 2 Tbsp. minced fresh cilantro
- 1/4 tsp. pepper
- 1/2 cup crumbled feta cheese

CHICKEN STIR-FRY WITH NOODLES

1. Cook orzo according to package directions. Meanwhile, in a large skillet, saute garlic in oil for 1 minute. Add tomatoes and lemon juice. Bring to a boil. Reduce heat; stir in shrimp. Simmer, uncovered, for 4-5 minutes or until shrimp turn pink.

2. Drain orzo. Add the orzo, cilantro and pepper to the shrimp mixture; heat through. Sprinkle with the feta cheese.

Nutrition Facts: 1 cup equals 406 calories, 12 g fat (3 g saturated fat), 180 mg cholesterol, 307 mg sodium, 40 g carbohydrate, 9 g fiber, 33 g protein. **Diabetic Exchanges:** 4 lean meat, 2 starch, 1 fat.

Simple Chicken Soup F

PREP/TOTAL TIME: 20 min.   YIELD: 6 servings

SUE WEST • ALVORD, TEXAS

I revised a recipe that my family loved so it would be lighter and easier to make. It's a hearty and healthy meal served with a green salad and fresh bread.

- 2 cans (14-1/2 oz. *each*) reduced-sodium chicken broth
- 1 Tbsp. dried minced onion
- 1 pkg. (16 oz.) frozen mixed vegetables
- 2 cups cubed cooked chicken breast
- 2 cans (10-3/4 oz. *each*) reduced-fat reduced-sodium condensed cream of chicken soup, undiluted

1. In a large saucepan, bring broth and onion to a boil. Reduce heat. Add the vegetables; cover and cook for 6-8 minutes or until crisp-tender. Stir in chicken and soup; heat through.

Nutrition Facts: 1-1/3 cups equals 195 calories, 3 g fat (1 g saturated fat), 44 mg cholesterol, 820 mg sodium, 21 g carbohydrate, 3 g fiber, 19 g protein.

> When chicken pieces are on sale, try to buy several packages and bake all of it at once. Bake the chicken skin side up on foil-lined pans. When cooled, remove the skin and bones, cube the meat and freeze **the chicken** in measured portions to use in quick suppers.

CHICKEN CHOW MEIN

Chicken Chow Mein

PREP/TOTAL TIME: 30 min. YIELD: 2 servings

BETH DAUENHAUER • PUEBLO, COLORADO

When we go out for Chinese food, my husband always orders chicken chow mein. I created this recipe using richer-flavored tamari sauce rather than soy.

- 1 Tbsp. cornstarch
- 2/3 cup reduced-sodium chicken broth
- 1 tsp. reduced-sodium soy sauce
- 1/2 tsp. salt
- 1/4 tsp. ground ginger
- 1/4 lb. sliced fresh mushrooms
- 2/3 cup thinly sliced celery
- 1/4 cup sliced onion
- 1/4 cup thinly sliced green pepper
- 2 Tbsp. julienned carrot
- 1 tsp. canola oil
- 1 garlic clove, minced
- 1 cup cubed cooked chicken breast
- 1 cup cooked brown rice
- 2 Tbsp. chow mein noodles

1. In a small bowl, combine the cornstarch, broth, soy sauce, salt and ginger until smooth; set aside.

2. In a large skillet or wok, stir-fry the mushrooms, celery, onion, pepper and carrot in oil for 5 minutes. Add garlic; stir-fry 1-2 minutes longer or until vegetables are crisp-tender.

3. Stir cornstarch mixture and add to the pan. Bring to a boil; cook and stir for 2 minutes or until thickened. Add chicken; heat through. Serve with rice; sprinkle with chow mein noodles.

Nutrition Facts: 1 cup chow mein with 1/2 cup cooked brown rice and 1 Tbsp. chow mein noodles equals 307 calories, 7 g fat (1 g saturated fat), 54 mg cholesterol, 984 mg sodium, 35 g carbohydrate, 4 g fiber, 27 g protein. **Diabetic Exchanges:** 3 lean meat, 2 starch, 1 vegetable, 1/2 fat.

Vegetable Pizza Ⓜ

PREP/TOTAL TIME: 30 min. YIELD: 8 slices

BEVERLY LITTLE • MARIETTA, GEORGIA

An assortment of fresh veggies tops this delicious meatless pizza. Feel free to use any vegetables you like. I often add a few sliced black olives.

- 1 tube (13.8 oz.) refrigerated pizza crust
- 1/2 cup sliced fresh mushrooms
- 1/2 cup chopped onion
- 1/2 cup chopped fresh broccoli
- 1/2 cup chopped green pepper
- 1/2 cup chopped fresh baby spinach
- 1 cup meatless spaghetti sauce
- 2 plum tomatoes, thinly sliced
- 2 cups (8 oz.) shredded part-skim mozzarella cheese

1. Unroll pizza crust into a 15-in. x 10-in. x 1-in. baking pan coated with cooking spray; flatten dough and build up edges slightly. Bake at 400° for 8 minutes.

2. Meanwhile, in a nonstick skillet coated with cooking spray, saute the mushrooms, onion, broccoli, green pepper and spinach until crisp-tender.

3. Spread spaghetti sauce over crust. Top with sauteed vegetables, tomatoes and cheese. Bake for 15-20 minutes or until crust is golden brown and cheese is melted. Let pizza stand for 10 minutes before serving.

Nutrition Facts: 1 serving equals 263 calories, 10 g fat (6 g saturated fat), 33 mg cholesterol, 644 mg sodium, 24 g carbohydrate, 2 g fiber, 18 g protein. **Diabetic Exchanges:** 1-1/2 starch, 1 medium-fat meat.

Mom's Sloppy Tacos

PREP/TOTAL TIME: 30 min. YIELD: 6 servings

KAMI JONES • AVONDALE, ARIZONA

No matter how hectic the weeknight, there's always time to serve your family a healthy meal with recipes this easy and good!

- 1-1/2 lbs. extra-lean ground beef (95% lean)
- 1 can (15 oz.) tomato sauce
- 3/4 tsp. garlic powder
- 1/2 tsp. salt
- 1/4 tsp. pepper
- 1/4 tsp. cayenne pepper
- 12 taco shells, warmed

Optional toppings: shredded lettuce and cheese, chopped tomatoes, avocado and olives

1. In a large skillet, cook beef over medium heat until no longer pink. Stir in the tomato sauce, garlic powder, salt, pepper and cayenne. Bring to a boil. Reduce heat; simmer, uncovered, for 10 minutes.

2. Fill each taco shell with 1/4 cup beef mixture and toppings of your choice.

Nutrition Facts: 2 tacos (calculated without optional toppings) equals 264 calories, 10 g fat (4 g saturated fat), 65 mg cholesterol, 669 mg sodium, 17 g carbohydrate, 1 g fiber, 25 g protein. **Diabetic Exchanges:** 3 lean meat, 1 starch, 1 fat.

MOM'S SLOPPY TACOS

Honey-Mustard Chicken Sandwiches

PREP/TOTAL TIME: 20 min. **YIELD:** 4 servings

CHRISTINA LEVRANT • HENDERSON, NEVADA

These hearty, mouthwatering sandwiches are homemade "fast food" and more delicious than the kind you go out for.

1/4	cup Dijon mustard
2	Tbsp. honey
1	tsp. dried oregano
1	tsp. water
1/4	tsp. garlic powder
1/8 to 1/4	tsp. cayenne pepper
4	boneless skinless chicken breast halves (4 oz. *each*)
4	sandwich buns, split
1	cup shredded lettuce
8	thin tomato slices

1. In a small bowl, combine the first six ingredients. Broil chicken 4 in. from the heat for 4-7 minutes on each side or until a thermometer reads 170°, brushing occasionally with mustard mixture. Serve on buns with lettuce and tomato.

Nutrition Facts: 1 sandwich equals 391 calories, 7 g fat (2 g saturated fat), 63 mg cholesterol, 813 mg sodium, 49 g carbohydrate, 2 g fiber, 32 g protein. **Diabetic Exchanges:** 3 starch, 3 lean meat.

Favorite Layered Salad

PREP/TOTAL TIME: 20 min. **YIELD:** 8 servings

JODI ANDERSON • OVERBROOK, KANSAS

Perfect for potlucks, this salad offers the best that summer produce has to offer, and it looks so beautiful layered in a glass bowl. It's almost too pretty to dig into—almost!

2	cups torn romaine
2	cups fresh baby spinach
1	cup sliced fresh mushrooms
1	cup grape tomatoes
1/2	cup shredded carrot
1	medium red onion, halved and sliced
1	medium sweet red pepper, chopped
1	medium cucumber, sliced
1	cup frozen peas, thawed
1/2	cup Miracle Whip Light
3	Tbsp. sugar
1/2	cup shredded cheddar cheese
3	Tbsp. crumbled cooked bacon

1. In a 3-qt. trifle bowl or glass bowl, combine romaine and spinach. Layer with mushrooms, tomatoes, carrot, onion, pepper, cucumber and peas.

2. Combine the Miracle Whip and sugar; spread over the peas. Sprinkle with the cheese and bacon. Chill until serving.

Nutrition Facts: 1-1/2 cups equals 131 calories, 6 g fat (2 g saturated fat), 14 mg cholesterol, 293 mg sodium, 16 g carbohydrate, 3 g fiber, 5 g protein. **Diabetic Exchanges:** 1 vegetable, 1 fat, 1/2 starch.

FAVORITE LAYERED SALAD

HONEY-MUSTARD CHICKEN SANDWICHES

Asian Chicken with Pasta

PREP/TOTAL TIME: 25 min. **YIELD:** 6 servings

REBECCA SAMS • OAK HARBOR, OHIO

Mild flavors make this a dish even picky eaters will like. The coleslaw mix brings a pleasing crunch to the veggie-filled recipe.

- 1/2 lb. uncooked angel hair pasta
- 1 lb. chicken tenderloins, cut into 1-in. cubes
- 1/3 cup prepared balsamic vinaigrette
- 1/3 cup prepared Italian salad dressing
- 1 pkg. (12 oz.) broccoli coleslaw mix
- 1/2 lb. sliced fresh mushrooms
- 3/4 cup julienned sweet red pepper
- 1/2 cup sliced onion
- 1/2 tsp. garlic powder
- 1/2 tsp. ground ginger
- 1/4 tsp. salt
- 1/8 tsp. pepper

1. Cook pasta according to package directions. Meanwhile, in a large skillet, saute chicken in vinaigrette and salad dressing until no longer pink. Remove and keep warm.

2. In the same skillet, saute the coleslaw mix, mushrooms, red pepper and onion until tender. Add the seasonings. Stir in the chicken; heat through. Drain pasta. Add to chicken mixture; toss to coat.

Nutrition Facts: 1-1/2 cups equals 320 calories, 8 g fat (1 g saturated fat), 44 mg cholesterol, 474 mg sodium, 38 g carbohydrate, 4 g fiber, 25 g protein. **Diabetic Exchanges:** 3 lean meat, 2 starch, 1 vegetable, 1 fat.

Garden Vegetable Wraps

PREP/TOTAL TIME: 25 min. **YIELD:** 4 servings

BARBARA BLAKE • WEST BRATTLEBORO, VERMONT

My husband and I love these light, tasty wraps for lunch. I found the recipe years ago, and it was an instant hit.

- 1/2 cup reduced-fat garlic-herb cheese spread
- 4 flour tortillas (10 in.)
- 1-1/4 cups chopped seeded tomatoes
- 1-1/4 cups julienned fresh spinach
- 3/4 cup chopped sweet red pepper
- 2 bacon strips, cooked and crumbled
- 1/4 tsp. coarsely ground pepper

1. Spread 2 Tbsp. cheese spread over each tortilla. Top with tomatoes, spinach, red pepper, bacon and pepper. Roll up tightly.

Nutrition Facts: 1 wrap equals 314 calories, 10 g fat (5 g saturated fat), 21 mg cholesterol, 614 mg sodium, 37 g carbohydrate, 8 g fiber, 12 g protein. **Diabetic Exchanges:** 2-1/2 starch, 2 fat, 1 vegetable.

SWEET & SPICY SALMON FILLETS

Sweet & Spicy Salmon Fillets [C]

PREP/TOTAL TIME: 25 min. **YIELD:** 4 servings

SUSAN BORDERS • GALENA, OHIO

Tender and moist, this baked salmon has a hit of heat, and a mango salsa lends sweetness. Stir any leftover salsa into chili.

    4   salmon fillets (6 oz. *each*)
  1/2   tsp. garlic powder
  1/2   tsp. cayenne pepper
  3/4   cup mango salsa

1. Place salmon on a 15-in. x 10-in. baking pan coated with cooking spray. Sprinkle with garlic powder and cayenne. Spoon salsa over top.

2. Bake at 375° for 12-15 minutes or until fish flakes easily with a fork.

Nutrition Facts: 1 fillet equals 281 calories, 16 g fat (3 g saturated fat), 85 mg cholesterol, 355 mg sodium, 2 g carbohydrate, trace fiber, 29 g protein. **Diabetic Exchanges:** 4 lean meat, 2 fat.

Better Than Fried Shrimp [F][S][C]

PREP/TOTAL TIME: 30 min. **YIELD:** 2-1/2 dozen

CHER SCHWARTZ • ELLISVILLE, MISSOURI

Coating with panko bread crumbs, spraying with cooking spray and then baking give this shrimp a wonderful crunch without all the saturated fat and calories of deep-frying.

  1-1/2   cups panko (Japanese) bread crumbs
      2   egg whites
      1   Tbsp. fat-free milk
      3   Tbsp. all-purpose flour
      3   tsp. seafood seasoning
    1/4   tsp. salt
    1/4   tsp. pepper
     30   uncooked large shrimp, peeled and deveined

Olive oil-flavored cooking spray

1. Place bread crumbs in a shallow bowl. In another shallow bowl, combine egg whites and milk. In a third shallow bowl, combine flour, seafood seasoning, salt and pepper. Dip shrimp in the flour mixture, egg mixture, then bread crumbs.

2. Place shrimp on a baking sheet coated with cooking spray; spritz shrimp with cooking spray.

3. Bake at 400° for 8-12 minutes or until shrimp turn pink and coating is golden brown, turning once.

Nutrition Facts: 1 shrimp equals 28 calories, 1 g fat (trace saturated fat), 20 mg cholesterol, 86 mg sodium, 2 g carbohydrate, trace fiber, 3 g protein.

Pear Chutney Chicken

PREP/TOTAL TIME: 30 min. **YIELD:** 4 servings

SHEILA O'CONNELL BERG • LUCAS VALLEY, CALIFORNIA

With the unique combination of flavors in this recipe, dinner is sure to satisfy. My freezer is rarely without servings of this dish that my grandson calls "Pear Chix." We love it!

      1   can (15-1/4 oz.) sliced pears
      4   boneless skinless chicken breast halves
          (4 oz. *each*)
      2   Tbsp. all-purpose flour
    1/4   tsp. pepper
      2   Tbsp. olive oil
    1/2   cup chopped onion
    1/2   cup mango chutney
      1   to 2 Tbsp. lemon juice
    3/4   to 1 tsp. curry powder

1. Drain pears, reserving 1/4 cup juice; set pears and juice aside.

2. Flatten chicken to 1/4-in. thickness.

3. In a large resealable bag, combine flour and pepper. Add chicken in batches and shake to coat.

4. In a large skillet, cook chicken in oil over medium heat for 5-6 minutes on each side or until no longer pink. Remove and keep warm.

5. In the same skillet, combine the onion, chutney, lemon juice, curry powder and reserved pear juice. Bring to a boil.

6. Add chicken and pears. Reduce heat; simmer, uncovered, for 3-5 minutes or until heated through. Serve immediately.

Nutrition Facts: 1 serving equals 395 calories, 9 g fat (2 g saturated fat), 63 mg cholesterol, 404 mg sodium, 51 g carbohydrate, 1 g fiber, 24 g protein.

PEAR CHUTNEY CHICKEN

Feta Shrimp Tacos

PREP/TOTAL TIME: 30 min. YIELD: 4 servings

ATHENA RUSSELL • FLORENCE, SOUTH CAROLINA

Taco seasoning and feta cheese work remarkably well together in these refreshing tacos. It's a good thing you get two per serving, because you won't want to stop at one!

- 2 cups shredded red cabbage
- 1/4 cup finely chopped sweet onion
- 1 banana pepper, finely chopped
- 1/4 cup Miracle Whip Light
- 1 Tbsp. cider vinegar
- 1 Tbsp. stone-ground mustard
- 1/4 tsp. pepper
- 1 lb. uncooked medium shrimp, peeled and deveined
- 1 Tbsp. reduced-sodium taco seasoning
- 1 Tbsp. olive oil
- 8 whole wheat tortillas (8 in.)
- 3/4 cup crumbled feta cheese

Sliced avocado, optional

1. In a small bowl, combine the cabbage, onion and banana pepper. In another small bowl, whisk the Miracle Whip, vinegar, mustard and pepper. Pour over cabbage mixture and toss to coat. Chill mixture until serving.

2. Sprinkle shrimp with taco seasoning. In a large nonstick skillet, saute shrimp in oil for 3-4 minutes or until shrimp turn pink. Place shrimp on tortillas; top with cheese, coleslaw and avocado if desired.

Nutrition Facts: 2 tacos (calculated without avocado) equals 527 calories, 18 g fat (4 g saturated fat), 153 mg cholesterol, 1,021 mg sodium, 55 g carbohydrate, 6 g fiber, 31 g protein.

FETA SHRIMP TACOS

Strawberry Puff Pancake M

PREP/TOTAL TIME: 30 min. YIELD: 4 servings

BRENDA MORTON • HALE CENTER, TEXAS

I've cut this recipe to 2 eggs and 1/2 cup milk for my husband and me, and it works just fine. It's yummy with strawberry or blueberry topping. You could even garnish it with whipped topping for a light dessert.

- 2 Tbsp. butter
- 3 eggs
- 3/4 cup fat-free milk
- 1 tsp. vanilla extract
- 3/4 cup all-purpose flour
- 1/8 tsp. salt
- 1/8 tsp. ground cinnamon
- 1/4 cup sugar
- 1 Tbsp. cornstarch
- 1/2 cup water
- 1 cup sliced fresh strawberries

Confectioners' sugar

1. Place butter in a 9-in. pie plate; place in a 400° oven for 4-5 minutes or until melted. Meanwhile, in a small bowl, whisk the eggs, milk and vanilla. In another small bowl, combine the flour, salt and cinnamon; whisk into egg mixture until blended.

2. Pour into prepared pie plate. Bake for 15-20 minutes or until sides are crisp and golden brown.

3. In a small saucepan, combine sugar and cornstarch. Stir in water until smooth; add strawberries. Cook and stir over medium heat until thickened. Coarsely mash strawberries. Serve with pancake. Dust with confectioners' sugar.

Nutrition Facts: 1 slice with 1/3 cup sauce (calculated without confectioners' sugar) equals 277 calories, 10 g fat (5 g saturated fat), 175 mg cholesterol, 187 mg sodium, 38 g carbohydrate, 2 g fiber, 9 g protein. **Diabetic Exchanges:** 2-1/2 starch, 1 medium-fat meat, 1 fat.

Spinach Tomato Linguine M

PREP/TOTAL TIME: 25 min. YIELD: 4 servings

ROSEMARY AVERKAMP • GENOA, WISCONSIN

Chock-full of garden freshness, this colorful toss makes an excellent meatless entree or even a side dish. Sometimes I substitute penne pasta and add cooked chicken for a heartier main meal. Using garlic-flavored feta cheese is a great touch.

- 8 oz. uncooked linguine
- 3 cups chopped seeded plum tomatoes
- 1 pkg. (10 oz.) frozen chopped spinach, thawed and squeezed dry
- 1/2 cup chopped green onions
- 1 tsp. olive oil
- 1/4 tsp. salt
- 1/4 tsp. garlic salt
- 4 oz. crumbled feta cheese

1. Cook linguine according to package directions. Meanwhile, in a large nonstick skillet, saute the tomatoes, spinach and onions in oil until tomatoes

TANGERINE CASHEW SNAPPER

are softened. Sprinkle with salt and garlic salt. Reduce heat. Stir in the cheese; until heated through.

2. Drain linguine; transfer to a serving bowl. Add tomato mixture; toss to coat.

Nutrition Facts: 1 cup equals 357 calories, 11 g fat (5 g saturated fat), 25 mg cholesterol, 646 mg sodium, 52 g carbohydrate, 6 g fiber, 15 g protein. **Diabetic Exchanges:** 2-1/2 starch, 2 vegetable, 1 lean meat, 1 fat.

Tangerine Cashew Snapper

PREP/TOTAL TIME: 30 min. **YIELD:** 4 servings

CRYSTAL BRUNS • ILIFF, COLORADO

Loads of delicious toppings make this fast-to-fix supper option stunning to both the palate and the eye!

- 4 tangerines
- 2 Tbsp. lime juice
- 2 Tbsp. reduced-sodium soy sauce
- 1 Tbsp. brown sugar
- 2 tsp. minced fresh gingerroot
- 1 tsp. sesame oil
- 1/8 tsp. crushed red pepper flakes
- 4 red snapper fillets (4 oz. *each*)
- 1/3 cup chopped unsalted cashews
- 2 green onions, thinly sliced

1. Peel, slice and remove seeds from 2 tangerines; chop the fruit and place in a small bowl. Squeeze juice from remaining tangerines; add to bowl. Stir in the lime juice, soy sauce, brown sugar, ginger, sesame oil and pepper flakes.

2. Place fillets in a 13-in. x 9-in. baking dish coated with cooking spray. Pour tangerine mixture over fillets; sprinkle with cashews and green onions. Bake, uncovered, at 425° for 15-20 minutes or until fish flakes easily with a fork.

Nutrition Facts: 1 fillet with about 2 Tbsp. sauce equals 260 calories, 8 g fat (2 g saturated fat), 40 mg cholesterol, 358 mg sodium, 22 g carbohydrate, 2 g fiber, 26 g protein. **Diabetic Exchanges:** 3 lean meat, 1 fruit, 1 fat.

CHICKEN SAUSAGE GYROS

Chicken Sausage Gyros

PREP/TOTAL TIME: 20 min. YIELD: 4 servings

KERRI GEORGE • BERNE, INDIANA

Surprise your family after a day at the beach with this fast, filling meal in minutes. Casual and hearty, the whole wheat pitas are packed with veggies—and flavor.

1	pkg. (12 oz.) fully cooked spinach and feta chicken sausage links or flavor of your choice, cut into 1/4-in. slices
1	cup (8 oz.) reduced-fat sour cream
1/4	cup finely chopped cucumber
1-1/2	tsp. red wine vinegar
1-1/2	tsp. olive oil
1/2	tsp. garlic powder
4	whole wheat pita breads (6 in.)
1	plum tomato, sliced
1/2	small onion, thinly sliced

1. In a large skillet coated with cooking spray, cook sausage over medium heat until heated through.

2. Meanwhile, in a small bowl, combine the sour cream, cucumber, vinegar, oil and garlic powder. Serve chicken sausage on pita breads with tomato, onion and cucumber sauce.

Nutrition Facts: 1 gyro with 1/4 cup sauce equals 418 calories, 15 g fat (6 g saturated fat), 75 mg cholesterol, 873 mg sodium, 42 g carbohydrate, 5 g fiber, 27 g protein. **Diabetic Exchanges:** 3 starch, 3 lean meat, 1-1/2 fat.

Cheese Ravioli with Pumpkin Alfredo Sauce

PREP/TOTAL TIME: 30 min. YIELD: 6 servings

CHERI NEUSTIFTER • STURTEVANT, WISCONSIN

When I first made this recipe, everyone thought: Pumpkin on pasta? Ewww! But once they tasted it, they couldn't believe how much they liked it! The unusual blend of flavors is warm, comforting and delicious.

- 1 pkg. (25 oz.) frozen cheese ravioli
- 3 Tbsp. all-purpose flour
- 2 cups fat-free milk
- 1 can (14-1/2 oz.) reduced-sodium chicken broth
- 3 garlic cloves, minced
- 2 Tbsp. butter
- 1/2 cup shredded Parmesan cheese
- 1/2 cup canned pumpkin
- 1/4 cup minced fresh parsley
- 1-1/2 tsp. minced fresh sage
- Dash ground nutmeg
- 1/4 cup pine nuts, toasted
- 1/4 cup chopped walnuts, toasted

1. Cook ravioli according to package directions. Meanwhile, in a large bowl, whisk the flour, milk and broth.

2. In a large skillet, saute garlic in butter until tender. Stir in the milk mixture, cheese, pumpkin, parsley, sage and nutmeg. Cook, uncovered, over medium heat for 10-15 minutes or until thickened, stirring occasionally.

3. Drain ravioli and gently stir into sauce. Sprinkle with nuts.

Nutrition Facts: 1 cup equals 420 calories, 16 g fat (6 g saturated fat), 29 mg cholesterol, 662 mg sodium, 50 g carbohydrate, 4 g fiber, 19 g protein.

Scrambled Egg Muffins C

PREP/TOTAL TIME: 30 min. YIELD: 1 dozen

CATHY LARKINS • MARSHFIELD, MISSOURI

After enjoying scrambled egg muffins at a local restaurant, I came up with this savory version that my husband likes even better. Freeze the extras to reheat on busy mornings.

- 1/2 lb. bulk pork sausage
- 12 eggs
- 1/2 cup chopped onion
- 1/4 cup chopped green pepper
- 1/2 tsp. salt
- 1/4 tsp. garlic powder
- 1/4 tsp. pepper
- 1/2 cup shredded cheddar cheese

1. In a large skillet, cook sausage over medium heat until no longer pink; drain.

2. In a large bowl, beat eggs. Add the onion, green pepper, salt, garlic powder and pepper. Stir in sausage and cheese.

3. Spoon by 1/3 cupfuls into muffin cups coated with cooking spray. Bake at 350° for 20-25 minutes or until a knife inserted near the center comes out clean.

Nutrition Facts: 1 muffin equals 133 calories, 10 g fat (4 g saturated fat), 224 mg cholesterol, 268 mg sodium, 2 g carbohydrate, trace fiber, 9 g protein.

CHEESE RAVIOLI WITH PUMPKIN ALFREDO SAUCE

SCRAMBLED EGG MUFFINS

Skewerless Stovetop Kabobs

PREP/TOTAL TIME: 30 min. **YIELD:** 4 servings

JENNIFER MITCHELL • ALTOONA, PENNSYLVANIA

My family loves this fast and simple recipe so much, we never have any leftovers. It's also great on the grill. In addition, it's a fine way to use a few items from your garden.

1	pork tenderloin (1 lb.), cut into 3/4-in. cubes
3/4	cup fat-free Italian salad dressing, *divided*
2	large green peppers, cut into 3/4-in. pieces
2	small zucchini, cut into 1/2-in. slices
1/2	pound medium fresh mushrooms, halved
1	large sweet onion, cut into wedges
1	cup cherry tomatoes
1/4	tsp. pepper
1/8	tsp. seasoned salt

1. In a large nonstick skillet, saute pork in 1/4 cup dressing until no longer pink. Remove and keep warm. In the same pan, cook the peppers, zucchini, mushrooms, onion, tomatoes, pepper and seasoned salt in remaining salad dressing until vegetables are tender. Return pork to skillet; heat through.

Nutrition Facts: 2 cups equals 236 calories, 5 g fat (2 g saturated fat), 65 mg cholesterol, 757 mg sodium, 22 g carbohydrate, 4 g fiber, 27 g protein. **Diabetic Exchanges:** 3 lean meat, 2 starch.

Cran-Apple Turkey Skillet F

PREP/TOTAL TIME: 20 min. **YIELD:** 6 servings

LISA RENSHAW • KANSAS CITY, MISSOURI

This quick and easy skillet meal has such wide appeal that it will become one of your favorite go-to recipes. The end result is a one-dish rendition of a Thanksgiving feast. Best of all, it comes together in just half an hour!

2	medium apples, peeled and thinly sliced
3/4	cup apple cider *or* unsweetened apple juice
3/4	cup reduced-sodium chicken broth
1/3	cup dried cranberries
1/8	tsp. ground nutmeg
3	cups cubed cooked turkey breast
1	pkg. (6 oz.) corn bread stuffing mix

1. In a large skillet, combine the apples, apple cider, broth, cranberries and nutmeg. Bring to a boil. Reduce heat; cover and simmer for 4-5 minutes or until apples are tender, stirring occasionally.

2. Stir in turkey and stuffing mix. Cover and cook for 2-3 minutes or until heated through.

Nutrition Facts: 1 cup equals 267 calories, 2 g fat (trace saturated fat), 60 mg cholesterol, 630 mg sodium, 36 g carbohydrate, 2 g fiber, 25 g protein. **Diabetic Exchanges:** 3 lean meat, 1 starch, 1 fruit.

SKEWERLESS STOVETOP KABOBS

CRAN-APPLE TURKEY SKILLET

Gingered Spaghetti Salad

PREP/TOTAL TIME: 30 min. **YIELD:** 8 servings

CINDY HEINBAUGH • AURORA, COLORADO

With a wonderful blend of bright flavors and colors, this cold pasta salad—bursting with yummy vegetables—is ideal for warm summer days. Try it alongside a whole wheat roll for a complete meal!

- 1 pkg. (16 oz.) spaghetti
- 1 cup frozen shelled edamame
- 3 cups cubed cooked chicken breast
- 1 English cucumber, chopped
- 1 medium sweet red pepper, chopped
- 1 small sweet yellow pepper, chopped
- 1 small red onion, chopped
- 1 tsp. minced fresh gingerroot
- 1 cup reduced-fat sesame ginger salad dressing
- 3 green onions, chopped

1. In a Dutch oven, cook spaghetti according to package directions, adding edamame during the last 5 minutes of cooking. Drain and rinse in cold water.

2. Place in a large bowl. Stir in the chicken, cucumber, peppers, red onion and ginger.

3. Drizzle with dressing; toss to coat. Sprinkle with green onions.

Nutrition Facts: 1-3/4 cups equals 364 calories, 5 g fat (1 g saturated fat), 40 mg cholesterol, 431 mg sodium, 53 g carbohydrate, 3 g fiber, 25 g protein.

Breaded Fish Sandwiches

PREP/TOTAL TIME: 30 min. YIELD: 4 servings

MILDRED CARUSO • BRIGHTON, TENNESSEE

The seasoned breading of this hearty sandwich turns mild-flavored cod or halibut into a taste sensation, and the creamy sauce just keeps it going!

- 1/2 cup dry bread crumbs
- 1/2 tsp. garlic powder
- 1/2 tsp. paprika
- 1/2 tsp. cayenne pepper
- 1/4 tsp. lemon-pepper seasoning
-   4 halibut *or* cod fillets (6 oz. *each*)
-   4 whole wheat hamburger buns, split
-   1 cup shredded lettuce
- 1/4 cup shredded carrots
-   1 Tbsp. grated onion, optional

SAUCE:
- 1/4 cup plain yogurt
-   1 Tbsp. lemon juice
- 1/2 tsp. dill weed
- 1/4 tsp. garlic powder
- 1/4 tsp. grated lemon peel
- 1/4 tsp. prepared horseradish

1. In a shallow bowl, combine the first five ingredients. Coat fillets with bread crumb mixture.

2. Using long-handled tongs, moisten a paper towel with cooking oil and lightly coat the grill rack. Grill halibut, covered, over medium heat or broil 4 in. from the heat for 4-5 minutes on each side or until fish flakes easily with a fork.

3. Grill buns, cut side down, over medium heat for 30-60 seconds or until toasted.

4. Meanwhile, in a small bowl, combine the lettuce, carrots and onion if desired; set aside. In another small bowl, combine the sauce ingredients; spread over bun bottoms. Top with halibut and vegetable mixture; replace bun tops.

Nutrition Facts: 1 sandwich equals 337 calories, 7 g fat (1 g saturated fat), 56 mg cholesterol, 356 mg sodium, 28 g carbohydrate, 4 g fiber, 41 g protein. **Diabetic Exchanges:** 5 lean meat, 2 starch.

Easy Greek Pizza

PREP/TOTAL TIME: 30 min. YIELD: 6 servings

JENNIFER BECK • MERIDIAN, IDAHO

Mix up the weeknight doldrums with this change-of-pace dinner. I created this recipe when trying to use up leftovers from a dinner party. If you prefer to go meatless, it's great without the chicken breast, too.

1 prebaked 12-in. pizza crust
1/2 cup pizza sauce
1 tsp. lemon-pepper seasoning, *divided*
2 cups shredded cooked chicken breast
1-1/2 cups chopped fresh spinach
1 small red onion, thinly sliced and separated into rings
1/4 cup sliced ripe olives
3/4 cup shredded part-skim mozzarella cheese
1/2 cup crumbled feta cheese

1. Place crust on an ungreased baking sheet; spread with pizza sauce and sprinkle with 1/2 tsp. lemon-pepper seasoning. Top with chicken, spinach, onion, olives, cheeses and remaining lemon-pepper seasoning.

2. Bake at 450° for 12-15 minutes or until edges are lightly browned and cheese is melted.

Nutrition Facts: 1 slice equals 321 calories, 9 g fat (4 g saturated fat), 49 mg cholesterol, 719 mg sodium, 32 g carbohydrate, 2 g fiber, 26 g protein. **Diabetic Exchanges:** 3 lean meat, 2 starch, 1/2 fat.

Chicken Cutlets With Citrus Cherry Sauce

PREP/TOTAL TIME: 30 min. YIELD: 4 servings

CHARLENE CHAMBERS • ORMOND BEACH, FLORIDA

You'll love the sweet-tart tanginess of this restaurant-quality chicken dish. Served with a salad, this is a meal to remember. It's also good with pork cutlets and dried cranberries instead of chicken and cherries.

4 boneless skinless chicken breast halves (6 oz. *each*)
1/2 tsp. salt
1/4 tsp. pepper
1/4 cup all-purpose flour

1/2 cup ruby red grapefruit juice
1/2 cup orange juice
1/3 cup dried cherries
2 tsp. Dijon mustard
1 Tbsp. butter
1 Tbsp. canola oil

1. Flatten chicken breasts to 1/2-in. thickness; sprinkle with salt and pepper. Place flour in a large resealable plastic bag. Add the chicken, a few pieces at a time, and shake to coat; set aside.

2. In a small saucepan, combine the juices, cherries and mustard. Bring to a boil; cook until liquid is reduced to 1/2 cup.

3. In a large skillet over medium heat, cook chicken in butter and oil for 5-7 minutes on each side or until juices run clear. Serve with sauce.

Nutrition Facts: 1 chicken breast half with 2 Tbsp. sauce equals 316 calories, 10 g fat (3 g saturated fat), 102 mg cholesterol, 458 mg sodium, 18 g carbohydrate, trace fiber, 35 g protein. **Diabetic Exchanges:** 5 lean meat, 1 starch, 1 fat.

Place boneless chicken breasts between two pieces of waxed paper or plastic wrap or in a resealable plastic bag. Starting in the center and working out to the edges, pound lightly with the **flat side of a meat mallet** until the chicken is even in thickness.

CHICKEN CUTLETS WITH CITRUS CHERRY SAUCE

EASY GREEK PIZZA

Pastrami Deli Wraps

PREP/TOTAL TIME: 20 min. YIELD: 4 servings

NILA GRAHL • GURNEE, ILLINOIS

I sometimes add horseradish when making these wonderful wraps for my husband and me. These work well for larger crowds, too, and the ingredients are easy to multiply.

- 1/4 cup reduced-fat spreadable cream cheese
- 1/4 cup coarsely chopped roasted sweet red pepper
- 4 spinach tortillas (8 in.)
- 4 lettuce leaves
- 4 slices deli pastrami
- 4 slices reduced-fat provolone cheese
- 1/4 cup thinly sliced red onion
- 1 small sweet red pepper, julienned
- 1/2 cup chopped cucumber

1. Place cream cheese and roasted pepper in a small food processor. Cover and process until blended. Spread over tortillas. Layer with remaining ingredients; roll up. Secure with toothpicks.

Nutrition Facts: 1 wrap equals 271 calories, 10 g fat (4 g saturated fat), 29 mg cholesterol, 697 mg sodium, 29 g carbohydrate, 1 g fiber, 15 g protein. **Diabetic Exchanges:** 2 medium-fat meat, 1-1/2 starch, 1 vegetable, 1 fat.

Taco-Stuffed Pepper Cups

PREP/TOTAL TIME: 30 min. YIELD: 4 servings

PAT HABIGER • SPEARVILLE, KANSAS

When green, red or yellow bell peppers are plentiful, they create a colorful container for this spicy taco mixture that's ready in record time.

- 2 medium green peppers
- 1/2 lb. ground beef *or* lean ground turkey
- 2 Tbsp. chopped onion
- 1 can (16 oz.) kidney beans, rinsed and drained
- 1 can (8 oz.) tomato sauce
- 3 Tbsp. taco seasoning
- 1/4 cup sour cream
- 1/4 cup shredded cheddar cheese
- 1/4 cup chopped tomato

1. Cut tops off peppers and remove seeds. In a large kettle, cook peppers in boiling water for 3-5 minutes. Drain and rinse in cold water; set aside.

2. In a large skillet, cook beef and onion over medium heat until meat is no longer pink; drain. Stir in the beans, tomato sauce and taco seasoning; bring to a boil. Reduce heat; simmer, uncovered, for 5-6 minutes or until heated through.

3. Spoon into peppers. Place in an ungreased 8-in. square baking dish. Bake, uncovered, at 350° for 10-12 minutes or until peppers are tender. Top with sour cream, cheese and tomatoes.

Nutrition Facts: 1 stuffed pepper half (prepared with ground turkey, fat-free sour cream and reduced-fat cheddar cheese) equals 261 calories, 6 g fat (2 g saturated fat), 52 mg cholesterol, 823 mg sodium, 31 g carbohydrate, 7 g fiber, 21 g protein. **Diabetic Exchanges:** 2 lean meat, 2 vegetable, 1-1/2 starch, 1 fat.

Mushroom Bean Burritos M

PREP/TOTAL TIME: 30 min. YIELD: 6 servings

TRISHA KRUSE • EAGLE, IDAHO

The whole family will love this. The filling can be used for tacos, nachos, enchiladas or salads.

- 2 medium sweet red peppers, thinly sliced
- 2 medium onions, sliced
- 1 lb. small fresh mushrooms, quartered
- 1/4 cup water
- 1/4 cup vegetable broth
- 3 garlic cloves, minced
- 1 can (16 oz.) vegetarian refried beans

PASTRAMI DELI WRAPS

MUSHROOM BEAN BURRITOS

3/4 cup salsa

1 Tbsp. chili powder

1 tsp. chipotle hot pepper sauce

6 whole wheat tortillas (8 in.), warmed

3/4 cup shredded reduced-fat cheddar cheese

1. In a large nonstick skillet coated with cooking spray, saute peppers and onions until crisp-tender. Stir in the mushrooms, water, broth and garlic. Bring to a boil. Reduce heat; simmer, uncovered, for 8-10 minutes or until vegetables are tender and liquid has evaporated.

2. Stir in the beans, salsa, chili powder and pepper sauce; heat through.

3. Spoon 1 cup filling off center on each tortilla. Sprinkle with cheese. Fold sides and ends over filling and roll up.

Nutrition Facts: 1 burrito equals 310 calories, 7 g fat (2 g saturated fat), 10 mg cholesterol, 798 mg sodium, 47 g carbohydrate, 9 g fiber, 15 g protein.

Caribbean Chicken Tenderloins

PREP/TOTAL TIME: 20 min. YIELD: 4 servings

LAURA MCALLISTER • MORGANTON, NORTH CAROLINA

This recipe is so fast and tasty. The light and sweet sauce perfectly offsets the bold jerk seasoning.

1 lb. chicken tenderloins

2 tsp. Caribbean jerk seasoning

3 tsp. olive oil, *divided*

2-1/2 cups cut fresh asparagus (2-in. pieces)

1 cup pineapple tidbits, drained

4 green onions, chopped

2 tsp. cornstarch

1 cup unsweetened pineapple juice

1 Tbsp. spicy brown mustard

2 cups hot cooked rice

1. Rub chicken with jerk seasoning. In a large skillet coated with cooking spray, cook chicken in 1 tsp. oil over medium heat for 3-4 minutes on each side or until juices run clear. Remove and keep warm.

2. In the same skillet, saute the asparagus, pineapple and onions in remaining oil for 2-3 minutes or until tender. Combine the cornstarch, pineapple juice and mustard until smooth; gradually stir into the pan. Bring to a boil; cook and stir for 2 minutes or until thickened. Serve with chicken and rice.

Nutrition Facts: 3 oz. cooked chicken with 1/2 cup asparagus mixture and 1/2 cup rice equals 314 calories, 4 g fat (1 g saturated fat), 67 mg cholesterol, 247 mg sodium, 40 g carbohydrate, 2 g fiber, 29 g protein. **Diabetic Exchanges:** 3 lean meat, 2 starch, 1/2 fruit, 1/2 fat.

To prepare **asparagus,** rinse stalks in cold water. Snap the stalk ends as far down as they will easily break when bent, or cut off the tough white portion. Use a veggie peeler to remove the tough skin of larger stalks.

Mediterranean Chicken

PREP/TOTAL TIME: 30 min. **YIELD:** 4 servings

KARA ZILIS • OAK FOREST, ILLINOIS

I've discovered that my friends and family love this flavorful twist on a classic chicken entree. Stewed tomatoes, green beans and brown rice increase the nutritional value, but it tastes just as good as the original.

- 4 boneless skinless chicken breast halves (4 oz. *each*)
- 1 Tbsp. olive oil
- 1 can (14-1/2 oz.) no-salt-added stewed tomatoes
- 1 can (14-1/2 oz.) cut green beans, drained
- 1 cup water
- 1 tsp. dried oregano
- 1/4 tsp. garlic powder
- 1-1/2 cups instant brown rice
- 12 pitted Greek olives, halved
- 1/2 cup crumbled feta cheese

1. In a large nonstick skillet, brown chicken in oil on each side. Stir in the tomatoes, green beans, water, oregano and garlic powder. Bring to a boil; reduce heat. Cover and simmer for 10 minutes.

2. Stir in rice. Return to a boil. Cover and simmer 8-10 minutes longer or until a meat thermometer reads 170° and rice is tender. Stir in olives; sprinkle with cheese.

Nutrition Facts: 1 chicken breast half with 1 cup rice mixture and 2 Tbsp. cheese equals 394 calories, 12 g fat (3 g saturated fat), 70 mg cholesterol, 724 mg sodium, 37 g carbohydrate, 6 g fiber, 30 g protein. **Diabetic Exchanges:** 3 lean meat, 2 starch, 2 vegetable, 1 fat.

Zesty Hamburger Soup

PREP/TOTAL TIME: 30 min.
YIELD: 10 servings (3-3/4 qt.)

KELLY MILAN • LAKE JACKSON, TEXAS

You won't face early afternoon hunger when this hearty soup is part of your lunch. Freeze leftovers in small batches so a meal for one or two is just moments away.

- 1 lb. lean ground beef (90% lean)
- 2 cups sliced celery
- 1 cup chopped onion
- 2 tsp. minced garlic
- 4 cups hot water
- 2 medium red potatoes, peeled and cubed
- 2 cups frozen corn
- 1-1/2 cups uncooked small shell pasta
- 4 pickled jalapeno slices
- 4 cups V8 juice
- 2 cans (10 oz. *each*) diced tomatoes with green chilies
- 1 to 2 Tbsp. sugar

1. In a Dutch oven, cook the beef, celery and onion over medium heat until meat is no longer pink. Add garlic; cook 1 minute longer. Drain. Stir in the water, potatoes, corn, pasta and jalapeno.

2. Bring to a boil. Reduce heat; cover and simmer for 10-15 minutes or until pasta is tender. Stir in the remaining ingredients. Cook and stir until heated through.

Nutrition Facts: 1-1/2 cups equals 222 calories, 5 g fat (2 g saturated fat), 28 mg cholesterol, 542 mg sodium, 33 g carbohydrate, 4 g fiber, 14 g protein. **Diabetic Exchanges:** 2 vegetable, 1-1/2 starch, 1 lean meat.

Grilled Mixed Green Salad C M

PREP/TOTAL TIME: 25 min. **YIELD:** 12 servings

JANICE ELDER • CHARLOTTE, NORTH CAROLINA

Grilling the lettuce adds smoky flavor and takes a simple salad to a whole new level. The fruits and nuts offer different dimensions of flavor and texture.

    2 heads Belgian endive, halved lengthwise
    2 bunches romaine, halved lengthwise
    1 head radicchio, quartered lengthwise
    5 Tbsp. olive oil, *divided*
  1/2 tsp. salt
  1/4 tsp. pepper
    2 Tbsp. balsamic vinegar
    1 cup fresh blueberries
    1 medium apple, thinly sliced
  1/4 cup chopped walnuts, toasted
  1/4 cup shaved Parmesan cheese

1. Brush the endive, romaine and radicchio with 3 Tbsp. oil. Sprinkle with salt and pepper.

2. Using long-handled tongs, moisten a paper towel with cooking oil and lightly coat the grill rack. Grill the greens, uncovered, over medium heat for 30 seconds on each side or until heated through.

3. Chop the greens and place in a large serving bowl. Whisk vinegar and remaining oil; drizzle over greens and toss to coat. Top with blueberries, apple, walnuts and cheese.

Nutrition Facts: 1 cup equals 117 calories, 8 g fat (1 g saturated fat), 1 mg cholesterol, 157 mg sodium, 10 g carbohydrate, 5 g fiber, 4 g protein. **Diabetic Exchanges:** 1 vegetable, 1 fat, 1/2 starch.

Skillet Ranch Burgers

PREP/TOTAL TIME: 30 min. **YIELD:** 4 servings

DEBRA JUSTICE • MOODY, TEXAS

Lean ground turkey keeps these burgers light, while jalapenos and ranch dressing mix add great zestiness.

  1/2 cup soft bread crumbs
    1 small onion, finely chopped
    1 small green pepper, finely chopped
    2 jalapeno peppers, seeded and finely chopped
  1/4 cup egg substitute
1-1/4 tsp. ranch salad dressing mix
    1 tsp. garlic powder
  1/2 tsp. hot pepper sauce
    1 lb. lean ground turkey
    4 whole wheat hamburger buns, split
    4 lettuce leaves
    4 slices tomato
    4 slices onion
SAUCE:
  1/2 cup fat-free sour cream
    1 tsp. ranch salad dressing mix

1. In a large bowl, combine the first eight ingredients. Crumble turkey over mixture and mix well. Shape into four patties.

2. In a large nonstick skillet coated with cooking spray, cook patties over medium heat for 6-8 minutes on each side or until a meat thermometer reads 165° and juices run clear.

3. Serve on buns with lettuce, tomato and onion. Combine sour cream and dressing mix; spoon over burgers.

Editor's Note: When cutting hot peppers, disposable gloves are recommended. Avoid touching your face.

Nutrition Facts: 1 burger equals 373 calories, 12 g fat (3 g saturated fat), 95 mg cholesterol, 772 mg sodium, 39 g carbohydrate, 5 g fiber, 29 g protein. **Diabetic Exchanges:** 3 lean meat, 2 starch, 1 vegetable.

GRILLED MIXED GREEN SALAD

SKILLET RANCH BURGERS

Meat 'n' Potato Kabobs

PREP/TOTAL TIME: 30 min. YIELD: 4 servings

HEALTHY COOKING TEST KITCHEN

Even the pickiest eaters at your table won't be able to resist these kabobs, which are as pretty as they are tasty. The surprising secret ingredient? A bit of cola!

1	lb. beef top sirloin steak, cut into 1-in. cubes
1-1/2	tsp. steak seasoning, *divided*
1	tsp. minced garlic
1	cup cola
3	small red potatoes, cubed
1	Tbsp. water
1	cup cherry tomatoes
1	medium sweet orange pepper, cut into 1-in. pieces
1	tsp. canola oil
1	cup pineapple chunks

1. Sprinkle beef cubes with 1 tsp. steak seasoning and garlic; place in a large resealable plastic bag. Add cola. Seal bag and turn to coat; set aside.

2. Place the potatoes and water in a microwave-safe dish; cover and microwave on high for 4 minutes or until tender. Drain. Add the tomatoes, orange pepper, oil and remaining steak seasoning; toss gently to coat.

3. Drain and discard marinade. Alternately thread the beef, vegetables and pineapple onto eight metal or soaked wooden skewers. Grill, covered, over medium-hot heat or broil 4-6 in. from the heat for 4 minutes on each side or until meat reaches desired doneness (for medium-rare, a meat thermometer should read 145°; medium, 160°; well-done, 170°).

Editor's Note: This recipe was tested in a 1,100-watt microwave. This recipe was tested with McCormick's Montreal Steak Seasoning. Look for it in the spice aisle.

Nutrition Facts: 1 kabob (prepared with diet cola) equals 251 calories, 7 g fat (2 g saturated fat), 63 mg cholesterol, 311 mg sodium, 23 g carbohydrate, 3 g fiber, 24 g protein. **Diabetic Exchanges:** 3 lean meat, 1 starch, 1/2 fruit.

Tortellini Primavera Ⓜ

PREP/TOTAL TIME: 30 min. YIELD: 5 servings

SUSIE PIETROWSKI • BELTON, TEXAS

This decadent tortellini with spinach, mushrooms and tomatoes always brings compliments. Dressed up with fresh Parmesan cheese, no one even notices it's meatless!

1	pkg. (19 oz.) frozen cheese tortellini
1/2	lb. sliced fresh mushrooms
1	small onion, chopped
2	tsp. butter
2	garlic cloves, minced
2/3	cup fat-free milk
1	pkg. (8 oz.) fat-free cream cheese, cubed
1	pkg. (10 oz.) frozen chopped spinach, thawed and squeezed dry
1	tsp. Italian seasoning
1	large tomato, chopped
1/4	cup shredded Parmesan cheese

1. Cook tortellini according to package directions. Meanwhile, in a large nonstick skillet coated with cooking spray, saute mushrooms and onion in butter until tender. Add garlic; cook 1 minute longer. Stir in milk; heat through. Stir in cream cheese until blended. Add spinach and Italian seasoning; heat through.

2. Drain tortellini; toss with sauce and tomato. Sprinkle with Parmesan cheese.

Nutrition Facts: 1-1/4 cups equals 341 calories, 10 g fat (5 g saturated fat), 28 mg cholesterol, 671 mg sodium, 41 g carbohydrate, 4 g fiber, 23 g protein. **Diabetic Exchanges:** 2-1/2 starch, 2 lean meat, 1 vegetable.

MEAT 'N' POTATO KABOBS

TORTELLINI PRIMAVERA

SPICY SHRIMP WRAPS

Spicy Shrimp Wraps

PREP/TOTAL TIME: 20 min. **YIELD:** 6 servings

FRANKIE ALLEN MANN • WARRIOR, ALABAMA

These hearty grab-and-go wraps are packed with spicy flavor and sweetened with mango. They'll win over family and friends in less time than they take to assemble.

- 1 cup salsa
- 1 medium ripe mango, peeled, pitted and diced
- 1 Tbsp. ketchup
- 1 envelope reduced-sodium taco seasoning
- 1 Tbsp. olive oil
- 1 lb. uncooked medium shrimp, peeled and deveined
- 6 flour tortillas (10 in.), warmed
- 1-1/2 cups coleslaw mix
- 6 Tbsp. reduced-fat sour cream

1. In a small bowl, combine the salsa, mango and ketchup; set aside. In a large resealable plastic bag, combine taco seasoning and oil; add shrimp. Seal bag and shake to coat.

2. In a nonstick skillet or wok, cook shrimp over medium-high heat for 2-3 minutes or until shrimp turn pink. Top tortillas with coleslaw mix, salsa mixture and shrimp. Fold bottom third of tortilla up over filling; fold sides over. Serve with sour cream.

Nutrition Facts: 1 wrap equals 374 calories, 9 g fat (2 g saturated fat), 97 mg cholesterol, 1,010 mg sodium, 46 g carbohydrate, 7 g fiber, 20 g protein. **Diabetic Exchanges:** 3 starch, 2 lean meat, 1 fat.

Tuna Caesar Sandwiches

PREP/TOTAL TIME: 20 min. **YIELD:** 4 servings

GLORIA BRADLEY • NAPERVILLE, ILLINOIS

I've always loved tuna sandwiches because they're such a cinch to make. Plus, they're versatile; you can add so many different ingredients to tuna.

- 2 cans (5 oz. *each*) white water-packed tuna, drained and flaked
- 1/4 cup marinated quartered artichoke hearts, drained and chopped
- 1/4 cup finely chopped onion
- 1/4 cup reduced-fat mayonnaise
- 3 Tbsp. grated Parmesan cheese
- 2 tsp. lemon juice
- 1 tsp. Dijon mustard
- 8 slices whole wheat bread, toasted
- 16 cucumber slices
- 8 slices tomato
- 2 cups shredded lettuce

1. In a small bowl, combine the first seven ingredients. Spread over four slices of toast. Top with cucumber, tomato, lettuce and remaining toast.

Nutrition Facts: 1 sandwich equals 338 calories, 12 g fat (3 g saturated fat), 38 mg cholesterol, 797 mg sodium, 30 g carbohydrate, 5 g fiber, 27 g protein. **Diabetic Exchanges:** 3 lean meat, 2 starch, 1 fat.

SENSATIONAL SPICED SALMON

Sensational Spiced Salmon C

PREP/TOTAL TIME: 25 min. YIELD: 4 servings

MICHELE DOUCETTE
STEPHENVILLE, NEWFOUNDLAND AND LABRADOR

A sweet and spicy rub gives this quick salmon entree fantastic flavor. Paired with a green veggie and rice, it's a delightful weeknight dinner that's special enough for company.

2	Tbsp. brown sugar
4	tsp. chili powder
2	tsp. grated lemon peel
3/4	tsp. ground cumin
1/2	tsp. salt
1/4	tsp. ground cinnamon
4	salmon fillets (4 oz. *each*)

1. Combine the first six ingredients; rub over salmon. Place in an 11-in. x 7-in. baking dish coated with cooking spray. Bake, uncovered, at 350° for 15-20 minutes or until fish flakes easily with a fork.

Nutrition Facts: 1 fillet equals 244 calories, 13 g fat (3 g saturated fat), 67 mg cholesterol, 392 mg sodium, 9 g carbohydrate, 1 g fiber, 23 g protein. **Diabetic Exchanges:** 3 lean meat, 1/2 starch.

Lasagna Soup

PREP/TOTAL TIME: 30 min. YIELD: 8 servings

SHERYL OLENICK • DEMAREST, NEW JERSEY

All the traditional flavors of lasagna come together in this heartwarming meal-in-a-bowl.

1	lb. lean ground beef (90% lean)
1	large green pepper, chopped
1	medium onion, chopped
2	garlic cloves, minced
2	cans (14-1/2 oz. *each*) reduced-sodium beef broth
2	cans (14-1/2 oz. *each*) diced tomatoes
1	can (8 oz.) tomato sauce
1	cup frozen corn
1/4	cup tomato paste
2	tsp. Italian seasoning
1/4	tsp. pepper
2-1/2	cups uncooked spiral pasta
1/2	cup shredded Parmesan cheese

1. In a large saucepan, cook the beef, green pepper and onion over medium heat until meat is no longer pink. Add garlic; cook 1 minute longer. Drain.

2. Stir in the broth, tomatoes, tomato sauce, corn, tomato paste, Italian seasoning and pepper. Bring to a boil. Stir in pasta. Return to a boil. Reduce heat; cover and simmer for 10-12 minutes or until pasta is tender. Sprinkle with cheese.

Nutrition Facts: 1-1/3 cups equals 280 calories, 7 g fat (3 g saturated fat), 41 mg cholesterol, 572 mg sodium, 35 g carbohydrate, 4 g fiber, 20 g protein. **Diabetic Exchanges:** 2 lean meat, 2 vegetable, 1-1/2 starch.

Gnocchi with White Beans [M]

PREP/TOTAL TIME: 30 min. YIELD: 6 servings

JULIANNE MEYERS • HINESVILLE, GEORGIA

Warm tummies and hearts on frosty nights with this yummy skillet dish full of spinach, tomatoes, beans, gnocchi, melty cheese and Italian flavors. It makes a fast and easy supper-in-one.

- 1 medium onion, chopped
- 1 Tbsp. olive oil
- 2 garlic cloves, minced
- 1 pkg. (16 oz.) potato gnocchi
- 1 pkg. (6 oz.) fresh baby spinach
- 1 can (15 oz.) white kidney or cannellini beans, rinsed and drained
- 1 can (14-1/2 oz.) Italian diced tomatoes, undrained
- 1/4 tsp. pepper
- 1/2 cup shredded part-skim mozzarella cheese
- 3 Tbsp. grated Parmesan cheese

1. In a large skillet, saute onion in oil until tender. Add garlic; cook 1 minute longer. Add gnocchi; cook and stir for 5-6 minutes or until golden brown. Stir in spinach; cook until spinach is wilted.

2. Add the beans, tomatoes and pepper; heat through. Sprinkle with cheeses; cover and remove from the heat. Let stand for 3-4 minutes or until cheese is melted.

Editor's Note: Look for potato gnocchi in the pasta or frozen foods section.

Nutrition Facts: 1 cup equals 307 calories, 6 g fat (2 g saturated fat), 13 mg cholesterol, 789 mg sodium, 50 g carbohydrate, 6 g fiber, 13 g protein.

Hearty Pita Tacos

PREP/TOTAL TIME: 30 min. YIELD: 6 servings

JAMIE VALOCCHI • MESA, ARIZONA

You don't need to skimp on flavor when trying to eat healthy. Our 9-year-old daughter enjoys helping us make these tasty tacos and enjoys eating them even more.

- 1 lb. lean ground beef (90% lean)
- 1 small sweet red pepper, chopped
- 2 green onions, chopped
- 1 can (16 oz.) kidney beans, rinsed and drained
- 3/4 cup frozen corn
- 2/3 cup taco sauce
- 1 can (2-1/4 oz.) sliced ripe olives, drained
- 1/2 tsp. garlic salt
- 1/4 tsp. onion powder
- 1/4 tsp. dried oregano
- 1/4 tsp. paprika
- 1/4 tsp. pepper
- 6 whole wheat pita pocket halves
- 6 Tbsp. shredded reduced-fat cheddar cheese

Sliced avocado and additional taco sauce, optional

1. In a large skillet, cook the beef, red pepper and onions over medium heat until meat is no longer pink; drain. Stir in the beans, corn, taco sauce, olives and seasonings; heat through.

2. Spoon 3/4 cup beef mixture into each pita half. Sprinkle with cheese. Serve with avocado and additional taco sauce if desired.

Nutrition Facts: 1 filled pita half (calculated without avocado and optional ingredients) equals 339 calories, 10 g fat (4 g saturated fat), 52 mg cholesterol, 787 mg sodium, 38 g carbohydrate, 8 g fiber, 26 g protein. **Diabetic Exchanges:** 3 lean meat, 2-1/2 starch.

HEARTY PITA TACOS

GNOCCHI WITH WHITE BEANS

Beef Stroganoff

PREP/TOTAL TIME: 30 min. **YIELD:** 5 servings

PATTY RODY • PUYALLUP, WASHINGTON

Creamy and comforting, you'll crave this hearty Beef Stroganoff no matter what the weather.

5	Tbsp. all-purpose flour, *divided*
1/2	tsp. salt
1	lb. beef top sirloin steak, cut into thin strips
4	Tbsp. butter, *divided*
1	cup sliced fresh mushrooms
1/2	cup chopped sweet onion
1	garlic clove, minced
1	Tbsp. tomato paste
1-1/4	cups beef broth
1	cup (8 oz.) sour cream
2	Tbsp. sherry *or* beef broth

Hot cooked egg noodles *or* brown rice

1. In a large resealable plastic bag, combine 2 Tbsp. flour and salt. Add beef, a few pieces at a time, and shake to coat. In a large skillet over medium-high heat, brown beef in 2 Tbsp. butter. Add mushrooms and onion; cook and stir until vegetables are tender. Add garlic; cook 1 minute longer. Remove and keep warm.

2. In the same skillet, melt remaining butter. Stir in tomato paste and remaining flour until smooth. Gradually add broth; bring to a boil. Cook and stir for 2 minutes or until thickened.

3. Carefully return beef mixture to the pan. Add sour cream and sherry; heat through (do not boil). Serve with noodles or rice.

Nutrition Facts: 1 cup (calculated without noodles) equals 338 calories, 21 g fat (13 g saturated fat), 107 mg cholesterol, 581 mg sodium, 11 g carbohydrate, 1 g fiber, 21 g protein.

Hearty Vegetarian Chili ⓜ

PREP/TOTAL TIME: 30 min. **YIELD:** 9 servings (2-1/4 qt.)

PAM IVBULS • OMAHA, NEBRASKA

Rich and flavorful, this chili is absolutely packed with fun veggies like mushrooms, beans and sun-dried tomatoes. It's so filling, you'll fool any meat lover.

1-3/4	cups chopped baby portobello mushrooms
1	medium onion, finely chopped
1/2	cup chopped sun-dried tomatoes (not packed in oil)
2	Tbsp. olive oil
2	garlic cloves, minced
1	pkg. (12 oz.) frozen vegetarian meat crumbles
2	cans (16 oz. *each*) chili beans, undrained
2	cans (14-1/2 oz. *each*) no-salt-added diced tomatoes
1/2	cup water
1/2	cup vegetable broth
4-1/2	tsp. chili powder
2	tsp. brown sugar
1/2	tsp. celery salt
1/2	tsp. ground cumin
1	medium ripe avocado, peeled and finely chopped
9	Tbsp. reduced-fat sour cream

1. In a Dutch oven, saute the mushrooms, onion and sun-dried tomatoes in oil until vegetables are tender. Add garlic; cook 1 minute longer. Add meat crumbles; heat through.

2. Stir in the chili beans, tomatoes, water, broth, chili powder, brown sugar, celery salt and cumin. Bring to a boil. Reduce heat; simmer, uncovered, for 10 minutes. Ladle chili into bowls. Top each with avocado and sour cream.

Editor's Note: Vegetarian meat crumbles are a nutritious protein source made from soy. Look for them in the natural foods freezer section.

Nutrition Facts: 1 serving equals 275 calories, 10 g fat (2 g saturated fat), 5 mg cholesterol, 768 mg sodium, 37 g carbohydrate, 12 g fiber, 17 g protein. **Diabetic Exchanges:** 2 lean meat, 2 vegetable, 1-1/2 starch, 1 fat.

BEEF STROGANOFF

HEARTY VEGETARIAN CHILI

Black Bean Chicken with Rice

PREP/TOTAL: 25 min. **YIELD:** 4 servings

MOLLY NEWMAN • PORTLAND, OREGON

This family favorite only requires a few ingredients I tend to keep on hand, so it's easy to fix on even the busiest weeknight. The corn, black beans and salsa give this complete meal a Southwest-style kick.

3	tsp. chili powder
1	tsp. ground cumin
1	tsp. pepper
1/4	tsp. salt
4	boneless skinless chicken breast halves (4 oz. *each*)
2	tsp. canola oil
1	can (15 oz.) black beans, rinsed and drained
1	cup frozen corn
1	cup salsa
2	cups cooked brown rice

1. Combine the chili powder, cumin, pepper and salt; rub over chicken. In a large nonstick skillet coated with cooking spray, brown chicken in oil on both sides. Stir in the beans, corn and salsa. Cover and cook over medium heat for 10-15 minutes or until a meat thermometer reads 170°.

2. Slice chicken; serve with rice and bean mixture.

Nutrition Facts: 1 chicken breast half with 3/4 cup bean mixture and 1/2 cup rice equals 400 calories, 7 g fat (1 g saturated fat), 63 mg cholesterol, 670 mg sodium, 52 g carbohydrate, 8 g fiber, 32 g protein.

Giant Mushroom Burger

PREP/TOTAL TIME: 30 min. **YIELD:** 6 servings

JANICE DELAGRANGE • MT. AIRY, MARYLAND

I add mushrooms and onion to well-seasoned lean ground beef before forming it into one giant, crowd-pleasing patty. After grilling it, all I need to do is slice and serve.

1-1/2	lbs. lean ground beef (90% lean)
1	can (4 oz.) mushroom stems and pieces, drained
1/4	cup egg substitute
1/2	cup chopped onion
1/4	cup ketchup
1	tsp. Italian seasoning
1	tsp. fennel seed, crushed
1/4	tsp. pepper
1/4	tsp. Worcestershire sauce

1. In a large bowl, combine all the ingredients. Pat into a 9-in. circle on a large sheet of waxed paper. Invert onto a greased wire grill basket; peel off waxed paper.

2. Grill, covered, over medium heat or broil 4 in. from the heat for 10-13 minutes on each side or until a meat thermometer reads 160° and meat juices run clear. Cut into six wedges.

Editor's Note: If you do not have a grill basket or wok, use a disposable foil pan. Poke holes in the bottom of the pan with a meat fork to allow liquid to drain.

Nutrition Facts: 1 serving equals 224 calories, 11 g fat (4 g saturated fat), 41 mg cholesterol, 305 mg sodium, 6 g carbohydrate, 1 g fiber, 25 g protein. **Diabetic Exchanges:** 3 lean meat, 1 vegetable.

Lactose-Free Potato Soup

PREP/TOTAL TIME: 30 min. YIELD: 6 servings

LISANNE HEYWARD • RICHMOND, VIRGINIA

This is a great way for my husband and me to have rich, creamy soup without worrying about my lactose intolerance. Try it—you won't believe it's dairy-free!

- 3 medium onions, chopped
- 2 celery ribs, chopped
- 2 Tbsp. canola oil
- 4 cups reduced-sodium chicken broth
- 4 medium potatoes, peeled and cubed

1. In a large saucepan, saute onions and celery in oil until tender. Add broth and potatoes; bring to a boil. Reduce heat; cover and simmer for 15-20 minutes or until potatoes are tender.

2. Cool slightly. In a blender, process half of the soup until smooth. Return to pan; heat through.

Nutrition Facts: 1 cup equals 166 calories, 5 g fat (trace saturated fat), 0 cholesterol, 396 mg sodium, 27 g carbohydrate, 3 g fiber, 5 g protein. **Diabetic Exchanges:** 1 starch, 1 vegetable, 1 fat.

Broiled Apricot Chicken C

PREP/TOTAL TIME: 30 min. YIELD: 6 servings

SUSAN WARREN • NORTH MANCHESTER, INDIANA

What a tasty treatment for lean, tender chicken breasts! A little sweetness blends perfectly with the bold taste of horseradish. This works well on the grill, too.

- 1 cup apricot nectar
- 3 Tbsp. brown sugar
- 2 Tbsp. ketchup
- 2 tsp. cornstarch
- 1 tsp. grated orange peel
- 1 tsp. horseradish mustard
- 6 boneless skinless chicken breast halves (6 oz. each)

LACTOSE-FREE POTATO SOUP

1. In a small saucepan, combine the first six ingredients. Bring to a boil. Cook and stir for 1 minute or until thickened.

2. Place chicken on a broiler pan coated with cooking spray. Broil 4 in. from the heat for 6-8 minutes on each side or until chicken juices run clear, basting frequently with apricot mixture.

Nutrition Facts: 1 chicken breast half equals 241 calories, 4 g fat (1 g saturated fat), 94 mg cholesterol, 158 mg sodium, 15 g carbohydrate, trace fiber, 34 g protein. **Diabetic Exchanges:** 5 very lean meat, 1 starch.

Easy Chicken Broccoli Pasta

PREP/TOTAL TIME: 25 min. YIELD: 4 servings

RENEE PAJESTKA • BRUNSWICK, OHIO

This is so easy to throw together in a pinch. It's wonderful served with crusty bread and a nice veggie salad.

- 2 cups uncooked penne pasta
- 2 cups frozen broccoli florets
- 1 lb. boneless skinless chicken breasts, cut into 1-in. cubes
- 1/4 tsp. salt
- 1/4 tsp. pepper
- 1 Tbsp. canola oil
- 1 small sweet red pepper, chopped
- 1/2 cup white wine or reduced-sodium chicken broth
- 1 cup reduced-fat Alfredo sauce

1. Cook pasta according to package directions, adding the broccoli during the last 5 minutes of cooking.

2. Meanwhile, sprinkle chicken with salt and pepper. In a large nonstick skillet, saute chicken in oil until lightly browned. Add pepper; saute 3-5 minutes longer or until chicken is no longer pink and pepper is tender.

3. Drain pasta mixture; add to the pan. Reduce heat to low. Stir in wine, then Alfredo sauce; cook and stir until heated through.

Nutrition Facts: 1-1/2 cups equals 400 calories, 13 g fat (5 g saturated fat), 88 mg cholesterol, 654 mg sodium, 33 g carbohydrate, 2 g fiber, 31 g protein.

Spanish Rice Supper

PREP/TOTAL TIME: 30 min. YIELD: 6 servings

CATHY FLIKKEMA • SALT LAKE CITY, UTAH

Mom made this when I was growing up, and now both of my children love it!

- 1 lb. lean ground beef
- 3 cups instant brown rice
- 1 can (29 oz.) tomato puree
- 1-1/2 cups water
- 1 can (4 oz.) chopped green chilies
- 1 can (2-1/4 oz.) sliced ripe olives, drained
- 1 envelope chili seasoning
- 1/2 cup shredded reduced-fat cheddar cheese

1. In a large skillet, cook beef over medium heat until no longer pink; drain. Stir in the rice, tomato

puree, water, chilies, olives and chili seasoning. Bring to a boil. Reduce the heat; cover and simmer for 10-12 minutes or until rice is tender.

2. Remove from the heat. Sprinkle with cheese; cover and let stand until cheese is melted.

Nutrition Facts: 1-1/3 cups equals 380 calories, 10 g fat (4 g saturated fat), 44 mg cholesterol, 741 mg sodium, 47 g carbohydrate, 4 g fiber, 24 g protein.

Hoisin Shrimp & Broccoli

PREP/TOTAL TIME: 30 min. **YIELD:** 4 servings

MARY KISINGER • CALGARY, ALBERTA

This healthy dish looks impressive and is a snap to prepare. I hope you adore it as much as I do.

    1 Tbsp. cornstarch
  1/3 cup reduced-sodium chicken broth
4-1/2 tsp. reduced-sodium soy sauce
4-1/2 tsp. hoisin sauce
    1 tsp. sesame oil
    3 cups fresh broccoli florets
    1 Tbsp. canola oil
    4 green onions, chopped
    3 garlic cloves, minced
    1 tsp. minced fresh gingerroot
    1 lb. uncooked medium shrimp, peeled and
       deveined
    2 cups hot cooked rice

1. In a small bowl, combine cornstarch and broth until smooth. Stir in the soy sauce, hoisin sauce and sesame oil; set aside.

2. In a large nonstick skillet or wok, stir-fry the broccoli in canola oil until crisp-tender. Add the onions, garlic and ginger; stir-fry for 3-4 minutes or until vegetables are tender. Add the shrimp; stir-fry 4-5 minutes longer or until shrimp turn pink.

3. Stir the cornstarch mixture and add to the pan. Bring to a boil; cook and stir for 2 minutes or until thickened. Serve with rice.

Nutrition Facts: 3/4 cup shrimp mixture with 1/2 cup rice equals 289 calories, 7 g fat (1 g saturated fat), 138 mg cholesterol, 524 mg sodium, 33 g carbohydrate, 2 g fiber, 23 g protein. **Diabetic Exchanges:** 3 very lean meat, 1-1/2 starch, 1 vegetable, 1 fat.

For an easy way to lend Asian flair to dishes without adding a lot of calories, consider a few teaspoons of **hoisin sauce.** Found in the ethnic or Asian aisle of most grocery stores, the thick sauce is a wonderful way to flavor everything from appetizers to entrees.

MUSHROOM POT ROAST

SKILLET BEEF STROGANOFF

MAKEOVER PHILLY STEAK
AND CHEESE STROMBOLI

Beef Entrees

Have a meat-and-potato lover in your family? Consider the lip-smacking specialties in this chapter. You'll find more than four dozen beefy main courses so satisfying, no one will guess they're lighter!

Mushroom Pot Roast C

PREP: 25 min. **COOK:** 6 hours **YIELD:** 10 servings

ANGIE STEWART • TOPEKA, KANSAS

Wow! The wine-warmed flavors in this recipe are amazing! Packed with wholesome veggies and tender beef, this is one company-special dish all ages will like. Serve with mashed potatoes to enjoy every last drop of the rich, beefy gravy.

- 1 boneless beef chuck roast (3 to 4 lbs.)
- 1/2 tsp. salt
- 1/4 tsp. pepper
- 1 Tbsp. canola oil
- 1-1/2 lb. sliced fresh shiitake mushrooms
- 2-1/2 cups thinly sliced onions
- 1-1/2 cups reduced-sodium beef broth
- 1-1/2 cups dry red wine *or* additional reduced-sodium beef broth
- 1 can (8 oz.) tomato sauce
- 3/4 cup chopped peeled parsnips
- 3/4 cup chopped celery
- 3/4 cup chopped carrots
- 8 garlic cloves, minced
- 2 bay leaves
- 1-1/2 tsp. dried thyme
- 1 tsp. chili powder
- 1/4 cup cornstarch
- 1/4 cup water
- Mashed potatoes

1. Sprinkle roast with salt and pepper. In a Dutch oven, brown roast in oil on all sides. Transfer to a 6-qt. slow cooker. Add the mushrooms, onions, broth, wine, tomato sauce, parsnips, celery, carrots, garlic, bay leaves, thyme and chili powder. Cover and cook on low for 6-8 hours or until meat is tender.

2. Remove meat and vegetables to a serving platter; keep warm. Discard bay leaves. Skim fat from cooking juices; transfer juices to a small saucepan. Bring liquid to a boil. Combine cornstarch and water until smooth; gradually stir into the pan. Bring to a boil; cook and stir for 2 minutes or until thickened. Serve with mashed potatoes, meat and vegetables.

Nutrition Facts: 4 oz. cooked beef with 2/3 cup vegetables and 1/2 cup gravy (calculated without potatoes) equals 310 calories, 14 g fat (5 g saturated fat), 89 mg cholesterol, 363 mg sodium, 14 g carbohydrate, 3 g fiber, 30 g protein. **Diabetic Exchanges:** 4 lean meat, 2 vegetable, 1-1/2 fat.

Makeover Philly Steak And Cheese Stromboli

PREP: 30 min. **BAKE:** 25 min. + standing
YIELD: 8 servings

BARBIE MILLER • OAKDALE, MINNESOTA

It's just not Christmas Eve at our house without this traditional stromboli—and now it's lower in fat and calories!

- 2 large green peppers, julienned
- 1/2 lb. sliced fresh mushrooms
- 1 large onion, halved and sliced
- 2 Tbsp. canola oil
- 1/2 tsp. garlic powder
- 1/4 tsp. pepper
- 1 loaf (1 lb.) frozen whole wheat bread dough, thawed
- 12 oz. reduced-fat process cheese (Velveeta), sliced
- 1/2 lb. shaved deli roast beef, chopped
- 1 egg white
- 1 tsp. water
- 1/4 cup shredded part-skim mozzarella cheese

1. In a large nonstick skillet, saute the peppers, mushrooms and onion in oil until tender. Stir in garlic powder and pepper; set aside.

2. On a baking sheet coated with cooking spray, roll dough into a 15-in. x 10-in. rectangle. Layer half of the sliced cheese, all of roast beef and vegetable mixture lengthwise over half of dough to within 1/2 in. of edges. Top with remaining sliced cheese. Fold dough over filling; pinch the seams to seal and tuck ends under.

3. Combine egg white and water; brush over dough. Cut slits in top. Bake at 350° for 20-25 minutes or until golden brown. Sprinkle with mozzarella cheese. Bake 5 minutes longer or until cheese is melted. Let stand for 10 minutes before cutting.

Nutrition Facts: 1 slice equals 331 calories, 12 g fat (3 g saturated fat), 33 mg cholesterol, 1,055 mg sodium, 38 g carbohydrate, 5 g fiber, 23 g protein.

Basil Burgers with Sun-Dried Tomato Mayonnaise

PREP: 25 min. GRILL: 10 min. YIELD: 6 servings

VIRGINIA KOCHIS • SPRINGFIELD, VIRGINIA

I often end up with a bumper crop of basil, and here's a favorite way to use some of it. These burgers feature great Italian flavor. And who can resist their gooey, cheesy centers or the scrumptious topping?

1/4	cup sun-dried tomatoes (not packed in oil)
1	cup boiling water
1	cup fat-free mayonnaise
2	tsp. Worcestershire sauce
1/4	cup fresh basil leaves, coarsely chopped
2	tsp. Italian seasoning
2	garlic cloves, minced
1/2	tsp. pepper
1/4	tsp. salt
1-1/2	lb. lean ground beef (90% lean)
3/4	cup shredded part-skim mozzarella cheese
6	whole wheat hamburger buns, split

Additional fresh basil leaves, optional

1. In a small bowl, combine tomatoes and water. Let stand for 5 minutes; drain. In a food processor, combine mayonnaise and tomatoes; cover and process until blended. Chill until serving.

2. In a large bowl, combine the Worcestershire sauce, basil, Italian seasoning, garlic, pepper and salt. Crumble beef over mixture and mix well. Shape into 12 thin patties. Place 2 Tbsp. cheese on six patties; top with the remaining patties and press edges firmly to seal.

3. Moisten a paper towel with cooking oil; using long-handled tongs, lightly coat the grill rack. Grill burgers, covered, over medium heat or broil 4 in. from the heat for 5-7 minutes on each side or until a thermometer reads 160° and juices run clear. Serve on buns with mayonnaise mixture and additional basil if desired.

Nutrition Facts: 1 burger equals 368 calories, 15 g fat (6 g saturated fat), 83 mg cholesterol, 816 mg sodium, 30 g carbohydrate, 5 g fiber, 30 g protein. **Diabetic Exchanges:** 4 lean meat, 2 starch, 1/2 fat.

Mexican Meat Loaf

PREP: 25 min. BAKE: 55 min. + standing
YIELD: 8 servings

MARY RELYEA • CANASTOTA, NEW YORK

Welcome your family in from the cold with this moist and delicious meat loaf that offers wonderful taco flavor. This is down-home comfort food at its healthy best!

1	large onion, chopped
1	large sweet red pepper, chopped
3	garlic cloves, minced
1	Tbsp. olive oil
1	cup dry bread crumbs
2	tsp. chili powder
1	tsp. salt
1	tsp. dried oregano
1/2	tsp. ground cumin
1/2	tsp. pepper
1	can (14-1/2 oz.) diced tomatoes with mild green chilies, *divided*
1/3	cup plain yogurt
1	egg, lightly beaten
2	lbs. lean ground beef (90% lean)

1. In a large nonstick skillet, saute the onion, red pepper and garlic in oil until tender. Transfer to a large bowl. Stir in the bread crumbs, chili powder, salt, oregano, cumin, pepper, 2/3 cup diced tomatoes with green chilies, yogurt and egg. Crumble beef over mixture and mix well.

2. Shape into a loaf and place in an 11-in. x 7-in. baking dish coated with cooking spray. Spoon the remaining diced tomatoes over top. Bake, uncovered, at 350° for 55-60 minutes or until no pink remains and a thermometer reads 160°. Drain if necessary; let stand for 15 minutes before slicing.

Nutrition Facts: 1 slice equals 296 calories, 13 g fat (5 g saturated fat), 98 mg cholesterol, 672 mg sodium, 18 g carbohydrate, 3 g fiber, 26 g protein. **Diabetic Exchanges:** 3 lean meat, 1 starch, 1/2 fat.

Chili Mac Casserole

PREP: 20 min. BAKE: 25 min. YIELD: 6 servings

JANET KANZLER • YAKIMA, WASHINGTON

With wagon wheel pasta and popular Tex-Mex ingredients, this beefy main dish is sure to be a hit with adults and kids. Simply add a mixed green salad with any light dressing you like for a complete dinner.

BASIL BURGERS WITH SUN-DRIED TOMATO MAYONNAISE

CHILI MAC CASSEROLE

1 cup uncooked wagon wheel pasta
1 lb. lean ground beef (90% lean)
1/2 cup chopped onion
1/2 cup chopped green pepper
1 can (15 oz.) turkey chili with beans
1 can (14-1/2 oz.) stewed tomatoes, undrained
1 cup crushed baked tortilla chip scoops
1 cup (4 oz.) shredded reduced-fat cheddar cheese, *divided*
1/4 cup uncooked instant rice
1 tsp. chili powder
1/4 tsp. salt
1/8 tsp. pepper

1. Cook pasta according to package directions. Meanwhile, in a large nonstick skillet, cook the beef, onion and green pepper over medium heat until meat is no longer pink; drain. Stir in the chili, tomatoes, chips, 1/2 cup cheese, rice, chili powder, salt and pepper. Drain pasta; add to beef mixture.

2. Transfer to a 2-qt. baking dish coated with cooking spray. Sprinkle with remaining cheese. Bake, uncovered, at 350° for 25-30 minutes or until cheese is melted.

Nutrition Facts: 1 cup equals 358 calories, 11 g fat (5 g saturated fat), 60 mg cholesterol, 847 mg sodium, 36 g carbohydrate, 4 g fiber, 28 g protein. **Diabetic Exchange:** 3 lean meat, 2 starch, 1 vegetable.

To **chop an onion**, peel and cut it in half from the root to the top. Leaving the root attached, cut vertically through the onion, leaving the root end uncut. Then, simply cut across the onion, discarding the root end.

Easy Burgundy Stew C

PREP: 20 min. BAKE: 3 hours YIELD: 7 servings

COLEEN BALCH • CLAY, NEW YORK

Watching your salt intake? This satisfying stew has almost 2/3 less sodium than many off-the-shelf "beef stew cup" products. To lower the sodium even further, replace the diced tomatoes with no-salt-added diced tomatoes.

- 1 boneless beef chuck roast (2 lbs.), cut into 1-in. cubes
- 1 can (14-1/2 oz.) diced tomatoes, undrained
- 1/2 lb. sliced fresh mushrooms
- 4 medium carrots, sliced
- 2 medium onions, sliced
- 2 celery ribs, chopped
- 1 cup Burgundy wine *or* reduced-sodium beef broth
- 1 Tbsp. minced fresh thyme *or* 1 tsp. dried thyme
- 1/2 tsp. salt
- 1/2 tsp. ground mustard
- 1/4 tsp. pepper
- 3 Tbsp. all-purpose flour
- 1 cup water

1. In an ovenproof Dutch oven, combine the first 11 ingredients. Combine flour and water until smooth. Gradually stir into stew. Cover and bake at 325° for 3 hours or until meat and vegetables are tender, stirring every 30 minutes.

Nutrition Facts: 1 cup equals 287 calories, 13 g fat (5 g saturated fat), 84 mg cholesterol, 332 mg sodium, 15 g carbohydrate, 4 g fiber, 28 g protein. **Diabetic Exchanges:** 3 lean meat, 2 vegetable, 1 fat.

Veggie Steak Fajitas

PREP/TOTAL TIME: 25 min. YIELD: 4 servings

BECKY TONEY • TARPON SPRINGS, FLORIDA

I used to live in Mexico and love re-creating the flavors I enjoyed there. This is one of my favorite quick meals!

- 1 beef top sirloin steak (1 lb.), thinly sliced
- 2 tsp. ground cumin
- 1/8 tsp. salt
- 3 tsp. canola oil, *divided*
- 1 large onion, julienned
- 1 small sweet red pepper, julienned
- 1 small green pepper, julienned

2 Tbsp. minced fresh cilantro
4 whole wheat tortillas (8 in.), warmed
Optional ingredients: Shredded lettuce, chopped tomato and reduced-fat sour cream

1. Sprinkle beef with cumin and salt. In a large skillet, saute beef in 2 tsp. oil until no longer pink. Remove and set aside.

2. In the same skillet, saute onion and peppers in remaining oil until tender. Stir in cilantro. Return beef to the pan; heat through.

3. Spoon onto whole wheat tortillas; fold in the sides. Serve with shredded lettuce, chopped tomato and sour cream if desired.

Nutrition Facts: 1 fajita (calculated without optional ingredients) equals 344 calories, 11 g fat (2 g saturated fat), 46 mg cholesterol, 299 mg sodium, 28 g carbohydrate, 4 g fiber, 29 g protein. **Diabetic Exchanges:** 3 lean meat, 1-1/2 starch, 1 vegetable, 1 fat.

Salisbury Steak with Gravy

PREP: 15 min. **BAKE:** 50 min. **YIELD:** 4 servings

DANELLE WEIHER • VERNDALE, MINNESOTA

This recipe was shared at a WeightWatchers meeting I attended, and my whole family really enjoys it. I like that it's so tasty and quick to prepare.

1/2 cup fat-free milk
14 fat-free saltines, crushed
2 Tbsp. dried minced onion
2 tsp. dried parsley flakes
1 lb. lean ground beef (90% lean)
1 jar (12 oz.) fat-free beef gravy
2 Tbsp. ketchup
2 tsp. Worcestershire sauce
1/4 tsp. pepper

1. In a large bowl, combine the milk, saltines, onion and parsley. Crumble beef over mixture and mix well. Shape into four patties. Place in an 8-in. square baking dish coated with cooking spray.

2. In a small bowl, combine the gravy, ketchup, Worcestershire and pepper; pour over patties. Bake, uncovered, at 350° for 50-55 minutes or until a thermometer reads 160°.

Nutrition Facts: 1 salisbury steak equals 266 calories, 9 g fat (4 g saturated fat), 77 mg cholesterol, 727 mg sodium, 21 g carbohydrate, 1 g fiber, 24 g protein. **Diabetic Exchanges:** 3 lean meat, 1-1/2 starch.

Skillet Beef Stroganoff C

PREP: 25 min. **COOK:** 1-1/4 hours **YIELD:** 6 servings

ALJENE WENDLING • SEATTLE, WASHINGTON

This has been a favorite of mine for 40 years. I like using horseradish, which gives the dish an extra zing.

5 cups sliced fresh mushrooms
1 large onion, sliced
1 Tbsp. reduced-fat butter
1/3 to 1/2 cup hot water
1 Tbsp. prepared horseradish

1/2 tsp. salt
1/8 tsp. pepper
1/4 cup all-purpose flour
1 beef flank steak (1-1/4 lb.), cut into 2-in. strips
1 cup (8 oz.) reduced-fat sour cream
Hot cooked noodles

1. In a large skillet, saute mushrooms and onion in butter until tender. With a slotted spoon, transfer to a large bowl; stir in the water, horseradish, salt and pepper. Set aside.

2. Place flour in a large resealable plastic bag. Add beef, a few pieces at a time. Seal bag; shake to coat.

3. In the same skillet, brown the beef in batches. Return all of the beef to the pan; top with the mushroom mixture.

4. Bring to a boil. Reduce heat; cover and simmer for 1-1/4 to 1-1/2 hours or until beef is tender, stirring occasionally. Remove from the heat; stir in sour cream. Serve with noodles.

Editor's Note: This recipe was tested with Land O'Lakes light stick butter.

Nutrition Facts: 2/3 cup (calculated without noodles) equals 246 calories, 11 g fat (6 g saturated fat), 62 mg cholesterol, 302 mg sodium, 11 g carbohydrate, 1 g fiber, 24 g protein. **Diabetic Exchanges:** 3 lean meat, 1 starch, 1 fat.

To perk up your own **beef stroganoff** recipe, add an envelope of ranch salad dressing/dip mix to the sour cream before stirring it into the rice or noodles. You can also sprinkle in a few teaspoons of dill weed.

SKILLET BEEF STROGANOFF

Gingered Beef Stir-Fry

PREP/TOTAL TIME: 20 min.   **YIELD:** 4 servings

DEBBIE WILLIAMS • ASHLAND, OHIO

Stir-fry is popular in our home because it's so quick to fix. My oldest son especially likes this version. With pleasant ginger flavor, sweet red peppers and bright green snap peas, it makes a complete, satisfying dinner.

1-1/2	tsp. sugar
1	tsp. cornstarch
1/4	cup cold water
3	Tbsp. reduced-sodium soy sauce
2	tsp. sesame oil, *divided*
1	beef flank steak (1 lb.), cut into thin strips
1	jar (8 oz.) whole baby corn, drained
1/4	cup julienned sweet red pepper
2	tsp. minced fresh gingerroot
2	tsp. minced garlic
1/4	lb. fresh sugar snap peas
3	cups hot cooked rice

1. In a small bowl, combine sugar and cornstarch. Stir in the water, soy sauce and 1 tsp. oil until smooth; set aside. In a large nonstick skillet or wok, stir-fry beef in remaining oil for 4-5 minutes or until no longer pink.

2. Add the corn, red pepper, ginger and garlic; stir-fry for 2-3 minutes or until vegetables are crisp-tender. Add peas; stir-fry 30 seconds longer. Stir soy sauce mixture and add to the pan. Bring to a boil; cook and stir for 2 minutes or until thickened. Serve with rice.

Nutrition Facts: 1 cup beef mixture with 3/4 cup rice equals 377 calories, 12 g fat (4 g saturated fat), 48 mg cholesterol, 618 mg sodium, 41 g carbohydrate, 2 g fiber, 25 g protein. **Diabetic Exchanges:** 3 lean meat, 2 starch, 1 vegetable, 1/2 fat.

Lasagna Corn Carne

PREP: 30 min.   **BAKE:** 45 min. + standing
YIELD: 12 servings

MARY LOU WILLS • LA PLATA, MARYLAND

Packed with lean ground beef and nutritious veggies, this filling dish is as good as it is good for you!

1	lb. lean ground beef (90% lean)
1	jar (16 oz.) salsa
1	can (16 oz.) kidney beans, rinsed and drained
1	can (14-3/4 oz.) cream-style corn
1	large onion, chopped
1	medium green pepper, chopped
1	celery rib, chopped
3	garlic cloves, minced
1	Tbsp. minced fresh basil *or* 1 tsp. dried basil
1	tsp. salt
1	tsp. chili powder
12	lasagna noodles, cooked, rinsed and drained
2	cups (8 oz.) shredded part-skim mozzarella cheese
1/2	cup grated Parmesan cheese

1. In a large skillet, cook beef over medium heat until no longer pink; drain. Add the salsa, beans, vegetables, garlic and seasonings. Bring to a boil. Reduce heat; cover and simmer for 15 minutes.

2. Spread a fourth of the meat sauce in a 13-in. x 9-in. baking dish coated with cooking spray; top with four noodles. Repeat layers once. Top with half of the remaining sauce; sprinkle with half of the cheeses. Layer with remaining noodles, sauce and cheeses.

GINGERED BEEF STIR-FRY

LASAGNA CORN CARNE

3. Cover and bake at 350° for 30 minutes. Uncover; bake 15-20 minutes longer or until heated through. Let stand for 15 minutes before cutting.

Nutrition Facts: 1 piece equals 292 calories, 8 g fat (4 g saturated fat), 37 mg cholesterol, 674 mg sodium, 36 g carbohydrate, 4 g fiber, 20 g protein. **Diabetic Exchanges:** 2-1/2 starch, 2 lean meat.

Fiesta Grilled Flank Steak C

PREP: 20 min. + marinating **GRILL:** 15 min.
YIELD: 4 servings

ROXANNE CHAN • ALBANY, CALIFORNIA

Whether you broil this tasty steak or slap it on the grill, the acid in the marinade's lime and pineapple juice will help tenderize it. Pair this with sweet potatoes for a colorful, hearty summer hit!

- 1/2 cup unsweetened pineapple juice
- 1 Tbsp. lime juice
- 1/2 tsp. garlic salt
- 1/2 tsp. ground cumin
- 1 beef flank steak (1 lb.)
- 1 cup cubed fresh pineapple
- 1/2 cup salsa verde
- 1 medium ripe avocado, peeled and cubed
- 1 green onion, finely chopped
- 1 Tbsp. minced fresh cilantro

1. In a large resealable plastic bag, combine the pineapple juice, lime juice, garlic salt and cumin. Score the surface of the beef, making diamond shapes 1/4 in. deep; place in bag. Seal bag and turn to coat; refrigerate for 8 hours or overnight.

2. In a small bowl, combine the pineapple, salsa, avocado, green onion and cilantro. Cover and chill until serving.

3. Drain beef and discard marinade. Using long-handled tongs, moisten a paper towel with cooking oil and lightly coat the grill rack. Grill steak, covered, over medium heat or broil 4 in. from the heat for 6-8 minutes on each side or until meat reaches desired doneness (for medium-rare, a thermometer should read 145°; medium, 160°; well-done, 170°).

4. Let stand for 5 minutes; thinly slice across the grain. Serve with salsa.

Nutrition Facts: 3 oz. cooked beef with 1/2 cup salsa equals 274 calories, 15 g fat (4 g saturated fat), 54 mg cholesterol, 322 mg sodium, 12 g carbohydrate, 4 g fiber, 24 g protein. **Diabetic Exchanges:** 3 lean meat, 1 fat, 1/2 fruit.

Beef & Blue Cheese Tart

PREP: 20 min. **BAKE:** 15 min. **YIELD:** 6 servings

JUDY BATSON • TAMPA, FLORIDA

This elegant yet rustic recipe goes together in minutes and is so simple. It's just perfect for entertaining!

1/2	lb. lean ground beef (90% lean)
1-3/4	cups sliced fresh mushrooms
1/2	medium red onion, thinly sliced
1/4	tsp. salt
1/4	tsp. pepper
1	tube (13.8 oz.) refrigerated pizza crust
1/2	cup reduced-fat sour cream
2	tsp. Italian seasoning
1/2	tsp. garlic powder
3/4	cup crumbled blue cheese

1. In a large skillet, cook the beef, mushrooms and onion over medium heat until meat is no longer pink; drain. Stir in salt and pepper; set aside.

2. On a lightly floured surface, roll crust into a 15-in. x 12-in. rectangle. Carefully transfer to a parchment paper-lined baking sheet.

3. In a small bowl, combine the sour cream, Italian seasoning and garlic powder; spread over crust to within 2 in. of edges. Spoon beef mixture over top. Fold up edges of crust over the filling, leaving the center uncovered.

4. Bake at 425° for 15-18 minutes or until crust is golden. Using the parchment paper, slide tart onto a wire rack. Sprinkle with blue cheese; let stand for 5 minutes before slicing.

Nutrition Facts: 1 slice equals 328 calories, 12 g fat (5 g saturated fat), 43 mg cholesterol, 803 mg sodium, 35 g carbohydrate, 1 g fiber, 19 g protein. **Diabetic Exchanges:** 2 starch, 2 lean meat, 2 fat.

Chipotle Beef & Rice

PREP/TOTAL TIME: 30 min. **YIELD:** 4 servings

AYSHA SCHURMAN • AMMON, IDAHO

Made completely in the skillet, this savory, moist mix of ground beef, lime, salsa, peppers and cheese offers creamy comfort. Chipotle pepper adds just the right amount of heat.

1	lb. extra-lean ground beef (95% lean)
1/3	cup chopped green onions
1/3	cup chopped green pepper
2	cups cooked brown rice
1	cup salsa
1	cup (8 oz.) fat-free sour cream
2	Tbsp. finely chopped pickled pepper rings
1	Tbsp. lime juice
1	tsp. ground chipotle pepper
3/4	cup shredded reduced-fat cheddar cheese, *divided*

1. In a large skillet, cook the beef, onions and pepper over medium heat until beef is no longer pink; drain.

2. Stir in the rice, salsa, sour cream, pepper rings, lime juice, chipotle pepper and 1/2 cup cheese. Cook and stir until heated through. Sprinkle with remaining cheese. Cover and let stand for 5 minutes or until cheese is melted.

Nutrition Facts: 1-1/2 cups equals 403 calories, 11 g fat (6 g saturated fat), 90 mg cholesterol, 495 mg sodium, 39 g carbohydrate, 2 g fiber, 35 g protein. **Diabetic Exchanges:** 4 lean meat, 2-1/2 starch, 1/2 fat.

One-For-All Marinated Beef C

PREP: 10 min. + marinating **GRILL:** 6 min. + standing **YIELD:** 6 servings

SUE SAUER • DEER RIVER, MINNESOTA

I use this mouthwatering marinade not just for beef but for everything I grill—from pork chops to chicken. The marinade's main ingredient, orange juice, is low in calories, and it makes a good tenderizer.

3/4	cup orange juice
1/4	cup reduced-sodium soy sauce
2	Tbsp. brown sugar
2	Tbsp. prepared mustard
1	Tbsp. canola oil
2	garlic cloves, minced
1	beef flank steak (1-1/2 lbs.)

1. In a large resealable plastic bag, combine the first six ingredients; add steak. Seal bag and turn to coat; refrigerate for 4 hours or overnight.

2. Drain and discard marinade. Using long-handled tongs, moisten a paper towel with cooking oil and lightly coat the grill rack. Grill steak, covered, over medium heat or broil 4 in. from the heat for 6-8 minutes on each side or until meat reaches desired doneness (for medium-rare, a thermometer should read 145°; medium, 160°; well-done, 170°). Let stand for 10 minutes before slicing.

Nutrition Facts: 3 oz. cooked beef equals 206 calories, 10 g fat (4 g saturated fat), 56 mg cholesterol, 305 mg sodium, 4 g carbohydrate, 1 g fiber, 23 g protein. **Diabetic Exchanges:** 3 lean meat, 1 fat.

Beefy Tomato Rice Skillet

PREP/TOTAL TIME: 25 min. **YIELD:** 6 servings

ELLYN GRAEBERT • YUMA, ARIZONA

I put this together one day with what I had on hand. It's quick on busy nights or in the summer when we're camping.

1	lb. ground beef
1	cup chopped celery
2/3	cup chopped onion
1/2	cup chopped green pepper
1	can (11 oz.) whole kernel corn, drained
1	can (10-3/4 oz.) condensed tomato soup, undiluted
1	cup water
1	tsp. Italian seasoning
1	cup uncooked instant rice

1. In a large skillet over medium heat, cook the beef, celery, onion and pepper until meat is no longer pink and vegetables are tender; drain.

2. Add the corn, soup, water and Italian seasoning; bring to a boil. Stir in rice; cover and remove from the heat. Let stand for 10 minutes or until rice is tender.

Nutrition Facts: 1 cup equals 266 calories, 7 g fat (3 g saturated fat), 37 mg cholesterol, 506 mg sodium, 30 g carbohydrate, 2 g fiber, 17 g protein. **Diabetic Exchanges:** 2 lean meat, 2 vegetable, 1 starch, 1 fat.

ONE-FOR-ALL MARINATED BEEF

BEEFY TOMATO RICE SKILLET

Beef Kabobs with Chutney Sauce

PREP: 15 min. + marinating **GRILL:** 5 min.
YIELD: 8 kabobs (about 1/2 cup sauce)

JUDY THOMPSON • ANKENY, IOWA

I created this speedy grilled entree for our daughter, who's a fan of Indian food. The mango chutney and subtle curry give the beef a sweet yet spicy flavor.

- 1/4 cup mango chutney
- 1 Tbsp. water
- 1 Tbsp. cider vinegar
- 1 tsp. curry powder
- 1/4 tsp. cayenne pepper
- 1 lb. beef top sirloin steak, cut into 1/4-in. strips

CHUTNEY SAUCE:
- 1/2 cup plain yogurt
- 3 Tbsp. mango chutney
- 1 tsp. lemon juice
- 1/2 tsp. curry powder
- 1/4 tsp. ground cumin
- 1/8 tsp. cayenne pepper

> Add flavor to beef with **marinades.** Always marinate in the refrigerator in a glass container or plastic resealable storage bag. If a marinade is also used as a basting sauce, reserve some before adding it to the uncooked beef.

1. In a large resealable plastic bag, combine the first five ingredients; add the beef. Seal bag and turn to coat; refrigerate overnight.

2. In a small bowl, combine the sauce ingredients. Cover and refrigerate until serving.

3. Drain and discard marinade. Thread beef onto eight metal or soaked wooden skewers.

4. Moisten a paper towel with cooking oil; using long-handled tongs, lightly coat the grill rack. Grill kabobs, covered, over medium heat or broil 4 in. from the heat for 4-6 minutes or until meat reaches desired doneness, turning occasionally. Serve beef with sauce.

Nutrition Facts: 2 skewers with 2 Tbsp. sauce equals 258 calories, 6 g fat (2 g saturated fat), 50 mg cholesterol, 321 mg sodium, 23 g carbohydrate, trace fiber, 25 g protein. **Diabetic Exchanges:** 3 lean meat, 1-1/2 starch.

Hungarian Goulash

PREP: 20 min. **COOK:** 7 hours **YIELD:** 12 servings

MARCIA DOYLE • POMPANO BEACH, FLORIDA

Talk about your heirloom recipes! My grandmother made this for my mother when she was a child, and my mother made it for us to enjoy. Sour cream gives it a creamy richness.

- 3 medium onions, chopped
- 2 medium carrots, chopped
- 2 medium green peppers, chopped
- 3 lb. beef stew meat, cut into 1-in. cubes
- 1/2 tsp. plus 1/4 tsp. salt, *divided*
- 1/2 tsp. plus 1/4 tsp. pepper, *divided*
- 2 Tbsp. olive oil
- 1-1/2 cups reduced-sodium beef broth
- 1/4 cup all-purpose flour
- 3 Tbsp. paprika
- 2 Tbsp. tomato paste
- 1 tsp. caraway seeds
- 1 garlic clove, minced

Dash sugar
- 12 cups uncooked whole wheat egg noodles
- 1 cup (8 oz.) reduced-fat sour cream

1. Place the onions, carrots and green peppers in a 5-qt. slow cooker. Sprinkle meat with 1/2 tsp. salt and 1/2 tsp. pepper. In a large skillet, brown meat in oil in batches. Transfer to slow cooker.

2. Add broth to skillet, stirring to loosen browned bits from pan. Combine the flour, paprika, tomato paste, caraway seeds, garlic, sugar and remaining salt and pepper; stir into skillet. Bring to a boil; cook and stir for 2 minutes or until thickened. Pour over the meat. Cover and cook on low for 7-9 hours or until the meat is tender.

3. Meanwhile, cook noodles according to package directions. Stir sour cream into slow cooker. Drain noodles; serve with goulash.

Nutrition Facts: 2/3 cup goulash with 1 cup noodles equals 388 calories, 13 g fat (4 g saturated fat), 78 mg cholesterol, 285 mg sodium, 41 g carbohydrate, 7 g fiber, 31 g protein. **Diabetic Exchanges:** 3 lean meat, 2 starch, 1 vegetable, 1 fat.

BEEF KABOBS WITH CHUTNEY SAUCE

Grilled Sirloin Teriyaki C

PREP: 10 min. + marinating **GRILL:** 10 min.
YIELD: 2 servings

AGNES WARD • STRATFORD, ONTARIO

The marinade for this very tender Asian-style beef also works well with fish, chicken and pork. It's perfect for two!

3	Tbsp. reduced-sodium soy sauce
4-1/2	tsp. brown sugar
1	Tbsp. rice vinegar
1-1/2	tsp. minced fresh gingerroot
1	garlic clove, minced
1/8	tsp. crushed red pepper flakes
1	beef top sirloin steak (1 in. thick and 1/2 lb.)

1. In a large resealable plastic bag, combine the first six ingredients. Add the steak; seal bag and turn to coat. Refrigerate for 8 hours or overnight.

2. Drain and discard marinade. Using long-handled tongs, moisten a paper towel with cooking oil and lightly coat the grill rack. Grill beef, covered, over medium heat or broil 4 in. from the heat for 4-5 minutes on each side or until meat reaches desired doneness (for medium-rare, a thermometer should read 145°; medium, 160°; well-done, 170°).

Nutrition Facts: 3 oz. cooked beef equals 163 calories, 5 g fat (2 g saturated fat), 46 mg cholesterol, 279 mg sodium, 4 g carbohydrate, trace fiber, 25 g protein. **Diabetic Exchange:** 3 lean meat.

TERIYAKI BEEF TENDERLOIN

Teriyaki Beef Tenderloin C

PREP: 10 min. + marinating **BAKE:** 45 min. + standing
YIELD: 8 servings

LILY JULOW • GAINESVILLE, FLORIDA

A beautiful glaze coats this fantastic tenderloin that's as easy as it is delicious. All you have to do is throw some ingredients together and let the marinade do all the work.

> 1 cup sherry or reduced-sodium beef broth
> 1/2 cup reduced-sodium soy sauce
> 1 envelope onion soup mix
> 1/4 cup packed brown sugar
> 1 beef tenderloin roast (2 lbs.)
> 2 Tbsp. water

1. In a large bowl, combine the sherry, soy sauce, soup mix and brown sugar. Pour 1 cup into a large resealable plastic bag; add tenderloin. Seal bag and turn to coat; refrigerate for 5 hours or overnight. Cover and refrigerate remaining marinade.

2. Drain and discard marinade. Place tenderloin on a rack in a shallow roasting pan. Bake, uncovered, at 425° for 45-50 minutes or until meat reaches desired doneness (for medium-rare, a thermometer should read 145°; medium, 160°; well-done, 170°), basting often with 1/3 cup reserved marinade. Let stand for 10-15 minutes.

3. Meanwhile, in a small saucepan, bring water and remaining marinade to a rolling boil for 1 minute or until sauce is slightly reduced. Slice beef; serve with sauce.

Nutrition Facts: 3 oz. cooked beef with 1 Tbsp. sauce equals 242 calories, 11 g fat (4 g saturated fat), 72 mg cholesterol, 695 mg sodium, 7 g carbohydrate, trace fiber, 24 g protein. **Diabetic Exchanges:** 3 lean meat, 1/2 starch.

Little Meat Loaves C

PREP: 15 min. **BAKE:** 45 min. **YIELD:** 8 servings

PAUL SOPER • SIERRA VISTA, ARIZONA

I've wanted to reduce the fat in my meat loaf for many years, and I finally came up with this recipe. By starting with lean ground beef and not adding any egg yolks, I reduced the total fat considerably. Making individual loaves cuts the cooking time by almost half.

> 3 egg whites
> 1/2 cup fat-free plain yogurt
> 1 can (6 oz.) tomato paste
> 1 Tbsp. Worcestershire sauce
> 1/2 cup quick-cooking oats
> 1 small onion, chopped
> 2 Tbsp. dried parsley flakes
> 1 tsp. salt
> 1 tsp. poultry seasoning
> 1/2 tsp. garlic powder
> 1/2 tsp. pepper
> 2 lbs. lean ground beef (90% lean)
> 1/2 cup ketchup

1. In a large bowl, combine the first 11 ingredients. Crumble beef over mixture and mix well. Shape into eight loaves.

2. Place on a rack coated with cooking spray in a shallow baking pan. Bake, uncovered, at 350° for 30 minutes. Spoon ketchup over the loaves. Bake 15 minutes longer or until a thermometer reads 160° and meat is no longer pink.

Nutrition Facts: 1 meat loaf equals 264 calories, 11 g fat (4 g saturated fat), 42 mg cholesterol, 633 mg sodium, 15 g carbohydrate, 2 g fiber, 27 g protein. **Diabetic Exchanges:** 3 lean meat, 1 starch, 1/2 fat.

Black Bean and Beef Tostadas

PREP/TOTAL TIME: 30 min. **YIELD:** 4 servings

SUSAN BROWN • KANSAS CITY, KANSAS

Simple ingredients add up to one of our family's favorites. It's also easy to double for casual get-togethers!

> 8 oz. lean ground beef (90% lean)
> 1 can (10 oz.) diced tomatoes and green chilies, undrained
> 1 can (15 oz.) black beans, rinsed and drained
> 1 can (16 oz.) refried beans
> 8 tostada shells

Optional toppings: shredded lettuce, shredded reduced-fat Mexican cheese blend, sour cream *and/or* salsa

1. In a large skillet, cook beef over medium heat until no longer pink; drain. Stir in tomatoes. Bring to a boil. Reduce heat; simmer, uncovered, for 6-8 minutes or until liquid is reduced to 2 Tbsp. Stir in black beans; heat through.

2. Spread refried beans over tostada shells. Top with beef mixture. Serve with toppings of your choice.

Nutrition Facts: 2 tostadas (calculated without toppings) equals 390 calories, 11 g fat (3 g saturated fat), 44 mg cholesterol, 944 mg sodium, 49 g carbohydrate, 12 g fiber, 24 g protein. **Diabetic Exchanges:** 3 starch, 3 lean meat.

BLACK BEAN AND BEEF TOSTADAS

Savory Marinated Flank Steak C

PREP: 10 min. + marinating **GRILL:** 15 min.
YIELD: 6 servings

LISA RUEHLOW • BLAINE, MINNESOTA

Kitchen staples come together quickly in this flavor-packed marinade that really perks up flank steak.

    3 Tbsp. canola oil
    2 Tbsp. lemon juice
    2 Tbsp. Worcestershire sauce
    1 Tbsp. dried minced garlic
    1 Tbsp. Greek seasoning
    1 Tbsp. brown sugar
    1 tsp. onion powder
    1 beef flank steak (1-1/2 lbs.)

1. In a large resealable plastic bag, combine the first seven ingredients; add the steak. Seal bag and turn to coat; refrigerate for 6 hours or overnight.

2. Drain and discard marinade. Moisten a paper towel with cooking oil; using long-handled tongs, lightly coat the grill rack. Grill steak, covered, over medium heat or broil 4 in. from heat for 6-8 minutes on each side or until steak reaches desired doneness (for medium-rare, a thermometer should read 145°; medium, 160°; well-done, 170°).

3. To serve, thinly slice across the grain.

Nutrition Facts: 3 oz. cooked beef equals 196 calories, 11 g fat (4 g saturated fat), 54 mg cholesterol, 269 mg sodium, 2 g carbohydrate, trace fiber, 22 g protein. **Diabetic Exchanges:** 3 lean meat, 1/2 fat.

Hearty Beans and Rice

PREP: 10 min. **COOK:** 25 min. **YIELD:** 5 servings

BARB MUSGROVE • FORT ATKINSON, WISCONSIN

Filling, fast-fixing and fabulous flavor make this satisfying dish destined to become a family favorite.

       1 lb. lean ground beef (90% lean)
       1 can (15 oz.) black beans, rinsed and drained
       1 can (14-1/2 oz.) diced tomatoes with mild green chilies, undrained
    1-1/3 cups frozen corn, thawed
       1 cup water
     1/4 tsp. salt
    1-1/2 cups instant brown rice

1. In a large saucepan, cook beef over medium heat until no longer pink; drain. Stir in the beans, tomatoes, corn, water and salt. Bring to a boil. Stir in rice; return to a boil. Reduce heat; cover and simmer for 5 minutes. Remove from the heat; let stand, covered, for 5 minutes.

Nutrition Facts: 1-1/4 cups equals 376 calories, 9 g fat (3 g saturated fat), 56 mg cholesterol, 647 mg sodium, 47 g carbohydrate, 7 g fiber, 26 g protein. **Diabetic Exchanges:** 3 starch, 3 lean meat, 1 vegetable.

Makeover Traditional Lasagna

PREP: 45 min. **BAKE:** 70 min. + standing
YIELD: 12 servings

MICHELLE BEHAN • LITTLETON, COLORADO

Here's a special recipe that's so good, it's become our family's Christmas Eve tradition. This light version allows us to enjoy it without the guilt!

    1 lb. extra-lean ground beef (95% lean)
    1 pkg. (14 oz.) breakfast turkey sausage links, casings removed and crumbled
    3 cans (8 oz. *each*) no-salt-added tomato sauce
    1 can (6 oz.) tomato paste

SAVORY MARINATED FLANK STEAK

HEARTY BEANS AND RICE

2 garlic cloves, minced

2 tsp. sugar

1-1/2 tsp. Italian seasoning

1/2 tsp. pepper

9 whole wheat lasagna noodles

3 eggs, lightly beaten

2 cups (16 oz.) 2% cottage cheese

1 carton (15 oz.) reduced-fat ricotta cheese

1/2 cup grated Parmesan cheese

3 Tbsp. minced fresh parsley

1-1/2 cups (6 oz.) shredded part-skim mozzarella cheese

6 slices provolone cheese

1. In a large skillet, cook beef and sausage over medium heat until meat is no longer pink; drain. Add the tomato sauce, tomato paste, garlic, sugar, Italian seasoning and pepper. Bring to a boil. Reduce heat; cover and simmer for 15 minutes. Meanwhile, cook noodles according to package directions; drain.

2. In a small bowl, combine the eggs, cottage cheese, ricotta cheese, Parmesan and parsley. Spread 1 cup meat sauce into a 13-in. x 9-in. baking dish coated with cooking spray. Layer with three noodles, half of the cheese mixture, 1-1/3 cups sauce and 1/2 cup mozzarella cheese. Repeat layers. Top with remaining noodles and sauce.

3. Cover and bake at 350° for 55-60 minutes or until bubbly. Top with provolone and remaining mozzarella cheese. Bake, uncovered, 15-20 minutes longer or until the cheese is melted. Let stand for 15 minutes before cutting.

Nutrition Facts: 1 piece equals 361 calories, 15 g fat (7 g saturated fat), 133 mg cholesterol, 634 mg sodium, 23 g carbohydrate, 3 g fiber, 32 g protein.

A half cup of creamed cottage cheese contains about 115 calories, while 1% cottage cheese has about 80 calories. A half cup of **ricotta cheese** made with whole milk contains about 215 calories, while ricotta made partly with skim milk has only 170 calories per half cup.

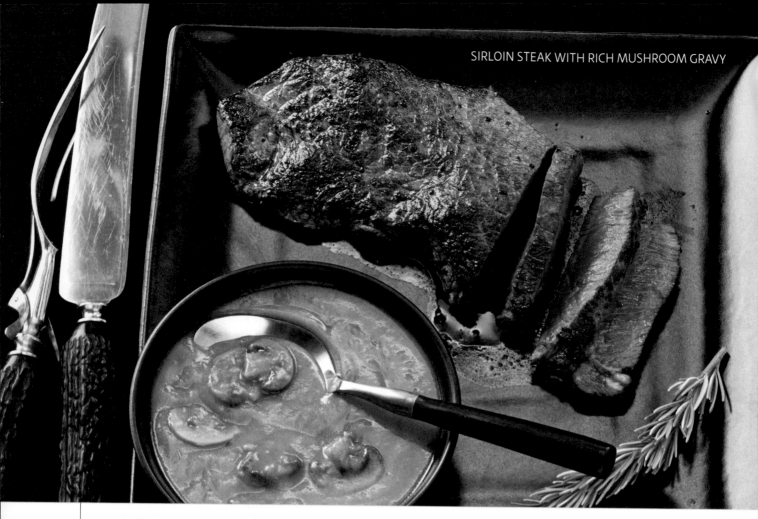

Sirloin Steak with Rich Mushroom Gravy **C**

PREP/TOTAL TIME: 30 min. YIELD: 4 servings

HEALTHY COOKING TEST KITCHEN

Toasting the flour to a light tan color gives this gravy a full flavor and thickness—without a lot of additional fat. The gravy can be thinned with broth to taste.

- 1/4 cup all-purpose flour
- 1 cup reduced-sodium beef broth
- 1 beef top sirloin steak (1-1/4 lbs.)
- 1/2 tsp. salt
- 1/4 tsp. pepper
- 1 Tbsp. canola oil
- 1/2 lb. sliced fresh mushrooms
- 1 garlic clove, minced
- 1/2 tsp. dried rosemary, crushed
- 1/8 tsp. salt
- 1/4 cup sherry or additional reduced-sodium beef broth
- 1 Tbsp. butter

1. In a large skillet over medium-high heat, cook and stir flour for 4-5 minutes or until light tan in color. Immediately transfer to a small bowl; whisk in broth until smooth. Set aside.

2. Sprinkle beef with salt and pepper. In the same skillet, cook beef in oil over medium heat for 5-6 minutes on each side or until meat reaches desired doneness (for medium-rare, a thermometer should read 145°; medium, 160°; well-done, 170°). Remove and keep warm.

3. In the same skillet, saute mushrooms until tender. Add the garlic, rosemary and salt; saute 1 minute longer. Stir in the sherry. Stir flour mixture; add to the pan. Bring to a boil; cook and stir for 1 minute or until thickened. Stir in butter until melted. Serve with steak.

Nutrition Facts: 4 oz. cooked beef with 1/2 cup gravy equals 289 calories, 12 g fat (4 g saturated fat), 66 mg cholesterol, 565 mg sodium, 9 g carbohydrate, 1 g fiber, 33 g protein. **Diabetic Exchanges:** 4 lean meat, 1 vegetable, 1 fat.

Mexican Beef & Pasta

PREP/TOTAL TIME: 30 min. YIELD: 8 servings

CHRISTINE RICHARDSON • MAPLE GROVE, MINNESOTA

Your family will love the hearty flavors of this skillet supper. You'll love that it's fast home cooking done light and chock-full of healthier ingredients. Topped with crushed corn chips for extra crunch, it's a must-try recipe.

- 3 cups uncooked whole wheat spiral pasta
- 1 lb. lean ground beef (90% lean)
- 1 small onion, chopped
- 2 cans (14-1/2 oz. *each*) no-salt-added diced tomatoes, undrained
- 1 can (15 oz.) black beans, rinsed and drained

1 cup frozen corn, thawed
1 cup chunky salsa
1 can (4 oz.) chopped green chilies
1 can (2-1/4 oz.) sliced ripe olives, drained
3 Tbsp. taco seasoning
1/2 cup reduced-fat sour cream
Crushed tortilla chips, optional

1. Cook pasta according to package directions; drain. Meanwhile, in a large skillet, cook beef and onion over medium heat until meat is no longer pink; drain.

2. Stir in the pasta, tomatoes, beans, corn, salsa, green chilies, olives and taco seasoning. Bring to a boil. Reduce heat; simmer, uncovered, for 8-10 minutes or until heated through. Top with sour cream and crushed chips if desired.

Nutrition Facts: 1-1/4 cups beef mixture with 1 Tbsp. reduced-fat sour cream (calculated without chips) equals 305 calories, 7 g fat (3 g saturated fat), 40 mg cholesterol, 737 mg sodium, 40 g carbohydrate, 7 g fiber, 20 g protein. **Diabetic Exchanges:** 2 starch, 2 lean meat, 2 vegetable.

Makeover Beef & Sausage Lasagna

PREP: 45 min. **BAKE:** 45 min. + standing
YIELD: 12 servings

JACOB KITZMAN • SEATTLE, WASHINGTON

Here's a healthier version of my popular meat-lover's lasagna. This recipe really trims the cholesterol and saturated fat, so I can enjoy it a bit more often...which is a good thing!

3/4 lb. lean ground beef (90% lean)
3/4 lb. Italian turkey sausage links, casings removed
1 medium onion, chopped
1 medium green pepper, chopped
1 jar (26 oz.) spaghetti sauce
1 pkg. (8 oz.) reduced-fat cream cheese, cubed
1 cup (8 oz.) 1% cottage cheese
1 egg, lightly beaten

1 Tbsp. minced fresh parsley
6 whole wheat lasagna noodles, cooked and drained
1 cup (4 oz.) shredded reduced-fat Italian cheese blend
3 tsp. Italian seasoning, *divided*
1 cup (4 oz.) shredded part-skim mozzarella cheese

1. In a large skillet, cook the beef, sausage, onion and green pepper over medium heat until meat is no longer pink; drain. Set aside 1 cup spaghetti sauce; stir remaining sauce into meat mixture. Bring to a boil. Reduce heat; simmer, uncovered, for 8-10 minutes or until thickened.

2. In a small saucepan, melt cream cheese over medium heat. Remove from the heat. Stir in the cottage cheese, egg and parsley.

3. Spread meat sauce into a 13-in. x 9-in. baking dish coated with cooking spray. Top with three noodles, Italian cheese blend, 1-1/2 tsp. Italian seasoning and cream cheese mixture. Layer with remaining noodles and reserved spaghetti sauce; sprinkle with mozzarella and remaining Italian seasoning.

4. Cover and bake at 350° for 35 minutes. Bake, uncovered, for 10-15 minutes or until bubbly. Let stand for 15 minutes before cutting.

Nutrition Facts: 1 piece equals 298 calories, 15 g fat (7 g saturated fat), 78 mg cholesterol, 772 mg sodium, 17 g carbohydrate, 3 g fiber, 23 g protein. **Diabetic Exchanges:** 3 lean meat, 1-1/2 fat, 1 starch.

MEXICAN BEEF & PASTA

MAKEOVER BEEF & SAUSAGE LASAGNA

Chili Tortilla Bake

PREP: 20 min. **BAKE:** 25 min. **YIELD:** 6 servings

CELINE WELDY • CAVE CREEK, ARIZONA

Young and old alike enjoy this dish. I'll sometimes assemble it the night before. With only 20 minutes of prep, this quick-to-fix oven entree is ideal for weeknight dining.

- 1 lb. extra-lean ground beef (95% lean)
- 2 cans (8 oz. *each*) no-salt-added tomato sauce
- 1 can (15 oz.) black beans, rinsed and drained
- 1 cup frozen corn
- 1 can (4 oz.) chopped green chilies
- 2 Tbsp. dried minced onion
- 2 Tbsp. chili powder
- 1 tsp. ground cumin
- 1/2 tsp. garlic powder
- 1/2 tsp. dried oregano
- 6 whole wheat tortillas (8 in.)
- 1 cup (4 oz.) shredded reduced-fat cheddar cheese

1. In a large skillet, cook beef over medium heat until no longer pink. Stir in the tomato sauce, beans, corn, green chilies, onion, chili powder, cumin, garlic powder and oregano; heat through.

2. In an 11-in. x 7-in. baking dish coated with cooking spray, layer half of the tortillas, beef mixture and cheese. Repeat layers. Bake, uncovered, at 350° for 25-30 minutes or until bubbly.

Nutrition Facts: 1 piece equals 413 calories, 11 g fat (4 g saturated fat), 56 mg cholesterol, 590 mg sodium, 47 g carbohydrate, 8 g fiber, 28 g protein.

CHILI TORTILLA BAKE

CHIPOTLE SHREDDED BEEF

Chipotle Shredded Beef

PREP: 25 min. **COOK:** 8 hours **YIELD:** 10 servings

DARCY WILLIAMS • OMAHA, NEBRASKA

This beef is delicious all rolled up in a tortilla, served with corn salsa and eaten as a burrito. You could also serve it over rice, over mashed potatoes or in buns.

1	small onion, chopped
1	tsp. canola oil
1	can (28 oz.) diced tomatoes, undrained
1/4	cup cider vinegar
6	garlic cloves, minced
2	chipotle peppers in adobo sauce, chopped
2	Tbsp. brown sugar
2	bay leaves
2	tsp. adobo sauce
1/2	tsp. ground cumin
1/2	tsp. paprika
1/2	tsp. pepper
1/4	tsp. ground cinnamon
1	boneless beef chuck roast (2-1/2 lbs.)
5	cups cooked brown rice

Shredded reduced-fat cheddar cheese and reduced-fat sour cream, optional

1. In a large skillet coated with cooking spray, saute onion in oil until tender. Stir in the tomatoes, vinegar, garlic, peppers, brown sugar, bay leaves, adobo sauce and seasonings. Bring to a boil; reduce heat, simmer, uncovered for 4-6 minutes or until thickened.

2. Place roast in a 5-qt. slow cooker; add tomato mixture. Cover and cook on low heat for 8-9 hours or until meat is tender.

3. Discard bay leaves. Remove meat and shred with two forks. Skim fat from juices; return meat to slow cooker. Using a slotted spoon, serve meat with rice. Top with cheese and sour cream if desired.

Nutrition Facts: 2/3 cup beef mixture with 1/2 cup cooked brown rice (calculated without optional ingredients) equals 345 calories, 13 g fat (4 g saturated fat), 74 mg cholesterol, 194 mg sodium, 31 g carbohydrate, 3 g fiber, 26 g protein.

When **shredding beef** for sandwiches, remove the meat from the pan and reserve the cooking liquid if called for. Place the meat in a shallow pan. With two forks, pull the meat in opposite directions to create thin shreds. Return the beef to the pan or use it as the recipe directs.

Bean Beef Burgers

PREP/TOTAL TIME: 30 min. **YIELD:** 6 servings

JENNIFER KUNZ • AUSTIN, TEXAS

When it comes to health, I know how important it is to boost fiber with something as simple as whole grains. So if you want to enjoy a burger without the fat and, as a bonus, sneak in more fiber, give these a try.

1	cup water
1/2	cup bulgur
1	can (15 oz.) black beans, rinsed and drained
3	green onions, sliced
1	Tbsp. stone-ground mustard
1	garlic clove, halved
1/4	tsp. salt
1/4	tsp. pepper
1	egg, lightly beaten
1/2	lb. lean ground beef (90% lean)
1	Tbsp. canola oil
6	whole wheat hamburger buns, split

Spinach leaves, sliced red onion and tomato

1. In a small saucepan, bring water to a boil. Stir in bulgur. Reduce heat; cover and simmer for 15-20 minutes or until tender. In a food processor, combine the beans, onions, mustard and garlic. Cover and pulse until blended. Stir in salt and pepper.

2. In a large bowl, combine the egg, bulgur and bean mixture. Crumble beef over mixture and mix well. Shape into six patties.

3. In a large nonstick skillet, cook patties in oil in batches for 4-5 minutes on each side or until a meat thermometer reads 160° and juices run clear. Serve on buns with spinach, onion and tomato.

Nutrition Facts: 1 burger (calculated without spinach, onion and tomato) equals 307 calories, 8 g fat (2 g saturated fat), 54 mg cholesterol, 517 mg sodium, 42 g carbohydrate, 9 g fiber, 17 g protein. **Diabetic Exchanges:** 2 starch, 2 lean meat, 1 fat.

Round Steak Sauerbraten

PREP: 20 min. **COOK:** 7 hours **YIELD:** 10 servings

LINDA BLOOM • MCHENRY, ILLINOIS

It takes only minutes to ready round steak for the slow cooker; then it simmers to a tasty tenderness most of the day. The flavorful beef strips and sauce are nice over hot rice, too.

1	envelope brown gravy mix
2	Tbsp. plus 1-1/2 tsp. brown sugar
2-1/2	cups cold water, *divided*
1	cup chopped onion
2	Tbsp. white vinegar
2	tsp. Worcestershire sauce
4	bay leaves
2-1/2	lbs. boneless beef top round steak, cut into 3-in. x 1/2-in. strips
2	tsp. salt
1	tsp. pepper
1/4	cup cornstarch
10	cups hot cooked egg noodles

1. In a 5-qt. slow cooker, combine the gravy mix, brown sugar, 2 cups water, onion, vinegar, Worcestershire sauce and bay leaves.

BEAN BEEF BURGERS

ROUND STEAK SAUERBRATEN

2. Sprinkle beef with salt and pepper; stir into gravy mixture. Cover and cook on low for 6-1/2 to 7 hours or until meat is tender.

3. Combine cornstarch and remaining water until smooth; stir into beef mixture. Cover and cook on high for 30 minutes or until thickened. Discard bay leaves. Serve with noodles.

Nutrition Facts: 3/4 cup beef mixture with 1 cup noodles equals 331 calories, 6 g fat (2 g saturated fat), 96 mg cholesterol, 741 mg sodium, 37 g carbohydrate, 2 g fiber, 32 g protein. **Diabetic Exchanges:** 3 lean meat, 2-1/2 starch.

Barley Beef Skillet

PREP: 20 min. **COOK:** 1 hour **YIELD:** 4 servings

KIT TUNSTALL • BOISE, IDAHO

Even my 3-year-old loves this family favorite. It's very filling, inexpensive and full of veggies. It's also really good spiced up with chili powder, cayenne or a dash of Tabasco.

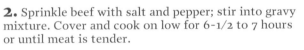

- 1 lb. lean ground beef (90% lean)
- 1/4 cup chopped onion
- 1 garlic clove, minced
- 1 can (14-1/2 oz.) reduced-sodium beef broth
- 1 can (8 oz.) tomato sauce
- 1 cup water
- 2 small carrots, chopped
- 1 small tomato, seeded and chopped
- 1 small zucchini, chopped
- 1 cup medium pearl barley
- 2 tsp. Italian seasoning
- 1/4 tsp. salt
- 1/8 tsp. pepper

1. In a large skillet, cook beef and onion over medium heat until meat is no longer pink. Add garlic; cook 1 minute longer. Drain. Add the broth, tomato sauce and water; bring to a boil. Stir in the remaining ingredients. Reduce heat; cover and simmer for 45-50 minutes or until barley is tender.

Nutrition Facts: 1-1/2 cups equals 400 calories, 10 g fat (4 g saturated fat), 73 mg cholesterol, 682 mg sodium, 48 g carbohydrate, 10 g fiber, 30 g protein.

Keep in mind that the more fat there is in the meat, the more shrinkage there is during cooking. So if you're making burgers out of regular **ground beef**, shape the patties to be slightly larger than the buns.

Eggplant Zucchini Bolognese

PREP: 30 min. COOK: 20 min. YIELD: 8 servings

TRISHA KRUSE • EAGLE, IDAHO

I roast the veggies while the pasta cooks, making this a quick dish for weeknights. This meal-in-one blends rustic comfort with fresh flavors.

    1   pkg. (16 oz.) penne pasta
    1   small eggplant, peeled and cut into 1-in. pieces
    1   medium zucchini, cut into 1/4-in. slices
    1   medium yellow summer squash, cut into
        1/4-in. slices
    1   cup chopped onion
    2   Tbsp. olive oil
    2   tsp. minced garlic
    1   tsp. salt
  1/2   tsp. pepper
    1   lb. lean ground beef (90% lean)
    1   can (28 oz.) tomato puree
    1   Tbsp. Italian seasoning
    1   Tbsp. brown sugar
    8   tsp. grated Parmesan cheese

1. Cook pasta according to package directions. In a large bowl, combine the eggplant, zucchini, squash, onion, oil, garlic, salt and pepper. Transfer to two 15-in. x 10-in. x 1-in. baking pans coated with cooking spray. Bake at 425° for 20-25 minutes or until tender.

2. Meanwhile, in a large skillet, cook beef over medium heat until no longer pink; drain. Stir in the tomato puree, Italian seasoning and brown sugar. Drain pasta; stir in tomato mixture and roasted vegetables. Sprinkle with cheese.

Nutrition Facts: 1-1/2 cups equals 395 calories, 10 g fat (3 g saturated fat), 36 mg cholesterol, 378 mg sodium, 56 g carbohydrate, 5 g fiber, 22 g protein.

Homemade Taco Seasoning Mix

PREP/TOTAL TIME: 20 min. YIELD: 4 servings per batch

HEALTHY COOKING TEST KITCHEN

This seasoning mix is right on. It tastes like purchased mixes but is cheaper and has nearly half the sodium. Your heart and wallet will surely thank you!

  1/4   cup all-purpose flour
  1/4   cup chili powder
    3   Tbsp. dried minced onion
    1   Tbsp. garlic powder
2-1/2   tsp. salt
    2   tsp. dried oregano
    2   tsp. ground cumin
1-1/2   tsp. cayenne pepper
    1   tsp. ground coriander

ADDITIONAL INGREDIENTS:
    1   lb. lean ground beef (90% lean)
  3/4   cup water
    4   whole wheat tortillas (8 in.), warmed

1. Combine the first nine ingredients. Store in an airtight container in a cool dry place for up to 1 year. Yield: 4 batches (about 1 cup total).

2. To prepare tacos: In a large skillet, cook beef over medium heat until no longer pink; drain. Add 1/4 cup taco seasoning mix and water. Bring to a boil; cook and stir for 2 minutes. Fill each tortilla with 1/2 cup beef mixture.

Nutrition Facts: 1 taco equals 338 calories, 13 g fat (4 g saturated fat), 71 mg cholesterol, 619 mg sodium, 26 g carbohydrate, 3 g fiber, 27 g protein.

Slow-Cooked Caribbean Pot Roast

PREP: 30 min. **COOK:** 6 hours **YIELD:** 10 servings

JENN TIDWELL • FAIR OAKS, CALIFORNIA

I put this dish together throughout the fall and winter seasons, but considering how simple it is to prepare, anytime is a great time to enjoy it!

2	medium sweet potatoes, cubed
2	large carrots, sliced
1/4	cup chopped celery
1	boneless beef chuck roast (2-1/2 lbs.)
1	Tbsp. canola oil
1	large onion, chopped
2	garlic cloves, minced
1	Tbsp. all-purpose flour
1	Tbsp. sugar
1	Tbsp. brown sugar
1	tsp. ground cumin
3/4	tsp. salt
3/4	tsp. ground coriander
3/4	tsp. chili powder
1/2	tsp. dried oregano
1/8	tsp. ground cinnamon
3/4	tsp. grated orange peel
3/4	tsp. baking cocoa
1	can (15 oz.) tomato sauce

1. Place potatoes, carrots and celery in a 5-qt. slow cooker. In a large skillet, brown the meat in oil on all sides. Transfer meat to slow cooker.

2. In the same skillet, saute onion in drippings until tender. Add garlic; cook 1 minute longer. Combine the flour, sugar, brown sugar, seasonings, orange peel and cocoa. Stir in tomato sauce; add to skillet and heat through. Pour over beef. Cover and cook on low for 6-8 hours or until beef and vegetables are tender.

Nutrition Facts: 3 oz. cooked beef with 1/2 cup vegetable mixture equals 278 calories, 12 g fat (4 g saturated fat), 74 mg cholesterol, 453 mg sodium, 16 g carbohydrate, 3 g fiber, 25 g protein. **Diabetic Exchanges:** 3 lean meat, 1 starch, 1 vegetable, 1/2 fat.

Broiled Sirloin Steaks

PREP/TOTAL TIME: 20 min. **YIELD:** 4 servings

KAROL CHANDLER-EZELL • NACOGDOCHES, TEXAS

A butcher gave me great advice on cooking different types of meat. Broiling after marinating works really well on very lean cuts like this. Let the steaks rest for a couple of minutes before serving to preserve moistness.

2	Tbsp. lime juice
1	tsp. onion powder
1	tsp. garlic powder
1/4	tsp. ground mustard
1/4	tsp. dried oregano
1/4	tsp. dried thyme
4	beef top sirloin steaks (5 oz. *each*)
1	cup sliced fresh mushrooms

1. In a small bowl, combine the first six ingredients; rub over both sides of steaks.

2. Broil 4 in. from the heat for 7 minutes. Turn steaks; top with mushrooms. Broil 7-8 minutes longer or until meat reaches desired doneness (for medium-rare, a meat thermometer should read 145°; medium, 160°; well-done, 170°) and the mushrooms are tender.

Nutrition Facts: 1 steak with 3 Tbsp. mushrooms equals 187 calories, 7 g fat (3 g saturated fat), 80 mg cholesterol, 60 mg sodium, 3 g carbohydrate, trace fiber, 28 g protein. **Diabetic Exchange:** 4 lean meat.

BROILED SIRLOIN STEAKS

SLOW-COOKED CARIBBEAN POT ROAST

Biscuit-Topped Shepherd's Pies

PREP: 30 min. BAKE: 10 min. YIELD: 6 servings

JOSEPHINE PIRO • EASTON, PENNSYLVANIA

Here's a moist, hearty, comforting and cozy meal-in-one to warm your family on chilly fall days. No ramekins? Just spoon into an 8-in. square baking dish. You'll love this.

- 1 lb. lean ground beef (90% lean)
- 1 medium onion, chopped
- 1 celery rib, finely chopped
- 1 pkg. (16 oz.) frozen peas and carrots, thawed and drained
- 1 can (15 oz.) Italian tomato sauce
- 1/4 tsp. pepper
- 1 cup reduced-fat biscuit/baking mix
- 2 Tbsp. grated Parmesan cheese
- 1/4 tsp. dried rosemary, crushed
- 1/2 cup fat-free milk
- 2 Tbsp. butter, melted

1. In a large nonstick skillet, cook the beef, onion and celery over medium heat until meat is no longer pink; drain. Add the vegetables, tomato sauce and pepper; cook and stir for 5-6 minutes or until heated through. Spoon into six 8-oz. ramekins coated with cooking spray; set aside.

2. In a small bowl, combine the biscuit mix, cheese and rosemary. Stir in milk and butter just until moistened. Spoon dough over meat mixture; place ramekins on a baking sheet.

3. Bake at 425° for 10-12 minutes or until biscuits are golden brown.

Nutrition Facts: 1 serving equals 311 calories, 12 g fat (5 g saturated fat), 59 mg cholesterol, 771 mg sodium, 31 g carbohydrate, 5 g fiber, 22 g protein. **Diabetic Exchanges:** 2 lean meat, 1-1/2 starch, 1 vegetable, 1 fat.

Spicy Goulash

PREP: 25 min. COOK: 5-1/2 hours YIELD: 12 servings

MELISSA POLK • WEST LAFAYETTE, INDIANA

Ground cumin, chili powder and a can of Mexican diced tomatoes jazz up my goulash recipe. Even the elbow macaroni is prepared in the slow cooker.

- 1 lb. lean ground beef (90% lean)
- 4 cans (14-1/2 oz. *each*) Mexican diced tomatoes, undrained
- 2 cans (16 oz. *each*) kidney beans, rinsed and drained
- 2 cups water
- 1 medium onion, chopped
- 1 medium green pepper, chopped
- 1/4 cup red wine vinegar
- 2 Tbsp. chili powder
- 1 Tbsp. Worcestershire sauce
- 2 tsp. beef bouillon granules
- 1 tsp. dried basil
- 1 tsp. dried parsley flakes
- 1 tsp. ground cumin
- 1/4 tsp. pepper
- 2 cups uncooked elbow macaroni

1. In a large skillet, cook beef over medium heat until no longer pink; drain. Transfer to a 5-qt. slow cooker. Stir in the tomatoes, beans, water, onion, green pepper, vinegar, chili powder, Worcestershire sauce, bouillon and seasonings.

2. Cover and cook on low for 5-6 hours or until heated through.

BISCUIT-TOPPED SHEPHERD'S PIES

SPICY GOULASH

3. Stir in macaroni; cover and cook 30 minutes longer or until macaroni is tender.

Nutrition Facts: 1 cup equals 223 calories, 4 g fat (2 g saturated fat), 19 mg cholesterol, 741 mg sodium, 34 g carbohydrate, 7 g fiber, 15 g protein.

Pineapple Beef Stir-Fry

PREP: 20 min. + marinating **COOK:** 15 min.
YIELD: 4 servings

JACKIE DRAKE • TROUTMAN, NORTH CAROLINA

Packed with veggies, tender beef and pineapple tidbits, this sweet-and-sour stir-fry is ideal for blustery weeknights or activity-packed weekends.

1	cup unsweetened pineapple juice
1/4	cup white wine or reduced-sodium chicken broth
2	Tbsp. brown sugar
2	Tbsp. reduced-sodium soy sauce
1/4	tsp. cayenne pepper
1	beef top sirloin steak (1 lb.), cut into thin strips
2	Tbsp. cornstarch
1-1/2	tsp. olive oil, *divided*
2	large carrots, sliced
1	small onion, halved and sliced
1	medium green pepper, julienned
1/2	cup fresh snow peas
3/4	cup unsweetened pineapple tidbits
2	cups cooked brown rice

1. In a small bowl, combine the first five ingredients. Pour 2/3 cup marinade into a large resealable plastic bag; add the beef. Seal bag and turn to coat; refrigerate for 30 minutes. Cover and refrigerate remaining marinade.

2. In a small bowl, combine cornstarch and reserved marinade until smooth; set aside.

3. Drain and discard marinade. In a large nonstick skillet or wok, stir-fry beef in 1 tsp. oil for 2-3 minutes or until no longer pink. Remove with a slotted spoon and keep warm.

4. Stir-fry carrots and onion in remaining oil for 4 minutes. Add green pepper and snow peas; stir-fry 2-3 minutes longer or until vegetables are crisp-tender.

5. Stir cornstarch mixture and add to the pan. Bring to a boil; cook and stir for 2 minutes or until thickened. Add beef and pineapple; heat through. Serve with rice.

Nutrition Facts: 1 cup stir-fry with 1/2 cup rice equals 388 calories, 7 g fat (2 g saturated fat), 46 mg cholesterol, 324 mg sodium, 51 g carbohydrate, 5 g fiber, 29 g protein.

One-dish meals like stir-fries often call for thin strips of meat, which can be difficult to cut. To make the job easier, **partially freeze** larger cuts before slicing. The meat should be solid enough to slice evenly within 30 minutes.

AFRICAN BEEF CURRY

African Beef Curry

PREP: 15 min. **COOK:** 1-1/2 hours **YIELD:** 4 servings

HEATHER EWALD • BOTHELL, WASHINGTON

This African Beef Curry is a popular dish with my family and friends. It's from my Aunt Linda, who was a missionary in Nigeria for 45 years. The stew is served on a bed of rice and sprinkled with toppings. I put the bowls of toppings on my large turntable, and everyone can take whatever they want. In addition to the coconut, peanuts and raisins, you could also top the stew with chopped cucumbers, pineapple tidbits or mandarin orange slices.

- 1 lb. beef stew meat, cut into 1/2-in. cubes
- 1 can (14-1/2 oz.) diced tomatoes, undrained
- 1 small onion, chopped
- 1 small sweet red pepper, chopped
- 1 small green pepper, chopped
- 1 to 2 Tbsp. curry powder
- 1/2 tsp. salt

Hot cooked rice

Raisins, chopped salted peanuts and flaked coconut, optional

1. In a large saucepan, combine the first seven ingredients. Bring to a boil. Reduce heat; cover and simmer for 1-1/2 to 2 hours or until meat is tender.

2. Serve with rice. Garnish with raisins, peanuts and coconut if desired.

Nutrition Facts: 1 cup (calculated without rice or garnishes) equals 205 calories, 8 g fat (3 g saturated fat), 70 mg cholesterol, 474 mg sodium, 10 g carbohydrate, 3 g fiber, 23 g protein. **Diabetic Exchanges:** 3 lean meat, 2 vegetable.

Beef Cabbage Rolls

PREP: 30 min. **BAKE:** 65 min. **YIELD:** 4 servings

HEALTHY COOKING TEST KITCHEN

A tiny bit of cinnamon adds a unique, slightly sweet taste to these savory stuffed cabbage rolls. Serve them with a side of broccoli for a delectable meal.

- 1/3 cup uncooked brown rice
- 1 medium head cabbage
- 1 medium onion, chopped
- 2 egg whites
- 3 Tbsp. dried currants
- 2 Tbsp. pine nuts
- 2 Tbsp. lemon juice
- 1/2 tsp. dried oregano
- 1/4 tsp. pepper
- 1/8 tsp. salt
- 1/8 tsp. ground cinnamon
- 3/4 lb. lean ground beef (90% lean)
- 2 cans (8 oz. *each*) no-salt-added tomato sauce
- 2 Tbsp. brown sugar
- 1/4 tsp. dried thyme

1. Cook rice according to package directions.

2. Meanwhile, cook cabbage in boiling water just until outer leaves pull away easily from head. Set aside 8 large leaves for rolls. Refrigerate remaining cabbage for another use. Cut out the thick vein from the bottom of each reserved leaf, making a V-shaped cut.

3. In a small nonstick skillet coated with cooking spray, saute onion until tender. In a large bowl, combine the rice, onion, egg whites, currants, pine nuts, lemon juice, oregano, pepper, salt and cinnamon. Crumble beef over mixture and mix well.

4. Place about 1/3 cup beef mixture on each cabbage leaf. Fold in sides, beginning from the cut end. Roll up completely to enclose filling. Place seam side down in a 13-in. x 9-in. baking dish coated with cooking spray. Combine the tomato sauce, brown sugar and thyme; pour over rolls.

5. Cover and bake at 350° for 1 hour or until cabbage is tender and a meat thermometer reads 160°. Uncover; bake 5-10 minutes longer or until sauce reaches desired consistency.

Nutrition Facts: 2 cabbage rolls equals 335 calories, 10 g fat (3 g saturated fat), 53 mg cholesterol, 198 mg sodium, 39 g carbohydrate, 4 g fiber, 22 g protein. **Diabetic Exchanges:** 2-1/2 starch, 2 lean meat, 1/2 fat.

Italian Pot Roast

PREP: 30 min. **COOK:** 6 hours **YIELD:** 8 servings

KAREN BURDELL • LAFAYETTE, COLORADO

I'm always collecting recipes from newspapers and magazines, and this one just sounded too good not to try! I love the slow cooker convenience and the blend of healthful ingredients and aromatic spices.

6	whole peppercorns
4	whole cloves
3	whole allspice
1	cinnamon stick (3 in.)
1	boneless beef chuck roast (2 lbs.)
2	tsp. olive oil
2	celery ribs, sliced
2	medium carrots, sliced
1	large onion, chopped
4	garlic cloves, minced
1	cup sherry or reduced-sodium beef broth
1	can (28 oz.) crushed tomatoes
1/4	tsp. salt

Hot cooked egg noodles, optional

1. Place the peppercorns, cloves, allspice and cinnamon stick on a double thickness of cheesecloth; bring up corners of cloth and tie with string to form a bag. Set aside.

2. In a large skillet, brown meat in oil on all sides; transfer to a 4-qt. slow cooker. Top with celery, carrots and spice bag.

3. In the same pan, saute onion in drippings until tender. Add garlic; cook 1 minute longer. Add sherry, stirring to loosen browned bits from pan. Bring to a boil; cook and stir until liquid is reduced to 2/3 cup. Stir in tomatoes and salt; pour over vegetables.

4. Cover and cook on low for 6-7 hours or until meat and vegetables are tender. Remove meat to a serving platter; keep warm. Discard spice bag. Skim fat from vegetable mixture; serve with beef.

Nutrition Facts: 3 oz. cooked meat with 2/3 cup vegetable mixture (calculated without egg noodles) equals 251 calories, 12 g fat (4 g saturated fat), 74 mg cholesterol, 271 mg sodium, 11 g carbohydrate, 3 g fiber, 24 g protein. **Diabetic Exchanges:** 3 lean meat, 2 vegetable, 1/2 fat.

Stovetop Meat Loaves

PREP: 20 min. **COOK:** 15 min. **YIELD:** 2 servings

EMILY SUND • GENESEO, ILLINOIS

Who says meat loaf has to bake in the oven for hours? For this convenient recipe, all you need is your stovetop and 35 minutes. Topped with a zesty sauce, it's a fast and easy entree to make for one or two people.

3	Tbsp. 2% milk
2	Tbsp. quick-cooking oats
1	Tbsp. chopped onion
1/4	tsp. salt
1/2	lb. lean ground beef
1/2	tsp. cornstarch
1/2	cup Italian tomato sauce
1/4	cup cold water

1. In a small bowl, combine the milk, oats, onion and salt. Crumble beef over mixture and mix well. Shape into two loaves.

2. In a small nonstick skillet, brown loaves on both sides; drain. Combine the cornstarch, tomato sauce and water until smooth. Pour over meat loaves. Bring to a boil. Reduce heat to medium-low; cover and cook for 15-20 minutes or until meat is no longer pink.

Nutrition Facts: 1 meat loaf equals 259 calories, 10 g fat (4 g saturated fat), 71 mg cholesterol, 922 mg sodium, 16 g carbohydrate, 2 g fiber, 25 g protein. **Diabetic Exchanges:** 3 lean meat, 1 starch.

STOVETOP MEAT LOAVES

Quinoa-Stuffed Peppers

PREP: 35 min. BAKE: 35 min. YIELD: 4 servings

JOYCE MOYNIHAN • LAKEVILLE, MINNESOTA

Quinoa adds crunch, corn lends sweetness and color, and red pepper flakes ratchet up the heat in these tender stuffed peppers. Whole wheat rolls or breadsticks and a pitcher of iced tea make for a standout supper.

- 1 can (14-1/2 oz.) diced tomatoes, undrained
- 1 cup water
- 1/2 cup quinoa, rinsed
- 4 large green peppers
- 3/4 lb. lean ground beef (90% lean)
- 1 large onion, finely chopped
- 3 garlic cloves, minced
- 3 tsp. dried parsley flakes
- 2 tsp. paprika
- 1/2 tsp. salt
- 1/4 to 1/2 tsp. crushed red pepper flakes
- 1/4 tsp. pepper
- 2 cans (8 oz. *each*) no-salt-added tomato sauce, *divided*
- 3/4 cup frozen corn, thawed
- 1/2 cup shredded reduced-fat cheddar cheese

1. Drain tomatoes reserving juice; set aside.

2. In a small saucepan, bring water to a boil. Add quinoa. Reduce heat; simmer, uncovered, for 15-20 minutes or until liquid is absorbed.

3. Meanwhile, cut peppers in half lengthwise and remove seeds. In a Dutch oven, cook peppers in boiling water for 3-5 minutes. Drain and rinse in cold water; invert onto paper towels.

4. In a large skillet, cook the beef, onion, garlic, parsley, paprika, salt, pepper flakes and pepper over medium heat until meat is no longer pink. Stir in one can tomato sauce, corn, quinoa and tomatoes; heat through.

5. Spoon into pepper halves. Place in a 13-in. x 9-in. baking dish coated with cooking spray. Combine the reserved tomato juice and remaining tomato sauce; pour over peppers.

6. Cover and bake at 350° for 30-35 minutes or until peppers are tender. Sprinkle with cheese; bake 5 minutes longer or until cheese is melted.

Editor's Note: Look for quinoa in the cereal, rice or organic food aisle.

Nutrition Facts: 2 stuffed pepper halves equals 386 calories, 11 g fat (5 g saturated fat), 52 mg cholesterol, 622 mg sodium, 47 g carbohydrate, 9 g fiber, 26 g protein.

Hearty Beef Ravioli

PREP/TOTAL TIME: 30 min. YIELD: 6 servings

HEALTHY COOKING TEST KITCHEN

You're only 30 minutes away from a great new pasta dish that's got a Tex-Mex twist. Just add a fresh salad and a slice of crusty bread, and dinner's done in no time!

- 1 pkg. (25 oz.) frozen beef ravioli
- 1/2 lb. extra-lean ground beef (95% lean)
- 1 medium green pepper, chopped
- 1 can (14-1/2 oz.) no-salt-added diced tomatoes
- 1 can (8 oz.) no-salt-added tomato sauce
- 2 Tbsp. reduced-sodium taco seasoning
- 3/4 cup shredded reduced-fat cheddar cheese
- 1 can (2-1/4 oz.) sliced ripe olives, drained

1. Cook ravioli according to package directions.

2. Meanwhile, in a large nonstick skillet, cook beef and green pepper over medium heat until meat is no longer pink. Stir in the tomatoes, tomato sauce and taco seasoning. Bring to a boil. Reduce heat; simmer, uncovered, for 5-7 minutes or until slightly thickened.

3. Drain pasta. Serve with sauce. Sprinkle each serving with 2 Tbsp. cheese and about 1 Tbsp. olives.

Nutrition Facts: 1 serving equals 375 calories, 10 g fat (5 g saturated fat), 44 mg cholesterol, 695 mg sodium, 49 g carbohydrate, 4 g fiber, 21 g protein.

QUINOA-STUFFED PEPPERS

HEARTY BEEF RAVIOLI

Terrific Teriyaki Burgers

PREP: 20 min. **GRILL:** 15 min. **YIELD:** 6 servings

MARGARET WILSON • SUN CITY, CALIFORNIA

Golden flecks of pineapple give these burgers a touch of sweetness, while the gingerroot adds some spice. Ground chicken works well in this recipe, too.

1/4 cup ketchup

2 Tbsp. reduced-sodium soy sauce

1 Tbsp. brown sugar

1 Tbsp. unsweetened crushed pineapple

1-1/2 tsp. minced fresh gingerroot

1 garlic clove, minced

1/2 tsp. sesame oil

BURGERS:

1 egg white, lightly beaten

1/3 cup dry bread crumbs

3 green onions, chopped

2 Tbsp. unsweetened crushed pineapple

3/4 lb. ground beef

3/4 lb. lean ground turkey

6 slices unsweetened pineapple

6 hamburger buns, split and toasted

6 lettuce leaves

6 slices tomato

1. In a small bowl, combine the ketchup, soy sauce, brown sugar, pineapple, ginger, garlic and sesame oil; set aside.

2. In a large bowl, combine the egg white, bread crumbs, onions, crushed pineapple and 3 Tbsp. reserved ketchup mixture. Crumble beef and turkey over mixture and mix well. Shape into six burgers.

3. Using long-handled tongs, moisten a paper towel with cooking oil and lightly coat the grill rack. Grill burgers, covered, over medium heat or broil 4 in. from the heat for 5-7 minutes on each side or until a meat thermometer reads 165° and juices run clear, brushing occasionally with remaining ketchup mixture.

4. Grill or broil pineapple slices for 2-3 minutes on each side or until heated through. Serve burgers and pineapple on buns with lettuce and tomato.

Nutrition Facts: 1 burger equals 386 calories, 12 g fat (4 g saturated fat), 79 mg cholesterol, 677 mg sodium, 41 g carbohydrate, 2 g fiber, 27 g protein. **Diabetic Exchanges:** 3 lean meat, 2 starch, 1/2 fruit.

Fresh **gingerroot** is available in your grocer's produce section. It should have a smooth skin. If wrinkled and cracked, the root is dry and past its prime.

Slow-Cooked Meat Loaf C

PREP: 15 min. COOK: 3 hours YIELD: 8 servings

SHARON DELANEY-CHRONIS • SOUTH MILWAUKEE, WISCONSIN

What could be easier than this recipe for an Italian-inspired meat loaf made in the slow cooker? No fuss, easy cleanup and great taste—it's all right here!

  1   cup soft bread crumbs
1-1/2   cups spaghetti sauce, *divided*
  1   egg, lightly beaten
  2   Tbsp. dried minced onion
  1   tsp. salt
1/2   tsp. garlic powder
1/2   tsp. Italian seasoning
1/4   tsp. pepper
  2   lbs. lean ground beef (90% lean)

1. Cut four 20-in. x 3-in. strips of heavy-duty foil; crisscross so they resemble spokes of a wheel. Place strips on the bottom and up the sides of a 3-qt. slow cooker. Coat strips with cooking spray.

2. In a large bowl, combine the bread crumbs, 1 cup spaghetti sauce, egg, onion and seasonings. Crumble beef over mixture and mix well. Shape into a loaf; place in the center of the strips.

3. Spoon remaining spaghetti sauce over meat loaf. Cover and cook on low for 3-4 hours or until a meat thermometer reads 160°. Using foil strips as handles, remove meat loaf to a platter.

Nutrition Facts: 1 slice equals 243 calories, 12 g fat (4 g saturated fat), 98 mg cholesterol, 635 mg sodium, 8 g carbohydrate, 1 g fiber, 24 g protein. **Diabetic Exchanges:** 3 lean meat, 1 fat, 1/2 starch.

Baked Barbecued Brisket

PREP: 20 min. BAKE: 3-1/2 hours YIELD: 16-20 servings

JOAN HALLFORD • NORTH RICHLAND HILLS, TEXAS

This simple brisket recipe never fails me. I always hope there will be a few slices left over for sandwiches the next day.

  1   Tbsp. all-purpose flour
  1   fresh beef brisket (5 lbs.)
  2   to 4 tsp. liquid smoke, optional
1/2   tsp. celery seed
1/4   tsp. pepper
  1   cup chili sauce
1/4   cup barbecue sauce

1. Place flour in a large oven roasting bag; shake to coat bag. Rub brisket with liquid smoke if desired, celery seed and pepper; place in bag. Place in a roasting pan. Combine chili sauce and barbecue sauce; pour over brisket. Seal bag.

2. With a knife, cut six 1/2-in. slits in top of bag. Bake at 325° for 3-1/2 to 4 hours or until meat is tender. Let stand for 5 minutes. Carefully remove brisket from bag. Thinly slice meat across the grain.

Editor's Note: This is a fresh beef brisket, not corned beef.

Nutrition Facts: 3 oz. cooked beef equals 159 calories, 5 g fat (2 g saturated fat), 48 mg cholesterol, 250 mg sodium, 4 g carbohydrate, trace fiber, 23 g protein. **Diabetic Exchange:** 3 lean meat.

Makeover Beef Stroganoff

PREP/TOTAL TIME: 30 min. **YIELD:** 6 servings

CANDACE CLARK • CONNELL, WASHINGTON

This recipe lightens up a classic comfort dish, slashing calories, saturated fat, sodium and cholesterol without sacrificing one bit of satisfying flavor.

- 1/2 cup plus 1 Tbsp. all-purpose flour, *divided*
- 1/2 tsp. pepper, *divided*
- 1 beef top round steak (1-1/2 lbs.), cut into thin strips
- 2 Tbsp. canola oil
- 1 cup sliced fresh mushrooms
- 1 small onion, chopped
- 1 garlic clove, minced
- 1 can (14-1/2 oz.) reduced-sodium beef broth
- 1/2 tsp. salt
- 1 cup (8 oz.) reduced-fat sour cream
- 3 cups cooked yolk-free noodles

1. In a large resealable plastic bag, combine 1/2 cup flour and 1/4 tsp. pepper. Add beef, a few pieces at a time, and shake to coat.

2. In a large nonstick skillet over medium-high heat, cook beef in oil in batches until no longer pink. Remove and keep warm. In the same skillet, saute mushrooms and onion in drippings until tender. Add garlic; cook 1 minute longer.

3. Combine remaining flour and broth until smooth; whisk into skillet. Bring to a boil; cook and stir for 2 minutes or until thickened. Add the beef, salt and remaining pepper; heat through. Add sour cream; heat through (do not boil). Serve with noodles.

Nutrition Facts: 1 cup beef Stroganoff with 1/2 cup noodles equals 351 calories, 12 g fat (4 g saturated fat), 78 mg cholesterol, 393 mg sodium, 25 g carbohydrate, 2 g fiber, 33 g protein. **Diabetic Exchanges:** 3 lean meat, 2 fat, 1-1/2 starch.

So-Easy Spaghetti Sauce F

PREP: 30 min. **COOK:** 5 hours
YIELD: About 2-1/4 qt.

CATHY JOHNSON • SOMERSET, PENNSYLVANIA

Let the slow cooker do all the work for this hearty spaghetti sauce. All you need to do is cook the pasta and bake up some crusty garlic bread.

- 1 lb. lean ground beef (90% lean)
- 1 medium onion, finely chopped
- 1/4 cup finely chopped celery
- 1 can (29 oz.) tomato sauce
- 2-1/2 cups tomato juice
- 1 can (14-1/2 oz.) diced tomatoes, undrained
- 1 can (12 oz.) tomato paste
- 2 tsp. sugar
- 2 tsp. chili powder
- 1 tsp. salt
- 1 tsp. garlic powder
- 1 tsp. dried basil
- 1 tsp. dried oregano
- 1/2 tsp. pepper
- 4 bay leaves

Hot cooked spaghetti

Grated Parmesan cheese, optional

1. In a large skillet, cook the beef, onion and celery over medium heat until meat is no longer pink; drain. In a 4- or 5-qt. slow cooker, combine the tomato sauce, tomato juice, tomatoes, tomato paste, sugar, seasonings and beef mixture.

2. Cover and cook on low for 5-6 hours or until heated through. Discard bay leaves. Serve with spaghetti; sprinkle with cheese if desired.

Nutrition Facts: 3/4 cup (calculated without spaghetti and cheese) equals 125 calories, 3 g fat (1 g saturated fat), 19 mg cholesterol, 744 mg sodium, 16 g carbohydrate, 4 g fiber, 10 g protein. **Diabetic Exchanges:** 1 lean meat, 1 vegetable, 1/2 starch, 1/2 fat.

SO-EASY SPAGHETTI SAUCE

MAKEOVER BEEF STROGANOFF

Hamburger Noodle Casserole

PREP: 30 min. **BAKE:** 35 min. **YIELD:** 10 servings

MARTHA HENSON • WINNSBORO, TEXAS

Whenever I need a hearty dish that serves a crowd, I turn to this casserole. It's a hit with people in any age group.

5	cups uncooked yolk-free noodles
1-1/4	lbs. lean ground beef (90% lean)
2	garlic cloves, minced
3	cans (8 oz. *each*) tomato sauce
1/2	tsp. sugar
1/2	tsp. salt
1/8	tsp. pepper
1	pkg. (8 oz.) reduced-fat cream cheese
1	cup reduced-fat ricotta cheese
1/4	cup fat-free sour cream
3	green onions, thinly sliced, *divided*
2/3	cup shredded reduced-fat cheddar cheese

1. Cook noodles according to package directions. Meanwhile, in a large nonstick skillet over medium heat, cook beef until meat is no longer pink. Add garlic; cook 1 minute longer. Drain. Stir in the tomato sauce, sugar, salt and pepper; heat through. Drain noodles; stir into beef mixture.

2. In a small bowl, beat the cream cheese, ricotta cheese and sour cream until blended. Stir in half of the onions.

3. Spoon half of the noodle mixture into a 13-in. x 9-in. baking dish coated with cooking spray. Top with cheese mixture and remaining noodle mixture.

4. Cover and bake at 350° for 30 minutes. Uncover; sprinkle with cheddar cheese. Bake 5-10 minutes longer or until heated through and cheese is melted. Sprinkle with remaining onions.

Nutrition Facts: 1 cup equals 290 calories, 12 g fat (7 g saturated fat), 56 mg cholesterol, 650 mg sodium, 23 g carbohydrate, 2 g fiber, 22 g protein. **Diabetic Exchanges:** 2 lean meat, 1-1/2 starch, 1 fat.

Whiskey Sirloin Steak C

PREP: 10 min. + marinating **BROIL:** 15 min.
YIELD: 4 servings

HEALTHY COOKING TEST KITCHEN

Moist, tender and slightly sweet from the marinade, this juicy steak boasts wonderful flavor and oh-so-easy preparation. Serve with potatoes and a green vegetable for a complete meal.

1/4	cup whiskey *or* apple cider
1/4	cup reduced-sodium soy sauce
1	Tbsp. sugar
1	garlic clove, thinly sliced
1/2	tsp. ground ginger
1	beef top sirloin steak (1 in. thick and 1 lb.)

1. In a large resealable plastic bag, combine the first five ingredients; add the beef. Seal bag and turn to coat; refrigerate for 8 hours or overnight.

2. Drain and discard marinade. Place beef on a broiler pan coated with cooking spray. Broil 4-6 in. from the heat for 7-8 minutes on each side or until meat reaches desired doneness (for medium-rare, a meat thermometer should read 145°; medium, 160°; well-done, 170°).

Nutrition Facts: 3 oz. cooked beef equals 168 calories, 5 g fat (2 g saturated fat), 46 mg cholesterol, 353 mg sodium, 2 g carbohydrate, trace fiber, 25 g protein. **Diabetic Exchange:** 3 lean meat.

HAMBURGER NOODLE CASSEROLE

WHISKEY SIRLOIN STEAK

Flank Steak Pitas

PREP: 15 min. + marinating **GRILL:** 15 min. + standing
YIELD: 4 servings

TAMMY KAMINSKI • STANWOOD, WASHINGTON

This sandwich packs so much flavor, you'll be satisfied without eating a huge serving. The marinade makes the most of tasty ingredients, so you won't even miss the cheese or mayo.

1/4	cup balsamic vinegar
2	Tbsp. water
2	Tbsp. reduced-sodium soy sauce
1	Tbsp. hoisin sauce
2	garlic cloves, minced
1	tsp. Thai chili sauce
3/4	tsp. pepper
1/2	tsp. sesame oil
1	beef flank steak (1 lb.)
4	whole pita breads
4	pieces leaf lettuce, torn
1/4	tsp. sesame seeds

1. In a small bowl, combine the first eight ingredients. Pour 1/4 cup marinade into a large resealable plastic bag; add the beef. Seal bag and turn to coat. Refrigerate for at least 8 hours or overnight. Cover and refrigerate remaining marinade.

2. Drain and discard marinade. Grill, covered, over medium heat for 6-8 minutes on each side or until meat reaches desired doneness (for medium-rare, a meat thermometer should read 145°; medium, 160°; well-done, 170°). Let stand for 10 minutes.

3. Meanwhile, grill pitas, uncovered, over medium heat for 1-2 minutes on each side or until warm. Thinly slice beef across the grain. In a large bowl, toss the beef, lettuce and reserved marinade. Serve in pitas; sprinkle with sesame seeds.

Nutrition Facts: 1 filled pita equals 362 calories, 10 g fat (4 g saturated fat), 54 mg cholesterol, 703 mg sodium, 39 g carbohydrate, 2 g fiber, 28 g protein. **Diabetic Exchanges:** 3 lean meat, 2-1/2 starch.

Beef and Spinach Lasagna

PREP: 10 min. **BAKE:** 40 min. + standing
YIELD: 12 servings

CAROLYN SCHMELING • BROOKFIELD, WISCONSIN

Using no-cook noodles gives you a jump start on assembling this hearty main dish. It cuts nicely after standing a few minutes, revealing tantalizing layers.

1	lb. lean ground beef (90% lean)
1	medium onion, chopped
2	jars (26 oz. *each*) meatless spaghetti sauce
4	garlic cloves, minced
1	tsp. dried basil
1	tsp. dried oregano
1	pkg. (10 oz.) frozen chopped spinach, thawed and squeezed dry
2	cups ricotta cheese
2	cups (8 oz.) shredded part-skim mozzarella cheese, *divided*
9	no-cook lasagna noodles

1. In a large skillet, cook beef and onion over medium heat until meat is no longer pink; drain. Stir in the spaghetti sauce, garlic, basil and oregano. Bring to a boil. Reduce heat; cover and simmer for 10 minutes. In a large bowl, combine the spinach, ricotta and 1 cup mozzarella cheese until combined.

2. Spread 1-1/2 cups meat sauce into a greased 13-in. x 9-in. baking dish. Top with three noodles. Spread 1-1/2 cups sauce to edges of noodles. Top with half of the spinach mixture. Repeat layers. Top with remaining noodles, sauce and remaining mozzarella cheese.

3. Cover and bake at 375° for 30 minutes. Uncover; bake 10-15 minutes longer or until bubbly. Let stand for 10 minutes before cutting.

Nutrition Facts: 1 piece (prepared with lean ground beef) equals 281 calories, 11 g fat (6 g saturated fat), 50 mg cholesterol, 702 mg sodium, 26 g carbohydrate, 3 g fiber, 20 g protein.

Hawaiian Beef Sliders

PREP: 30 min. + marinating **GRILL:** 10 min.
YIELD: 6 servings

MARY RELYEA • CANASTOTA, NEW YORK

Sweet and savory with just a hint of heat, these dynamite burgers are packed with flavor. Pineapple and bacon may sound like an unusual combination, but once you take a bite, you'll discover that they're the perfect match.

1	can (20 oz.) unsweetened crushed pineapple
1	tsp. pepper
1/4	tsp. salt
1-1/2	lbs. lean ground beef (90% lean)
1/4	cup reduced-sodium soy sauce
2	Tbsp. ketchup
1	Tbsp. white vinegar
2	garlic cloves, minced
1/4	tsp. crushed red pepper flakes
18	minature whole wheat buns

Baby spinach leaves

3	center-cut bacon strips, cooked and crumbled

Sliced jalapeno peppers, optional

1. Drain pineapple, reserving juice and 1-1/2 cups pineapple (save remaining pineapple for another use). In a large bowl, combine 3/4 cup reserved crushed pineapple, pepper and salt. Crumble beef over mixture and mix well. Shape into 18 patties; place in two 11-in. x 7-in. dishes.

2. In a small bowl, combine the soy sauce, ketchup, vinegar, garlic, pepper flakes and reserved pineapple juice. Pour half of marinade into each dish; cover and refrigerate for 1 hour, turning once.

3. Drain and discard marinade. Using long-handled tongs, moisten a paper towel with cooking oil and lightly coat the grill rack.

4. Grill patties, covered, over medium heat or broil 4 in. from the heat for 4-5 minutes on each side or until a meat thermometer reads 160° and juices run clear.

5. Grill buns, uncovered, for 1-2 minutes or until toasted. Serve burgers on buns with spinach, remaining pineapple, bacon and jalapeno peppers if desired.

Editor's Note: If miniature whole wheat buns are not available in your area, you can also use whole wheat hot dog buns cut into thirds.

Nutrition Facts: 3 sliders (calculated without peppers) equals 350 calories, 12 g fat (4 g saturated fat), 74 mg cholesterol, 444 mg sodium, 34 g carbohydrate, 4 g fiber, 27 g protein.
Diabetic Exchanges: 3 lean meat, 1-1/2 starch, 1/2 fruit.

Beef Tenderloin With Roasted Vegetables

PREP: 20 min. + marinating **BAKE:** 1 hour + standing
YIELD: 8-10 servings

JANET SINGLETON • BELLEVUE, OHIO

I appreciate this recipe because it includes a side dish of roasted potatoes, Brussels sprouts and carrots. I prepare this entree for celebrations throughout the year.

1	beef tenderloin roast (3 lbs.)
3/4	cup dry white wine *or* beef broth
3/4	cup reduced-sodium soy sauce
4	tsp. minced fresh rosemary
4	tsp. Dijon mustard
1-1/2	tsp. ground mustard
3	garlic cloves, peeled and sliced
1	lb. Yukon Gold potatoes, cut into 1-in. wedges
1	lb. Brussels sprouts, halved
1	lb. fresh baby carrots

1. Place tenderloin in a large resealable plastic bag. Combine the wine, soy sauce, rosemary, Dijon mustard, ground mustard and garlic. Pour half of the marinade over tenderloin; seal bag and turn to coat. Refrigerate for 4-12 hours, turning several times. Cover and rcfrigerate remaining marinade.

2. Place the potatoes, Brussels sprouts and carrots in a greased 13-in. x 9-in. baking dish; add reserved marinade and toss to coat. Cover and bake at 425° for 30 minutes; stir.

3. Drain and discard marinade from tenderloin. Place tenderloin over vegetables. Bake, uncovered, for 30-45 minutes or until meat reaches desired doneness (for medium-rare, a meat thermometer should read 145°; medium, 160°; well-done, 170°).

4. Remove beef and let stand for 15 minutes. Check vegetables for doneness. If additional roasting is needed, cover with foil and bake for 10-15 minutes or until tender. Slice beef and serve with vegetables.

Nutrition Facts: 1 serving equals 283 calories, 8 g fat (3 g saturated fat), 60 mg cholesterol, 627 mg sodium, 16 g carbohydrate, 3 g fiber, 33 g protein. **Diabetic Exchanges:** 4 lean meat, 1 vegetable, 1/2 starch.

Taco Salad Tacos

PREP: 30 min. YIELD: 4 servings

CHERYL PLAINTE • PRUDENVILLE, MICHIGAN

I was making tacos one night and noticed I was out of spicy taco sauce. Using a combination of spices and fat-free Catalina salad dressing saved our family's taco night.

- 1 pound extra-lean ground beef (95% lean)
- 1 medium onion, chopped
- 1 tablespoon chili powder
- 1 teaspoon garlic powder
- 1 teaspoon reduced-sodium beef bouillon granules
- 1 teaspoon ground cumin
- 1/4 teaspoon salt

SALAD:
- 3 cups torn romaine
- 1 large tomato, seeded and chopped
- 1 medium sweet orange pepper, chopped
- 3 green onions, chopped
- 8 taco shells, warmed
- 1/2 cup fat-free Catalina salad dressing

Shredded reduced-fat Colby-Monterey Jack cheese and reduced-fat sour cream, optional

1. In a large skillet, cook beef and onion over medium heat until mcat is no longer pink. Stir in the chili powder, garlic powder, bouillon, cumin and salt; remove from the heat.

2. In a large bowl, combine the romaine, tomato, orange pepper and green onions. Spoon beef mixture into taco shells; top with salad mixture. Drizzle with dressing. Serve with cheese and sour cream if desired.

Nutrition Facts: 2 tacos (calulated without cheese and sour cream) equals 334 calories, 11 g fat (4 g saturated fat), 65 mg cholesterol, 722 mg sodium, 33 g carbohydrate, 6 g fiber, 26 g protein. **Diabetic Exchanges:** 3 lean meat, 2 vegetable, 1-1/2 starch.

Portobello Burgundy Beef

PREP: 20 min. COOK: 35 min. YIELD: 4 servings

MELANIE COLEMAN • PITTSBURG, CALIFORNIA

Nothing feels light about this rustic dish! Each bite is filled with mushrooms, beef and carrots wrapped in a savory, Burgundy-flavored sauce. This is comfort food at its finest!

- 1/4 cup plus 1 Tbsp. all-purpose flour, *divided*
- 1 tsp. dried marjoram, *divided*
- 1/2 tsp. salt, *divided*
- 1 beef top round steak (1 lb.), cut into 1/2-in. cubes
- 1 Tbsp. olive oil
- 2 cups sliced baby portobello mushrooms
- 3 garlic cloves, minced
- 3 medium carrots, cut into 1/2-in. pieces
- 1 can (14-1/2 oz.) reduced-sodium beef broth, *divided*
- 1/2 cup Burgundy wine or additional reduced-sodium beef broth
- 1 bay leaf
- 4 cups cooked egg noodles

1. Place 1/4 cup flour, 1/2 tsp. marjoram and 1/4 tsp. salt in a large resealable plastic bag. Add beef, a few pieces at a time, and shake to coat. In a large nonstick skillet coated with cooking spray, brown beef in oil.

2. Add mushrooms and garlic; saute until mushrooms are tender. Stir in the carrots, 1-1/2 cups broth, wine, bay leaf, remaining marjoram and salt. Bring to a boil. Reduce heat; cover and simmer for 15-20 minutes or until carrots are tender.

3. Combine remaining flour and broth; stir into pan. Bring to a boil; cook and stir for 2 minutes or until thickened. Discard bay leaf. Serve with noodles.

Nutrition Facts: 1 cup beef mixture with 1 cup noodles equals 384 calories, 9 g fat (2 g saturated fat), 98 mg cholesterol, 484 mg sodium, 39 g carbohydrate, 3 g fiber, 34 g protein. **Diabetic Exchanges:** 3 lean meat, 2 starch, 1 vegetable, 1/2 fat.

PORTOBELLO BURGUNDY BEEF

PAT'S PECAN CHICKEN

CHICKEN TACOS WITH AVOCADO SALSA

HOMEMADE CHICKEN
ALFREDO PIZZAS

Chicken Favorites

From hurried weeknight suppers to special Sunday dinners, the perfect chicken dish is always at your fingertips with this popular chapter. No one will guess they're eating healthy when these classics are on the menu.

Homemade Chicken Alfredo Pizzas

PREP: 30 min. + standing **BAKE:** 15 min.
YIELD: 2 pizzas (6 slices each)

CATHERINE NICKELSON • SCANDIA, MINNESOTA

Give these mouthwatering Alfredo pizzas a try next time you need to feed a crowd but want something healthier than delivery pizza. Even with their from-scratch crust and sauce, you'll be surprised by how simply they come together.

- 1 pkg. (1/4 oz.) quick-rise yeast
- 1 cup warm water (120° to 130°)
- 1 tsp. sugar
- 1-1/2 tsp. salt, *divided*
- 2-1/2 to 3 cups all-purpose flour
- 2 Tbsp. cornmeal
- 1 Tbsp. olive oil
- 2 garlic cloves, minced
- 2 Tbsp. butter
- 1 tsp. dried parsley flakes
- 1/4 tsp. pepper
- 4-1/2 tsp. all-purpose flour
- 1-1/2 cups 2% milk
- 3 cups cubed cooked chicken breasts
- 2 large tomatoes, chopped
- 2 cups chopped fresh baby spinach
- 4 cups (16 oz.) shredded part-skim mozzarella cheese
- 1/2 cup shredded Italian cheese blend
- 1 tsp. Italian seasoning

1. In a large bowl, dissolve yeast in warm water. Add the sugar, 1/2 tsp. salt and 2-1/2 cups flour. Beat until smooth. Stir in enough remaining flour to form a soft dough (dough will be sticky).

2. Turn onto a lightly floured surface; knead until smooth and elastic, about 6-8 minutes. Cover and let rest for 10 minutes.

3. Sprinkle cornmeal over two 12-in. pizza pans coated with cooking spray. Divide dough in half. On a floured surface, roll each portion into a 13-in. circle. Transfer to prepared pans. Build up edges slightly. Prick dough

thoroughly with a fork; brush with oil. Bake at 425° for 5-8 minutes or until edges are lightly browned.

4. In a small saucepan, saute garlic in butter until tender. Stir in the parsley, pepper and remaining salt. Combine flour and milk until smooth. Stir into pan. Bring to a boil; cook and stir for 2 minutes or until slightly thickened.

5. Spread over crusts; top with chicken, tomatoes, spinach, cheeses and Italian seasoning. Bake 10-12 minutes longer or until crusts are lightly browned and cheeses are melted.

Nutrition Facts: 1 slice equals 328 calories, 13 g fat (7 g saturated fat), 62 mg cholesterol, 568 mg sodium, 27 g carbohydrate, 1 g fiber, 26 g protein.

Pat's Pecan Chicken C

PREP: 20 min. **BAKE:** 20 min. **YIELD:** 4 servings

PATRICIA BROWN • BATTLE CREEK, MICHIGAN

Parmesan, pecans, oregano and basil blend beautifully in this crunchy, crusted chicken. The recipe couldn't be much easier, and no one will know it's lower in calories.

- 1/2 cup fat-free milk
- 1-1/4 cups soft bread crumbs
- 1/2 cup finely chopped pecans
- 1/4 cup grated Parmesan cheese
- 3 tsp. dried oregano
- 3 tsp. dried basil
- 1 tsp. garlic powder
- 4 boneless skinless chicken breast halves (4 oz. *each*)
- 2 tsp. canola oil

1. Place milk in a shallow bowl. In another shallow bowl, combine the bread crumbs, pecans, cheese and seasonings. Dip the chicken in milk, then roll it in the crumb mixture. In a large nonstick skillet, brown chicken in oil.

2. Transfer to a baking sheet coated with cooking spray. Bake, uncovered, at 350° for 20-25 minutes or until a meat thermometer reads 170°.

Nutrition Facts: 1 chicken breast half equals 229 calories, 11 g fat (2 g saturated fat), 65 mg cholesterol, 143 mg sodium, 6 g carbohydrate, 1 g fiber, 25 g protein. **Diabetic Exchanges:** 3 lean meat, 2 fat.

Chicken Fajita Pizza

PREP/TOTAL TIME: 30 min. **YIELD:** 6 servings

CARRIE SHAUB • MOUNT JOY, PENNSYLVANIA

This recipe has always been a hit! Even my kids like it—and it's such a great way to sneak in extra vegetables.

1	pkg. (13.8 oz.) refrigerated pizza crust
8	oz. boneless skinless chicken breasts, cut into thin strips
1	tsp. canola oil, *divided*
1	medium onion, sliced
1	medium sweet red pepper, sliced
1	medium green pepper, sliced
1	tsp. chili powder
1/2	tsp. ground cumin
1	garlic clove, minced
1/4	cup chunky salsa
2	cups (8 oz.) shredded reduced-fat Mexican cheese blend
1	Tbsp. minced fresh cilantro

Sour cream and additional salsa, optional

1. Unroll dough into a 15-in. x 10-in. x 1-in. baking pan coated with cooking spray; flatten dough and build up edges slightly. Bake at 425° for 8-10 minutes or until edges are lightly browned.

2. Meanwhile, in a large nonstick skillet coated with cooking spray, cook chicken over medium heat in 1/2 tsp. oil for 4-6 minutes or until no longer pink; remove and keep warm.

3. In the same pan, saute the onion, peppers, chili powder and cumin in remaining oil until crisp-tender. Add the garlic; cook 1 minute longer. Stir in the salsa and chicken.

4. Sprinkle half of the cheese over prepared crust; top with chicken mixture and remaining cheese.

CHICKEN FAJITA PIZZA

Bake for 8-10 minutes or until crust is golden brown and cheese is melted. Sprinkle with cilantro. Serve with sour cream and additional salsa if desired.

Nutrition Facts: 1 piece (calculated without optional ingredients) equals 351 calories, 12 g fat (4 g saturated fat), 48 mg cholesterol, 767 mg sodium, 38 g carbohydrate, 2 g fiber, 25 g protein. **Diabetic Exchanges:** 3 lean meat, 2 starch, 1 vegetable, 1/2 fat.

Lemon-Olive Chicken with Orzo

PREP/TOTAL TIME: 30 min. **YIELD:** 4 servings

NANCY BROWN • DAHINDA, ILLINOIS

This quick recipe is a healthy all-in-one meal. I just add a tossed salad for a menu the entire family loves!

4	boneless skinless chicken thighs (about 1 lb.)
1	Tbsp. olive oil
1	can (14-1/2 oz.) reduced-sodium chicken broth
2/3	cup uncooked whole wheat orzo pasta
4	lemon wedges
1/2	cup pitted Greek olives, sliced
1	Tbsp. lemon juice
1	tsp. dried oregano
1/4	tsp. salt
1/4	tsp. pepper

1. In a large nonstick skillet, brown chicken in oil; drain and set aside. Add broth to skillet, stirring to loosen browned bits from pan.

2. Bring to a boil. Stir in the orzo, lemon wedges, olives, lemon juice, oregano, salt and pepper. Return to a boil. Reduce heat; simmer, uncovered, for 5 minutes, stirring occasionally.

3. Return chicken to the skillet. Cover and cook for 5-7 minutes or until chicken juices run clear and pasta is tender.

Nutrition Facts: 1 serving equals 346 calories, 17 g fat (3 g saturated fat), 76 mg cholesterol, 784 mg sodium, 22 g carbohydrate, 5 g fiber, 26 g protein. **Diabetic Exchanges:** 3 lean meat, 2 fat, 1 starch.

Chicken Sausages With Peppers C

PREP/TOTAL TIME: 30 min. **YIELD:** 4 servings

DEBORAH SCHAEFER • DURAND, MICHIGAN

Ready in just half an hour, this is one savory main course you will turn to time and again!

1	small onion, halved and sliced
1	small sweet orange pepper, julienned
1	small sweet red pepper, julienned
1	Tbsp. olive oil
1	garlic clove, minced
1	pkg. (12 oz.) fully cooked apple chicken sausage links *or* flavor of your choice, cut into 1-in. pieces

1. In a large nonstick skillet, saute onion and peppers in oil until crisp-tender. Add garlic; cook 1 minute longer. Stir in sausages; heat through.

FAVORITE JAMBALAYA

Nutrition Facts: 1 cup equals 208 calories, 11 g fat (2 g saturated fat), 60 mg cholesterol, 483 mg sodium, 14 g carbohydrate, 1 g fiber, 15 g protein. **Diabetic Exchanges:** 2 lean meat, 1 vegetable, 1/2 starch, 1/2 fat.

Favorite Jambalaya

PREP: 20 min.   COOK: 25 min.   YIELD: 6 servings

HEALTHY COOKING TEST KITCHEN

This zesty jambalaya trumps most ready-made jambalaya mixes. Not only does our recipe include fresh vegetables, but we use our own seasonings to boost flavor.

1/2	lb. boneless skinless chicken breasts, cubed
1/4	lb. smoked turkey sausage, halved lengthwise and sliced
1	large onion, chopped
1	medium green pepper, chopped
1	celery rib, chopped
1	Tbsp. canola oil
2	garlic cloves, minced
2	cans (14-1/2 oz. *each*) no-salt-added diced tomatoes, undrained
1	bay leaf
1	tsp. Cajun seasoning
1	tsp. dried thyme
1/4	tsp. cayenne pepper
1/4	tsp. pepper
1	lb. uncooked medium shrimp, peeled and deveined
3	cups hot cooked brown rice

1. In a nonstick Dutch oven, saute the chicken, sausage, onion, green pepper and celery in oil until chicken is no longer pink. Add garlic; cook 1 minute longer. Stir in the tomatoes, bay leaf, Cajun seasoning, thyme, cayenne and pepper.

2. Bring to a boil. Reduce heat; cover and simmer for 15 minutes. Add shrimp; cook 5-6 minutes longer or until shrimp turn pink. Discard bay leaf. Serve with the rice.

Nutrition Facts: 1 cup jambalaya with 1/2 cup rice equals 302 calories, 6 g fat (1 g saturated fat), 125 mg cholesterol, 450 mg sodium, 34 g carbohydrate, 5 g fiber, 27 g protein. **Diabetic Exchanges:** 3 lean meat, 2 vegetable, 1 starch.

Lentil & Chicken Sausage Stew

PREP: 15 min. **COOK:** 8 hours **YIELD:** 6 servings

JAN VALDEZ • CHICAGO, ILLINOIS

No matter how chilly the weather, this hearty and healthy soup will warm up your family right down to their toes! It's packed with veggies and the comforting flavors of autumn. Serve with cornbread or rolls to soak up every last drop.

- 1 carton (32 oz.) reduced-sodium chicken broth
- 1 can (28 oz.) diced tomatoes, undrained
- 3 fully cooked spicy chicken sausage links (3 oz. *each*), cut into 1/2-in. slices
- 1 cup dried lentils, rinsed
- 1 medium onion, chopped
- 1 medium carrot, chopped
- 1 celery rib, chopped
- 2 garlic cloves, minced
- 1/2 tsp. dried thyme

1. In a 4- or 5-qt. slow cooker, combine all ingredients. Cover and cook on low for 8-10 hours or until lentils are tender.

Nutrition Facts: 1-1/2 cups equals 231 calories, 4 g fat (1 g saturated fat), 33 mg cholesterol, 803 mg sodium, 31 g carbohydrate, 13 g fiber, 19 g protein. **Diabetic Exchanges:** 2 lean meat, 2 vegetable, 1 starch.

Mango Barbecued Jerk Chicken Thighs c

PREP: 20 min. + marinating COOK: 20 min.
YIELD: 4 servings

KAREN CAMBIOTTI • STROUDSBURG, PENNSYLVANIA

I like my food bursting with flavor, so I love to experiment with all different ethnic recipes. Sweet, tangy barbecue sauce goes well with the heat of the jerk-seasoned marinade in this recipe. Ease of prep plus an appealing presentation make it great for entertaining. And friends always come back for seconds!

  2 Tbsp. orange juice
1-1/2 tsp. lime juice
1-1/2 tsp. olive oil
  1 Tbsp. Caribbean jerk seasoning
  1 garlic clove, minced
  4 boneless skinless chicken thighs (about 1 lb.)

BARBECUE SAUCE:
  3 Tbsp. mango chutney
1-1/2 tsp. lime juice
1-1/2 tsp. honey
  1 tsp. Dijon mustard
1/4 tsp. Chinese five-spice powder
1/4 tsp. minced fresh gingerroot
  1 Tbsp. minced fresh cilantro
1-1/2 tsp. sesame seeds, toasted
  1 tsp. grated orange peel

1. In a large resealable plastic bag, combine the first five ingredients; add the chicken. Seal bag and turn to coat; refrigerate for 8 hours or overnight.

2. For barbecue sauce, in a small bowl, combine the chutney, lime juice, honey, mustard, five-spice powder and ginger; set aside. In another small bowl, combine the cilantro, sesame seeds and orange peel; set aside.

3. Drain and discard marinade. Broil chicken 4-6 in. from the heat for 7 minutes. Turn and broil for 6 minutes. Baste with half of the barbecue sauce. Broil 3-5 minutes longer or until chicken juices run clear. Place on a serving dish. Sprinkle cilantro mixture over chicken. Serve with remaining sauce.

Nutrition Facts: 1 chicken thigh equals 232 calories, 9 g fat (2 g saturated fat), 76 mg cholesterol, 297 mg sodium, 14 g carbohydrate, trace fiber, 21 g protein. **Diabetic Exchanges:** 3 lean meat, 1 starch.

Curried Chicken and Rice Ring

PREP: 30 min. BAKE: 35 min. YIELD: 6 servings

HEALTHY COOKING TEST KITCHEN

Here's an impressive change-of-pace entree that's sure to liven up meals. Best of all, it's a meal-in-one specialty! Simply add a healthy green salad, and dinner is ready.

  1 cup reduced-sodium chicken broth
1/2 cup uncooked long grain rice
1-1/2 cups cubed cooked chicken breast
  1 cup frozen peas and carrots, thawed and drained
  6 Tbsp. reduced-fat mayonnaise
  2 green onions, chopped
  1 tsp. salt
1/2 tsp. pepper
1/2 tsp. curry powder
1/4 tsp. garlic powder
1/4 tsp. ground turmeric
1/4 tsp. ground coriander
 12 sheets phyllo dough (14 in. x 9 in.)
Butter-flavored cooking spray

1. In a small saucepan, bring broth and rice to a boil. Reduce heat; cover and simmer for 15-18 minutes or until liquid is absorbed and rice is tender.

2. In a large bowl combine the rice, chicken, peas and carrots, mayonnaise, green onion and seasonings.

3. Coat a 10-in. fluted tube pan with cooking spray. Drape one sheet of phyllo over pan and push down over hole. Repeat twice, rotating sheets to cover sides of pan and letting edges of dough hang over sides. Spritz with butter-flavored spray; repeat.

4. Spoon filling into pan. Top with remaining phyllo in the same manner. Fold edges over into pan; spray with butter-flavored cooking spray. Bake at 375° for 30-35 minutes or until lightly browned. Let the ring stand for 10 minutes before removing from the pan to a serving platter.

Nutrition Facts: 1 piece equals 248 calories, 8 g fat (1 g saturated fat), 32 mg cholesterol, 740 mg sodium, 30 g carbohydrate, 2 g fiber, 15 g protein.

CURRIED CHICKEN AND RICE RING

Tuscan Chicken C

PREP: 25 min. COOK: 15 min. YIELD: 4 servings

CARLA WELLS • SOMERSET, KENTUCKY

I created this recipe one night when I was looking for a new way to prepare chicken. It's moist, tender, saucy and healthy, too. I recently lost 30-some pounds, and this is one dish I prepare often.

- 4 boneless skinless chicken breast halves (6 oz. *each*)
- 1/4 tsp. pepper
- 2 Tbsp. olive oil
- 1 *each* medium green, sweet red and yellow peppers, julienned
- 2 thin slices prosciutto *or* deli ham, chopped
- 2 garlic cloves, minced
- 1 can (14-1/2 oz.) diced tomatoes, undrained
- 1/4 cup reduced-sodium chicken broth
- 2 Tbsp. minced fresh basil *or* 2 tsp. dried basil
- 1 tsp. minced fresh oregano *or* 1/4 tsp. dried oregano

1. Sprinkle chicken with pepper. In a large nonstick skillet, brown chicken in oil. Remove and keep warm. In the same skillet, saute peppers and prosciutto until peppers are tender. Add garlic; cook 1 minute longer.

2. Add the tomatoes, broth, basil, oregano and chicken. Bring to a boil. Reduce heat; cover and simmer for 12-15 minutes or until a thermometer reads 170°.

Nutrition Facts: 1 chicken breast half with 1 cup vegetable mixture equals 304 calories, 12 g fat (2 g saturated fat), 100 mg cholesterol, 389 mg sodium, 11 g carbohydrate, 3 g fiber, 38 g protein. **Diabetic Exchanges:** 5 lean meat, 2 vegetable, 1 fat.

TUSCAN CHICKEN

Sassy Chicken & Peppers C

PREP/TOTAL TIME: 25 min. YIELD: 2 servings

DORIS HEATH • FRANKLIN, NORTH CAROLINA

Sharing supper with a friend who's watching his or her weight? Taco seasoning, salsa and a squirt of lime add up to a nice summery flavor for chicken—but a slim 239 calories for you!

- 2 boneless skinless chicken breast halves (4 oz. *each*)
- 2 tsp. taco seasoning
- 4 tsp. canola oil, *divided*
- 1 small onion, halved and sliced
- 1/2 small green bell pepper, julienned
- 1/2 small sweet red pepper, julienned
- 1/4 cup salsa
- 1 Tbsp. lime juice

1. Sprinkle the chicken with seasoning. In a small nonstick skillet, cook chicken in 2 tsp. oil over medium heat for 4-5 minutes on each side or until juices run clear. Remove and keep warm.

2. Saute onion and peppers in remaining oil until crisp-tender; stir in salsa and lime juice. Spoon mixture over chicken.

Nutrition Facts: 1 serving equals 239 calories, 12 g fat (1 g saturated fat), 63 mg cholesterol, 377 mg sodium, 8 g carbohydrate, 1 g fiber, 24 g protein. **Diabetic Exchanges:** 3 lean meat, 2 fat, 1 vegetable.

Chicken with Berry Wine Sauce C

PREP: 35 min. GRILL: 10 min. YIELD: 4 servings

ELIZABETH WRIGHT • RALEIGH, NORTH CAROLINA

An impressive ruby-red sauce makes this grilled entree a natural choice for summer entertaining.

- 1 cup fresh strawberries, halved
- 1 cup fresh raspberries
- 1 cup merlot *or* red grape juice
- 2 Tbsp. sugar
- 4 boneless skinless chicken breast halves (6 oz. *each*)
- 1/2 tsp. salt
- 1/2 tsp. pepper

Thinly sliced fresh basil leaves

1. In a small saucepan, combine the strawberries, raspberries, merlot and sugar. Bring to a boil. Reduce heat; simmer, uncovered, for 25-30 minutes or until thickened, stirring occasionally.

2. Meanwhile, moisten a paper towel with cooking oil; using long-handled tongs, lightly coat the grill rack. Sprinkle the chicken with salt and pepper. Grill chicken, covered, over medium heat or broil 4 in. from the heat for 4-7 minutes on each side or until a thermometer reads 170°.

3. Serve with berry sauce; garnish with basil.

Nutrition Facts: 1 chicken breast half with 2 Tbsp. sauce equals 251 calories, 4 g fat (1 g saturated fat), 94 mg cholesterol, 378 mg sodium, 13 g carbohydrate, 3 g fiber, 35 g protein. **Diabetic Exchanges:** 5 lean meat, 1/2 starch, 1/2 fruit.

Spicy Chicken and Rice

PREP: 20 min. COOK: 5-1/2 hours YIELD: 8 servings

JESSICA COSTELLO • WESTMINSTER, MASSACHUSETTS

As a working mom with two kids, I have little time to prepare something hearty during the week. This recipe is easily tossed together in the morning and fabulous to come home to after a long day. Both my picky eaters love it!

- 4 boneless skinless chicken breast halves (6 oz. *each*)
- 2 cans (14-1/2 oz. *each*) diced tomatoes with mild green chilies, undrained
- 2 medium green peppers, chopped
- 1 medium onion, chopped
- 1 garlic clove, minced
- 1 tsp. smoked paprika
- 3/4 tsp. salt
- 1/2 tsp. ground cumin
- 1/2 tsp. ground chipotle pepper
- 6 cups cooked brown rice
- 1 can (15 oz.) black beans, rinsed and drained
- 1/2 cup shredded cheddar cheese
- 1/2 cup reduced-fat sour cream

1. Place chicken in a 4- or 5-qt. slow cooker. In a large bowl, combine the tomatoes, green peppers, onion, garlic, paprika, salt, cumin and chipotle pepper; pour over chicken. Cover and cook on low for 5-6 hours or until chicken is tender.

2. Shred chicken with two forks and return to the slow cooker. Stir in rice and beans; heat through. Garnish with cheese and sour cream.

Nutrition Facts: 1-1/3 cups chicken mixture with 1 Tbsp. cheese and 1 Tbsp. sour cream equals 389 calories, 7 g fat (3 g saturated fat), 59 mg cholesterol, 817 mg sodium, 53 g carbohydrate, 7 g fiber, 27 g protein.

Chicken Pasta Skillet

PREP/TOTAL TIME: 30 min. YIELD: 6 servings

HEATHER MCCLINTOCK • COLUMBUS, OHIO

I was inspired to come up with a healthier mac and cheese dish—something with a little fiber and some veggies. My husband doesn't like health food, but he loved this!

3	cups uncooked whole wheat spiral pasta
2	cups fresh broccoli florets
2	Tbsp. butter
2	Tbsp. plus 1 tsp. all-purpose flour
1-1/4	cups reduced-sodium chicken broth
1/2	cup fat-free half-and-half
4	oz. reduced-fat process cheese (Velveeta), cubed
1	tsp. garlic-herb seasoning blend
1/4	tsp. salt
2-1/2	cups cubed cooked chicken breast
1/2	cup shredded cheddar cheese

1. In a large saucepan, cook pasta according to package directions, adding the broccoli during the last 2 minutes of cooking; drain.

2. In a large skillet, melt butter. Combine flour and broth until smooth; stir into pan. Add half-and-half. Bring to a boil; cook and stir for 1 minute or until thickened. Add the process cheese, seasoning blend and salt; stir until smooth. Stir in pasta mixture and chicken; heat through.

3. Remove from the heat; sprinkle with cheddar cheese. Cover and let stand for 5-10 minutes or until cheese is melted.

Nutrition Facts: 1-1/4 cups equals 335 calories, 11 g fat (6 g saturated fat), 72 mg cholesterol, 671 mg sodium, 29 g carbohydrate, 4 g fiber, 29 g protein. **Diabetic Exchanges:** 3 lean meat, 2 starch, 1 fat.

Garden Chicken Cacciatore [C]

PREP: 15 min. COOK: 8-1/2 hours YIELD: 12 servings

MARTHA SCHIRMACHER • STERLING HEIGHTS, MICHIGAN

Here's the perfect Italian meal to serve company. While simmering, it frees you up to visit with your guests and always receives rave reviews. Mangia!

12	boneless skinless chicken thighs (about 3 lbs.)
2	medium green peppers, chopped
1	can (14-1/2 oz.) diced tomatoes with basil, oregano and garlic, undrained
1	can (6 oz.) tomato paste
1	medium onion, sliced
1/2	cup reduced-sodium chicken broth
1/4	cup dry red wine *or* additional reduced-sodium chicken broth
3	garlic cloves, minced
3/4	tsp. salt
1/8	tsp. pepper
2	Tbsp. cornstarch
2	Tbsp. water

1. Place chicken in a 4-qt. slow cooker. In a small bowl, combine the green peppers, tomatoes, tomato paste, onion, broth, wine, garlic, salt and pepper. Cover and cook on low for 8-10 hours or until chicken is tender.

2. Combine the cornstarch and water until the mixture is smooth; gradually stir into slow cooker. Cover and cook on high 30 minutes longer or until the sauce is thickened.

Nutrition Facts: 1 chicken thigh with scant 1/2 cup sauce equals 207 calories, 9 g fat (2 g saturated fat), 76 mg cholesterol, 410 mg sodium, 8 g carbohydrate, 1 g fiber, 23 g protein. **Diabetic Exchanges:** 3 lean meat, 1 vegetable, 1/2 fat.

> Garlic that's been finely chopped by hand and garlic that's been put through a press can be used **interchangeably** in recipes. Choose whichever is most convenient for you.

GARDEN CHICKEN CACCIATORE

Spinach-Stuffed Chicken Rolls C

PREP: 30 min. COOK: 20 min. YIELD: 4 servings

VIRGINIA ANTHONY • JACKSONVILLE, FLORIDA

I've been making this pretty, festive-looking dish for years and people often ask for the recipe. Convenient for company, it can be made ahead of time right up to the point of dusting with flour and browning.

- 1/3 cup sun-dried tomatoes (not packed in oil)
- 1 cup boiling water
- 4 boneless skinless chicken breast halves (4 oz. *each*)
- 1-1/2 tsp. minced fresh rosemary *or* 1/2 tsp. dried rosemary, crushed
- 1/2 tsp. pepper
- 1/4 tsp. salt
- 1 pkg. (10 oz.) frozen chopped spinach, thawed and squeezed dry
- 1 Tbsp. golden raisins
- 1 Tbsp. reduced-fat cream cheese
- 2 tsp. pine nuts
- 2 Tbsp. all-purpose flour
- 2 tsp. olive oil
- 1 cup reduced-sodium chicken broth
- 1/2 cup minced fresh basil
- 3 garlic cloves, minced
- 1-1/2 tsp. cornstarch
- 1 Tbsp. cold water
- 2 medium tomatoes, chopped

1. Place dried tomatoes in a small bowl. Cover with boiling water; let stand for 5 minutes. Drain, reserving 1/2 cup water; chop tomatoes and set aside.

2. Flatten chicken to 1/4-in. thickness; sprinkle with rosemary, pepper and salt. In a small bowl, combine the spinach, raisins, cream cheese, pine nuts and sun-dried tomatoes. Spread 1/4 cup spinach mixture over each chicken breast. Roll up and secure with toothpicks. Place flour in a shallow bowl; coat chicken with flour.

3. In a large nonstick skillet coated with cooking spray over medium heat, brown chicken in oil. Add the broth, basil, garlic and reserved water. Bring to a boil. Reduce heat; cover and simmer for 10-12 minutes or until a thermometer reads 170°.

4. Combine cornstarch and cold water until smooth. Stir into pan. Bring to a boil; cook and stir for 1 minute or until thickened. Add tomatoes; heat through. Discard toothpicks.

Nutrition Facts: 1 stuffed chicken roll with 1/3 cup tomato mixture equals 226 calories, 7 g fat (2 g saturated fat), 65 mg cholesterol, 512 mg sodium, 14 g carbohydrate, 4 g fiber, 28 g protein. **Diabetic Exchanges:** 3 lean meat, 2 vegetable, 1 fat.

Baked Caesar Chicken C

PREP: 10 min. BAKE: 30 min. YIELD: 4 servings

KIRSTEN NORGAARD • ASTORIA, OREGON

Easy, fast to fix and delicious, this meal maker is a winner!

- 4 boneless skinless chicken breast halves (6 oz. *each*)
- 1/2 cup fat-free creamy Caesar salad dressing
- 1 medium ripe avocado, peeled and cubed
- 1/4 cup shredded Parmesan cheese, *divided*

1. Place chicken in an 11-in. x 7-in. baking dish coated with cooking spray.

2. In a small bowl, combine the salad dressing, avocado and 2 Tbsp. cheese; spoon over chicken. Bake, uncovered, at 375° for 30-35 minutes or until a thermometer reads 170°. Sprinkle with the remaining cheese.

Nutrition Facts: 1 chicken breast half equals 320 calories, 12 g fat (3 g saturated fat), 98 mg cholesterol, 530 mg sodium, 15 g carbohydrate, 4 g fiber, 38 g protein. **Diabetic Exchanges:** 5 lean meat, 1 starch, 1 fat.

Curried Chicken And Rice Bundles

PREP: 30 min. BAKE: 15 min. YIELD: 6 servings

HEALTHY COOKING TEST KITCHEN

Looking to liven up a special menu? Consider these tasty bundles! Their cute presentation is sure to impress, but the savory filling is what will keep folks talking.

- 1 cup reduced-sodium chicken broth
- 1/2 cup uncooked long grain rice
- 1-1/2 cups cubed cooked chicken breast

BAKED CAESAR CHICKEN

CURRIED CHICKEN AND RICE BUNDLES

1 cup frozen peas and carrots, thawed and drained
6 Tbsp. reduced-fat mayonnaise
2 green onions, chopped
1 tsp. salt
1/2 tsp. pepper
1/2 tsp. curry powder
1/4 tsp. garlic powder
1/4 tsp. ground turmeric
1/4 tsp. ground coriander
12 sheets phyllo dough (14 in. x 9 in.)
Butter-flavored cooking spray
6 whole chives

1. In a small saucepan, bring broth and rice to a boil. Reduce heat; cover and simmer for 15-18 minutes or until liquid is absorbed and rice is tender.

2. In a large bowl, combine the rice, chicken, peas and carrots, mayonnaise, green onions and seasonings.

3. Place one sheet of phyllo on a work surface; spritz with butter-flavored spray. Top with another sheet of phyllo; spritz with spray. Place 1/2 cup of the rice filling in the center. Bring the corners together and twist; tie bundle closed with a chive. Repeat with the remaining ingredients.

4. Place on a baking sheet coated with cooking spray. Bake at 375° for 12-15 minutes or until bundles are lightly browned.

Nutrition Facts: 1 bundle equals 248 calories, 8 g fat (1 g saturated fat), 32 mg cholesterol, 740 mg sodium, 30 g carbohydrate, 2 g fiber, 15 g protein.

Chicken with Celery Root Puree

PREP: 30 min. COOK: 15 min. YIELD: 4 servings

TASTE OF HOME TEST KITCHEN

Celeriac, or celery root, is a root veggie that combines well with other seasonal ingredients and adds nice texture and flavor to this puree.

- 4 boneless skinless chicken breast halves (6 oz. *each*)
- 1/2 tsp. pepper
- 1 Tbsp. canola oil, *divided*
- 1 large celery root, peeled and chopped
- 2 cups chopped peeled butternut squash
- 1 small onion, chopped
- 2 garlic cloves, minced
- 1 can (5-1/2 oz.) unsweetened apple juice
- 1/4 tsp. salt

1. Sprinkle chicken with pepper. In a large nonstick skillet coated with cooking spray, brown chicken in 2 tsp. oil. Remove and keep warm. In the same skillet, saute the celery root, squash and onion in remaining oil until squash is crisp-tender. Add garlic; cook 1 minute longer.

2. Add the apple juice, salt and chicken. Bring to a boil. Reduce heat; cover and simmer for 12-15 minutes or until a thermometer reads 170°.

3. Remove chicken and keep warm. Transfer vegetable mixture to a food processor. Cover and process until smooth. Return to the pan; heat through. Serve with chicken.

Nutrition Facts: 1 chicken breast half with 2/3 cup puree equals 328 calories, 8 g fat (1 g saturated fat), 94 mg cholesterol, 348 mg sodium, 28 g carbohydrate, 5 g fiber, 37 g protein. **Diabetic Exchanges:** 5 lean meat, 2 starch, 1/2 fat.

Provolone Chicken Pizza

PREP/TOTAL TIME: 25 min. YIELD: 6 servings

SHELLY BEVINGTON-FISHER • HERMISTON, OREGON

Just pick up a ready-made pizza crust and rotisserie chicken on the way home, and enjoy a fresh, cheesy pizza in less time than it takes to order one that's not even half as good!

- 1 prebaked 12-in. thin whole wheat pizza crust
- 1/2 cup reduced-fat ranch salad dressing
- 6 slices reduced-fat provolone cheese
- 2 cups shredded cooked chicken breast
- 1 medium tomato, thinly sliced
- 2 green onions, thinly sliced
- 1 Tbsp. grated Parmesan cheese

1. Place crust on an ungreased 12-in. pizza pan or baking sheet; spread with salad dressing. Top with provolone cheese, chicken, tomato and onions. Sprinkle with Parmesan cheese. Bake at 450° for 10-12 minutes or until cheese is melted and edges are lightly browned.

Nutrition Facts: 1 slice equals 306 calories, 12 g fat (4 g saturated fat), 52 mg cholesterol, 636 mg sodium, 26 g carbohydrate, 4 g fiber, 25 g protein. **Diabetic Exchanges:** 3 lean meat, 1-1/2 starch, 1 fat.

Asian Chicken Pasta Salad

PREP/TOTAL TIME: 30 min. YIELD: 6 servings

NICOLE FILIZETTI • JACKSONVILLE, FLORIDA

Packed with veggies, chicken, whole wheat pasta and just the right amount of heat, this main-dish salad is definitely special.

- 3 cups uncooked whole wheat spiral pasta
- 2 cups cubed cooked chicken breast
- 2 cups fresh broccoli florets
- 1-1/2 cups fresh sugar snap peas, trimmed and halved
- 1 can (8 oz.) bamboo shoots
- 1 small sweet red pepper, chopped
- 3 Tbsp. rice vinegar
- 3 Tbsp. peanut oil
- 3 Tbsp. reduced-sodium soy sauce
- 2 Tbsp. sesame oil
- 3 garlic cloves, minced
- 2 tsp. minced fresh gingerroot
- 1/2 tsp. crushed red pepper flakes
- 1/2 tsp. pepper

1. Cook pasta according to package directions. Meanwhile, in a large bowl, combine the chicken, broccoli, peas, bamboo shoots and red pepper.

2. In a small bowl, whisk the remaining ingredients. Pour over chicken mixture; toss to coat. Drain pasta and rinse in cold water; add to salad.

Nutrition Facts: 1-2/3 cups equals 321 calories, 14 g fat (2 g saturated fat), 36 mg cholesterol, 344 mg sodium, 29 g carbohydrate, 6 g fiber, 21 g protein. **Diabetic Exchanges:** 2 lean meat, 2 fat, 1-1/2 starch, 1 vegetable.

ASIAN CHICKEN PASTA SALAD

Thai Chicken Pasta Salad

PREP/TOTAL TIME: 30 min.   **YIELD:** 8 servings

BETH DAUENHAUER • PUEBLO, COLORADO

This healthier twist on traditional pad thai has only one-third the sodium of similar name-brand products—and it's ready to serve in just 30 minutes!

- 3/4 cup reduced-fat creamy peanut butter
- 3 Tbsp. water
- 3 Tbsp. lime juice
- 3 Tbsp. molasses
- 4-1/2 tsp. reduced-sodium soy sauce
- 3 garlic cloves, minced
- 1-1/2 tsp. rice vinegar
- 1-1/2 tsp. sesame oil
- 1/4 tsp. crushed red pepper flakes

SALAD:
- 12 oz. uncooked whole wheat spaghetti
- 2 large carrots, julienned
- 8 cups finely shredded Chinese or napa cabbage
- 2 cups shredded cooked chicken breast
- 2/3 cup minced fresh cilantro
- 3 Tbsp. unsalted dry roasted peanuts, chopped

1. For dressing, in a small bowl, whisk the first nine ingredients until smooth; set aside.

2. In a large saucepan, cook spaghetti according to package directions, adding the carrots during the last 2 minutes of cooking; drain. Transfer to a large bowl; stir in cabbage and chicken.

3. Whisk dressing and pour over spaghetti mixture; toss to coat. Sprinkle with cilantro and peanuts. Serve immediately or chill before serving.

Nutrition Facts: 1-1/2 cups equals 400 calories, 12 g fat (2 g saturated fat), 27 mg cholesterol, 298 mg sodium, 51 g carbohydrate, 9 g fiber, 25 g protein.

THAI CHICKEN PASTA SALAD

Italian Baked Chicken

PREP: 15 min. + marinating   **BAKE:** 20 min.
YIELD: 2 servings

LADONNA REED • PONCA CITY, OKLAHOMA

This scrumptious chicken entree is low in fat but bursting with flavor from the marinade and bread crumb coating. The meat is tender and moist—and so easy to prepare.

- 3/4 cup fat-free ranch salad dressing
- 4 garlic cloves, minced
- 2 boneless skinless chicken breast halves (5 oz. *each*)
- 1/2 cup seasoned bread crumbs
- 3 Tbsp. grated Parmesan cheese
- 1/4 tsp. pepper

1. In a large resealable plastic bag, combine salad dressing and garlic; add the chicken. Seal bag and turn to coat; refrigerate for at least 30 minutes.

2. Meanwhile, in a small shallow bowl, combine the bread crumbs, Parmesan cheese and pepper. Drain and discard marinade. Roll chicken in crumb mixture. Place in an 8-in. square baking dish coated with cooking spray. Bake, uncovered, at 325° for 20-25 minutes or until chicken juices run clear.

Nutrition Facts: 1 chicken breast half equals 297 calories, 6 g fat (2 g saturated fat), 82 mg cholesterol, 813 mg sodium, 26 g carbohydrate, 1 g fiber, 33 g protein. **Diabetic Exchanges:** 4 lean meat, 1-1/2 starch.

Chicken with Cherry Pineapple Sauce

PREP/TOTAL TIME: 25 min.   **YIELD:** 4 servings

SALLY MALONEY • DALLAS, GEORGIA

Sweet and colorful, this tender, lower-fat chicken dish is simply fantastic! The quick prep time, fresh flavors and cherries will make it a family favorite in no time.

- 4 boneless skinless chicken breast halves (4 oz. *each*)
- 1/2 tsp. garlic salt
- 1/4 tsp. ground ginger
- 2 tsp. canola oil
- 1 can (8 oz.) unsweetened pineapple chunks
- 1/2 cup sweet-and-sour sauce
- 1/4 cup dried cherries
- 2 green onions, sliced

1. Sprinkle chicken with garlic salt and ginger. In a large nonstick skillet coated with cooking spray, brown chicken in oil.

2. Drain pineapple, reserving 1/4 cup juice. In a small bowl, combine the sauce, cherries and reserved juice; pour over chicken. Bring to a boil. Reduce heat; cover and simmer for 8-10 minutes or until a thermometer reads 170°, turning chicken once. Stir in pineapple and onions; heat through.

Nutrition Facts: 1 chicken breast half with about 1/4 cup sauce equals 238 calories, 5 g fat (1 g saturated fat), 63 mg cholesterol, 473 mg sodium, 24 g carbohydrate, 1 g fiber, 24 g protein. **Diabetic Exchanges:** 3 lean meat, 1/2 starch, 1/2 fruit, 1/2 fat.

CHICKEN WITH CHERRY PINEAPPLE SAUCE

Italian Restaurant Chicken C

PREP: 25 min. **BAKE:** 50 min. **YIELD:** 6 servings

PATRICIA NIEH • PORTOLA VALLEY, CALIFORNIA

Here's a nutritious dish that's a favorite with family and friends. While the chicken and sauce cook, I make pasta to serve with it. The moist, tender, richly seasoned chicken is something special!

- 1 broiler/fryer chicken (3 lbs.), cut up and skin removed
- 1/2 tsp. salt
- 1/4 tsp. pepper
- 2 Tbsp. olive oil
- 1 small onion, finely chopped
- 1/4 cup finely chopped celery
- 1/4 cup finely chopped carrot
- 3 garlic cloves, minced
- 1/2 cup dry red wine or reduced-sodium chicken broth
- 1 can (28 oz.) crushed tomatoes
- 1 bay leaf
- 1 tsp. minced fresh rosemary or 1/4 tsp. dried rosemary, crushed
- 1/4 cup minced fresh basil

1. Sprinkle chicken with salt and pepper. In an ovenproof Dutch oven, brown chicken in oil in batches. Remove and keep warm.

2. In the same pan, saute the onion, celery, carrot and garlic in pan drippings until tender. Add wine, stirring to loosen browned bits from pan.

3. Stir in the tomatoes, bay leaf, rosemary and chicken; bring to a boil.

4. Cover and bake at 325° for 50-60 minutes or until chicken is tender. Discard bay leaf; sprinkle with basil.

Nutrition Facts: 3 oz. cooked chicken with 2/3 cup sauce equals 254 calories, 11 g fat (2 g saturated fat), 73 mg cholesterol, 442 mg sodium, 12 g carbohydrate, 3 g fiber, 27 g protein. **Diabetic Exchanges:** 3 lean meat, 2 vegetable, 1 fat.

Makeover Bacon Chicken Alfredo

PREP: 30 min. **COOK:** 15 min. **YIELD:** 8 servings

IRENE SULLIVAN • LAKE MILLS, WISCONSIN

This healthier version of Bacon Chicken Alfredo offers all the creamy comfort and rich homey flavor of the original, but slashes the calories, cholesterol and sodium.

- 1 pkg. (16 oz.) whole wheat fettuccine
- 8 bacon strips, chopped
- 1 lb. boneless skinless chicken breasts, cubed
- 1/2 tsp. salt, *divided*
- 1/4 tsp. pepper
- 2 garlic cloves, minced
- 1 Tbsp. butter
- 3 Tbsp. cornstarch
- 3 cups 2% milk
- 1 cup half-and-half cream
- 1 pkg. (10 oz.) frozen chopped spinach, thawed and squeezed dry
- 1 cup grated Parmigiano-Reggiano cheese, *divided*
- 1/2 tsp. Italian seasoning

1. Cook fettuccine according to package directions. Meanwhile, in a large skillet, cook bacon over medium heat until crisp. Remove to paper towels to drain.

2. Sprinkle chicken with 1/4 tsp. salt and pepper. Cook chicken and garlic in butter over medium heat for 4-6 minutes or until meat is no longer pink; remove and keep warm.

3. Combine cornstarch and milk until smooth; stir into skillet. Add cream and remaining salt. Bring to a boil; cook and stir for 2 minutes or until thickened. Add the spinach, chicken, 3/4 cup cheese, Italian seasoning and half of the bacon; cook and stir until cheese is melted.

4. Drain fettuccine; add to chicken mixture. Cook and stir until heated through. Sprinkle with remaining cheese and bacon.

Nutrition Facts: 1 cup equals 465 calories, 14 g fat (7 g saturated fat), 72 mg cholesterol, 584 mg sodium, 51 g carbohydrate, 7 g fiber, 32 g protein.

MAKEOVER BACON CHICKEN ALFREDO

Chicken Tacos with Avocado Salsa

PREP/TOTAL TIME: 30 min. YIELD: 4 servings.

CHRISTINE SCHENHER • EXETER, CALIFORNIA

I make these to accommodate various food allergies in our family. Served with a simple green salad, it's a meal my family enjoys together.

1	pound boneless skinless chicken breasts, cut into 1/2-inch strips
1/3	cup water
1	tablespoon chili powder
1	teaspoon sugar
1	teaspoon onion powder
1	teaspoon paprika
1	teaspoon ground cumin
1	teaspoon dried oregano
1/2	teaspoon salt
1/2	teaspoon garlic powder
1	medium ripe avocado, peeled and cubed
1	cup fresh or frozen corn
1	cup cherry tomatoes, quartered
2	teaspoons lime juice
8	taco shells, warmed

1. In a large nonstick skillet coated with cooking spray, brown chicken. Add the water, chili powder, sugar, onion powder, paprika, cumin, oregano, salt and garlic powder. Cook over medium heat for 5-6 minutes or until chicken is no longer pink, stirring occasionally.

2. Meanwhile, in a small bowl, gently combine the avocado, corn, tomatoes and lime juice. Spoon chicken mixture into taco shells; top with avocado salsa.

Nutrition Facts: 2 tacos equals 354 calories, 15 g fat (3 g saturated fat), 63 mg cholesterol, 474 mg sodium, 30 g carbohydrate, 6 g fiber, 27 g protein. **Diabetic Exchanges:** 3 lean meat, 2 starch, 1 fat.

CHICKEN TACOS WITH AVOCADO SALSA

Chicken Casserole Supreme

PREP: 40 min. BAKE: 20 min. YIELD: 6 servings

JUDY WILSON • SUN CITY WEST, ARIZONA

This casserole is so satisfying on a cold night, and it gets even better the next day. I added apples and raisins on a whim and discovered they really set this apart from other dishes.

1	cup reduced-sodium chicken broth
1	medium apple, peeled and chopped
1/2	cup golden raisins
1	Tbsp. butter
1	pkg. (6 oz.) reduced-sodium stuffing mix
1	lb. boneless skinless chicken breasts, cubed
1/4	tsp. salt
1/4	tsp. pepper
1	cup sliced fresh mushrooms
1	small onion, chopped
1	Tbsp. olive oil
3	garlic cloves, minced
1-1/2	cups (12 oz.) fat-free sour cream
1	can (10-3/4 oz.) reduced-fat reduced-sodium condensed cream of mushroom soup, undiluted
4	cups frozen broccoli florets, thawed

1. In a large saucepan, combine the broth, apple and raisins. Bring to a boil. Reduce heat; simmer, uncovered, for 3-4 minutes or until apple is tender. Stir in butter and stuffing mix. Remove from the heat; cover and let stand for 5 minutes.

2. Sprinkle chicken with salt and pepper. In a large skillet, cook the chicken, mushrooms and onion in oil over medium heat until chicken is no longer pink. Add garlic; cook 1 minute longer. Remove from the heat. Stir in sour cream and soup.

3. Transfer to a 13-in. x 9-in. baking dish coated with cooking spray. Layer with broccoli and stuffing mixture. Bake, uncovered, at 350° for 20-25 minutes or until heated through.

Nutrition Facts: 2 cups equals 390 calories, 8 g fat (2 g saturated fat), 59 mg cholesterol, 771 mg sodium, 52 g carbohydrate, 3 g fiber, 26 g protein.

Chicken Kabobs With Peach Glaze F S

PREP: 30 min. GRILL: 10 min. YIELD: 4 servings

SHARON RICCI • MENDON, NEW YORK

Chicken, peaches and veggies are treated to a delightful glaze. These kabobs pack in flavor. Pair with a dish of couscous or rice, and dinner's served!

1	Tbsp. cornstarch
1/4	tsp. curry powder
1/8	tsp. ground cinnamon
1/8	tsp. chili powder
2	cans (5-1/2 oz. *each*) peach nectar, *divided*
1	lb. boneless skinless chicken breasts, cut into 1-in. cubes
2	medium peaches, cut into chunks
4	green onions, cut into 1-in. pieces

1 small green pepper, cut into 1-in. pieces

1 small sweet red pepper, cut into 1-in. pieces

1. In a small saucepan, combine the cornstarch, curry, cinnamon and chili powder. Gradually stir in the peach nectar. Bring to a boil; cook and stir for 2 minutes or until thickened.

2. On eight metal or soaked wooden skewers, alternately thread the chicken, peaches, onions and peppers. Using long-handled tongs, moisten a paper towel with cooking oil and lightly coat the grill rack.

3. Grill kabobs, covered, over medium heat or broil 4 in. from the heat for 10-15 minutes or until juices run clear, turning occasionally and basting with nectar mixture.

Nutrition Facts: 2 kabobs equals 205 calories, 3 g fat (1 g saturated fat), 63 mg cholesterol, 65 mg sodium, 21 g carbohydrate, 2 g fiber, 24 g protein. **Diabetic Exchanges:** 3 lean meat, 1 vegetable, 1 fruit.

Chicken Marinara with Pasta

PREP: 20 min. + marinating **COOK:** 20 min.
YIELD: 6 servings

JOANIE FUSON • INDIANAPOLIS, INDIANA

My son Logan, 11, and I created this basic but very good dish. It was the first meal he made all by himself (with supervision, of course). Best of all, it was a real hit with the three friends he invited for dinner.

1-1/2 lbs. boneless skinless chicken breasts

1/2 cup reduced-fat Italian salad dressing

1 medium onion, chopped

1 Tbsp. olive oil

2 garlic cloves, minced

1 can (15 oz.) crushed tomatoes

1 can (14-1/2 oz.) diced tomatoes, undrained

1 Tbsp. minced fresh parsley *or* 1 tsp. dried parsley flakes

1 tsp. minced fresh oregano *or* 1/4 tsp. dried oregano

1 tsp. brown sugar

1/4 tsp. salt

1/4 tsp. pepper

9 oz. uncooked whole wheat spaghetti

1/4 cup grated Parmesan cheese

6 Tbsp. shredded part-skim mozzarella cheese

1. Flatten chicken to 1/2-in. thickness; place in a large resealable plastic bag. Add salad dressing. Seal bag and turn to coat; refrigerate for 30 minutes.

2. Meanwhile, in a large nonstick skillet coated with cooking spray, saute onion in oil until tender. Add garlic; cook 1 minute longer. Stir in the tomatoes, parsley, oregano, brown sugar, salt and pepper. Bring to a boil. Reduce heat; simmer, uncovered, for 10-15 minutes or until slightly thickened, stirring occasionally.

3. Drain and discard marinade. Using long-handled tongs, moisten a paper towel with cooking oil and lightly coat the grill rack. Grill the chicken, covered, over medium heat or broil 4 in. from the heat for 4-6 minutes on each side or until it's no longer pink. When chicken is cool enough to handle, cut into 1/4-in. strips.

4. Meanwhile, cook spaghetti according to package directions. Stir Parmesan cheese into sauce. Drain spaghetti. Serve with chicken and sauce; sprinkle with mozzarella cheese.

Nutrition Facts: 1 serving equals 389 calories, 8 g fat (2 g saturated fat), 70 mg cholesterol, 438 mg sodium, 44 g carbohydrate, 8 g fiber, 35 g protein. **Diabetic Exchanges:** 4 lean meat, 2 starch, 2 vegetable.

Sweet 'n' Sour Chicken F

PREP: 15 min. **BAKE:** 20 min. **YIELD:** 4 servings

CHRISTINE MCDONALD • RIVERDALE, UTAH

This entree was served at a special dinner hosted by my Sunday school teacher. The ingredients are simple, but the chicken is tender and tasty. I frequently serve it over brown rice, and I'm often asked for the recipe.

4	boneless skinless chicken breast halves (4 oz. *each*)
2/3	cup water
1/3	cup sugar
1/4	cup cider vinegar
1/4	cup reduced-sodium soy sauce
1	medium sweet red pepper, cut into 1-in. pieces
1	medium green pepper, cut into 1-in. pieces
2	Tbsp. cornstarch
3	Tbsp. cold water

Hot cooked brown rice

1. Place chicken in an 11-in. x 7-in. baking dish; set aside. In a small saucepan, bring the water, sugar, vinegar and soy sauce to a boil, stirring constantly. Add peppers; return to a boil. Combine cornstarch and cold water until smooth; gradually stir into pepper mixture. Bring to a boil; cook and stir for 1-2 minutes or until thickened. Pour over chicken.

2. Bake, uncovered, at 350° for 10-13 minutes on each side or until a meat thermometer reaches 170°. Serve with rice.

Nutrition Facts: 1 serving (calculated without rice) equals 231 calories, 2 g fat (trace saturated fat), 66 mg cholesterol, 683 mg sodium, 25 g carbohydrate, 1 g fiber, 28 g protein. **Diabetic Exchanges:** 3 lean meat, 1 starch, 1 vegetable.

Slow Cooker Chicken Stew

PREP: 15 min. **COOK:** 6 hours **YIELD:** 6 servings

ANGELA BUCHANAN • LONGMONT, COLORADO

I like to sprinkle this with toasted almonds or cashews and serve with hot couscous. Flavored with cinnamon and a touch of sweetness from the apricots, this stew tastes like you fussed. It's great for potlucks, too!

6	bone-in chicken thighs (about 2-1/4 lbs.), skin removed
1	large onion, chopped
2	medium carrots, sliced
3/4	cup unsweetened apple juice
1	garlic clove, minced
1	tsp. salt
1/2	tsp. ground cinnamon
1/2	tsp. pepper
1	cup chopped dried apricots

Hot cooked couscous

1. Place the chicken, onion and carrots in a 3- or 4-qt. slow cooker coated with cooking spray. In a small bowl, combine the apple juice, garlic, salt, cinnamon and pepper; pour over vegetables.

2. Cover and cook on low for 6-8 hours or until chicken is tender.

3. Remove chicken from slow cooker; shred meat with two forks. Skim fat from cooking juices; stir in apricots. Return shredded chicken to slow cooker; heat through. Serve with couscous.

Nutrition Facts: 1-1/3 cups (calculated without couscous) equals 279 calories, 10 g fat (3 g saturated fat), 87 mg cholesterol, 497 mg sodium, 23 g carbohydrate, 3 g fiber, 25 g protein. **Diabetic Exchanges:** 3 lean meat, 1 vegetable, 1 fruit.

Chicken Enchilada Casserole

PREP: 30 min. BAKE: 30 min. YIELD: 6 servings

AMY JOHNSON • NEW BRAUNFELS, TEXAS

This family-friendly recipe offers a new take on classic enchiladas. If you like yours with a little extra oomph, sprinkle some seeded, fresh chopped jalapenos and cilantro on top.

1	large onion, chopped
1	medium green pepper, chopped
1	tsp. butter
3	cups shredded cooked chicken breast
2	cans (4 oz. *each*) chopped green chilies
1/4	cup all-purpose flour
1-1/2 to 2	tsp. ground coriander
2-1/2	cups reduced-sodium chicken broth
1	cup (8 oz.) reduced-fat sour cream
1	cup (4 oz.) reduced-fat Monterey Jack or reduced-fat Mexican cheese blend, *divided*
12	corn tortillas (6 in.), warmed

1. In a small skillet, saute onion and green pepper in butter until tender. In a large bowl, combine the chicken, green chilies and onion mixture.

2. In a small saucepan, combine flour and coriander. Add broth; stir until smooth. Cook and stir over medium heat until mixture comes to a boil. Cook and stir 1-2 minutes longer or until thickened. Remove from the heat; stir in sour cream and 1/2 cup cheese. Stir 3/4 cup sauce into chicken mixture.

3. Place 1/3 cup chicken mixture down the center of each tortilla. Roll up and place seam side down in a 13-in. x 9-in. baking dish coated with cooking spray. Pour remaining sauce over top; sprinkle with remaining cheese. Bake, uncovered, at 350° for 30-35 minutes or until heated through.

Nutrition Facts: 2 enchiladas equals 383 calories, 12 g fat (6 g saturated fat), 82 mg cholesterol, 710 mg sodium, 37 g carbohydrate, 5 g fiber, 33 g protein. **Diabetic Exchanges:** 4 lean meat, 2 starch, 1 fat.

Buying skinned and boned chicken breasts can cut up to **15 minutes off** your cooking time. Save money by buying larger packages, then rewrap individually or in family-size portions and freeze.

SLOW COOKER CHICKEN STEW

CHICKEN ENCHILADA CASSEROLE

Tropical Chicken Packets

PREP: 15 min. GRILL: 20 min. YIELD: 4 servings

JACQUELINE CORREA • LANDING, NEW JERSEY

Yum! These quick-and-easy chicken packets are destined to become your family's new favorite. The chicken is tender and laced with sweet pineapple and tropical flavors. Cleanup's a breeze—these would be perfect for camping.

4	boneless skinless chicken breast halves (6 oz. *each*)
1/8	tsp. pepper
1	can (20 oz.) unsweetened pineapple chunks, drained
1	medium sweet red pepper, julienned
1	small onion, sliced and separated into rings
1/4	cup packed brown sugar
1/4	cup reduced-sodium teriyaki sauce
1	tsp. minced fresh gingerroot

1. Sprinkle chicken breasts with pepper; place each on a double thickness of heavy-duty foil (about 18 in. x 12 in.). Top with pineapple, red pepper and onion. Combine the remaining ingredients; spoon over vegetables. Fold foil around mixture and seal tightly.

2. Grill, covered, over medium heat for 20-25 minutes or until chicken juices run clear. Open foil carefully to allow steam to escape.

Nutrition Facts: 1 packet equals 324 calories, 4 g fat (1 g saturated fat), 94 mg cholesterol, 410 mg sodium, 35 g carbohydrate, 2 g fiber, 36 g protein. **Diabetic Exchanges:** 5 lean meat, 1 starch, 1 fruit.

Shredded Barbecue Chicken over Grits

PREP: 20 min. COOK: 25 min. YIELD: 6 servings

ERIN RENOUF MYLROIE • SANTA CLARA, UTAH

There's nothing like juicy meat over steaming grits. And the pumpkin in these grits makes them taste like a spicy, comforting bowl of fall flavors. Your gang will come running to the table for this one.

1	lb. boneless skinless chicken breasts
1/4	tsp. pepper
1	can (14-1/2 oz.) reduced-sodium chicken broth, *divided*
1	cup hickory smoke-flavored barbecue sauce
1/4	cup molasses
1	Tbsp. ground ancho chili pepper
1/2	tsp. ground cinnamon
2-1/4	cups water
1	cup quick-cooking grits
1	cup canned pumpkin
3/4	cup shredded pepper jack cheese
1	medium tomato, seeded and chopped
6	Tbsp. reduced-fat sour cream
2	green onions, chopped
2	Tbsp. minced fresh cilantro

1. Sprinkle chicken with pepper; place in a large nonstick skillet coated with cooking spray.

2. In a large bowl, combine 1 cup broth, barbecue sauce, molasses, chili pepper and cinnamon; pour over chicken. Bring to a boil. Reduce heat; cover and simmer for 20-25 minutes or until a meat thermometer reads 170°. Shred meat with two forks and return to the skillet.

SHREDDED BARBECUE CHICKEN OVER GRITS

TROPICAL CHICKEN PACKETS

MARVELOUS CHICKEN ENCHILADAS

3. Meanwhile, in a large saucepan, bring water and remaining broth to a boil. Slowly stir in grits and pumpkin. Reduce heat; cook and stir for 5-7 minutes or until thickened. Stir in cheese until melted.

4. Divide grits among six serving bowls; top each with 1/2 cup chicken mixture. Serve with tomato, sour cream, green onions and cilantro.

Nutrition Facts: 1 serving equals 345 calories, 9 g fat (4 g saturated fat), 62 mg cholesterol, 718 mg sodium, 42 g carbohydrate, 4 g fiber, 25 g protein. **Diabetic Exchanges:** 3 lean meat, 2-1/2 starch, 1 fat.

Marvelous Chicken Enchiladas

PREP: 30 min. **BAKE:** 25 min. **YIELD:** 6 enchiladas

REBEKAH SABO • ROCHESTER, NEW YORK

I love Mexican food, and this is one of my favorites. Try using Monterey Jack cheese in place of the cheddar for a slightly milder flavor.

1	lb. boneless skinless chicken breasts, cut into thin strips
4	tsp. chili powder
2	tsp. olive oil
2	Tbsp. all-purpose flour
1-1/2	tsp. ground coriander
1	tsp. baking cocoa
1	cup fat-free milk
1	cup frozen corn, thawed
4	green onions, chopped
1	can (4 oz.) chopped green chilies, drained
1/2	tsp. salt
1/2	cup minced fresh cilantro, *divided*
6	whole wheat tortillas (8 in.)
1/2	cup salsa
1/2	cup tomato sauce
1/2	cup shredded reduced-fat cheddar cheese

1. Sprinkle chicken with chili powder. In a large nonstick skillet coated with cooking spray, cook chicken in oil over medium heat until no longer pink. Sprinkle with flour, coriander and cocoa; stir until blended.

2. Gradually stir in milk. Bring to a boil; cook and stir for 2 minutes or until thickened. Add the corn, onions, chilies and salt; cook and stir 2 minutes longer or until heated through. Remove from the heat. Stir in 1/4 cup cilantro.

3. Spread 2/3 cup filling down the center of each tortilla. Roll up and place seam side down in a 13-in. x 9-in. baking dish coated with cooking spray.

4. In a small bowl, combine the salsa, tomato sauce and remaining cilantro; pour over enchiladas. Sprinkle with cheese. Cover and bake at 375° for 25 minutes or until heated through.

Nutrition Facts: 1 enchilada equals 336 calories, 9 g fat (2 g saturated fat), 49 mg cholesterol, 749 mg sodium, 37 g carbohydrate, 4 g fiber, 25 g protein. **Diabetic Exchanges:** 3 lean meat, 2-1/2 starch, 1/2 fat.

Chicken Florentine Burgers

PREP: 25 min. + cooling **GRILL:** 10 min.
YIELD: 6 servings

MARY CANNATARO • CHICAGO, ILLINOIS

Just try convincing your guests that a recipe this scrumptious is healthier, too. These moist monster burgers are packed with veggies, cheese and loads of great grilled flavor.

1-1/2	cups chopped sweet onions
1-1/2	cups dry white wine *or* reduced-sodium chicken broth
3	garlic cloves, minced
1	pkg. (10 oz.) frozen chopped spinach, thawed and squeezed dry
2/3	cup dry bread crumbs
1/4	cup plus 6 Tbsp. shredded Gruyere or Swiss cheese, *divided*
1	Tbsp. Dijon mustard
1/2	tsp. salt
1/2	tsp. pepper
3/4	lb. ground chicken
3/4	lb. extra-lean ground turkey
6	whole wheat hamburger buns, split
6	slices tomato
1	cup fresh baby spinach

1. Place the onion, wine and garlic in a small saucepan. Bring to a boil; cook until wine is reduced to about 1/4 cup. Cool to room temperature.

2. In a large bowl, combine the spinach, bread crumbs, 1/4 cup cheese, mustard, salt, pepper and onion mixture. Crumble meat over mixture and mix well. Shape into six patties.

3. Using long-handled tongs, moisten a paper towel with cooking oil and lightly coat the grill rack. Grill burgers, covered, over medium heat or broil 4 in. from the heat for 5-7 minutes on each side or until a meat thermometer reads 165° and juices run clear. Serve on buns with tomato, spinach and remaining cheese.

Nutrition Facts: 1 burger equals 407 calories, 12 g fat (4 g saturated fat), 72 mg cholesterol, 740 mg sodium, 41 g carbohydrate, 7 g fiber, 36 g protein.

Baked Chicken Cordon Bleu `C`

PREP: 15 min. **BAKE:** 35 min. **YIELD:** 4 servings

SARAH CHRISTENSON • SAN DIEGO, CALIFORNIA

With only six ingredients, this entree has lots of flavor. This tempting dish is easy enough for a weeknight, but special enough for guests as well.

4	boneless skinless chicken breast halves (6 oz. *each*)
1/4	tsp. salt
1/4	tsp. pepper
4	thin slices prosciutto *or* deli ham
1/2	cup shredded Asiago cheese
1/4	cup seasoned bread crumbs

1. Flatten chicken to 1/4-in. thickness; sprinkle with salt and pepper. Top each with prosciutto and cheese. Roll up and tuck in ends; secure with toothpicks.

2. Transfer to an 11-in. x 7-in. baking dish coated with cooking spray. Sprinkle with bread crumbs. Bake, uncovered, at 350° for 35-45 minutes or until juices run clear.

Nutrition Facts: 1 serving equals 291 calories, 10 g fat (4 g saturated fat), 119 mg cholesterol, 645 mg sodium, 6 g carbohydrate, trace fiber, 43 g protein. **Diabetic Exchanges:** 6 lean meat, 1/2 fat.

Apricot-Almond Chicken Breasts

PREP: 10 min. **BAKE:** 30 min. **YIELD:** 4 servings

TRISHA KRUSE • EAGLE, IDAHO

This chicken dish is so delicious, I constantly get asked for the recipe—even my picky eaters clamor for it! It takes only minutes to prepare, so on busy weeknights I can put a healthy supper on the table.

- 4 boneless skinless chicken breast halves (6 oz. *each*)
- 1/2 tsp. salt
- 1/4 tsp. pepper
- 3/4 cup apricot preserves
- 1/4 cup reduced-sodium chicken broth
- 1 Tbsp. honey mustard
- 1/4 cup sliced almonds

1. Sprinkle chicken with salt and pepper. Place in a 13-in. x 9-in. baking dish coated with cooking spray. Bake, uncovered, at 350° for 15 minutes.

2. In a small bowl, combine the preserves, broth and mustard. Pour over the chicken; sprinkle with almonds. Bake 15-20 minutes longer or until chicken juices run clear.

Nutrition Facts: 1 chicken breast half equals 372 calories, 7 g fat (1 g saturated fat), 94 mg cholesterol, 468 mg sodium, 42 g carbohydrate, 1 g fiber, 36 g protein. **Diabetic Exchanges:** 5 lean meat, 3 starch, 1/2 fat.

Balsamic Roast Chicken C

PREP: 20 min. **BAKE:** 2-1/4 hours + standing
YIELD: 12 servings (1-1/2 cups onion sauce)

TRACY TYLKOWSKI • OMAHA, NEBRASKA

When the aroma from this dish fills your house, your family will think you spent all day cooking. But this elegant, Sunday-special entree, flavored with rosemary, wine and balsamic vinegar, is surprisingly simple to make.

- 1 roasting chicken (6 to 7 lbs.)
- 2 Tbsp. minced fresh rosemary *or* 2 tsp. dried rosemary, crushed
- 3 garlic cloves, minced
- 1 tsp. salt
- 1 tsp. pepper
- 2 medium red onions, chopped
- 1/2 cup dry red wine *or* reduced-sodium chicken broth
- 1/2 cup balsamic vinegar

1. Pat chicken dry. In a small bowl, combine the rosemary, garlic, salt and pepper; rub under skin of chicken. Place onions in a shallow roasting pan; top with chicken. Combine wine and balsamic vinegar; pour over chicken.

2. Bake, uncovered, at 350° for 2-1/4 to 2-3/4 hours or until a meat thermometer reads 180°, basting occasionally with pan juices. (Cover loosely with foil if chicken browns too quickly.)

3. Let stand for 15 minutes before carving. Remove and discard skin before serving. Pour onion sauce into a small bowl; skim fat. Serve with chicken.

Nutrition Facts: 3 oz. cooked chicken with 2 Tbsp. onion sauce equals 182 calories, 7 g fat (2 g saturated fat), 77 mg cholesterol, 275 mg sodium, 4 g carbohydrate, trace fiber, 25 g protein. **Diabetic Exchange:** 4 lean meat.

BALSAMIC ROAST CHICKEN

APRICOT-ALMOND CHICKEN BREASTS

Chicken Thighs With Sausage C

PREP: 25 min. COOK: 6 hours YIELD: 8 servings

JOANNA IOVINO • COMMACK, NEW YORK

Whether you're serving your family or special guests, this comforting entree hits the spot on cold winter nights.

- 2 medium carrots, chopped
- 2 celery ribs, chopped
- 1 large onion, finely chopped
- 8 bone-in chicken thighs (about 3 lbs.), skin removed
- 1 pkg. (14 oz.) smoked turkey sausage, cut into 1/2-in. slices
- 1/4 cup ketchup
- 6 garlic cloves, minced
- 1 Tbsp. Louisiana-style hot sauce
- 1 tsp. dried basil
- 1 tsp. paprika
- 1 tsp. dried thyme
- 1 tsp. browning sauce, optional
- 1/2 tsp. dried oregano
- 1/2 tsp. pepper
- 1/4 tsp. ground allspice

1. In a 4- or 5-qt. slow cooker, combine the carrots, celery and onion. Top with chicken and sausage.

2. In a small bowl, combine the ketchup, garlic, hot sauce, basil, paprika, thyme, browning sauce if desired, oregano, pepper and allspice. Spoon over meats. Cover and cook on low for 6-8 hours or until chicken is tender.

Nutrition Facts: 1 chicken thigh with 1/3 cup sausage mixture equals 280 calories, 12 g fat (4 g saturated fat), 118 mg cholesterol, 675 mg sodium, 8 g carbohydrate, 1 g fiber, 33 g protein. **Diabetic Exchanges:** 5 lean meat, 1/2 starch.

Rich Fettuccine Alfredo

PREP: 20 min. COOK: 20 min. YIELD: 6 servings

HEALTHY COOKING TEST KITCHEN

Everyone will love this super-creamy, warm and cozy entree on a chilly evening. But no one will ever guess that something this cheesy and delicious could also be lighter! Try it—you'll see what we mean.

- 8 oz. uncooked whole wheat fettuccine
- 2 bacon strips, coarsely chopped
- 1/2 lb. sliced fresh mushrooms
- 1 small onion, chopped
- 1 small sweet red pepper, chopped
- 2 garlic cloves, minced
- 4 oz. fat-free cream cheese, cubed
- 2 Tbsp. cornstarch
- 2 cups whole milk
- 3 cups cubed cooked chicken breast
- 1/3 cup shredded Parmigiano-Reggiano cheese
- 1/2 tsp. salt
- 1/2 cup shredded part-skim mozzarella cheese

1. Cook fettuccine according to package directions. Meanwhile, in a large ovenproof skillet, cook bacon over medium heat until crisp. Using a slotted spoon, remove to paper towels to drain.

2. Saute the mushrooms, onion and pepper in drippings until tender. Add the garlic; cook 1 minute longer. Stir in cream cheese until melted.

3. Combine cornstarch and milk until smooth; stir into skillet. Bring to a boil; cook and stir for 2 minutes or until thickened. Add the chicken, Parmigiano-Reggiano cheese and salt; cook and stir until cheese is melted.

CHICKEN THIGHS WITH SAUSAGE

RICH FETTUCCINE ALFREDO

GRILLED CARIBBEAN LIME CHICKEN

4. Drain fettuccine; add to chicken mixture. Heat through. Sprinkle with mozzarella cheese and reserved bacon. Broil 4-6 in. from the heat for 2-3 minutes or until cheese is melted.

Nutrition Facts: 1-1/3 cups equals 417 calories, 12 g fat (5 g saturated fat), 77 mg cholesterol, 561 mg sodium, 38 g carbohydrate, 5 g fiber, 38 g protein.

Grilled Caribbean Lime Chicken C

PREP: 20 min. + marinating **GRILL:** 10 min.
YIELD: 8 servings

MARY SHIVERS • ADA, OKLAHOMA

With its amazing tropical salsa, this entree is a showstopper. Add leftover salsa to quesadillas, pork tenderloin or serve it with tortilla chips.

1/2 cup lime juice
1/4 cup olive oil
4 garlic cloves, minced
2 tsp. Greek seasoning
8 boneless skinless chicken breast halves (6 oz. *each*)

SALSA:
2 large tomatoes, seeded and chopped
1 cup diced fresh pineapple
2/3 cup cubed avocado
2 green onions, thinly sliced
1 Tbsp. lime juice
1 Tbsp. cider vinegar
1/2 tsp. salt
1/2 tsp. pepper

1. In a large resealable plastic bag, combine the lime juice, oil, garlic and Greek seasoning; add the chicken. Seal the bag and turn it to coat; refrigerate for 2 hours. In a small bowl, combine the salsa ingredients. Chill until serving.

2. Using long-handled tongs, moisten a paper towel with cooking oil and lightly coat the grill rack. Grill chicken, covered, over medium heat or broil 4 in. from the heat for 5-8 minutes on each side or until a meat thermometer reads 170°. Serve with salsa.

Nutrition Facts: 1 chicken breast half with 1/3 cup salsa equals 260 calories, 10 g fat (2 g saturated fat), 94 mg cholesterol, 371 mg sodium, 7 g carbohydrate, 2 g fiber, 35 g protein.
Diabetic Exchanges: 5 lean meat, 1 fat, 1/2 starch.

Cheese that has been commercially grated or shredded contains **anti-caking agents** that prevent it from blending well into sauces. However, freshly grated or shredded Parmesan cheese has good melting properties.

ASIAN CHICKEN WITH GINGERED VEGETABLES

Asian Chicken with Gingered Vegetables ⓒ

PREP: 15 min. + chilling GRILL: 15 min. YIELD: 4 servings

TERESA RALSTON • NEW ALBANY, OHIO

My gang loves this light, colorful and quick meal. Grilled pineapple sprinkled with cinnamon makes a yummy dessert.

  1 Tbsp. brown sugar
  1 tsp. garlic powder
1/2 tsp. ground ginger
1/2 tsp. Chinese five-spice powder
1/2 tsp. pepper
  4 boneless skinless chicken breast halves (6 oz. *each*)
  2 cups fresh sugar snap peas, trimmed
  1 medium carrot, julienned
  2 Tbsp. orange juice
  2 Tbsp. reduced-sodium soy sauce
  2 tsp. minced fresh gingerroot

1. Combine the first five ingredients; rub over chicken. Cover and refrigerate for 30 minutes.

2. Using long-handled tongs, moisten a paper towel with cooking oil and lightly coat the grill rack. Grill chicken, covered, over medium heat or broil 4 in. from the heat for 6-8 minutes on each side or until a meat thermometer reads 170°.

3. Meanwhile, in a large nonstick skillet coated with cooking spray, combine the remaining ingredients. Cook and stir over medium-high heat for 5-8 minutes or until vegetables are tender. Serve with chicken.

Nutrition Facts: 1 chicken breast half with 1/2 cup vegetables equals 249 calories, 4 g fat (1 g saturated fat), 94 mg cholesterol, 400 mg sodium, 13 g carbohydrate, 3 g fiber, 38 g protein. **Diabetic Exchanges:** 5 lean meat, 1 vegetable.

Crunchy Onion Barbecue Chicken ⓒ

PREP: 10 min. BAKE: 25 min. YIELD: 4 servings

JANE HOLEY • CLAYTON, MICHIGAN

I threw this recipe together one night when I had two chicken breasts to use up. After adding French-fried onions and baked-on barbecue sauce, I was thrilled with the moist and tasty result. My husband was, too!

1/2 cup barbecue sauce
1-1/3 cups French-fried onions, crushed
1/4 cup grated Parmesan cheese
1/2 tsp. pepper
  4 boneless skinless chicken breast halves (6 oz. *each*)

1. Place barbecue sauce in a shallow bowl. In another shallow bowl, combine the onions, cheese and pepper. Dip both sides of chicken in barbecue sauce, then one side in onion mixture.

2. Place chicken, crumb side up, on a baking sheet coated with cooking spray. Bake at 400° for 22-27 minutes or until a meat thermometer reads 170°.

Nutrition Facts: 1 chicken breast half equals 286 calories, 10 g fat (3 g saturated fat), 97 mg cholesterol, 498 mg sodium, 9 g carbohydrate, trace fiber, 36 g protein. **Diabetic Exchanges:** 5 lean meat, 1 fat, 1/2 starch.

Broccoli Chicken Alfredo

PREP: 20 min. **COOK:** 15 min. **YIELD:** 4 servings

TERRIE FONTENOT • FRESNO, TEXAS

What a fast and simple weeknight supper! This lighter take on Alfredo pasta offers all the comforting flavor families long for—but in a reduced-fat meal. Broccoli and whole wheat pasta boost nutrition.

2	cups uncooked whole wheat penne pasta
3	cups frozen chopped broccoli
1	lb. boneless skinless chicken breasts, cut into 1/2-in. cubes
2	garlic cloves, minced
1	cup reduced-fat Alfredo sauce
1/4	cup grated Parmesan cheese
1/4	tsp. pepper

1. Cook pasta according to package directions, adding the broccoli during the last 5 minutes of cooking.

2. Meanwhile, in a large nonstick skillet coated with cooking spray, saute chicken until lightly browned. Add garlic; saute 1-2 minutes longer or until chicken is no longer pink and garlic is tender.

3. Drain pasta mixture; add to the pan. Stir in the Alfredo sauce, cheese and pepper; cook and stir until heated through.

Nutrition Facts: 1-1/2 cups equals 470 calories, 11 g fat (6 g saturated fat), 92 mg cholesterol, 599 mg sodium, 51 g carbohydrate, 10 g fiber, 39 g protein.

Simple Sesame Chicken ⬛C

PREP: 15 min. **COOK:** 10 min./batch **YIELD:** 6 servings

LYNN JONAS • MADISON, WISCONSIN

Returning home after 20 years as a missionary in the Philippines, I tried to make food reminiscent of what we had there and came up with these flavorful strips. This recipe became a family favorite and is often requested at potlucks!

1/3	cup all-purpose flour
1/2	tsp. salt
1/4	tsp. pepper
1-2/3	cups Caesar salad croutons, crushed
1/4	cup sesame seeds
2	eggs, lightly beaten
1-1/2	lbs. boneless skinless chicken breasts, cut into 1-in. strips
2	tsp. butter
2	tsp. canola oil

1. In a shallow bowl, combine the flour, salt and pepper. In another shallow bowl, combine crushed croutons and sesame seeds. Place eggs in a third shallow bowl. Coat chicken with flour mixture, then dip in eggs and coat with crouton mixture.

2. In a large nonstick skillet coated with cooking spray, cook chicken in butter and oil in batches over medium heat for 4-6 minutes on each side or until no longer pink.

Nutrition Facts: 1 serving equals 255 calories, 11 g fat (3 g saturated fat), 120 mg cholesterol, 319 mg sodium, 11 g carbohydrate, 1 g fiber, 27 g protein. **Diabetic Exchanges:** 3 lean meat, 1 starch, 1 fat.

SIMPLE SESAME CHICKEN

BROCCOLI CHICKEN ALFREDO

Makeover Italian Chicken

PREP: 25 min. **BAKE:** 25 min. **YIELD:** 6 servings

SARAH KLIER • GRAND RAPIDS, MICHIGAN

Simple ingredient substitutions add up to a tasty makeover that boasts only about half the fat and a fourth fewer calories than the original. We like math that's easy!

2-1/2 cups sliced fresh mushrooms
  2 Tbsp. butter
  6 boneless skinless chicken breast halves (6 oz. *each*)
  2 Tbsp. Italian salad dressing mix
  1 can (10-3/4 oz.) reduced-fat reduced-sodium condensed cream of mushroom soup, undiluted
  1 carton (8 oz.) reduced-fat spreadable chive and onion cream cheese
1/3 cup dry white wine *or* reduced-sodium chicken broth
1/4 cup fat-free milk
  3 cups uncooked yolk-free whole wheat noodles
  1 Tbsp. minced chives

1. In a large nonstick skillet coated with cooking spray, saute the mushrooms in butter until tender. Remove mushrooms with a slotted spoon and keep warm; set aside.

2. Sprinkle chicken with salad dressing mix. In the same skillet, brown chicken on both sides. Transfer to a 13-in. x 9-in. baking dish coated with cooking spray. Stir the soup, cream cheese, wine, milk and reserved mushrooms into skillet; heat through. Spoon mixture over the chicken.

3. Cover and bake at 350° for 25-30 minutes or until a meat thermometer reads 170°.

4. Meanwhile, cook noodles according to package directions; drain. Serve with chicken and sauce; sprinkle with chives.

Nutrition Facts: 1 chicken breast half with 1/2 cup noodles and 1/3 cup sauce equals 417 calories, 16 g fat (8 g saturated fat), 133 mg cholesterol, 860 mg sodium, 26 g carbohydrate, 3 g fiber, 41 g protein.

Orange Barley Chicken

PREP: 30 min. **COOK:** 45 min. **YIELD:** 8 servings

HELEN GLAZIER • SEATTLE, WASHINGTON

My mother used to prepare orange chicken with rice back in the '60s, and it was so good. My version uses pearl barley instead of rice, and I added parsnips for flavor and baby carrots for color.

  1 cup all-purpose flour
  1 tsp. celery salt
1/2 tsp. pepper
  1 broiler/fryer chicken (3 to 4 lbs.), cut up and skin removed
  2 tsp. olive oil
  1 medium onion, thinly sliced
  1 Tbsp. butter
  3 cups reduced-sodium chicken broth
  3 cups orange juice
  2 medium parsnips, peeled and chopped
1-1/2 cups medium pearl barley
1-1/2 cups sliced fresh mushrooms
1-1/2 cups fresh baby carrots
  2 bay leaves

1. In a large resealable plastic bag, combine the flour, celery salt and pepper. Add chicken, a few pieces at a time, and shake to coat.

2. In a Dutch oven, brown chicken in oil in batches. Remove and keep warm. In the same pan, saute onion in butter until tender. Add the broth, orange juice, parsnips, barley, mushrooms, carrots, bay leaves and chicken. Bring to a boil. Reduce heat; cover and cook for 45-50 minutes or until barley is tender, turning chicken occasionally.

3. Remove from the heat; let stand for 5 minutes. Discard bay leaves.

Nutrition Facts: 1 serving equals 386 calories, 8 g fat (2 g saturated fat), 59 mg cholesterol, 361 mg sodium, 55 g carbohydrate, 8 g fiber, 25 g protein.

Sesame Cilantro Chicken

PREP: 10 min. **BAKE:** 25 min. **YIELD:** 4 servings

BRITTANY BOWEN • FLAGSTAFF, ARIZONA

Slightly sweet, super juicy and drizzled with a wonderfully Asian-inspired sauce, this chicken is definitely delicious enough to serve guests. Wild rice would make an easy side.

  4 boneless skinless chicken breast halves (6 oz. *each*)
1/2 cup honey
  2 Tbsp. reduced-sodium soy sauce
1/4 tsp. garlic powder
1/8 tsp. ground ginger
  1 Tbsp. minced fresh cilantro
  1 Tbsp. sesame seeds, toasted

MAKEOVER ITALIAN CHICKEN

1. Place chicken in an 11-in. x 7-in. baking dish coated with cooking spray. Combine the honey, soy sauce, garlic powder, ginger and cilantro; spoon 1/4 cup honey mixture over chicken. Set aside the remaining mixture.

2. Cover and bake at 375° for 20 minutes. Uncover; bake 5-10 minutes longer or until a meat thermometer reads 170°. Spoon reserved mixture over chicken; sprinkle with sesame seeds.

Nutrition Facts: 1 serving equals 328 calories, 5 g fat (1 g saturated fat), 94 mg cholesterol, 398 mg sodium, 36 g carbohydrate, trace fiber, 35 g protein. **Diabetic Exchanges:** 5 lean meat, 2 starch.

Mexicali Chicken C

PREP/TOTAL TIME: 30 min. **YIELD:** 4 servings

AVANELL HEWITT • NORTH RICHLAND HILLS, TEXAS

This recipe has been a family favorite for many years. It's great served with Spanish rice and refried beans. Cilantro may be added to the salsa, if desired.

1	medium tomato, finely chopped
1	small onion, finely chopped
2	jalapeno peppers, seeded and chopped
2	Tbsp. lime juice
1	garlic clove, minced
1/4	tsp. salt
1/8	tsp. pepper

4	boneless skinless chicken breast halves (4 oz. *each*)
1	to 2 tsp. reduced-sodium taco seasoning
4	bacon strips, halved
4	slices reduced-fat provolone cheese
1	medium lime, cut into four wedges

1. In a small bowl, combine the tomato, onion, jalapenos, lime juice, garlic, salt and pepper. Chill until serving.

2. Sprinkle chicken with taco seasoning; set aside. In a large skillet, cook bacon over medium heat until crisp. Remove to paper towels; drain.

3. If grilling the chicken, using long-handled tongs, moisten a paper towel with cooking oil and lightly coat the grill rack. Grill chicken, covered, over medium heat or broil 4 in. from the heat for 4-7 minutes on each side or until a meat thermometer reads 170°.

4. Top with bacon and cheese; cook 1 minute longer or until cheese is melted. Serve with salsa; squeeze lime wedges over top.

Editor's Note: When cutting hot peppers, disposable gloves are recommended. Avoid touching your face.

Nutrition Facts: 1 serving equals 227 calories, 9 g fat (4 g saturated fat), 80 mg cholesterol, 532 mg sodium, 5 g carbohydrate, 1 g fiber, 31 g protein. **Diabetic Exchanges:** 4 lean meat, 1 vegetable, 1/2 fat.

TURKEY AND BLACK BEAN ENCHILADAS

TURKEY DIVAN

FAVORITE SKILLET LASAGNA

Turkey Specialties

Packed with health benefits, this bird's not just for Thanksgiving anymore. From warm-weather roll-ups to comforting casseroles, the dishes that follow are sure to get a thumbs-up rating from everyone at your table.

Favorite Skillet Lasagna

PREP/TOTAL TIME: 30 min. **YIELD:** 5 servings

LORIE MINER • KAMAS, UTAH

Whole wheat noodles and zucchini pump up nutrition in this delicious, family-friendly dinner. Topped with dollops of ricotta cheese, it has an extra touch of decadence. No one will believe this one's lighter.

- 1/2 lb. Italian turkey sausage links, casings removed
- 1 small onion, chopped
- 1 jar (14 oz.) spaghetti sauce
- 2 cups uncooked whole wheat egg noodles
- 1 cup water
- 1/2 cup chopped zucchini
- 1/2 cup fat-free ricotta cheese
- 2 Tbsp. grated Parmesan cheese
- 1 Tbsp. minced fresh parsley *or* 1 tsp. dried parsley flakes
- 1/2 cup shredded part-skim mozzarella cheese

1. In a large nonstick skillet, cook sausage and onion over medium heat until no longer pink; drain. Stir in the spaghetti sauce, egg noodles, water and zucchini. Bring to a boil. Reduce heat; cover and simmer for 8-10 minutes or until pasta is tender, stirring occasionally.

2. Combine the ricotta, Parmesan and parsley. Drop by tablespoonfuls over pasta mixture. Sprinkle with mozzarella cheese; cover and cook 3-5 minutes longer or until cheese is melted.

Nutrition Facts: 1 cup equals 250 calories, 10 g fat (3 g saturated fat), 41 mg cholesterol, 783 mg sodium, 24 g carbohydrate, 3 g fiber, 17 g protein. **Diabetic Exchanges:** 2 lean meat, 1-1/2 starch, 1 fat.

Hearty Pasta Casserole

PREP: 45 min. **BAKE:** 35 min. **YIELD:** 8 servings

HEALTHY COOKING TEST KITCHEN

Loaded with colorful, flavorful roasted veggies, this recipe became an instant hit with the Test Kitchen staff. This rustic Italian-inspired casserole is also the perfect main dish "to go" because it transports easily and retains heat well. If you and your family are crunched for time during the week, this bake is a great make-ahead, too!

- 2 cups cubed peeled butternut squash
- 1/2 lb. fresh Brussels sprouts, halved
- 1 medium onion, cut into wedges
- 2 tsp. olive oil
- 1 pkg. (13-1/4 oz.) whole wheat penne pasta
- 1 lb. Italian turkey sausage links, casings removed
- 2 garlic cloves, minced
- 2 cans (14-1/2 oz. *each*) Italian stewed tomatoes
- 2 Tbsp. tomato paste
- 1-1/2 cups (6 oz.) shredded part-skim mozzarella cheese, *divided*
- 1/3 cup shredded Asiago cheese, *divided*

1. In a large bowl, combine the squash, Brussels sprouts and onion; drizzle with oil and toss to coat. Spread vegetables in a single layer in two 15-in. x 10-in. x 1-in. baking pans coated with cooking spray. Bake, uncovered, at 425° for 30-40 minutes or until vegetables are tender.

2. Meanwhile, cook pasta according to package directions. In a large nonstick skillet, cook sausage over medium heat until meat is no longer pink. Add garlic; cook 1 minute longer; drain. Add tomatoes and tomato paste; cook and stir over medium heat until slightly thickened, about 5 minutes.

3. Drain pasta and return to the pan. Add sausage mixture, 1 cup mozzarella, 1/4 cup Asiago and roasted vegetables.

4. Transfer to a 13-in. x 9-in. baking dish coated with cooking spray. Cover and bake at 350° for 30-40 minutes or until heated through. Uncover; sprinkle with remaining cheeses. Bake 5 minutes longer or until cheese is melted.

Nutrition Facts: 1-1/4 cups equals 416 calories, 13 g fat (5 g saturated fat), 47 mg cholesterol, 816 mg sodium, 53 g carbohydrate, 7 g fiber, 24 g protein.

To keep **fresh parsley** in the refrigerator for several weeks, wash the bunch in warm water, shake off excess moisture, wrap in a paper towel and seal in a plastic bag.

Terrific Turkey Chili

PREP: 10 min. **COOK:** 35 min.
YIELD: 6 servings (about 2 qt.)

KIM SEEGER • BROOKLYN PARK, MINNESOTA

This satisfying medley is full of tomato flavor and also provides a good dose of fiber. To keep things light, top it with reduced-fat cheese, cilantro and green onions.

- 1 lb. lean ground turkey
- 1 cup chopped onion
- 1 cup chopped green pepper
- 2 tsp. minced garlic
- 1 can (28 oz.) crushed tomatoes
- 1 can (16 oz.) kidney beans, rinsed and drained
- 1 can (11-1/2 oz.) tomato juice
- 1 can (6 oz.) tomato paste
- 1 can (4 oz.) chopped green chilies
- 2 Tbsp. brown sugar
- 1 Tbsp. dried parsley flakes
- 1 Tbsp. ground cumin
- 3 tsp. chili powder
- 2 tsp. dried oregano
- 1-1/2 tsp. pepper

1. In a large saucepan, cook the turkey, onion, green pepper over medium heat until meat is no longer pink. Add garlic; cook 1 minute longer. Drain.

TERRIFIC TURKEY CHILI

2. Stir in the remaining ingredients. Bring to a boil. Reduce heat; cover and simmer for 25 minutes or until heated through.

3. Serve desired amount. Cool the remaining chili; transfer to freezer containers. May be frozen for up to 3 months.

To use frozen chili: Thaw in the refrigerator. Place in a saucepan; heat through.

Nutrition Facts: 1-1/3 cups equals 315 calories, 8 g fat (2 g saturated fat), 60 mg cholesterol, 706 mg sodium, 43 g carbohydrate, 11 g fiber, 23 g protein. **Diabetic Exchanges:** 3 starch, 2 lean meat.

Slow Cooker Turkey Breast F C

PREP: 10 min. **COOK:** 5 hours **YIELD:** 14 servings

MARIA JUCO • MILWAUKEE, WISCONSIN

Try this wonderfully flavored, easy-fixing, tender, slow cooker entree when you're craving turkey.

- 1 bone-in turkey breast (6 to 7 lbs.), skin removed
- 1 Tbsp. olive oil
- 1 tsp. dried minced garlic
- 1 tsp. seasoned salt
- 1 tsp. paprika
- 1 tsp. Italian seasoning
- 1 tsp. pepper

1. Brush turkey with oil. Combine the remaining ingredients; rub over turkey. Transfer to a 6-qt. slow cooker. Cover and cook on low for 5-6 hours or until turkey is tender.

Nutrition Facts: 4 oz. cooked turkey equals 174 calories, 2 g fat (trace saturated fat), 101 mg cholesterol, 172 mg sodium, trace carbohydrate, trace fiber, 37 g protein. **Diabetic Exchange:** 4 lean meat.

Turkey Sausage Jambalaya

PREP: 20 min. **COOK:** 20 min. **YIELD:** 4 servings

JAMES MCNAUGHTON • QUINCY, FLORIDA

Creole cooking is delicious but frequently calls for lots of high-fat meats and oils. This is a spicy adaptation of an old favorite that is tasty, healthy and fast.

- 3/4 lb. reduced-fat smoked turkey sausage, cut into 1/4-in. slices
- 1 small onion, chopped
- 1 small green pepper, chopped
- 1 Tbsp. canola oil
- 1 garlic clove, minced
- 1-1/2 cups water
- 1/2 cup uncooked long grain rice
- 1/4 tsp. salt
- 1/4 tsp. cayenne pepper
- 1/4 tsp. hot pepper sauce
- 1 can (14-1/2 oz.) diced tomatoes with green chilies, undrained
- 1/4 lb. uncooked medium shrimp, peeled and deveined

BARBECUED TURKEY SANDWICHES

1. In a large saucepan, saute the sausage, onion and green pepper in oil until vegetables are tender. Add garlic; cook 1 minute longer. Stir in the water, rice, salt, cayenne and hot pepper sauce. Bring to a boil.

2. Reduce heat; cover and simmer for 15 minutes or until rice is tender. Add tomatoes and shrimp; cook and stir until shrimp turn pink.

Spicy Sausage Jambalaya: Substitute fully cooked andouille sausage for the turkey sausage. Increase garlic to 2 cloves. Add 1 bay leaf, 1/2 tsp. paprika and 1/4 tsp. dried thyme to the saucepan along with the rice. Proceed with recipe as directed. Discard bay leaf before serving.

Nutrition Facts: 1 cup equals 288 calories, 6 g fat (1 g saturated fat), 72 mg cholesterol, 1,311 mg sodium, 38 g carbohydrate, 3 g fiber, 18 g protein.

Barbecued Turkey Sandwiches

PREP/TOTAL TIME: 25 min.   YIELD: 6 servings

JAMARR JAMES • ELKINS PARK, PENNSYLVANIA

Try these sweet, tangy turkey sandwiches for a fun change from sloppy joes. You could also make them with pork or chicken. One of my best recipes ever!

  1 medium onion, finely chopped
  2 tsp. canola oil

3/4 cup chili sauce
1/2 cup water
  2 Tbsp. Worcestershire sauce
  1 Tbsp. brown sugar
  3 cups shredded cooked turkey breast
  6 whole wheat hamburger buns, split

1. In a large saucepan, saute onion in oil until tender. Stir in the chili sauce, water, Worcestershire sauce and brown sugar. Bring to a boil. Reduce heat; simmer, uncovered, for 5 minutes. Stir in turkey; heat through. Serve on buns.

Nutrition Facts: 1 sandwich equals 279 calories, 4 g fat (1 g saturated fat), 60 mg cholesterol, 762 mg sodium, 36 g carbohydrate, 4 g fiber, 25 g protein. **Diabetic Exchanges:** 3 lean meat, 2 starch.

To remove **onion odors,** when you've finished chopping onions, sprinkle your hands with table salt, rub them together for a few moments, then wash them. Presto! No more smelly hands.

Turkey Meatballs and Sauce

PREP: 30 min. **COOK:** 6 hours **YIELD:** 8 servings

JANE MCMILLAN • DANIA BEACH, FLORIDA

My sweetie and I have fought the battle of the bulge forever. This is my less-fattening take on meatballs. They're slow-cooker easy and so flavorful!

- 1/4 cup egg substitute
- 1/2 cup seasoned bread crumbs
- 1/3 cup chopped onion
- 1/2 tsp. pepper
- 1/4 tsp. salt-free seasoning blend
- 1-1/2 lb. lean ground turkey

SAUCE:
- 1 can (15 oz.) tomato sauce
- 1 can (14-1/2 oz.) diced tomatoes, undrained
- 1 small zucchini, chopped
- 1 medium green pepper, chopped
- 1 medium onion, chopped
- 1 can (6 oz.) tomato paste
- 2 bay leaves
- 2 garlic cloves, minced
- 1 tsp. dried oregano
- 1 tsp. dried basil
- 1 tsp. dried parsley flakes
- 1/4 tsp. crushed red pepper flakes
- 1/4 tsp. pepper
- 1 pkg. (16 oz.) whole wheat spaghetti

1. In a large bowl, combine the egg substitute, bread crumbs, onion, pepper and seasoning blend. Crumble turkey over mixture and mix well. Shape into 1-in. balls; place on a rack coated with cooking spray in a shallow baking pan. Bake, uncovered, at 400° for 15 minutes or until no longer pink.

2. Meanwhile, in a 4- or 5-qt. slow cooker, combine the tomato sauce, tomatoes, zucchini, green pepper, onion, tomato paste, bay leaves, garlic and seasonings. Stir in meatballs. Cover and cook on low for 6 hours. Meanwhile, cook spaghetti according to package directions; serve with sauce.

Nutrition Facts: 4 meatballs with 3/4 cup sauce and 1 cup spaghetti equals 416 calories, 8 g fat (2 g saturated fat), 67 mg cholesterol, 533 mg sodium, 61 g carbohydrate, 10 g fiber, 28 g protein.

Mexican Turkey Hash Brown Bake

PREP: 20 min. **BAKE:** 35 min. **YIELD:** 6 servings

TIM ASH • SALEM, INDIANA

Here's an easy, stick-to-your-ribs casserole that really delivers on nutrition and flavor!

- 1 lb. lean ground turkey
- 1/4 cup chopped onion
- 3 garlic cloves, minced
- 1 pkg. (32 oz.) frozen cubed hash brown potatoes, thawed
- 1 can (10 oz.) enchilada sauce
- 1 can (8 oz.) tomato sauce
- 1 can (4 oz.) chopped green chilies
- 1 Tbsp. reduced-sodium taco seasoning
- 1 cup (4 oz.) shredded cheddar cheese

Reduced-fat sour cream, optional

1. In a large skillet, cook the turkey, onion and garlic over medium heat until meat is no longer pink. Add the hash browns, enchilada sauce, tomato sauce, chilies and taco seasoning; heat through. Transfer to a 13-in. x 9-in. baking dish coated with cooking spray.

2. Cover and bake at 375° for 30 minutes. Sprinkle with cheese; bake, uncovered, 5-10 minutes longer or until cheese is melted. Serve with sour cream if desired.

Nutrition Facts: 1-1/3 cups (calculated without sour cream) equals 330 calories, 12 g fat (6 g saturated fat), 80 mg cholesterol, 799 mg sodium, 35 g carbohydrate, 4 g fiber, 23 g protein. **Diabetic Exchanges:** 3 lean meat, 2 starch, 1 fat.

Makeover Sausage & Potato Bake

PREP: 30 min. **BAKE:** 65 min. **YIELD:** 8 servings

SHANNON JONES • ASHLAND, VIRGINIA

This hearty dish makes an awesome breakfast bake, so we enjoy it on Christmas morning!

- 1 lb. lean ground turkey
- 1 small onion, chopped
- 1 tsp. fennel seed
- 1/4 tsp. salt
- 1/4 tsp. pepper
- 1/4 tsp. cayenne pepper
- 1/8 tsp. ground nutmeg
- 1 garlic clove, minced
- 1 can (10-3/4 oz.) condensed cream of potato soup, undiluted
- 3/4 cup 2% milk
- 2 lb. potatoes, peeled and thinly sliced
- 1 cup (4 oz.) shredded sharp cheddar cheese
- 1 cup (4 oz.) shredded part-skim mozzarella cheese

1. In a large nonstick skillet, cook the turkey, onion, fennel seed, salt, pepper, cayenne and nutmeg over medium heat until turkey is no longer pink. Add garlic; cook 1 minute longer. Drain. In a small bowl, combine soup and milk.

2. In a 2-qt. baking dish coated with cooking spray, layer half of the potatoes, soup mixture, sausage mixture and cheeses. Top with remaining potatoes, soup mixture and sausage mixture.

3. Cover and bake at 350° for 60-70 minutes or until bubbly and potatoes are tender. Sprinkle with remaining cheeses. Bake, uncovered, 5-10 minutes longer or until cheese is melted.

Nutrition Facts: 1 cup equals 281 calories, 12 g fat (6 g saturated fat), 71 mg cholesterol, 483 mg sodium, 23 g carbohydrate, 2 g fiber, 19 g protein.

Flavor your Italian sausage with **fennel seed.** Crush the seed, then heat it in a small amount of water and mix it into the sausage. It permeates the meat quicker this way and gives it a rich, sweet taste.

MAKEOVER SAUSAGE & POTATO BAKE

Savory Turkey Potpies

PREP: 25 min. **BAKE:** 20 min. **YIELD:** 8 servings

JUDY WILSON • SUN CITY WEST, ARIZONA

This is the ultimate in comfort food on a cold, rainy day with a crisp green salad. You can use chicken in place of turkey. Instead of the green salad, I sometimes serve a small ramekin of cranberry sauce.

1	small onion, chopped
1/4	cup all-purpose flour
3	cups chicken stock
3	cups cubed cooked turkey breast
1	package (16 oz.) frozen peas and carrots
2	medium red potatoes, cooked and cubed
3	tablespoons minced fresh parsley
1	tablespoon minced fresh thyme
1/4	teaspoon pepper
1	sheet refrigerated pie pastry

Additional fresh parsley or thyme leaves, optional

1	egg
1	teaspoon water
1/2	teaspoon kosher salt

1. In a Dutch oven coated with cooking spray, saute onion until tender. In a small bowl, whisk flour and stock until smooth; gradually stir into Dutch oven. Bring to a boil; cook and stir for 2 minutes or until thickened. Remove from the heat. Add the turkey, peas and carrots, potatoes, parsley, thyme and pepper; stir gently.

2. Divide turkey mixture among eight 10-oz. ramekins. On a lightly floured surface, unroll pastry. Cut out eight 3-in. circles. Gently press parsley into pastries if desired. Place over turkey mixture. Beat egg and water; brush over tops. Sprinkle with salt.

3. Place ramekins on a baking sheet. Bake at 425° for 20-25 minutes or until crusts are golden brown.

Nutrition Facts: 1 potpie equals 279 calories, 9 g fat (3 g saturated fat), 77 mg cholesterol, 495 mg sodium, 28 g carbohydrate, 3 g fiber, 22 g protein. **Diabetic Exchanges:** 2 starch, 2 lean meat, 1/2 fat.

Turkey Sloppy Joes

PREP: 15 min. **COOK:** 4 hours **YIELD:** 8 servings

MARYLOU LARUE • FREELAND, MICHIGAN

This tangy sandwich filling is so easy to prepare in the slow cooker, and it goes over well at gatherings large and small. I frequently take it to potlucks, and I'm always asked for my secret ingredient.

1	lb. lean ground turkey
1	small onion, chopped
1/2	cup chopped celery
1/4	cup chopped green pepper
1	can (10-3/4 oz.) reduced-sodium condensed tomato soup, undiluted
1/2	cup ketchup
2	Tbsp. prepared mustard
1	Tbsp. brown sugar
1/4	tsp. pepper
8	hamburger buns, split

1. In a large skillet coated with cooking spray, cook the turkey, onion, celery and green pepper over medium heat until meat is no longer pink; drain. Stir in the tomato soup, ketchup, mustard, brown sugar and pepper.

2. Transfer to a 3-qt. slow cooker. Cover and cook on low for 4 hours. Serve on buns.

Nutrition Facts: 1 sandwich equals 247 calories, 7 g fat (2 g saturated fat), 45 mg cholesterol, 553 mg sodium, 32 g carbohydrate, 2 g fiber, 14 g protein. **Diabetic Exchanges:** 2 starch, 1-1/2 lean meat.

Roasted Turkey a l'Orange ⬛S ⬛C

PREP: 40 min. **BAKE:** 3-1/2 hours + standing **YIELD:** 28 servings

ROBIN HAAS • CRANSTON, RHODE ISLAND

My niece says this is the best turkey she's ever had—she even requests it in the middle of summer!

1	whole garlic bulb, cloves separated and peeled
1	large navel orange
1/4	cup orange marmalade
2	Tbsp. lemon juice
1	Tbsp. honey
2	tsp. dried parsley flakes
1	tsp. paprika
1	tsp. dried oregano
1/2	tsp. salt
1/2	tsp. dried thyme
1/2	tsp. pepper
1	turkey (14 lb.)

SAVORY TURKEY POTPIES

ROASTED TURKEY A L'ORANGE

4 celery ribs, quartered
4 large carrots, quartered
1 large onion, quartered
1 large potato, peeled and cut into 2-in. cubes
1 large sweet potato, peeled and cut into 2-in. cubes

1. Mince four garlic cloves; transfer to a small bowl. Juice half of the orange; add to bowl. Stir in the marmalade, lemon juice, honey, parsley, paprika, oregano, salt, thyme and pepper. With fingers, carefully loosen skin from the turkey; rub 1/2 cup marmalade mixture under the skin.

2. Thinly slice remaining orange half; place under the skin. Brush turkey with remaining marmalade mixture. Place remaining garlic cloves inside the cavity. Tuck the wings under turkey; tie the drumsticks together.

3. Combine the celery, carrots, onion and potatoes in a roasting pan. Place the turkey, breast side up, over the vegetables.

4. Bake at 325° for 3-1/2 to 4 hours or until a thermometer reads 180°, basting occasionally with pan drippings. Cover loosely with foil if turkey browns too quickly. Cover and let stand for 20 minutes before carving.

Nutrition Facts: 4 oz. cooked turkey (calculated without skin and vegetables) equals 207 calories, 6 g fat (2 g saturated fat), 86 mg cholesterol, 123 mg sodium, 4 g carbohydrate, trace fiber, 33 g protein. **Diabetic Exchange:** 4 lean meat.

You can store whole or partial **garlic bulbs** in a cool, dry, dark place in a well-ventilated container, like a mesh bag, for up to 2 months. Leaving the cloves on the bulb with the papery skin attached will help prevent them from drying out.

Quinoa Turkey Chili

PREP: 40 min. **COOK:** 35 min.
YIELD: 9 servings (2-1/4 qt.)

SHARON GILJUM • SAN DIEGO, CALIFORNIA

This heart-healthy chili is not only tasty, it's a vitamin and protein powerhouse!

1	cup quinoa, rinsed
3-1/2	cups water, *divided*
1/2	lb. lean ground turkey
1	large sweet onion, chopped
1	medium sweet red pepper, chopped
4	garlic cloves, minced
1	Tbsp. chili powder
1	Tbsp. ground cumin
1/2	tsp. ground cinnamon

2	cans (15 oz. *each*) black beans, rinsed and drained
1	can (28 oz.) crushed tomatoes
1	medium zucchini, chopped
1	chipotle pepper in adobo sauce, chopped
1	Tbsp. adobo sauce
1	bay leaf
1	tsp. dried oregano
1/2	tsp. salt
1/4	tsp. pepper
1	cup frozen corn, thawed
1/4	cup minced fresh cilantro

1. In a large saucepan, bring quinoa and 2 cups water to a boil. Reduce heat; cover and simmer for 12-15 minutes or until water is absorbed. Remove from the heat; fluff with a fork and set aside.

2. Meanwhile, in a large saucepan coated with cooking spray, cook the turkey, onion, red pepper and garlic over medium heat until meat is no longer pink and vegetables are tender; drain. Stir in the chili powder, cumin and cinnamon; cook 2 minutes longer.

3. Add the black beans, tomatoes, zucchini, chipotle pepper, adobo sauce, bay leaf, oregano, salt, pepper and remaining water. Bring to a boil. Reduce heat; cover and simmer for 30 minutes. Stir in corn and quinoa; heat through. Discard the bay leaf; stir in the cilantro.

Editor's Note: Look for quinoa in the cereal, rice or organic food aisle.

Nutrition Facts: 1 cup equals 264 calories, 5 g fat (1 g saturated fat), 20 mg cholesterol, 514 mg sodium, 43 g carbohydrate, 9 g fiber, 15 g protein. **Diabetic Exchanges:** 2 starch, 2 lean meat, 2 vegetable.

Enchilada Stuffed Shells

PREP: 20 min. BAKE: 30 min. YIELD: 5 servings

REBECCA STOUT • CONROE, TEXAS

I served this entree to my husband, my sister and my brother-in-law, who is a hard-to-please eater. He said he liked it and even took leftovers for his lunch the next day; I was just thrilled!

15	uncooked jumbo pasta shells
1	lb. lean ground turkey
1	can (10 oz.) enchilada sauce
1/2	tsp. dried minced onion
1/4	tsp. dried basil
1/4	tsp. dried oregano
1/4	tsp. ground cumin
1/2	cup fat-free refried beans
1	cup (4 oz.) shredded reduced-fat cheddar cheese

1. Cook pasta according to package directions; drain and rinse in cold water. In a nonstick skillet, cook turkey over medium heat until no longer pink; drain. Stir in enchilada sauce and seasonings; set aside.

2. Place a rounded teaspoonful of refried beans in each pasta shell, then fill with the turkey mixture. Place in an 11-in. x 7-in. baking dish coated with cooking spray.

3. Cover and bake at 350° for 25 minutes. Uncover; sprinkle with cheese. Bake 5 minutes longer or until cheese is melted.

Nutrition Facts: 3 stuffed shells equals 379 calories, 15 g fat (6 g saturated fat), 89 mg cholesterol, 591 mg sodium, 33 g carbohydrate, 2 g fiber, 28 g protein. **Diabetic Exchanges:** 3 lean meat, 2 starch, 1 fat.

Italian Turkey Tenders

PREP: 25 min. BAKE: 20 min. YIELD: 6 servings

MARY SHIVERS • ADA, OKLAHOMA

Flavorful and crispy, this healthier version of a kids' favorite should delight the whole family. Seasoned bread crumbs or ranch dressing would make tasty variations.

1	egg, beaten
1/2	cup fat-free creamy Italian salad dressing
1/2	cup all-purpose flour
1-1/4	cups dry bread crumbs
1	tsp. dried parsley flakes
1	tsp. Italian seasoning
3/4	tsp. salt
1/2	tsp. onion powder
1/2	tsp. garlic powder
1/2	tsp. dried oregano
1/2	tsp. pepper
2	lb. boneless skinless turkey breast halves, cut into 1-in. strips

Cooking spray

1. In a shallow bowl, whisk egg and salad dressing. Place flour in another shallow bowl. In a third shallow bowl, combine bread crumbs and seasonings. Coat turkey with flour, then dip in egg mixture and coat with bread crumb mixture.

2. Place on baking sheets coated with cooking spray. Spritz turkey with cooking spray. Bake at 375° for 20-25 minutes or until juices run clear, turning once.

Nutrition Facts: 1 serving equals 329 calories, 4 g fat (1 g saturated fat), 129 mg cholesterol, 766 mg sodium, 29 g carbohydrate, 2 g fiber, 42 g protein.

Dry bread crumbs may be purchased or made from very dry bread or crackers. Simply place **dry bread slices** in a plastic bag and crush with a rolling pin.

ITALIAN TURKEY TENDERS

Lightened-Up Gumbo

PREP: 30 min. **COOK:** 20 min. **YIELD:** 6 servings

HEALTHY COOKING TEST KITCHEN

Full of flavor and color, this gumbo tastes like the real deal, except that it's a healthier option!

1/2	cup all-purpose flour
3	cups reduced-sodium chicken broth
1	small onion, chopped
1	celery rib, chopped
1	small green pepper, chopped
1	Tbsp. canola oil
2	garlic cloves, minced
8	oz. smoked turkey sausage, sliced
1	cup frozen sliced okra
2	bay leaves
1	tsp. Creole seasoning
1/4	tsp. salt
1/4	tsp. pepper
1	lb. uncooked medium shrimp, peeled and deveined
1	cup cubed cooked chicken breast
3	cups cooked brown rice

1. In a large skillet over medium-high heat, cook and stir flour for 6-7 minutes or until light brown in color. Immediately transfer to a small bowl; whisk in broth until smooth.

2. In the same skillet, saute the onion, celery and green pepper in oil until tender. Add garlic; cook 1 minute longer. Stir flour mixture; add to the pan. Bring to a boil; cook and stir for 2 minutes or until mixture is thickened.

3. Add the sausage, okra, bay leaves, Creole seasoning, salt and pepper. Simmer, uncovered, for 4-5 minutes or until okra is tender. Stir in shrimp and chicken. Cook and stir 5-6 minutes longer or until shrimp turn pink. Discard bay leaves. Serve with rice.

Nutrition Facts: 1-1/3 cups gumbo with 1/2 cup rice equals 336 calories, 7 g fat (1 g saturated fat), 134 mg cholesterol, 981 mg sodium, 35 g carbohydrate, 3 g fiber, 31 g protein. **Diabetic Exchanges:** 4 lean meat, 2 starch, 1/2 fat.

Sausage Penne Bake

PREP: 35 min. **BAKE:** 20 min. **YIELD:** 8 servings

BARBARA KEMPEN • CAMBRIDGE, MINNESOTA

No one will guess a dish this cheesy and filling could be healthy, but this one's chock-full of eggplant, whole wheat pasta, tomatoes and fabulous flavor.

2	cups uncooked whole wheat penne pasta
3/4	lb. Italian turkey sausage links, casings removed
1	small eggplant, peeled and cut into 1/2-in. cubes
1	medium onion, chopped
1/2	cup dry red wine *or* chicken broth
3	garlic cloves, minced
1	can (28 oz.) crushed tomatoes
2	cups (8 oz.) shredded part-skim mozzarella cheese, *divided*
3	Tbsp. chopped ripe olives
2	tsp. dried basil
1/4	tsp. pepper
1/2	cup grated Parmesan cheese

1. Cook pasta according to package directions. Meanwhile, in a large skillet, cook the sausage, eggplant and onion over medium heat until meat is no longer pink; drain.

2. Stir in wine and garlic, stirring to loosen browned bits from pan. Add tomatoes. Bring to a boil. Reduce heat; simmer, uncovered, for 10 minutes or until slightly thickened. Drain pasta. Add the pasta, 1-1/2 cups mozzarella cheese, olives, basil and pepper to the skillet.

3. Transfer to a 3-qt. baking dish coated with cooking spray. Sprinkle with Parmesan cheese and remaining mozzarella cheese. Bake, uncovered, at 350° for 20-25 minutes or until heated through.

Nutrition Facts: 1 cup equals 325 calories, 11 g fat (5 g saturated fat), 46 mg cholesterol, 623 mg sodium, 35 g carbohydrate, 7 g fiber, 23 g protein. **Diabetic Exchanges:** 3 lean meat, 1-1/2 starch, 1 vegetable, 1 fat.

Italian Turkey Burgers

PREP: 15 min. **BAKE:** 20 min. **YIELD:** 6 servings

BRENDA DIMARCO • WHITEFORD, MARYLAND

We eat burgers a lot in warm weather. I cut down on fat and calories by using ground turkey, then spicing it up. My husband is picky about burgers, but he loves these!

1/2	cup sun-dried tomatoes (not packed in oil)
3/4	cup boiling water

LIGHTENED-UP GUMBO

ITALIAN TURKEY BURGERS

1 egg white, beaten
1/2 cup dry bread crumbs
1 small onion, finely chopped
1/4 cup ketchup
1 Tbsp. minced fresh basil *or* 1 tsp. dried basil
1 Tbsp. minced fresh parsley
1 Tbsp. spicy brown mustard
2 garlic cloves, minced
1 tsp. dried oregano
1/4 tsp. Italian seasoning
1 lb. lean ground turkey
1/2 lb. extra-lean ground turkey
3 slices reduced-fat provolone cheese, halved
6 whole wheat hamburger buns, split
Ketchup and mustard, optional

1. Place tomatoes in a small bowl; add boiling water. Cover and let stand for 5 minutes.

2. In a large bowl, combine the egg white, bread crumbs, onion, ketchup, basil, parsley, mustard, garlic, oregano and Italian seasoning. Drain and chop tomatoes; add to egg white mixture. Crumble turkey over mixture and mix well. Shape into six burgers.

3. Place in a 15-in. x. 10-in. x 1-in. baking pan coated with cooking spray. Bake at 350° for 16-20 minutes or until a thermometer reads 165° and juices run clear. Top with cheese; bake 1-2 minutes longer or until melted. Serve on buns with ketchup and mustard if desired.

Nutrition Facts: 1 burger (calculated without optional condiments) equals 362 calories, 11 g fat (3 g saturated fat), 80 mg cholesterol, 698 mg sodium, 35 g carbohydrate, 5 g fiber, 31 g protein. **Diabetic Exchanges:** 4 lean meat, 2 starch.

Packed in oil or dry packed, **sun-dried tomatoes** are available in most grocery stores today. The dry-packed varieties are usually soaked in a liquid to soften them before they're used in recipes.

ITALIAN SAUSAGE MARINARA WITH PENNE

Italian Sausage Marinara with Penne

PREP: 30 min. COOK: 1 hour YIELD: 8 servings

TERESA KRIESE • EAU CLAIRE, WISCONSIN

Fill your house with the wonderful aroma of this rich, bold-flavored sauce. It's my first original recipe and a family favorite from the start. We love its zesty blend of veggies and Italian turkey links.

1 pkg. (19-1/2 oz.) Italian turkey sausage links, cut into 1/2-in. slices

3 small zucchini, cut into 1/2-in. slices

1 medium sweet yellow pepper, julienned

1 cup sliced fresh mushrooms

2 Tbsp. olive oil

2 garlic cloves, minced

1/2 cup dry red wine *or* reduced-sodium chicken broth

1 can (28 oz.) Italian crushed tomatoes

1 can (14-1/2 oz.) fire-roasted diced tomatoes, undrained

1/3 cup grated Parmesan cheese

4-1/2 tsp. Louisiana-style hot sauce

3 tsp. Italian seasoning

1 tsp. sugar

1/4 tsp. salt

4 cups uncooked whole wheat penne pasta

1. In a Dutch oven, saute sausage until no longer pink; drain. Remove and set aside. In the same pan, saute the zucchini, pepper and mushrooms in oil until tender. Add garlic; cook 1 minute longer. Add wine, stirring to loosen browned bits from pan.

2. Add the crushed tomatoes, diced tomatoes, cheese, hot sauce, Italian seasoning, sugar and salt. Stir in sausage. Bring to a boil. Reduce heat; simmer, uncovered, for 1 hour or until slightly thickened.

3. Meanwhile, cook pasta according to package directions; drain. Serve with sauce.

Nutrition Facts: 1 cup sauce with 1 cup pasta equals 441 calories, 12 g fat (2 g saturated fat), 44 mg cholesterol, 991 mg sodium, 56 g carbohydrate, 8 g fiber, 24 g protein.

Open-Faced Fennel Turkey Burgers

PREP: 20 min. + chilling **COOK:** 15 min.
YIELD: 5 servings

HEALTHY COOKING TEST KITCHEN

Fresh fennel and crunchy vegetables pump up the flavor and nutrition of these mouthwatering burgers. They're topped with chopped tomatoes and served on toasted Italian bread.

- 1/2 cup chopped fennel bulb
- 1/2 cup chopped sweet onion
- 1/2 cup chopped green pepper
- 2 tsp. butter
- 1/4 cup seasoned bread crumbs
- 1/4 tsp. plus 1/8 tsp. salt, *divided*
- 1/4 tsp. pepper
- 1 pkg. (20 oz.) lean ground turkey
- 1 cup chopped tomato
- 2 Tbsp. minced fresh parsley
- 2 tsp. olive oil
- 5 slices Italian bread (3/4 in. thick), toasted
- Chopped fennel fronds, optional

1. In a large nonstick skillet, saute fennel, onion and green pepper in butter until crisp-tender. Transfer to a large bowl; cool slightly. Add the bread crumbs, 1/4 tsp. salt and pepper. Crumble turkey over mixture and mix well. Shape into five patties. Cover and refrigerate for at least 1 hour.

2. In a small bowl, combine the tomato, parsley, oil and remaining salt; set aside.

3. Using long handled tongs, moisten a paper towel with cooking oil and lightly coat the grill rack. Grill burgers, covered, over medium heat or broil 4 in. from the heat for 6-8 minutes or until a thermometer reads 165° and the juices run clear. Serve on toast with the tomato mixture. Sprinkle with fennel fronds if desired.

Nutrition Facts: 1 burger with 1 toast slice and 3 Tbsp. tomato mixture equals 321 calories, 14 g fat (4 g saturated fat), 94 mg cholesterol, 571 mg sodium, 24 g carbohydrate, 2 g fiber, 24 g protein. **Diabetic Exchanges:** 3 lean meat, 1 starch, 1 vegetable, 1/2 fat.

OPEN-FACED FENNEL TURKEY BURGERS

Turkey Burgers with Sweet Onion Relish

PREP: 25 min. **GRILL:** 10 min. **YIELD:** 6 servings

REBECCA MAGNUSON • SAN DIEGO, CALIFORNIA

People really like this. The sweet onion relish is a little different, which makes this a great meal for entertaining. I often form the turkey mix for these burgers into hot dog shapes for a fun alternative.

- 1 large sweet onion, chopped
- 1/4 cup tomato sauce
- 3 Tbsp. water
- 2 Tbsp. ketchup
- 1 Tbsp. sugar
- 1 garlic clove, minced
- 1/4 tsp. dried oregano
- 1/4 tsp. crushed red pepper flakes

BURGERS:
- 2 egg whites
- 1-1/2 tsp. poultry seasoning
- 1/4 tsp. pepper
- 1-1/2 lbs. lean ground turkey
- 6 whole wheat hamburger buns, split

1. In a small skillet, combine the first eight ingredients. Cook, uncovered, over medium heat for 10-15 minutes or until onions are tender, stirring occasionally. Set aside.

2. For burgers, in a large bowl, combine the egg whites, poultry seasoning and pepper. Crumble turkey over mixture and mix well. Shape into six patties.

3. Using long-handled tongs, moisten a paper towel with cooking oil and lightly coat the grill rack. Grill burgers, covered, over medium heat or broil 4 in. from the heat for 5-7 minutes on each side or until a meat thermometer reads 165° and juices run clear. Serve on buns with relish.

Nutrition Facts: 1 burger with 4 tsp. relish equals 317 calories, 11 g fat (3 g saturated fat), 90 mg cholesterol, 437 mg sodium, 29 g carbohydrate, 4 g fiber, 25 g protein. **Diabetic Exchanges:** 3 lean meat, 2 starch.

Pizza Pepperoni Pasta

PREP: 25 min. **BAKE:** 25 min. **YIELD:** 8 servings

AMY BIPES • TOPEKA, KANSAS

Turkey pepperoni adds classic Italian flavor to this family-friendly main dish that's done in a flash. It's ideal for busy weeknights or for satisfying a potluck crowd. Serve with a green salad and breadsticks, and dinner's done.

- 3 cups uncooked whole wheat spiral pasta
- 1 lb. lean ground turkey
- 1 medium onion, chopped
- 2-1/2 cups garden-style spaghetti sauce
- 1 can (14-1/2 oz.) diced tomatoes, undrained
- 1/2 tsp. dried basil
- 1/2 tsp. dried oregano
- 1/2 tsp. Worcestershire sauce
- 1/8 tsp. pepper
- 3 Tbsp. grated Parmesan cheese
- 4 oz. sliced turkey pepperoni
- 1/2 cup shredded part-skim mozzarella cheese

1. Cook pasta according to package directions.

2. Meanwhile, in a large nonstick skillet, cook turkey and onion over medium heat until the meat is no longer pink; drain. Stir in the spaghetti sauce, tomatoes, basil, oregano, Worcestershire sauce and pepper; set aside.

3. Drain pasta. Transfer to a 13-in. x 9-in. baking dish coated with cooking spray; sprinkle with Parmesan cheese. Top with spaghetti sauce mixture and pepperoni. Sprinkle with mozzarella cheese.

4. Cover and bake at 350° for 25-30 minutes or until heated through.

Nutrition Facts: 1-1/4 cups equals 299 calories, 10 g fat (3 g saturated fat), 71 mg cholesterol, 752 mg sodium, 30 g carbohydrate, 5 g fiber, 22 g protein. **Diabetic Exchanges:** 3 lean meat, 1-1/2 starch, 1 fat.

Turkey and Black Bean Enchiladas

PREP: 30 min. **BAKE:** 15 min. **YIELD:** 8 servings

SARAH BURLESON • SPRUCE PINE, NORTH CAROLINA

Hearty and satisfying, these slimmed-down enchiladas with whole-wheat tortillas feature a moist and delicious filling you're sure to love.

- 2 cans (15 oz. *each*) black beans, rinsed and drained, *divided*
- 1 lb. lean ground turkey
- 1 medium green pepper, chopped

TURKEY BURGERS WITH SWEET ONION RELISH

1 small onion, chopped

1 can (15 oz.) enchilada sauce, *divided*

1 cup (4 oz.) shredded reduced-fat Mexican cheese blend, *divided*

8 whole wheat tortillas (8 in.), warmed

1. In a small bowl, mash 1 can black beans; set aside. In a large nonstick skillet, cook the turkey, pepper and onion over medium heat until meat is no longer pink; drain. Add the mashed beans, remaining beans, half of the enchilada sauce and 1/2 cup cheese; heat through.

2. Place 2/3 cupfuls of bean mixture down the center of each tortilla. Roll up and place seam side down in two 11-in. x 7-in. baking dishes coated with cooking spray. Pour remaining enchilada sauce over the top; sprinkle with remaining cheese. Bake, uncovered, at 425° for 15-20 minutes or until heated through.

Nutrition Facts: 1 enchilada equals 363 calories, 11 g fat (3 g saturated fat), 55 mg cholesterol, 808 mg sodium, 42 g carbohydrate, 7 g fiber, 24 g protein.

Baked Mostaccioli

PREP: 35 min. **BAKE:** 30 min. **YIELD:** 6 servings

DONNA EBERT • RICHFIELD, WISCONSIN

I often serve this for dinner parties and always get tons of compliments. It's easier than it seems!

8 oz. uncooked mostaccioli

1/2 lb. lean ground turkey

1 small onion, chopped

1 can (14-1/2 oz.) diced tomatoes, undrained

1 can (6 oz.) tomato paste

1/3 cup water

1 tsp. dried oregano

1/2 tsp. salt

1/8 tsp. pepper

2 cups (16 oz.) fat-free cottage cheese

1 tsp. dried marjoram

1-1/2 cups (6 oz.) shredded part-skim mozzarella cheese

1/4 cup grated Parmesan cheese

1. Cook mostaccioli according to package directions. Meanwhile, in a large saucepan, cook turkey and onion over medium heat until meat is no longer pink; drain if necessary.

2. Stir in the tomatoes, tomato paste, water, oregano, salt and pepper. Bring to a boil. Reduce heat; cover and simmer for 15 minutes.

3. In a small bowl, combine cottage cheese and marjoram; set aside. Drain mostaccioli.

4. Spread 1/2 cup meat sauce into an 11-in. x 7-in. baking dish coated with cooking spray. Layer with half of the mostaccioli, meat sauce and mozzarella cheese. Top with the cottage cheese mixture. Layer with the remaining mostaccioli, meat sauce and mozzarella cheese. Sprinkle with grated Parmesan cheese (dish will be full).

5. Bake, uncovered, at 350° for 30-40 minutes or until bubbly and heated through.

Nutrition Facts: 1-1/3 cups equals 278 calories, 7 g fat (3 g saturated fat), 39 mg cholesterol, 607 mg sodium, 32 g carbohydrate, 3 g fiber, 23 g protein. **Diabetic Exchanges:** 3 medium-fat meat, 2 vegetable, 1-1/2 starch.

Coconut-Crusted
Turkey Strips

PREP/TOTAL TIME: 30 min. **YIELD:** 6 servings

AGNES WARD • STRATFORD, ONTARIO

These Coconut-Crusted Turkey Strips with a plum dipping sauce are just the thing to serve for a light supper or extra-special appetizer. My granddaughter made them last year, and they were a big hit with everyone.

- 2 egg whites
- 2 tsp. sesame oil
- 1/2 cup flaked coconut, toasted
- 1/2 cup dry bread crumbs
- 2 Tbsp. sesame seeds, toasted
- 1/2 tsp. salt
- 1-1/2 lbs. turkey breast tenderloins, cut into 1/2-in. strips

Cooking spray

DIPPING SAUCE:
- 1/2 cup plum sauce
- 1/3 cup unsweetened pineapple juice
- 1-1/2 tsp. prepared mustard
- 1 tsp. cornstarch

1. In a shallow bowl, whisk egg whites and oil. In another shallow bowl, combine the coconut, bread crumbs, sesame seeds and salt. Dip turkey in egg mixture, then coat with coconut mixture.

2. Place on baking sheets coated with cooking spray; spritz turkey with cooking spray. Bake at 425° for 4-6 minutes on each side or until golden brown and juices run clear.

3. Meanwhile, in a small saucepan, combine the sauce ingredients. Bring to a boil; cook and stir for 2 minutes or until thickened. Serve with turkey strips.

Nutrition Facts: 3 oz. cooked turkey with 2 Tbsp. sauce equals 278 calories, 8 g fat (3 g saturated fat), 56 mg cholesterol, 519 mg sodium, 22 g carbohydrate, 1 g fiber, 30 g protein. **Diabetic Exchanges:** 3 lean meat, 1 starch, 1/2 fat.

Moist & Tender
Turkey Breast C

PREP: 10 min. **COOK:** 4 hours **YIELD:** 12 servings

HEIDI VAWDREY • RIVERTON, UTAH

This easy dish will be very popular in your home. Everyone will look forward to the leftovers.

- 1 bone-in turkey breast (6 to 7 lbs.)
- 4 fresh rosemary sprigs
- 4 garlic cloves, peeled

1 Tbsp. brown sugar
1/2 tsp. coarsely ground pepper
1/4 tsp. salt

1. Place turkey breast in a 6-qt. slow cooker. Place rosemary and garlic around the turkey. Combine the brown sugar, pepper and salt; sprinkle over turkey. Cover and cook on low for 4-6 hours or until the turkey is tender.

Nutrition Facts: 7 oz. cooked turkey equals 318 calories, 12 g fat (3 g saturated fat), 122 mg cholesterol, 154 mg sodium, 2 g carbohydrate, trace fiber, 47 g protein.

Curry Turkey Stir-Fry

PREP/TOTAL TIME: 25 min. **YIELD:** 4 servings

LAUREEN RUSH • ELK RIVER, MINNESOTA

Chicken also works well in this satisfying meal-in-one. If you're in a hurry, use instant brown rice.

1/2 tsp. cornstarch
2 Tbsp. reduced-sodium soy sauce
1 Tbsp. minced fresh cilantro
1 Tbsp. honey
1 tsp. curry powder
1 tsp. scsame or canola oil
1 garlic clove, minced
1/8 tsp. crushed red pepper flakes, optional
1 large sweet red pepper, julienned
1 Tbsp. canola oil
3 green onions, cut into 3-in. pieces
2 cups cubed cooked turkey breast
2 cups cooked brown rice

1. In a small bowl, combine the cornstarch, soy sauce, cilantro, honey, curry, sesame oil, garlic and pepper flakes if desired until blended; set aside.

2. In a large skillet or wok, stir-fry the red pepper in oil for 2 minutes or until crisp-tender. Add green onions; stir-fry 1-2 minutes longer or until the vegetables are tender.

3. Stir cornstarch mixture and add to the pan. Bring to a boil; cook and stir for 2 minutes or until thickened. Add turkey; heat through. Serve with rice.

Nutrition Facts: 3/4 cup stir-fry with 1/2 cup rice equals 287 calories, 7 g fat (1 g saturated fat), 60 mg cholesterol, 351 mg sodium, 31 g carbohydrate, 3 g fiber, 25 g protein. **Diabetic Exchanges:** 3 lean meat, 1-1/2 starch, 1 fat.

Sausage Spinach Pizza

PREP: 35 min. + rising **BAKE:** 10 min.
YIELD: 2 pizzas (8 slices each)

ELENA FALK • VERSAILLES, OHIO

My husband loves this pizza, and it's the best way for him to get his fix while staying in his carb range. Putting cheese and seasonings in the crust lets you get by with less on top.

1 pkg. (1/4 oz.) active dry yeast
1 cup warm water (110° to 115°)
2-1/4 cups all-purpose flour
2 Tbsp. olive oil

1 Tbsp. sugar
2 tsp. Italian seasoning
1/2 tsp. salt
1/2 cup shredded Asiago cheese
3/4 lb. Italian turkey sausage links, thinly sliced
1 can (14-1/2 oz.) Italian diced tomatoes, undrained
2 cups fresh baby spinach
6 slices reduced-fat provolone cheese, halved

1. In a large bowl, dissolve yeast in water. Add the flour, oil, sugar, Italian seasoning and salt; beat on medium speed for 3 minutes or until smooth. Stir in Asiago cheese.

2. Turn onto a lightly floured surface; knead until smooth and elastic, about 5-6 minutes. Place in a bowl coated with cooking spray, turning once to coat the top. Cover and let rise in a warm place until doubled, about 1 hour.

3. Punch dough down; divide in half. On a floured surface, roll each portion into a 13-in. circle. Transfer to two 12-in. pizza pans coated with cooking spray. Build up edges slightly. Prick dough thoroughly with a fork. Bake at 425° for 5-8 minutes or until edges are lightly browned.

4. Meanwhile, in a large nonstick skillet, cook sausage over medium heat until no longer pink; drain. Place tomatoes in a food processor; cover and pulse until finely chopped.

5. Spread the tomatoes over crusts; layer with spinach, sausage and provolone cheese. Bake at 425° for 8-12 minutes or until the crusts and cheese are lightly browned.

Nutrition Facts: 2 slices equals 314 calories, 12 g fat (4 g saturated fat), 39 mg cholesterol, 729 mg sodium, 34 g carbohydrate, 2 g fiber, 17 g protein. **Diabetic Exchanges:** 2 starch, 2 lean meat, 1 vegetable, 1/2 fat.

SAUSAGE SPINACH PIZZA

Spicy Turkey Tacos

PREP/TOTAL TIME: 25 min. **YIELD:** 4 servings

KENDRA DOSS • KANSAS CITY, MISSOURI

So easy, so healthy and so good—I love these whenever I'm in the mood for a little Mexican food. With a hint of cinnamon, these tacos have an unusual blend of seasonings that's exotic and mouthwatering.

  8 taco shells
  1 lb. extra-lean ground turkey
  1 small red onion, finely chopped
  1 cup salsa
  1/2 tsp. dried oregano
  1/2 tsp. paprika
  1/2 tsp. ground cinnamon
  1/2 tsp. ground cumin
  2 cups shredded lettuce
  1/2 cup shredded pepper Jack cheese
  1/4 cup fat-free sour cream

Cubed avocado and additional salsa, optional

1. Heat taco shells according to package directions.

2. Meanwhile, in a large nonstick skillet, cook turkey and onion over medium heat until meat is no longer pink. Stir in salsa and spices; heat through.

3. Fill each taco shell with 1/3 cup turkey mixture. Serve with lettuce, cheese, sour cream and optional ingredients if desired.

Nutrition Facts: 2 tacos (calculated without optional ingredients) equals 324 calories, 11 g fat (4 g saturated fat), 63 mg cholesterol, 502 mg sodium, 23 g carbohydrate, 2 g fiber, 35 g protein. **Diabetic Exchanges:** 4 lean meat, 1 starch, 1 vegetable, 1 fat.

Turkey Spiral Skillet

PREP: 15 min. **COOK:** 25 min. **YIELD:** 8 servings

MANDY PHELPS • GRESHAM, OREGON

Family-friendly and everyday delicious, this dish is a little healthier and lighter twist on classic beef and pasta dishes. It's fast and full of flavor.

  1 pkg. (16 oz.) whole wheat spiral pasta
  1 lb. extra-lean ground turkey
  1 medium sweet orange pepper, finely chopped
  1 cup sliced fresh mushrooms
  1 small onion, finely chopped
  3 garlic cloves, minced
  1 can (14-1/2 oz.) Italian stewed tomatoes, undrained
  1 jar (14 oz.) spaghetti sauce
  1/4 tsp. pepper
  1 can (2-1/4 oz.) sliced ripe olives, drained
  2 Tbsp. grated Parmesan cheese

1. Cook pasta according to package directions.

2. Meanwhile, in a large nonstick skillet, cook the turkey, orange pepper, mushrooms, onion and garlic until turkey is no longer pink; drain. Add the tomatoes, spaghetti sauce and pepper. Bring to a boil. Reduce heat; simmer, uncovered, for 10-15 minutes or until slightly thickened, stirring occasionally.

3. Drain pasta; add to skillet. Stir in olives; heat through. Sprinkle with cheese just before serving.

Nutrition Facts: 1-1/2 cups equals 351 calories, 5 g fat (1 g saturated fat), 25 mg cholesterol, 542 mg sodium, 53 g carbohydrate, 9 g fiber, 26 g protein.

Sausage Spinach Pasta Bake

PREP: 35 min. **BAKE:** 25 min. **YIELD:** 10 servings

KIM FORNI • CLAREMONT, NEW HAMPSHIRE

I've fixed this many times and like to make it differently on occasion. I've swapped in other meats, such as chicken sausage, veal or ground pork, and added summer squash, zucchini, green beans and mushrooms, depending on what's in season. Also, fresh herbs really perk up the flavors.

SPICY TURKEY TACOS

TURKEY SPIRAL SKILLET

TURKEY DIVAN

1 pkg. (16 oz.) whole wheat spiral pasta
1 lb. Italian turkey sausage links, casings removed
1 medium onion, chopped
5 garlic cloves, minced
1 can (28 oz.) crushed tomatoes
1 can (14-1/2 oz.) diced tomatoes, undrained
1 tsp. dried oregano
1 tsp. dried basil
1/4 tsp. pepper
1 pkg. (10 oz.) frozen chopped spinach, thawed and squeezed dry
1/2 cup half-and-half cream
2 cups (8 oz.) shredded part-skim mozzarella cheese
1/2 cup grated Parmesan cheese

1. Cook pasta according to package directions.

2. Meanwhile, in a large skillet, cook turkey and onion over medium heat until meat is no longer pink. Add garlic. Cook 1 minute longer; drain. Stir in the tomatoes, oregano, basil and pepper. Bring to a boil. Reduce heat; simmer, uncovered, for 10 minutes.

3. Drain pasta; stir into turkey mixture. Add spinach and cream; heat through. Transfer to a 13-in. x 9-in. baking dish coated with cooking spray. Sprinkle with cheeses. Bake, uncovered, at 350° for 25-30 minutes or until golden brown.

Nutrition Facts: 1-1/3 cups equals 377 calories, 11 g fat (5 g saturated fat), 50 mg cholesterol, 622 mg sodium, 45 g carbohydrate, 8 g fiber, 25 g protein. **Diabetic Exchanges:** 3 lean meat, 2 starch, 2 vegetable, 1/2 fat.

Turkey Divan

PREP/TOTAL TIME: 30 min. **YIELD:** 8 servings

HEALTHY COOKING TEST KITCHEN

It looks and tastes decadent, but at just 291 calories per serving, this classic entree isn't much of a splurge. Pair it with a side salad and slice of whole grain bread for a complete meal.

1-1/2 cups water
16 fresh asparagus spears, trimmed
2 egg whites
1 egg
2 Tbsp. fat-free milk
1-1/4 cups seasoned bread crumbs
1 pkg. (17.6 oz.) turkey breast cutlets
1/4 cup butter, cubed
8 slices deli ham
8 slices reduced-fat Swiss cheese

1. In a large skillet, bring water to a boil. Add asparagus; cover and boil for 3 minutes. Drain and pat dry.

2. In a shallow bowl, beat the egg whites, egg and milk. Place bread crumbs in another shallow bowl. Dip turkey in egg mixture, then coat with crumbs.

3. In a large skillet, cook turkey in butter in batches for 2-3 minutes on each side or until meat is no longer pink. Layer with a ham slice, two asparagus spears and cheese. Cover and cook for 1 minute or until cheese is melted. Transfer to a platter; keep warm.

Nutrition Facts: 1 serving equals 291 calories, 12 g fat (6 g saturated fat), 100 mg cholesterol, 595 mg sodium, 16 g carbohydrate, 1 g fiber, 31 g protein. **Diabetic Exchanges:** 3 lean meat, 2 fat, 1 starch.

Italian Turkey Roll-Ups

PREP/TOTAL TIME: 20 min. **YIELD:** 6 servings

KAY HEDRICK • GIBSONVILLE, NORTH CAROLINA

These quick-and-easy wraps, with a fresh combination of creamy Havarti, turkey and veggies, have it all. They taste light, healthful and delectable, but they will definitely fill you up, too. Serve with a salad, fruit or a bowl of soup.

1	pkg. (8 oz.) fat-free cream cheese
1	Tbsp. Italian seasoning
1/2	tsp. onion powder
1/4	tsp. garlic powder
6	whole wheat tortillas (8 in.), room temperature
6	slices deli turkey
3	oz. Havarti cheese, cut into six slices
1-1/2	cups shredded lettuce
3	plum tomatoes, thinly sliced
1	medium carrot, shredded
1	small cucumber, thinly sliced
3	thin slices red onion, separated into rings

1. In a small bowl, beat the cream cheese, Italian seasoning, onion powder and garlic powder until smooth. Spread 1 heaping Tbsp. over each tortilla. Layer each with a slice of turkey and cheese. Top with remaining ingredients. Roll up tightly and secure with toothpicks.

Nutrition Facts: 1 roll-up equals 271 calories, 8 g fat (3 g saturated fat), 24 mg cholesterol, 662 mg sodium, 29 g carbohydrate, 3 g fiber, 18 g protein. **Diabetic Exchanges:** 2 medium-fat meat, 1 starch, 1 vegetable.

Turkey Spaghetti Sauce **F** **C**

PREP: 25 min. **COOK:** 40 min. **YIELD:** 7-1/2 cups

JENNIFER KOLB • OVERLAND PARK, KANSAS

This is rich, homey and flavorful, but lower in sodium than jarred meat sauce.

1	lb. Italian turkey sausage links, casings removed
1/2	lb. extra-lean ground turkey
1-3/4	cups sliced fresh mushrooms
1	medium green pepper, chopped
1	medium onion, chopped
1	can (29 oz.) tomato puree
1	can (14-1/2 oz.) diced tomatoes, undrained
1	can (6 oz.) tomato paste
2	bay leaves
1	Tbsp. dried oregano
1	tsp. garlic powder
1	tsp. dried basil
1/2	tsp. salt
1/4	tsp. pepper

Hot cooked multigrain spaghetti

1. Crumble sausage and turkey into a large nonstick skillet coated with cooking spray. Add mushrooms, green pepper and onion. Cook and stir over medium heat until meat is no longer pink; drain. Stir in the puree, tomatoes, tomato paste, bay leaves and seasonings. Bring to a boil. Reduce heat; simmer, uncovered, for 30 minutes.

2. Discard bay leaves. Serve desired amount with spaghetti. Cool remaining sauce; transfer to freezer containers. Freeze for up to 3 months.

3. To use frozen sauce: Thaw in the refrigerator overnight. Place in a saucepan and heat through.

Nutrition Facts: 1/2 cup (calculated without spaghetti) equals 103 calories, 3 g fat (1 g saturated fat), 24 mg cholesterol, 325 mg sodium, 9 g carbohydrate, 2 g fiber, 10 g protein. **Diabetic Exchanges:** 2 vegetable, 1 lean meat.

Makeover Sweet Potato Sausage Skillet

PREP: 20 min. **COOK:** 15 min. **YIELD:** 8 servings

NATALIE SIMONS • AKRON, OHIO

This skillet supper is a real flavor sensation. The Healthy Cooking Test Kitchen transformed it into a much-better-for-you version that you can be proud to serve.

- 3 cups uncooked whole wheat spiral pasta
- 2 medium sweet potatoes, peeled and cut into 1/2-in. cubes
- 1 Tbsp. water
- 8 oz. smoked turkey sausage, cut into 1/4-in. slices
- 1 medium green pepper, chopped
- 1 small onion, chopped
- 1 Tbsp. olive oil
- 1 garlic clove, minced
- 1 can (14-1/2 oz.) diced tomatoes, undrained
- 1 cup half-and-half cream
- 1/4 tsp. salt
- 1/4 tsp. pepper
- 3/4 cup shredded cheddar cheese

1. Cook pasta according to package directions. Meanwhile, place potatoes and water in a microwave-safe bowl. Cover and microwave on high for 4-5 minutes or until potatoes are almost tender.

2. In a large nonstick skillet, cook the sausage, green pepper and onion in oil over medium heat for 5 minutes or until vegetables are tender. Add garlic; cook 1 minute longer.

3. Stir in the tomatoes, cream, salt, pepper and potatoes; heat through. Drain pasta; stir into skillet. Sprinkle with cheese. Cover and let stand for 5 minutes or until cheese is melted.

Nutrition Facts: 1-1/4 cups equals 253 calories, 10 g fat (5 g saturated fat), 44 mg cholesterol, 500 mg sodium, 28 g carbohydrate, 4 g fiber, 12 g protein. **Diabetic Exchanges:** 1-1/2 starch, 1 medium-fat meat, 1 vegetable, 1 fat.

Family-Favorite Taco Salad C

PREP/TOTAL TIME: 20 min. **YIELD:** 6 servings

LYNNE GRAVES • PALISADE, MINNESOTA

This lighter, healthier version of classic Southwestern fare is a tradition with my family. I love the fact that it's delicious and such a fast-to-fix meal on busy weeknights.

- 1-1/2 lbs. lean ground turkey
- 1 can (14-1/2 oz.) diced tomatoes, undrained
- 2 tsp. dried minced onion
- 2 tsp. chili powder
- 1 tsp. garlic powder
- 1 tsp. seasoned salt
- 1/2 tsp. ground cumin
- 1/4 tsp. pepper
- 6 cups shredded lettuce
- 1/2 cup shredded reduced-fat Mexican cheese blend
- 6 Tbsp. fat-free sour cream, optional

1. In a large nonstick skillet, cook turkey over medium heat until meat is no longer pink; drain. Stir in tomatoes and seasonings; heat through.

2. Divide lettuce among six plates; top each with 2/3 cup turkey mixture, 4 tsp. cheese and 1 Tbsp. sour cream if desired.

Nutrition Facts: 1 serving (calculated without sour cream) equals 239 calories, 12 g fat (4 g saturated fat), 99 mg cholesterol, 551 mg sodium, 9 g carbohydrate, 2 g fiber, 25 g protein. **Diabetic Exchanges:** 3 lean meat, 1 vegetable, 1 fat.

MAKEOVER SWEET POTATO SAUSAGE SKILLET

FAMILY-FAVORITE TACO SALAD

Turkey Mole with Rice

PREP: 20 min. COOK: 15 min. YIELD: 4 servings

TRISHA KRUSE • EAGLE, IDAHO

This is a wonderful Tex-Mex dish. A smoky chipotle pepper makes the sauce extra special!

1-1/2 cups chunky salsa
1/4 cup plus 2 Tbsp. unsalted peanuts, *divided*
1 chipotle pepper in adobo sauce
1 Tbsp. lime juice
1/4 tsp. baking cocoa
1 pkg. (20 oz.) turkey breast tenderloins, cut into 1-in. pieces
2 tsp. olive oil
1/3 cup reduced-sodium chicken broth
2 cups cooked brown rice
2 Tbsp. minced fresh cilantro

1. In a food processor, combine the salsa, 1/4 cup peanuts, chipotle pepper, lime juice and cocoa; cover and process until blended.

2. In a large skillet, cook turkey in oil over medium heat for 6-8 minutes or until no longer pink. Add broth and salsa mixture. Bring to a boil. Reduce heat; simmer, uncovered for 10 minutes. Serve with rice; sprinkle with cilantro and remaining nuts.

Nutrition Facts: 1 cup chicken mixture with 1/2 cup rice and 1-1/2 tsp. peanuts equals 393 calories, 12 g fat (2 g saturated fat), 69 mg cholesterol, 514 mg sodium, 32 g carbohydrate, 3 g fiber, 39 g protein. **Diabetic Exchanges:** 5 lean meat, 2 fat, 1-1/2 starch, 1 vegetable.

TURKEY MOLE WITH RICE

Healthy Turkey Burgers

PREP/TOTAL TIME: 20 min. YIELD: 4 servings

CATHERINE VANSTEENKISTE • RAY, MICHIGAN

Even though they're new to his palate, my 81-year-old dad loves these! Savory and sweet, these easy, fun burgers will lure you away from your pub favorite with just one bite.

1/4 cup egg substitute
1/4 cup seasoned bread crumbs
1/4 cup dried cranberries *or* cherries
3 Tbsp. crumbled feta cheese
1 lb. lean ground turkey
4 whole wheat hamburger buns, split

1. In a large bowl, combine the egg substitute, bread crumbs, cranberries and feta cheese. Crumble turkey over mixture and mix well. Shape into four patties.

2. Using long-handled tongs, moisten a paper towel with cooking oil and lightly coat the grill rack. Grill the patties, covered, over medium heat or broil 4 in. from the heat for 5-7 minutes on each side or until a meat thermometer reads 165° and juices run clear. Serve on buns.

Nutrition Facts: 1 burger equals 354 calories, 13 g fat (3 g saturated fat), 92 mg cholesterol, 502 mg sodium, 34 g carbohydrate, 4 g fiber, 27 g protein.

Zippy Turkey and Rice

PREP: 45 min. BAKE: 35 min. YIELD: 8 servings

THOMAS LINDGREN • HACKENSACK, MINNESOTA

Hearty and healthful, this yummy casserole is chock-full of rice, beans, tomatoes and cheese. Serve it with fresh fruit or a side salad for a comforting, satisfying meal.

1 cup uncooked brown rice
1 lb. lean ground turkey
1 large onion, chopped
1 can (14-1/2 oz.) diced tomatoes with mild green chilies, undrained
2/3 cup picante sauce
2 tsp. chili powder
2 tsp. ground cumin
1 can (16 oz.) kidney beans, rinsed and drained
1 cup (4 oz.) shredded reduced-fat cheddar cheese, *divided*

1. Cook rice according to package directions.

2. Meanwhile, in a large nonstick skillet, cook turkey and onion over medium heat until meat is no longer pink; drain. Stir in the tomatoes, picante sauce, chili powder and cumin; heat though. Remove from the heat, stir in kidney beans, 1/2 cup cheese and cooked rice. Transfer to a 13-in. x 9-in. baking dish coated with cooking spray.

3. Cover and bake at 350° for 30 minutes. Uncover; sprinkle with remaining cheese. Bake 5-10 minutes longer or until cheese is melted.

Nutrition Facts: 1-1/4 cups equals 294 calories, 9 g fat (3 g saturated fat), 55 mg cholesterol, 593 mg sodium, 35 g carbohydrate, 5 g fiber, 20 g protein. **Diabetic Exchanges:** 3 lean meat, 1-1/2 starch, 1 vegetable.

HERBED TURKEY TETRAZZINI

Herbed Turkey Tetrazzini

PREP: 30 min. BAKE: 25 min. YIELD: 12 servings

BRIGITTE GARRINGER • COPPER CANYON, TEXAS

There are many versions of this old-fashioned casserole. Mine offers a little more zip due to the thyme and lemon peel. It's a nice way to use up those turkey leftovers.

 6 cups uncooked egg noodles
1/3 cup sliced green onions
 2 Tbsp. olive oil
 1 lb. sliced fresh mushrooms
 3 Tbsp. minced fresh parsley
 1 Tbsp. minced fresh thyme *or* 1 tsp. dried thyme
 2 bay leaves
 1 garlic clove, minced
 2 tsp. grated lemon peel
1/4 cup butter
1/4 cup all-purpose flour
 2 cups chicken broth
 1 egg yolk, lightly beaten
 1 cup milk
 4 cups cubed cooked turkey
Salt and pepper to taste

1/3 cup dry bread crumbs
1/3 cup grated Parmesan cheese
1/2 cup sliced almonds, toasted

1. Cook noodles according to package directions. Meanwhile, in a Dutch oven, saute onions in oil for 3 minutes. Add the mushrooms, parsley, thyme and bay leaves. Cook until mushrooms are lightly browned. Add garlic; cook 1 minute longer. Discard bay leaves.

2. Transfer mushroom mixture to a small bowl; stir in lemon peel and set aside. Drain noodles; set aside.

3. In the Dutch oven, melt butter over medium heat. Stir in flour until smooth. Whisk in broth. Bring to a boil; cook and stir for 2 minutes or until thickened. Combine egg yolk and milk; stir into white sauce. Cook and stir 2 minutes longer.

4. Stir in mushroom mixture and turkey; heat through. Fold in noodles. Season with salt and pepper.

5. Spoon into a greased 13-in. x 9-in. baking dish. Toss bread crumbs and cheese; sprinkle over the top. Bake, uncovered, at 350° for 25-30 minutes or until lightly browned. Sprinkle with almonds.

Nutrition Facts: 1-1/3 cups equals 326 calories, 14 g fat (5 g saturated fat), 91 mg cholesterol, 296 mg sodium, 28 g carbohydrate, 2 g fiber, 22 g protein.

PORK CHOPS WITH HERB PESTO

HAM TETRAZZINI

BAJA PORK TACOS

Pork, Ham & More

Today's health-conscious cooks know the value of setting a hearty, homemade meal on the table. They also know that pork can be a great way to satisfy a hungry crew while keeping fat and calories at bay!

Baja Pork Tacos

PREP: 10 min. COOK: 8 hours YIELD: 12 servings

ARIELLA WINN • MESQUITE, TEXAS

This delicious recipe is my copycat version of the most excellent Mexican food we ever had in Flagstaff, Arizona. The original recipe used beef instead of pork, but this comes mighty close to the same flavor.

    1   boneless pork sirloin roast (3 lbs.)
    5   cans (4 oz. *each*) chopped green chilies
    2   Tbsp. reduced-sodium taco seasoning
    1   Tbsp. ground cumin
    24 corn tortillas (6 in.), warmed
    3   cups shredded lettuce
1-1/2   cups (6 oz.) shredded part-skim mozzarella
        cheese

1. Cut roast in half; place in a 3- or 4-qt. slow cooker. In a small bowl, combine the chilies, taco seasoning and cumin; pour over pork. Cover and cook on low for 8-9 hours or until meat is tender.

2. Remove pork; cool slightly. Skim fat from cooking juices. Shred meat with two forks; return to the slow cooker and heat through. Spoon 1/4 cup onto each tortilla; top each with 2 tablespoons lettuce and 1 tablespoon cheese.

Nutrition Facts: 2 tacos equals 326 calories, 10 g fat (4 g saturated fat), 76 mg cholesterol, 469 mg sodium, 28 g carbohydrate, 4 g fiber, 30 g protein. **Diabetic Exchanges:** 3 lean meat, 2 starch, 1 fat.

Teriyaki Pork

PREP: 10 min. + marinating COOK: 20 min.
YIELD: 4 servings

MOLLY GEE • PLAINWELL, MICHIGAN

I like to season tender pork loin and an assortment of crisp-tender vegetables with a garlicky soy sauce marinade for this savory, no-fuss stir-fry.

    3/4   cup reduced-sodium chicken broth, *divided*
    1/3   cup reduced-sodium soy sauce
    2   Tbsp. red wine vinegar
    2   tsp. honey
    2   tsp. garlic powder

    1   lb. boneless pork loin chops, cut into thin
          strips
    1   Tbsp. canola oil
    2   cups fresh broccoli florets
    3   medium carrots, sliced
    3   celery ribs, sliced
    4   cups shredded cabbage
    6   green onions, sliced
    1   Tbsp. cornstarch
Hot cooked brown rice, optional

1. In a small bowl, combine 1/4 cup broth, soy sauce, vinegar, honey and garlic powder. Pour 1/3 cup marinade into a large resealable plastic bag; add the pork. Seal bag and turn to coat; refrigerate for 1 hour. Cover and refrigerate remaining marinade.

2. Drain and discard marinade. In large nonstick skillet or wok, stir-fry pork in oil for 2-3 minutes or until no longer pink. Remove and keep warm.

3. In the same pan, stir-fry the broccoli and carrots in reserved marinade for 2 minutes. Add the celery; stir-fry for 2 minutes. Add the cabbage and the green onions; stir-fry 2-3 minutes longer or until the vegetables are crisp-tender.

4. Combine cornstarch and remaining broth until smooth; stir into vegetable mixture. Bring to a boil; cook and stir until thickened. Return pork to the pan; heat through. Serve with rice if desired.

Nutrition Facts: 1-1/2 cups (calculated without rice) equals 302 calories, 11 g fat (3 g saturated fat), 63 mg cholesterol, 802 mg sodium, 20 g carbohydrate, 5 g fiber, 30 g protein. **Diabetic Exchanges:** 3 lean meat, 1 starch, 1/2 fat.

Pork products are naturally salty, so keep the sodium down in your final dishes by using seasonings such as garlic and onion powders. These seasonings tend to **absorb moisture** from the air, especially during warm weather months. Store them in airtight spice jars to keep them as free from moisture and humidity as possible.

Pork Tenderloin with Raspberry Dijon Sauce

PREP/TOTAL TIME: 25 min. YIELD: 4 servings

LISA VARNER • CHARLESTON, SOUTH CAROLINA

Try this tempting pork tenderloin with its peppery, slightly sweet raspberry tang for a fast, full-flavored entree your whole family will enjoy.

1	pork tenderloin (1 lb.), cut into 1/2-in. slices
1	tsp. garlic pepper blend
2	tsp. canola oil
1/2	cup seedless raspberry jam
2	Tbsp. red wine vinegar
2	tsp. Dijon mustard

1. Flatten pork slices to 1/4-in. thickness; sprinkle with pepper blend. In a large nonstick skillet coated with cooking spray over medium heat, cook pork in oil in batches for 2-3 minutes on each side or until juices run clear. Remove and keep warm.

2. In the same skillet, add the jam, vinegar and mustard, stirring to loosen browned bits. Bring to a boil. Reduce heat; simmer, uncovered, for 1 minute or until thickened. Serve with pork.

Nutrition Facts: 3 oz. cooked pork with 2 Tbsp. sauce equals 256 calories, 6 g fat (1 g saturated fat), 63 mg cholesterol, 175 mg sodium, 27 g carbohydrate, 0 fiber, 22 g protein. **Diabetic Exchanges:** 3 lean meat, 1-1/2 starch, 1/2 fat.

Onion-Dijon Pork Chops

PREP/TOTAL TIME: 25 min. YIELD: 4 servings

HEALTHY COOKING TEST KITCHEN

Coated in a flavorful sauce, these chops are cooked to tender perfection. Serve with rice and carrots for a full meal.

4	boneless pork loin chops (5 oz. *each*)
1/4	tsp. salt
1/4	tsp. pepper
3/4	cup thinly sliced red onion
1/4	cup water
1/4	cup cider vinegar
3	Tbsp. brown sugar
2	Tbsp. honey Dijon mustard

1. Sprinkle pork chops with salt and pepper. In a large nonstick skillet coated with cooking spray, cook pork over medium heat for 4-6 minutes on each side or until lightly browned. Remove and keep warm.

2. Add the remaining ingredients to the skillet, stirring to loosen browned bits from pan. Bring to a boil; cook and stir for 2 minutes or until thickened. Return chops to the pan. Reduce heat; cover and simmer for 4-5 minutes or until a thermometer reads 160°.

Nutrition Facts: 1 pork chop with 2 Tbsp. onion mixture equals 261 calories, 9 g fat (3 g saturated fat), 69 mg cholesterol, 257 mg sodium, 17 g carbohydrate, 1 g fiber, 28 g protein. **Diabetic Exchanges:** 4 lean meat, 1 starch.

Pork Chops with Cranberry Dijon Sauce c

PREP/TOTAL TIME: 30 min. YIELD: 4 servings

LISA HERRING BRIDGES • ATLANTA, GEORGIA

Here's a rich-tasting dish with bold flavors that blend so well together. Quick yet special, it's a terrific choice for both family and unexpected guests.

PORK TENDERLOIN WITH RASPBERRY DIJON SAUCE

ONION-DIJON PORK CHOPS

1 medium apple, peeled and thinly sliced
2 Tbsp. dried cranberries
2 Tbsp. Dijon mustard
1 Tbsp. cider vinegar
1 Tbsp. honey
1 tsp. Worcestershire sauce
1/8 tsp. dried thyme
1/8 tsp. rubbed sage
1/8 tsp. dried rosemary, crushed
1/8 tsp. pepper
Dash salt

Dash ground nutmeg
4 boneless pork loin chops (4 oz. *each*)
1 Tbsp. butter

1. In a small bowl, combine the first 12 ingredients. In a large skillet coated with cooking spray, brown pork chops in butter. Stir in fruit mixture. Bring to a boil. Reduce heat; cover and simmer for 3-4 minutes on each side or until a thermometer reads 160°.

Nutrition Facts: 1 serving equals 229 calories, 9 g fat (4 g saturated fat), 62 mg cholesterol, 283 mg sodium, 13 g carbohydrate, 1 g fiber, 22 g protein. **Diabetic Exchanges:** 3 lean meat, 1 starch, 1/2 fat.

GLAZED PORK MEDALLIONS

Glazed Pork Medallions [C]

PREP/TOTAL TIME: 30 min. **YIELD:** 4 servings

MICHELE FLAGEL • SHELLSBURG, IOWA

After my husband was told to lower his cholesterol, he was sure he'd never taste good food again. He was so surprised by this entree, which proves you don't have to eat fish every night to keep fat down.

- 1 pork tenderloin (1-1/4 lbs.)
- 1/4 tsp. salt
- 1/3 cup reduced-sugar orange marmalade
- 2 tsp. cider vinegar
- 2 tsp. Worcestershire sauce
- 1/2 tsp. minced fresh gingerroot
- 1/8 tsp. crushed red pepper flakes

1. Cut pork into 1-in. slices and flatten to 1/4-in. thickness; sprinkle with salt. In a large nonstick skillet coated with cooking spray, cook pork in batches over medium-high heat until juices run clear. Reduce heat to low; return all meat to the pan. Combine the remaining ingredients; pour over pork and turn to coat. Heat through.

Nutrition Facts: 4 oz. cooked pork equals 200 calories, 5 g fat (2 g saturated fat), 79 mg cholesterol, 231 mg sodium, 9 g carbohydrate, trace fiber, 28 g protein. **Diabetic Exchanges:** 4 lean meat, 1/2 fruit, 1/2 fat.

Spiced Orange Glaze for Ham [F][S][C]

PREP/TOTAL TIME: 5 min. **YIELD:** 2/3 cup

SUE GRONHOLZ • BEAVER DAM, WISCONSIN

Add something new to your traditional ham with this easy glaze. It covers an 8- to 10-lb. ham and provides about 20 servings. The blend of citrus and spice makes it especially lovely for the holidays.

- 1/4 cup packed brown sugar
- 1/4 cup orange juice
- 2 Tbsp. honey
- 1 Tbsp. stone-ground mustard
- 2 tsp. dried basil
- 1 tsp. grated orange peel
- 1/8 tsp. ground cloves

1. In a small bowl, combine all ingredients. Brush over ham during the last 30 minutes of cooking.

Nutrition Facts: 1-1/2 tsp. equals 20 calories, trace fat (trace saturated fat), 0 cholesterol, 17 mg sodium, 5 g carbohydrate, trace fiber, trace protein. **Diabetic Exchange:** Free food.

Pork Roast with Gravy [C]

PREP: 10 min. **COOK:** 50 min. **YIELD:** 8 servings

JEAN VIRZI LOWREY • DUBACH, LOUISIANA

I've been making this juicy roast for 40 years. Lower in calories, it's a favorite of mine.

- 1 boneless pork sirloin roast (2-1/2 lbs.)
- 1-1/2 tsp. canola oil
- 3/4 cup white wine or chicken broth

- 2 Tbsp. brown sugar
- 2 Tbsp. reduced-sodium soy sauce
- 1 tsp. minced fresh gingerroot
- 1 garlic clove, minced
- 1/2 tsp. chicken bouillon granules
- 4-1/2 tsp. cornstarch
- 4-1/2 tsp. cold water

1. In a Dutch oven, brown roast in oil on all sides. In a small bowl, combine the wine, brown sugar, soy sauce, ginger, garlic and bouillon; pour over roast.

2. Bring to a boil. Reduce heat to low; cover and cook for 45-60 minutes or until a thermometer reads 160°, basting occasionally with pan juices.

3. Remove roast to a serving platter; keep warm. Pour drippings and loosened browned bits into a 2-cup measuring cup; skim fat. Add enough water to measure 1-1/2 cups. Return to the pan.

4. Combine cornstarch and water until smooth; gradually stir into the pan. Bring to a boil; cook and stir for 1-2 minutes or until thickened. Serve with the roast.

Nutrition Facts: 4 oz. cooked pork with 3 Tbsp. gravy equals 241 calories, 9 g fat (3 g saturated fat), 85 mg cholesterol, 262 mg sodium, 5 g carbohydrate, trace fiber, 29 g protein. **Diabetic Exchange:** 4 lean meat.

> Dried herbs don't spoil, but they lose flavor and potency over time. For maximum flavor in your cooking, replace herbs that are more than a year old. Store **dried herbs** in airtight containers and keep them away from heat and light.

PORK ROAST WITH GRAVY

Tangy Pineapple Glaze ⟨F⟩⟨S⟩⟨C⟩

PREP/TOTAL TIME: 5 min. YIELD: 1 cup

JOAN HALLFORD • NORTH RICHLAND HILLS, TEXAS

A few basic ingredients can easily dress up a ham. This glaze will cover an 8- to 10-lb. ham and provides about 20 servings.

- 1 can (8 oz.) unsweetened crushed pineapple, drained
- 1/2 cup apricot jam
- 1 Tbsp. spicy brown mustard
- 2 tsp. prepared horseradish

1. In a small bowl, combine all ingredients. Brush over ham during the last 30 minutes of cooking.

Nutrition Facts: 2-1/2 tsp. equals 27 calories, trace fat (trace saturated fat), 0 cholesterol, 15 mg sodium, 7 g carbohydrate, trace fiber, trace protein. **Diabetic Exchange:** 1/2 starch.

Peachy Pork with Rice

PREP/TOTAL TIME: 30 min. YIELD: 4 servings

MELISSA MOLAISON • HAWKINSVILLE, GEORGIA

Peach preserves sweeten the spicy salsa in this delicious dish that's nice enough for company. Adjust the heat level to taste by using mild or spicy salsa and seasoning.

- 1-1/2 cups instant brown rice
- 1 pork tenderloin (1 lb.), cut into 1-in. cubes
- 2 Tbsp. olive oil
- 2 Tbsp. reduced-sodium taco seasoning
- 1 cup salsa
- 3 Tbsp. peach preserves

1. Cook rice according to package directions. Meanwhile, place pork in a large bowl; drizzle with oil. Sprinkle with taco seasoning; toss to coat.

2. In a large nonstick skillet coated with cooking spray, cook pork for 8-10 minutes or until no longer

pink. Stir in salsa and preserves; heat through. Serve with rice.

Nutrition Facts: 1 cup pork mixture with 1/2 cup rice equals 387 calories, 12 g fat (2 g saturated fat), 63 mg cholesterol, 540 mg sodium, 42 g carbohydrate, 2 g fiber, 25 g protein. **Diabetic Exchanges:** 3 lean meat, 2-1/2 starch, 1-1/2 fat.

Pork with Blueberry Herb Sauce

PREP: 25 min. COOK: 10 min. YIELD: 4 servings

LIBBY WALP • CHICAGO, ILLINOIS

A different and delicious way to use blueberries, this tangy, sweet-savory sauce would also be great over chicken. The blend of berries and balsamic vinegar is wonderful!

- 1 garlic clove, minced
- 1 tsp. pepper
- 1/2 tsp. salt
- 1/8 tsp. cayenne pepper
- 4 boneless pork loin chops (6 oz. *each*)
- 2 cups fresh blueberries
- 1/4 cup packed brown sugar
- 2 Tbsp. minced fresh parsley
- 1 Tbsp. balsamic vinegar
- 2 tsp. butter
- 1 tsp. minced fresh thyme *or* 1/4 tsp. dried thyme
- 1 tsp. fresh sage *or* 1/4 tsp. dried sage leaves

1. In a small bowl, combine the garlic, pepper, salt and cayenne; sprinkle over pork.

2. In a large ovenproof skillet coated with cooking spray, brown pork chops. Bake uncovered, at 350° for 10-15 minutes or until a thermometer reads 160°. Remove pork and keep warm.

3. In the same skillet, add the remaining ingredients. Cook and stir over medium heat until thickened, about 8 minutes. Serve with pork.

Nutrition Facts: 1 pork chop with 1/4 cup sauce equals 343 calories, 12 g fat (5 g saturated fat), 87 mg cholesterol, 364 mg sodium, 25 g carbohydrate, 2 g fiber, 33 g protein. **Diabetic Exchanges:** 5 lean meat, 1 starch, 1/2 fruit.

PEACHY PORK WITH RICE

PORK WITH BLUEBERRY HERB SAUCE

Spice-Rubbed Ham C

PREP: 15 min. **BAKE:** 3-1/4 hours + standing
YIELD: 24 servings

SHARON TIPTON • WINTER GARDEN, FLORIDA

Now this is a ham—sweet and smoky, with just enough clove and ginger flavor to let you know you're in for a holiday treat.

    1   fully cooked semi-boneless ham (8 to 10 lbs.)
    1/2 cup spicy brown mustard
    1/4 cup packed brown sugar
    1/4 tsp. ground ginger
    1/4 tsp. ground cinnamon
    Whole cloves

1. Place ham on a rack in a shallow roasting pan. Score the surface of the ham, making diamond shapes 1/2 in. deep. Combine the mustard, brown sugar, ginger and cinnamon; rub over surface of ham. Insert a clove in each diamond.

2. Bake, uncovered, at 325° for 1-1/2 hours. Cover and bake 1-3/4 to 2 hours longer or until a thermometer reads 140°. Cover loosely with foil if ham browns too quickly. Discard cloves. Let stand for 10 minutes before slicing.

Nutrition Facts: 3 oz. cooked ham equals 139 calories, 4 g fat (1 g saturated fat), 66 mg cholesterol, 858 mg sodium, 3 g carbohydrate, trace fiber, 22 g protein. **Diabetic Exchange:** 3 lean meat.

When a label reads that a ham is "fully cooked" it means that the meat is cooked and smoked and/or cured. The **ham** can be eaten without being warmed, but it is generally heated to an internal temperature of 140° for optimal flavor.

PORK CHOPS
WITH APRICOT GLAZE

Pork Chops
With Apricot Glaze

PREP/TOTAL TIME: 30 min. **YIELD:** 6 servings

KATHY HARDING • RICHMOND, MISSOURI

Wow! What an impressive-looking main course. No one will guess it came together in about a half hour!

1-1/2 tsp. ground ginger
   1 tsp. salt
  1/2 tsp. garlic powder
  1/2 tsp. pepper
   6 boneless pork loin chops (6 oz. *each*)
   1 cup apricot preserves
   2 Tbsp. hoisin sauce
  1/2 tsp. crushed red pepper flakes
   2 green onions, chopped
   3 Tbsp. chopped unsalted peanuts

1. Combine the ginger, salt, garlic powder and pepper; rub over chops. In a small saucepan, combine the preserves, hoisin sauce and pepper flakes. Cook and stir over medium heat until preserves are melted. Set aside 1/2 cup sauce for brushing.

2. Moisten a paper towel with cooking oil; using long-handled tongs, lightly coat the grill rack. Grill pork, covered, over medium heat or broil 4-5 in. from the heat for 4-5 minutes on each side or until a thermometer reads 145°, basting frequently with sauce. Let stand 5 minutes before serving. Brush with reserved sauce before serving; sprinkle with green onions and peanuts.

Nutrition Facts: 1 pork chop equals 399 calories, 12 g fat (4 g saturated fat), 82 mg cholesterol, 549 mg sodium, 39 g carbohydrate, 1 g fiber, 34 g protein.

Raspberry Chipotle Glaze for Ham F S C

PREP/TOTAL TIME: 15 min.
YIELD: 1-2/3 cups (enough for an 8- to 10-lb. ham)

MARY LOU WAYMAN • SALT LAKE CITY, UTAH

A wonderfully different combination of flavors creates my terrific glaze. It easily covers an 8- to 10-lb. ham and provides about 20 servings.

- 1 jar (12 oz.) seedless raspberry jam
- 2 Tbsp. white vinegar
- 2 chipotle peppers in adobo sauce, drained, seeded and minced
- 2 to 3 garlic cloves, minced
- 2 tsp. coarsely ground pepper

1. In a small saucepan, combine the jam, vinegar, peppers and garlic. Bring to a boil. Reduce heat; simmer, uncovered, for 5 minutes. Brush over ham during the last 30 minutes of cooking. Sprinkle with pepper before serving.

Nutrition Facts: 4 tsp. equals 45 calories, trace fat (0 saturated fat), 0 cholesterol, 10 mg sodium, 11 g carbohydrate, trace fiber, trace protein. **Diabetic Exchange:** 1 starch.

Ham Noodle Casserole

PREP: 15 min. **BAKE:** 20 min. **YIELD:** 6 servings

SHERI SWITZER • CRAWFORDVILLE, INDIANA

My mom used to make the original version of this mild curry casserole, which I loved. It didn't fit my healthier eating habits until I made a few changes. Now our entire family can enjoy it without the guilt.

- 6 cups uncooked no-yolk medium noodles
- 1 can (10-3/4 oz.) reduced-fat reduced-sodium condensed cream of celery soup, undiluted
- 1 cup cubed fully cooked lean ham
- 2/3 cup cubed reduced-fat process American cheese
- 1/2 cup fat-free milk
- 1/4 cup thinly sliced green onions
- 1/2 tsp. curry powder

1. Cook noodles according to package directions; drain and place in a large bowl. Stir in the remaining ingredients.

2. Transfer to a 2-1/2-qt. baking dish coated with cooking spray. Cover and bake at 375° for 20-30 minutes or until heated through.

Nutrition Facts: 1 cup equals 241 calories, 4 g fat (2 g saturated fat), 20 mg cholesterol, 725 mg sodium, 35 g carbohydrate, 3 g fiber, 15 g protein. **Diabetic Exchanges:** 2-1/2 starch, 1 lean meat.

Pineapple Pork Tenderloin

PREP: 10 min. + marinating **GRILL:** 30 min.
YIELD: 4 servings

DONNA NOEL • GRAY, MAINE

Just a handful of ingredients creates this easy, elegant entree that pairs juicy, grilled pineapple slices and ginger-flavored pork tenderloin. It's sure to be popular with all ages. It's simply delicious!

- 1 cup unsweetened pineapple juice
- 1/4 cup minced fresh gingerroot
- 1/4 cup reduced-sodium soy sauce
- 4 garlic cloves, minced
- 1 tsp. ground mustard
- 2 pork tenderloins (3/4 lb. *each*)
- 1 fresh pineapple, cut into 12 slices

1. In a small bowl, combine the first five ingredients. Pour 2/3 cup marinade into a large resealable plastic bag. Add the pork; seal bag and turn to coat. Refrigerate for 8 hours or overnight. Cover and refrigerate remaining marinade.

2. Drain and discard marinade. Moisten a paper towel with cooking oil; using long-handled tongs, lightly coat the grill rack.

3. Prepare grill for indirect heat, using a drip pan. Place pork over drip pan and grill, covered, over indirect medium-hot heat for 25-30 minutes or until a thermometer reads 160°, basting occasionally with the reserved marinade. Let stand for 5 minutes before slicing.

4. Meanwhile, grill pineapple slices for 2-3 minutes on each side or until heated through; serve with pork.

Nutrition Facts: 5 oz. cooked pork with 3 pineapple slices equals 295 calories, 6 g fat (2 g saturated fat), 95 mg cholesterol, 523 mg sodium, 23 g carbohydrate, 2 g fiber, 36 g protein. **Diabetic Exchanges:** 5 lean meat, 1 fruit.

Keep tenderloin in the freezer for last-minute meals since it thaws and cooks quickly. Thaw the **pork tenderloin** using the "defrost" cycle of your microwave according to the manufacturer's directions.

PINEAPPLE PORK TENDERLOIN

Makeover Linguine With Ham & Swiss Cheese

PREP: 15 min. **BAKE:** 45 min. **YIELD:** 8 servings

MIKE TCHOU • PEPPER PIKE, OHIO

This rich linguine casserole recipe eliminates nearly half the saturated fat from the original, but keeps the creamy texture and distinctive Swiss cheese flavor.

  8 oz. uncooked multigrain linguine, broken in half
  2 cups cubed fully cooked lean ham
1-3/4 cups (7 oz.) shredded Swiss cheese, *divided*
  1 can (10-3/4 oz.) reduced-fat reduced-sodium condensed cream of mushroom soup, undiluted
  1 cup (8 oz.) reduced-fat sour cream
  1 medium onion, chopped
  1 small green pepper, finely chopped

1. Cook linguine according to package directions. Meanwhile, in a large bowl, combine the ham, 1-1/2 cups cheese, soup, sour cream, onion and green pepper. Drain the pasta; add to the ham mixture and stir to coat.

2. Transfer to a 13-in. x 9-in. baking dish coated with cooking spray. Cover and bake at 350° for 35 minutes. Uncover; sprinkle with remaining cheese. Bake 10-15 minutes longer or until cheese is melted.

Nutrition Facts: 1 cup equals 293 calories, 12 g fat (7 g saturated fat), 47 mg cholesterol, 665 mg sodium, 29 g carbohydrate, 4 g fiber, 19 g protein. **Diabetic Exchanges:** 2 starch, 2 lean meat, 1 fat.

> Feel free to get creative with this **casserole.** Use cream of onion soup or toss in a handful of frozen peas or fresh sliced mushrooms.

MAKEOVER LINGUINE WITH HAM & SWISS CHEESE

Pork Chops with Cherry Sauce

PREP/TOTAL TIME: 25 min. **YIELD:** 2 servings

KENDRA DOSS • KANSAS CITY, MISSOURI

Enjoy the rich flavor of this dish, which is just right for two. The spice rub also works well on lamb or beef.

  1 Tbsp. finely chopped shallot
  1 tsp. olive oil
  1 cup fresh *or* frozen pitted dark sweet cherries, halved
1/3 cup ruby port wine
  1 tsp. balsamic vinegar
1/8 tsp. salt

PORK CHOPS:
  1 tsp. coriander seeds, crushed
3/4 tsp. ground mustard
1/4 tsp. salt
1/4 tsp. pepper
  2 bone-in pork loin chops (7 oz. *each*)
  2 tsp. olive oil

1. In a small saucepan, saute the shallot in oil until tender. Stir in the cherries, wine, vinegar and salt. Bring to a boil; cook until liquid is reduced by half, about 10 minutes.

2. Meanwhile, in a small bowl, combine the coriander, mustard, salt and pepper; rub over chops. In a large skillet, cook chops in oil over medium heat for 4-6 minutes on each side or until a thermometer reads 160°. Serve with sauce.

Nutrition Facts: 1 pork chop with 1/3 cup sauce equals 356 calories, 16 g fat (4 g saturated fat), 86 mg cholesterol, 509 mg sodium, 16 g carbohydrate, 2 g fiber, 32 g protein. **Diabetic Exchanges:** 4 lean meat, 1-1/2 fat, 1 fruit.

Oven-Barbecued Pork Tenderloins [c]

PREP: 5 min. **BAKE:** 35 min. **YIELD:** 6 servings

RUBY WILLIAMS • BOGALUSA, LOUISIANA

Pork tenderloin is one of the leanest cuts of meat. This luscious heirloom recipe is a wonderful way to serve it with very little preparation time.

  3 Tbsp. ketchup
  2 Tbsp. cider vinegar
  1 Tbsp. maple syrup
  2 tsp. Dijon mustard
  1 tsp. Worcestershire sauce
1/8 tsp. cayenne pepper
  2 pork tenderloins (3/4 lb. *each*)

1. In a small bowl, combine the first six ingredients. Place tenderloins on a rack in a shallow roasting pan; spoon some of the sauce over pork.

2. Bake, uncovered, at 425° for 35-40 minutes or until a thermometer reads 160°, basting occasionally with remaining sauce.

3. Let stand for 5 minutes before slicing.

CRUMB-CRUSTED PORK ROAST
WITH ROOT VEGETABLES

Nutrition Facts: 3 oz. cooked pork equals 151 calories, 4 g fat (1 g saturated fat), 63 mg cholesterol, 185 mg sodium, 5 g carbohydrate, trace fiber, 23 g protein. **Diabetic Exchange:** 3 lean meat.

Crumb-Crusted Pork Roast with Root Vegetables

PREP: 25 min. **BAKE:** 1-1/2 hours + standing
YIELD: 8 servings

HEALTHY COOKING TEST KITCHEN

Perfect for fall, this hearty meal combines sweet roasted veggies with a savory crumb coating.

1	boneless pork loin roast (2 to 3 lbs.)
4-1/2 tsp.	honey
1 Tbsp.	molasses
1-1/2 tsp.	spicy brown mustard
2 tsp.	rubbed sage
1 tsp.	dried thyme
1 tsp.	dried rosemary, crushed
1/2 cup	soft whole wheat bread crumbs
2 Tbsp.	grated Parmesan cheese
1	large celery root, peeled and cut into 1/2-in. cubes
1	large rutabaga, peeled and cut into 1/2-in. cubes
1	large sweet potato, peeled and cut into 1/2-in. cubes
1	large onion, cut into wedges
2 Tbsp.	canola oil
1/2 tsp.	salt
1/4 tsp.	pepper

1. Place roast on a rack in a shallow roasting pan coated with cooking spray. In a small bowl, combine the honey, molasses and mustard; brush over roast. In another small bowl, combine the sage, thyme and rosemary; set aside. Combine the bread crumbs, Parmesan cheese and 2 tsp. of the herb mixture; press onto roast.

2. In a resealable plastic bag, combine the celery root, rutabaga, sweet potato, onion, oil, salt, pepper and remaining herb mixture; toss to coat. Arrange vegetables around roast.

3. Bake, uncovered, at 350° for 1-1/2 to 1-3/4 hours or until a thermometer reads 160°. Transfer to a warm serving platter. Let stand for 10-15 minutes before slicing.

Nutrition Facts: 3 oz. cooked pork with 3/4 cup vegetables equals 302 calories, 10 g fat (2 g saturated fat), 57 mg cholesterol, 313 mg sodium, 29 g carbohydrate, 5 g fiber, 25 g protein. **Diabetic Exchanges:** 3 lean meat, 2 starch, 1/2 fat.

SPICY PORK
TENDERLOIN

Spicy Pork Tenderloin

PREP: 20 min. + chilling **GRILL:** 25 min.
YIELD: 4 servings (2 cups salsa)

CAROLYN CARTELLI • PARSIPPANY, NEW JERSEY

Cool, sweet mango salsa melds with the spicy rub on this pork tenderloin for a delicious, bold-flavored main dish. The colors and presentation are elegant.

1	pork tenderloin (1 lb.)
1	Tbsp. olive oil
2	tsp. coarsely ground pepper
1-1/2	tsp. paprika
1/2	tsp. salt
1/2	tsp. garlic powder
1/2	tsp. chili powder
1/2	tsp. ground cinnamon
1/4	tsp. cayenne pepper

MANGO SALSA:

1	medium mango, peeled and cubed
2	Tbsp. minced fresh cilantro
2	Tbsp. lime juice
1	Tbsp. honey

1. Rub pork with oil. Combine the pepper, paprika, salt, garlic powder, chili powder, cinnamon and cayenne; rub over pork. Refrigerate for 30 minutes.

2. Using long-handled tongs, moisten a paper towel with cooking oil and lightly coat the grill rack. Prepare grill for indirect heat using a drip pan. Place pork over drip pan and grill, covered, over indirect medium-hot heat for 25-30 minutes or until a thermometer reads 160°. Let stand for 5 minutes before slicing.

3. In a small bowl, combine the mango, cilantro, lime juice and honey; serve with pork.

Nutrition Facts: 3 oz. cooked pork with 1/2 cup salsa equals 222 calories, 8 g fat (2 g saturated fat), 63 mg cholesterol, 345 mg sodium, 16 g carbohydrate, 2 g fiber, 23 g protein. **Diabetic Exchanges:** 3 lean meat, 1/2 starch, 1/2 fruit, 1/2 fat.

Pork Chops Charcuterie C

PREP: 25 min. **COOK:** 25 min. **YIELD:** 4 servings

MONIQUE HOOKER • DESOTO, WISCONSIN

The peppery Dijon-mustard sauce spooned over these tender chops makes for a recipe special enough to serve guests.

- 4 boneless pork loin chops (5 oz. *each*)
- 1 to 3 tsp. pepper
- 4-1/2 tsp. olive oil
- 1 small onion, finely chopped
- 4 shallots, finely chopped
- 1 cup reduced-sodium beef broth
- 1/2 cup white wine *or* additional reduced-sodium beef broth
- 2 Tbsp. Dijon mustard
- 2 Tbsp. chopped celery leaves *or* minced fresh parsley

1. Sprinkle pork chops with pepper. In a large nonstick skillet coated with cooking spray, brown chops in oil. Remove and keep warm. In the same skillet, saute onion and shallots until tender. Add broth and wine, stirring to loosen browned bits from skillet. Bring to a boil. Reduce heat; simmer, uncovered, for 3 minutes.

2. Return chops to skillet. Cover and cook 8-10 minutes longer or until meat is tender. Place chops on a serving platter and keep warm. Stir mustard into skillet. Return to a boil. Reduce heat; simmer, uncovered, for 12-15 minutes or until sauce is thickened. Spoon sauce over chops; sprinkle with celery leaves.

Nutrition Facts: 1 pork chop with 1/4 cup sauce equals 292 calories, 13 g fat (4 g saturated fat), 70 mg cholesterol, 339 mg sodium, 11 g carbohydrate, 1 g fiber, 29 g protein. **Diabetic Exchanges:** 4 lean meat, 1 starch, 1 fat.

> Cuts of pork vary little in tenderness. Use dry-heat cooking methods (broiling, grilling, roasting and stir-frying) when a **firm texture** is desired.

PORK CHOPS CHARCUTERIE

Honey-Glazed Ham C

PREP: 10 min. COOK: 4-1/2 hours YIELD: 14 servings

JACQUIE STOLZ • LITTLE SIOUX, IOWA

Here's an easy solution for feeding a large group. The simple ham is perfect for family dinners where time in the kitchen is as valuable as space in the oven.

1	boneless fully cooked ham (4 lbs.)
1-1/2	cups ginger ale
1/4	cup honey
1/2	tsp. ground mustard
1/2	tsp. ground cloves
1/4	tsp. ground cinnamon

Sour cream, optional

1. Cut ham in half; place in a 5-qt. slow cooker. Pour ginger ale over ham. Cover and cook on low for 4-5 hours or until heated through.

2. Combine honey, mustard, cloves and cinnamon; stir until smooth. Spread over ham; cook 30 minutes longer. Garnish with the sour cream if desired.

Nutrition Facts: 4 oz. ham equals 166 calories, 5 g fat (2 g saturated fat), 66 mg cholesterol, 1,347 mg sodium, 8 g carbohydrate, trace fiber, 24 g protein.

HONEY-GLAZED HAM

Pork Chops with Scalloped Potatoes

PREP: 30 min. COOK: 8 hours YIELD: 6 servings

ELIZABETH JOHNSTON • GLENDALE, ARIZONA

This is a wonderful dish. My sister gave me the recipe as a casserole baked in the oven, but I've also fixed it in the slow cooker and on the stovetop. Everyone who has tasted it loves it. It's a homey meal that feels Sunday-special.

4	medium potatoes, peeled and thinly sliced
6	bone-in pork loin chops (7 oz. *each*)
1	Tbsp. canola oil
2	large onions, sliced and separated into rings
2	tsp. butter
3	Tbsp. all-purpose flour
1/4	tsp. salt
1/4	tsp. pepper
1	can (14-1/2 oz.) reduced-sodium chicken broth
1	cup fat-free milk

1. Place potatoes in a 5- or 6-qt. slow cooker coated with cooking spray. In a large nonstick skillet, brown pork chops in oil in batches.

2. Place chops over potatoes. Saute onions in drippings until tender; place over chops. Melt butter in skillet. Combine the flour, salt, pepper and broth until smooth. Stir into pan. Add milk. Bring to a boil; cook and stir for 2 minutes or until thickened.

3. Pour sauce over onions. Cover and cook on low for 8-10 hours or until pork is tender. Skim fat and thicken cooking juices if desired.

Nutrition Facts: 1 pork chop with 3/4 cup potatoes equals 372 calories, 12 g fat (4 g saturated fat), 90 mg cholesterol, 389 mg sodium, 29 g carbohydrate, 2 g fiber, 35 g protein. **Diabetic Exchanges:** 4 lean meat, 2 starch, 1 fat.

PORK CHOPS WITH SCALLOPED POTATOES

GLAZED PORK WITH STRAWBERRY COUSCOUS

Glazed Pork with Strawberry Couscous

PREP: 15 min. **BAKE:** 1 hour 20 min. + standing
YIELD: 10 servings

BERNICE JANOWSKI • STEVENS POINT, WISCONSIN

This is a delicious dish I often serve guests. I typically save it for when mint and strawberries are plentiful in my garden.

    2 tsp. dried marjoram
    1 tsp. salt
    1 tsp. seasoned pepper
    1 bone-in pork loin roast (5 lbs.)
  1/2 cup seedless strawberry jam
  1/2 cup orange juice, divided
    1 can (14-1/2 oz.) chicken broth
    1 pkg. (10 oz.) plain couscous
    1 cup fresh strawberries, quartered
  1/4 cup minced fresh mint
    2 tsp. grated orange peel

1. Line the bottom of a large shallow roasting pan with foil; set aside. Combine the marjoram, salt and pepper; rub over roast. Place in pan. Bake, uncovered, at 350° for 1 hour.

2. Combine jam and 1/4 cup orange juice; brush half over pork. Bake 20-30 minutes longer or until a meat thermometer reads 160°, basting with remaining jam mixture every 10 minutes. Let stand for 10 minutes before slicing.

3. Meanwhile, in a small saucepan, bring broth to a boil. Stir in couscous. Cover and remove from the heat; let stand for 5 minutes or until liquid is absorbed. Fluff with a fork; stir in the strawberries, mint, orange peel and remaining orange juice. Serve with pork.

Nutrition Facts: 4 oz. cooked meat with 1/2 cup couscous mixture equals 383 calories, 11 g fat (4 g saturated fat), 92 mg cholesterol, 493 mg sodium, 35 g carbohydrate, 2 g fiber, 36 g protein. **Diabetic Exchanges:** 4 lean meat, 2 starch, 1 fat.

Have leftover pork? Freeze it in a resealable storage bag. Each time you have **extra pork,** add it to the bag. When the bag is full, set the contents in a slow cooker and cover with your favorite barbecue sauce. Set to low and cook until heated through. Shred the pork for sandwiches.

Apple Pork Roast c

PREP: 35 min.   **BAKE:** 1-1/4 hours + standing
YIELD: 10 servings

FLORENCE LAPOINTE • DRYDEN, ONTARIO

This is a delicious way to make a pork roast, and it's my husband's favorite. The gravy is very tasty without all of the fat. The flavors of apple and apricot lend a delightful touch.

1	boneless pork loin roast (3 lbs.)
2	garlic cloves, sliced
2	Tbsp. Dijon mustard
1	tsp. red wine vinegar
3/4	tsp. dried thyme
1/2	tsp. rubbed sage
3/4	cup reduced-sodium beef broth
3/4	cup unsweetened apple juice
1/4	cup apricot jam
1-1/2	cups chopped peeled apples
1	Tbsp. cornstarch
1	Tbsp. reduced-fat sour cream

1. Cut eight to ten 1-in. slits in top of roast; insert garlic slices. In a large nonstick skillet coated with cooking spray, brown roast on all sides. Transfer to a roasting pan.

2. In a small bowl, combine the mustard, vinegar, thyme and sage; brush over roast. In a small saucepan, combine the broth, apple juice and jam. Cook and stir over medium heat until jam is melted; pour over roast. Arrange apples around roast.

3. Cover and bake at 350° for 1-1/4 to 1-1/2 hours or until a meat thermometer reads 160°, basting occasionally. Remove roast to a warm serving platter; let stand for 10 minutes before slicing.

4. Meanwhile, skim fat from pan juices. Set aside 1/2 cup juices; pour remaining juices and apples into a large saucepan. Combine cornstarch and sour cream until smooth; stir into reserved pan juices. Stir into saucepan. Bring to a boil over medium heat; cook and stir for 2 minutes or until slightly thickened. Serve with roast.

Nutrition Facts: 4 oz. cooked pork with 1/4 cup gravy equals 278 calories, 10 g fat (4 g saturated fat), 84 mg cholesterol, 158 mg sodium, 11 g carbohydrate, 1 g fiber, 33 g protein. **Diabetic Exchanges:** 4 lean meat, 1 starch.

Simple Sweet Pork Chops

PREP: 10 min.   **BAKE:** 40 min.   **YIELD:** 6 servings

SHERRI MELOTIK • OAK CREEK, WISCONSIN

Simple enough to whip up for busy weeknights, these tender pork chops are all juiced up with sweet pineapple and just the right touch of jalapeno. They're perfect for the whole family.

6 boneless pork loin chops (6 oz. *each*)
1 can (20 oz.) unsweetened pineapple chunks, undrained
3 Tbsp. brown sugar
1 jalapeno pepper, seeded and finely chppped
1 Tbsp. reduced-sodium soy sauce
1/2 tsp. chili powder
1/4 tsp. garlic powder

1. Place pork chops in a 13-in. x 9-in. baking dish coated with cooking spray. Combine remaining ingredients; pour over chops. Cover and bake at 350° for 30 minutes. Bake, uncovered, 10-15 minutes longer or until a meat thermometer reads 160°.

Editor's Note: When cutting hot peppers, disposable gloves are recommended. Avoid touching your face.

Nutrition Facts: 1 pork chop with about 1/3 cup sauce equals 303 calories, 10 g fat (4 g saturated fat), 82 mg cholesterol, 161 mg sodium, 19 g carbohydrate, 1 g fiber, 33 g protein. **Diabetic Exchanges:** 5 lean meat, 1 fruit.

Jambalaya

PREP: 20 min. COOK: 6-1/4 hours YIELD: 12 servings

SHERRY HUNTWORK • GRETNA, NEBRASKA

Sausage, chicken and shrimp keep this dish hearty and satisfying. Made easy with canned items and other kitchen staples, it's ideal for casual get-togethers.

1 lb. smoked Polish sausage, cut into 1/2-in. slices
1/2 lb. boneless skinless chicken breasts, cut into 1-in. cubes
1 can (14-1/2 oz.) beef broth
1 can (14-1/2 oz.) diced tomatoes, undrained
2 celery ribs, chopped
1/3 cup tomato paste
4 garlic cloves, minced
1 Tbsp. dried parsley flakes
1-1/2 tsp. dried basil
1 tsp. cayenne pepper
1/2 tsp. salt
1/2 tsp. dried oregano
1 lb. cooked medium shrimp, peeled and deveined
2 cups cooked rice

1. In a 5-qt. slow cooker, combine the first 12 ingredients. Cover and cook on low for 6-7 hours or until chicken is no longer pink.

2. Stir in shrimp and rice. Cover and cook 15 minutes longer or until heated through.

Nutrition Facts: 1 cup equals 228 calories, 11 g fat (4 g saturated fat), 95 mg cholesterol, 693 mg sodium, 12 g carbohydrate, 1 g fiber, 18 g protein.

Ham Tetrazzini

PREP: 15 min. COOK: 4 hours YIELD: 5 servings

SUSAN BLAIR • STERLING, MICHIGAN

I modified a recipe that came with my slow cooker to reduce the fat without sacrificing taste. I've served this at parties, family dinners and potlucks. Everyone is pleasantly surprised to find they're eating healthy.

1 can (10-3/4 oz.) reduced-sodium condensed cream of mushroom soup, undiluted
1 cup sliced fresh mushrooms
1 cup cubed fully cooked ham
1/2 cup fat-free evaporated milk
2 Tbsp. white wine *or* water
1 tsp. prepared horseradish
1 pkg. (7 oz.) spaghetti
1/2 cup shredded Parmesan cheese

1. In a 3-qt. slow cooker, combine the soup, mushrooms, ham, milk, wine and horseradish. Cover and cook on low for 4 hours.

2. Cook spaghetti according to package directions; drain. Add the spaghetti and cheese to slow cooker; toss to coat.

Nutrition Facts: 1 cup equals 290 calories, 6 g fat (3 g saturated fat), 24 mg cholesterol, 759 mg sodium, 39 g carbohydrate, 2 g fiber, 16 g protein. **Diabetic Exchanges:** 2-1/2 starch, 1 lean meat, 1/2 fat.

HAM TETRAZZINI

JAMBALAYA

Pork Chop Cacciatore

PREP: 30 min. COOK: 8 hours YIELD: 6 servings

TRACY HIATT GRICE • SOMERSET, WISCONSIN

It's hard to believe the wonderful flavor of these tender chops could come from such an easy recipe! Pair it with noodles and a simple green salad, and dinner's served.

  6 bone-in pork loin chops (7 oz. *each*)
3/4 tsp. salt, *divided*
1/4 tsp. pepper
  1 Tbsp. olive oil
  1 cup sliced fresh mushrooms
  1 small onion, chopped
  1 celery rib, chopped
  1 small green pepper, chopped
  2 garlic cloves, minced
  1 can (14-1/2 oz.) diced tomatoes
1/2 cup water, *divided*
1/2 tsp. dried basil
  2 Tbsp. cornstarch
4-1/2 cups cooked egg noodles

1. Sprinkle chops with 1/2 tsp. salt and pepper. In a large skillet, brown chops in oil in batches. Transfer to a 4- or 5-qt. slow cooker coated with cooking spray. Saute the mushrooms, onion, celery and green pepper in drippings until tender. Add the garlic; cook 1 minute longer. Stir in the tomatoes, 1/4 cup water, basil and remaining salt; pour over chops.

2. Cover and cook on low for 8-9 hours or until pork is tender. Remove meat to a serving platter; keep warm. Skim fat from cooking juices if necessary;

transfer to a small saucepan. Bring liquid to a boil. Combine cornstarch and remaining water until smooth. Gradually stir into the pan. Bring to a boil; cook and stir for 2 minutes or until thickened. Serve with meat and noodles.

Nutrition Facts: 1 pork chop with 3/4 cup noodles and 1/2 cup sauce equals 371 calories, 12 g fat (4 g saturated fat), 110 mg cholesterol, 458 mg sodium, 29 g carbohydrate, 3 g fiber, 35 g protein. **Diabetic Exchanges:** 4 lean meat, 1-1/2 starch, 1 vegetable, 1/2 fat.

Pizza Lover's Pie

PREP: 20 min. BAKE: 20 min. YIELD: 8 servings

CAROL GILLESPIE • CHAMBERSBURG, PENNSYLVANIA

Love pizza? Then you'll adore the tasty spin this recipe puts on it. Plus, it's virtually effortless to tailor for picky eaters.

1/4 lb. bulk pork sausage
1/2 cup chopped green pepper
1/4 cup chopped onion
  1 loaf (1 lb.) frozen bread dough, thawed and halved
  2 cups (8 oz.) shredded part-skim mozzarella cheese
1/2 cup grated Parmesan cheese
  1 can (8 oz.) pizza sauce
  8 slices pepperoni
  1 can (4 oz.) mushroom stems and pieces, drained
1/4 tsp. dried oregano

1. In a large skillet, cook the sausage, pepper and onion over medium heat until meat is no longer pink; drain. Set aside.

2. Roll half of dough into a 12-in. circle. Transfer to a greased 9-in. deep-dish pie plate. Layer with half of the mozzarella cheese, Parmesan cheese and pizza sauce. Top with the sausage mixture, pepperoni, mushrooms and 1/8 teaspoon oregano.

PORK CHOP CACCIATORE

PIZZA LOVER'S PIE

PORK CHOPS WITH HERB PESTO

3. Roll out remaining dough to fit top of pie. Place over filling; seal edges. Layer with remaining pizza sauce, cheeses and oregano.

4. Bake at 400° for 18-22 minutes or until crust is golden brown.

Nutrition Facts: 1 piece equals 305 calories, 12 g fat (5 g saturated fat), 27 mg cholesterol, 743 mg sodium, 32 g carbohydrate, 3 g fiber, 17 g protein. **Diabetic Exchanges:** 2 starch, 2 medium-fat meat.

Pork Chops With Herb Pesto c

PREP: 15 min. + marinating GRILL: 10 min.
YIELD: 4 servings

LISA BYNUM • BRANDON, MISSISSIPPI

You won't believe how much a handful of fresh garden herbs can pump up the flavor of ordinary pork chops when you try this easy entree. These juicy chops would be fantastic alongside garlic mashed potatoes.

  4 bone-in pork loin chops (3/4 in. thick and 7 oz. *each*)
1/4 tsp. salt
1/8 tsp. pepper
  2 Tbsp. water
  1 Tbsp. *each* minced fresh rosemary, sage, thyme, parsley and basil
  1 Tbsp. olive oil
  3 garlic cloves, minced

1. Sprinkle pork with salt and pepper. In a small bowl, combine the water, herbs, oil and garlic; brush over both sides of chops. Cover and refrigerate for at least 1 hour.

2. Using long-handled tongs, moisten a paper towel with cooking oil and lightly coat the grill rack. Grill chops, covered, over medium heat or broil 4 in. from the heat for 4-5 minutes on each side or until a meat thermometer reads 160°.

Nutrition Facts: 1 pork chop equals 241 calories, 12 g fat (4 g saturated fat), 86 mg cholesterol, 212 mg sodium, 1 g carbohydrate, trace fiber, 30 g protein. **Diabetic Exchanges:** 4 lean meat, 1 fat.

Slow-Cooked Pork and Beans

PREP: 15 min. COOK: 6 hours YIELD: 12 servings

PATRICIA HAGER • NICHOLASVILLE, KENTUCKY

I like to get this dish started before leaving for work in the morning. When I get home, my supper's ready! It's a hearty slow cooker meal that is also good for a potluck. A generous helping of tender pork and beans is perfect alongside a slice of warm corn bread.

  1 boneless whole pork loin roast (3 lbs.)
  1 medium onion, sliced
  3 cans (15 oz. *each*) pork and beans
1-1/2 cups barbecue sauce
1/4 cup packed brown sugar
  1 tsp. garlic powder

1. Cut roast in half; place in a 5-qt. slow cooker. Top with onion. In a large bowl, combine the beans, barbecue sauce, brown sugar and garlic powder; pour over meat. Cover and cook on low for 6 hours or until meat is tender.

2. Remove roast; shred with two forks. Return meat to slow cooker; heat through.

Nutrition Facts: 1 cup equals 217 calories, 6 g fat (2 g saturated fat), 56 mg cholesterol, 404 mg sodium, 16 g carbohydrate, 2 g fiber, 24 g protein.

Tangy Barbecued Pork Chops ⓒ

PREP: 35 min. **BAKE:** 25 min. **YIELD:** 6 servings

NELLA PARKER • HERSEY, MICHIGAN

This tasty pork dish makes a great entree and has become a family tradition over the years. It's lower in carbs, and the sweet, tangy sauce is fantastic served over chicken, too. I make extra sauce when I'm serving mashed potatoes.

  1 medium onion, sliced
1/2 cup water
  3 Tbsp. cider vinegar
  2 Tbsp. sugar
  1 Tbsp. prepared mustard
  1 lemon slice
1/4 tsp. salt
1/4 tsp. pepper
1/8 tsp. crushed red pepper flakes
1/2 cup ketchup
  2 Tbsp. Worcestershire sauce
  1 tsp. liquid smoke, optional
  6 bone-in pork loin chops (7 oz. *each*)
  1 Tbsp. canola oil

1. In a small saucepan, combine the first nine ingredients. Bring to a boil. Reduce heat: simmer, uncovered, for 20 minutes. Stir in the ketchup, Worcestershire sauce and liquid smoke if desired; heat through. Discard lemon.

2. Meanwhile, in a large skillet, brown pork chops in oil in batches. Transfer to a 13-in. x 9-in. baking dish coated with cooking spray; pour sauce over chops.

3. Cover and bake at 350° for 25-30 minutes or until a meat thermometer reads 160°.

Nutrition Facts: 1 chop equals 279 calories, 11 g fat (3 g saturated fat), 86 mg cholesterol, 500 mg sodium, 13 g carbohydrate, 1 g fiber, 31 g protein. **Diabetic Exchanges:** 4 lean meat, 1 starch.

Creamy Pepperoni Ziti

PREP: 15 min. **BAKE:** 25 min. **YIELD:** 9 servings

CHARLANE GATHY • LEXINGTON, KENTUCKY

You can easily feed a crowd with this simple dish that's ready in about 40 minutes. Its comforting flair will make it a fast favorite at your next potluck or weeknight dinner.

  1 pkg. (16 oz.) ziti or small tube pasta
  1 can (10-3/4 oz.) condensed cream of mushroom soup, undiluted
3/4 cup shredded part-skim mozzarella cheese
3/4 cup chopped pepperoni
1/2 cup *each* chopped onion, mushrooms, green pepper and tomato
1/2 cup half-and-half cream
1/4 cup chicken broth
1/4 tsp. salt
1/4 tsp. garlic powder
1/4 tsp. pepper
1/2 cup grated Parmesan cheese

1. Cook pasta according to package directions; drain. In a large bowl, combine the pasta, soup, mozzarella cheese, pepperoni, onion, mushrooms, green pepper, tomato, cream, broth and seasonings.

2. Transfer to a greased 13-in. x 9-in. baking dish. Sprinkle with Parmesan cheese. Cover and bake at 350° for 20 minutes. Uncover; bake 5-10 minutes longer or until bubbly.

Nutrition Facts: 1 cup equals 340 calories, 12 g fat (6 g saturated fat), 27 mg cholesterol, 696 mg sodium, 43 g carbohydrate, 2 g fiber, 15 g protein. **Diabetic Exchanges:** 3 starch, 1 high-fat meat, 1/2 fat.

Old-Fashioned Lamb Stew

PREP: 20 min. **COOK:** 3 hours **YIELD:** 10-12 servings

MICHELLE WISE • SPRING MILLS, PENNSYLVANIA

This hearty stew is chock-full of tender lamb chunks and lots of vegetables. Sometimes, I prepare this recipe in my slow cooker.

- 1/4 cup all-purpose flour
- 1 tsp. salt
- 1/2 tsp. pepper
- 3 lbs. boneless lamb, cut into 3-in. pieces
- 2 Tbsp. canola oil
- 1 can (28 oz.) diced tomatoes, undrained
- 1 medium onion, cut into eighths
- 1 Tbsp. dried parsley flakes
- 2 tsp. dried rosemary, crushed
- 1/4 tsp. garlic powder
- 4 large carrots, cut into 1/2-in. pieces
- 4 medium potatoes, peeled and cut into 1-in. pieces
- 1 pkg. (10 oz.) frozen peas
- 1 can (4 oz.) mushroom stems and pieces, drained

1. In a large resealable plastic bag, combine flour, salt and pepper; add lamb and toss to coat. In a Dutch oven, brown the lamb in oil; drain. Add tomatoes, onion, parsley, rosemary and garlic powder. Cover and simmer for 2 hours.

2. Add carrots and potatoes; cover and cook 1 hour longer or until the meat is tender. Add peas and mushrooms; heat through. Thicken if desired.

Nutrition Facts: 1 cup equals 273 calories, 8 g fat (2 g saturated fat), 74 mg cholesterol, 426 mg sodium, 22 g carbohydrate, 4 g fiber, 27 g protein.

Sausage Pizza

PREP: 20 min. **BAKE:** 15 min. **YIELD:** 8 slices

HEALTHY COOKING TEST KITCHEN

Spicy sausage, onions, mushrooms and plenty of cheese make this pizza from our home economists a real keeper. It beats the delivery variety every time—and there's no wait! Bake up two or more and keep one on hand for busy nights.

- 1 loaf (1 lb.) frozen bread dough, thawed
- 3/4 lb. bulk hot Italian sausage
- 1/2 cup sliced onion
- 1/2 cup sliced fresh mushrooms
- 1/2 cup chopped green pepper
- 1/2 cup pizza sauce
- 2 cups (8 oz.) shredded part-skim mozzarella cheese

1. With greased fingers, pat dough onto an ungreased 12-in. pizza pan. Prick dough thoroughly with a fork. Bake at 400° for 10-12 minutes or until lightly browned. Meanwhile, in a large skillet, cook the sausage, onion, mushrooms and green pepper over medium heat until sausage is no longer pink; drain.

2. Spread pizza sauce over crust. Top with sausage mixture; sprinkle with cheese. Bake at 400° for 12-15 minutes or until golden brown. Or wrap pizza and freeze for up to 2 months.

3. To use frozen pizza: Unwrap and place on a pizza pan; thaw in the refrigerator. Bake at 400° for 18-22 minutes or until golden brown.

Nutrition Facts: 1 slice (prepared with turkey sausage and reduced-fat cheese) equals 311 calories, 11 g fat (4 g saturated fat), 39 mg cholesterol, 754 mg sodium, 33 g carbohydrate, 2 g fiber, 20 g protein. **Diabetic Exchanges:** 2 starch, 1-1/2 lean meat, 1-1/2 fat.

To quickly use a huge supply of **garden tomatoes**, wash and core them, then puree them in the blender with lemon juice, onion and celery for a delicious vegetable juice. You can even simmer several batches until slightly thickened for a healthy spaghetti sauce or until very thick for pizza sauce. Freeze the extras.

SAUSAGE PIZZA

Applesauce-Glazed Pork Chops

PREP/TOTAL TIME: 30 min. YIELD: 4 servings

BRENDA CAMPBELL • OLYMPIA, WASHINGTON

Perfect for hectic weeknights, this half-hour entree easily satisfies. The tender chops get special treatment from an effortless sauce.

- 4 bone-in pork loin chops (7 oz. each)
- 1 cup unsweetened applesauce
- 1/4 cup packed brown sugar
- 1 Tbsp. barbecue sauce
- 1 Tbsp. Worcestershire sauce
- 1 garlic clove, minced
- 1/2 tsp. salt
- 1/2 tsp. pepper

1. Place pork chops in a 13-in. x 9-in. baking dish coated with cooking spray. In a small bowl, combine the remaining ingredients; spoon over chops.

2. Bake, uncovered, at 350° for 20-25 minutes or until a meat thermometer reads 160°.

Nutrition Facts: 1 pork chop with 1/3 cup sauce equals 291 calories, 9 g fat (3 g saturated fat), 86 mg cholesterol, 442 mg sodium, 22 g carbohydrate, 1 g fiber, 30 g protein. **Diabetic Exchanges:** 4 lean meat, 1 starch, 1/2 fruit.

APPLESAUCE-GLAZED PORK CHOPS

Makeover Rigatoni With Bacon and Asparagus

PREP: 25 min. COOK: 20 min. YIELD: 8 servings

JOANIE FUSON • INDIANAPOLIS, INDIANA

Wouldn't it be great to find a company-worthy dish that not only impresses with its taste, but with its nutrition numbers, too? That's just what I got when I asked the Healthy Cooking team to lighten up my rigatoni dish.

- 1 pkg. (16 oz.) spiral pasta
- 1 lb. fresh asparagus, trimmed and coarsely chopped
- 8 bacon strips
- 1 garlic clove, minced
- 2 Tbsp. butter
- 1 Tbsp. olive oil
- 2/3 cup half-and-half cream
- 1/2 cup shredded part-skim mozzarella cheese
- 1/2 tsp. salt
- 1/4 cup minced fresh parsley
- 1/8 tsp. coarsely ground pepper
- 1/4 cup grated Parmigiano-Reggiano cheese

1. Cook pasta according to package directions.

2. Meanwhile, in a Dutch oven, bring 2 cups water to a boil. Add asparagus; cover and boil for 3 minutes. Drain and immediately place asparagus in ice water. Drain and pat dry.

3. In the same pan, cook bacon over medium heat until crisp. Remove to paper towels to drain. Crumble bacon and set aside.

4. Saute garlic in butter and oil until tender. Stir in cream. Bring to a boil. Reduce heat; simmer, uncovered, for 3-4 minutes or until slightly thickened.

5. Stir in mozzarella cheese until melted. Drain pasta; add to pan. Stir in the salt, asparagus, parsley and reserved bacon. Sprinkle with pepper and Parmigiano-Reggiano cheese.

MAKEOVER RIGATONI WITH BACON AND ASPARAGUS

ASIAN PORK TENDERLOIN

Nutrition Facts: 1-1/4 cups equals 345 calories, 13 g fat (6 g saturated fat), 32 mg cholesterol, 428 mg sodium, 44 g carbohydrate, 2 g fiber, 15 g protein.

Asian Pork Tenderloin c

PREP: 10 min. + marinating BAKE: 20 min.
YIELD: 6 servings

APRIL LANE • GREENEVILLE, TENNESSEE

This quick-to-prepare entree bursts with flavor. Throw together the marinade before work, so it's ready to toss together when you walk through the door at night.

1/3	cup packed brown sugar
1/3	cup reduced-sodium soy sauce
2	Tbsp. lemon juice
2	Tbsp. sesame oil
2	Tbsp. Worcestershire sauce
4	garlic cloves, minced
1	Tbsp. ground mustard
1	tsp. pepper
2	pork tenderloins (3/4 lb. *each*)

1. In a small bowl, combine the first eight ingredients. Pour 1/2 cup marinade into a large resealable plastic bag. Add the pork; seal bag and turn to coat. Refrigerate for 8 hours or overnight. Cover and refrigerate remaining marinade.

2. Drain and discard marinade. Place pork on a rack in a shallow roasting pan. Bake at 450° for 20-25 minutes or until a meat thermometer reads 160°, basting occasionally with reserved marinade. Let stand for 5 minutes before slicing.

Nutrition Facts: 3 oz. cooked pork equals 218 calories, 8 g fat (2 g saturated fat), 63 mg cholesterol, 510 mg sodium, 12 g carbohydrate, trace fiber, 24 g protein. **Diabetic Exchanges:** 3 lean meat, 1 starch.

Mustard Bourbon Kabobs c

PREP: 10 min. + marinating GRILL: 10 min.
YIELD: 4 servings

BARBARA WHITE • KATY, TEXAS

You'll love the tangy and subtly sweet blend of mustard and bourbon in these tasty, no-fuss kabobs. Make a little extra marinade and serve them with a side of brown rice.

6	Tbsp. brown sugar
6	Tbsp. Dijon mustard
3	Tbsp. bourbon *or* apple cider
3	Tbsp. reduced-sodium soy sauce
1	pork tenderloin (1 lb.), cut into 3/4-in. cubes

1. In a small bowl, combine the brown sugar, mustard, bourbon and soy sauce. Pour 3/4 cup marinade into a large resealable plastic bag; add pork. Seal bag and turn to coat; refrigerate for 8 hours or overnight. Cover and refrigerate remaining marinade.

2. Drain and discard marinade. Thread pork onto four metal or soaked wooden skewers. Using long-handled tongs, moisten a paper towel with cooking oil and lightly coat the grill rack.

3. Grill kabobs, covered, over medium heat or broil 4 in. from the heat for 8-10 minutes or until juices run clear, turning and basting occasionally with the reserved marinade.

Nutrition Facts: 1 kabob equals 172 calories, 4 g fat (1 g saturated fat), 63 mg cholesterol, 355 mg sodium, 8 g carbohydrate, 0 fiber, 23 g protein. **Diabetic Exchanges:** lean meat, 1/2 starch.

Grilled Spicy Pork Tenderloin [c]

PREP: 15 min. + marinating **GRILL:** 25 min.
YIELD: 4 servings

MARY ANN LEE • CLIFTON PARK, NEW YORK

Tender and full of flavor, this juicy tenderloin couldn't be much more convenient on busy work nights. Make ahead the night before, marinate during the day, then grill when you get home.

  2 Tbsp. brown sugar
3/4 tsp. salt
3/4 tsp. dried thyme
1/4 tsp. onion powder
1/4 tsp. garlic powder
1/4 tsp. ground mustard
1/4 tsp. ground cumin
1/4 tsp. dried oregano
1/4 tsp. ground allspice
1/4 tsp. pepper
  1 pork tenderloin (1 lb.)
SAUCE:
1/2 cup cola
  1 Tbsp. brown sugar
1/4 tsp. ground cinnamon
1/4 tsp. chili powder

1. In a small bowl, combine the first 10 ingredients; rub over pork. Cover and refrigerate for 8 hours or overnight.

2. In a small bowl, combine sauce ingredients. Using long-handled tongs, moisten a paper towel with cooking oil and lightly coat the grill rack. Prepare sauce ingredients; set aside.

3. Prepare grill for indirect heat using a drip pan. Place pork over drip pan and grill, covered, over indirect medium-hot heat for 25-30 minutes or until a meat thermometer reads 160°, basting occasionally with reserved sauce. Let roast stand for 5 minutes before slicing.

Nutrition Facts: 3 oz. cooked pork equals 188 calories, 4 g fat (1 g saturated fat), 63 mg cholesterol, 495 mg sodium, 14 g carbohydrate, 1 g fiber, 23 g protein. **Diabetic Exchanges:** 3 lean meat, 1 starch.

Pork Chops with Parmesan Sauce [c]

PREP/TOTAL TIME: 20 min. **YIELD:** 4 servings

HEALTHY COOKING TEST KITCHEN

Here's a new family favorite! Moist and tender chops make a speedy and comforting weeknight meal. They're dressed with a smooth, creamy sauce seasoned with Parmesan, onion and a hint of nutmeg, parsley and thyme.

  4 boneless pork loin chops (4 oz. *each*)
1/2 tsp. salt
1/4 tsp. pepper
  1 Tbsp. butter
  2 Tbsp. all-purpose flour
  1 cup fat-free milk
1/3 cup grated Parmesan cheese

2 Tbsp. grated onion
3 tsp. minced fresh parsley
1/4 tsp. dried thyme
1/4 tsp. ground nutmeg

1. Sprinkle pork chops with salt and pepper. In a large nonstick skillet coated with cooking spray, cook chops in butter over medium heat until meat juices run clear; remove and keep warm.

2. Combine flour and milk until smooth; stir into pan. Bring to a boil; cook and stir for 2 minutes or until thickened. Stir in remaining ingredients; heat through. Serve with chops.

Nutrition Facts: 1 pork chop with 3 Tbsp. sauce equals 244 calories, 11 g fat (5 g saturated fat), 69 mg cholesterol, 475 mg sodium, 7 g carbohydrate, trace fiber, 27 g protein. **Diabetic Exchanges:** 4 lean meat, 1/2 starch, 1/2 fat.

Honey Lemon Schnitzel

PREP/TOTAL TIME: 25 min. **YIELD:** 4 servings

CAROLE FRASER • NORTH YORK, ONTARIO

These pork cutlets are coated in a sweet sauce with honey, lemon juice and butter. They're certainly good enough for company, but perfect for a quick weeknight meal, too. Very seldom are there any leftovers.

2 Tbsp. all-purpose flour
1/2 tsp. salt
1/2 tsp. pepper
4 pork sirloin cutlets (4 oz. *each*)
2 Tbsp. butter
1/4 cup lemon juice
1/4 cup honey

1. In a large resealable plastic bag, combine the flour, salt and pepper. Add pork, two pieces at a time, and shake to coat. In a large skillet, cook pork in butter over medium heat for 3-4 minutes on each side or until juices run clear. Remove and keep warm.

2. Add lemon juice and honey to the skillet; cook and stir for 3 minutes or until thickened. Return pork to pan; cook 2-3 minutes longer or until heated through.

Nutrition Facts: 1 cutlet equals 298 calories, 13 g fat (6 g saturated fat), 88 mg cholesterol, 393 mg sodium, 22 g carbohydrate, trace fiber, 24 g protein.

Pork Chops with Orange Sauce c

PREP: 15 min. + marinating **BROIL:** 15 min.
YIELD: 4 servings

MARY CHANDLER • GRAND TOWER, ILLINOIS

Tangy orange and pineapple juices flavor the marinade that dresses up these tender, juicy chops. Add mashed potatoes or rice and a simple side salad for a fuss-free supper.

1 cup orange juice
1/2 cup unsweetened pineapple juice
1/4 cup reduced-sodium soy sauce
2 Tbsp. honey
2 garlic cloves, minced
1/2 tsp. grated orange peel
1/4 tsp. pepper
4 bone-in pork loin chops (7 oz. *each*)
1 Tbsp. cornstarch

1. In a small bowl, combine the first seven ingredients. Pour a scant 1 cup into a large resealable plastic bag; add pork chops. Seal bag and turn to coat; refrigerate for 8 hours or overnight. Cover and refrigerate remaining marinade for sauce.

2. Drain and discard marinade. Using long-handled tongs, moisten a paper towel with cooking oil and lightly coat the grill rack.

3. Grill chops, covered, over medium heat or broil 4 in. from the heat for 4-5 minutes on each side or until a meat thermometer reads 160°.

4. Meanwhile, in a small saucepan, combine cornstarch and reserved marinade. Bring to a boil; cook and stir for 2 minutes or until thickened. Serve with chops.

Nutrition Facts: 1 pork chop with 3 Tbsp. sauce equals 269 calories, 8 g fat (3 g saturated fat), 86 mg cholesterol, 451 mg sodium, 15 g carbohydrate, trace fiber, 31 g protein. **Diabetic Exchanges:** 4 lean meat, 1 starch.

HONEY LEMON SCHNITZEL

PORK CHOPS WITH ORANGE SAUCE

Caraway Pork Chops And Red Cabbage

PREP: 20 min. COOK: 20 min. YIELD: 4 servings

JUDY REBMAN • FREDERICK, ILLINOIS

My husband loves cooked red cabbage. This is my healthy spin on a savory one-skillet supper that my 18-year-old son also enjoys. I serve it with mashed potatoes.

4	boneless pork loin chops (5 oz. *each*)
1-1/4 tsp.	caraway seeds, *divided*
1 tsp.	rotisserie chicken seasoning
1 tsp.	brown sugar
1 Tbsp.	canola oil
4 cups	shredded red cabbage
1	medium apple, peeled and thinly sliced
1/2	small onion, sliced
1 Tbsp.	water
1 Tbsp.	red wine vinegar
1/2 tsp.	salt
1/2 tsp.	reduced-sodium chicken bouillon granules
4 Tbsp.	apple jelly

1. Season pork chops with 1 tsp. caraway seeds, chicken seasoning and brown sugar. In a large nonstick skillet coated with cooking spray, brown chops in oil. Remove and keep warm.

2. Add the cabbage, apple, onion, water, vinegar, salt, bouillon granules and remaining caraway seeds to the skillet. Cover and cook over medium heat for 10 minutes, stirring occasionally.

3. Place chops over cabbage mixture; top each with 1 Tbsp. apple jelly. Cover and cook 10-12 minutes longer or until meat is tender.

Nutrition Facts: 1 pork chop with 3/4 cup cabbage mixture equals 319 calories, 12 g fat (3 g saturated fat), 68 mg cholesterol, 523 mg sodium, 25 g carbohydrate, 2 g fiber, 29 g protein. **Diabetic Exchanges:** 4 lean meat, 1 starch, 1 vegetable, 1 fat.

Zesty Herbed Lamb Chops [C]

PREP/TOTAL TIME: 30 min. YIELD: 4 servings

CORA ANDERSON • SEATTLE, WASHINGTON

I sometimes serve this sauce with seared scallops or grilled salmon or halibut. It's really good either way. I also modify the recipe when there are fresh herbs in season. I've made a version with basil instead of mint, and I sometimes swap thyme for oregano for a more subtle flavor.

1/2 cup	fresh mint leaves
1/4 cup	minced fresh oregano
1/4 cup	packed fresh parsley sprigs, stems removed
1/4 cup	lemon juice
3 Tbsp.	water
6	garlic cloves
1 Tbsp.	olive oil
1/4 tsp.	salt

Dash pepper

LAMB CHOPS:

8	lamb loin chops (3 oz. *each*)
1/2 tsp.	salt
1/2 tsp.	pepper
1 Tbsp.	olive oil

CARAWAY PORK CHOPS AND RED CABBAGE

ZESTY HERBED LAMB CHOPS

JEWELED BUFFET HAM

1. In a food processor, combine the first nine ingredients; cover and pulse until blended. Set aside half of the sauce. Brush remaining sauce over chops; sprinkle with salt and pepper.

2. In a large skillet coated with cooking spray, cook chops in oil over medium heat for 7-10 minutes on each side or until meat reaches desired doneness (for medium-rare, a meat thermometer should read 145°; medium, 160°; well-done, 170°). Serve with reserved mint sauce.

Nutrition Facts: 2 lamb chops with 4 tsp. sauce equals 236 calories, 14 g fat (3 g saturated fat), 68 mg cholesterol, 509 mg sodium, 5 g carbohydrate, 1 g fiber, 22 g protein.

Jeweled Buffet Ham

PREP: 10 min. **BAKE:** 2-1/2 hours **YIELD:** 15 servings

AGNES WARD • STRATFORD, ONTARIO

Cranberry sauce and mandarin oranges make a beautiful, aromatic glaze for this spiral-sliced cooked ham. This recipe will be a crowd-pleaser any time of the year, but it's wonderful during the holidays due to the lovely cranberry-and-orange flavor that it offers. Best of all, it only takes a few moments of prep work before popping it into the oven!

  1 bone-in fully cooked spiral-sliced ham (7 lbs.)
  1 can (14 oz.) whole-berry cranberry sauce

  1 can (11 oz.) mandarin oranges, drained
  1 can (8 oz.) jellied cranberry sauce
1/2 cup orange juice
1/2 tsp. garlic powder
1/8 tsp. hot pepper sauce

1. Place ham on a rack in a shallow roasting pan. Bake, uncovered, at 325° for 2 hours.

2. In a large saucepan, combine the remaining ingredients. Cook and stir over medium heat until heated through.

3. Brush ham with some of the glaze; bake 30-60 minutes longer or until a meat thermometer reads 140°, brushing occasionally with remaining glaze.

Nutrition Facts: 6 oz. ham equals 329 calories, 5 g fat (1 g saturated fat), 47 mg cholesterol, 1,915 mg sodium, 34 g carbohydrate, 1 g fiber, 38 g protein.

To keep your **ham** from drying out in the oven, be sure to brush on extra glaze as needed, and loosely cover it with a "tent" of aluminum foil.

Ham & Asparagus Casserole

PREP: 25 min. **BAKE:** 25 min. **YIELD:** 4 servings

RACHEL KOWASIC • CONNELLSVILLE, PENNSYLVANIA

I'm always looking for ways to add veggies to main dishes, and this comforting casserole was a success!

3-3/4	cups uncooked yolk-free whole wheat noodles
2-1/2	cups cut fresh asparagus (1-in. pieces)
1	medium onion, chopped
1	Tbsp. reduced-fat butter
1/4	cup all-purpose flour
1/2	tsp. dried thyme
1/8	tsp. pepper
1	cup fat-free milk
1	cup reduced-sodium chicken broth
1	Tbsp. lemon juice
1-1/2	cups cubed fully cooked lean ham
1/4	cup minced fresh parsley
1/3	cup French-fried onions
2	Tbsp. shredded Parmesan cheese

1. Cook noodles according to package directions. Meanwhile, in a large saucepan, bring 2 cups of water to a boil. Add asparagus. Cover and cook for 3-5 minutes or until crisp-tender; drain and set aside.

2. In a large skillet, saute the chopped onion in butter until tender. Combine the flour, thyme and pepper; gradually whisk in milk and broth until smooth. Add milk mixture to the skillet. Bring to a boil; cook and stir for 1-2 minutes or until thickened. Remove from the heat; stir in lemon juice.

3. Drain noodles; add the ham, parsley, sauce and asparagus. Transfer to a 13-in. x 9-in. baking dish coated with cooking spray. Top with the fried onions and cheese.

4. Cover and bake at 350° for 20 minutes or until bubbly. Uncover and bake 5-10 minutes longer or until golden brown.

Editor's Note: This recipe was tested with Land O'Lakes light stick butter.

Nutrition Facts: 1-1/2 cups equals 343 calories, 8 g fat (3 g saturated fat), 27 mg cholesterol, 946 mg sodium, 50 g carbohydrate, 7 g fiber, 22 g protein.

Cajun Herb Mix F S C

PREP/TOTAL TIME: 5 min. **YIELD:** about 2/3 cup

HEALTHY COOKING TEST KITCHEN

Low-salt foods can help decrease your risk for high blood pressure. Try this spicy salt-free rub on pork to boost flavor, not sodium. It's also great on chicken.

5	Tbsp. paprika
2	Tbsp. dried minced onion
2	Tbsp. dried minced garlic
1	Tbsp. cayenne pepper
1-1/2	tsp. dried oregano
1-1/2	tsp. dried basil
1-1/2	tsp. white pepper

1. In a small bowl, combine all ingredients. Store mixture in an airtight container for up to six months. Rub over meat before cooking.

Nutrition Facts: 1 tsp. equals 6 calories, trace fat (trace saturated fat), 0 cholesterol, 1 mg sodium, 1 g carbohydrate, trace fiber, trace protein. **Diabetic Exchange:** Free food.

HAM & ASPARAGUS CASSEROLE

CAJUN HERB MIX

Southwestern Pasta & Cheese

PREP: 30 min. **BAKE:** 20 min. **YIELD:** 8 servings

NAOMI REED • MCMINNVILLE, OREGON

I gave mac 'n' cheese a twist by adding some favorite ingredients. My family absolutely loves this side dish!

3-1/3	cups uncooked bow tie pasta
1	medium sweet red pepper, chopped
8	green onions, chopped
1	Tbsp. olive oil
1/4	cup all-purpose flour
1	tsp. chili powder
1	tsp. minced chipotle pepper in adobo sauce
1/2	tsp. salt
1/2	tsp. ground cumin
2-1/4	cups fat-free milk
1	cup (4 oz.) shredded sharp cheddar cheese, *divided*
4	center-cut bacon strips, cooked and crumbled
2	Tbsp. minced fresh cilantro

1. Cook pasta according to package directions.

2. Meanwhile, in a large skillet, saute pepper and onions in oil until tender. Stir in the flour, chili powder, chipotle pepper, salt and cumin until blended. Gradually stir in milk. Bring to a boil; cook and stir for 2 minutes or until thickened. Stir in 1/4 cup cheese until melted.

3. Drain pasta; toss with sauce. Stir in bacon and cilantro. Transfer to a 2-qt. baking dish coated with cooking spray. Sprinkle with remaining cheese. Bake, uncovered, at 400° for 20-25 minutes or until bubbly.

Nutrition Facts: 3/4 cup equals 240 calories, 8 g fat (4 g saturated fat), 20 mg cholesterol, 327 mg sodium, 32 g carbohydrate, 2 g fiber, 12 g protein. **Diabetic Exchanges:** 2 starch, 1 lean meat, 1 fat.

Ham & Spinach Couscous

PREP/TOTAL TIME: 20 min. **YIELD:** 4 servings

LISA SHANNON • CULLMAN, ALABAMA

A simple way to dress up couscous, this colorful, foolproof dish makes a lovely one-pot meal when time's tight. For extra flair, toss in some sliced mushrooms, peas, chopped onion, diced carrot or even some chopped broccoli.

2	cups water
1	cup chopped fully cooked ham
1	cup chopped fresh spinach
1/2	tsp. garlic salt
1	cup uncooked couscous
1/4	cup shredded cheddar cheese

1. In a large saucepan, combine the water, ham, spinach and garlic salt. Bring to a boil. Stir in couscous. Remove from the heat; cover and let stand for 5-10 minutes or until water is absorbed. Fluff with a fork. Sprinkle with cheese.

Nutrition Facts: 1 cup equals 248 calories, 6 g fat (3 g saturated fat), 26 mg cholesterol, 727 mg sodium, 36 g carbohydrate, 2 g fiber, 14 g protein. **Diabetic Exchanges:** 2 starch, 1 lean meat, 1 fat.

Irish Stew

PREP: 15 min. **COOK:** 1-1/2 hours
YIELD: 8 servings (2-1/2 qt.)

HEALTHY COOKING TEST KITCHEN

Lamb, a great protein source, adds plenty of mouthwatering flavor to this traditional stew. Can't find lamb at the grocery store? You can substitute beef stew meat instead with equally pleasing results.

> 1/3 cup plus 1 Tbsp. all-purpose flour, *divided*
> 1-1/2 lbs. lamb stew meat, cut into 1-in. cubes
> 3 Tbsp. olive oil, *divided*
> 3 medium onions, chopped
> 3 garlic cloves, minced
> 4 cups reduced-sodium beef broth
> 2 medium potatoes, peeled and cubed
> 4 medium carrots, cut into 1-in. pieces
> 1 cup frozen peas
> 1 tsp. salt
> 1 tsp. dried thyme
> 1/2 tsp. pepper
> 1/2 tsp. Worcestershire sauce
> 2 Tbsp. water

1. Place 1/3 cup flour in a large resealable plastic bag. Add lamb, a few pieces at a time, and shake to coat. In a Dutch oven, brown lamb in batches in 2 Tbsp. oil. Remove and set aside.

2. In the same pan, saute onions and garlic in remaining oil until tender. Add broth, stirring to loosen browned bits from pan. Add meat. Bring to a boil. Reduce heat; cover and simmer for 1 hour or until meat is tender.

3. Add potatoes and carrots; cover and cook for 20 minutes. Stir in peas; cook 5-10 minutes longer or until vegetables are tender. Add seasonings and Worcestershire sauce. Combine remaining flour with water until smooth. Stir into the pan. Bring to a boil; cook and stir for 2 minutes or until thickened.

Nutrition Facts: 1-1/4 cups equals 271 calories, 10 g fat (2 g saturated fat), 58 mg cholesterol, 618 mg sodium, 24 g carbohydrate, 4 g fiber, 22 g protein. **Diabetic Exchanges:** 2 lean meat, 1 starch, 1 vegetable, 1 fat.

Pork Medallions In Mustard Sauce C

PREP/TOTAL TIME: 30 min. **YIELD:** 4 servings

TAHNIA FOX • TRENTON, MICHIGAN

Mustard and apple juice liven up lean pork tenderloin, creating a dish that's ideal for family and special guests alike.

> 1/2 cup reduced-sodium chicken broth
> 2 Tbsp. apple juice concentrate
> 4-1/2 tsp. whole grain mustard
> 1 lb. pork tenderloin, cut into 1/2-in. slices
> 1/4 tsp. salt
> 1/4 tsp. pepper
> 1 Tbsp. olive oil
> 2 garlic cloves, minced
> 1 tsp. cornstarch
> 2 Tbsp. cold water
> 1 Tbsp. minced fresh parsley

1. In a small bowl, combine the broth, juice concentrate and mustard; set aside.

2. Sprinkle pork with salt and pepper. In a large nonstick skillet, brown pork in oil. Remove pork and set aside.

3. Add garlic to the pan; saute for 1 minute. Add reserved broth mixture, stirring to loosen browned bits from pan. Bring to a boil. Reduce heat; simmer, uncovered, for 6-8 minutes or until liquid is reduced to about 1/3 cup.

4. Return pork to the pan; cover and cook over low heat for 3-4 minutes or until meat is no longer pink. Combine cornstarch and water until smooth; add to the pan. Bring to a boil; cook and stir for 2 minutes or until thickened. Sprinkle with parsley.

Nutrition Facts: 3 oz. cooked pork equals 193 calories, 7 g fat (2 g saturated fat), 63 mg cholesterol, 356 mg sodium, 6 g carbohydrate, 1 g fiber, 23 g protein. **Diabetic Exchanges:** 3 lean meat, 1/2 starch, 1/2 fat.

Best-Ever Lamb Chops C

PREP: 10 min. + chilling **BROIL:** 10 min.
YIELD: 4 servings

KIM MUNDY • VISALIA, CALIFORNIA

My mom just loved a good lamb chop, and this easy recipe was her favorite way to have them. I've also grilled these chops with great results.

1 tsp. *each* dried basil, marjoram and thyme
1/2 tsp. salt
8 lamb loin chops (3 oz. *each*)
Mint jelly, optional

1. Combine herbs and salt; rub over lamb chops. Cover and refrigerate for 1 hour.

2. Broil 4-6 in. from the heat for 5-8 minutes on each side or until meat reaches desired doneness (for medium-rare, a meat thermometer should read 145°; medium, 160°; well-done, 170°). Serve chops with jelly if desired.

Nutrition Facts: 2 lamb chops (calculated without jelly) equals 157 calories, 7 g fat (2 g saturated fat), 68 mg cholesterol, 355 mg sodium, trace carbohydrate, trace fiber, 22 g protein. **Diabetic Exchanges:** 3 lean meat, 1/2 fat.

Pork Tenderloin With Cherry Relish S C

PREP: 10 min. + chilling **COOK:** 2 min.
YIELD: 8 servings (1 cup relish)

HEALTHY COOKING TEST KITCHEN

We gave pork tenderloin an herb rub to keep flavor high and sodium low, then paired it with a dried-cherry relish, rich in antioxidants, for a tasty meal.

1 tsp. garlic powder
1 tsp. *each* dried oregano, tarragon and rosemary, crushed
2 pork tenderloins (1 lb. *each*), trimmed

RELISH:
1 large red onion, sliced
2 Tbsp. olive oil
3 Tbsp. sugar
1/2 cup dried cherries
1/4 cup red wine vinegar
1/4 tsp. dried rosemary, crushed

1. In a small bowl, combine garlic powder and herbs; rub over pork. Cover and refrigerate for 30 minutes.

2. For relish, in a large saucepan, saute onion in oil until tender. Add sugar; cook and stir over medium heat for 10 minutes or until onion is browned. Add the cherries, vinegar and rosemary. Bring to a boil. Reduce heat; cover and simmer for 10 minutes. Cool to room temperature.

3. Place pork on a rack in a shallow roasting pan lined with foil. Bake at 425° for 25-30 minutes or until a meat thermometer reads 160°. Let stand for 10 minutes before slicing. Serve with relish.

Nutrition Facts: 3 oz. cooked pork with 2 Tbsp. relish equals 217 calories, 7 g fat (2 g saturated fat), 63 mg cholesterol, 46 mg sodium, 14 g carbohydrate, 1 g fiber, 23 g protein. **Diabetic Exchanges:** 3 lean meat, 1/2 starch, 1/2 fruit, 1/2 fat.

PORK TENDERLOIN WITH CHERRY RELISH

BEST-EVER LAMB CHOPS

THAI SHRIMP SOUP

GLAZED SALMON SALAD

PINEAPPLE PICO TUNA STEAKS

Fish & Seafood

Light and refreshing, seafood is a natural choice for those looking to cut calories and eat healthy. Turn here for change-of-pace menu options you'll adore...most of which pare down carbs and come together in no time!

Pineapple Pico Tuna Steaks

PREP: 10 min. + marinating **GRILL:** 10 min.
YIELD: 4 servings

SALLY SIBTHORPE • SHELBY TOWNSHIP, MICHIGAN

Bursting with flavor from a quick and easy marinade, these tuna steaks are topped with pico de gallo made of pineapple, tomatoes, lime juice and a nice kick of jalapeno.

- 1/2 cup tequila
- 3 Tbsp. brown sugar
- 2 Tbsp. lime juice
- 1 Tbsp. chili powder
- 1 Tbsp. olive oil
- 1 tsp. salt
- 4 tuna steaks (6 oz. *each*)

PICO DE GALLO:
- 1 cup chopped fresh pineapple
- 1 plum tomato, finely chopped
- 1/3 cup finely chopped onion
- 1/4 cup minced fresh cilantro
- 2 Tbsp. minced seeded jalapeno pepper
- 2 Tbsp. lime juice
- 1 Tbsp. olive oil
- 2 tsp. grated lime peel
- 1/2 tsp. salt

1. In a large resealable plastic bag, combine the first six ingredients. Add the tuna; seal bag and turn to coat. Refrigerate for 30 minutes. Meanwhile, in a small bowl, combine pico de gallo ingredients. Cover and refrigerate until serving.

2. Drain and discard marinade. Using long-handled tongs, moisten a paper towel with cooking oil and lightly coat the grill rack. For medium-rare, grill tuna, covered, over high heat or broil 3-4 in. from the heat for 3-4 minutes on each side or until slightly pink in the center. Serve with pico de gallo.

Editor's Note: Wear disposable gloves when cutting hot peppers; the oils can burn skin. Avoid touching your face.

Nutrition Facts: 1 tuna steak with 1/2 cup salsa equals 385 calories, 9 g fat (1 g saturated fat), 77 mg cholesterol, 974 mg sodium, 20 g carbohydrate, 2 g fiber, 41 g protein. **Diabetic Exchanges:** 5 lean meat, 1/2 starch, 1/2 fat.

Thai Shrimp Soup C

PREP: 20 min. **COOK:** 20 min. **YIELD:** 8 servings (2 qt.)

JESSIE GREARSON-SAPAT • FALMOUTH, MAINE

This tasty, crowd-pleasing soup comes together in minutes, and I like the fact that the ingredients are available in my little local grocery store.

- 1 medium onion, chopped
- 1 Tbsp. olive oil
- 3 cups reduced-sodium chicken broth
- 1 cup water
- 1 Tbsp. brown sugar
- 1 Tbsp. minced fresh gingerroot
- 1 Tbsp. fish *or* soy sauce
- 1 Tbsp. red curry paste
- 1 lemon grass stalk
- 1 lb. uncooked large shrimp, peeled and deveined
- 1-1/2 cups frozen shelled edamame
- 1 can (14 oz.) light coconut milk
- 1 can (8-3/4 oz.) whole baby corn, drained and cut in half
- 1/2 cup bamboo shoots
- 1/4 cup fresh basil leaves, torn
- 1/4 cup minced fresh cilantro
- 2 Tbsp. lime juice
- 1-1/2 tsp. grated lime peel
- 1 tsp. curry powder

1. In a Dutch oven, saute onion in oil until tender. Add the broth, water, brown sugar, ginger, fish sauce, curry paste and lemon grass. Bring to a boil. Reduce heat; carefully stir in shrimp and edamame. Cook, uncovered, for 5-6 minutes or until shrimp turn pink.

2. Add the coconut milk, corn, bamboo shoots, basil, cilantro, lime juice, lime peel and curry powder; heat through. Discard lemon grass.

Nutrition Facts: 1 cup equals 163 calories, 7 g fat (3 g saturated fat), 69 mg cholesterol, 505 mg sodium, 9 g carbohydrate, 2 g fiber, 14 g protein. **Diabetic Exchanges:** 2 lean meat, 1 vegetable, 1 fat.

Creole Baked Tilapia F C

PREP/TOTAL TIME: 25 min. YIELD: 4 servings

CAROLYN COLLINS • FREEPORT, TEXAS

Since I'm originally from Louisiana, I love Creole cooking. This is quick and easy as well as healthy. It's great served with your favorite rice dish. Enjoy!

- 4 tilapia fillets (6 oz. *each*)
- 1 can (8 oz.) tomato sauce
- 1 small green pepper, thinly sliced
- 1/2 cup chopped red onion
- 1 tsp. Creole seasoning

1. Place tilapia in an ungreased 13-in. x 9-in. baking dish. In a small bowl, combine the tomato sauce, green pepper, onion and Creole seasoning; pour over the fillets.

2. Bake, uncovered, at 350° for 20-25 minutes or until fish flakes easily with a fork.

Editor's Note: The following spices may be substituted for 1 tsp. Creole seasoning: 1/4 tsp. each salt, garlic powder and paprika; and a pinch each of dried thyme, ground cumin and cayenne pepper.

Nutrition Facts: 1 fish fillet with 1/3 cup topping equals 166 calories, 2 g fat (1 g saturated fat), 83 mg cholesterol, 488 mg sodium, 6 g carbohydrate, 1 g fiber, 33 g protein. **Diabetic Exchanges:** 5 lean meat, 1 vegetable.

CREOLE BAKED TILAPIA

Glazed Salmon Salad C

PREP: 20 min. BAKE: 20 min. YIELD: 4 servings

ELIZABETH DEHART • WEST JORDAN, UTAH

Honey and smoked paprika lend delightful flavors and a bright color to this beautiful dish. It has a special feeling but is quick enough for weeknights, too.

- 4 salmon fillets (4 oz. *each*)
- 1 Tbsp. olive oil
- 2 tsp. smoked paprika
- 2 tsp. honey
- 1 garlic clove, minced
- 1/2 tsp. salt
- 1/2 tsp. pepper
- 1/4 tsp. crushed red pepper flakes

SALAD:
- 4 cups fresh baby spinach
- 1/2 cup shredded carrot
- 1/4 cup chopped red onion
- 1/4 cup olive oil
- 2 Tbsp. cider vinegar
- 1-1/2 tsp. finely chopped shallot
- 1 tsp. Dijon mustard

1. Place salmon in an 11-in. x 7-in. baking dish coated with cooking spray.

2. In a small bowl, combine the oil, paprika, honey, garlic, salt, pepper and pepper flakes; brush over salmon. Bake, uncovered, at 350° for 20-25 minutes or until fish flakes easily with a fork. Cut salmon into 1-in. pieces.

3. In a large bowl, combine the spinach, carrot and onion. Divide among four serving plates; top with salmon. In a small bowl, combine the oil, vinegar, shallot and mustard; drizzle over the salads. Serve the salads immediately.

Nutrition Facts: 1 serving equals 362 calories, 28 g fat (4 g saturated fat), 57 mg cholesterol, 417 mg sodium, 8 g carbohydrate, 2 g fiber, 21 g protein.

GLAZED SALMON SALAD

Broiled Parmesan Tilapia [C]

PREP/TOTAL TIME: 20 min. YIELD: 6 servings

TRISHA KRUSE • EAGLE, IDAHO

Even picky families will change their minds about eating fish with this toasty, cheesy Parmesan-coated dish. I serve it with mashed cauliflower and a green salad for a low-carb meal everyone loves.

    6   tilapia fillets (6 oz. *each*)
  1/4   cup grated Parmesan cheese
  1/4   cup reduced-fat mayonnaise
    2   Tbsp. lemon juice
    1   Tbsp. butter, softened
    1   garlic clove, minced
    1   tsp. minced fresh basil *or* 1/4 tsp. dried basil
  1/2   tsp. seafood seasoning

1. Place fillets on a broiler pan coated with cooking spray. In a small bowl, combine the remaining ingredients; spread over fillets.

2. Broil 3-4 in. from the heat for 10-12 minutes or until fish flakes easily with a fork.

Nutrition Facts: 1 fillet equals 207 calories, 8 g fat (3 g saturated fat), 94 mg cholesterol, 260 mg sodium, 2 g carbohydrate, trace fiber, 33 g protein. **Diabetic Exchanges:** 5 lean meat, 1 fat.

Scallops with Citrus Glaze [C]

PREP/TOTAL TIME: 20 min. YIELD: 4 servings

PATRICIA NIEH • PORTOLA VALLEY, CALIFORNIA

These scallops are especially scrumptious when served on steamed rice with a green veggie on the side.

   12   sea scallops (about 1-1/2 lbs.)
  1/2   tsp. pepper
  1/4   tsp. salt
    2   Tbsp. olive oil, *divided*
    4   garlic cloves, minced
  1/2   cup orange juice
  1/4   cup lemon juice
    1   Tbsp. reduced-sodium soy sauce
  1/2   tsp. grated orange peel

1. Sprinkle scallops with pepper and salt. In a large skillet, saute scallops in 1 Tbsp. oil until firm and opaque. Remove and keep warm.

2. In the same skillet, cook garlic in remaining oil for 1 minute. Add the juices, soy sauce and orange peel. Bring to a boil; cook and stir for 5 minutes or until thickened. Serve with scallops.

Nutrition Facts: 3 scallops with 2 tsp. glaze equals 235 calories, 8 g fat (1 g saturated fat), 56 mg cholesterol, 574 mg sodium, 10 g carbohydrate, trace fiber, 29 g protein. **Diabetic Exchanges:** 4 lean meat, 1-1/2 fat.

FIRECRACKER GRILLED SALMON

Firecracker Grilled Salmon **C**

PREP: 20 min. + marinating **GRILL:** 5 min.
YIELD: 4 servings

MELISSA ROGERS • TUSCALOOSA, ALABAMA

Let this sensational salmon perk up dinner tonight. With a super flavorful glaze that kicks you right in the taste buds, this dish is anything but boring!

2	Tbsp. balsamic vinegar
2	Tbsp. reduced-sodium soy sauce
1	green onion, thinly sliced
1	Tbsp. olive oil
1	Tbsp. maple syrup
2	garlic cloves, minced
1	tsp. ground ginger
1	tsp. crushed red pepper flakes
1/2	tsp. sesame oil
1/4	tsp. salt
4	salmon fillets (6 oz. *each*)

1. In a small bowl, combine the first ten ingredients. Pour 1/4 cup marinade into a large resealable plastic bag. Add the salmon; seal bag and turn to coat. Refrigerate for up to 30 minutes. Cover and refrigerate remaining marinade. Drain and discard the marinade.

2. Using long-handled tongs, moisten a paper towel with cooking oil and lightly coat the grill rack. Place salmon skin side down on grill rack. Grill, covered, over high heat or broil 3-4 in. from the heat for 5-10 minutes or until fish flakes easily with a fork, basting occasionally with remaining marinade.

Nutrition Facts: 1 fillet equals 306 calories, 18 g fat (4 g saturated fat), 85 mg cholesterol, 367 mg sodium, 4 g carbohydrate, trace fiber, 29 g protein. **Diabetic Exchanges:** 5 lean meat, 1 fat.

Spicy Mango Scallops

PREP/TOTAL TIME: 30 min. **YIELD:** 4 servings

NICOLE FILIZETTI • JACKSONVILLE, FLORIDA

This sweet and spicy seafood combo gives off enough heat to make the whole family warm up to its great flavors! Be sure to buy the larger sea scallops for this recipe; cooking times would be off for the smaller bay scallops.

12	sea scallops (1-1/2 lbs.)
1	Tbsp. peanut oil
1	medium red onion, chopped
1	garlic clove, minced
1/4	to 1/2 tsp. crushed red pepper flakes
1/2	cup unsweetened pineapple juice
1/4	cup mango chutney
2	cups hot cooked basmati rice

Minced fresh cilantro

1. In a large skillet, saute scallops in oil for 1-1/2 to 2 minutes on each side or until firm and opaque. Remove and keep warm.

2. In the same skillet, saute onion until tender. Add garlic and pepper flakes; cook 1 minute longer. Stir in pineapple juice. Bring to a boil; cook until liquid is reduced by half. Remove from the heat. Add chutney and scallops; stir to coat. Serve with rice; drizzle with sauce. Sprinkle with cilantro.

Nutrition Facts: 3 scallops with 1/2 cup cooked rice and 2 Tbsp. sauce equals 371 calories, 5 g fat (1 g saturated fat), 56 mg cholesterol, 447 mg sodium, 47 g carbohydrate, 1 g fiber, 31 g protein. **Diabetic Exchanges:** 4 lean meat, 3 starch, 1/2 fat.

Curried Halibut Skillet

PREP/TOTAL TIME: 25 min. **YIELD:** 4 servings

KAREN KUEBLER • DALLAS, TEXAS

My friend in England told me coconut is all the rage there, so I've been experimenting with it in main dishes here at home. This is one of my most successful recipes.

4	halibut fillets (4 oz. *each*)
1/2	tsp. salt
4	tsp. curry powder
2	Tbsp. olive oil, *divided*
1	large sweet onion, chopped
1	can (14-1/2 oz.) diced tomatoes, undrained
2	Tbsp. lime juice
1-1/2	tsp. grated lime peel
1	tsp. minced fresh gingerroot
1/4	cup flaked coconut, toasted
1/4	cup minced fresh cilantro

1. Sprinkle fillets with salt; coat with curry. In a large nonstick skillet coated with cooking spray, brown fillets in 1 Tbsp. oil; remove and set aside.

2. In the same pan, saute onion in remaining oil for 1 minute. Stir in the tomatoes, lime juice, lime peel and ginger. Bring to a boil. Return fillets to the pan; cover and simmer for 10-12 minutes or until fish flakes easily with a fork. Serve with tomato mixture; sprinkle with coconut and cilantro.

Nutrition Facts: 1 serving equals 270 calories, 12 g fat (3 g saturated fat), 36 mg cholesterol, 510 mg sodium, 16 g carbohydrate, 3 g fiber, 26 g protein. **Diabetic Exchanges:** 3 lean meat, 2 vegetable, 1-1/2 fat.

Spicy Shrimp Kabobs ▪F

PREP: 15 min. + marinating **GRILL:** 5 min.
YIELD: 4 servings

MICHELE TUNGETT • ROCHESTER, ILLINOIS

Shrimp lovers will adore these spicy, juicy kabobs. Adjust the cayenne to suit your preference for more or less heat. They are so quick and easy!

1/4	cup tomato sauce
2	Tbsp. minced fresh basil or 2 tsp. dried basil
2	Tbsp. red wine vinegar
3	garlic cloves, minced
1	Tbsp. olive oil
1/4	tsp. salt
1/4	tsp. cayenne pepper
1	lb. uncooked medium shrimp, peeled and deveined
1-1/2	cups pineapple chunks
1	medium onion, cut into wedges

1. In a large resealable plastic bag, combine the first seven ingredients. Add the shrimp; seal bag and turn to coat. Refrigerate for up to 2 hours.

2. Drain and discard marinade. On eight metal or soaked wooden skewers, alternately thread the shrimp, pineapple and onion. Using long-handled tongs, moisten a paper towel with cooking oil and lightly coat the grill rack. Grill kabobs, covered, over medium heat or broil 4 in. from the heat for 2-3 minutes on each side or until shrimp turn pink.

Nutrition Facts: 2 kabobs equals 187 calories, 3 g fat (1 g saturated fat), 138 mg cholesterol, 245 mg sodium, 20 g carbohydrate, 2 g fiber, 20 g protein. **Diabetic Exchanges:** 3 lean meat, 1 fruit.

CURRIED HALIBUT SKILLET

SPICY SHRIMP KABOBS

Crusty Red Snapper

PREP: 25 min. **BAKE:** 20 min. **YIELD:** 6 servings

KELLY REMINGTON • ARCATA, CALIFORNIA

This is an amazing dish. It's so easy, yet so elegant. The veggies steam the fish from the bottom, and covering the fillets with a crunchy topping keeps them moist.

- 2 medium tomatoes, chopped
- 1 *each* medium green, sweet yellow and red pepper, chopped
- 1 cup chopped leeks (white portion only)
- 1/2 cup chopped celery leaves
- 2 garlic cloves, minced
- 6 red snapper fillets (4 oz. *each*)

TOPPING:
- 1/2 cup panko (Japanese) bread crumbs
- 1/2 cup coarsely crushed baked Parmesan and Tuscan herb potato chips
- 1/4 cup grated Parmesan cheese
- 1/2 tsp. salt
- 1/2 tsp. paprika
- 1/4 tsp. cayenne pepper
- 1/4 tsp. pepper
- 2 Tbsp. butter, melted

1. In a 15-in. x 10-in. x 1-in. baking pan coated with cooking spray, combine the tomatoes, peppers, leeks, celery leaves and garlic; arrange fillets over vegetable mixture.

2. In a small bowl, combine the bread crumbs, chips, cheese, salt, paprika, cayenne and pepper; stir in butter. Sprinkle over the fillets. Bake, uncovered, at 425° for 18-22 minutes or until the fish flakes easily with a fork.

Nutrition Facts: 1 fillet with 2/3 cup vegetable mixture equals 237 calories, 7 g fat (3 g saturated fat), 53 mg cholesterol, 396 mg sodium, 16 g carbohydrate, 3 g fiber, 26 g protein. **Diabetic Exchanges:** 3 lean meat, 1 vegetable, 1 fat, 1/2 starch.

Grilled Salmon with Marmalade Dijon Glaze

PREP/TOTAL TIME: 20 min. **YIELD:** 4 servings

JUDY GREBETZ • RACINE, WISCONSIN

This tender salmon takes just a handful of ingredients and is pretty enough to serve guests.

- 1/2 cup orange marmalade
- 1 Tbsp. Dijon mustard
- 1/2 tsp. salt
- 1/2 tsp. garlic powder
- 1/4 tsp. pepper
- 1/8 tsp. ground ginger
- 4 salmon fillets (6 oz. *each*)

1. In a small bowl, combine the first six ingredients; set aside 1/4 cup. Brush remaining glaze over salmon.

2. Moisten a paper towel with cooking oil; using long-handled tongs, lightly coat the grill rack. Place salmon skin side down on grill rack.

3. Grill, covered, over medium heat or broil 4 in. from the heat for 10-12 minutes or until fish flakes easily with a fork, basting occasionally with the remaining glaze.

Nutrition Facts: 1 fillet equals 368 calories, 16 g fat (3 g saturated fat), 85 mg cholesterol, 493 mg sodium, 28 g carbohydrate, trace fiber, 29 g protein. **Diabetic Exchanges:** 4 lean meat, 1-1/2 starch, 1-1/2 fat.

CRUSTY RED SNAPPER

GRILLED SALMON WITH MARMALADE DIJON GLAZE

Feta Shrimp with Linguine

PREP/TOTAL TIME: 30 min. **YIELD:** 4 servings

CHARLENE CHAMBERS • ORMOND BEACH, FLORIDA

Great Mediterranean flavors, full-fat feta cheese and a little heat make this one recipe to die for! I serve it with crusty bread, a green salad and red wine.

8	oz. uncooked multigrain linguine
4	garlic cloves, minced
1	tsp. olive oil
1	can (28 oz.) diced tomatoes, undrained
1/4	cup sun-dried tomatoes (not packed in oil), chopped
1/4	cup Greek olives, coarsely chopped
1/4	tsp. salt
1/4	tsp. pepper
1	lb. uncooked medium shrimp, peeled and deveined
1/4	cup minced fresh parsley
2	Tbsp. lemon juice
1/4	tsp. crushed red pepper flakes
1/2	cup crumbled feta cheese

1. Cook linguine according to package directions. Meanwhile, in a large skillet, saute garlic in oil for 1 minute. Add the diced tomatoes, sun-dried tomatoes, olives, salt and pepper. Bring to a boil. Reduce heat; simmer, uncovered, for 8-10 minutes or until thickened, stirring occasionally.

2. Add the shrimp to the tomato mixture; cook, uncovered, for 5-6 minutes or until shrimp turn pink. Stir in the parsley, lemon juice and pepper flakes. Drain pasta; serve with shrimp mixture. Sprinkle with feta cheese.

Nutrition Facts: 1-1/4 cups shrimp mixture with 1 cup cooked linguine and 2 Tbsp. feta cheese equals 404 calories, 8 g fat (2 g saturated fat), 145 mg cholesterol, 881 mg sodium, 58 g carbohydrate, 10 g fiber, 30 g protein.

Soy-Glazed Scallops ⓒ

PREP: 25 min. + marinating **BROIL:** 5 min.
YIELD: 4 servings

APRIL KORANDO • AVA, ILLINOIS

These yummy broiled scallops are a great source of vitamin B12 and heart-healthy minerals such as magnesium.

1/4	cup lemon juice
2	Tbsp. canola oil
2	Tbsp. reduced-sodium soy sauce
2	Tbsp. honey
2	garlic cloves, minced
1/2	tsp. ground ginger
12	sea scallops (about 1-1/2 lbs.)

1. In a small bowl, combine the first six ingredients. Pour 1/3 cup marinade into a large resealable plastic bag. Add the scallops; seal bag and turn to coat. Refrigerate for 20 minutes.

2. Place remaining marinade in a small saucepan. Bring to a boil. Reduce heat; simmer, uncovered, for 8-10 minutes or until slightly thickened.

3. Drain and discard marinade. Thread scallops onto four metal or soaked wooden skewers. Broil 4 in. from the heat for 2-4 minutes on each side or until scallops are firm and opaque, basting occasionally with remaining marinade.

Nutrition Facts: 3 scallops equals 250 calories, 8 g fat (1 g saturated fat), 54 mg cholesterol, 567 mg sodium, 15 g carbohydrate, trace fiber, 28 g protein. **Diabetic Exchanges:** 4 lean meat, 1 fat, 1/2 starch.

Chipotle Salmon with Strawberry Mango Salsa

PREP/TOTAL TIME: 25 min. **YIELD:** 4 servings

NAYLET LAROCHELLE • MIAMI, FLORIDA

I've made this recipe several times for family dinners and have always received compliments. Even the kids like this sweet berry salsa with the spicy, savory salmon.

- 2 Tbsp. brown sugar
- 3 garlic cloves, minced
- 2 tsp. finely chopped chipotle peppers in adobo sauce
- 1/4 tsp. salt
- 4 salmon fillets (6 oz. *each*)

SALSA:
- 2 cups chopped fresh strawberries
- 2/3 cup chopped peeled mango
- 1/3 cup chopped red onion
- 2 Tbsp. lime juice
- 1 Tbsp. minced fresh cilantro
- 1 Tbsp. minced fresh mint
- 2 tsp. olive oil

1. In a small bowl, combine the brown sugar, garlic, chipotle peppers and salt; rub over salmon.

2. Moisten a paper towel with cooking oil; using long-handled tongs, lightly coat the grill rack. Place salmon skin side down on grill rack. Grill salmon, covered, over high heat or broil 3-4 in. from heat for 5-10 minutes or until the fish flakes easily with a fork.

3. In a small bowl, combine the salsa ingredients; serve with salmon.

Nutrition Facts: 1 salmon fillet with 1/2 cup salsa equals 368 calories, 18 g fat (4 g saturated fat), 85 mg cholesterol, 255 mg sodium, 21 g carbohydrate, 3 g fiber, 30 g protein. **Diabetic Exchanges:** 5 lean meat, 1-1/2 fat, 1/2 starch, 1/2 fruit.

Grapefruit Shrimp Salad C

PREP/TOTAL TIME: 15 min. **YIELD:** 4 servings

JOANNE BEAUPRE • MANCHESTER, CONNECTICUT

A simple combination of shrimp, avocado and grapefruit add up to one simply fabulous salad.

- 1 head Bibb or Boston lettuce
- 1 large grapefruit, peeled and sectioned
- 1 medium ripe avocado, peeled and thinly sliced
- 1 lb. cooked medium shrimp, peeled and deveined

CITRUS VINAIGRETTE:
- 2 Tbsp. orange juice
- 2 Tbsp. red wine vinegar
- 1 Tbsp. olive oil
- 2 tsp. Dijon mustard
- 1/4 tsp. salt

1. Place lettuce on four serving plates. Arrange the grapefruit, avocado and shrimp over lettuce. In a small bowl, whisk the vinaigrette ingredients. Drizzle over each salad.

Nutrition Facts: 1 serving equals 266 calories, 12 g fat (2 g saturated fat), 221 mg cholesterol, 445 mg sodium, 14 g carbohydrate, 4 g fiber, 26 g protein. **Diabetic Exchanges:** 3 lean meat, 2 fat, 1 vegetable, 1/2 fruit.

Grilled Tilapia with Raspberry Chipotle Chutney

PREP: 40 min. GRILL: 5 min. YIELD: 4 servings

MEGAN DICOU • BENTONVILLE, ARKANSAS

I eat a lot of fish and am always looking for healthy, tasty ways to prepare it. This recipe has become a family favorite because of the great flavors—and it's so easy to prepare, especially if you make the chutney ahead. I serve it with herbed couscous.

- 1   medium red onion, chopped
- 1   medium sweet red pepper, chopped
- 2   tsp. olive oil
- 3   garlic cloves, minced
- 2   tsp. minced fresh gingerroot
- 1-1/2 cups fresh raspberries
- 3/4 cup reduced-sodium chicken broth
- 1/4 cup honey
- 2   Tbsp. cider vinegar
- 1   Tbsp. minced chipotle peppers in adobo sauce
- 1/2 tsp. salt, *divided*
- 1/2 tsp. pepper, *divided*
- 4   tilapia fillets (6 oz. *each*)

1. In a large saucepan, saute onion and pepper in oil until tender. Add garlic and ginger; cook 1 minute longer. Stir in the raspberries, broth, honey, vinegar, chipotle peppers, 1/4 tsp. salt and 1/4 tsp. pepper. Bring to a boil. Reduce heat; simmer, uncovered, for 25-30 minutes or until thickened.

2. Meanwhile, sprinkle fillets with remaining salt and pepper. Using long-handled tongs, moisten a paper towel with cooking oil and lightly coat the grill rack. Grill fish, covered, over high heat or broil 3-4 in. from the heat for 3-5 minutes or until fish flakes easily with a fork. Serve with chutney.

Nutrition Facts: 1 fillet with 1/4 cup chutney equals 277 calories, 4 g fat (1 g saturated fat), 83 mg cholesterol, 491 mg sodium, 29 g carbohydrate, 5 g fiber, 33 g protein. **Diabetic Exchanges:** 5 lean meat, 2 starch, 1/2 fat.

Grilled Salmon Packets

PREP/TOTAL TIME: 25 min. YIELD: 4 servings

MIKE MILLER • CRESTON, IOWA

I don't like plain salmon, but this has a nice stir-fried flavor! It's a healthy meal-in-one favorite.

- 4   salmon fillets (6 oz. each)
- 3   cups fresh sugar snap peas
- 1   small sweet red pepper, cut into strips
- 1   small sweet yellow pepper, cut into strips
- 1/4 cup reduced-fat Asian toasted sesame salad dressing

1. Place each salmon fillet on a double thickness of heavy-duty foil (about 12 in. square). Combine sugar snap peas and peppers; spoon over salmon. Drizzle with dressing. Fold foil around mixture and seal tightly.

2. Grill, covered, over medium heat for 15-20 minutes or until fish flakes easily with a fork. Open foil carefully to allow steam to escape.

Nutrition Facts: 1 salmon fillet with 1 cup vegetables equals 350 calories, 17 g fat (3 g saturated fat), 85 mg cholesterol, 237 mg sodium, 14 g carbohydrate, 4 g fiber, 34 g protein. **Diabetic Exchanges:** 4 lean meat, 2 vegetable, 2 fat.

GRILLED SALMON PACKETS

GRILLED TILAPIA WITH RASPBERRY CHIPOTLE CHUTNEY

Halibut Steaks With Papaya Mint Salsa S C

PREP/TOTAL TIME: 20 min. **YIELD:** 4 servings

SONYA LABBE • LOS ANGELES, CALIFORNIA

An amazing mix of fresh, zesty salsa and good, smoky flavor—plus 161 mg of magnesium—makes this dish the catch of the day!

- 1 medium papaya, peeled, seeded and chopped
- 1/4 cup chopped red onion
- 1/4 cup fresh mint leaves
- 1 tsp. finely chopped chipotle pepper in adobo sauce
- 1 Tbsp. olive oil
- 1 Tbsp. honey
- 4 halibut steaks (6 oz. *each*)
- 1 Tbsp. olive oil

1. In a small bowl, combine the papaya, onion, mint, chipotle pepper, oil and honey. Cover and refrigerate until serving.

2. In a large skillet, cook halibut in oil for 4-6 minutes on each side or until fish flakes easily with a fork. Serve with salsa.

Nutrition Facts: 1 halibut steak with 1/2 cup salsa equals 300 calories, 11 g fat (2 g saturated fat), 54 mg cholesterol, 105 mg sodium, 13 g carbohydrate, 2 g fiber, 36 g protein. **Diabetic Exchanges:** 5 lean meat, 1 starch, 1 fat.

HALIBUT STEAKS WITH PAPAYA MINT SALSA

Colorful Crab Stir-Fry

PREP/TOTAL TIME: 30 min. **YIELD:** 4 servings

LEE DENEAU • LANSING, MICHIGAN

My love for seafood has carried over from childhood, when we used to fish together as a family. So I was happy to find this change-of-pace recipe that combines stir-fry with seafood. It tastes like a special treat but is a breeze to prepare.

- 2 tsp. cornstarch
- 1 tsp. chicken bouillon granules
- 3/4 cup water
- 1/2 tsp. reduced-sodium soy sauce
- 1 cup sliced fresh carrots
- 1 Tbsp. canola oil
- 1 cup fresh *or* frozen snow peas
- 1/2 cup julienned sweet red pepper
- 1 tsp. minced fresh gingerroot
- 1 tsp. minced garlic
- 1 pkg. (8 oz.) imitation crabmeat

Hot cooked rice, optional

1. In a small bowl, combine the cornstarch, bouillon, water and soy sauce until smooth; set aside. In a large skillet or wok, stir-fry carrots in oil. Add the peas, red pepper, ginger and garlic; stir-fry 1-2 minutes longer or until vegetables are crisp-tender.

2. Stir cornstarch mixture and gradually add to the pan. Bring to a boil; cook and stir for 2 minutes or until thickened. Add crab; heat through. Serve with rice if desired.

Nutrition Facts: 3/4 cup (calculated without rice) equals 126 calories, 4 g fat (trace saturated fat), 7 mg cholesterol, 562 mg sodium, 16 g carbohydrate, 2 g fiber, 7 g protein. **Diabetic Exchanges:** 3 vegetable, 1 lean meat.

COLORFUL CRAB STIR-FRY

Baked Italian Tilapia C

PREP: 10 min. **BAKE:** 40 min. **YIELD:** 4 servings

KIMBERLY MCGEE • MOSHEIM, TENNESSEE

It's easy to include healthful fish in your weekly menus with recipes as tasty and simple as this one!

4	tilapia fillets (6 oz. *each*)
1/4	tsp. pepper
1	can (14-1/2 oz.) diced tomatoes with basil, oregano and garlic, drained
1	large onion, halved and julienned
1	medium green pepper, halved and julienned
1/4	cup shredded Parmesan cheese

1. Place tilapia in a 13-in. x 9-in. baking dish coated with cooking spray; sprinkle with the pepper. Spoon the tomatoes over tilapia; top with the onion and the green pepper.

2. Cover and bake at 350° for 30 minutes. Uncover; sprinkle with cheese.

3. Bake 10-15 minutes longer or until fish flakes easily with a fork.

Nutrition Facts: 1 serving equals 215 calories, 4 g fat (2 g saturated fat), 86 mg cholesterol, 645 mg sodium, 12 g carbohydrate, 2 g fiber, 36 g protein. **Diabetic Exchanges:** 4 lean meat, 2 vegetable.

If you're looking for fish that doesn't taste "fishy," try widely available **tilapia.** It offers a delightfully mild flavor that works well with many herbs and seasonings. It's a great way to get your family accustomed to main courses featuring fish and seafood.

EGG FOO YONG

Egg Foo Yong [C]

PREP: 15 min. COOK: 5 min./batch YIELD: 4 servings

SHERRI MELOTIK • OAK CREEK, WISCONSIN

Forget the Chinese takeout! You'll have fun making this colorful, crunchy and delicious version of an Asian classic at home in just about 20 minutes.

  1 can (14 oz.) chop suey vegetables, drained
1/2 lb. peeled and deveined cooked small shrimp, coarsely chopped
  4 green onions, thinly sliced
  4 eggs, beaten
  2 Tbsp. canola oil

GREEN PEA SAUCE:
  2 Tbsp. cornstarch
  1 tsp. chicken bouillon granules
  2 cups water
1-1/2 tsp. reduced-sodium soy sauce
1/2 cup frozen peas, thawed

1. In a large bowl, combine the chop suey vegetables, shrimp and green onions. Stir in eggs.

2. In a large nonstick skillet, heat 1 tsp. oil. Drop vegetable mixture by 1/4 cupfuls into skillet. Cook in batches until browned on both sides, using remaining oil as needed.

3. In a small saucepan, combine cornstarch and bouillon. Gradually stir in the water and soy sauce. Bring to a boil; cook and stir for 2 minutes or until sauce is thickened.

4. Stir peas into the sauce; heat through. Serve with egg foo yong.

Nutrition Facts: 3 patties with 1/2 cup sauce equals 242 calories, 13 g fat (2 g saturated fat), 298 mg cholesterol, 497 mg sodium, 10 g carbohydrate, 2 g fiber, 20 g protein. **Diabetic Exchanges:** 3 lean meat, 1-1/2 fat, 1/2 starch.

Walnut-Crusted Salmon [C]

PREP/TOTAL TIME: 25 min. **YIELD:** 4 servings

EDIE DESPAIN • LOGAN, UTAH

Whenever I can get salmon for a good price, I always turn to this simple and delicious recipe. It's wonderful served with mashed potatoes and fresh green beans.

- 4 salmon fillets (4 oz. *each*)
- 4 tsp. Dijon mustard
- 4 tsp. honey
- 2 slices whole wheat bread
- 3 Tbsp. finely chopped walnuts
- 2 tsp. canola oil
- 1/2 tsp. dried thyme

1. Place salmon on a baking sheet coated with cooking spray. Combine mustard and honey; brush over salmon. Place bread in a food processor; cover and process until crumbly. Transfer to a small bowl. Add the walnuts, oil and thyme; press onto salmon.

2. Bake at 400° for 12-15 minutes or until fish flakes easily with a fork and topping is lightly browned.

Nutrition Facts: 1 fillet equals 326 calories, 19 g fat (3 g saturated fat), 67 mg cholesterol, 253 mg sodium, 13 g carbohydrate, 1 g fiber, 25 g protein. **Diabetic Exchanges:** 3 lean meat, 1 starch, 1/2 fat.

Poached Salmon with Grapefruit Salsa [C]

PREP/TOTAL TIME: 30 min. **YIELD:** 4 servings

PATRICIA NIEH • PORTOLA VALLEY, CALIFORNIA

Family and friends often request this recipe ahead of time when they know they'll be dining with me. I gladly fill their requests because this is so easy, the dish is delicious—and it especially pleases those who are counting calories.

- 5 cups strong brewed green tea
- 4 fresh basil sprigs
- 4 fresh thyme sprigs
- 4 fresh cilantro sprigs
- 3 Tbsp. lemon juice
- 3 Tbsp. minced fresh gingerroot
- 4 salmon fillets (4 oz. *each*)

SALSA:
- 1 large pink grapefruit, sectioned and chopped
- 4 green onions, thinly sliced
- 1 Tbsp. minced fresh cilantro
- 1 Tbsp. finely chopped crystallized ginger
- 1/4 tsp. salt

1. In a large skillet, combine the first six ingredients. Bring to a boil. Reduce heat; add salmon and poach, uncovered, for 8-10 minutes or until fish flakes easily with a fork.

2. Meanwhile, in a small bowl, combine the salsa ingredients. Remove salmon with a slotted spoon. Serve with salsa.

Nutrition Facts: 1 salmon fillet with 1/4 cup salsa equals 220 calories, 11 g fat (2 g saturated fat), 57 mg cholesterol, 209 mg sodium, 11 g carbohydrate, 1 g fiber, 20 g protein. **Diabetic Exchanges:** 3 lean meat, 1 starch.

> When sectioning **grapefruit**, it can be hard to remove the white pith. Place the whole fruit in boiling water. Remove from heat; let stand 5 minutes before draining. Peel and section when it's cool enough to handle.

POACHED SALMON WITH GRAPEFRUIT SALSA

WALNUT-CRUSTED SALMON

Individual Tuna Casseroles

PREP: 30 min. **BAKE:** 25 min. **YIELD:** 6 servings

CHERYL WOODSON • LIBERTY, MISSOURI

Tuna casserole gets updated with this unique and flavorful recipe. Friends and family will love the appeal, not to mention that it's lower in saturated fat and calories.

- 1-1/2 cups uncooked whole wheat penne pasta
- 1 can (12 oz.) white water-packed tuna, drained
- 1 can (10-3/4 oz.) reduced-fat reduced-sodium condensed cream of mushroom soup, undiluted
- 1-1/4 cups water-packed artichoke hearts, rinsed, drained and chopped
- 1/2 cup reduced-fat sour cream
- 1/4 cup roasted sweet red peppers, drained and chopped
- 3 Tbsp. chopped onion
- 3 Tbsp. sun-dried tomatoes (not packed in oil), chopped
- 2 Tbsp. Greek olives, chopped
- 1 Tbsp. snipped fresh dill or 1 tsp. dill weed
- 1 Tbsp. capers, drained
- 2 garlic cloves, minced
- 1 tsp. grated lemon peel
- 1/2 tsp. crushed red pepper flakes
- 1/2 cup dry bread crumbs
- 1/4 cup grated Parmesan cheese
- 1/2 tsp. Italian seasoning

1. Cook pasta according to package directions.

2. Meanwhile, in a large bowl, combine the tuna, soup, artichokes, sour cream, peppers, onion, sun-dried tomatoes, olives, dill, capers, garlic, lemon peel and pepper flakes. Drain the pasta; stir into the tuna mixture. Divide among six 10-oz. ramekins or custard cups.

3. In a small bowl, combine the bread crumbs, cheese and Italian seasoning. Sprinkle over tuna mixture. Place ramekins on a baking sheet. Bake, uncovered at 350° for 25-30 minutes or until golden brown.

Nutrition Facts: 1 serving equals 321 calories, 7 g fat (3 g saturated fat), 35 mg cholesterol, 801 mg sodium, 38 g carbohydrate, 4 g fiber, 24 g protein.

INDIVIDUAL TUNA CASSEROLES

TILAPIA WITH GRAPEFRUIT SALSA

Tilapia with Grapefruit Salsa

PREP: 25 min. + marinating **COOK:** 10 min.
YIELD: 2 servings

EMILY SEEFELDT • RED WING, MINNESOTA

Not only is tilapia a tender and attractive fish, but it's a snap to find these fillets in single serving sizes. Ideal for two, this favorite is draped in a spicy grapefruit salsa.

1/3 cup unsweetened grapefruit juice
1/2 tsp. ground cumin
  1 garlic clove, minced
1/4 tsp. grated grapefruit peel
1/8 tsp. salt
1/8 tsp. pepper
Dash to 1/8 tsp. cayenne pepper
  2 tilapia fillets (6 oz. *each*)
1/2 cup canned black beans, rinsed and drained
1/3 cup chopped pink grapefruit sections
1/4 cup chopped red onion

  1 Tbsp. minced fresh cilantro
  1 to 2 tsp. chopped jalapeno pepper
  2 tsp. butter

1. For marinade, in a small bowl, combine the first seven ingredients. Set aside 1 Tbsp. Place tilapia in a large resealable plastic bag; add remaining marinade. Seal bag and turn to coat. Refrigerate for 1 hour.

2. In a small bowl, combine the beans, grapefruit sections, onion, cilantro, jalapeno and reserved marinade. Cover and refrigerate until serving.

3. Drain and discard marinade. In a small skillet over medium heat, cook tilapia in butter for 4-5 minutes on each side or until fish flakes easily with a fork. Serve with salsa.

Editor's Note: When cutting hot peppers, disposable gloves are recommended. Avoid touching your face.

Nutrition Facts: 1 fillet with 1/2 cup salsa equals 264 calories, 6 g fat (3 g saturated fat), 93 mg cholesterol, 369 mg sodium, 18 g carbohydrate, 4 g fiber, 36 g protein. **Diabetic Exchanges:** 5 lean meat, 1 starch, 1 fat.

Grilled Shrimp with Cilantro Dipping Sauce ⓒ

PREP: 25 min. + marinating **GRILL:** 5 min.
YIELD: 4 servings

ELIZABETH LUBIN • HUNTINGTON BEACH, CALIFORNIA

I came up with this recipe when my daughter grew a beautiful jalapeno plant last summer. I already had cilantro in the garden, so it seemed like a great combination for a tasty sauce.

- 2 Tbsp. minced fresh cilantro
- 2 Tbsp. olive oil
- 1 Tbsp. minced fresh chives
- 1 garlic clove, minced
- 1 pound uncooked medium shrimp, peeled and deveined

DIPPING SAUCE:
- 1 cup fresh cilantro leaves
- 1 cup fat-free mayonnaise
- 1 jalapeno pepper, seeded
- 1 garlic clove, peeled
- 1 Tbsp. white vinegar
- 1 tsp. sugar

Dash cayenne pepper

1. In a large resealable plastic bag, combine the cilantro, oil, chives and garlic. Add the shrimp; seal bag and turn to coat. Cover and refrigerate for 1 hour.

2. In a blender, combine the sauce ingredients; cover and process until blended. Chill until serving.

3. Thread shrimp onto four metal or soaked wooden skewers. Grill, covered, over medium heat for 2-3 minutes on each side or until shrimp turn pink. Serve with sauce.

Editor's Note: When cutting hot peppers, disposable gloves are recommended. Avoid touching your face.

Nutrition Facts: 1 skewer with 1/4 cup sauce equals 208 calories, 10 g fat (2 g saturated fat), 144 mg cholesterol, 615 mg sodium, 11 g carbohydrate, 1 g fiber, 19 g protein.

Salmon Spirals With Cucumber Sauce ⓒ

PREP: 20 min. + marinating **GRILL:** 10 min.
YIELD: 4 skewers (1-1/3 cups sauce)

ROSALIND POPE • GREENSBORO, NORTH CAROLINA

When you serve up this dish, it'll be hard to tell which impresses your guests more: the delicious flavor or the classy presentation.

- 1 salmon fillet (1 lb.)
- 8 fresh dill sprigs
- 1/4 cup lime juice
- 1 Tbsp. olive oil
- 2 tsp. Dijon mustard

SAUCE:
- 1 cup (8 oz.) fat-free plain yogurt
- 1/4 cup fat-free mayonnaise
- 2 Tbsp. finely chopped seeded peeled cucumber
- 2 Tbsp. snipped fresh dill
- 1 Tbsp. lemon juice

1. Remove skin from fillet and discard. Cut fillet lengthwise into four strips. Place two dill sprigs on each strip; roll up. Thread salmon onto four metal or soaked wooden skewers.

2. In a large resealable plastic bag, combine the lime juice, oil and mustard; add the salmon. Seal bag and turn to coat; refrigerate salmon for 30 minutes, turning occasionally.

3. Drain and discard marinade. Using long-handled tongs, moisten a paper towel with cooking oil and

GRILLED SHRIMP WITH CILANTRO DIPPING SAUCE

SALMON SPIRALS WITH CUCUMBER SAUCE

CRAB MACARONI CASSEROLE

lightly coat the grill rack. Grill the salmon, covered, over high heat or broil 3-4 in. from the heat for 4-5 minutes on each side or until the fish flakes easily with a fork.

4. Meanwhile, in a small bowl, combine the sauce ingredients. Serve with salmon.

Nutrition Facts: 1 skewer with 1/3 cup sauce equals 253 calories, 13 g fat (3 g saturated fat), 70 mg cholesterol, 233 mg sodium, 8 g carbohydrate, trace fiber, 25 g protein.

Open-Faced Crab Melts

PREP/TOTAL TIME: 10 min. YIELD: 4 servings

FLORENCE MCCLELLAND • FREDONIA, NEW YORK

Not only do these versatile sandwiches make a change-of-pace lunch, but you can serve them at everything from fancy teas to last-minute suppers. Add some chili sauce and a little prepared horseradish to the crab mixture to mix things up a bit.

4	English muffins, split
1/3	cup mayonnaise
1	Tbsp. lemon juice
1/2	tsp. pepper
1/4	tsp. dried tarragon
1	can (6 oz.) crabmeat, drained, flaked and cartilage removed
1	cup (4 oz.) shredded cheddar cheese

1. Broil English muffins 4-6 in. from the heat for 2-3 minutes or until golden brown.

2. In a large bowl, combine the mayonnaise, lemon juice, pepper and tarragon; stir in crab. Spread over each muffin half; sprinkle with cheddar cheese. Broil for 2-3 minutes or until cheese is melted.

Nutrition Facts: 1 serving (1 each) equals 411 calories, 24 g fat (8 g saturated fat), 75 mg cholesterol, 676 mg sodium, 28 g carbohydrate, 2 g fiber, 19 g protein.

Crab Macaroni Casserole

PREP: 25 min. BAKE: 20 min. YIELD: 6 servings

JASON EGNER • EDGERTON, WISCONSIN

Cold winter evenings are much more tolerable with this comforting casserole. Whole wheat macaroni boosts nutrition, while the melted cheese topping makes it rich and so satisfying. We like it best with a veggie side.

2	cups uncooked whole wheat elbow macaroni
3	Tbsp. chopped onion
2	Tbsp. butter
3	Tbsp. all-purpose flour
1-1/2	cups fat-free milk
2	cans (6 oz. *each*) lump crabmeat, drained
1	cup (8 oz.) reduced-fat sour cream
1/2	cup shredded Swiss cheese
1/2	tsp. salt
1/2	tsp. ground mustard
1	cup (4 oz.) shredded fat-free cheddar cheese, *divided*

1. Cook macaroni according to package directions.

2. Meanwhile, in a large skillet, saute onion in butter until tender. Combine flour and milk until smooth; stir into pan. Bring to a boil; cook and stir for 1-2 minutes or until thickened. Remove from the heat. Drain macaroni. Add the crabmeat, sour cream, Swiss cheese, salt, mustard, macaroni and 1/4 cup cheddar cheese to the skillet.

3. Transfer to an 11-in. x 7-in. baking dish coated with cooking spray. Sprinkle with remaining cheddar cheese. Bake, uncovered, at 350° for 20-25 minutes or until heated through.

Nutrition Facts: 1 cup equals 380 calories, 11 g fat (6 g saturated fat), 86 mg cholesterol, 619 mg sodium, 38 g carbohydrate, 4 g fiber, 31 g protein. **Diabetic Exchanges:** 3 lean meat, 2 starch, 1-1/2 fat.

Spicy Shrimp Fettuccine

PREP: 20 min. COOK: 15 min. YIELD: 6 servings

TRISHA KRUSE • EAGLE, IDAHO

Pasta gets a kick from red pepper flakes in this change-of-pace dish featuring shrimp, garlic and basil served in a tomato sauce.

- 9 oz. uncooked whole wheat fettuccine
- 4 garlic cloves, minced
- 3 Tbsp. olive oil
- 1-1/2 lbs. uncooked medium shrimp, peeled and deveined
- 2 cups reduced-sodium tomato juice
- 1/2 cup tomato sauce
- 1/2 to 1 tsp. crushed red pepper flakes
- 1/4 tsp. salt
- 1/4 tsp. pepper
- 4 tsp. cornstarch
- 1/4 cup white wine *or* reduced-sodium chicken broth
- 2 Tbsp. minced fresh basil

1. Cook fettuccine according to package directions.

2. Meanwhile, in a large nonstick skillet, saute garlic in oil until tender. Stir in the shrimp, tomato juice, tomato sauce, pepper flakes, salt and pepper. In a small bowl, combine cornstarch and wine until smooth; stir into skillet. Bring to a boil. Reduce heat; simmer, uncovered, for 5-6 minutes or until shrimp turn pink and sauce is thickened.

3. Drain fettuccine; stir into skillet. Sprinkle with basil just before serving.

Nutrition Facts: 1-1/3 cups equals 348 calories, 9 g fat (1 g saturated fat), 138 mg cholesterol, 374 mg sodium, 38 g carbohydrate, 5 g fiber, 26 g protein. **Diabetic Exchanges:** 3 lean meat, 2 starch, 1 vegetable, 1 fat.

Veggie Tuna Burgers

PREP/TOTAL TIME: 30 min. YIELD: 6 servings

LAURA DAVIS • RUSTON, LOUISIANA

You don't have to be a health nut to enjoy the flavor of these moist and nutritious burgers. They're an easy way to get my children to eat their vegetables.

- 1/4 cup finely chopped onion
- 1 garlic clove, minced
- 1 cup *each* shredded zucchini, yellow summer squash and carrots
- 1 egg, lightly beaten
- 2 cups soft whole wheat bread crumbs
- 1 can (6 oz.) light water-packed tuna, drained and flaked
- 1/4 tsp. salt
- 1/4 tsp. pepper
- 1 tsp. butter
- 6 hamburger buns, split
- 6 slices reduced-fat cheddar cheese
- 6 lettuce leaves
- 6 slices tomato

1. In a large nonstick skillet coated with cooking spray, saute onion and garlic for 1 minute. Add the zucchini, yellow squash and carrots; saute until tender. Drain and cool to room temperature.

2. In a large bowl, combine the egg, bread crumbs, tuna, salt and pepper. Add vegetable mixture. Shape into six 3-1/2-in. patties.

3. Coat the same skillet again with cooking spray; cook patties in butter for 3-5 minutes on each side or until lightly browned. Serve on buns with cheese, lettuce and tomato.

Nutrition Facts: 1 burger equals 275 calories, 8 g fat (4 g saturated fat), 58 mg cholesterol, 643 mg sodium, 32 g carbohydrate, 3 g fiber, 20 g protein. **Diabetic Exchanges:** 2 starch, 2 lean meat, 1 vegetable.

Shrimp and Pineapple Fried Rice

PREP/TOTAL TIME: 30 min. YIELD: 6 servings

LYNNE VAN WAGENEN • SALT LAKE CITY, UTAH

Pineapple chunks give fried rice a tropical twist, while shrimp and cashews turn this simple favorite into a restaurant-quality meal everyone will love.

- 2 eggs
- 1 small onion, chopped
- 1 tsp. canola oil
- 3 garlic cloves, minced
- 3 cups cooked instant brown rice
- 1 can (20 oz.) unsweetened pineapple chunks, drained
- 1/2 lb. cooked medium shrimp, peeled and deveined
- 1/2 cup chopped cashews
- 1/2 cup frozen peas, thawed
- 2 green onions, sliced
- 3 Tbsp. reduced-sodium soy sauce
- 1 Tbsp. hoisin sauce
- 1 tsp. sugar
- 1 tsp. sesame oil
- 1/4 tsp. pepper

1. In a small bowl, whisk eggs. Heat a large nonstick skillet coated with cooking spray over medium heat. Add eggs; cook and stir until set; remove from the skillet and keep warm.

2. In the same skillet, saute onion in oil until tender. Add garlic; cook 1 minute longer. Stir in the rice, pineapple, shrimp, cashews, peas and green onions; heat through. Combine the soy sauce, hoisin sauce, sugar, sesame oil and pepper; stir into rice mixture. Stir in eggs.

Nutrition Facts: 1-1/3 cups equals 342 calories, 10 g fat (2 g saturated fat), 128 mg cholesterol, 521 mg sodium, 46 g carbohydrate, 4 g fiber, 16 g protein.

Scrumptious California Salmon

PREP: 35 min. BAKE: 10 min. YIELD: 4 servings

DUSTIN ANDERSON • FILLMORE, CALIFORNIA

California cuisine is all about balancing flavors. This recipe brings out the sweetness in citrus and honey and balances it with a pop of ancho chili pepper and balsamic vinegar.

- 3 garlic cloves, minced
- 1 tsp. minced shallot
- 1 cup orange juice
- 1 Tbsp. balsamic vinegar
- 3 Tbsp. honey
- 1 Tbsp. ground ancho chili pepper
- 1/4 tsp. salt
- 1/8 tsp. pepper
- 1 salmon fillet (1 lb.)
- 2 tsp. canola oil
- 2 Tbsp. minced fresh cilantro

1. In a small saucepan coated with cooking spray, saute garlic and shallot until tender. Add orange juice and vinegar. Bring to a boil. Reduce heat; simmer, uncovered, for 20-25 minutes or until reduced to 1/4 cup. Stir in the honey, chili pepper, salt and pepper.

2. In a large ovenproof skillet, brown salmon in oil on both sides. Brush with 1/4 cup sauce. Bake, uncovered, at 400° for 8-10 minutes or until fish flakes easily with a fork.

3. Brush with remaining sauce and sprinkle with fresh cilantro.

Nutrition Facts: 3 oz. cooked salmon equals 317 calories, 15 g fat (3 g saturated fat), 67 mg cholesterol, 217 mg sodium, 21 g carbohydrate, trace fiber, 23 g protein.

SCRUMPTIOUS CALIFORNIA SALMON

SHRIMP AND PINEAPPLE FRIED RICE

Salmon with Tomato Shallot Sauce C

PREP: 20 min. COOK: 15 min. YIELD: 4 servings

KIMBERLY CUTLER • FLORENCE, ARIZONA

Light and refreshing, this is a great treatment for salmon that perfectly suits any occasion. Capers add a delightful burst of tangy saltiness.

4	salmon fillets (4 oz. *each*)
1	Tbsp. grated lemon peel
1/2	tsp. white pepper
1/8	tsp. salt
3/4	cup chopped shallots
2	tsp. olive oil
1	garlic clove, minced
1	tsp. capers, drained
3/4	cup dry white wine *or* reduced-sodium chicken broth
2	medium tomatoes, seeded and chopped
1/2	tsp. dried basil

1. Sprinkle fillets with lemon peel, white pepper and salt; set aside.

2. In a large nonstick skillet, saute the shallots in oil until tender. Add garlic and capers; cook 1 minute longer. Stir in wine; add reserved salmon.

3. Reduce heat; cover and cook for 8-10 minutes or until fish flakes easily with a fork. Add tomatoes and basil; heat through.

Nutrition Facts: 1 fillet with 1/3 cup sauce equals 297 calories, 15 g fat (3 g saturated fat), 67 mg cholesterol, 171 mg sodium, 10 g carbohydrate, 1 g fiber, 24 g protein.

Spicy Shrimp & Peppers with Pasta

PREP: 20 min. COOK: 25 min. YIELD: 4 servings

AMY MILLS • SEBRING, FLORIDA

Spice up any weeknight with this filling and tasty family dish. It goes together in no time and features tender shrimp, veggies, whole wheat pasta and just the right amount of heat.

1	cup sliced baby portobello mushrooms
1	medium sweet yellow pepper, cut into 1/2-in. pieces
1	medium green pepper, cut into 1/2-in. pieces
1	shallot, minced
2	Tbsp. olive oil
1	garlic clove, minced
1/2	tsp. crushed red pepper flakes
1	can (28 oz.) crushed tomatoes
1	tsp. Italian seasoning
1/2	tsp. salt
6	oz. uncooked multigrain linguine
1	pound uncooked medium shrimp, peeled and deveined
3	Tbsp. minced fresh parsley *or* 1 Tbsp. dried parsley flakes

1. In a large nonstick skillet coated with cooking spray, saute the mushrooms, peppers and shallot in oil until tender. Add garlic and pepper flakes; cook 1 minute longer.

2. Stir in the tomatoes, Italian seasoning and salt. Bring to a boil. Reduce heat; simmer, uncovered, for 12-15 minutes or until vegetables are tender.

3. Meanwhile, cook linguine according to package directions. Add shrimp to sauce; cook and stir for 5-7 minutes or until shrimp turn pink.

4. Drain linguine; stir into sauce. Heat through. Sprinkle with parsley.

Nutrition Facts: 2 cups equals 385 calories, 10 g fat (1 g saturated fat), 138 mg cholesterol, 697 mg sodium, 53 g carbohydrate, 10 g fiber, 28 g protein.

SPICY SHRIMP & PEPPERS WITH PASTA

SALMON WITH TOMATO SHALLOT SAUCE

Snapper with Zucchini & Mushrooms C

PREP: 25 min. **COOK:** 10 min. **YIELD:** 4 servings

LISA GLOGOW • ALISO VIEJO, CALIFORNIA

Looking for a way to keep your family's meals light and high in veggie content? This recipe is it. Colorful tomatoes, mushrooms and zucchini make a surprisingly filling topping for this fish. It's yummy with pork, too.

3 cups diced zucchini

2 cups halved fresh mushrooms

3/4 cup chopped sweet onion

2 Tbsp. olive oil, *divided*

3 garlic cloves, minced

1 can (14-1/2 oz.) diced tomatoes, undrained

2 tsp. minced fresh basil *or* 1/2 tsp. dried basil

2 tsp. minced fresh oregano *or* 1/2 tsp. dried oregano

1/4 tsp. salt

1/4 tsp. pepper

1/4 tsp. crushed red pepper flakes, optional

4 red snapper *or* orange roughy fillets (6 oz. *each*)

1. In a large nonstick skillet coated with cooking spray, saute the zucchini, mushrooms and onion in 1 Tbsp. oil until crisp-tender. Add garlic; cook 1 minute longer. Stir in the tomatoes, basil, oregano, salt, pepper and pepper flakes if desired. Bring to a boil. Reduce heat; cover and simmer for 12-15 minutes or until vegetables are tender.

2. Meanwhile, in another large nonstick skillet coated with cooking spray, cook the fillets in remaining oil over medium heat for 4-6 minutes on each side or until fish flakes easily with a fork. Serve with the vegetable mixture.

Nutrition Facts: 1 fillet with 1 cup vegetables equals 253 calories, 8 g fat (1 g saturated fat), 102 mg cholesterol, 414 mg sodium, 14 g carbohydrate, 4 g fiber, 32 g protein. **Diabetic Exchanges:** 4 lean meat, 2 vegetable, 1-1/2 fat.

To choose the **freshest zucchini,** look for a firm, heavy squash with a moist stem end and a shiny, unblemished skin. Smaller zucchini are generally sweeter and more tender than their larger counterparts.

APRICOT-PINEAPPLE GLAZED SHRIMP

Apricot-Pineapple Glazed Shrimp

PREP: 30 min. GRILL: 10 min. YIELD: 14 appetizers

TRISHA KRUSE • EAGLE, IDAHO

This is one of my favorite grill recipes. The glaze is sweet, tangy and addictive, and the shrimp tastes fantastic over rice, on salad or as an appetizer.

1	cup apricot preserves
1/4	cup finely chopped dried apricots
2	Tbsp. finely chopped onion
1	Tbsp. rice vinegar
1	Tbsp. Dijon mustard
1	garlic clove, halved
1/4	tsp. salt
28	uncooked jumbo shrimp, peeled and deveined
2	cups cubed fresh pineapple (about 14 pieces)
1	medium sweet red pepper, cut into 14 pieces

1. Place first seven ingredients in a food processor. Cover and process until blended; set aside half of sauce for serving.

2. On each of 14 metal or soaked wooden appetizer skewers, thread shrimp, pineapple and red pepper. Grill, covered, over medium heat for 3-4 minutes on each side or until shrimp turn pink, basting frequently with remaining sauce. Serve with reserved sauce.

Nutrition Facts: 1 kabob with about 2-1/2 tsp. sauce equals 120 calories, 1 g fat (trace saturated fat), 62 mg cholesterol, 139 mg sodium, 21 g carbohydrate, 1 g fiber, 9 g protein.
Diabetic Exchanges: 1-1/2 starch, 1 lean meat.

Baked Salmon Cakes

PREP/TOTAL TIME: 30 min. YIELD: 4 servings

NIKKI HADDAD • GERMANTOWN, MARYLAND

Baked in muffin pans and served with sauce on the side, these cute cakes make a fantastic light meal. You can also bake a double batch and freeze some for a quick, healthful supper later in the month.

1	can (14-3/4 oz.) salmon, drained, bones and skin removed
1-1/2	cups soft whole wheat bread crumbs
1/2	cup finely chopped sweet red pepper
1/2	cup egg substitute
3	green onions, thinly sliced
1/4	cup finely chopped celery
1/4	cup minced fresh cilantro
3	Tbsp. fat-free mayonnaise
1	Tbsp. lemon juice
1	garlic clove, minced
1/8 to 1/4	tsp. hot pepper sauce

SAUCE:

2	Tbsp. fat-free mayonnaise
1/4	tsp. capers, drained
1/4	tsp. dill weed

Dash lemon juice

1. In a large bowl, combine the first 11 ingredients. Place 1/3 cup salmon mixture into eight muffin cups coated with cooking spray. Bake at 425° for 10-15 minutes or until a meat thermometer reads 160°.

2. Meanwhile, combine the sauce ingredients. Serve with salmon.

Nutrition Facts: 2 salmon cakes with 1-1/2 tsp. sauce equals 266 calories, 9 g fat (2 g saturated fat), 48 mg cholesterol, 914 mg sodium, 17 g carbohydrate, 3 g fiber, 28 g protein.

Salmon & Slaw Sliders

PREP/TOTAL TIME: 30 min. **YIELD:** 4 servings

EDRIE O'BRIEN • DENVER, COLORADO

This recipe first came about using leftover salmon and slaw. Now we plan to make it all the time. It's a nice alternative to burgers and always well-received at parties. The salmon can also be broiled.

- 1/2 cup chopped cabbage
- 1/2 cup chopped fennel bulb
- 1 green onion, chopped
- 1/4 cup fat-free mayonnaise, *divided*
- 1 Tbsp. fat-free plain yogurt
- 1-3/4 tsp. salt-free seasoning blend, *divided*
- 4 salmon fillets (4 oz. *each*)

Cooking spray

- 4 whole wheat dinner rolls, split

1. In a small bowl, combine the cabbage, fennel and onion. Combine 2 Tbsp. mayonnaise, yogurt and 1/4 tsp. seasoning blend; pour over cabbage mixture and toss to coat. Chill until serving.

2. Spritz salmon with cooking spray; sprinkle with remaining seasoning blend.

3. Using long-handled tongs, moisten a paper towel with cooking oil and lightly coat the grill rack. Grill fillets, covered, over medium heat or broil 4 in. from the heat for 10-12 minutes or until fish flakes easily with a fork. Remove and keep warm.

4. Grill rolls, cut side down, over medium heat for 30-60 seconds or broil 4 in. from the heat until toasted. Spread with remaining mayonnaise; top each with a fillet and 1/4 cup coleslaw. Replace roll tops.

Nutrition Facts: 1 sandwich equals 335 calories, 15 g fat (3 g saturated fat), 86 mg cholesterol, 388 mg sodium, 22 g carbohydrate, 2 g fiber, 26 g protein.

Grilled Tuna Steaks ⓒ

PREP: 10 min. + marinating **GRILL:** 10 min. **YIELD:** 4 servings

JAN HUNTINGTON • PAINESVILLE, OHIO

After enjoying yellowfin tuna at a restaurant in southwest Florida, I came up with this recipe so I could enjoy the flavor of my favorite fish at home.

- 2 Tbsp. lemon juice
- 1 Tbsp. olive oil
- 2 garlic cloves, minced
- 2 tsp. minced fresh thyme *or* 1/2 tsp. dried thyme
- 4 tuna steaks (6 oz. *each*)
- 1/4 tsp. salt
- 1/4 tsp. pepper

1. In a large resealable plastic bag, combine the lemon juice, oil, garlic and thyme. Add the tuna; seal bag and turn to coat. Refrigerate for up to 30 minutes, turning occasionally.

2. Remove tuna from bag; sprinkle with salt and pepper. Drain and discard marinade. Using long-handled tongs, moisten a paper towel with cooking oil and lightly coat the grill rack.

3. Grill tuna, covered, over medium-hot heat or broil 4 in. from the heat for 3-4 minutes on each side for medium-rare or until slightly pink in the center.

Nutrition Facts: 1 tuna steak equals 218 calories, 5 g fat (1 g saturated fat), 77 mg cholesterol, 211 mg sodium, 1 g carbohydrate, trace fiber, 40 g protein. **Diabetic Exchanges:** 5 lean meat, 1/2 fat.

GRILLED TUNA STEAKS

SALMON & SLAW SLIDERS

Shrimp Lo Mein

PREP: 25 min. **COOK:** 15 min. **YIELD:** 4 servings

SHERRI STARKIN • LYLE, WASHINGTON

This recipe is simple, fast, healthy and very adaptable. You can change the seafood or vegetables to your taste.

- 1 pound uncooked medium shrimp, peeled and deveined
- 2 garlic cloves, sliced

Dash blackened seasoning

- 6 oz. uncooked multigrain linguine
- 4 tsp. cornstarch
- 1/3 cup water
- 1/4 cup ketchup
- 2 Tbsp. reduced-sodium soy sauce
- 2 Tbsp. sherry *or* reduced-sodium chicken broth
- 2 tsp. honey
- 1/4 tsp. ground ginger
- 1/4 tsp. crushed red pepper flakes
- 2 Tbsp. olive oil, *divided*
- 1 celery rib, sliced
- 1 medium carrot, chopped
- 1/2 cup sliced fresh mushrooms
- 1/4 cup fresh broccoli florets
- 2 Tbsp. chopped cashews
- 1 can (8 oz.) unsweetened pineapple chunks, drained

1. In a small bowl, combine the shrimp, garlic and blackened seasoning; set aside. Cook linguine according to package directions.

2. Meanwhile, in a small bowl, combine the cornstarch, water, ketchup, soy sauce, sherry, honey, ginger and pepper flakes until blended; set aside.

3. In a large nonstick skillet or wok, stir-fry shrimp in 1 Tbsp. oil for 2-3 minutes or until no longer pink. Remove with a slotted spoon and keep warm.

4. Stir-fry celery and carrot in remaining oil for 5 minutes. Add the mushrooms, broccoli and cashews; stir-fry 4-6 minutes longer or until vegetables are crisp-tender.

5. Stir cornstarch mixture and add to the pan. Bring to a boil; cook and stir for 2 minutes or until thickened. Drain linguine; stir into skillet. Add shrimp and pineapple; heat through.

Nutrition Facts: 1 cup equals 401 calories, 11 g fat (2 g saturated fat), 138 mg cholesterol, 678 mg sodium, 53 g carbohydrate, 6 g fiber, 25 g protein.

Orange Tilapia In Parchment F C

PREP/TOTAL TIME: 30 min. **YIELD:** 4 servings

TIFFANY DIEBOLD • NASHVILLE, TENNESSEE

Sweet orange juice and spicy cayenne pepper give this no-fuss dish fabulous flavor. A bonus? Cleanup is a breeze!

- 1/4 cup orange juice
- 4 tsp. grated orange peel
- 1/4 tsp. salt
- 1/4 tsp. cayenne pepper
- 1/4 tsp. pepper
- 4 tilapia fillets (6 oz. *each*)
- 1/2 cup julienned carrot
- 1/2 cup julienned zucchini

1. In a small bowl, combine the first five ingredients; set aside. Cut parchment paper or heavy-duty foil into four 18-in. x 12-in. lengths; place a fish fillet on each. Top with carrot and zucchini; drizzle with reserved orange juice mixture.

2. Fold parchment paper over fish. Working from the bottom inside corner, fold up about 3/4 in. of the paper and crimp both layers to seal. Repeat, folding edges up and crimping, until a half-moon-shaped packet is formed. Repeat for remaining packets. Place on baking sheets.

3. Bake at 450° for 12-15 minutes or until fish flakes easily with a fork. Open packets carefully to allow steam to escape.

Nutrition Facts: 1 packet equals 158 calories, 2 g fat (1 g saturated fat), 83 mg cholesterol, 220 mg sodium, 4 g carbohydrate, 1 g fiber, 32 g protein. **Diabetic Exchange:** 5 lean meat.

Rosemary Shrimp With Spaghetti

PREP/TOTAL TIME: 30 min. **YIELD:** 4 servings

CANDACE HAVELY • STERLING, COLORADO

I came up with this recipe on a busy weeknight when I was pressed for time. Now it's my go-to dish whenever I need a quick, nutritious meal. Serve it with garlic bread so you can scoop every last bit of goodness off your plate.

- 8 oz. uncooked whole wheat spaghetti
- 1 pound uncooked medium shrimp, peeled and deveined
- 2 garlic cloves, minced
- 1-1/2 tsp. minced fresh rosemary *or* 1/2 tsp. dried rosemary, crushed
- 1 Tbsp. olive oil
- 2 cups fresh baby spinach
- 2 Tbsp. lemon juice

SHRIMP LO MEIN

CRISPY COD WITH VEGGIES

1/4 tsp. salt
1/4 tsp. pepper
1/4 cup crumbled feta cheese

1. Cook spaghetti according to package directions.

2. Meanwhile, in a large nonstick skillet, cook the shrimp, garlic and rosemary in oil over medium heat for 4-5 minutes or until shrimp turn pink. Add spinach; cook and stir until spinach is wilted.

3. Drain spaghetti; add to the pan. Stir in the lemon juice, salt and pepper; heat through. Sprinkle with feta cheese; remove from the heat. Cover and let stand for 3-5 minutes or until cheese is melted.

Nutrition Facts: 1-1/2 cups equals 349 calories, 7 g fat (2 g saturated fat), 142 mg cholesterol, 366 mg sodium, 46 g carbohydrate, 8 g fiber, 29 g protein.

Crispy Cod with Veggies

PREP: 15 min. **BAKE:** 25 min. **YIELD:** 2 servings

HEALTHY COOKING TEST KITCHEN

Take the chill off brisk evenings and warm the body and soul with this light, nourishing entree from our Test Kitchen pros. Round out the meal with a loaf of crusty bread.

2 cups broccoli coleslaw mix
1/2 cup chopped fresh tomato
4 tsp. chopped green onion
2 garlic cloves, minced
2 cod fillets (6 oz. *each*)
Pepper to taste
1/4 cup crushed potato sticks
3 Tbsp. seasoned bread crumbs
2 Tbsp. grated Parmesan cheese
4 tsp. butter, melted

1. In a large bowl, combine the coleslaw mix, tomato, onion and garlic; spread into an 11-in. x 7-in. baking pan coated with cooking spray. Top with cod fillets; sprinkle with pepper.

2. Combine the potato sticks, bread crumbs, cheese and butter; sprinkle over fillets. Bake, uncovered, at 450° for 25-30 minutes or until the fish flakes easily with a fork.

Nutrition Facts: 1 fillet with 1 cup vegetables equals 316 calories, 12 g fat (6 g saturated fat), 89 mg cholesterol, 445 mg sodium, 18 g carbohydrate, 3 g fiber, 34 g protein. **Diabetic Exchanges:** 5 very lean meat, 2 fat, 1 vegetable, 1/2 starch.

Hoisin Salmon Fillets C

PREP: 10 min. + marinating **GRILL:** 10 min.
YIELD: 6 servings

JERI FAROUGH • PERRYVILLE, MISSOURI

Fabulous Asian flavor in no time flat—this moist salmon is special enough for guests, easy enough for weekdays. I usually serve the entree with steamed brown rice, broccoli and a fresh fruit salad.

3	green onions, chopped
1/3	cup reduced-sodium soy sauce
1/4	cup hoisin sauce
3	Tbsp. lemon juice
1	Tbsp. grated lemon peel
1/2	tsp. pepper
6	salmon fillets (4 oz. *each*)

1. In a large resealable plastic bag, combine the first six ingredients. Add the salmon; seal bag and turn to coat. Refrigerate for 30 minutes, turning occasionally.

2. Drain and discard marinade. Using long-handled tongs, moisten a paper towel with cooking oil and lightly coat the grill rack. Place salmon skin side down on grill rack.

3. Grill, covered, over medium heat or broil 4 in. from the heat for 10-12 minutes or until fish flakes easily with a fork.

Nutrition Facts: 1 salmon fillet equals 224 calories, 12 g fat (3 g saturated fat), 67 mg cholesterol, 401 mg sodium, 3 g carbohydrate, trace fiber, 23 g protein. **Diabetic Exchanges:** 3 lean meat, 2 fat.

Lime-Marinated Orange Roughy F S C

PREP: 10 min. + marinating **BROIL:** 10 min.
YIELD: 4 servings

PAM CORDER • MONROE, LOUISIANA

This dish is simple, flavorful and not fattening at all. And since it's so quick, you can have company over and spend all your time visiting.

4	orange roughy fillets (6 oz. *each*)
1/3	cup water
1/3	cup lime juice
2	Tbsp. honey
1	Tbsp. canola oil
1/2	tsp. dill weed

1. Place fillets in a 13-in. x 9-in. baking dish. In a small bowl, combine the remaining ingredients; set aside 3 Tbsp. marinade. Pour remaining marinade over fillets; turn to coat. Cover and refrigerate for 1 hour.

2. Drain and discard marinade. Transfer fillets to a broiler pan coated with cooking spray. Broil 4-6 in. from the heat for 4-6 minutes on each side or until fish flakes easily with a fork, basting frequently with reserved marinade.

Nutrition Facts: 1 fillet equals 169 calories, 3 g fat (trace saturated fat), 102 mg cholesterol, 123 mg sodium, 6 g carbohydrate, trace fiber, 28 g protein. **Diabetic Exchanges:** 4 lean meat, 1/2 starch, 1/2 fat.

Grilled Tilapia with Lemon Basil Vinaigrette C

PREP/TOTAL TIME: 25 min. **YIELD:** 4 servings

BETH COOPER • COLUMBUS, OHIO

We aren't big fish eaters, but a friend made this for us, and we couldn't believe how wonderful it was! Now we eat it regularly.

- 3 Tbsp. lemon juice
- 3 Tbsp. minced fresh basil, *divided*
- 2 Tbsp. olive oil
- 2 garlic cloves, minced
- 2 tsp. capers, drained
- 1/2 tsp. grated lemon peel
- 4 tilapia fillets (6 oz. *each*)
- 1/2 tsp. salt
- 1/4 tsp. pepper

1. For vinaigrette, in a small bowl, whisk the lemon juice, 2 Tbsp. basil, olive oil, garlic, capers and lemon peel; set aside 2 Tbsp. for sauce. Sprinkle fillets with salt and pepper. Brush both sides of fillets with remaining vinaigrette.

2. Using long-handled tongs, moisten a paper towel with cooking oil and lightly coat the grill rack. Grill, covered, over medium heat or broil 4 in. from the heat for 3-4 minutes on each side or until fish flakes easily with a fork. Brush with reserved vinaigrette and sprinkle with remaining basil.

Nutrition Facts: 1 fillet equals 206 calories, 8 g fat (2 g saturated fat), 83 mg cholesterol, 398 mg sodium, 2 g carbohydrate, trace fiber, 32 g protein. **Diabetic Exchanges:** 5 lean meat, 1-1/2 fat.

Feta Shrimp Skillet

PREP: 20 min. **COOK:** 20 min. **YIELD:** 4 servings

SONALI RUDER • NEW YORK, NEW YORK

A Mediterranean-style blend of feta, wine, garlic and oregano seasons this bold, beautiful dish. Serve it with crusty bread to soak up the delightful sauce.

- 1 medium onion, finely chopped
- 1 Tbsp. olive oil
- 3 garlic cloves, minced
- 2 cans (14-1/2 oz. *each*) diced tomatoes, undrained
- 1/4 cup white wine, optional
- 1 tsp. dried oregano
- 1/2 tsp. pepper
- 1/4 tsp. salt
- 1 pound uncooked medium shrimp, peeled and deveined
- 2 Tbsp. minced fresh parsley
- 3/4 cup crumbled feta cheese

1. In a large nonstick skillet, saute onion in oil until tender. Add garlic; cook 1 minute longer. Stir in the tomatoes, wine if desired, oregano, pepper and salt. Bring to a boil. Reduce heat; simmer, uncovered, for 5-7 minutes or until sauce is slightly thickened.

2. Stir in shrimp and parsley. Cook and stir over medium heat for 5-6 minutes or until shrimp turn pink. Remove from the heat; sprinkle with cheese. Cover and let stand for 5-10 minutes or until cheese is softened.

Nutrition Facts: 1-1/4 cups (calculated without wine) equals 240 calories, 8 g fat (3 g saturated fat), 149 mg cholesterol, 748 mg sodium, 16 g carbohydrate, 5 g fiber, 25 g protein. **Diabetic Exchanges:** 3 lean meat, 1 starch, 1 fat.

FETA SHRIMP SKILLET

GRILLED TILAPIA WITH LEMON BASIL VINAIGRETTE

Red Clam Sauce

PREP: 25 min. COOK: 3 hours YIELD: 4 servings

JOANN BROWN • LATROBE, PENNSYLVANIA

This recipe tastes like it's been slaved over all day. Instead, it cooks while you do other things. What a great way to jazz up pasta sauce!

- 1 medium onion, chopped
- 2 garlic cloves, minced
- 1 Tbsp. canola oil
- 2 cans (6-1/2 oz. each) chopped clams, undrained
- 1 can (14-1/2 oz.) diced tomatoes, undrained
- 1 can (6 oz.) tomato paste
- 1/4 cup minced fresh parsley
- 1 bay leaf
- 1 tsp. sugar
- 1 tsp. dried basil
- 1/2 tsp. dried thyme
- 6 oz. linguine, cooked and drained

1. In a small skillet, saute onion and garlic in oil until tender. Transfer to a 1-1/2- or 2-qt. slow cooker. Stir in the clams, tomatoes, tomato paste, parsley, bay leaf, sugar, basil and thyme. Cover and cook on low for 3-4 hours or until heated through. Discard bay leaf. Serve with linguine.

Nutrition Facts: 1 cup sauce with 3/4 cup cooked linguine equals 305 calories, 5 g fat (trace saturated fat), 15 mg cholesterol, 553 mg sodium, 53 g carbohydrate, 7 g fiber, 15 g protein.

Mini Scallop Casseroles

PREP: 30 min. BAKE: 20 min. YIELD: 4 servings

VIVIAN MANARY • NEPEAN, ONTARIO

Tiny and tender bay scallops take center stage in these cute individual dishes. They're reminiscent of potpies, very creamy and packed with flavorful veggies in every bite.

- 3 celery ribs, chopped
- 1 cup sliced fresh mushrooms
- 1 medium green pepper, chopped
- 1 small onion, chopped
- 2 Tbsp. butter
- 1/3 cup all-purpose flour
- 1/4 tsp. salt
- 1/4 tsp. pepper
- 2 cups fat-free milk
- 1 lb. bay scallops

TOPPING:
- 1 cup soft bread crumbs
- 1 Tbsp. butter, melted
- 1/4 cup shredded cheddar cheese

1. In a large skillet, saute the celery, mushrooms, green pepper and onion in butter until tender. Stir in the flour, salt and pepper until blended; gradually add milk. Bring to a boil; cook and stir for 2 minutes or until thickened.

2. Reduce heat; add scallops. Cook, stirring occasionally, for 3-4 minutes or until scallops are firm and opaque.

3. Divide mixture among four 10-oz. ramekins or custard cups. In a small bowl, combine crumbs and butter; sprinkle over scallop mixture. Bake, uncovered, at 350° for 15-20 minutes or until bubbly. Sprinkle with cheese; bake 5 minutes longer or until the cheese is melted.

Nutrition Facts: 1 serving equals 332 calories, 12 g fat (7 g saturated fat), 70 mg cholesterol, 588 mg sodium, 27 g carbohydrate, 2 g fiber, 28 g protein. **Diabetic Exchanges:** 3 very lean meat, 2 fat, 1 starch, 1 vegetable, 1/2 fat-free milk.

Grilled Tilapia with Mango C

PREP/TOTAL TIME: 20 min. YIELD: 4 servings

GREGG MAY • COLUMBUS, OHIO

This is a different twist on tilapia that I created for my wife. She enjoyed the combination of mango with the Parmesan. There's nothing like eating this out on the deck with a cold glass of iced tea.

- 4 tilapia fillets (6 oz. each)
- 1 Tbsp. olive oil
- 1/2 tsp. salt
- 1/2 tsp. dill weed

RED CLAM SAUCE

GRILLED TILAPIA WITH MANGO

1/4 tsp. pepper
1 Tbsp. grated Parmesan cheese
1 medium lemon sliced
1 medium mango, peeled and thinly sliced

1. Coat grill rack with cooking spray before starting the grill. Brush fillets with oil; sprinkle with salt, dill and pepper.

2. Grill tilapia, covered, over medium heat for 5 minutes. Turn tilapia; top with cheese, lemon and mango. Grill 4-6 minutes longer or until fish flakes easily with a fork.

Nutrition Facts: 1 serving equals 213 calories, 5 g fat (1 g saturated fat), 84 mg cholesterol, 377 mg sodium, 10 g carbohydrate, 1 g fiber, 32 g protein. **Diabetic Exchanges:** 5 very lean meat, 1/2 fruit, 1/2 fat.

Company-Ready Crusted Salmon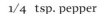

PREP: 20 min. **BAKE:** 20 min. **YIELD:** 6 servings

SUSAN ROBENSON • HOT SPRINGS, ARKANSAS

My husband had high cholesterol, so I created this heart-healthy entree. Now I serve it to guests all the time...even those who don't like fish rave and ask for the recipe! Best of all it's a tasty meal-in-one. All I have to do is add a salad and dinner is ready.

2 pkg. (6 oz. each) fresh baby spinach
1 salmon fillet (1-1/2 lbs.)
1 tsp. olive oil
3 Tbsp. honey
3 Tbsp. Dijon mustard
1/4 cup cornflakes
2 Tbsp. sliced almonds
2 Tbsp. chopped pecans
1/4 cup fat-free mayonnaise
Hot cooked couscous, optional

1. Place spinach in a 13-in. x 9-in. baking dish coated with cooking spray; top with salmon. Drizzle oil over spinach.

2. Combine honey and mustard. Remove 2 Tbsp. mixture; brush over salmon. Place the cornflakes, almonds and pecans in a small food processor; cover and process until ground. Press onto salmon. Stir mayonnaise into remaining honey mixture; refrigerate until serving.

3. Bake, uncovered, at 450° for 18-22 minutes or until fish flakes easily with a fork. Drizzle with reserved sauce. Serve with couscous if desired.

Nutrition Facts: about 3 oz. cooked salmon with 1/4 cup spinach and 1 Tbsp. sauce equals 296 calories, 15 g fat (3 g saturated fat), 68 mg cholesterol, 381 mg sodium, 15 g carbohydrate, 2 g fiber, 25 g protein.

Walnut Ginger Salmon C

PREP: 10 min. + marinating **BROIL:** 10 min.
YIELD: 4 servings

BECKY WALCH • MANTECA, CALIFORNIA

Pantry ingredients combine for a delightful marinade that lightly glazes this tender, moist salmon.

- 1 Tbsp. brown sugar
- 1 Tbsp. Dijon mustard
- 1 Tbsp. soy sauce
- 1 tsp. ground ginger
- 4 skinless salmon fillets (4 oz. *each*)
- 1/4 cup chopped walnuts

1. In a large resealable plastic bag, combine the brown sugar, mustard, soy sauce and ginger; add the salmon. Seal bag and turn to coat; refrigerate for 30 minutes, turning occasionally.

2. Drain and discard marinade. Place salmon on a foil-lined baking sheet coated with cooking spray. Broil 4-6 in. from the heat for 7-9 minutes or until fish flakes easily with a fork, sprinkling with walnuts during the last 2 minutes of cooking.

Nutrition Facts: 1 fillet equals 270 calories, 17 g fat (3 g saturated fat), 67 mg cholesterol, 292 mg sodium, 4 g carbohydrate, trace fiber, 25 g protein. **Diabetic Exchanges:** 3 medium-fat meat, 1 fat.

Pan-Seared Shrimp

PREP/TOTAL TIME: 30 min. **YIELD:** 4 servings

PATRICIA ZARTMAN • YORK, PENNSYLVANIA

Garlic, parsley and wine punch up the buttery flavor of this simple shrimp recipe, giving it a decadent and special feel. Best of all it comes together in just half an hour, so it's perfect for company and for hectic weeknights alike. Serve it with steamed spinach for a fabulous meal.

- 1 lb. uncooked medium shrimp, peeled and deveined
- 2 garlic cloves, minced
- 2 Tbsp. olive oil
- 1/3 cup white wine or reduced-sodium chicken broth
- 1/2 tsp. seafood seasoning
- 2 cups hot cooked rice
- 2 Tbsp. minced fresh parsley

1. In a large skillet, saute shrimp and garlic in oil for 3 minutes. Add wine and seasoning; cook and stir 3-5 minutes longer or until shrimp turn pink. Serve with rice; sprinkle with parsley.

Nutrition Facts: 1/2 cup shrimp with 1/2 cup rice equals 262 calories, 9 g fat (1 g saturated fat), 138 mg cholesterol, 238 mg sodium, 24 g carbohydrate, trace fiber, 21 g protein.
Diabetic Exchanges: 3 very lean meat, 1-1/2 starch, 1 fat.

Shrimp Curry

PREP/TOTAL TIME: 30 min. YIELD: 4 servings

AGNES WARD • STRATFORD, ONTARIO

Here's a tasty way to add seafood to your diet. It's great with chicken, too. Either way, your family will request this satisfying supper again and again!

- 1/4 cup finely chopped onion
- 1-1/2 tsp. curry powder
- 2 Tbsp. butter
- 3 Tbsp. all-purpose flour
- 1 cup reduced-sodium chicken broth
- 1 cup fat-free milk
- 1 lb. uncooked medium shrimp, peeled and deveined
- 3/4 tsp. sugar
- 1/2 tsp. salt
- 1/8 tsp. ground ginger
- 1/2 tsp. lemon juice
- 2 cups hot cooked rice

1. In a large skillet, saute onion and curry in butter until tender. Stir in the flour until blended; gradually add broth and milk. Bring to a boil; cook and stir for 2 minutes or until thickened.

2. Reduce heat; add the shrimp, sugar, salt and ginger. Cook and stir over medium heat until shrimp turn pink. Remove from the heat; stir in lemon juice. Serve with rice.

Nutrition Facts: 3/4 cup shrimp mixture with 1/2 cup rice equals 305 calories, 8 g fat (4 g saturated fat), 154 mg cholesterol, 640 mg sodium, 33 g carbohydrate, 1 g fiber, 24 g protein.

Pistachio-Crusted Fish Fillets [c]

PREP/TOTAL TIME: 25 min. YIELD: 4 servings

MARIE STUPIN • ROANOKE, VIRGINA

What a fresh, fun, absolutely delicious way to fix orange roughy in a hurry! I really adore the nutty crunch of the pistachio and parsley crust.

- 1 egg white, beaten
- 1/2 cup pistachios, finely chopped
- 1/3 cup dry bread crumbs
- 1/4 cup minced fresh parsley
- 1/2 tsp. pepper
- 1/4 tsp. salt
- 4 orange roughy fillets (6 oz. *each*)
- 4 tsp. butter, melted

1. Place egg white in a shallow bowl. In another shallow bowl, combine the pistachios, bread crumbs, parsley, pepper and salt. Dip fillets in egg white, then pistachio mixture.

2. Place fish on a baking sheet coated with cooking spray. Drizzle with butter. Bake at 450° for 8-10 minutes or until fish flakes easily with a fork.

Nutrition Facts: 1 fillet equals 295 calories, 13 g fat (3 g saturated fat), 112 mg cholesterol, 444 mg sodium, 11 g carbohydrate, 2 g fiber, 34 g protein.

Light-But-Hearty Tuna Casserole

PREP: 20 min. BAKE: 25 min. YIELD: 4 servings

HEIDI CAROFANO • BROOKLYN, NEW YORK

My boyfriend grew up loving his mom's tuna casserole and says he can't tell this is light!

- 3 cups uncooked yolk-free noodles
- 1 can (10-3/4 oz.) reduced-fat reduced-sodium condensed cream of mushroom soup, undiluted
- 1/2 cup fat-free milk
- 2 Tbsp. reduced-fat mayonnaise
- 1/2 tsp. ground mustard
- 1 can (6 oz.) solid white tuna, drained
- 1 jar (6 oz.) sliced mushrooms, drained
- 1/4 cup chopped roasted sweet red pepper

TOPPING:
- 1/4 cup dry bread crumbs
- 1 Tbsp. butter, melted
- 1/2 tsp. paprika
- 1/4 tsp. Italian seasoning
- 1/4 tsp. pepper

1. Cook noodles according to package directions.

2. In a large bowl, combine the soup, milk, mayonnaise and mustard. Stir in the tuna, mushrooms and red pepper. Drain noodles; add to soup mixture and stir until blended. Transfer to an 8-in. square baking dish coated with cooking spray. Combine topping ingredients; sprinkle over casserole. Bake at 400° for 25-30 minutes or until bubbly.

Nutrition Facts: 1-1/2 cups equals 322 calories, 9 g fat (3 g saturated fat), 32 mg cholesterol, 843 mg sodium, 39 g carbohydrate, 4 g fiber, 18 g protein.

LIGHT-BUT-HEARTY TUNA CASSEROLE

CORN BREAD-TOPPED FRIJOLES

CURRIED QUINOA AND CHICKPEAS

PESTO VEGGIE PIZZA

For some, meat-free dinners are a way of life. For others, they simply mix up dinnertime lineups occasionally. Consider these entrees when you want to try something new yet keep your commitment to eating right.

Pesto Veggie Pizza M

PREP: 30 min. + standing BAKE: 10 min.
YIELD: 6 servings

DANA DIRKS • SAN DIEGO, CALIFORNIA

When I started thinking of recipes I could submit to a healthy-cooking contest, I thought about what my family really likes to eat and what I like to cook, and the answer was...pizza!

1	pkg. (1/4 oz.) active dry yeast
1	cup warm water (110° to 115°)
1/3	cup grated Parmesan cheese
2	Tbsp. canola oil
1	Tbsp. sugar
1	Tbsp. dried basil
1/2	tsp. salt
3/4	cup all-purpose flour
1	to 1-1/2 cups whole wheat flour
3-1/2	cups fresh baby spinach
1/4	cup prepared pesto
1-3/4	cups coarsely chopped fresh broccoli
3/4	cup chopped green pepper
2	green onions, chopped
4	garlic cloves, minced
2	cups (8 oz.) shredded part-skim mozzarella cheese

1. In a small bowl, dissolve yeast in warm water. Add Parmesan cheese, oil, sugar, basil, salt, all-purpose flour and 3/4 cup whole wheat flour. Beat until smooth. Stir in enough remaining whole wheat flour to form a soft dough (dough will be sticky).

2. Turn onto a lightly floured surface; knead until smooth and elastic, about 6-8 minutes. Cover and let rest for 10 minutes.

3. Roll dough into a 16-in. x 12-in. rectangle. Transfer to a baking sheet coated with cooking spray; build up edges slightly. Prick dough with a fork. Bake at 375° for 8-10 minutes or until lightly browned.

4. Meanwhile, in a large saucepan, bring 1/2 in. of water to a boil. Add spinach; cover and boil for 3-5 minutes or until wilted. Drain and place in a food processor. Add pesto; cover and process until mixture is blended.

5. Spread over pizza crust. Top with broccoli, green pepper, green onions, garlic and mozzarella cheese. Bake 10-12 minutes longer or until cheese is melted.

Nutrition Facts: 1 piece equals 364 calories, 17 g fat (6 g saturated fat), 29 mg cholesterol, 543 mg sodium, 35 g carbohydrate, 5 g fiber, 19 g protein. **Diabetic Exchanges:** 2 starch, 2 medium-fat meat, 2 fat, 1 vegetable.

Curried Quinoa And Chickpeas M

PREP: 15 min. COOK: 25 min. YIELD: 4 servings

SUZANNE BANFIELD • BASKING RIDGE, NEW JERSEY

Quinoa contains more protein than other grains, and that protein is of unusually high quality for a plant food. That makes this a great, filling main dish. The blend of flavors and colors will bring everyone at the table back for more.

1-1/2	cups water
1/2	cup orange juice
1	can (15 oz.) chickpeas or garbanzo beans, rinsed and drained
2	medium tomatoes, seeded and chopped
1	medium sweet red pepper, julienned
1	cup quinoa, rinsed
1	small red onion, finely chopped
1/2	cup raisins
1	tsp. curry powder
1/2	cup minced fresh cilantro

1. In a large saucepan, bring water and orange juice to a boil. Stir in chickpeas, tomatoes, red pepper, quinoa, onion, raisins and curry. Return to a boil. Reduce heat; cover and simmer for 15-20 minutes or until liquid is absorbed.

2. Remove from the heat; fluff with a fork. Sprinkle with cilantro.

Editor's Note: Look for quinoa in the cereal, rice or organic food aisle.

Nutrition Facts: 1-1/2 cups equals 355 calories, 5 g fat (trace saturated fat), 0 cholesterol, 155 mg sodium, 70 g carbohydrate, 9 g fiber, 12 g protein.

Zucchini Enchiladas M

PREP: 1-1/2 hours **BAKE:** 30 min. **YIELD:** 12 servings

ANGELA LEINENBACH • MECHANICSVLLE, VIRGINIA

I love this recipe because it helps me serve a healthy but tasty meal to my family. Plus, zucchini is so plentiful in my garden, and this dish makes a great way to use it up.

1	medium sweet yellow pepper, chopped
1	medium green pepper, chopped
1	large sweet onion, chopped
2	Tbsp. olive oil
2	garlic cloves, minced
2	cans (15 oz. *each*) tomato sauce
2	cans (14-1/2 oz. *each*) no-salt-added diced tomatoes, undrained
2	Tbsp. chili powder
2	tsp. sugar
2	tsp. dried marjoram
1	tsp. dried basil
1	tsp. ground cumin
1/4	tsp. salt
1/4	tsp. cayenne pepper
1	bay leaf
3	lb. zucchini, shredded (about 8 cups)
24	corn tortillas (6 in.), warmed
4	cups (16 oz.) shredded reduced-fat cheddar cheese

2	cans (2-1/4 oz. *each*) sliced ripe olives, drained
1/2	cup minced fresh cilantro

Reduced-fat sour cream, optional

1. In a large saucepan, saute peppers and onion in oil until tender. Add garlic; cook 1 minute longer. Stir in the tomato sauce, tomatoes, chili powder, sugar, marjoram, basil, cumin, salt, cayenne and bay leaf. Bring to a boil. Reduce heat; simmer, uncovered, for 30-35 minutes or until slightly thickened. Discard bay leaf.

2. Place 1/3 cup zucchini down the center of each tortilla; top with 2 Tbsp. cheese and 1 Tbsp. olives. Roll up and place seam side down in two 13-in. x 9-in. baking dishes coated with cooking spray. Pour sauce over the top; sprinkle with remaining cheese.

3. Bake, uncovered, at 350° for 30-35 minutes or until heated through. Sprinkle with cilantro. Serve with sour cream if desired.

Nutrition Facts: 2 enchiladas (calculated without sour cream) equals 326 calories, 13 g fat (6 g saturated fat), 27 mg cholesterol, 846 mg sodium, 42 g carbohydrate, 7 g fiber, 16 g protein. **Diabetic Exchanges:** 2 starch, 2 medium-fat meat, 2 vegetable, 1/2 fat.

Southwestern Frittata C M

PREP/TOTAL TIME: 25 min. **YIELD:** 4 servings

MARY RELYEA • CANASTOTA, NEW YORK

This tasty egg dish makes a great breakfast entree but could easily be served for lunch or dinner, too. Fresh eggs are jazzed up with red tomatoes, onion and green bell pepper, then treated to a topping of savory mozzarella cheese. What a fantastic way to spice up your meals.

4	eggs
1	Tbsp. fat-free milk
1/4	tsp. salt
1/4	tsp. ground mustard
1/4	tsp. pepper

Dash to 1/8 tsp. cayenne pepper

1/2	cup chopped onion
1/2	cup chopped green pepper
1/2	tsp. minced garlic
1	tsp. olive oil
1	large tomato, chopped
2	Tbsp. sliced ripe olives, drained
1/2	cup shredded part-skim mozzarella cheese

1. In a small bowl, whisk the eggs, milk, salt, mustard, pepper and cayenne; set aside.

2. In a large skillet over medium heat, cook the onion, green pepper and garlic in oil until tender. Add tomato and olives; heat through.

3. Pour egg mixture over vegetables. As eggs set, lift edges, letting uncooked portion flow underneath. When eggs are set, sprinkle with cheese. Remove from the heat. Cover and let stand for 1-2 minutes or until cheese is melted. Cut into four wedges.

Nutrition Facts: 1 slice equals 152 calories, 9 g fat (3 g saturated fat), 221 mg cholesterol, 320 mg sodium, 7 g carbohydrate, 1 g fiber, 11 g protein.

ZUCCHINI ENCHILADAS

Fiery Stuffed Poblanos M

PREP: 50 min. + standing BAKE: 20 min.
YIELD: 8 servings

AMBER MASSEY • FORT WORTH, TEXAS

I love Southwest-inspired cuisine, but since it's often laden with fatty meat and cheese, I tend to steer clear. As a future dietitian, I try to come up with healthy twists on recipes. That's how my stuffed chili dish was born.

- 8 poblano peppers
- 1 can (15 oz.) black beans, rinsed and drained
- 1 medium zucchini, chopped
- 1 small red onion, chopped
- 4 garlic cloves, minced
- 1 can (15-1/4 oz.) whole kernel corn, drained
- 1 can (14-1/2 oz.) fire-roasted diced tomatoes, undrained
- 1 cup cooked brown rice
- 1 Tbsp. ground cumin
- 1 to 1-1/2 tsp. ground ancho chili pepper
- 1/4 tsp. salt
- 1/4 tsp. pepper
- 1 cup (4 oz.) shredded reduced-fat Mexican cheese blend, *divided*
- 3 green onions, chopped
- 1/2 cup reduced-fat sour cream

1. Broil peppers 3 in. from the heat until skins blister, about 5 minutes. With tongs, rotate peppers a quarter turn. Broil and rotate until all sides are blistered and blackened. Immediately place peppers in a large bowl; cover and let stand for 20 minutes.

2. Meanwhile, in a small bowl, coarsely mash beans; set aside. In a large nonstick skillet coated with cooking spray, cook and stir zucchini and onion until tender. Add garlic; cook 1 minute longer. Add the corn, tomatoes, rice, seasonings and beans. Remove from the heat; stir in 1/2 cup cheese. Set aside.

3. Peel off and discard charred skins from poblanos. Cut a lengthwise slit down each pepper, leaving the stem intact; remove membranes and seeds. Fill each pepper with 2/3 cup filling.

4. Place peppers in a 13-in. x 9-in. baking dish coated with cooking spray. Bake, uncovered, at 375° for 18-22 minutes or until heated through, sprinkling with green onions and remaining cheese during last 5 minutes of baking. Garnish with sour cream.

Nutrition Facts: 1 stuffed pepper with 1 Tbsp. sour cream equals 223 calories, 5 g fat (2 g saturated fat), 15 mg cholesterol, 579 mg sodium, 32 g carbohydrate, 7 g fiber, 11 g protein.
Diabetic Exchanges: 2 vegetable, 1 starch, 1 lean meat, 1 fat.

Ravioli with Snap Peas & Mushrooms Ⓜ

PREP/TOTAL TIME: 30 min. YIELD: 8 servings

CHARLENE CHAMBERS • ORMOND BEACH, FLORIDA

Topped with the toasty texture and flavor of hazelnuts, this pasta makes an easy, earthy weeknight dinner. I like to serve it with an herbed lettuce salad and white wine.

- 1 pkg. (20 oz.) refrigerated cheese ravioli
- 1 lb. fresh sugar snap peas, trimmed
- 1/2 lb. sliced fresh mushrooms
- 3 shallots, chopped
- 2 garlic cloves, minced
- 1 Tbsp. butter
- 2 cups fat-free evaporated milk
- 8 fresh sage leaves, thinly sliced or 2 tsp. rubbed sage
- 1 tsp. lemon-pepper seasoning
- 1 tsp. grated lemon peel
- 1/4 tsp. white pepper
- 1/4 cup shredded Parmesan cheese
- 1/4 cup hazelnuts, coarsely chopped and toasted

1. In a large saucepan, cook ravioli according to the package directions, adding the peas during the last 3 minutes of cooking; drain.

2. Meanwhile, in a large skillet, saute the mushrooms, shallots and garlic in butter until tender. Stir in the milk, sage, lemon-pepper, lemon peel and white pepper. Bring to a boil. Reduce heat; simmer, uncovered, for 2 minutes or until slightly thickened.

3. Add ravioli and peas to skillet; heat through. Sprinkle with cheese and hazelnuts.

Nutrition Facts: 1 cup equals 347 calories, 11 g fat (5 g saturated fat), 36 mg cholesterol, 470 mg sodium, 44 g carbohydrate, 4 g fiber, 20 g protein. **Diabetic Exchanges:** 2-1/2 starch, 1 medium-fat meat, 1 vegetable, 1 fat.

Curried Tofu with Rice Ⓜ

PREP: 15 min. COOK: 20 min. YIELD: 4 servings

CRYSTAL BRUNS • ILIFF, COLORADO

Tofu takes the place of meat in this bold dish with lots of curry and cilantro flavor.

- 1 pkg. (12.3 oz.) extra-firm tofu, drained and cubed
- 1 tsp. seasoned salt

1 Tbsp. canola oil
1 small onion, chopped
3 garlic cloves, minced
1/2 cup light coconut milk
1/4 cup minced fresh cilantro
1 tsp. curry powder
1/4 tsp. salt
1/4 tsp. pepper
2 cups cooked brown rice

1. Sprinkle tofu with seasoned salt. In a large nonstick skillet coated with cooking spray, saute tofu in oil until lightly browned. Remove and keep warm.

2. In the same skillet, saute onion and garlic for 1-2 minutes or until crisp-tender. Stir in the coconut milk, cilantro, curry, salt and pepper. Bring to a boil. Reduce heat; simmer, uncovered, for 4-5 minutes or until sauce is slightly thickened. Stir in tofu; heat through. Serve with rice.

Nutrition Facts: 1/2 cup tofu mixture with 1/2 cup rice equals 240 calories, 11 g fat (3 g saturated fat), 0 cholesterol, 540 mg sodium, 27 g carbohydrate, 3 g fiber, 10 g protein. **Diabetic Exchanges:** 1-1/2 starch, 1 medium-fat meat, 1 fat.

Corn Bread-Topped Frijoles

PREP: 20 min. COOK: 3 hours YIELD: 8 servings

SUZANNE CALDWELL • ARTESIA, NEW MEXICO

My family often requests this economical slow-cooker favorite. It's loaded with fresh Southwestern flavors. One batch makes several servings, but it never lasts long at our house!

1 medium onion, chopped
1 medium green pepper, chopped
1 Tbsp. canola oil
2 garlic cloves, minced
1 can (16 oz.) kidney beans, rinsed and drained
1 can (15 oz.) pinto beans, rinsed and drained
1 can (14-1/2 oz.) diced tomatoes, undrained

1 can (8 oz.) tomato sauce
1 tsp. chili powder
1/2 tsp. pepper
1/8 tsp. hot pepper sauce

CORN BREAD TOPPING:
1 cup all-purpose flour
1 cup yellow cornmeal
1 Tbsp. sugar
1-1/2 tsp. baking powder
1/2 tsp. salt
2 eggs, lightly beaten
1-1/4 cups fat-free milk
1 can (8-1/4 oz.) cream-style corn
3 Tbsp. canola oil

1. In a large skillet, saute onion and green pepper in oil until tender. Add garlic; cook 1 minute longer. Transfer to a greased 5-qt. slow cooker.

2. Stir in the beans, tomatoes, tomato sauce, chili powder, pepper and pepper sauce. Cover and cook on high for 1 hour.

3. In a large bowl, combine the flour, cornmeal, sugar, baking powder and salt. Combine the eggs, milk, corn and oil; add to dry ingredients and mix well. Spoon evenly over bean mixture.

4. Cover and cook on high 2 hours longer or until a toothpick inserted near the center of corn bread comes out clean.

Nutrition Facts: 1 serving equals 367 calories, 9 g fat (1 g saturated fat), 54 mg cholesterol, 708 mg sodium, 59 g carbohydrate, 9 g fiber, 14 g protein.

CURRIED TOFU WITH RICE

CORN BREAD-TOPPED FRIJOLES

Veggie Bean Tacos M

PREP: 20 min. COOK: 20 min. YIELD: 6 servings

TONYA BURKHARD-JONES • DAVIS, ILLINOIS

Here's a delicious way to use up your summer bounty of vegetables. Fresh tomatoes, corn and zucchini star in these sensational tacos. Avocado, salsa verde and black beans round out the flavor.

- 2 cups fresh corn
- 2 Tbsp. canola oil, *divided*
- 4 medium tomatoes, seeded and chopped
- 3 small zucchini, chopped
- 1 large red onion, chopped
- 3 garlic cloves, minced
- 1 cup black beans, rinsed and drained
- 1 tsp. minced fresh oregano *or* 1/4 tsp. dried oregano
- 1/2 tsp. salt
- 1/4 tsp. pepper
- 12 corn tortillas (6 in.), warmed
- 3/4 cup shredded Monterey Jack cheese
- 1/4 cup salsa verde
- 1 medium ripe avocado, peeled and thinly sliced

Reduced-fat sour cream, optional

1. In a large skillet, saute corn in 1 Tbsp. oil until lightly browned. Remove and keep warm. In the same skillet, saute tomatoes, zucchini and onion in remaining oil until tender. Add garlic; cook 1 minute longer. Stir in the beans, oregano, salt, pepper and corn; heat through.

2. Divide filling among tortillas. Top with cheese, salsa, avocado and sour cream if desired.

Nutrition Facts: 2 tacos (calculated without sour cream) equals 378 calories, 16 g fat (4 g saturated fat), 13 mg cholesterol, 517 mg sodium, 52 g carbohydrate, 10 g fiber, 13 g protein.

Bow Ties with Walnut-Herb Pesto M

PREP/TOTAL TIME: 20 min. YIELD: 6 servings

DIANE NEMITZ • LUDINGTON, MICHIGAN

A homemade pesto turns whole wheat pasta into a sensational meatless main course. If you've never made pesto before, this is an easy recipe to start with. Skip the red pepper flakes if you don't like that much extra spice.

- 4 cups uncooked whole wheat bow tie pasta
- 1 cup fresh arugula
- 1/2 cup packed fresh parsley sprigs
- 1/2 cup loosely packed basil leaves
- 1/4 cup grated Parmesan cheese
- 1/2 tsp. salt
- 1/8 tsp. crushed red pepper flakes
- 1/4 cup chopped walnuts
- 1/3 cup olive oil
- 1 plum tomato, seeded and chopped

1. Cook pasta according to the package directions. Meanwhile, place the arugula, parsley, basil, cheese, salt and pepper flakes in a food processor; cover and pulse until chopped. Add walnuts; cover and process until blended. While processing, gradually add oil in a steady stream.

2. Drain pasta, reserving 3 Tbsp. cooking water. In a large bowl, toss pasta with pesto, tomato and reserved water.

Nutrition Facts: 1 cup equals 323 calories, 17 g fat (3 g saturated fat), 3 mg cholesterol, 252 mg sodium, 34 g carbohydrate, 6 g fiber, 10 g protein. **Diabetic Exchanges:** 2-1/2 fat, 2 starch.

VEGGIE BEAN TACOS

BOW TIES WITH WALNUT-HERB PESTO

GREEK PITA PIZZAS

Greek Pita Pizzas M

PREP/TOTAL TIME: 25 min. **YIELD:** 6 servings

TRISHA KRUSE • EAGLE, IDAHO

Colorful, crunchy and packed with fresh veggies and flavor, these quick pizzas taste just like a Greek salad. Whole wheat pitas were never more delicious!

6	whole wheat pita breads (6 in.)
1-1/2	cups meatless spaghetti sauce
1	can (14 oz.) water-packed artichoke hearts, rinsed, drained and quartered
2	cups fresh baby spinach, chopped
1-1/2	cups sliced fresh mushrooms
1/2	cup crumbled feta cheese
1	small green pepper, thinly sliced
1/4	cup thinly sliced red onion
1/4	cup sliced ripe olives
3	Tbsp. grated Parmesan cheese
1/4	tsp. pepper

1. Place the pita breads on an ungreased baking sheet; spread with the spaghetti sauce. Top with the remaining ingredients.

2. Bake at 350° for 8-12 minutes or until cheese is melted. Serve immediately.

Nutrition Facts: 1 pizza equals 273 calories, 5 g fat (2 g saturated fat), 7 mg cholesterol, 969 mg sodium, 48 g carbohydrate, 7 g fiber, 13 g protein. **Diabetic Exchanges:** 2 starch, 1 medium-fat meat, 1 vegetable.

Don't be afraid to get creative with **the crust** for this recipe. While the Nutrition Facts will change, you can always set the toppings over English muffin halves or whole wheat tortillas. Consider placing the toppings over a packaged crust for one large pizza.

FOUR-CHEESE BAKED PENNE

Four-Cheese Baked Penne M

PREP: 30 min. + cooling BAKE: 20 min.
YIELD: 6 servings

JANET ELROD • NEWNAN, GEORGIA

This cheesy pasta dish is comforting, hearty, delicious and—surprise —meatless. Filling whole grains, low-fat protein and a touch of heat make this recipe a keeper! Serve with a salad and crusty bread.

4	cups uncooked whole wheat penne pasta
1	medium onion, chopped
2	tsp. olive oil
4	garlic cloves, minced
1	can (15 oz.) crushed tomatoes
1	can (8 oz.) tomato sauce
3	Tbsp. minced fresh parsley *or* 1 Tbsp. dried parsley flakes
1	tsp. dried oregano
1	tsp. dried rosemary, crushed
1/2	tsp. crushed red pepper flakes
1/4	tsp. pepper
1-1/2	cups (12 oz.) 2% cottage cheese
1-1/4	cups (5 oz.) shredded part-skim mozzarella cheese, *divided*
1	cup part-skim ricotta cheese
1/4	cup grated Parmesan cheese

1. Cook penne according to package directions.

2. Meanwhile, in a large skillet, saute onion in oil until tender. Add garlic; cook 1 minute longer. Stir in the tomatoes, tomato sauce, parsley, oregano, rosemary, pepper flakes and pepper. Bring to a boil. Remove from the heat; cool for 15 minutes.

3. Drain penne; add to sauce. Stir in the cottage cheese, 1/2 cup mozzarella and all of the ricotta. Transfer to a 13-in. x 9-in. baking dish coated with cooking spray. Top with Parmesan cheese and remaining mozzarella.

4. Bake, uncovered, at 400° for 20-25 minutes or until bubbly.

Nutrition Facts: 1-1/3 cups equals 523 calories, 12 g fat (6 g saturated fat), 37 mg cholesterol, 682 mg sodium, 72 g carbohydrate, 11 g fiber, 32 g protein.

Spanako-Pasta M

PREP: 20 min. COOK: 15 min. YIELD: 4 servings

LINDSAY WILLIAMS • HASTINGS, MINNESOTA

I love spanakopita, so I made it into a wonderful creamy pasta dish. If you don't have fresh dill, try 2 tablespoons of dried.

4-1/2	cups uncooked whole wheat spiral pasta
1	medium onion, chopped
2	tsp. olive oil
2	garlic cloves, minced

2 Tbsp. all-purpose flour

3/4 cup reduced-sodium chicken broth *or* vegetable broth

3/4 cup fat-free milk

1 pkg. (10 oz.) frozen chopped spinach, thawed and squeezed dry

1/4 cup grated Parmesan cheese

2 oz. reduced-fat cream cheese

2 Tbsp. lemon juice

2 Tbsp. snipped fresh dill

1/4 tsp. ground nutmeg

1/4 tsp. salt

Dash cayenne pepper

3/4 cup crumbled feta cheese

1. Cook pasta according to package directions. Meanwhile, in a large skillet, saute onion in oil until tender. Add garlic; cook 1 minute longer. Stir in flour until blended; gradually add broth and milk. Bring to a boil; cook and stir for 2 minutes or until thickened.

2. Add the spinach, Parmesan cheese, cream cheese, lemon juice, dill, nutmeg, salt and cayenne; heat through. Drain pasta, reserving 1 cup liquid. Toss pasta with spinach mixture, adding some of the reserved pasta liquid if needed. Sprinkle with the feta cheese.

Nutrition Facts: 1-1/2 cups equals 435 calories, 12 g fat (6 g saturated fat), 27 mg cholesterol, 667 mg sodium, 61 g carbohydrate, 11 g fiber, 23 g protein.

Spinach Cheese Manicotti Ⓜ

PREP: 55 min. **BAKE:** 55 min. **YIELD:** 7 servings

JULIE LOWER • KATY, TEXAS

No one will even miss the meat in this hearty, delicious meal. Cream cheese and cottage cheese "beef up" the filling and give this lasagna-like dish a creamy base.

1 large onion, chopped

2 garlic cloves, minced

1 Tbsp. olive oil

3 cans (8 oz. *each*) no-salt-added tomato sauce

2 cans (6 oz. *each*) tomato paste

1-1/2 cups water

1/2 cup dry red wine *or* vegetable broth

2 Tbsp. Italian seasoning

2 tsp. sugar

2 tsp. dried oregano

FILLING:

1 pkg. (8 oz.) fat-free cream cheese

1-1/4 cups (10 oz.) 2% cottage cheese

1 pkg. (10 oz.) frozen chopped spinach, thawed and squeezed dry

1/4 cup grated Parmesan cheese

2 eggs, lightly beaten

1/2 tsp. salt

1 pkg. (8 oz.) manicotti shells

1 cup (4 oz.) shredded part-skim mozzarella cheese

1. In a large saucepan, saute onion and garlic in oil until tender. Stir in the tomato sauce, tomato paste, water, wine, Italian seasoning, sugar and oregano. Bring to a boil. Reduce heat; simmer, uncovered, for 15-20 minutes, stirring occasionally.

2. Meanwhile, for filling, in a large bowl, beat cream cheese until smooth. Stir in the cottage cheese, spinach, Parmesan cheese, eggs and salt.

3. Stuff cream cheese mixture into uncooked manicotti shells. Spread 1 cup sauce into a 13-in. x 9-in. baking dish coated with cooking spay. Arrange manicotti over sauce. Pour remaining sauce over top.

4. Cover and bake at 350° for 50-55 minutes or until pasta is tender. Uncover; sprinkle with mozzarella cheese. Bake 5-10 minutes longer or until the cheese is melted.

Nutrition Facts: 2 stuffed manicotti equals 389 calories, 9 g fat (4 g saturated fat), 80 mg cholesterol, 722 mg sodium, 50 g carbohydrate, 5 g fiber, 25 g protein.

SPANAKO-PASTA

SPINACH CHEESE MANICOTTI

Bean 'n' Rice Burritos

PREP/TOTAL TIME: 25 min.   YIELD: 8 servings

KIM HARDISON • MAITLAND, FLORIDA

I love that these hearty, zippy burritos can be whipped up in a jiffy. They're ideal for weeknights.

1-1/2	cups water
1-1/2	cups uncooked instant brown rice
1	medium green pepper, diced
1/2	cup chopped onion
1	Tbsp. olive oil
1	tsp. minced garlic
1	Tbsp. chili powder
1	tsp. ground cumin
1/8	tsp. crushed red pepper flakes
1	can (15 oz.) black beans, rinsed and drained
8	flour tortillas (8 in.), warmed
1	cup salsa

Reduced-fat shredded cheddar cheese and reduced-fat sour cream, optional

1. In a small saucepan, bring water to a boil. Add rice. Return to a boil. Reduce heat; cover and simmer for 5 minutes. Remove from the heat. Let stand for 5 minutes or until water is absorbed.

2. Meanwhile, in a large skillet, saute green pepper and onion in oil for 3-4 minutes or until tender. Add garlic; cook 1 minute longer. Stir in the chili powder, cumin and pepper flakes until combined. Add beans and rice; cook and stir for 4-6 minutes or until the mixture is heated through.

3. Spoon about 1/2 cup of filling off-center on each tortilla; top with 2 Tbsp. salsa. Fold sides and ends over filling and roll up. Serve with cheese and sour cream if desired.

Nutrition Facts: 1 burrito (calculated without cheese and sour cream) equals 290 calories, 6 g fat (1 g saturated fat), 0 cholesterol, 504 mg sodium, 49 g carbohydrate, 4 g fiber, 9 g protein.

Eggplant Parmesan

PREP: 40 min.   COOK: 25 min.   YIELD: 8 servings

LACI HOOTEN • MCKINNEY, TEXAS

Because my recipe calls for baking the eggplant instead of frying it, it's much healthier. The prep time is a little longer than for some recipes, but the Italian flavors and rustic elegance are well worth it.

3	eggs, beaten
2-1/2	cups panko (Japanese) bread crumbs
3	medium eggplants, cut into 1/4-in. slices
2	jars (4-1/2 oz. *each*) sliced mushrooms, drained
1/2	tsp dried basil
1/8	tsp. dried oregano
2	cups (8 oz.) shredded part-skim mozzarella cheese
1/2	cup grated Parmesan cheese
1	jar (28 oz.) spaghetti sauce

1. Place eggs and bread crumbs in separate shallow bowls. Dip eggplant in eggs, then coat in crumbs. Place on baking sheets coated with cooking spray. Bake at 350° for 15-20 minutes or until tender and golden brown, turning once.

2. In a small bowl, combine the mushrooms, basil and oregano. In another small bowl, combine mozzarella and Parmesan cheeses.

3. Spread 1/2 cup sauce into a 13-in. x 9-in. baking dish coated with cooking spray. Layer with a third of the mushroom mixture, eggplant, 3/4 cup sauce and a third of the cheese mixture. Repeat layers twice.

4. Bake, uncovered, at 350° for 25-30 minutes or until heated through and cheese is melted.

Nutrition Facts: 1 serving equals 305 calories, 12 g fat (5 g saturated fat), 102 mg cholesterol, 912 mg sodium, 32 g carbohydrate, 9 g fiber, 18 g protein. **Diabetic Exchanges:** 2 starch, 2 vegetable, 1 medium-fat meat.

BEAN 'N' RICE BURRITOS

EGGPLANT PARMESAN

CREAMY MAKEOVER
MACARONI AND CHEESE

Creamy Makeover Macaroni and Cheese M

PREP: 30 min. BAKE: 25 min. YIELD: 10 servings

APRIL TAYLOR • FORT RILEY, KANSAS

Your family will love the rich, creamy flavor of this mac and cheese dish—and you'll feel good knowing there is less saturated fat than most recipes.

- 1 pkg. (16 oz.) elbow macaroni
- 2 Tbsp. butter
- 1/3 cup all-purpose flour
- 2 cups fat-free half-and-half
- 2 cups fat-free milk
- 1/2 tsp. garlic powder
- 1/2 tsp. pepper
- 1/4 tsp. salt
- 3 cups (12 oz.) shredded reduced-fat sharp cheddar cheese

TOPPING:
- 1 medium onion, chopped
- 2 Tbsp. butter
- 5 cups cubed bread
- 1/2 cup shredded reduced-fat cheddar cheese

1. Cook macaroni according to package directions. Meanwhile, in a large saucepan, melt butter over medium heat.

2. Combine flour and half-and-half; stir into pan. Add milk and seasonings. Bring to a gentle boil; remove from the heat. Stir in cheese until melted. Drain macaroni; add to the cheese sauce and stir to coat.

3. Transfer to a 13-in. x 9-in. baking dish coated with cooking spray. In a large skillet, saute onion in butter until tender. Add bread; saute 2-3 minutes longer. Sprinkle bread mixture and cheese over macaroni mixture. Bake, uncovered, at 350° for 25-30 minutes or until heated through.

Nutrition Facts: 1 cup equals 432 calories, 15 g fat (9 g saturated fat), 41 mg cholesterol, 526 mg sodium, 55 g carbohydrate, 2 g fiber, 21 g protein.

Using milk and half-and-half that's fat free, reducing the butter and taking advantage of reduced-fat cheeses, our Test Kitchen **cut the fat** from the original version of this dish by 27 g, including 19 g of saturated fat.

Hearty Shepherd's Pie M

PREP: 50 min. BAKE: 30 min. YIELD: 6 servings

KIMBERLY HAMMOND • KINGWOOD, TEXAS

Mushrooms, carrots, celery, peas and potatoes pack this full-flavored meal-maker. You'll never even miss the meat.

- 6 garlic cloves
- 1/4 tsp. olive oil
- 1-1/2 lb. medium potatoes, peeled and cubed
- 3 Tbsp. vegetable broth
- 1/4 tsp. salt
- 1/8 tsp. pepper

FILLING:
- 1 medium onion, chopped
- 1 Tbsp. olive oil
- 2 garlic cloves, minced
- 1 lb. sliced baby portobello mushrooms
- 8 oz. frozen vegetarian meat crumbles
- 2 medium carrots, sliced
- 2 celery ribs, chopped
- 3/4 cup vegetable broth, *divided*
- 2 Tbsp. minced fresh rosemary *or* 2 tsp. dried rosemary, crushed
- 1 Tbsp. reduced-sodium soy sauce
- 1/2 tsp. salt
- 1/4 tsp. pepper
- 2 Tbsp. all-purpose flour
- 1 cup frozen peas

1. Place garlic on a double thickness of heavy-duty foil. Drizzle with oil. Wrap foil around garlic. Bake at 425° for 15-20 minutes. Cool for 10-15 minutes.

2. Place potatoes in a Dutch oven and cover with water. Bring to a boil. Reduce heat; cover and cook for 10-15 minutes or until tender; drain. Mash potatoes with broth, salt and pepper; squeeze softened garlic into potatoes and mix well.

3. In a large nonstick skillet coated with cooking spray, saute onion in oil until tender. Add garlic; cook 1 minute longer. Stir in the mushrooms, meat crumbles, carrots and celery; cook and stir for 5 minutes. Add 1/2 cup broth, rosemary, soy sauce, salt and pepper; cover and cook for 10 minutes.

4. Combine flour and remaining broth until smooth. Gradually stir into the pan. Bring to a boil; cook and stir for 1 minute or until thickened. Stir in peas.

5. Transfer vegetable mixture to an 8-in. square baking dish coated with cooking spray; cover with potato mixture. Bake, uncovered, at 350° for 30-35 minutes or until heated through.

Editor's Note: Vegetarian meat crumbles are a nutritious protein source made from soy. Look for them in the natural foods freezer section.

Nutrition Facts: 1-1/2 cups equals 223 calories, 5 g fat (1 g saturated fat), trace cholesterol, 753 mg sodium, 34 g carbohydrate, 6 g fiber, 13 g protein. **Diabetic Exchanges:** 2 vegetable, 1 starch, 1 lean meat, 1 fat.

Provolone Ziti Bake M

PREP: 20 min. BAKE: 65 min. YIELD: 8 servings

VICKY PALMER • ALBUQUERQUE, NEW MEXICO

As easy as it is filling and delicious, this Italian meal appeals to everyone—and they won't even miss the meat.

  1 medium onion, chopped
  1 Tbsp. olive oil
  3 garlic cloves, minced
  2 cans (28 oz. *each*) Italian crushed tomatoes
1-1/2 cups water
  1/2 cup dry red wine *or* reduced-sodium chicken broth
  1 Tbsp. sugar
  1 tsp. dried basil
  1 pkg. (16 oz.) ziti *or* small tube pasta
  8 slices provolone cheese

1. In a Dutch oven, saute onion in oil until tender. Add garlic; cook 1 minute longer. Stir in the tomatoes, water, wine, sugar and basil. Bring to a boil; remove from the heat. Stir in ziti.

2. Transfer to a 13-in. x 9-in. baking dish coated with cooking spray. Cover and bake at 350° for 1 hour. Top with cheese. Bake, uncovered, 4-6 minutes longer or until the ziti is tender and the cheese is melted.

Nutrition Facts: 1-1/2 cups equals 381 calories, 8 g fat (4 g saturated fat), 15 mg cholesterol, 763 mg sodium, 60 g carbohydrate, 4 g fiber, 16 g protein.

Lentil Sweet Potato Curry M

PREP: 20 min. COOK: 35 min. YIELD: 6 servings

TRISHA KRUSE • EAGLE, IDAHO

This is one of those suppers you can start when you get home, then relax while it cooks. (Or help the kids with homework or hop on the stair-stepper.) Apple and brown sugar sweeten this delicious meatless meal.

  1 cup dried lentils, rinsed
  3 cups water, *divided*
  1 large onion, chopped
  1 Tbsp. olive oil
  2 medium carrots, chopped
  3 garlic cloves, minced
  2 medium sweet potatoes, peeled and chopped
  4 tsp. curry powder
3/4 tsp. salt
1/2 tsp. pepper
  2 medium tomatoes, chopped
  1 medium apple, peeled and chopped
  1 Tbsp. brown sugar
  3 cups hot cooked brown rice

1. In a small saucepan, combine lentils and 2 cups water; bring to a boil. Reduce heat; cover and simmer for 20-25 minutes or until tender. Drain.

2. Meanwhile, in a large saucepan, saute onion in oil until tender. Add carrots and garlic; cook 2 minutes longer. Stir in the sweet potatoes, curry, salt, pepper and remaining water. Bring to a boil. Reduce heat; cover and simmer for 10 minutes.

3. Add the tomatoes, apple and brown sugar; cover and cook 10-15 minutes longer or until apple is tender. Stir in lentils; heat through. Serve with rice.

Nutrition Facts: 1 cup lentil mixture with 1/2 cup rice equals 333 calories, 4 g fat (1 g saturated fat), 0 cholesterol, 325 mg sodium, 63 g carbohydrate, 15 g fiber, 13 g protein.

PROVOLONE ZITI BAKE

LENTIL SWEET POTATO CURRY

Enchilada Pie M

PREP: 40 min. COOK: 4 hours YIELD: 8 servings

JACQUELINE CORREA • LANDING, NEW JERSEY

This impressive, hearty dish is the perfect choice for vegetarians and meat eaters alike.

- 1 pkg. (12 oz.) frozen vegetarian meat crumbles
- 1 cup chopped onion
- 1/2 cup chopped green pepper
- 2 tsp. canola oil
- 1 can (16 oz.) kidney beans, rinsed and drained
- 1 can (15 oz.) black beans, rinsed and drained
- 1 can (10 oz.) diced tomatoes and green chilies, undrained
- 1/2 cup water
- 1-1/2 tsp. chili powder
- 1/2 tsp. ground cumin
- 1/4 tsp. pepper
- 6 whole wheat tortillas (8 in.)
- 2 cups (8 oz.) shredded reduced-fat cheddar cheese

1. Cut three 25-in. x 3-in. strips of heavy-duty foil; crisscross so they resemble spokes of a wheel. Place strips on the bottom and up the sides of a 5-qt. slow cooker. Coat strips with cooking spray.

2. In a large saucepan, cook the meat crumbles, onion and green pepper in oil until vegetables are tender. Stir in both cans of beans, tomatoes, water, chili powder, cumin and pepper. Bring to a boil. Reduce heat; simmer, uncovered, for 10 minutes.

3. In prepared slow cooker, layer about 3/4 cup bean mixture, one tortilla and 1/3 cup cheese. Repeat layers five times. Cover and cook on low for 4-5 hours or until heated through and cheese is melted.

4. Using foil strips as handles, remove the pie to a serving platter.

Editor's Note: Vegetarian meat crumbles are a nutritious protein source made from soy. Look for them in the natural foods freezer section.

Nutrition Facts: 1 piece equals 367 calories, 11 g fat (4 g saturated fat), 20 mg cholesterol, 818 mg sodium, 41 g carbohydrate, 9 g fiber, 25 g protein. **Diabetic Exchanges:** 3 starch, 2 lean meat, 1 fat.

ENCHILADA PIE

Southwest Spinach Strata ⓜ

PREP: 20 min. **BAKE:** 45 min. + standing
YIELD: 6 servings

DEBORAH BIGGS • OMAHA, NEBRASKA

With a mix of whole wheat and white bread, spinach and black beans, this main-dish strata has an amazing savory flavor the whole family will love. Pinto or cannellini beans may be substituted for black beans with fantastic success.

2-1/2 cups cubed day-old white bread

2-1/2 cups cubed day-old whole wheat bread

  2/3 cup black beans, rinsed and drained

    1 pkg. (10 oz.) frozen chopped spinach, thawed and squeezed dry

1-1/2 cups (6 oz.) shredded reduced-fat cheddar cheese

    1 cup Southwestern-style egg substitute

    2 cups fat-free milk

  1/4 cup minced fresh cilantro

  1/4 tsp. salt

    6 Tbsp. reduced-fat sour cream

    6 Tbsp. salsa

1. Place half of the bread cubes in an 8-in. square baking dish coated with cooking spray. Layer with beans, spinach and half of the cheese. Top with remaining bread cubes.

2. In a large bowl, whisk the egg substitute, milk, cilantro and salt. Pour over top. Let stand for 5 minutes.

3. Bake, uncovered, at 350° for 40 minutes. Sprinkle with remaining cheese. Bake 5 minutes longer or until cheese is melted and a knife inserted near the center comes out clean. Let stand for 10 minutes before cutting. Serve with sour cream and salsa.

Nutrition Facts: 1 piece with 1 Tbsp. sour cream and 1 Tbsp. salsa equals 264 calories, 9 g fat (5 g saturated fat), 27 mg cholesterol, 736 mg sodium, 28 g carbohydrate, 4 g fiber, 20 g protein. **Diabetic Exchanges:** 2 starch, 2 lean meat, 1/2 fat.

Spring Frittata C M

PREP: 35 min. BAKE: 30 min. YIELD: 6 servings

DIANE HIGGINS • TAMPA, FLORIDA

With roasted veggies, Asiago cheese and plenty of dill, this frittata is packed with spring flavors. It looks impressive, but it's really a snap to make.

- 1/2 cup chopped leek (white portion only)
- 1/2 cup cut fresh asparagus (1-in. pieces)
- 2 tsp. olive oil
- 1/4 tsp. salt
- 1/4 tsp. pepper
- 1 cup sliced fresh mushrooms
- 1 cup shredded Asiago cheese
- 4 eggs
- 1 cup egg substitute
- 1/4 cup fat-free milk
- 1 Tbsp. snipped fresh dill *or* 1 tsp. dill weed
- 1 Tbsp. minced fresh parsley *or* 1 tsp. dried parsley flakes

1. In small bowl, combine leek and asparagus. Drizzle with oil and sprinkle with salt and pepper; toss to coat. Transfer to a baking sheet coated with cooking spray. Bake at 400° for 20-25 minutes or until tender, stirring occasionally. Reduce heat to 350°.

2. Place mushrooms on the bottom of a 9-in. deep-dish pie plate coated with cooking spray. Top with roasted vegetables and cheese. In a large bowl, whisk the remaining ingredients; pour over cheese.

3. Bake for 30-35 minutes or until a knife inserted near the center comes out clean. Let stand for 5 minutes. Cut into wedges.

Nutrition Facts: 1 wedge equals 163 calories, 10 g fat (4 g saturated fat), 158 mg cholesterol, 282 mg sodium, 4 g carbohydrate, 1 g fiber, 14 g protein.

Vegetable-Stuffed Portobellos M

PREP: 20 min. BROIL: 15 min. YIELD: 4 servings

ELIZABETH DOSS • CALIFORNIA CITY, CALIFORNIA

I often substitute portobellos for hamburger patties, but in this open-faced recipe, they take the place of buns. My family loves this tasty, healthful dinner, and it's ready in no time.

- 1 can (15 oz.) white kidney *or* cannellini beans, rinsed and drained
- 2 Tbsp. olive oil, *divided*
- 1 Tbsp. water
- 1 tsp. dried rosemary, crushed
- 1 garlic clove, peeled and halved
- 1/4 tsp. salt
- 1/4 tsp. pepper
- 4 large portobello mushrooms (4 to 4-1/2 in.), stems removed
- 1 medium sweet red pepper, finely chopped
- 1 medium red onion, finely chopped
- 1 medium zucchini, finely chopped
- 1/2 cup shredded pepper jack cheese

1. In a food processor, combine the beans, 1 Tbsp. oil, water, rosemary, garlic, salt and pepper. Cover and process until pureed; set aside.

2. Place mushrooms on a broiler pan coated with cooking spray. Broil 4 in. from the heat for 6-8 minutes on each side or until mushrooms are tender.

3. Meanwhile, in a small nonstick skillet coated with cooking spray, saute the red pepper, red onion and zucchini in remaining oil until tender.

4. Spread about 1/3 cup reserved bean mixture over each mushroom; top with 1/2 cup vegetable mixture. Sprinkle with cheese. Broil 2-3 minutes longer or until cheese is melted.

Nutrition Facts: 1 stuffed mushroom equals 252 calories, 12 g fat (4 g saturated fat), 15 mg cholesterol, 378 mg sodium, 26 g carbohydrate, 7 g fiber, 11 g protein. **Diabetic Exchanges:** 2 lean meat, 2 vegetable, 1 starch, 1 fat.

SPRING FRITTATA

VEGETABLE-STUFFED PORTOBELLOS

BLACK BEAN VEGGIE BURRITOS

Black Bean Veggie Burritos

PREP: 30 min. **BAKE:** 25 min. **YIELD:** 8 servings

CARISSA SUMNER • ALEXANDRIA, VIRGINIA

Sweet potatoes give these baked burritos a unique twist. Packed with tender veggies, cheese and spices, they'll make a mouthwatering dinner any night.

- 1 large sweet potato, peeled and cut into 1/2-in. cubes
- 1 medium onion, finely chopped
- 1 Tbsp. water
- 1 can (15 oz.) black beans, rinsed and drained
- 1 cup frozen corn
- 1 medium green pepper, chopped
- 2 Tbsp. lemon juice
- 3 garlic cloves, minced
- 1 Tbsp. chili powder
- 2 tsp. dried oregano
- 1 tsp. ground cumin
- 8 whole wheat tortillas (8 in.), warmed
- 2 cups (8 oz.) shredded Monterey Jack cheese
- 1/2 cup fat-free plain yogurt
- 1/2 cup salsa

1. In a large microwave-safe bowl, combine the sweet potato, onion and water. Cover and microwave on high for 4-5 minutes or until potato is almost tender. Stir in the beans, corn, green pepper, lemon juice, garlic and seasonings.

2. Spoon a heaping 1/2 cup filling off center on each tortilla. Sprinkle with 1/4 cup cheese. Fold sides and ends over filling and roll up.

3. Place seam side down in a 13-in. x 9-in. baking dish coated with cooking spray. Cover and bake at 350° for 25-30 minutes or until heated through. Serve with yogurt and salsa.

Nutrition Facts: 1 burrito with 1 Tbsp. yogurt and 1 Tbsp. salsa equals 362 calories, 12 g fat (5 g saturated fat), 25 mg cholesterol, 505 mg sodium, 47 g carbohydrate, 7 g fiber, 16 g protein.

Makeover Macaroni And Cheese

PREP/TOTAL TIME: 30 min. **YIELD:** 8 servings

NANCY LANGROCK • SOUTHBURY, CONNECTICUT

Creamy and cheesy with comfort in every bite, this lightened-up classic is sure to become a family favorite at your house, too!

- 1 pkg. (16 oz.) elbow macaroni
- 2 Tbsp. all-purpose flour
- 2 cups fat-free milk
- 1 pkg. (16 oz.) reduced-fat process cheese (Velveeta), cubed
- 1 cup (4 oz.) shredded sharp cheddar cheese, *divided*

1. Cook macaroni according to package directions. Meanwhile, in a large saucepan, combine flour and milk until smooth. Bring to a boil; cook and stir for 2 minutes or until thickened. Stir in process cheese and 1/2 cup cheddar cheese until smooth. Drain macaroni; stir into cheese sauce.

2. Remove from the heat; sprinkle with remaining cheese. Cover and let stand for 5 minutes or until cheese is melted.

Nutrition Facts: 1 cup equals 403 calories, 11 g fat (6 g saturated fat), 36 mg cholesterol, 944 mg sodium, 54 g carbohydrate, 2 g fiber, 23 g protein.

Hash Brown Supreme C M

PREP: 20 min. COOK: 15 min. YIELD: 4 servings

JENNIFER BISTLINE • CONFLUENCE, PENNSYLVANIA

This is a great way to use up leftover fresh vegetables. In addition to the potatoes, use whatever you have on hand to brighten up the recipe. My family likes this meal best when it's garnished with sour cream. If you are not big on spicy foods, simply leave out the jalapeno pepper.

1	small onion, finely chopped
1/2	cup sliced fresh mushrooms
1/2	cup chopped green pepper
1	Tbsp. canola oil
3	cups frozen shredded hash brown potatoes
1	medium tomato, finely chopped
1/2	cup shredded reduced-fat cheddar cheese
2	Tbsp. sliced ripe olives
1	jalapeno pepper, seeded and sliced
1/4	tsp. seasoned salt
1/8	tsp. pepper
1	Tbsp. minced chives

1. In a large nonstick skillet, saute the onion, mushrooms and pepper in oil until tender. Add hash browns; cook over medium heat for 8-10 minutes or until potatoes are browned, stirring occasionally.

2. Stir in the tomato, cheese, olives, jalapeno, seasoned salt and pepper. Cover and cook for 2 minutes or until cheese is melted. Sprinkle with chives; cut into wedges.

Editor's Note: When cutting hot peppers, disposable gloves are recommended. Avoid touching your face.

Nutrition Facts: 1 wedge equals 142 calories, 7 g fat (2 g saturated fat), 10 mg cholesterol, 233 mg sodium, 15 g carbohydrate, 2 g fiber, 6 g protein. **Diabetic Exchanges:** 1 medium-fat meat, 1 vegetable, 1/2 starch.

Fettuccine with Mushrooms and Tomatoes M

PREP/TOTAL TIME: 30 min. YIELD: 6 servings

PHYLLIS SCHMALZ • KANSAS CITY, KANSAS

I can toss this dish together in just 30 minutes on a busy weeknight. And it's elegant enough to serve as a meatless entree for guests.

1	pkg. (12 oz.) fettuccine
1	lb. fresh mushrooms, halved
1	large onion, chopped
1	large green pepper, chopped
1	tsp. olive oil
4	garlic cloves, minced
3	Tbsp. all-purpose flour

3 cups 1% milk
1 tsp. salt
1/4 tsp. pepper
1/2 cup sun-dried tomatoes (not packed in oil), thinly sliced
1 cup (4 oz.) shredded reduced-fat Swiss cheese
1/4 cup grated Parmesan cheese

1. Cook fettuccine according to package directions. Meanwhile, in a large nonstick skillet, saute the mushrooms, onion and green pepper in oil for 4-6 minutes or until vegetables are tender. Add garlic; cook 1 minute longer.

2. In a small bowl, combine the flour, milk, salt and pepper until smooth; gradually stir into mushroom mixture. Add tomatoes. Bring to a boil; cook and stir for 2 minutes or until thickened. Stir in cheeses. Drain fettuccine; toss with sauce.

Nutrition Facts: 1-1/3 cups equals 387 calories, 8 g fat (4 g saturated fat), 17 mg cholesterol, 662 mg sodium, 60 g carbohydrate, 5 g fiber, 23 g protein.

Grilled Veggie Pizza Ⓜ

PREP: 30 min. **BAKE:** 10 min. **YIELD:** 6 servings

SUSAN MARSHALL • COLORADO SPRINGS, COLORADO

Excess summer bounty is perfect for this delightfully simple pizza. Grilling the veggies first brings out rich, caramelized flavors. Also try it with a sprinkling of olives or pine nuts before adding the cheese.

8 small fresh mushrooms, halved
1 small zucchini, cut into 1/4-in. slices
1 small sweet yellow pepper, sliced
1 small sweet red pepper, sliced
1 small onion, sliced
1 Tbsp. white wine vinegar
1 Tbsp. water
4 tsp. olive oil, *divided*
2 tsp. minced fresh basil *or* 1/2 tsp. dried basil
1/4 tsp. salt

1/4 tsp. pepper
1 prebaked 12-in. thin whole wheat pizza crust
1 can (8 oz.) pizza sauce
2 small tomatoes, chopped
2 cups (8 oz.) shredded part-skim mozzarella cheese

1. In a large bowl, combine the mushrooms, zucchini, peppers, onion, vinegar, water, 3 tsp. oil and seasonings. Transfer to a grill wok or basket. Grill, covered, over medium heat for 8-10 minutes or until tender, stirring once.

2. Prepare grill for indirect heat. Brush crust with remaining oil; spread with pizza sauce. Top with grilled vegetables, tomatoes and cheese. Grill, covered, over indirect medium heat for 10-12 minutes or until edges are lightly browned and cheese is melted. Rotate pizza halfway through cooking to ensure evenly browned crust.

Editor's Note: If you do not have a grill wok or basket, use a disposable foil pan. Poke holes in the bottom of the pan with a meat fork to allow liquid to drain.

Nutrition Facts: 1 slice equals 274 calories, 11 g fat (5 g saturated fat), 22 mg cholesterol, 634 mg sodium, 30 g carbohydrate, 5 g fiber, 17 g protein. **Diabetic Exchanges:** 2 starch, 2 medium-fat meat, 1 vegetable.

> Olive oil can be stored at room temperature or in the refrigerator for 1 year. When chilled, the oil turns cloudy and thick. **Chilled olive oil** will return to its original consistency when left at room temperature for a short period of time.

GRILLED VEGGIE PIZZA

FETTUCCINE WITH MUSHROOMS AND TOMATOES

Southwestern Bean Chowder M

PREP: 20 min. **COOK:** 35 min. **YIELD:** 8 servings (2 qt.)

JULIANNE MEYERS • HINESVILLE, GEORGIA

I'm really fortunate that my children are great eaters. They and my husband love this soup. My favorite beans for this are white kidney beans—they have a terrific texture.

>   2 cans (15 oz. *each*) white kidney *or* cannellini beans, rinsed and drained, *divided*
>   1 medium onion, chopped
>   1/4 cup chopped celery
>   1/4 cup chopped green pepper
>   1 Tbsp. olive oil
>   2 garlic cloves, minced
>   3 cups vegetable broth
> 1-1/2 cups frozen corn, thawed
>   1 medium carrot, shredded
>   1 can (4 oz.) chopped green chilies
>   1 Tbsp. ground cumin
>   1/2 tsp. chili powder
> 4-1/2 tsp. cornstarch
>   2 cups 2% milk
>   1 cup (4 oz.) shredded cheddar cheese
> Minced fresh cilantro and additional shredded cheddar cheese, optional

1. In a small bowl, mash one can beans with a fork; set aside.

2. In a Dutch oven, saute the onion, celery and pepper in oil until tender. Add garlic; cook 1 minute longer. Stir in the mashed beans, broth, corn, carrot, chilies, cumin, chili powder and remaining beans. Bring to a boil. Reduce heat; simmer, uncovered, for 20 minutes.

3. Combine cornstarch and milk until smooth. Stir into bean mixture. Bring to a boil; cook and stir for 2 minutes or until thickened. Stir in cheese until melted. Serve with cilantro and additional cheese if desired.

Nutrition Facts: 1 cup (calculated without additional cheese) equals 236 calories, 8 g fat (4 g saturated fat), 20 mg cholesterol, 670 mg sodium, 31 g carbohydrate, 6 g fiber, 11 g protein. **Diabetic Exchanges:** 2 starch, 1 lean meat, 1/2 fat.

Crispy Seasoned Polenta Squares M

PREP: 30 min. + cooling **COOK:** 10 min.
YIELD: 9 servings

SHELLY BEVINGTON-FISHER • HERMISTON, OREGON

Crisp polenta squares make a delightful side for a variety of main dishes. Sun-dried tomatoes and just the right amount of seasoning make them seem special...a dollop of sour cream adds the finishing touch!

>   4 cups water
>   1/2 cup chopped sun-dried tomatoes (not packed in oil)
>   1 tsp. salt
>   1 tsp. dried minced onion
>   1 tsp. dried minced garlic
>   1 cup cornmeal
>   1/2 cup grated Parmesan cheese
>   1/2 tsp. dried oregano
>   1 egg
>   1/4 cup fat-free milk
>   1/2 cup seasoned bread crumbs
>   2 tsp. dried cilantro flakes
>   1 Tbsp. olive oil
>   9 Tbsp. reduced-fat sour cream

1. In a large heavy saucepan, bring the water, tomatoes, salt, onion and garlic to a boil. Reduce heat to a gentle boil; slowly whisk in cornmeal. Cook and stir with a wooden spoon for 15-20 minutes or until polenta is thickened and pulls away cleanly from the

CRISPY SEASONED POLENTA SQUARES

SOUTHWESTERN BEAN CHOWDER

sides of the pan. Stir in cheese and oregano. Spread into a 9-in. square baking pan coated with cooking spray. Cool to room temperature, about 30 minutes.

2. Cut polenta into nine squares. In a shallow bowl, whisk egg and milk. In another shallow bowl, combine bread crumbs and cilantro. Dip polenta in the egg mixture, then bread crumb mixture.

3. In a large nonstick skillet coated with cooking spray, cook the polenta in oil in batches for 1-2 minutes on each side or until golden brown. Serve with sour cream.

Nutrition Facts: 1 square with 1 Tbsp. reduced-fat sour cream equals 134 calories, 5 g fat (2 g saturated fat), 18 mg cholesterol, 456 mg sodium, 18 g carbohydrate, 2 g fiber, 5 g protein. **Diabetic Exchanges:** 1 starch, 1 fat.

Vegetable Pad Thai M

PREP: 25 min. **COOK:** 15 min. **YIELD:** 6 servings

SARA LANDRY • BROOKLINE, MASSACHUSETTS

Classic flavors of Thailand abound in this fragrant and easy dish featuring peanuts, tofu and noodles. New to tofu? It beefs up protein in this satisfying entree—a delicious way to introduce it to your diet.

  1   pkg. (12 oz.) whole wheat fettuccine
1/4   cup rice vinegar
  3   Tbsp. reduced-sodium soy sauce
  2   Tbsp. brown sugar
  2   Tbsp. fish sauce *or* additional reduced-sodium soy sauce
  1   Tbsp. lime juice

Dash Louisiana-style hot sauce
  1   pkg. (12 oz.) extra-firm tofu, drained and cut into 1/2-in. cubes
  3   tsp. canola oil, *divided*
  2   medium carrots, grated
  2   cups fresh snow peas, halved
  3   garlic cloves, minced
  2   eggs, lightly beaten
  2   cups bean sprouts
  3   green onions, chopped
1/2   cup minced fresh cilantro
1/4   cup unsalted peanuts, chopped

1. Cook fettuccine according to package directions. Meanwhile, in a small bowl, combine the vinegar, soy sauce, brown sugar, fish sauce, lime juice and hot sauce until smooth; set aside.

2. In a large skillet or wok, stir-fry tofu in 2 tsp. oil until golden brown. Remove and keep warm. Stir-fry the carrots and snow peas in remaining oil for 1-2 minutes. Add the garlic, cook 1 minute longer or until the vegetables are crisp-tender. Add eggs; cook and stir until set.

3. Drain pasta; add to the vegetable mixture. Stir vinegar mixture and add to the skillet. Bring to a boil. Add the tofu, bean sprouts and onions; heat through. Sprinkle with cilantro and peanuts.

Nutrition Facts: 1-1/3 cups equals 383 calories, 11 g fat (2 g saturated fat), 71 mg cholesterol, 806 mg sodium, 61 g carbohydrate, 10 g fiber, 18 g protein.

Asian Quinoa F M

PREP: 20 min. **COOK:** 20 min. + standing
YIELD: 4 servings

SONYA LABBE • SANTA MONICA, CALIFORNIA

I love to cook and come up with new recipes. I serve this dish at least once a month and sometimes more. For a different twist, I'll occasionally add a scrambled egg or use soy sauce instead of the rice vinegar.

1	cup water
2	Tbsp. rice vinegar
2	Tbsp. plum sauce
2	garlic cloves, minced
1	tsp. minced fresh gingerroot
1	tsp. sesame oil
1/4	tsp. salt
1/4	tsp. crushed red pepper flakes
1/2	cup quinoa, rinsed
1	medium sweet red pepper, chopped
1/2	cup sliced water chestnuts, chopped
1/2	cup fresh sugar snap peas, trimmed and halved
2	green onions, thinly sliced

1. In a large saucepan, combine the first eight ingredients; bring to a boil. Add quinoa. Reduce heat; cover and simmer for 12-15 minutes or until water is absorbed.

2. Remove from the heat. Add the red pepper, water chestnuts, peas and onions; fluff with a fork. Cover and let stand for 10 minutes.

Editor's Note: Look for quinoa in the cereal, rice or organic food aisle.

Nutrition Facts: 2/3 cup equals 138 calories, 3 g fat (trace saturated fat), 0 cholesterol, 205 mg sodium, 25 g carbohydrate, 3 g fiber, 4 g protein.

Mexican Lentils and Rice M

PREP: 15 min. **COOK:** 40 min. **YIELD:** 4 servings

SHANNON KOENE • BLACKSBURG, VIRGINIA

You'll love this simple, quick-cooking, throw-in-the-pan-and-simmer meal!

1	medium onion, chopped
1	Tbsp. olive oil
2	garlic cloves, minced
1-1/2	cups vegetable broth
1/2	cup dried lentils, rinsed
3	tsp. chili powder
1-1/2	tsp. ground cumin
1	cup frozen corn
1	cup salsa
1/4	cup tomato paste
1	tsp. dried oregano
1	tsp. white vinegar
2	cups hot cooked brown rice
3/4	cup shredded reduced-fat sharp cheddar cheese

1. In a large saucepan, saute onion in oil until tender. Add garlic; cook 1 minute longer. Add the broth, lentils, chili powder and cumin. Bring to a boil. Reduce heat; cover and simmer for 20-25 minutes or until lentils are almost tender.

2. Stir in the corn, salsa, tomato paste, oregano and vinegar. Bring to a boil. Reduce heat; cover and simmer 10 minutes longer or until lentils are tender. Serve with rice; sprinkle with cheese.

Nutrition Facts: 1 cup lentil mixture with 1/2 cup brown rice and 3 Tbsp. cheese equals 387 calories, 10 g fat (4 g saturated fat), 15 mg cholesterol, 770 mg sodium, 60 g carbohydrate, 13 g fiber, 17 g protein.

Makeover Penne with Vodka Cream Sauce M

PREP: 15 min. COOK: 40 min. YIELD: 8 servings

DEBRA TORRES • CLARION, PENNSYLVANIA

This version of my original recipe is still creamy, rich and restaurant-quality special, but it now has less than half the original recipe's fat and cholesterol. It's tough to tell it apart from my full-fat version.

> 1 large onion, chopped
> 1 Tbsp. olive oil
> 4 garlic cloves, minced
> 2 cans (one 28 oz., one 14.5 oz.) diced tomatoes
> 1/4 cup vodka
> 1 pkg. (12 oz.) whole wheat penne pasta
> 2 tsp. prepared pesto
> 1/4 tsp. salt
> 1/4 tsp. crushed red pepper flakes
> 2 Tbsp. all-purpose flour
> 1/2 cup heavy whipping cream
> 1 cup whole milk
> 1/2 cup shredded Parmesan cheese

1. In a large saucepan, saute onion in oil until tender. Add garlic; cook 1 minute longer. Stir in tomatoes and vodka. Bring to a boil. Reduce heat; simmer, uncovered, for 30-35 minutes or until slightly thickened, stirring occasionally.

2. Meanwhile, cook the penne according to the package directions.

3. Stir the pesto, salt and pepper flakes into tomato mixture. In a small bowl, combine flour and cream

until smooth; stir into pan. Add milk. Bring to a boil; cook and stir for 2 minutes or until slightly thickened. Drain penne; serve with sauce. Sprinkle with cheese.

Nutrition Facts: 2/3 cup pasta with 2/3 cups sauce and 1 Tbsp. cheese equals 324 calories, 11 g fat (5 g saturated fat), 27 mg cholesterol, 379 mg sodium, 44 g carbohydrate, 7 g fiber, 12 g protein. **Diabetic Exchanges:** 2 starch, 2 fat, 1 lean meat, 1 vegetable.

Beans & Spinach M

PREP/TOTAL TIME: 25 min. YIELD: 6 servings

PATRICK AND HELEN REDDY • WILMINGTON, NORTH CAROLINA

One of our favorite appetizers at a local restaurant is made with white beans and escarole. It's nearly impossible to find escarole where we live, so we subbed in baby spinach and were pleasantly surprised by the result. Enjoy!

> 4 garlic cloves, sliced
> 2 Tbsp. olive oil
> 2 large onions, chopped
> 1 lb. fresh baby spinach
> 1 can (15 oz.) white kidney or cannellini beans, rinsed and drained
> 1/2 cup white wine or reduced-sodium chicken broth
> 3/4 tsp. salt
> 1/4 tsp. pepper

1. In a large nonstick skillet, saute garlic in oil until tender. Remove garlic and discard. Add onions to pan; saute until crisp-tender.

2. Stir in the remaining ingredients. Cook and stir over medium heat for 10-12 minutes or until spinach is wilted. Serve with a slotted spoon.

Nutrition Facts: 3/4 cup equals 138 calories, 5 g fat (1 g saturated fat), 0 cholesterol, 446 mg sodium, 17 g carbohydrate, 5 g fiber, 5 g protein. **Diabetic Exchanges:** 2 vegetable, 1 fat, 1/2 starch.

MAKEOVER PENNE WITH VODKA CREAM SAUCE

BEANS & SPINACH

Lactose-Free Spinach Lasagna Ⓜ

PREP: 45 min. **BAKE:** 35 min. + standing
YIELD: 12 servings

PEGGY KERN • RIVERSIDE, CALIFORNIA

Think you don't like tofu? It tastes just like ricotta cheese in this fabulous dish.

- 1-3/4 cups sliced fresh mushrooms
- 1/4 cup chopped onion
- 1 Tbsp. olive oil
- 1 pkg. (10 oz.) frozen chopped spinach, thawed and squeezed dry
- 2 garlic cloves, minced
- 2 cans (14-1/2 oz. *each*) diced tomatoes, undrained
- 1 can (8 oz.) tomato sauce
- 1 can (6 oz.) tomato paste
- 2 Tbsp. minced fresh basil *or* 2 tsp. dried basil
- 1 tsp. dried marjoram
- 9 uncooked lasagna noodles
- 1 pkg. (14 oz.) firm tofu, drained and cubed
- 2 eggs, lightly beaten
- 2 Tbsp. dried parsley flakes
- 1/2 tsp. salt
- 1/4 tsp. pepper
- 1-1/2 cups (6 oz.) shredded mozzarella-flavored soy cheese
- 1 cup (4 oz.) shredded cheddar-flavored soy cheese

1. In a large nonstick skillet coated with cooking spray, saute mushrooms and onion in oil until tender. Add spinach and garlic; cook 2 minutes longer. Stir in the tomatoes, tomato sauce, tomato paste, basil and marjoram. Bring to a boil. Reduce heat; cover and simmer for 15 minutes, stirring occasionally.

2. Meanwhile, cook lasagna noodles according to package directions; drain.

3. In a small bowl, combine the tofu, eggs, parsley, salt and pepper. Place three noodles in the bottom of a 13-in. x 9-in. baking dish coated with cooking spray. Layer with half of the tofu mixture, 1-1/2 cups spinach mixture, 1/2 cup mozzarella-flavored soy cheese and 1/3 cup cheddar-flavored soy cheese. Repeat layers. Top with remaining noodles and spinach mixture; sprinkle with remaining cheeses.

4. Cover and bake at 375° for 35-40 minutes or until heated through. Let the lasagna stand for 10 minutes before cutting.

Nutrition Facts: 1 piece equals 216 calories, 7 g fat (1 g saturated fat), 35 mg cholesterol, 531 mg sodium, 24 g carbohydrate, 3 g fiber, 14 g protein. **Diabetic Exchanges:** 2 vegetable, 1 medium-fat meat, 1 starch.

Two-Bean Veggie Pizza Ⓜ

PREP: 30 min. **BAKE:** 10 min. **YIELD:** 8 slices

LAURA LETNES • FARGO, NORTH DAKOTA

This is my much healthier version of a black bean pizza I had in Guatemala. It's so delicious!

- 1 medium onion, sliced
- 2 tsp. canola oil
- 3/4 cup canned kidney beans, rinsed and drained
- 3/4 cup canned black beans, rinsed and drained
- 1/2 cup salsa
- 1 Tbsp. hickory smoke-flavored barbecue sauce
- 1 sprig fresh parsley, stems removed
- 1 small garlic clove, peeled and halved
- 3/4 tsp. ground cumin
- 1/4 tsp. pepper

Dash hot pepper sauce

LACTOSE-FREE SPINACH LASAGNA

TWO-BEAN VEGGIE PIZZA

VEGGIE-CHEESE STUFFED SHELLS

1 prebaked 12-in. thin pizza crust
1 cup frozen corn, thawed
1 can (14-1/2 oz.) diced tomatoes, drained
3/4 cup shredded sharp cheddar cheese
3/4 cup shredded pepper jack cheese

1. In a small nonstick skillet, cook onion in oil over low heat for 15-20 minutes or until onion is golden brown, stirring occasionally.

2. Meanwhile, in a food processor, combine the beans, salsa, barbecue sauce, fresh parsley, garlic, cumin, pepper and pepper sauce; cover and process until pureed.

3. Place crust on a baking sheet; spread with the bean mixture. Top with caramelized onions, corn, tomatoes and cheeses. Bake at 450° for 8-10 minutes or until edges are lightly browned and cheese is melted.

Nutrition Facts: 1 slice equals 278 calories, 10 g fat (5 g saturated fat), 23 mg cholesterol, 561 mg sodium, 35 g carbohydrate, 4 g fiber, 13 g protein. **Diabetic Exchanges:** 2 starch, 1 lean meat, 1 vegetable, 1/2 fat.

Veggie-Cheese Stuffed Shells Ⓜ

PREP: 20 min. BAKE: 35 min. YIELD: 2 servings

SHARON DELANEY-CHRONIS • SOUTH MILWAUKEE, WISCONSIN

Need a great-tasting meatless dish you can count on? These pleasing pasta shells are packed with veggies, three kinds of cheese and comforting flavor.

6 uncooked jumbo pasta shells
2/3 cup reduced-fat ricotta cheese
1/2 cup shredded part-skim mozzarella cheese, *divided*
1/4 cup shredded carrot
1/4 cup shredded zucchini
2 Tbsp. grated Parmesan cheese
1/2 tsp. dried parsley flakes
1/2 tsp. dried oregano
1/8 tsp. garlic powder
1/8 tsp. pepper
3/4 cup meatless spaghetti sauce, *divided*

1. Cook the pasta according to package directions. Meanwhile, in a small bowl, combine the ricotta cheese, 1/4 cup mozzarella cheese, carrot, zucchini, Parmesan cheese, parsley, oregano, garlic powder and pepper.

2. Spread 1/4 cup spaghetti sauce in a 3-cup baking dish coated with cooking spray. Drain shells; stuff with cheese mixture. Place in prepared baking dish. Top with remaining spaghetti sauce.

3. Cover and bake at 350° for 25 minutes. Uncover; sprinkle with remaining mozzarella. Bake 10-15 minutes longer or until bubbly.

Nutrition Facts: 3 stuffed shells equals 326 calories, 10 g fat (6 g saturated fat), 40 mg cholesterol, 721 mg sodium, 37 g carbohydrate, 3 g fiber, 21 g protein. **Diabetic Exchanges:** 2 medium-fat meat, 2 vegetable, 1-1/2 starch.

Linguine with Edamame And Tomatoes Ⓜ

PREP/TOTAL TIME: 25 min. YIELD: 4 servings

DIANA RIOS • LYTLE, TEXAS

Featuring garden-fresh basil, cherry tomatoes and edamame, this bright and hearty pasta makes for a marvelous meatless meal on any busy weeknight.

8	oz. uncooked multigrain linguine
1-1/2	cups frozen shelled edamame
4	green onions, thinly sliced
1	Tbsp. olive oil
2	cups cherry tomatoes, halved
3	garlic cloves, minced
1	tsp. dried oregano
1/2	tsp. salt
1/4	cup white wine *or* reduced-sodium chicken broth
3/4	cup crumbled feta cheese
2	Tbsp. minced fresh basil

1. Cook linguine according to package directions, adding edamame during the last 5 minutes; drain, reserving 1/2 cup cooking liquid.

2. In a large nonstick skillet, saute onions in oil until tender. Add the tomatoes, garlic, oregano and salt. Add wine and reserved cooking liquid; cook and stir for 2 minutes.

3. Add linguine and edamame; cook and stir 2-3 minutes longer. Remove from the heat. Sprinkle with cheese and basil; toss to coat.

Nutrition Facts: 1-1/2 cups equals 370 calories, 11 g fat (3 g saturated fat), 11 mg cholesterol, 514 mg sodium, 54 g carbohydrate, 10 g fiber, 17 g protein.

Scrumptious Vegetable Lasagna Ⓜ

PREP: 30 min. BAKE: 40 min. + standing
YIELD: 12 servings

COLLEEN CASSADY • LANCASTER, NEW HAMPSHIRE

My sister insists that I make this every year for one of our holiday family get-togethers.

9	whole wheat lasagna noodles
2	medium yellow summer squash, cut into 1/4-in. slices
2	medium zucchini, cut into 1/4-in. slices
1	large green pepper, chopped
1/2	lb. sliced fresh mushrooms
1	large sweet onion, chopped
1	Tbsp. olive oil
1	jar (25 oz.) marinara sauce
1	carton (15 oz.) fat-free ricotta cheese
9	slices reduced-fat provolone cheese, halved
2	cups (8 oz.) shredded part-skim mozzarella cheese
1	cup grated Parmesan cheese

1. Cook noodles according to package directions.

2. Meanwhile, in a large nonstick skillet coated with cooking spray, saute the squash, zucchini, green pepper, mushrooms and onion in oil until tender.

3. Drain noodles. Rinse in cold water and drain again. Spread 1/4 cup marinara sauce in a 13-in. x 9-in. baking dish coated with cooking spray. Top with three noodles, a scant 1 cup marinara sauce, 2 cups vegetable mixture, 1/2 cup ricotta cheese, six halved slices of provolone cheese, 2/3 cup mozzarella cheese and 1/3 cup Parmesan cheese. Repeat layers twice.

4. Cover and bake at 375° for 30 minutes. Uncover; bake 10-15 minutes longer or until bubbly. Let stand for 10 minutes before cutting.

Nutrition Facts: 1 piece equals 269 calories, 9 g fat (5 g saturated fat), 30 mg cholesterol, 441 mg sodium, 27 g carbohydrate, 4 g fiber, 19 g protein. **Diabetic Exchanges:** 2 lean meat, 2 vegetable, 1 starch, 1 fat.

Black Bean Pasta ᖴ Ⅿ

PREP/TOTAL TIME: 25 min. YIELD: 6 servings

ASHLYNN AZAR • ALBUQUERQUE, NEW MEXICO

This filling vegetarian dish is loaded with flavor. I use fresh rosemary when I have it on hand.

9	oz. uncooked whole wheat fettuccine
1-3/4	cups sliced baby portobello mushrooms
1	Tbsp. olive oil
1	garlic clove, minced
1	can (15 oz.) black beans, rinsed and drained
1	can (14-1/2 oz.) diced tomatoes
1	tsp. dried rosemary, crushed
1/2	tsp. dried oregano
2	cups fresh baby spinach

1. Cook fettuccine according to package directions. Meanwhile, in a large skillet, saute mushrooms in oil until tender; add garlic, cook 2 minutes longer.

2. Stir in the black beans, tomatoes, rosemary and oregano. Cook and stir until heated through. Stir in the spinach until wilted. Drain fettuccine. Serve with bean mixture.

Nutrition Facts: 2/3 cup bean mixture with 2/3 cup pasta equals 255 calories, 3 g fat (trace saturated fat), 0 cholesterol, 230 mg sodium, 45 g carbohydrate, 9 g fiber, 12 g protein. **Diabetic Exchanges:** 3 starch, 1 lean meat, 1/2 fat.

Zucchini Tomato Frittata Ｃ Ⅿ

PREP: 20 min. COOK: 15 min. YIELD: 4 servings

KIM SOSEBEE • CLEVELAND, GEORGIA

"Frittata" is Italian for omelet, and this dinner entree is packed full of veggies. Egg substitute and low-fat cheese lighten it up, making for a healthy meal. It's great for a quick late-night bite.

1/3	cup sun-dried tomatoes (not packed in oil)
1	cup boiling water
1-1/2	cups egg substitute
1/2	cup 2% cottage cheese
2	green onions, chopped
1/4	cup minced fresh basil *or* 1 Tbsp. dried basil
1/8	tsp. crushed red pepper flakes
1	cup sliced zucchini
1	cup fresh broccoli florets
1	medium sweet red pepper, chopped
2	tsp. canola oil
2	Tbsp. grated Parmesan cheese

1. Place tomatoes in a small bowl. Cover with boiling water; let stand for 5 minutes. Drain and set aside.

2. In a large bowl, whisk the egg substitute, cottage cheese, onions, basil, pepper flakes and reserved tomatoes; set aside. In a 10-in. ovenproof skillet, saute the zucchini, broccoli and red pepper in oil until tender. Reduce heat; top with reserved egg mixture. Cover and cook for 4-6 minutes or until nearly set.

3. Uncover skillet. Sprinkle with Parmesan cheese. Broil 3-4 in. from the heat for 2-3 minutes or until eggs are completely set. Let stand for 5 minutes. Cut into wedges.

Nutrition Facts: 1 wedge equals 138 calories, 4 g fat (1 g saturated fat), 6 mg cholesterol, 484 mg sodium, 11 g carbohydrate, 3 g fiber, 15 g protein. **Diabetic Exchanges:** 2 lean meat, 2 vegetable.

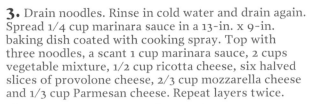

BLACK BEAN PASTA

ZUCCHINI TOMATO FRITTATA

Risotto-Stuffed Portobellos M

PREP: 45 min. **BAKE:** 20 min. **YIELD:** 4 servings

RIAN MACDONALD • POWDER SPRINGS, GEORGIA

I invented this dish one night when I was having last-minute guests. I ran to a local farm stand for some amazing produce and created this using fresh portobellos and leftover risotto. My friends still ask for the recipe!

> 1 can (14-1/2 oz.) reduced-sodium chicken *or* vegetable broth
> 1 cup water
> 2 celery ribs, finely chopped
> 2 medium carrots, finely chopped
> 1 large onion, finely chopped
> 1 Tbsp. olive oil
> 1 cup uncooked arborio rice
> 1/2 cup chopped shallots
> 1 garlic clove, minced
> 1 cup dry white wine or additional broth
> 1/2 cup grated Parmesan cheese
> 4 green onions, finely chopped
> 4 large portobello mushrooms (4 to 4-1/2 in.), stems removed

Cooking spray

> 1/4 tsp. salt
> 1/8 tsp. pepper
> 1/4 cup shredded part-skim mozzarella cheese

1. In a small saucepan, heat broth and water and keep warm. In a large nonstick skillet coated with cooking spray, saute the celery, carrots and onion in oil until crisp-tender. Add the rice, shallots and garlic; cook and stir for 2-3 minutes. Reduce heat; stir in wine. Cook and stir until all of the liquid is absorbed.

2. Add heated broth mixture, 1/2 cup at a time, stirring constantly. Allow the liquid to absorb between additions. Cook just until risotto is creamy and rice is almost tender. (Cooking time is about 20 minutes.) Remove from the heat; add Parmesan cheese and green onions. Stir until cheese is melted.

3. Spritz mushrooms with cooking spray; sprinkle with salt and pepper. Fill each with 1 cup risotto mixture and sprinkle with mozzarella cheese. Place in a 13-in. x 9-in. baking dish coated with cooking spray.

4. Bake, uncovered, at 350° for 20-25 minutes or until mushrooms are tender and cheese is melted.

Nutrition Facts: 1 stuffed mushroom equals 380 calories, 9 g fat (3 g saturated fat), 13 mg cholesterol, 680 mg sodium, 57 g carbohydrate, 4 g fiber, 14 g protein.

Instant Potato Gnocchi F S M

PREP/TOTAL TIME: 30 min. **YIELD:** 4 servings

SARAH OTT • BLANCHARDVILLE, WISCONSIN

This tasty gnocchi is much easier than it looks and contains almost no saturated fat. Just serve with your favorite jarred pasta sauce, and you're set!

> 1 cup mashed potato flakes
> 1 cup boiling water
> 1 egg, lightly beaten
> 1-1/2 cups all-purpose flour
> 1/2 tsp. dried basil
> 1/4 tsp. garlic powder
> 1/8 tsp. salt
> 1/8 tsp. pepper
> 6 cups water

Pasta sauce of your choice

Grated Parmesan cheese, optional

1. Place potato flakes in a large bowl. Stir in boiling water; add egg. Stir in flour and seasonings. On a lightly floured surface, knead 10-12 times, forming a soft dough.

2. Divide dough into four portions. On a floured surface, roll each portion into 1/2-in.-thick ropes; cut into 3/4-in. pieces. Press and roll each piece with a lightly floured fork.

3. In a large saucepan, bring water to a boil. Cook gnocchi in batches for 30-60 seconds or until they float. Remove with a slotted spoon. Serve with sauce; sprinkle with cheese if desired.

RISOTTO-STUFFED PORTOBELLOS

INSTANT POTATO GNOCCHI

Nutrition Facts: 1-1/2 cups (calculated without sauce and cheese) equals 250 calories, 2 g fat (trace saturated fat), 53 mg cholesterol, 126 mg sodium, 50 g carbohydrate, 2 g fiber, 8 g protein.

Mediterranean Chickpeas M

PREP/TOTAL TIME: 25 min. **YIELD:** 4 servings

ELAINE OBER • BROOKLINE, MASSACHUSETTS

Olives, oregano and artichoke hearts boost flavor in this colorful and hearty meatless main dish. It goes together in minutes with convenient pantry items. Try a little feta cheese on top for something extra special.

- 1 cup water
- 3/4 cup uncooked whole wheat couscous
- 1 medium onion, chopped
- 1 Tbsp. olive oil
- 2 garlic cloves, minced
- 1 can (15 oz.) garbanzo beans or chickpeas, rinsed and drained
- 1 can (14-1/2 oz.) no-salt-added stewed tomatoes, cut up
- 1 can (14 oz.) water-packed artichoke hearts, rinsed, drained and chopped
- 1/2 cup Greek olives, coarsely chopped
- 1 Tbsp. lemon juice
- 1/2 tsp. dried oregano
- Dash pepper
- Dash cayenne pepper

1. In a small saucepan, bring water to a boil. Stir in the couscous. Remove from the heat; cover and let stand for 5-10 minutes or until water is absorbed. Fluff with a fork.

2. Meanwhile, in a large nonstick skillet, saute onion in oil until tender. Add garlic; cook 1 minute longer. Sir in the garbanzo beans, tomatoes, artichokes, olives, lemon juice, oregano and peppers. Cook and stir until heated through. Serve with couscous.

Nutrition Facts: 1 cup garbanzo bean mixture with 2/3 cup couscous equals 340 calories, 10 g fat (1 g saturated fat), 0 cholesterol, 677 mg sodium, 51 g carbohydrate, 9 g fiber, 11 g protein.

Black Beans with Brown Rice M

PREP: 15 min. **COOK:** 20 min. **YIELD:** 5 servings

SHEILA MEYER • NORTH CANTON, OHIO

Your family will never miss the meat in this robust, vibrant and fresh-tasting main dish. Served over brown rice, it makes a healthy, stick-to-the-ribs dinner.

- 1 small green pepper, chopped
- 1/2 cup chopped sweet red pepper
- 1/2 cup chopped sweet yellow pepper
- 1/2 cup chopped red onion
- 2 Tbsp. canola oil
- 2 cans (15 oz. *each*) black beans, rinsed and drained
- 1 can (14-1/2 oz.) diced tomatoes, undrained
- 2 Tbsp. cider vinegar
- 1/2 tsp. garlic salt
- 1/8 tsp. pepper
- 1/8 tsp. cayenne pepper
- 2-1/2 cups hot cooked brown rice

1. In a large saucepan, saute peppers and onion in oil until tender. Stir in the beans, tomatoes, vinegar, garlic salt, pepper and cayenne. Bring to a boil. Reduce heat; simmer, uncovered, for 12-15 minutes or until it reaches the desired consistency, stirring occasionally. Serve with rice.

Nutrition Facts: 3/4 cup bean mixture with 1/2 cup rice equals 327 calories, 7 g fat (1 g saturated fat), 0 cholesterol, 614 mg sodium, 55 g carbohydrate, 11 g fiber, 12 g protein.

White Bean, Sweet Potato & Pepper Ragout M

PREP: 20 min. **COOK:** 25 min. **YIELD:** 4 servings

HEATHER SAVAGE • CORYDON, INDIANA

I try to serve a meatless meal two or three nights a week. It's a great way to keep up our intake of veggies—along with all the fiber and nutrients they provide. It even helps save money! This hearty comfort food is a family favorite.

- 1 large sweet red pepper, cut into 1-in. pieces
- 1 large green pepper, cut into 1-in. pieces
- 1 Tbsp. olive oil
- 1 large sweet potato, peeled, quartered and sliced
- 3 garlic cloves, minced
- 1/2 tsp. minced fresh rosemary *or* 1/4 tsp. dried rosemary, crushed
- 1/2 cup water
- 1/4 tsp. pepper
- 2 cans (15 oz. each) white kidney *or* cannellini beans, rinsed and drained
- 1 can (14-1/2 oz.) diced tomatoes, undrained
- 1/4 tsp. salt

1. In a Dutch oven over medium heat, cook and stir peppers in oil until tender. Add the sweet potato, garlic and rosemary; cook 4-5 minutes longer.

2. Stir in water and pepper. Bring to a boil. Reduce heat; cover and simmer for 5-7 minutes or until sweet potato is tender. Stir in the beans, tomatoes and salt; heat through.

Nutrition Facts: 1-3/4 cups equals 286 calories, 5 g fat (trace saturated fat), 0 cholesterol, 551 mg sodium, 51 g carbohydrate, 13 g fiber, 11 g protein.

WHITE BEAN, SWEET POTATO & PEPPER RAGOUT

Grilled Black Bean & Pineapple Burgers M

PREP: 30 min. + chilling **GRILL:** 10 min.
YIELD: 6 servings

CAROLE RESNICK • CLEVELAND, OHIO

This filling sandwich contains a whopping 11 g of fiber but only 5 g of fat per serving. Pineapple slices are a perfect topper for this tasty bean burger.

- 2 cans (15 oz. *each*) black beans, rinsed and drained
- 1 medium red onion, finely chopped
- 2 eggs, beaten
- 1/2 cup panko (Japanese) bread crumbs
- 1/2 cup crushed baked tortilla chip scoops
- 1/3 cup chopped green pepper
- 1 Tbsp. minced fresh cilantro
- 1 tsp. ground cumin
- 1 tsp. chili powder
- 1/2 tsp. hot pepper sauce
- 1/2 cup fat-free mayonnaise
- 4 tsp. chopped green onion
- 4 tsp. Dijon mustard
- 2 tsp. honey
- 1-1/2 tsp. orange juice
- 1/2 tsp. reduced-sodium soy sauce
- 6 slices unsweetened pineapple
- 6 whole wheat hamburger buns, split

1. In a large bowl, mash beans. Add the red onion, eggs, bread crumbs, chips, green pepper, cilantro, cumin, chili powder and pepper sauce. Shape into six patties. Refrigerate for 1 hour.

2. In a small bowl, combine the mayonnaise, green onion, mustard, honey, orange juice and soy sauce; refrigerate until serving.

3. Coat grill rack with cooking spray before starting the grill. Grill burgers, covered, over medium heat for 3-5 minutes on each side or until a thermometer reads 160°. Grill pineapple slices for 2-3 minutes on each side or until heated through. Place burgers and pineapple on buns; top each with 1 rounded tablespoon of sauce.

Nutrition Facts: 1 burger equals 357 calories, 5 g fat (1 g saturated fat), 73 mg cholesterol, 807 mg sodium, 65 g carbohydrate, 11 g fiber, 14 g protein.

GRILLED BLACK BEAN & PINEAPPLE BURGERS

Stuffed Portobellos C M

PREP: 15 min. BAKE: 20 min. YIELD: 4 servings

MALCOLM LEWIS • FREEVILLE, NEW YORK

I like to turn hearty portobellos into a flavorful meal. The addition of walnuts adds crunch to the savory topping. If you'd like, add raisins for a bit of sweetness.

4	large portobello mushrooms (about 5 in.)
3/4	cup shredded part-skim mozzarella cheese, *divided*
1/3	cup dry bread crumbs
1/3	cup chopped walnuts
1/3	cup finely chopped onion
1/3	cup golden raisins, optional
3	Tbsp. grated Parmesan cheese
1/4	tsp. salt
1/4	tsp. pepper
1	egg, lightly beaten
2	Tbsp. vegetable broth

1. Remove stems from mushrooms (discard or save for another use); set caps aside. In a small bowl, combine 1/4 cup mozzarella cheese, bread crumbs, walnuts, onion, raisins if desired, Parmesan cheese, salt and pepper. Stir in egg and broth until blended.

2. Spoon into the mushroom caps; sprinkle with remaining mozzarella cheese. Place in a 15-in. x 10-in. baking pan coated with cooking spray. Bake, uncovered, at 350° for 20-25 minutes or until the mushrooms are tender.

Nutrition Facts: 1 stuffed portobello (calculated without raisins) equals 221 calories, 12 g fat (4 g saturated fat), 68 mg cholesterol, 435 mg sodium, 14 g carbohydrate, 2 g fiber, 14 g protein. **Diabetic Exchanges:** 2 fat, 1 lean meat, 1 vegetable, 1/2 starch.

Black Bean 'n' Corn Quesadillas M

PREP/TOTAL TIME: 25 min. YIELD: 6 servings

SUSAN FRANKLIN • LITTLETON, COLORADO

Black beans partner up with another power food, spinach, in my easy quesadillas.

1	can (15 oz.) black beans, rinsed and drained, *divided*
1	small onion, finely chopped
2	tsp. olive oil
1	can (11 oz.) Mexicorn, drained
1	tsp. chili powder
1	tsp. ground cumin
1	pkg. (6 oz.) fresh baby spinach
8	flour tortillas (8 in.)
3/4	cup shredded reduced-fat Monterey Jack cheese or Mexican cheese blend

1. In a small bowl, mash 1 cup beans with a fork. In a large skillet, saute onion in oil until tender. Add the corn, chili powder, cumin, mashed beans and remaining beans; cook and stir until heated through. Stir in spinach just until wilted.

2. Place two tortillas on an ungreased baking sheet; spread each with a rounded 1/2 cup of bean mixture. Sprinkle each with 3 tablespoons of cheese; top with another tortilla. Repeat.

3. Bake at 400° for 8-10 minutes or until the cheese is melted. Cut each of the quesadillas into six wedges. Serve warm.

Nutrition Facts: 4 wedges equals 358 calories, 9 g fat (3 g saturated fat), 10 mg cholesterol, 900 mg sodium, 56 g carbohydrate, 5 g fiber, 15 g protein.

Black Bean Lasagna M

PREP: 25 min. **BAKE:** 40 min. + standing
YIELD: 12 servings

DUSTY DAVIS • SLIDELL, LOUISIANA

I came up with this lasagna to help my husband lower his cholesterol. It's one of our favorite meals.

- 9 lasagna noodles
- 1 large onion, chopped
- 3 garlic cloves, minced
- 1 tsp. canola oil
- 2 cans (16 oz. *each*) black beans, rinsed and drained
- 1 can (14-1/2 oz.) diced tomatoes, undrained
- 2 cans (6 oz. each) tomato paste
- 1 cup water
- 2 Tbsp. minced fresh cilantro
- 1/4 to 1/2 tsp. crushed red pepper flakes
- 4 egg whites, beaten
- 1 carton (15 oz.) reduced-fat ricotta cheese
- 1/2 cup grated Parmesan cheese
- 1/4 cup minced fresh parsley
- 2 cups (8 oz. *each*) shredded reduced-fat Mexican cheese blend

1. Cook noodles according to package directions. Meanwhile, in a large skillet over medium heat, cook onion and garlic in oil until tender. Add the beans, tomatoes, tomato paste, water, cilantro and pepper flakes. Bring to a boil. Reduce heat; simmer, uncovered, for 15 minutes or until slightly thickened.

2. In a small bowl, combine the egg whites, ricotta cheese, Parmesan cheese and parsley.

3. Drain noodles. Spread 1/2 cup bean mixture into a 13-in. x 9-in. baking dish coated with cooking spray. Layer with three noodles, a third of the ricotta mixture, a third of the remaining bean mixture and 2/3 cup cheese blend. Repeat layers twice.

4. Cover and bake at 350° for 30-35 minutes. Uncover; bake 10-15 minutes longer or until bubbly. Let stand for 10 minutes before cutting.

Nutrition Facts: 1 piece equals 279 calories, 7 g fat (4 g saturated fat), 25 mg cholesterol, 455 mg sodium, 36 g carbohydrate, 6 g fiber, 18 g protein. **Diabetic Exchanges:** 2 starch, 1-1/2 lean meat, 1 vegetable.

Zucchini Frittata C M

PREP: 25 min. **BAKE:** 25 min. **YIELD:** 4 servings

AMY CRANE • SWARTZ CREEK, MICHIGAN

Ideal for breakfast or dinner, this delicate frittata hits the spot without being too heavy. I like to prepare it with sharp cheddar cheese for extra flavor.

- 3 medium zucchini, thinly sliced
- 3 Tbsp. whole wheat flour
- 2 tsp. olive oil
- 6 egg whites
- 3 eggs
- 1/2 cup reduced-fat ricotta cheese
- 1/2 cup shredded cheddar cheese, *divided*
- 1/3 cup plain yogurt

1 Tbsp. dried parsley flakes
2 garlic cloves, minced
1/2 tsp. salt
1/4 tsp. white pepper
1/2 tsp. poppy seeds

1. Toss zucchini with flour. In a large nonstick skillet coated with cooking spray, saute zucchini in oil until crisp-tender and lightly browned. Remove from heat.

2. In a large bowl, whisk the egg whites, eggs, ricotta cheese, 1/4 cup cheddar cheese, yogurt, parsley, garlic, salt and pepper. Stir in zucchini. Transfer to a 9-in. pie plate coated with cooking spray. Sprinkle with poppy seeds and remaining cheddar cheese.

3. Bake at 350° for 25-30 minutes or until a knife inserted near the center comes out clean. Let stand for 5 minutes before cutting.

Nutrition Facts: 1 piece equals 238 calories, 12 g fat (6 g saturated fat), 185 mg cholesterol, 552 mg sodium, 13 g carbohydrate, 3 g fiber, 19 g protein. **Diabetic Exchanges:** 2 lean meat, 1 vegetable, 1 fat, 1/2 starch.

Mediterranean Pizza ▣

PREP/TOTAL TIME: 20 min. YIELD: 12 pieces

DEBORAH PREVOST • BARNET, VERMONT

Every year, my sisters and I have a "Sisters Day," which includes a special lunch. This fast and easy pizza is one of our favorites. Served with a garden salad, it makes a light and nutritious meal.

1 prebaked thin Italian whole wheat bread shell crust (10 oz.)
3 Tbsp. prepared pesto
2 medium tomatoes, thinly sliced
3/4 cup water-packed artichoke hearts, rinsed, drained and chopped
1/2 cup crumbled reduced-fat feta cheese
1/4 cup sliced ripe olives

1. Place the crust on an ungreased 12-in. pizza pan; spread with pesto. Top with tomatoes, artichokes, feta cheese and olives.

2. Bake at 450° for 10-12 minutes or until heated through.

Nutrition Facts: 2 pieces equals 206 calories, 8 g fat (3 g saturated fat), 6 mg cholesterol, 547 mg sodium, 27 g carbohydrate, 4 g fiber, 10 g protein. **Diabetic Exchanges:** 1-1/2 starch, 1-1/2 fat, 1 vegetable.

Zucchini Corn Bake ▣

PREP: 20 min. BAKE: 25 min. YIELD: 4 servings

DIANE CONSER • LAKEWOOD, NEW JERSEY

I found the original version of this recipe in a magazine and decided to lighten it. It's delicious!

1 medium zucchini, quartered lengthwise and sliced
1-3/4 cups frozen corn, thawed
1 small onion, chopped
1 Tbsp. plus 1 tsp. butter, *divided*
1 Tbsp. all-purpose flour
1/4 tsp. salt
1/4 tsp. pepper
1 cup fat-free milk
3/4 cup shredded reduced-fat cheddar cheese
1/4 cup dry bread crumbs
2 garlic cloves, minced
1/4 tsp. dried oregano

1. In a large nonstick skillet over medium heat, cook the zucchini, corn and onion in 1 tablespoon butter until crisp-tender. Stir in the flour, salt and pepper until blended.

2. Gradually add milk. Bring to a boil; cook and stir for 2 minutes or until thickened. Reduce heat; stir in cheese. Cook and stir for 1-2 minutes or until the cheese is melted. Transfer to a 1-qt. baking dish coated with cooking spray.

3. In a small skillet, saute the bread crumbs, garlic and oregano in remaining butter for 2-3 minutes or until crumbs are lightly browned. Sprinkle over vegetable mixture.

4. Bake, uncovered, at 350° for 25-30 minutes or until bubbly.

Nutrition Facts: 3/4 cup equals 229 calories, 10 g fat (6 g saturated fat), 27 mg cholesterol, 417 mg sodium, 29 g carbohydrate, 3 g fiber, 12 g protein. **Diabetic Exchanges:** 2 fat, 1-1/2 starch, 1 vegetable.

MEDITERRANEAN PIZZA

ZUCCHINI FRITTATA

Italian Garden Frittata C M

PREP/TOTAL TIME: 30 min. YIELD: 4 servings

SALLY MALONEY • DALLAS, GEORGIA

I like to serve this pretty frittata with melon wedges for a delightful breakfast or brunch.

- 6 egg whites
- 4 eggs
- 1/2 cup grated Romano cheese, *divided*
- 1 Tbsp. minced fresh sage
- 1/2 tsp. salt
- 1/4 tsp. pepper
- 1 small zucchini, sliced
- 2 green onions, sliced
- 1 tsp. olive oil
- 2 plum tomatoes, thinly sliced

1. In a large bowl, whisk the egg whites, eggs, 1/4 cup Romano cheese, sage, salt and pepper; set aside.

2. In a 10-in. ovenproof skillet coated with cooking spray, saute zucchini and onions in oil for 2 minutes. Add egg mixture; cover and cook for 4-6 minutes or until eggs are nearly set.

3. Uncover; top with tomato slices and remaining cheese. Broil 3-4 in. from the heat for 2-3 minutes or until eggs are completely set. Let stand for 5 minutes. Cut into wedges.

Nutrition Facts: 1 wedge equals 183 calories, 11 g fat (5 g saturated fat), 228 mg cholesterol, 655 mg sodium, 4 g carbohydrate, 1 g fiber, 18 g protein.

ITALIAN GARDEN FRITTATA

Black Bean Veggie Enchiladas M

PREP: 30 min. BAKE: 25 min. YIELD: 6 servings

NICOLE BARNETT • AURORA, COLORADO

I created this recipe one night when we were in the mood for enchiladas, but didn't want all the traditional version's fat and calories. I used ingredients I had on hand, and now this recipe's a family favorite!

- 1 small onion, chopped
- 1 small green pepper, chopped
- 1/2 cup sliced fresh mushrooms
- 1 garlic clove, minced
- 2 tsp. olive oil
- 1 can (15 oz.) black beans, rinsed and drained
- 3/4 cup frozen corn, thawed
- 1 can (4 oz.) chopped green chilies
- 2 Tbsp. reduced-sodium taco seasoning
- 1 tsp. dried cilantro flakes
- 6 whole wheat tortillas (8 in.), warmed
- 1/2 cup enchilada sauce
- 3/4 cup shredded reduced-fat Mexican cheese blend

1. In a large skillet, saute the onion, pepper, mushrooms and garlic in oil until crisp-tender. Add the beans, corn, chilies, taco seasoning and cilantro; saute 2-3 minutes longer.

2. Spoon 1/2 cup bean mixture down the center of each tortilla. Roll up and place seam side down in a 13-in. x 9-in. baking dish coated with cooking spray. Pour sauce over the top; sprinkle with cheese. Bake, uncovered, at 350° for 25-30 minutes or until heated through.

Nutrition Facts: 1 enchilada equals 292 calories, 8 g fat (2 g saturated fat),10 mg cholesterol, 759 mg sodium, 43 g carbohydrate, 6 g fiber, 13 g protein.

BLACK BEAN VEGGIE ENCHILADAS

Loaded Mexican Pizza M

PREP/TOTAL TIME: 25 min. YIELD: 6 slices

MARY BARKER • KNOXVILLE, TENNESSEE

My husband, Steve, is a picky eater, but this healthy pizza has lots of flavor and he actually looks forward to it. Try it for parties and other casual get-togethers.

- 1 can (15 oz.) black beans, rinsed and drained
- 1 medium red onion, chopped
- 1 small sweet yellow pepper, chopped
- 3 tsp. chili powder
- 3/4 tsp. ground cumin
- 3 medium tomatoes, chopped
- 1 jalapeno pepper, seeded and finely chopped
- 1 garlic clove, minced
- 1 prebaked thin Italian bread shell crust (10 oz.)
- 2 cups chopped fresh spinach
- 2 Tbsp. minced fresh cilantro

Hot pepper sauce to taste
- 1/2 cup shredded reduced-fat cheddar cheese
- 1/2 cup pepper Jack cheese

1. In a small bowl, mash black beans; stir in the onion, yellow pepper, chili powder and cumin. In another bowl, combine the tomatoes, jalapeno and garlic.

2. Place the crust on an ungreased 12-in. pizza pan; spread with bean mixture. Top with tomato mixture and spinach. Sprinkle with cilantro, hot pepper sauce and cheeses.

3. Bake at 400° for 12-15 minutes or until the cheese is melted.

Editor's Note: When cutting or seeding hot peppers, use rubber or plastic gloves to protect your hands. Avoid touching your face.

Nutrition Facts: 1 slice equals 297 calories, 9 g fat (4 g saturated fat), 17 mg cholesterol, 566 mg sodium, 41 g carbohydrate, 6 g fiber, 15 g protein. **Diabetic Exchanges:** 2-1/2 starch, 1 lean meat, 1 vegetable.

Roasted Veggie Tacos M

PREP: 20 min. BAKE: 15 min. YIELD: 6 servings

SHANNON KOENE • BLACKSBURG, VIRGINIA

When I tried making one vegetarian dish a week, my husband often said, "It would've been better with meat in it." But he doesn't even miss the beef in these tacos!

- 2 medium green peppers, julienned
- 3 plum tomatoes, cut into wedges
- 1 medium onion, halved and sliced
- 1 Tbsp. reduced-sodium taco seasoning
- 1 Tbsp. olive oil
- 1 can (16 oz.) fat-free refried beans, warmed
- 6 flour tortillas (8 in.), warmed
- 3/4 cup shredded reduced-fat cheddar cheese

1. In a large bowl, combine green peppers, tomatoes, onion, taco seasoning and oil. Arrange in a single layer in an ungreased 15-in. x 10-in. baking pan. Bake at 425° for 15-20 minutes or until tender, stirring once.

2. Spread about 1/4 cup refried beans over each tortilla; top with 1/3 cup vegetable mixture and 2 tablespoons cheese. Fold in half.

Nutrition Facts: 1 taco equals 316 calories, 8 g fat (3 g saturated fat), 10 mg cholesterol, 722 mg sodium, 48 g carbohydrate, 6 g fiber, 14 g protein.

Warm Roasted Beet Salad M

PREP: 30 min. BAKE: 40 min. YIELD: 6 servings

JILL ANDERSON • SLEEPY EYE, MINNESOTA

This recipe lets beets shine. It's a hearty salad that's beautiful on the plate. I often use hazelnut oil in the dressing, but olive oil or any nut oil works well, too.

8	whole fresh beets

Cooking spray

1-1/2	cups orange juice
1	shallot, chopped
2	Tbsp. olive oil
2	Tbsp. balsamic vinegar
1	tsp. minced fresh thyme *or* 1/4 tsp. dried thyme
1/2	tsp. grated orange peel
1/8	tsp. salt
1/8	tsp. pepper
6	cups fresh arugula *or* baby spinach
3	Tbsp. crumbled blue cheese
3	Tbsp. chopped hazelnuts, toasted

1. Scrub beets and cut into wedges; place on a baking sheet coated with cooking spray. Lightly coat beets with additional cooking spray. Bake at 350° for 40-50 minutes or until tender, turning occasionally.

2. Meanwhile, for dressing, place orange juice in a small saucepan. Bring to a boil. Reduce heat; simmer, uncovered, until liquid is syrupy and reduced to about 1/3 cup. Remove from the heat. Whisk in the shallot, oil, vinegar, thyme, orange peel, salt and pepper. Set aside to cool.

3. Just before serving, place arugula in a large bowl. Drizzle with 1/4 cup dressing and toss to coat. Divide mixture among six salad plates. Place beets in the same bowl; add remaining dressing and toss to coat. Arrange on plates. Sprinkle salads with blue cheese and hazelnuts.

Nutrition Facts: 1 serving equals 147 calories, 8 g fat (2 g saturated fat), 3 mg cholesterol, 167 mg sodium, 17 g carbohydrate, 2 g fiber, 4 g protein. **Diabetic Exchanges:** 2 vegetable, 1–1/2 fat, 1/2 fruit.

Chickpea 'n' Red Onion Burgers M

PREP/TOTAL TIME: 30 min. YIELD: 6 servings

LILLIAN JULOW • GAINESVILLE, FLORIDA

I like to make this burger when it's chilly outdoors, and the grill has been retired to the garage.

1	large red onion, thinly sliced
1/4	cup fat-free red wine vinaigrette
2	cans (15 oz. each) chickpeas *or* garbanzo beans, rinsed and drained
1/3	cup chopped walnuts
1/4	cup toasted wheat germ
1/4	cup packed fresh parsley sprigs
2	eggs
1	tsp. curry powder
1/2	tsp. pepper
1/3	cup fat-free mayonnaise
2	tsp. Dijon mustard

6 sesame seed hamburger buns, split

6 lettuce leaves

3 Tbsp. thinly sliced fresh basil leaves

1. In a small bowl, combine onion and vinaigrette; set aside. In a food processor, combine the chickpeas, walnuts, wheat germ and parsley; cover and pulse until blended. Add the eggs, curry and pepper; cover and process until smooth.

2. Shape into six patties. Place on a baking sheet coated with cooking spray. Bake at 375° for 10-15 minutes or until firm.

3. Combine mayonnaise and mustard; spread over cut sides of buns. Serve patties on buns with lettuce, basil and reserved onion mixture.

Nutrition Facts: 1 burger equals 386 calories, 12 g fat (2 g saturated fat), 72 mg cholesterol, 732 mg sodium, 54 g carbohydrate, 9 g fiber, 16 g protein.

Vegetarian Sloppy Joes M

PREP/TOTAL TIME: 25 min. **YIELD:** 6 servings

LINDA WINTER • OAK HARBOR, WASHINGTON

The meat won't be missed in this vegetarian version of sloppy joes. I like to preserve the flavor of a classic while adding important nutrients.

1 small onion, finely chopped

2 tsp. butter

1 pkg. (12 oz.) frozen vegetarian meat crumbles

1/2 tsp. pepper

2 Tbsp. all-purpose flour

1 can (8 oz.) no-salt-added tomato sauce

2/3 cup ketchup

6 hamburger buns, split and toasted

1. In a large nonstick skillet coated with cooking spray, saute onion in butter until tender. Stir in meat crumbles and pepper; heat through.

2. Sprinkle flour over mixture and stir until blended. Stir in tomato sauce and ketchup. Bring to a boil; cook and stir for 1-2 minutes or until thickened. Spoon 1/2 cup onto each bun.

Nutrition Facts: 1 sandwich equals 273 calories, 6 g fat (2 g saturated fat), 4 mg cholesterol, 815 mg sodium, 39 g carbohydrate, 5 g fiber, 15 g protein. **Diabetic Exchanges:** 2-1/2 starch, 2 lean meat.

Zucchini Tomato Bake C M

PREP: 30 min. **BAKE:** 25 min. **YIELD:** 6 servings

TINA REPAK • JOHNSTOWN, PENNSYLVANIA

Melted Swiss cheese and sour cream lend decadence to this flavorful side with garden-fresh ingredients.

1 medium onion, chopped

1 Tbsp. butter

3 medium zucchini (about 1 lb.), shredded and patted dry

3 medium tomatoes, seeded and chopped

1 cup (4 oz.) shredded reduced-fat Swiss cheese, *divided*

1/3 cup reduced-fat sour cream

1 tsp. paprika

1/2 tsp. salt

1/2 tsp. garlic powder

1/4 tsp. pepper

2 Tbsp. shredded Parmesan cheese

1. In a large nonstick skillet, saute onion in butter until tender. Transfer to a large bowl. Add the zucchini, tomatoes, 1/2 cup Swiss cheese, sour cream and seasonings; mix well.

2. Transfer to an 11-in. x 7-in. baking dish coated with cooking spray. Sprinkle with Parmesan cheese and remaining Swiss cheese. Bake, uncovered, at 350° for 25-30 minutes or until vegetables are tender.

Nutrition Facts: 1 serving equals 113 calories, 5 g fat (3 g saturated fat), 18 mg cholesterol, 321 mg sodium, 9 g carbohydrate, 2 g fiber, 9 g protein. **Diabetic Exchanges:** 2 vegetable, 1 lean meat, 1/2 fat.

ZUCCHINI TOMATO BAKE

VEGETARIAN SLOPPY JOES

MAKEOVER ROSEMARY MUFFINS

ROSEMARY-GARLIC FOCCACIA BREAD

IRISH SODA BREAD

The Bread Basket

Golden loaves of bread, sweet muffins, delicate scones perfect alongside warm tea...you can enjoy these aromatic delights and still keep your healthy-eating goals in check. Just consider the delightful recipes here.

Makeover Rosemary Muffins

PREP: 20 min. **BAKE:** 20 min. **YIELD:** 1 dozen

MARLEA RICE WARREN • ST. LOUIS PARK, MINNESOTA

The experts created light, full-flavored muffins that accompany any meal beautifully. While they are quite a bit lower in saturated fat, calories, sodium and cholesterol than the original, these tasty makeover muffins never let on that they're healthier than my original.

1-1/2	cups all-purpose flour
1-1/2	cups whole wheat flour
2	tsp. sugar
1	tsp. baking powder
3/4	tsp. baking soda
1/2	tsp. salt
2	eggs
1-1/2	cups (12 oz.) reduced-fat plain yogurt
1/2	cup fat-free milk
1/4	cup canola oil
1	Tbsp. Dijon mustard
1/2	cup crumbled goat cheese
1/2	cup chopped Greek olives
1	Tbsp. minced fresh rosemary *or* 1 tsp. dried rosemary, crushed

1. In a large bowl, combine the first six ingredients. In another bowl, combine the eggs, yogurt, milk, oil and mustard. Stir into dry ingredients just until moistened. Fold in the cheese, olives and rosemary.

2. Coat muffin cups with cooking spray; fill three-fourths full with batter. Bake at 375° for 20-25 minutes or until a toothpick inserted in muffin comes out clean. Cool for 5 minutes before removing from pan to a wire rack. Serve warm.

Nutrition Facts: 1 muffin equals 217 calories, 9 g fat (2 g saturated fat), 43 mg cholesterol, 394 mg sodium, 27 g carbohydrate, 2 g fiber, 8 g protein. **Diabetic Exchanges:** 2 starch, 1 fat.

Irish Soda Bread

PREP: 20 min. **BAKE:** 50 min. + cooling
YIELD: 1 loaf (16 slices)

PADMINI ROY-DIXON • COLUMBUS, OHIO

My husband's family is Irish. Wanting to impress my future mother-in-law, I baked this bread and took it along with me when I met her the first time. Needless to say, it worked!

3/4	cup raisins
1	cup boiling water
2	cups all-purpose flour
1	cup whole wheat flour
1/3	cup sugar
3	tsp. baking powder
1	tsp. baking soda
1	tsp. salt
1	egg
2	cups buttermilk
1/4	cup butter, melted

1. Place raisins in a small bowl. Cover with boiling water; let stand for 5 minutes. Drain and pat dry.

2. In a large bowl, combine the flours, sugar, baking powder, baking soda and salt.

3. In a small bowl, whisk the egg, buttermilk and butter. Stir into dry ingredients just until moistened. Fold in raisins.

4. Transfer to a 9-in. x 5-in. loaf pan coated with cooking spray. Bake at 350° for 50-60 minutes or until a toothpick inserted near the center comes out clean. Cool for 10 minutes before removing from pan to a wire rack.

Nutrition Facts: 1 slice equals 161 calories, 4 g fat (2 g saturated fat), 22 mg cholesterol, 359 mg sodium, 28 g carbohydrate, 2 g fiber, 4 g protein. **Diabetic Exchanges:** 2 starch, 1 fat.

Cinnamon Pull-Apart Loaf

PREP: 30 min. + rising **BAKE:** 25 min.
YIELD: 1 loaf (12 slices)

JUDY EDDY • BALDWIN CITY, KANSAS

If you like the fun of monkey bread, you'll adore this unique take on cinnamon bread. The flaky layers are heavenly topped with a creamy drizzle.

1	pkg. (1/4 oz.) active dry yeast
3/4	cup warm water (110° to 115°)
1/2	cup quick-cooking oats
1/2	cup whole wheat flour
1/4	cup packed brown sugar
2	Tbsp. butter, melted
1	egg
1	tsp. salt
1-3/4 to 2-1/4	cups all-purpose flour

FILLING:

3	Tbsp. butter, softened
1/3	cup sugar
2	tsp. ground cinnamon

GLAZE:

1	cup confectioners' sugar
6-1/2	tsp. half-and-half cream
4-1/2	tsp. butter, softened

1. In a large bowl, dissolve yeast in warm water. Add the oats, whole wheat flour, brown sugar, butter, egg, salt and 1 cup all-purpose flour. Beat on medium speed until smooth. Stir in enough remaining flour to form a soft dough (dough will be sticky).

2. Turn onto a lightly floured surface; knead until smooth and elastic, about 6-8 minutes. Place in a bowl coated with cooking spray, turning once to coat the top. Cover and let rise in a warm place until doubled, about 1 hour.

3. Punch dough down. Roll into an 18-in. x 12-in. rectangle; spread with butter. Combine the sugar and the cinnamon; sprinkle mixture over dough to within 1/2 in. of edges.

4. Cut into thirty-six 3-in. x 2-in. rectangles. Make two stacks of 18 rectangles. Place, cut sides up, in a 9-in. x 5-in. loaf pan coated with cooking spray. Cover and let rise until doubled, about 45 minutes.

5. Bake at 375° for 25-30 minutes or until golden brown. Cool for 10 minutes before removing from pan to a wire rack. For glaze, in a small bowl, beat the confectioners' sugar, cream and butter until smooth. Drizzle over warm loaf.

Nutrition Facts: 1 slice equals 240 calories, 7 g fat (4 g saturated fat), 35 mg cholesterol, 251 mg sodium, 40 g carbohydrate, 2 g fiber, 4 g protein.

Lime Coconut Biscotti F S C

PREP: 25 min. **BAKE:** 30 min. **YIELD:** 32 cookies

DIANA BURRINK • CRETE, ILLINOIS

My family loves this recipe! It's great with a morning cup of coffee, delicious as an afternoon snack or after-dinner dessert. Citrusy, crunchy and not too sweet, it always hits the spot.

3/4	cup sugar
1/4	cup canola oil
2	eggs
1/4	cup lime juice
1	tsp. vanilla extract
1/4	tsp. coconut extract
1-3/4	cups all-purpose flour
2/3	cup cornmeal
1-1/2	tsp. baking powder
1/4	tsp. salt
1	cup flaked coconut
1	tsp. grated lime peel

1. In a small bowl, beat sugar and oil until blended. Beat in the eggs, lime juice, and vanilla and coconut extracts. Combine the flour, cornmeal, baking powder and salt; gradually add to sugar mixture and mix well (dough will be sticky). Stir in coconut and lime peel.

2. Divide dough in half. With lightly floured hands, shape each half into a 12-in. x 2-in. rectangle on a parchment paper-lined baking sheet. Bake at 350° for 20-25 minutes or until set.

3. Place pan on a wire rack. When cool enough to handle, transfer to a cutting board; cut diagonally with a serrated knife into 3/4-in. slices. Place cut side down on ungreased baking sheets. Bake for 5-6 minutes on each side or until golden brown. Remove to wire racks to cool. Store in an airtight container.

Nutrition Facts: 1 cookie equals 89 calories, 3 g fat (1 g saturated fat), 13 mg cholesterol, 49 mg sodium, 14 g carbohydrate, 1 g fiber, 1 g protein. **Diabetic Exchanges:** 1 starch, 1/2 fat.

CINNAMON PULL-APART LOAF

GLUTEN-FREE
SANDWICH BREAD

Gluten-Free
Sandwich Bread ⓢ

PREP: 20 min. + rising **BAKE:** 30 min. + cooling
YIELD: 1 loaf (16 slices)

DORIS KINNEY • MERRIMACK, NEW HAMPSHIRE

*In my quest to find an enjoyable gluten-free bread, this recipe
emerged. It's moist and has no cardboard texture!*

1	Tbsp. active dry yeast
2	Tbsp. sugar
1	cup warm fat-free milk (110° to 115°)
2	eggs
3	Tbsp. canola oil
1	tsp. cider vinegar
2-1/2	cups gluten-free all-purpose baking flour
2-1/2	tsp. xanthan gum
1	tsp. unflavored gelatin
1/2	tsp. salt

1. Grease a 9-in. x 5-in. loaf pan and sprinkle with
gluten-free flour; set aside.

2. In a small bowl, dissolve yeast and sugar in warm
milk. In a stand mixer with a paddle attachment,
combine the eggs, oil, vinegar and yeast mixture.
Gradually beat in the flour, xanthan gum, gelatin and
salt. Beat on low speed for 1 minute. Beat on medium
for 2 minutes. (Dough will be softer than yeast bread
dough with gluten.)

3. Transfer to prepared pan. Smooth the top with a
wet spatula. Cover and let rise in a warm place until
dough reaches the top of pan, about 25 minutes.

4. Bake at 375° for 20 minutes; cover loosely with
foil. Bake 10-15 minutes longer or until golden brown.
Remove from pan to a wire rack to cool.

Editor's Note: Read all ingredient labels for possible gluten
content prior to use. Ingredient formulas can change, and
production facilities vary among brands. If you're concerned
that your brand may contain gluten, contact the company.

Nutrition Facts: 1 slice equals 110 calories, 4 g fat (trace
saturated fat), 27 mg cholesterol, 95 mg sodium, 17 g
carbohydrate, 2 g fiber, 4 g protein. **Diabetic Exchanges:**
1 starch, 1/2 fat.

MULTI-GRAIN CINNAMON ROLLS

Multi-Grain Cinnamon Rolls

PREP: 30 min. + rising **BAKE:** 15 min. **YIELD:** 1 dozen

JUDY EDDY • BALDWIN CITY, KANSAS

This simple and easy-to-work-with recipe is sure to become a family favorite. The wholesome cinnamon rolls will fill your kitchen with a wonderful, warm aroma.

- 1 pkg. (1/4 oz.) active dry yeast
- 3/4 cup warm water (110° to 115°)
- 1/2 cup quick-cooking oats
- 1/2 cup whole wheat flour
- 1/4 cup packed brown sugar
- 2 Tbsp. butter, melted
- 1 egg
- 1 tsp. salt
- 1-3/4 to 2-1/4 cups all-purpose flour

FILLING:
- 3 Tbsp. butter, softened
- 1/3 cup sugar
- 2 tsp. ground cinnamon

GLAZE:
- 1 cup confectioners' sugar
- 6-1/2 tsp. half-and-half cream
- 4-1/2 tsp. butter, softened

1. In a large bowl, dissolve yeast in warm water. Add the oats, whole wheat flour, brown sugar, butter, egg, salt and 1 cup all-purpose flour. Beat on medium speed until smooth. Stir in enough remaining flour to form a soft dough (dough will be sticky).

2. Turn onto a lightly floured surface; knead until smooth and elastic, about 6-8 minutes. Place in a bowl coated with cooking spray, turning once to coat the top. Cover and let rise in a warm place until doubled, about 1 hour.

3. Punch dough down. Roll into an 18-in. x 12-in. rectangle; spread with butter. Combine the sugar and cinnamon; sprinkle over dough to within 1/2 in. of edges.

4. Roll up jelly-roll style, starting with a short side; pinch seams to seal. Cut into 12 slices. Place cut sides down in a 13-in. x 9-in. baking pan coated with cooking spray. Cover and let rise until doubled, about 45 minutes.

5. Bake at 375° for 15-20 minutes or until golden brown. For icing, in a small bowl, beat the confectioners' sugar, cream and butter until smooth. Drizzle over warm rolls.

Nutrition Facts: 1 cinnamon roll equals 240 calories, 7 g fat (4 g saturated fat), 35 mg cholesterol, 251 mg sodium, 40 g carbohydrate, 2 g fiber, 4 g protein.

Gluten-Free Banana Walnut Muffins

PREP: 20 min. **BAKE:** 20 min. **YIELD:** 16 muffins

TRISH PANNELL • COLLEGE STATION, TEXAS

I've been cooking gluten-free since 2003, when my husband was diagnosed with celiac disease. Over the years, I've managed to perfect some recipes so when family and friends join us, they can't tell that what they're eating is gluten-free. This is one of those recipes.

1 cup mashed ripe bananas (2 medium)
3/4 cup sugar
2 eggs
1/2 cup unsweetened applesauce
1/4 cup canola oil
1/4 cup orange juice
1 tsp. vanilla extract
1-1/2 cups gluten-free all-purpose baking flour
3/4 tsp. baking soda
3/4 tsp. xanthan gum
1/2 tsp. salt
1/2 tsp. ground cinnamon
1/3 cup finely chopped walnuts

1. In a large bowl, beat the first seven ingredients until well blended. In a large bowl, combine the flour, baking soda, xanthan gum, salt and cinnamon; gradually beat into banana mixture until blended.

2. Coat muffin cups with cooking spray or use paper liners; fill three-fourths full with batter. Sprinkle with the walnuts. Bake at 350° for 20-25 minutes or until a toothpick inserted near the center comes out clean. Cool for 5 minutes before removing from pans to wire racks.

Editor's Note: Read all ingredient labels for possible gluten content prior to use. Ingredient formulas can change, and production facilities vary among brands. If you're concerned that your brand may contain gluten, contact the company.

Nutrition Facts: 1 muffin equals 148 calories, 6 g fat (1 g saturated fat), 26 mg cholesterol, 143 mg sodium, 23 g carbohydrate, 2 g fiber, 2 g protein. **Diabetic Exchanges:** 1-1/2 starch, 1 fat.

Makeover Maple Coffee Cake

PREP: 20 min. BAKE: 30 min. + cooling
YIELD: 12 servings

SHARON BOYNAK • LA PORTE, INDIANA

Downsizing the sugar and margarine, and switching to fat-free milk made all the difference in this coffee cake recipe—without sacrificing one tasty crumb of flavor!

1/3 cup butter, softened
3/4 cup sugar
2 eggs
1 cup fat-free milk
1/2 cup unsweetened applesauce
3 cups all-purpose flour
2-1/2 tsp. baking powder
1/2 tsp. salt
1/4 tsp. baking soda

FILLING:
1/2 cup finely chopped pecans
1/3 cup packed brown sugar
2 Tbsp. all-purpose flour
2 Tbsp. butter, melted
2 tsp. ground cinnamon

ICING:
1/4 cup confectioners' sugar
1-1/2 tsp. fat-free milk
1/4 tsp. maple flavoring

1. In a large bowl, beat butter and sugar until crumbly, about 2 minutes. Add eggs; mix well. Beat in milk and applesauce (mixture may appear curdled). Combine the flour, baking powder, salt and baking soda; add to butter mixture just until moistened. Spread half of the batter into a 13-in. x 9-in. baking pan coated with cooking spray.

2. Combine filling ingredients; sprinkle half of filling over the batter. Gently top with remaining batter and filling. Bake at 350° for 30-35 minutes or until a toothpick inserted near the center comes out clean. Cool on a wire rack.

3. Combine icing ingredients until smooth; drizzle over coffee cake.

Nutrition Facts: 1 piece equals 318 calories, 11 g fat (5 g saturated fat), 54 mg cholesterol, 281 mg sodium, 49 g carbohydrate, 1 g fiber, 6 g protein.

MAKEOVER MAPLE COFFEE CAKE

GLUTEN-FREE BANANA WALNUT MUFFINS

Maple-Walnut Coffee Cake

PREP: 25 min. **BAKE:** 35 min. + cooling
YIELD: 24 servings

ANGELA SPENGLER • CLOVIS, NEW MEXICO

Wake up the sleepy heads in your household with this moist, tender coffee cake that's both sweet and savory. Bacon and nuts in the crumbly topping blend with flavors of maple, nutmeg and cinnamon. Yum!

2-1/2	cups all-purpose flour
1	cup packed brown sugar
1/2	tsp. salt
1/3	cup cold butter
2	tsp. baking powder
1/2	tsp. baking soda
1/2	tsp. ground cinnamon
1/4	tsp. ground nutmeg
2	eggs
1-1/2	cups buttermilk
1/2	cup maple syrup
1/3	cup unsweetened applesauce
5	bacon strips, cooked and crumbled
1/2	cup chopped walnuts

1. In a large bowl, combine the flour, brown sugar and salt. Cut in butter until crumbly. Set aside 1/2 cup for topping. Combine the baking powder, baking soda, cinnamon and nutmeg; stir into the remaining flour mixture.

2. In a small bowl, whisk the eggs, buttermilk, syrup and applesauce until well blended. Gradually stir into flour mixture until combined.

3. Spread into a 13-in. x 9-in. baking pan coated with cooking spray. Sprinkle with reserved topping, then bacon and walnuts. Bake at 350° for 35-40 minutes or until a toothpick inserted near the center comes out clean. Cool on a wire rack.

Nutrition Facts: 1 piece equals 160 calories, 5 g fat (2 g saturated fat), 27 mg cholesterol, 183 mg sodium, 25 g carbohydrate, 1 g fiber, 3 g protein. **Diabetic Exchanges:** 1-1/2 starch, 1 fat.

MAPLE-WALNUT COFFEE CAKE

Multigrain Nutrition Loaves F

PREP: 30 min. + rising **BAKE:** 35 min. + cooling
YIELD: 3 loaves (16 slices each)

BARB TROY • NEW BERLIN, WISCONSIN

As a dietitian, I'm always hunting for healthful, homemade additions to my family's meals, and this is a delicious one.

6-1/2 to 7	cups all-purpose flour
1-1/2	cups whole wheat flour
1	cup bran flakes
1	cup quick-cooking oats
2	pkg. (1/4 oz. *each*) active dry yeast
2	tsp. salt
2-1/2	cups water
1-1/2	cups (12 oz.) 1% cottage cheese
1	cup raisins
1/2	cup molasses
2	Tbsp. butter
2	eggs

1. In a large mixing bowl, combine 2 cups all-purpose flour, whole wheat flour, bran flakes, oats, yeast and salt. In a small saucepan, heat the water, cottage cheese, raisins, molasses and butter to 120°-130°. Add to dry ingredients; beat until blended. Beat in eggs. Stir in enough remaining all-purpose flour to form a soft dough.

2. Turn onto a lightly floured surface; knead until smooth and elastic, about 6-8 minutes. Place in a bowl coated with cooking spray, turning once to coat the top. Cover and let rise in a warm place until doubled, about 1 hour.

3. Punch dough down. Turn onto a lightly floured surface; divide into thirds. Shape into loaves. Place in three 9-in. x 5-in. loaf pans coated with cooking spray. Cover and let rise until doubled, about 40 minutes.

4. Bake at 375° for 35-40 minutes or until golden brown. Remove from pans to wire racks.

Nutrition Facts: 1 slice equals 110 calories, 1 g fat (trace saturated fat), 10 mg cholesterol, 143 mg sodium, 21 g carbohydrate, 1 g fiber, 4 g protein. **Diabetic Exchange:** 1-1/2 starch.

Bananas Foster Bread

PREP: 20 min. + cooling **BAKE:** 50 min. + cooling
YIELD: 1 loaf (16 slices)

CHRISTEN CHALMERS • HOUSTON, TEXAS

This moist, tender bread has all the flavors of New Orleans' famous dessert. And the rum-flavored glaze is amazing!

5	Tbsp. butter, cubed
1	cup packed brown sugar, *divided*
1-1/2	cups mashed ripe bananas
3	Tbsp. dark rum
1-1/2	cups all-purpose flour
1/4	cup ground flaxseed
3/4	tsp. baking soda
1/2	tsp. salt
1/2	tsp. ground cinnamon

2 eggs
1/3 cup fat-free plain yogurt
GLAZE:
1/3 cup confectioners' sugar
1 Tbsp. butter, melted
1 Tbsp. dark rum

1. In a small saucepan, melt butter. Stir in 1/2 cup brown sugar and bananas. Bring to a boil. Reduce heat; simmer, uncovered, for 3-4 minutes or until slightly thickened. Remove from the heat. Stir in rum; set aside to cool.

2. In a large bowl, combine the flour, flax, baking soda, salt and cinnamon. In another large bowl, whisk the eggs, yogurt, banana mixture and remaining brown sugar. Stir into dry ingredients just until moistened.

3. Transfer to a 9-in. x 5-in. loaf pan coated with cooking spray. Bake at 350° for 50-55 minutes or until a toothpick inserted near the center comes out clean. Cool for 10 minutes before removing from pan to a wire rack to cool completely.

4. Combine the glaze ingredients; drizzle over bread.

Nutrition Facts: 1 slice equals 189 calories, 6 g fat (3 g saturated fat), 38 mg cholesterol, 181 mg sodium, 31 g carbohydrate, 1 g fiber, 3 g protein. **Diabetic Exchanges:** 2 starch, 1 fat.

Gluten-Free Cornmeal Muffins

PREP: 20 min. BAKE: 15 min. YIELD: 1 dozen

LAURA FALL-SUTTON • BUHL, IDAHO

I serve these muffins warm with butter, honey or even salsa. Reheat leftovers in foil in the oven...if there are any!

3/4 cup fat-free milk
1/4 cup honey
2 Tbsp. canola oil
1 egg
1 egg white
1-1/2 cups cornmeal
1/2 cup amaranth flour
2-1/2 tsp. baking powder
1/2 tsp. xanthan gum
1/2 tsp. salt
1 cup frozen corn, thawed
3/4 cup shredded reduced-fat Monterey Jack cheese *or* Mexican cheese blend

1. In a large bowl, beat the first five ingredients until well blended.

2. Combine the cornmeal, amaranth flour, baking powder, xanthan gum and salt; gradually beat into milk mixture until blended. Stir in corn and cheese.

3. Coat muffin cups with cooking spray or use foil liners; fill three-fourths full with batter. Bake at 375° for 15-18 minutes or until a toothpick inserted near the center comes out clean.

4. Cool for 5 minutes before removing from pan to a wire rack.

Editor's Note: Read all ingredient labels for possible gluten content prior to use. Ingredient formulas can change, and production facilities vary among brands. If you're concerned that your brand may contain gluten, contact the company.

Nutrition Facts: 1 muffin equals 169 calories, 5 g fat (1 g saturated fat), 23 mg cholesterol, 263 mg sodium, 27 g carbohydrate, 2 g fiber, 6 g protein. **Diabetic Exchanges:** 1-1/2 starch, 1 fat.

Cafe Mocha Mini Muffins ⬛S ⬛C

PREP/TOTAL TIME: 30 min. YIELD: 1-1/2 dozen

TINA SAWCHUK • ARDMORE, ALBERTA

These mini muffins freeze well, so it's always easy to keep some on hand. They're just the right size for a low-carb snack!

2	tsp. instant coffee granules
1/3	cup boiling water
1/4	cup quick-cooking oats
3	Tbsp. butter, softened
1/4	cup sugar
3	Tbsp. brown sugar
1	egg yolk
1/2	tsp. vanilla extract
1/2	cup all-purpose flour
1	Tbsp. baking cocoa
1/2	tsp. baking powder
1/8	tsp. baking soda
1/8	tsp. salt
1/2	cup miniature semisweet chocolate chips, *divided*

1. In a small bowl, dissolve coffee granules in water. Stir in the oats; set aside. In a small bowl, cream butter and sugars. Beat in egg yolk, vanilla and oat mixture. Combine the flour, cocoa, baking powder, baking soda and salt; add to oat mixture just until moistened. Stir in 1/3 cup chocolate chips.

2. Coat miniature muffin cups with cooking spray or use paper liners; fill three-fourths full with batter. Sprinkle with remaining chips. Bake at 350° for 12-15 minutes or until a toothpick inserted near the center comes out clean. Cool for 5 minutes before removing from pans to wire racks.

Editor's Note: Muffins may be frozen for up to 2 months.

Nutrition Facts: 1 muffin equals 81 calories, 4 g fat (2 g saturated fat), 17 mg cholesterol, 53 mg sodium, 12 g carbohydrate, 1 g fiber, 1 g protein. **Diabetic Exchanges:** 1 starch, 1/2 fat.

CAFE MOCHA MINI MUFFINS

Moist Mexican Corn Bread

PREP: 20 min. BAKE: 25 min. YIELD: 9 servings

KATHERINE THOMPSON • TYBEE ISLAND, GEORGIA

The name of this recipe says it all. The bread is perfect for scooping up that last drop of soup or stew.

1	cup all-purpose flour
1	cup cornmeal
1/4	cup ground flaxseed
1	Tbsp. sugar
2-1/2	tsp. baking powder
1	tsp. salt
2	eggs
1-1/2	cups fat-free milk
1	Tbsp. olive oil
1-1/2	cups frozen corn, thawed
1-1/2	cups (6 oz.) shredded reduced-fat Colby-Monterey Jack cheese, *divided*
1/2	cup finely chopped sweet red pepper

1. In a large bowl, combine the flour, cornmeal, flax, sugar, baking powder and salt. In a small bowl, whisk the eggs, milk and oil. Stir into dry ingredients just until moistened. Fold in the corn, 1 cup cheese and pepper.

2. Transfer to an 11-in. x 7-in. baking pan coated with cooking spray. Sprinkle with remaining cheese. Bake at 350° for 25-30 minutes or until a toothpick inserted near the center comes out clean. Serve warm.

Nutrition Facts: 1 piece equals 251 calories, 8 g fat (3 g saturated fat), 58 mg cholesterol, 563 mg sodium, 34 g carbohydrate, 3 g fiber, 12 g protein.

Parmesan Herb Loaf ⬛F

PREP: 10 min. + rising BAKE: 20 min.
YIELD: 1 loaf (12 slices)

SHIRLEY SIBIT RUDDER • BURKEVILLE, TEXAS

A frozen loaf of whole wheat bread makes this recipe a snap to toss together. Flavored with garlic, butter and Parmesan cheese, it's a wonderful addition to an Italian menu.

1	loaf (1 lb.) frozen whole wheat bread dough
1/4	cup shredded Parmesan cheese
1-1/2	tsp. dried parsley flakes
1-1/2	tsp. dried minced garlic
1/4	tsp. dill weed
1/4	tsp. salt
1	Tbsp. butter, melted

1. Place dough in an 8-in. x 4-in. loaf pan coated with cooking spray. Thaw according to package directions. In a small bowl, combine the cheese, parsley, garlic, dill and salt. Brush dough with butter; sprinkle with cheese mixture. Cover and let rise in a warm place until nearly doubled, about 2-1/2 hours.

2. Bake at 350° for 20-25 minutes or until golden brown. Remove from pan to a wire rack to cool.

Nutrition Facts: 1 slice equals 111 calories, 3 g fat (1 g saturated fat), 4 mg cholesterol, 250 mg sodium, 18 g carbohydrate, 2 g fiber, 6 g protein. **Diabetic Exchange:** 1 starch.

Swirl Cinnamon Bread ⬛S

PREP: 25 min. **BAKE:** 45 min. + cooling
YIELD: 1 loaf (12 slices)

MERYL SHEPPARD • GREENSBORO, NORTH CAROLINA

If you like cinnamon, you'll love this quick bread. It's crusty on top, soft and moist inside—and one of my most-requested recipes. I always make extra loaves for the holidays and give them to family and friends.

    2   cups all-purpose flour
3/4 cup sugar
1/2 tsp. baking soda
1/2 tsp. plus 1-1/2 tsp. ground cinnamon, *divided*
1/4 tsp. salt
    1   egg
    1   cup (8 oz.) reduced-fat plain yogurt
1/4 cup canola oil
    1   tsp. vanilla extract
1/4 cup packed brown sugar

1. In a large bowl, combine the flour, sugar, baking soda, 1/2 tsp. cinnamon and salt. In a small bowl, whisk the egg, yogurt, oil and vanilla. Stir into dry ingredients just until moistened. In a small bowl, combine brown sugar and remaining cinnamon.

2. Spoon a third of the batter into an 8-in. x 4-in. loaf pan coated with cooking spray. Top with a third of the brown sugar mixture. Repeat layers twice. Cut through batter with a knife to swirl the brown sugar mixture.

3. Bake at 350° for 45-55 minutes or until a toothpick inserted near the center comes out clean. Cool for 10 minutes before removing from pan to a wire rack.

Nutrition Facts: 1 slice equals 203 calories, 6 g fat (1 g saturated fat), 19 mg cholesterol, 124 mg sodium, 35 g carbohydrate, 1 g fiber, 4 g protein.

For quick breads, bake in a **light aluminum pan,** rather than a darker nonstick pan, and bake so the top of the loaf is in the center of the oven. Bake as directed. Cool for 10 minutes, then remove to a wire rack.

Holiday Herb-Cheese Rolls F

PREP: 45 min. + rising **BAKE:** 20 min. **YIELD:** 2 dozen

NANCY BOYD • MIDLOTHIAN, VIRGINIA

These low-fat hot rolls are flavored with garlic, dill and cheese—they're yummy even without butter! Or stuff with your favorite fixings for mini sandwiches.

    4   to 4-1/2 cups all-purpose flour
  1/4   cup sugar
    2   Tbsp. mashed potato flakes
    1   pkg. (1/4 oz.) active dry yeast
    2   tsp. salt
  1/2   tsp. dill weed
  1/4   tsp. garlic powder
    2   cups water
4-1/2   tsp. butter
    1   cup old-fashioned oats
    1   egg
  3/4   cup shredded part-skim mozzarella cheese

TOPPING:
    2   Tbsp. fat-free milk
4-1/2   tsp. grated Parmesan cheese
  1/2   tsp. garlic powder
  1/2   tsp. dill weed
  1/2   tsp. dried basil

1. In a large bowl, combine 1-1/2 cups flour, sugar, potato flakes, yeast, salt, dill and garlic powder. In a small saucepan, bring water and butter just to a boil.

2. In a small bowl, pour boiling liquid over oats. Let stand until mixture cools to 120°-130°, stirring occasionally. Add to dry ingredients; beat just until moistened. Add egg; beat until smooth. Stir in enough remaining flour to form a firm dough (dough will be sticky).

3. Turn onto a floured surface; knead until smooth and elastic, about 6-8 minutes. Knead in mozzarella cheese. Place in a large bowl coated with cooking spray, turning once to coat the top. Cover and let rise in a warm place until doubled, about 1-1/4 hours.

4. Punch dough down. Turn onto a lightly floured surface; divide into 24 pieces. Shape each into a ball. Place in a 13-in. x 9-in. baking pan coated with cooking spray; brush milk over rolls.

5. In a small bowl, combine the remaining ingredients; sprinkle over tops. Cover and let rise until nearly doubled, about 45 minutes. Bake at 375° for 20-25 minutes or until golden brown. Remove from pan to a wire rack.

Nutrition Facts: 1 roll equals 119 calories, 2 g fat (1 g saturated fat), 13 mg cholesterol, 228 mg sodium, 21 g carbohydrate, 1 g fiber, 4 g protein. **Diabetic Exchange:** 1-1/2 starch.

Honey Whole Wheat Bread F

PREP: 20 min. + rising **BAKE:** 35 min. + cooling
YIELD: 2 loaves (16 slices each)

ROBYN LINDBERG • KECHI, KANSAS

Here's a recipe that turns out two beautiful golden loaves.

    2   pkg. (1/4 oz. *each*) active dry yeast
    3   cups warm water (110° to 115°)
  1/2   cup nonfat dry milk powder
  1/2   cup honey
  1/3   cup wheat bran
  1/3   cup toasted wheat germ
  1/4   cup ground flaxseed

2 Tbsp. canola oil
2 tsp. salt
4 cups whole wheat flour
3-1/2 to 4 cups all-purpose flour

1. In a large bowl, dissolve yeast in warm water. Add the milk powder, honey, wheat bran, wheat germ, flax, oil, salt, whole wheat flour and 3 cups all-purpose flour. Beat until smooth. Stir in enough of the remaining flour to form a soft dough (dough will be sticky).

2. Turn onto a lightly floured surface; knead until smooth and elastic, about 6-8 minutes. Place in a bowl coated with cooking spray, turning once to coat the top. Cover and let rise in a warm place until doubled, about 1 hour.

3. Punch dough down and turn onto a floured surface; shape into two loaves. Place in two 9-in. x 5-in. loaf pans coated with cooking spay. Cover and let rise until doubled, about 30 minutes.

4. Bake at 350° for 35-40 minutes or until golden brown. Remove from pans to a wire rack to cool.

Nutrition Facts: 1 slice equals 139 calories, 2 g fat (trace saturated fat), trace cholesterol, 155 mg sodium, 28 g carbohydrate, 3 g fiber, 5 g protein. **Diabetic Exchange:** 2 starch.

Ginger Pear Bread

PREP: 25 min. **BAKE:** 45 min. + cooling
YIELD: 2 loaves (12 slices each)

CARLY CURTIN • ELLICOTT CITY, MARYLAND

A great way to use up extra pears, this bread is packed with juicy chunks of them, along with ginger, cinnamon, brown sugar and whole wheat flour. It's a healthier choice than many other baked items—and it freezes well, too.

4 medium pears, peeled and chopped
1 tsp. lemon juice
1-1/2 cups all-purpose flour
1 cup whole wheat flour
1 cup sugar
1/4 cup plus 2 tsp. packed brown sugar, *divided*
2 tsp. baking powder
1 tsp. baking soda
1 tsp. salt
1 tsp. ground ginger
1 tsp. ground cinnamon
3 eggs
3/4 cup canola oil
1 tsp. vanilla extract

1. In a large bowl, drizzle the pears with lemon juice; set aside.

2. In another large bowl, combine the flours, sugar, 1/4 cup brown sugar, baking powder, baking soda, salt, ginger and cinnamon. In a small bowl, whisk the eggs, oil and vanilla. Stir into dry ingredients just until moistened. Fold in pear mixture.

3. Transfer to two 8-in. x 4-in. loaf pans coated with cooking spray. Sprinkle with remaining brown sugar. Bake at 350° for 45-55 minutes or until a toothpick

inserted near the center comes out clean. Cool for 10 minutes before removing from pans to wire racks.

Nutrition Facts: 1 slice equals 175 calories, 8 g fat (1 g saturated fat), 26 mg cholesterol, 195 mg sodium, 25 g carbohydrate, 2 g fiber, 2 g protein. **Diabetic Exchanges:** 1-1/2 starch, 1-1/2 fat.

Cranberry Pistachio Biscotti F S C

PREP: 25 min. **BAKE:** 30 min. **YIELD:** about 2-1/2 dozen

DIANE GRUBER • SIOUX CITY, IOWA

This tasty biscotti is studded with dried cranberries and crunchy pistachios. It's delicious with tea or coffee.

3/4 cup sugar
1/4 cup canola oil
2 eggs
2 tsp. vanilla extract
1 tsp. almond extract
1-3/4 cups all-purpose flour
1 tsp. baking powder
1/4 tsp. salt
2/3 cup chopped pistachios
1/2 cup dried cranberries

1. In a small bowl, beat sugar and oil until blended. Beat in eggs, then extracts. Combine the flour, baking powder and salt; gradually add to sugar mixture and mix well (dough will be stiff). Stir in the pistachios and cranberries.

2. Divide dough in half. With floured hands, shape each half into a 12-in. x 2-in. rectangle on a parchment paper-lined baking sheet. Bake at 350° for 18-22 minutes or until set.

3. Place pan on wire rack. When cool enough to handle, transfer to a cutting board; cut diagonally with a serrated knife into 3/4-in. slices. Place cut side down on ungreased baking sheets. Bake for 12-14 minutes or until firm. Remove to wire racks to cool. Store in an airtight container.

Nutrition Facts: 1 cookie equals 85 calories, 3 g fat (trace saturated fat), 13 mg cholesterol, 46 mg sodium, 12 g carbohydrate, 1 g fiber, 2 g protein. **Diabetic Exchange:** 1 starch.

CRANBERRY PISTACHIO BISCOTTI

Twisted Cinnamon Ring

PREP: 30 min. + rising BAKE: 20 min.
YIELD: 1 ring (12 slices)

JUDY EDDY • BALDWIN CITY, KANSAS

Here's a fun take on a no-fuss dough I created! The presentation is lovely, and it's really quite simple!

   1 pkg. (1/4 oz.) active dry yeast
 3/4 cup warm water (110° to 115°)
 1/2 cup quick-cooking oats
 1/2 cup whole wheat flour
 1/4 cup packed brown sugar
   2 Tbsp. butter, melted
   1 egg
   1 tsp. salt
1-3/4 to 2-1/4 cups all-purpose flour

FILLING:
   3 Tbsp. butter, softened
 1/3 cup sugar
   2 tsp. ground cinnamon

GLAZE:
   1 cup confectioners' sugar
6-1/2 tsp. half-and-half cream
4-1/2 tsp. butter, softened

1. In a large bowl, dissolve yeast in warm water. Add the oats, whole wheat flour, brown sugar, butter, egg, salt and 1 cup all-purpose flour. Beat on medium speed until smooth. Stir in enough remaining flour to form a soft dough (dough will be sticky).

2. Turn onto a lightly floured surface; knead until smooth and elastic, about 6-8 minutes. Place in a bowl coated with cooking spray, turning once to coat the top. Cover and let rise in a warm place until doubled, about 1 hour.

3. Punch dough down. Roll into an 18-in. x 12-in. rectangle; spread with butter. Combine sugar and cinnamon; sprinkle over dough to within 1/2 in. of the edges.

TWISTED CINNAMON RING

4. Roll up jelly-roll style, starting with a long side; pinch seams to seal. Cut roll in half lengthwise. Place doughs side by side on a baking sheet coated with cooking spray. Twist together, cut side up, and shape into a ring. Pinch ends together. Cover and let rise until doubled, about 45 minutes.

5. Bake at 375° for 20-25 minutes or until golden brown. Remove from pan to a wire rack. For glaze, in a small bowl, beat the confectioners' sugar, cream and butter until smooth. Drizzle over ring.

Nutrition Facts: 1 slice equals 240 calories, 7 g fat (4 g saturated fat), 35 mg cholesterol, 251 mg sodium, 40 g carbohydrate, 2 g fiber, 4 g protein.

Walnut Apple Bread ⬛F⬛S

PREP: 40 min. + rising BAKE: 30 min. + cooling
YIELD: 2 loaves (16 slices each)

NANCY DAUGHERTY • CORTLAND, OHIO

Whenever I make this bread, it's like being in my Grandma's kitchen. Swirled with apples, walnuts and cinnamon, it's one of the best breads I've ever tasted.

   2 pkg. (1/4 oz.) active dry yeast
 1/2 cup warm water (110° to 115°)
 3/4 cup sugar
 1/2 cup warm 2% milk (110° to 115°)
 1/4 cup reduced-fat butter, softened
   2 eggs
   1 tsp. salt
   4 to 4-1/2 cups all-purpose flour

FILLING:
   2 cups chopped peeled apples
 1/2 cup chopped walnuts
 2/3 cup sugar
   1 Tbsp. all-purpose flour
   2 tsp. ground cinnamon
   2 Tbsp. reduced-fat butter, softened

GLAZE:
   1 cup confectioners' sugar
   2 Tbsp. apple cider *or* juice

1. In a large bowl, dissolve yeast in warm water. Add the sugar, milk, butter, eggs, salt and 2 cups flour. Beat until smooth. Stir in enough remaining flour to form a soft dough (dough will be sticky).

2. Turn onto a lightly floured surface; knead until smooth and elastic, about 6-8 minutes. Place in a bowl coated with cooking spray, turning once to coat the top. Cover and let rise in a warm place until doubled, about 1 hour.

3. For filling, in a small bowl, combine apples and walnuts. Combine the sugar, flour and cinnamon; stir into apple mixture. Punch dough down. Roll into a 14-in. x 12-in. rectangle. Spread butter to within 1/2 in. of edges; sprinkle with apple mixture. Roll up jelly-roll style, starting with a long side. Cut in half. Pinch seams to seal and tuck ends under.

4. Place loaves seam side down in two 9-in. x 5-in. loaf pans coated with cooking spray. Cover and let rise until doubled, about 30 minutes. With a sharp knife, make eight shallow slashes across top of each loaf.

5. Bake at 350° for 30-35 minutes or until golden brown. Remove from pans to wire racks to cool. In a small bowl, combine the glaze ingredients; drizzle over the bread.

Editor's Note: This recipe was tested with Land O'Lakes light stick butter.

Nutrition Facts: 1 slice equals 140 calories, 3 g fat (1 g saturated fat), 16 mg cholesterol, 99 mg sodium, 27 g carbohydrate, 1 g fiber, 3 g protein. **Diabetic Exchanges:** 1-1/2 starch, 1/2 fat.

Rhubarb-Lemon Coffee Cake

PREP: 25 min. **BAKE:** 35 min. + cooling
YIELD: 12 servings

STEPHANIE OTTEN • BYRON CENTER, MICHIGAN

And you thought rhubarb was just for pie—not so in the case of this tart and tasty coffee cake.

2-1/4 cups all-purpose flour
3/4 cup sugar
1/2 tsp. baking powder
1/2 tsp. baking soda
1/4 tsp. salt
1/3 cup butter, melted
2/3 cup vanilla yogurt
2 eggs
1 Tbsp. lemon juice
2 tsp. grated lemon peel
1 cup chopped fresh *or* frozen rhubarb
1 tsp. ground cinnamon
1/2 tsp. ground nutmeg

STREUSEL:
1/2 cup all-purpose flour
1/3 cup sugar
1 tsp. ground cinnamon
2 Tbsp. cold butter

GLAZE:
1/3 cup confectioners' sugar
2 tsp. lemon juice

1. In a large bowl, combine the flour, sugar, baking powder, baking soda and salt. In a small bowl, whisk the butter, yogurt, eggs, lemon juice and lemon peel. Stir into dry ingredients just until moistened.

2. Coat a 9-in. springform pan with cooking spray and sprinkle with flour. Spread half the batter into prepared pan. Add rhubarb to within 1/2 in. of the edges. Sprinkle with cinnamon and nutmeg. Top with remaining batter.

3. For streusel, combine the flour, sugar and cinnamon in a small bowl; cut in butter until crumbly. Sprinkle over batter. Bake at 350° for 35-45 minutes or until a toothpick inserted near the center comes out clean. Cool for 10 minutes.

4. For glaze, in a small bowl combine confectioners' sugar and lemon juice. Drizzle over warm cake. Cool for 1 hour.

Editor's Note: If using frozen rhubarb, measure rhubarb while still frozen, then thaw completely. Drain in a colander, but do not press liquid out.

Nutrition Facts: 1 slice equals 273 calories, 8 g fat (5 g saturated fat), 54 mg cholesterol, 187 mg sodium, 46 g carbohydrate, 1 g fiber, 5 g protein.

Sage Fontina Focaccia ⬛S ⬛C

PREP: 30 min. + rising **BAKE:** 10 min.
YIELD: 1 loaf (8 wedges)

BETH DAUENHAUER • PUEBLO, COLORADO

These rustic loaves have plenty of sage flavor—a tasty addition to just about any feast.

1-1/4 tsp. active dry yeast
   1/2 cup warm water (110° to 115°)
   1/2 tsp. honey
   3/4 to 1 cup all-purpose flour
   1/4 cup whole wheat flour
     1 Tbsp. olive oil
     2 tsp. minced fresh sage
   1/4 tsp. salt

TOPPING:
1-1/2 tsp. olive oil, *divided*
     8 fresh sage leaves
   1/2 cup shredded fontina cheese

1. In a large bowl, dissolve yeast in warm water. Stir in honey; let stand for 5 minutes. Add 3/4 cup all-purpose flour, whole wheat flour, oil, minced sage and salt. Beat on medium speed for 3 minutes or until smooth. Stir in enough remaining flour to form a soft dough (dough will be sticky).

2. Turn onto a lightly floured surface; knead until smooth and elastic, about 6-8 minutes. Place in a large bowl coated with cooking spray, turning once to coat the top. Cover and let rise in a warm place until doubled, about 1 hour.

3. Punch dough down. Cover and let rest for 5 minutes. Shape into an 8-in. circle; place on a baking sheet coated with cooking spray. Cover and let rise until doubled, about 30 minutes. Using the end of a wooden spoon handle, make several 1/4-in. indentations in the loaf.

4. For topping, brush dough with 1 tsp. oil. Top with sage leaves; brush leaves with remaining oil. Sprinkle with cheese. Bake at 400° for 8-10 minutes or until golden brown. Remove to a wire rack.

Nutrition Facts: 1 wedge equals 112 calories, 5 g fat (2 g saturated fat), 8 mg cholesterol, 131 mg sodium, 12 g carbohydrate, 1 g fiber, 4 g protein. **Diabetic Exchanges:** 1 starch, 1 fat.

Banana Nut Bread ⓢ

PREP: 20 min. **BAKE:** 50 min. + cooling
YIELD: 1 loaf (12 slices)

BRITTANY CARRINGTON • TEHACHAPI, CALIFORNIA

I made up this recipe when I was a vegetarian and didn't eat eggs. It's packed with fiber, omega-3s and soy protein yet tastes delicious! Silken tofu is a wonderful egg substitute.

- 1 cup all-purpose flour
- 1 cup whole wheat flour
- 1 tsp. baking powder
- 1/2 tsp. baking soda
- 1/4 tsp. salt
- 1 cup sugar
- 1 cup mashed ripe bananas (2 medium)
- 3/4 cup silken soft tofu
- 1/4 cup canola oil
- 1 tsp. vanilla extract
- 1/2 cup chopped walnuts

1. In a large bowl, combine the first five ingredients. In a small bowl, beat the sugar, bananas, tofu, oil and and vanilla. Beat into dry ingredients just until moistened. Fold in walnuts.

2. Transfer to an 8-in. x 4-in. loaf pan coated with cooking spray. Bake at 350° for 50-55 minutes or until a toothpick inserted near the center comes out clean. Cool for 10 minutes before removing from pan to a wire rack.

Nutrition Facts: 1 slice equals 234 calories, 9 g fat (1 g saturated fat), 0 cholesterol, 140 mg sodium, 37 g carbohydrate, 2 g fiber, 4 g protein.

> To test baking powder for freshness, place 1 teaspoon **baking powder** in a cup and add 1/3 cup hot tap water. If active bubbling occurs, the product is fine. If not, you should discard the powder and replace it.

BANANA NUT BREAD

ROSEMARY-GARLIC FOCACCIA BREAD

Rosemary-Garlic Focaccia Bread M

PREP: 30 min. + rising **BAKE:** 15 min.
YIELD: 1 loaf (12 wedges)

TAMMY BOLLMAN • MINATARE, NEBRASKA

This bread smells wonderful when it's baking in the oven. I make it mostly during the summer when rosemary is abundant in the garden, but also around the holidays when rosemary plants are available in the stores.

3/4	cup warm fat-free milk (70° to 80°)
1/4	cup water (70° to 80°)
1/4	cup butter, softened
1	egg
2-3/4	cups bread flour
2	Tbsp. sugar
2	tsp. kosher salt, *divided*
2	tsp. active dry yeast
4	tsp. olive oil
4	garlic cloves, minced
1	Tbsp. minced fresh rosemary

1. In bread machine pan, place the milk, water, butter, egg, flour, sugar, 1 tsp. salt and yeast in order suggested by manufacturer. Select dough setting (check dough after 5 minutes of mixing; add 1 to 2 Tbsp. of water or flour if needed).

2. When cycle is completed, turn dough onto a lightly floured surface. Punch dough down. Cover and let rest for 10 minutes. Shape into an 11-in. circle; place on a baking sheet coated with cooking spray. Cover and let rise until doubled, about 30 minutes.

Using the end of a wooden spoon handle, make several 1/4-in. indentations in dough.

3. Brush with oil. Sprinkle with garlic, rosemary and remaining salt. Bake at 400° for 15-20 minutes or until golden brown. Cut into wedges.

Editor's Note: We recommend you do not use a bread machine's time-delay feature for this recipe.

Nutrition Facts: 1 wedge equals 162 calories, 6 g fat (3 g saturated fat), 28 mg cholesterol, 353 mg sodium, 24 g carbohydrate, 1 g fiber, 5 g protein. **Diabetic Exchanges:** 1-1/2 starch, 1 fat.

Fruited Bran Muffins

PREP: 20 min. **BAKE:** 20 min. **YIELD:** 9 muffins

BETSY KING • DULUTH, MINNESOTA

Juicy blueberries and an apple make a nice addition to these hearty muffins. Bran cereal helps pump up fiber to 5 grams.

1-1/2	cups All-Bran
3/4	cup whole wheat flour
3	Tbsp. sugar
1/2	tsp. baking powder
1/2	tsp. baking soda
1/2	tsp. ground cinnamon
1	egg
3/4	cup buttermilk
1/4	cup mashed ripe banana
1/4	cup molasses
2	Tbsp. canola oil
1/2	cup chopped peeled tart apple
1/2	cup fresh or frozen blueberries

1. In a small bowl, combine the first six ingredients. In another bowl, combine the egg, buttermilk, banana, molasses and oil. Stir into dry ingredients just until moistened. Fold in apple and blueberries.

2. Coat muffin cups with cooking spray or use paper liners; fill three-fourths full with batter. Bake at 350° for 20-25 minutes or until a toothpick inserted near the center comes out clean. Cool for 5 minutes before removing from pan to a wire rack. Serve warm.

Editor's Note: If using frozen blueberries, use without thawing to avoid discoloring the batter.

Nutrition Facts: 1 muffin equals 160 calories, 5 g fat (1 g saturated fat), 24 mg cholesterol, 150 mg sodium, 30 g carbohydrate, 5 g fiber, 4 g protein. **Diabetic Exchanges:** 2 starch, 1/2 fat.

Old-Fashioned Biscuits

PREP: 20 min. BAKE: 15 min. YIELD: 4 biscuits

HEALTHY COOKING TEST KITCHEN

Fresh-from-the-oven biscuits can be yours in no time. Best of all, they don't have to break your commitment to eating right. Serve them with breakfast or with a steaming mug of coffee or tea. Either way, you'll love every bite!

- 1/2 cup all-purpose flour
- 1/2 cup cake flour
- 1 tsp. baking powder
- 1 tsp. sugar
- 1/4 tsp. salt
- 1/8 tsp. baking soda
- 3/4 oz. cold reduced-fat cream cheese
- 1 Tbsp. cold butter
- 1/4 cup plus 1/2 tsp. buttermilk, *divided*

1. In a small bowl, combine the flours, baking powder, sugar, salt and baking soda. Cut in cream cheese and butter until mixture resembles coarse crumbs. Stir in 1/4 cup buttermilk just until moistened. Turn onto a lightly floured surface; knead 5-6 times.

2. Pat or roll out to 1/2-in. thickness; cut with a floured 2-in. biscuit cutter.

3. Place 2 in. apart on a baking sheet coated with cooking spray. Brush with remaining buttermilk. Bake at 400° for 12-15 minutes or until golden brown. Serve warm.

Nutrition Facts: 1 biscuit equals 167 calories, 4 g fat (3 g saturated fat), 12 mg cholesterol, 355 mg sodium, 27 g carbohydrate, 1 g fiber, 4 g protein. **Diabetic Exchanges:** 2 starch, 1 fat.

Pumpkin Spice Bagels F

PREP: 30 min. + standing BAKE: 15 min.
YIELD: 9 servings

KRISTY REEVES • LEROY, KANSAS

Enjoy pumpkin pie flavor with these classic bagels. For a change, adjust the spices to suit your taste buds.

- 2/3 cup plus 2 Tbsp. water (70° to 80°), *divided*
- 1/2 cup canned pumpkin
- 1/3 cup packed brown sugar
- 1 tsp. salt
- 1-1/2 tsp. ground cinnamon
- 3/4 tsp. ground nutmeg
- 1/2 tsp. ground allspice
- 1/2 tsp. ground cloves
- 3 cups bread flour
- 1 pkg. (1/4 oz.) active dry yeast
- 1 egg white
- 1 Tbsp. cornmeal

1. In bread machine pan, place 2/3 cup water, pumpkin, brown sugar, salt, spices, flour and yeast in order suggested by manufacturer. Select dough setting (check dough after 5 minutes of mixing; add 1 to 2 Tbsp. of water or flour if needed).

2. When cycle is completed, turn dough onto a lightly floured surface. Shape into nine balls. Push thumb through centers to form a 1-in. hole. Stretch and shape dough to form an even ring. Cover and let rest for 10 minutes; flatten rings slightly.

3. Fill a Dutch oven two-thirds full with water; bring to a boil. Drop bagels, two at a time, into boiling water. Cook for 45 seconds; turn and cook 45 seconds longer. Remove with a slotted spoon; drain on paper towels.

4. Whisk egg white and remaining water; brush over bagels. Coat a baking sheet with cooking spray and sprinkle with cornmeal. Place bagels 2 in. apart on prepared pan. Bake at 400° for 15-20 minutes or until golden brown. Remove to wire racks to cool.

Nutrition Facts: 1 bagel equals 180 calories, trace fat (trace saturated fat), 0 cholesterol, 273 mg sodium, 40 g carbohydrate, 2 g fiber, 6 g protein.

PUMPKIN SPICE BAGELS

Italian Spinach Braid

PREP: 20 min. + rising BAKE: 20 min. YIELD: 6 servings

PAT JASPER • NORTHLAKE, ILLINOIS

I've been making this recipe for over 25 years. It's how I got my kids to eat spinach when they were little. This is the dish I'm asked to make the most.

1	loaf (1 lb.) frozen whole wheat bread dough, thawed
1	lb. lean ground beef (90% lean)
1	pkg. (10 oz.) frozen chopped spinach, thawed and squeezed dry
2/3	cup shredded part-skim mozzarella cheese
2	Tbsp. grated Romano cheese
3/4	tsp. dried minced garlic
3/4	tsp. fennel seed
3/4	tsp. dried oregano
1/2	tsp. salt
1	egg white, beaten

Pizza sauce, optional

1. Roll dough into a 12-in. x 9-in. rectangle. Transfer to a 15-in. x 10-in. x 1-in. baking pan coated with cooking spray. Cover and let rise in a warm place until doubled, about 1 hour.

2. Meanwhile, in a large skillet, cook beef over medium heat until no longer pink; drain. Transfer to a large bowl; add the spinach, cheeses, garlic, fennel seed, oregano and salt.

3. Spread beef mixture lengthwise down the center of dough. On each long side, cut 1-in.-wide strips 3 in. into center.

4. Starting at one end, fold alternating strips at an angle across filling. Pinch ends to seal. Brush with egg white. Bake at 350° for 20-25 minutes or until golden brown. Serve with pizza sauce if desired.

Nutrition Facts: 1 piece (calculated without pizza sauce) equals 366 calories, 12 g fat (4 g saturated fat), 57 mg cholesterol, 709 mg sodium, 38 g carbohydrate, 6 g fiber, 30 g protein. **Diabetic Exchanges:** 3 lean meat, 2-1/2 starch.

Makeover Zucchini Bread

PREP: 20 min. BAKE: 45 min. + cooling
YIELD: 2 loaves (12 slices each)

MARJORIE CURTIS • HADDAM, CONNECTICUT

This makeover bread has a golden top, lots of sweet cinnamon flavor and a slimmed-down nutritional profile. It's perfect for your next afternoon snack.

1-1/2	cups sugar
1/2	cup unsweetened applesauce
2	eggs
1/3	cup canola oil
3	tsp. vanilla extract
3	cups all-purpose flour
2-1/2	tsp. ground cinnamon
2	tsp. baking powder
1	tsp. salt
1/2	tsp. baking soda
2	cups shredded zucchini
3/4	cup chopped walnuts

1. In a large bowl, beat the sugar, applesauce, eggs, oil and vanilla until well blended. Combine the flour, cinnamon, baking powder, salt and baking soda; gradually beat into sugar mixture until blended. Stir in zucchini and walnuts.

2. Transfer to two 8-in. x 4-in. loaf pans coated with cooking spray. Bake at 350° for 45-55 minutes or until a toothpick inserted near the center comes out clean. Cool for 10 minutes before removing from pans to wire racks.

Nutrition Facts: 1 slice equals 168 calories, 6 g fat (1 g saturated fat), 18 mg cholesterol, 165 mg sodium, 26 g carbohydrate, 1 g fiber, 3 g protein. **Diabetic Exchanges:** 2 starch, 1 fat.

MAKEOVER ZUCCHINI BREAD

ITALIAN SPINACH BREAD

BLUEBERRY-CITRUS MINI LOAVES

Blueberry-Citrus Mini Loaves

PREP: 15 min. BAKE: 40 min. + cooling
YIELD: 2 loaves (6 slices each)

HEIDI LINDSEY • PRAIRIE DU SAC, WISCONSIN

Moist and packed with flavor, these healthful treats hit the spot. With subtle orange peel, blueberries and hearty whole wheat flour, they offer a delectable way to get your family going in the morning!

> 1 cup all-purpose flour
> 1 cup whole wheat pastry flour
> 3/4 cup sugar
> 1/2 tsp. salt
> 1/2 tsp. baking soda
> 1 egg
> 3/4 cup orange juice
> 1/4 cup canola oil
> 1 Tbsp. grated orange peel
> 1/2 cup fresh or frozen blueberries
> 1/4 cup chopped pecans

1. In a large bowl, combine the flours, sugar, salt and baking soda. In a small bowl, whisk the egg, orange juice, oil and orange peel. Stir into dry ingredients just until moistened. Fold in blueberries and pecans.

2. Transfer to two 5-3/4-in. x 3-in. x 2-in. loaf pans coated with cooking spray. Bake at 350° for 40-45 minutes or until a toothpick inserted near the center comes out clean. Cool for 10 minutes before removing from pans to wire racks.

Editor's Note: If using frozen blueberries, use without thawing to avoid discoloring the batter.

Nutrition Facts: 1 slice equals 189 calories, 7 g fat (1 g saturated fat), 18 mg cholesterol, 157 mg sodium, 29 g carbohydrate, 2 g fiber, 3 g protein.

Sweet Potato Biscuits

PREP/TOTAL TIME: 30 min. YIELD: 17 biscuits

DELYNNE RUTLEDGE • LOVELADY, TEXAS

Flaky and bursting with flavor from honey and sweet potatoes, these biscuits are wonderful any time, but they're best right from the oven.

> 2 cups all-purpose flour
> 1/3 cup yellow cornmeal
> 2-1/2 tsp. baking powder
> 1/2 tsp. salt
> 1/3 cup cold butter
> 1 cup mashed sweet potato
> 1/2 cup fat-free milk
> 2 Tbsp. honey

1. In a large bowl, combine the flour, cornmeal, baking powder and salt. Cut in butter until mixture resembles coarse crumbs. Stir in the sweet potato, milk and honey just until moistened. Turn onto a lightly floured surface; knead 5-8 times. Pat out to 1/2-in. thickness; cut with a floured 2-in. biscuit cutter.

2. Place 2 in. apart on an ungreased baking sheet. Bake at 400° for 14-18 minutes or until lightly browned. Serve warm.

Nutrition Facts: 1 biscuit equals 120 calories, 4 g fat (2 g saturated fat), 10 mg cholesterol, 162 mg sodium, 19 g carbohydrate, 1 g fiber, 2 g protein. **Diabetic Exchanges:** 1 starch, 1 fat.

Cranberry Orange Bagels F

PREP: 30 min. + standing BAKE: 20 min. YIELD: 9 bagels

KRISTY REEVES • LEROY, KANSAS

Dried cranberries and grated orange peel add bright flavor to these scrumptious morning treats. Switch up the taste, if you'd like, by using raisins and cinnamon.

- 1   cup plus 4 Tbsp. water (70° to 80°), *divided*
- 1/2 cup dried cranberries
- 1/3 cup packed brown sugar
- 4-1/2 tsp. grated orange peel
- 1   tsp. salt
- 1/4 tsp. ground cloves
- 3   cups bread flour
- 1   pkg. (1/4 oz.) active dry yeast
- 1   Tbsp. sugar
- 1   egg white
- 1   Tbsp. cornmeal

1. In bread machine pan, place 1 cup plus 2 Tbsp. water, cranberries, brown sugar, orange peel, salt, cloves, flour and yeast in order suggested by manufacturer. Select dough setting (check dough after 5 minutes of mixing; add 1 to 2 Tbsp. of water or flour if needed).

2. When cycle is completed, turn dough onto a lightly floured surface. Shape into nine balls. Push thumb through centers to form a 1-in. hole. Stretch and shape dough to form an even ring. Cover and let rest for 10 minutes; flatten rings slightly.

3. Fill a Dutch oven two-thirds full with water; add sugar and bring to a boil. Drop bagels, two at a time, into boiling water. Cook for 45 seconds; turn and cook 45 seconds longer. Remove with a slotted spoon; drain on paper towels.

4. Whisk egg white and remaining water; brush over bagels. Coat a baking sheet with cooking spray and sprinkle with cornmeal. Place bagels 2 in. apart on prepared pan. Bake at 400° for 18-22 minutes or until golden brown. Remove to wire racks to cool.

Nutrition Facts: 1 bagel equals 197 calories, trace fat (trace saturated fat), 0 cholesterol, 272 mg sodium, 45 g carbohydrate, 2 g fiber, 6 g protein.

Bountiful Loaves

PREP: 30 min. + rising BAKE: 25 min. + cooling
YIELD: 2 loaves (16 slices each)

JENNIFER FERRO • DRUMHELLER, ALBERTA

This healthy, rustic bread fills you up. It's delicious as is or with dried cranberries instead of raisins.

2 pkg. (1/4 oz. *each*) active dry yeast
3 tsp. sugar, *divided*
2-1/2 cups warm water (110° to 115°)
3 cups whole wheat flour
1 cup old-fashioned oats
1/2 cup oat bran
1/2 cup toasted wheat germ
1/2 cup ground flaxseed
1 egg
2 Tbsp. olive oil
2 tsp. salt
2-1/2 cups all-purpose flour
1/2 cup sunflower kernels
1/2 cup raisins

1. In a large bowl, dissolve yeast and 1 tsp. sugar in warm water; let stand for 5 minutes. Add the whole wheat flour, oats, oat bran, wheat germ, flaxseed, egg, oil, salt, 1 cup all-purpose flour and remaining sugar. Beat until smooth. Stir in the sunflower kernels, raisins and enough remaining flour to form a firm dough (dough will be sticky).

2. Turn onto a lightly floured surface; knead until smooth and elastic, about 6-8 minutes. Place in a bowl coated with cooking spray, turning once to coat the top. Cover and let rise in a warm place until doubled, about 1 hour.

3. Punch dough down. Turn onto a lightly floured surface; divide in half. Shape into two round loaves. Place on a baking sheet coated with cooking spray. Cover and let rise until nearly doubled, about 30 minutes.

4. Bake at 375° for 25-30 minutes or until golden brown. Remove from baking sheet to wire rack to cool.

Nutrition Facts: 1 slice equals 133 calories, 4 g fat (trace saturated fat), 7 mg cholesterol, 161 mg sodium, 23 g carbohydrate, 3 g fiber, 5 g protein. **Diabetic Exchanges:** 1-1/2 starch, 1/2 fat.

Basil Marmalade Scones

PREP: 20 min. BAKE: 15 min. YIELD: 8 scones

HANNAH WALLACE • WENATCHEE, WASHINGTON

Orange marmalade and fragrant basil give these delightful scones a slightly sweet, garden-fresh flavor. They're tender and moist and perfect with morning or afternoon tea.

2 cups all-purpose flour
3 Tbsp. sugar
2 tsp. baking powder
1/2 tsp. salt
3 Tbsp. cold butter
3 Tbsp. minced fresh basil or 1 Tbsp. dried basil
2 eggs
1/3 cup fat-free milk
1/3 cup orange marmalade

1. In a small bowl, combine the flour, sugar, baking powder and salt. Cut in butter until mixture resembles coarse crumbs. Stir in basil. Whisk eggs and milk; stir into crumb mixture just until moistened. Turn onto a floured surface; knead 5 times.

2. Divide dough in half. Transfer one portion to a baking sheet coated with cooking spray. Pat into a 7-in. circle. Spread marmalade to within 1/2 in. of edge. Pat remaining dough into a 7-in. circle. Place over marmalade; seal edges. Cut into eight wedges, but do not separate. Bake at 400° for 15-20 minutes or until golden brown. Serve warm.

Nutrition Facts: 1 scone equals 224 calories, 6 g fat (3 g saturated fat), 64 mg cholesterol, 308 mg sodium, 38 g carbohydrate, 1 g fiber, 5 g protein.

BASIL MARMALADE SCONES

BOUNTIFUL LOAVES

Double Corn Corn Bread

PREP: 15 min. **BAKE:** 40 min. + cooling
YIELD: 1 loaf (6 slices)

SILVANA NARDONE • BROOKLYN, NEW YORK

Looking for a delightful bread to dunk in a bowl of chowder or chili? Try this tasty recipe. It's one of my son's all-time favorites. He could eat it for breakfast, lunch and dinner.

- 1 cup gluten-free all-purpose baking flour
- 1 cup cornmeal
- 1/4 cup sugar
- 1 Tbsp. baking powder
- 1 tsp. baking soda
- 1 tsp. salt
- 2 eggs, lightly beaten
- 1 cup rice milk
- 1/4 cup canola oil
- 1 Tbsp. cider vinegar
- 1 cup frozen corn, thawed

1. In a large bowl, combine the flour, cornmeal, sugar, baking powder, baking soda and salt. In a small bowl, whisk the eggs, rice milk, oil and vinegar. Stir into dry ingredients just until moistened; stir in corn.

2. Transfer to an 8-in. x 4-in. loaf pan coated with cooking spray. Bake at 350° for 40-45 minutes or until top is lightly browned and a toothpick inserted near the center comes out clean. Cool on a wire rack.

Editor's Note: Read all ingredient labels for possible gluten content prior to use. Ingredient formulas can change, and production facilities vary among brands. If you're concerned that your brand may contain gluten, contact the company.

Nutrition Facts: 1 slice equals 334 calories, 13 g fat (1 g saturated fat), 71 mg cholesterol, 842 mg sodium, 51 g carbohydrate, 4 g fiber, 7 g protein.

DOUBLE CORN CORN BREAD

Peanut Butter-Banana Muffins F S C

PREP: 25 min. **BAKE:** 10 min./batch **YIELD:** 4 dozen

PATTY PUTTER • MARION, KANSAS

These bite-size muffins make a great treat. Banana and peanut butter are ideal partners and taste terrific with chocolate.

- 1 cup old-fashioned oats
- 1 cup whole wheat flour
- 1/2 cup all-purpose flour
- 1/2 cup sugar
- 1 tsp. baking powder
- 1/2 tsp. baking soda
- 1/2 tsp. salt
- 1 egg
- 3/4 cup fat-free milk
- 3/4 cup mashed ripe bananas
- 1/2 cup creamy peanut butter
- 1/3 cup unsweetened applesauce
- 1/2 tsp. vanilla extract
- 3/4 cup miniature semisweet chocolate chips

TOPPING:
- 1/3 cup packed brown sugar
- 1/3 cup dry roasted peanuts, coarsely chopped
- 1/3 cup miniature semisweet chocolate chips

1. In a large bowl, combine the first seven ingredients. In a small bowl, combine the egg, milk, bananas, peanut butter, applesauce and vanilla. Stir into dry ingredients just until moistened. Fold in chocolate chips.

2. Fill greased or paper-lined miniature muffin cups three-fourths full. For topping, in a small bowl, combine the brown sugar, peanuts and chocolate chips. Sprinkle over muffins. Bake at 350° for 10-13 minutes or until a toothpick inserted near the center comes out clean.

3. Cool for 5 minutes before removing from pans to wire racks. Serve warm.

Nutrition Facts: 1 muffin equals 80 calories, 3 g fat (1 g saturated fat), 4 mg cholesterol, 71 mg sodium, 12 g carbohydrate, 1 g fiber, 2 g protein. **Diabetic Exchange:** 1 starch.

Honey Lemon Muffins

PREP/TOTAL TIME: 30 min. **YIELD:** 10 muffins

RACHEL HART • WILDOMAR, CALIFORNIA

Honey's subtle essence comes through in every bite of these succulent little muffins, providing the perfect counterpoint to the bright taste of lemon.

- 1 cup all-purpose flour
- 1/2 cup whole wheat flour
- 1 tsp. baking powder
- 1/4 tsp. baking soda
- 1/4 tsp. salt
- 1 egg
- 1/2 cup honey
- 1/4 cup lemon juice

GLUTEN-FREE AUTUMN BREAD

1/4 cup butter, melted
1/2 tsp. grated lemon peel

DRIZZLE:
1/4 cup confectioners' sugar
  1 tsp. lemon juice
Additional grated lemon peel

1. In a large bowl, combine the flours, baking powder, baking soda and salt. In another bowl, combine the egg, honey, lemon juice, butter and lemon peel. Stir into dry ingredients just until moistened.

2. Coat muffin cups with cooking spray or use paper liners; fill one-half full with batter.

3. Bake at 375° for 15-18 minutes or until a toothpick inserted near the center comes out clean. Cool for 5 minutes before removing from pan to a wire rack.

4. In a small bowl, combine confectioners' sugar and lemon juice; drizzle over warm muffins. Sprinkle with additional lemon peel.

Nutrition Facts: 1 muffin equals 178 calories, 5 g fat (3 g saturated fat), 33 mg cholesterol, 171 mg sodium, 31 g carbohydrate, 1 g fiber, 3 g protein. **Diabetic Exchanges:** 2 starch, 1 fat.

Gluten-Free Autumn Bread

PREP: 20 min. **BAKE:** 50 min. + cooling
YIELD: 1 loaf (16 slices)

CHRISTINE LEVINE • WALDORF, MARYLAND
This moist, yummy loaf has a golden-brown crust and added sweetness from bananas, raisins and carrots.

  1 cup mashed ripe bananas (2 to 3 medium)
  1 cup packed brown sugar
1/4 cup unsweetened applesauce
1/4 cup canola oil
  2 eggs
  1 cup sorghum flour
  1 cup brown rice flour
1-1/2 tsp. baking powder
  1 tsp. baking soda
  1 tsp. xanthan gum
1/2 tsp. salt
1/2 tsp. ground cinnamon
  1 cup shredded carrots
1/2 cup raisins
1/3 cup chopped walnuts

1. In a large bowl, beat the bananas, brown sugar, applesauce, oil and eggs until well blended. Combine the flours, baking powder, baking soda, xanthan gum, salt and cinnamon; gradually beat into banana mixture until blended. Stir in the carrots, raisins and walnuts.

2. Transfer to a 9-in. x 5-in. loaf pan coated with cooking spray. Bake at 350° for 50-60 minutes or until a toothpick inserted near the center comes out clean. Cool for 10 minutes before removing from pan to a wire rack.

Editor's Note: Read all ingredient labels for possible gluten content prior to use. Ingredient formulas can change, and production facilities vary among brands. If you're concerned that your brand may contain gluten, contact the company.

Nutrition Facts: 1 slice equals 199 calories, 6 g fat (1 g saturated fat), 26 mg cholesterol, 212 mg sodium, 35 g carbohydrate, 2 g fiber, 3 g protein. **Diabetic Exchanges:** 2 starch, 1 fat, 1/2 fruit.

No-Knead Whole Wheat Rolls 🇫

PREP: 15 min. + rising BAKE: 10 min. YIELD: 1 dozen

DEBORAH PATRAUCHUK • SICAMOUS, BRITISH COLUMBIA

Tender and moist, these easy whole wheat rolls boast a great herb flavor!

1	pkg. (1/4 oz.) active dry yeast
1-1/4	cups warm water (110° to 115°)
2	cups all-purpose flour
1	cup whole wheat flour
2	Tbsp. butter, softened
1	Tbsp. honey
1	Tbsp. molasses
1	tsp. salt
1	tsp. Italian seasoning

1. In a large bowl, dissolve yeast in warm water. Add the remaining ingredients. Beat on medium speed for 3 minutes (dough will be sticky). Do not knead. Cover and let rise in a warm place until doubled, about 30 minutes.

2. Stir dough down. Set aside 1/4 cup batter. Fill muffin cups coated with cooking spray half full. Top each with 1 tsp. reserved batter. Cover and let rise until doubled, about 8-12 minutes.

3. Bake at 375° for 10-15 minutes or until golden brown. Cool for 1 minute before removing from pan to a wire rack.

Nutrition Facts: 1 roll equals 139 calories, 2 g fat (1 g saturated fat), 5 mg cholesterol, 212 mg sodium, 26 g carbohydrate, 2 g fiber, 4 g protein. **Diabetic Exchange:** 1-1/2 starch.

Swiss Cheese Muffins

PREP/TOTAL TIME: 30 min. YIELD: 1 dozen

MARY RELYEA • CANASTOTA, NEW YORK

Ideal as a snack, a quick breakfast or alongside a bowl of chili or stew, these tasty muffins hit the spot. Their savory yet mild flavors make them a hit with all ages. Best of all, I can whip them up and have them on the table in just half an hour!

2	cups all-purpose flour
1	Tbsp. sugar
3/4	tsp. salt

1/2 tsp. baking soda
2 eggs
1 cup (8 oz.) reduced-fat sour cream
2 Tbsp. canola oil
1/2 cup shredded Swiss cheese
2 green onions, chopped

1. In a small bowl, combine the flour, sugar, salt and baking soda. In another bowl, combine the eggs, sour cream and oil. Stir into dry ingredients just until moistened. Fold in cheese and onions.

2. Coat muffin cups with cooking spray or use paper liners; fill three-fourths full with batter. Bake at 375° for 15-18 minutes or until a toothpick inserted in muffin comes out clean. Cool for 5 minutes before removing from pan to a wire rack. Serve warm.

Nutrition Facts: 1 muffin equals 157 calories, 6 g fat (2 g saturated fat), 46 mg cholesterol, 237 mg sodium, 19 g carbohydrate, 1 g fiber, 6 g protein. **Diabetic Exchanges:** 1 starch, 1 fat.

Gluten-Free Banana Nut Muffins **S**

PREP: 20 min. BAKE: 20 min. YIELD: 1 dozen

GINGERLEMONGIRL • TASTEOFHOME.COM COMMUNITY

You don't have to be gluten-intolerant to appreciate the sweet essence of grains and bananas in these delectable muffins.

1-1/2 cups mashed ripe bananas (2 to 3 medium)
2/3 cup sugar
2 eggs
1/4 cup fat-free plain yogurt
2 Tbsp. plus 1-1/2 tsp. canola oil
1 tsp. vanilla extract
1/2 cup millet flour
1/2 cup sorghum flour
1/2 cup tapioca flour
1 Tbsp. ground flaxseed
2 tsp. baking powder
1/2 tsp. baking soda
1/4 tsp. xanthan gum
1/3 cup chopped walnuts

1. In a large bowl, beat the first six ingredients until well blended. In a large bowl, combine the flours, flax, baking powder, baking soda and xanthan gum; gradually beat into banana mixture until blended. Stir in walnuts.

2. Coat muffin cups with cooking spray or use paper liners; fill three-fourths full with batter. Bake at 350° for 18-22 minutes or until a toothpick inserted near the center comes out clean.

3. Cool for 5 minutes before removing from pan to a wire rack.

Editor's Note: Read all ingredient labels for possible gluten content prior to use. Ingredient formulas can change, and production facilities vary among brands. If you're concerned that your brand may contain gluten, contact the company.

Nutrition Facts: 1 muffin equals 191 calories, 6 g fat (1 g saturated fat), 35 mg cholesterol, 135 mg sodium, 32 g carbohydrate, 2 g fiber, 4 g protein. **Diabetic Exchanges:** 2 starch, 1 fat.

Rustic Rye Bread **F**

PREP: 20 min. + rising BAKE: 30 min. + cooling
YIELD: 2 loaves (12 slices each)

HOLLY WADE • HARRISONBURG, VIRGINIA

This gorgeous rye bread has just a touch of sweetness and the perfect amount of caraway seeds. With a crusty top and firm texture, it holds up well to sandwiches...but a pat of butter will do the job, too.

1 pkg. (1/4 oz.) active dry yeast
1-3/4 cups warm water (110° to 115°), *divided*
1/4 cup packed brown sugar
1/4 cup light molasses
3 Tbsp. caraway seeds
2 Tbsp. canola oil
3 tsp. salt
1-3/4 cups rye flour
3/4 cup whole wheat flour
1-3/4 to 2-1/4 cups all-purpose flour

1. In a large bowl, dissolve yeast in 1/4 cup warm water. Add the brown sugar, molasses, caraway seeds, oil, salt and remaining water; mix well. Add the rye flour, whole wheat flour and 1-3/4 cups all-purpose flour. Beat until smooth. Stir in enough remaining flour to form a firm dough.

2. Turn onto a lightly floured surface; knead until smooth and elastic, about 6-8 minutes. Place in a bowl coated with cooking spray, turning once to coat the top. Cover and let rise in a warm place until doubled, about 1 hour.

3. Punch dough down; shape into two round loaves. Place on a baking sheet coated with cooking spray. Cover and let rise until doubled, about 1 hour.

4. Bake at 350° for 30-35 minutes or until golden brown. Remove from pan to wire rack to cool.

Nutrition Facts: 1 slice equals 104 calories, 2 g fat (trace saturated fat), 0 cholesterol, 298 mg sodium, 21 g carbohydrate, 2 g fiber, 2 g protein. **Diabetic Exchange:** 1 starch.

RUSTIC RYE BREAD

Chocolate Ribbon Banana Loaf

PREP: 20 min. BAKE: 40 min. + cooling
YIELD: 1 loaf (12 slices)

SHARON GILJUM • SAN DIEGO, CALIFORNIA

With chocolate, bananas and peanut butter, this bread has it all. At less than 275 calories per slice, it's perfect for breakfast, dessert or an afternoon snack.

1/4	cup butter, softened
1	cup sugar
2	eggs
1	cup mashed ripe bananas (about 2 medium)
1/3	cup fat-free plain yogurt
1	tsp. vanilla extract
1-1/2	cups all-purpose flour
1/2	cup whole wheat pastry flour
3/4	tsp. baking soda
1/2	tsp. salt
1/2	tsp. ground cinnamon
1/2	cup peanut butter chips
1/2	cup semisweet chocolate chips, melted

1. In a large bowl, beat butter and sugar until crumbly, about 2 minutes. Add eggs, one at a time, beating well after each addition. Beat in the bananas, yogurt and vanilla. Combine the flours, baking soda, salt and cinnamon; gradually beat into the butter mixture. Stir in peanut butter chips.

2. Remove 1 cup batter to a small bowl; stir in chocolate until well blended. Pour half of the remaining plain batter into a 9-in. x 5-in. loaf pan coated with cooking spray; top with half of the chocolate batter. Repeat layers. Cut through batter with a knife to swirl.

3. Bake at 350° for 40-50 minutes or until a toothpick inserted near the center comes out clean. Cool for 10 minutes before removing from pan to a wire rack.

Nutrition Facts: 1 slice equals 272 calories, 9 g fat (5 g saturated fat), 45 mg cholesterol, 238 mg sodium, 44 g carbohydrate, 2 g fiber, 5 g protein.

Wheat Germ Streusel Banana Muffins

PREP: 20 min. BAKE: 20 min. YIELD: 10 muffins

TRISHA KRUSE • EAGLE, IDAHO

Using a mild oil like canola adds moisture and tenderness without changing flavor. You'll love the good, healthy feeling and great taste these muffins provide!

- 1 cup all-purpose flour
- 1/2 cup whole wheat flour
- 1/3 cup packed brown sugar
- 1 tsp. baking powder
- 1/2 tsp. baking soda
- 1/2 tsp. salt
- 1-1/3 cups mashed ripe bananas (about 3 medium)
- 1 egg
- 2 Tbsp. canola oil
- 2 Tbsp. unsweetened applesauce

STREUSEL:
- 1/4 cup packed brown sugar
- 2 Tbsp. toasted wheat germ
- 1/8 tsp. ground cinnamon
- 1 Tbsp. cold butter
- 2 Tbsp. finely chopped walnuts

1. In a large bowl, combine the flours, brown sugar, baking powder, baking soda and salt. In another bowl, beat the bananas, egg, oil and applesauce until well blended. Stir into dry ingredients just until moistened.

2. Coat muffin cups with cooking spray or use paper liners; fill two-thirds full with batter. For streusel, combine the brown sugar, wheat germ and cinnamon; cut in butter until crumbly. Stir in walnuts. Sprinkle over batter.

3. Bake at 375° for 18-22 minutes or until a toothpick inserted near the center comes out clean. Cool for 5 minutes before removing from pan to a wire rack.

Nutrition Facts: 1 muffin equals 203 calories, 6 g fat (1 g saturated fat), 24 mg cholesterol, 242 mg sodium, 36 g carbohydrate, 2 g fiber, 4 g protein.

Steamed Hawaiian Bread ⬛S

PREP: 20 min. COOK: 45 min. + standing
YIELD: 1 loaf (6 wedges)

ROXANNE CHAN • ALBANY, CALIFORNIA

For a moist and flavorful loaf of bread that won't overheat your kitchen, try this unique steaming method. You'll love the subtle sweetness of banana and coconut.

- 3/4 cup all-purpose flour
- 1/2 cup ground almonds, toasted
- 1/4 cup flaked coconut
- 1 tsp. baking powder
- 1/4 tsp. baking soda
- 1/3 cup coconut milk
- 1/4 cup honey
- 3 Tbsp. mashed ripe banana
- 1/4 tsp. coconut extract

1. In a large bowl, combine the first five ingredients. Combine the coconut milk, honey, banana and extract; stir into dry ingredients just until moistened. Pour into a 2-cup stoneware dish or bowl coated with cooking spray; cover with foil.

2. Place on a rack in a deep kettle; add 1 in. of hot water to the kettle. Bring to a gentle boil; cover and steam for 45-50 minutes or until a toothpick inserted near the center comes out clean, adding more water as needed.

3. Remove dish from kettle; let stand for 15 minutes before removing bread from dish.

Nutrition Facts: 1 wedge equals 197 calories, 8 g fat (4 g saturated fat), 0 cholesterol, 132 mg sodium, 29 g carbohydrate, 2 g fiber, 4 g protein.

STEAMED HAWAIIAN BREAD

WHEAT GERM STREUSEL BANANA MUFFINS

Cheese Flatbread C

PREP: 5 min. + rising BAKE: 20 min. YIELD: 16 servings

SHARON DELANEY-CHRONIS • SOUTH MILWAUKEE, WISCONSIN

The convenience of frozen bread dough and dried herbs makes this treat about as easy as it gets. To boost fiber, you can also use frozen whole wheat bread dough.

> 1   loaf (1 lb.) frozen bread dough, thawed
> 2   Tbsp. butter, softened
> 2   tsp. paprika
> 1/2 tsp. garlic powder
> 1/2 tsp. dried oregano
> 1/2 tsp. dried basil
> 1   cup (4 oz.) shredded part-skim mozzarella cheese

1. On a lightly floured surface, roll dough into a 16-in. x 11-in. rectangle. Transfer to a 15-in. x 10-in. x 1-in. baking pan coated with cooking spray; build up edges slightly. Spread with butter. Sprinkle with paprika, garlic powder, oregano and basil. Prick the dough several times with a fork; sprinkle with cheese. Cover and let rise for 30 minutes.

2. Bake at 375° for 20-25 minutes or until crust is golden brown and cheese is melted. Serve warm.

Nutrition Facts: 1 piece equals 111 calories, 4 g fat (2 g saturated fat), 8 mg cholesterol, 202 mg sodium, 14 g carbohydrate, 1 g fiber, 5 g protein. **Diabetic Exchanges:** 1 starch, 1/2 fat.

Banana Date-Nut Mini Muffins F S C

PREP: 15 min. BAKE: 15 min./batch YIELD: 4 dozen

LILLIAN JULOW • GAINESVILLE, FLORIDA

These little muffins have so much flavor, they don't need butter or jam to make them complete. Keep some in the freezer for fast snacks. Be sure to not overmix the wet and dry ingredients, so the muffins stay tender.

> 1   cup mashed ripe bananas (about 2 medium)
> 3/4 cup sugar
> 1/3 cup unsweetened applesauce
> 3   Tbsp. canola oil
> 1   egg
> 3/4 cup all-purpose flour
> 3/4 cup whole wheat flour
> 1/2 cup quick-cooking oats
> 1-1/2 tsp. baking powder
> 1/2 tsp. baking soda
> 1/3 cup chopped dates
> 1/4 cup finely chopped walnuts
> 1   tsp. grated lemon peel

1. In a large bowl, beat bananas, sugar, applesauce, oil and egg until well blended. Combine the flours, oats, baking powder and baking soda; gradually beat into banana mixture until blended. Stir in the dates, walnuts and lemon peel.

2. Coat miniature muffin cups with cooking spray or use paper liners; fill half full with batter. Bake at 350° for 12-14 minutes or until a toothpick comes out clean. Cool for 5 minutes before removing from pans to wire racks.

Nutrition Facts: 1 muffin equals 49 calories, 1 g fat (trace saturated fat), 4 mg cholesterol, 27 mg sodium, 9 g carbohydrate, 1 g fiber, 1 g protein. **Diabetic Exchange:** 1/2 starch.

Cranberry-Pecan Corn Muffins

PREP: 15 min. **COOK:** 20 min. **YIELD:** 1 dozen

LISA VARNER • GREENVILLE, SOUTH CAROLINA

I found a low-fat recipe for corn muffins and added cranberries and pecans to make a wonderful new dish. They have just the right flavor for the holidays or any time.

1-3/4 cups yellow cornmeal
  3/4 cup all-purpose flour
1-1/4 tsp. baking soda
  1/2 tsp. salt
1-1/2 cups (12 oz.) fat-free plain yogurt
    1 egg
  1/4 cup canola oil
  1/4 cup honey
  1/2 cup dried cranberries
  1/4 cup chopped pecans

1. In a large bowl, combine the cornmeal, flour, baking soda and salt. In another bowl, combine the yogurt, egg, oil and honey. Stir into dry ingredients just until moistened. Fold in cranberries and pecans. Coat muffin cups with cooking spray; fill three-fourths full with batter.

2. Bake at 375° for 18-20 minutes or until a toothpick inserted near the center comes out clean. Cool for 5 minutes before removing from pans to wire racks. Serve warm.

Nutrition Facts: 1 muffin equals 185 calories, 6 g fat (1 g saturated fat), 16 mg cholesterol, 217 mg sodium, 29 g carbohydrate, 2 g fiber, 4 g protein. **Diabetic Exchanges:** 2 starch, 1 fat.

Candy Cane Chocolate Loaves S

PREP: 25 min. **BAKE:** 50 min. + cooling
YIELD: 3 loaves (12 slices each)

SHELLY PLATTEN • AMHERST, WISCONSIN

Leftover candy canes after Christmas inspired me to combine them with a favorite chocolate bread recipe.

  1/4 cup butter, softened
1-2/3 cups packed brown sugar
    4 egg whites
    2 eggs
  3/4 cup strong brewed coffee
  1/2 cup reduced-fat vanilla yogurt
  1/4 cup canola oil
    1 Tbsp. vanilla extract

  1/4 tsp. peppermint extract
3-1/2 cups all-purpose flour
  3/4 cup baking cocoa
1-1/2 tsp. baking soda
  1/2 tsp. salt
1-1/2 cups buttermilk
    1 cup (6 oz.) miniature semisweet chocolate chips
TOPPING:
  1/3 cup vanilla or white chips
    3 Tbsp. crushed candy canes

1. In a large bowl, beat butter and brown sugar until crumbly, about 2 minutes. Add the egg whites, eggs, coffee, yogurt, oil and extracts until blended.

2. Combine the flour, cocoa, baking soda and salt; add to the butter mixture alternately with buttermilk, beating well after each addition. Fold in chocolate chips.

3. Transfer to three 8-in x 4-in. loaf pans coated with cooking spray. Bake at 350° for 50-55 minutes or until a toothpick inserted near the center comes out clean. Cool for 10 minutes before removing from pans to wire racks to cool completely.

4. For topping, in a microwave, melt vanilla chips; stir until smooth. Drizzle over loaves. Sprinkle with crushed candies.

Nutrition Facts: 1 slice equals 162 calories, 5 g fat (2 g saturated fat), 16 mg cholesterol, 124 mg sodium, 26 g carbohydrate, 1 g fiber, 3 g protein. **Diabetic Exchanges:** 1-1/2 starch, 1 fat.

CRANBERRY-PECAN CORN MUFFINS

Hazelnut Wheat Bread

PREP: 20 min. **BAKE:** 3 hours
YIELD: 1 loaf (2 pounds, 12 slices)

RUTH FANGER • MONROE, OREGON

I developed this recipe to match the flavors of our favorite store-bought bread, adapting it to a recipe in my bread machine manual. It makes a great-tasting loaf!

 1 cup water (70° to 80°)
 1 Tbsp. honey
 1 Tbsp. butter, softened
 3 Tbsp. toasted wheat germ
 2 Tbsp. mashed potato flakes
 1 Tbsp. nonfat dry milk powder
 1 Tbsp. ground flaxseed
 1 Tbsp. sesame seeds
 1 Tbsp. poppy seeds
 1 tsp. salt
1-1/4 cups whole wheat flour
 1 cup bread flour
 1/4 cup chopped hazelnuts
1-1/2 tsp. active dry yeast

1. In bread machine pan, place all ingredients in order suggested by manufacturer. Choose crust color and loaf size if available.

2. Bake according to bread machine directions (check dough after 5 minutes of mixing; add 1 to 2 Tbsp. of water or flour if needed).

Nutrition Facts: 1 slice equals 127 calories, 4 g fat (1 g saturated fat), 3 mg cholesterol, 213 mg sodium, 21 g carbohydrate, 3 g fiber, 5 g protein. **Diabetic Exchanges:** 1 starch, 1/2 fat.

Asparagus Scones

PREP: 25 min. **BAKE:** 20 min. + cooling
YIELD: 8 scones

MARY ANN DELL • PHOENIXVILLE, PENNSYLVANIA

Featuring fresh asparagus, these moist scones have a mild peppery bite and go great with soup for a light lunch. I sometimes substitute Parmesan and smoked mozzarella cheese for the cheddar.

1-3/4 cups cut fresh asparagus (1/4-in. pieces)
 2 cups all-purpose flour
 1 Tbsp. sugar
 2 tsp. baking powder
 1/2 tsp. salt
 1/4 tsp. baking soda
 1/4 tsp. pepper
 1/4 tsp. cayenne pepper
 1/4 cup cold butter
 3/4 cup plus 2 Tbsp. buttermilk, *divided*
 1/2 cup shredded reduced-fat cheddar cheese

1. In a large saucepan, bring 1/2 in. of water to a boil. Add asparagus; cover and boil for 3 minutes. Drain and immediately place asparagus in ice water. Drain and pat dry; set aside.

2. In a large bowl, combine the flour, sugar, baking powder, salt, baking soda, pepper and cayenne. Cut in butter until mixture resembles coarse crumbs. Stir in 3/4 cup buttermilk just until moistened. Stir in cheese and asparagus.

3. Turn onto a floured surface; knead 10 times. Transfer dough to a baking sheet coated with cooking spray. Pat into a 9-in. circle. Cut into eight wedges, but do not separate.

4. Brush with remaining buttermilk. Bake at 425° for 18-20 minutes or until golden brown. Cool scones on a wire rack.

Nutrition Facts: 1 scone equals 211 calories, 8 g fat (5 g saturated fat), 21 mg cholesterol, 419 mg sodium, 29 g carbohydrate, 2 g fiber, 7 g protein. **Diabetic Exchanges:** 2 starch, 1-1/2 fat.

Pumpkin Oat Bran Muffins

PREP: 15 min. BAKE: 20 min. YIELD: 9 muffins

IRENE ROBINSON • CINCINNATI, OHIO

The aroma from these muffins is especially wonderful in the fall. They're healthy and yummy and disappear quite quickly. They also freeze well.

1-1/2 cups oat bran
1/2 cup all-purpose flour
1/2 cup packed brown sugar
2 tsp. baking powder
1 tsp. pumpkin pie spice
1/2 tsp. salt
2 egg whites
1 cup canned pumpkin
1/2 cup fat-free milk
2 Tbsp. canola oil

1. In a small bowl, combine the first six ingredients. In another bowl, whisk the egg whites, pumpkin, milk and oil until well blended. Stir into dry ingredients just until moistened.

2. Coat muffin cups with cooking spray; fill half full. Bake at 400° for 20-25 minutes or until a toothpick comes out clean. Cool for 5 minutes before removing from pan to wire rack.

Nutrition Facts: 1 muffin equals 155 calories, 4 g fat (trace saturated fat), trace cholesterol, 246 mg sodium, 30 g carbohydrate, 4 g fiber, 5 g protein. **Diabetic Exchanges:** 2 starch, 1/2 fat.

Yogurt Wheat Bread ▪F

PREP: 30 min. + rising BAKE: 35 min.
YIELD: 1 loaf (16 slices)

CAROL FORCUM • MARION, ILLINOIS

I make my own yogurt and use it in cooking and baking as well as for snacking. You can use homemade yogurt or store-bought in this healthy wheat bread. It's a great way to keep things light.

1/2 cup plain yogurt
1 pkg. (1/4 oz.) active dry yeast
1 cup warm water (110° to 115°)
1 cup whole wheat flour
1/4 cup toasted wheat germ
1 Tbsp. sugar
1 Tbsp. olive oil
1 tsp. salt
1-2/3 to 2 cups bread flour

1. Let yogurt stand at room temperature for 15 minutes. In a large mixing bowl, dissolve yeast in warm water. Add the whole wheat flour, wheat germ, sugar, oil, salt and yogurt. Stir in enough bread flour to form a firm dough.

2. Turn onto a lightly floured surface; knead until smooth and elastic, about 6-8 minutes. Place in a bowl coated with cooking spray, turning once to coat the top. Cover and let rise in a warm place until doubled, about 1 hour.

3. Punch dough down. Turn onto a lightly floured surface; shape into a loaf. Place in a 9-in. x 5-in. loaf pan coated with cooking spray. Cover and let rise until doubled, about 40 minutes.

4. Bake at 375° for 35-40 minutes or until golden brown. Remove from pan to a wire rack to cool.

Nutrition Facts: 1 slice equals 92 calories, 1 g fat (trace saturated fat), 1 mg cholesterol, 152 mg sodium, 17 g carbohydrate, 2 g fiber, 4 g protein. **Diabetic Exchange:** 1 starch.

YOGURT WHEAT BREAD

PUMPKIN OAT BRAN MUFFINS

Cheese Straws F S C

PREP/TOTAL TIME: 30 min. YIELD: 4 dozen

ANN NACE • PERKASIE, PENNSYLVANIA

You'll have a hard time eating just one of these cheesy, buttery treats. They make a fun appetizer or side for soups or salads. Try twisting the sticks for an extra-fancy look.

- 1 cup all-purpose flour
- 1-1/2 tsp. baking powder
- 1/2 tsp. salt
- 1/2 cup shredded reduced-fat cheddar cheese
- 2 Tbsp. plus 1-1/2 tsp. cold butter
- 1/3 cup fat-free milk
- 2 tsp. paprika

1. In a small bowl, combine the flour, baking powder and salt; stir in cheese. Cut in butter until mixture resembles coarse crumbs. Gradually add milk, tossing with a fork until dough forms a ball.

2. On a lightly floured surface, roll dough into a 12-in. square. Cut in half lengthwise; cut each half widthwise into 1/2-in. strips. Sprinkle with paprika.

3. Place 1 in. apart on baking sheets coated with cooking spray. Bake at 425° for 6-8 minutes or until golden brown. Serve warm.

Nutrition Facts: 1 cheese straw equals 19 calories, 1 g fat (1 g saturated fat), 2 mg cholesterol, 52 mg sodium, 2 g carbohydrate, trace fiber, 1 g protein.

Southwest Surprise Bread F

PREP: 30 min. + rising BAKE: 40 min. + cooling
YIELD: 2 loaves (16 slices each)

SANDRA LEE HERR • STEVENS, PENNSYLVANIA

Fat-free refried beans are the surprise ingredient in these soft, high-rising loaves with just a hint of heat. Beans increase the bread's protein content and are so good! We serve this instead of garlic bread with Mexican dishes.

- 2 pkg. (1/4 oz. *each*) active dry yeast
- 2 cups warm 2% milk (110° to 115°)
- 1 can (16 oz.) spicy fat-free refried beans
- 2 Tbsp. sugar
- 2 Tbsp. butter, melted
- 2 tsp. salt
- 5 to 6 cups all-purpose flour

1. In a large mixing bowl, dissolve yeast in warm milk. Add the beans, sugar, butter, salt and 2 cups flour. Beat until smooth. Stir in enough remaining flour to form a firm dough.

2. Turn onto a lightly floured surface; knead until smooth and elastic, about 6-8 minutes. Place in a bowl coated with cooking spray, turning once to coat the top. Cover and let rise in a warm place until doubled, about 1 hour.

3. Punch dough down. Turn onto a lightly floured surface; divide in half. Shape into loaves. Place in two 9-in. x 5-in. loaf pans coated with cooking spray. Cover and let rise until doubled, about 30 minutes. Bake at 350° for 40-45 minutes or until golden brown. Remove from pans to wire racks to cool.

Nutrition Facts: 1 slice equals 104 calories, 1 g fat (1 g saturated fat), 3 mg cholesterol, 219 mg sodium, 19 g carbohydrate, 1 g fiber, 4 g protein. **Diabetic Exchange:** 1 starch.

Apricot-Banana Quick Bread

PREP: 20 min. BAKE: 1 hour + cooling
YIELD: 1 loaf (16 slices)

DIXIE TERRY • GOREVILLE, ILLINOIS

Bananas and apricots lend sweet flavor to this bread, while wheat germ gives it a dose of nutrition.

- 1/4 cup butter, softened
- 3/4 cup sugar
- 2 eggs
- 1 cup mashed ripe bananas
- 1-2/3 cups all-purpose flour
- 2/3 cup toasted wheat germ
- 2 tsp. baking powder
- 1/4 tsp. salt
- 1/4 tsp. baking soda
- 1 cup finely chopped dried apricots
- 2 tsp. grated lemon peel

CHEESE STRAWS

SOUTHWEST SURPRISE BREAD

MILK-FREE CORN BREAD

1. In a large mixing bowl, beat butter and sugar until crumbly, about 2 minutes. Add eggs, one at a time, beating well after each addition. Beat in bananas. Combine the flour, wheat germ, baking powder, salt and baking soda; gradually beat into the banana mixture. Stir in apricots and lemon peel.

2. Transfer to a 9-in. x 5-in. loaf pan coated with cooking spray.

3. Bake at 350° for 60-70 minutes or until a toothpick inserted near the center comes out clean. Cool for 10 minutes before removing from pan to a wire rack.

Nutrition Facts: 1 slice equals 168 calories, 4 g fat (2 g saturated fat), 34 mg cholesterol, 150 mg sodium, 30 g carbohydrate, 2 g fiber, 4 g protein. **Diabetic Exchanges:** 1-1/2 starch, 1/2 fruit, 1/2 fat.

Honey-Wheat Oatmeal Bread F

PREP: 10 min. BAKE: 3 hours
YIELD: 1 loaf (2 pounds, 20 slices)

WANNETTA EHNES • EAGLE BEND, MINNESOTA

This wholesome bread is great for the bread machine and uses less fat. Serve it with dinner or toasted for breakfast.

1-1/4 cups water (70° to 80°)
  1/2 cup honey
    2 Tbsp. canola oil
1-1/2 tsp. salt
    1 cup quick-cooking oats
1-1/2 cups bread flour
1-1/2 cups whole wheat flour
1 pkg. (1/4 oz.) active dry yeast

1. In bread machine pan, place all ingredients in order suggested by manufacturer. Select basic bread setting. Choose crust color and loaf size if available.

2. Bake according to bread machine directions (check dough after 5 minutes of mixing; add 1 to 2 tablespoons of water or flour if needed).

Nutrition Facts: 1 slice equals 115 calories, 2 g fat (trace saturated fat), 0 cholesterol, 178 mg sodium, 23 g carbohydrate, 2 g fiber, 3 g protein. **Diabetic Exchange:** 1-1/2 starch.

Milk-Free Corn Bread

PREP/TOTAL TIME: 30 min. YIELD: 9 servings

ANGIE PHILKILL • FORT GRATIOT, MICHIGAN

My children have food allergies, so I always take this bread with me when we're invited to dinner. It goes great with most any meal and my kids absolutely adore its hearty wedges. Best of all, I can whip it up and pull it out of the oven in just half an hour. What a time saver!

    1 cup all-purpose flour
    1 cup cornmeal
  1/4 cup sugar
    2 tsp. baking powder
  1/4 tsp. salt
    1 egg
    1 cup rice drink
    2 Tbsp. canola oil
    2 Tbsp. unsweetened applesauce

1. In a small bowl, combine the first five ingredients. In another bowl, whisk the egg, rice drink, oil and applesauce. Stir into dry ingredients just until moistened. Transfer to a 9-in. square baking pan coated with cooking spray.

2. Bake at 425° for 15-20 minutes or until a toothpick inserted near the center comes out clean. Serve warm.

Nutrition Facts: 1 piece equals 178 calories, 4 g fat (trace saturated fat), 24 mg cholesterol, 173 mg sodium, 31 g carbohydrate, 2 g fiber, 4 g protein. **Diabetic Exchanges:** 2 starch, 1/2 fat.

PINEAPPLE-APPLE CHICKEN SALAD

AVOCADO TURKEY WRAPS

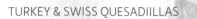
TURKEY & SWISS QUESADIILLAS

Table for Two

Now it's easier than ever for empty nesters, newlyweds and single cooks to prepare healthy fare without having to deal with lots of leftovers. Simply consider these sensational dishes, sized right for small households.

Turkey & Swiss Quesadillas

PREP/TOTAL TIME: 20 min. YIELD: 2 servings

KAREN O'SHEA • SPARKS, NEVADA

Light, lean and nutritious, this quick supper idea goes together in just minutes.

- 2 Tbsp. reduced-fat Parmesan peppercorn ranch salad dressing
- 1 Tbsp. Dijon mustard
- 2 whole wheat tortillas (8 in.)
- 2 slices reduced-fat Swiss cheese, halved
- 1/2 medium ripe avocado, peeled and thinly sliced
- 6 oz. sliced cooked turkey breast

Diced sweet red pepper, optional

1. In a small bowl, combine salad dressing and mustard; spread over one side of each tortilla. Place tortillas, spread side up, on a griddle coated with cooking spray.

2. Layer cheese, avocado and turkey over half of each tortilla. Fold over and cook over low heat for 1-2 minutes on each side or until cheese is melted. Garnish with red pepper if desired.

Nutrition Facts: 1 quesadilla equals 421 calories, 16 g fat (3 g saturated fat), 86 mg cholesterol, 566 mg sodium, 32 g carbohydrate, 5 g fiber, 38 g protein. **Diabetic Exchanges:** 4 lean meat, 2 starch, 2 fat.

Avocado Turkey Wraps

PREP/TOTAL TIME: 15 min. YIELD: 2 servings

HEALTHY COOKING TEST KITCHEN

These delicious sandwiches are perfect for brown-bag lunches. With sliced turkey, avocado and cheese, they'll add extra flavor to noontime meals. If you like, substitute tomato slices with a well-drained chunky salsa.

- 2 whole wheat tortillas (8 in.), room temperature
- 2 Tbsp. fat-free mayonnaise
- 1/4 lb. thinly sliced deli turkey
- 8 thin slices tomato
- 2 tsp. finely chopped jalapeno pepper
- 1/4 cup shredded reduced-fat cheddar cheese
- 2 tsp. minced fresh cilantro
- 1/2 medium ripe avocado, peeled and thinly sliced

1. Spread tortillas with mayonnaise. Top each with turkey, tomato, jalapeno, cheese, cilantro and avocado. Roll up and cut in half.

Editor's Note: Wear disposable gloves when cutting hot peppers; the oils can burn skin. Avoid touching your face.

Nutrition Facts: 1 wrap equals 342 calories, 15 g fat (4 g saturated fat), 37 mg cholesterol, 1,079 mg sodium, 34 g carbohydrate, 6 g fiber, 18 g protein.

Pineapple-Apple Chicken Salad

PREP/TOTAL TIME: 10 min. YIELD: 2 servings

PRISCILLA COTE • NEW HARTFORD, NEW YORK

This just might be the fastest chicken salad recipe ever! The fruit gives it a sweet touch, the almonds lend crunch, and the curry adds depth of flavor and color. Using a snack-size cup of pineapple means you won't have leftovers after you make this. You can replace the apple with a chopped pear if you like.

- 1 cup cubed cooked chicken breast
- 1/2 medium apple, chopped
- 1 snack-size cup (4 oz.) pineapple tidbits, drained
- 1/4 cup reduced-fat mayonnaise
- 2 Tbsp. slivered almonds
- 1/4 to 1/2 tsp. curry powder
- 2 cups torn mixed salad greens

1. In a large bowl, combine the first six ingredients. Serve with greens.

Nutrition Facts: 1 cup chicken salad with 1 cup salad greens equals 301 calories, 16 g fat (2 g saturated fat), 64 mg cholesterol, 302 mg sodium, 17 g carbohydrate, 4 g fiber, 23 g protein. **Diabetic Exchanges:** 3 lean meat, 2-1/2 fat, 1 vegetable, 1/2 fruit.

> Any cooked chicken can be used when making chicken salad, regardless of cooking method or seasonings. Just remove all chicken skin to keep fat at bay. When mixing your own **chicken salad,** get creative with healthy additions such as diced cucumber, peas and red onion.

Skillet Tacos

PREP/TOTAL TIME: 30 min. **YIELD:** 2 servings

MARIA GOBEL • GREENFIELD, WISCONSIN

If you like Mexican food, you'll be whipping up this fast and healthy version of tacos often. It's a great meal-in-one dish!

1/4	lb. lean ground turkey
2	Tbsp. chopped onion
2	Tbsp. chopped green pepper
1	can (8 oz.) tomato sauce
1/2	cup uncooked elbow macaroni
1/2	cup water
1/4	cup picante sauce
2	Tbsp. shredded fat-free cheddar cheese
1/4	cup crushed baked tortilla chip scoops
1/4	cup chopped avocado

Iceberg lettuce wedges and fat-free sour cream, optional

1. In a large nonstick skillet coated with cooking spray, cook the turkey, onion and green pepper over medium heat until turkey is no longer pink.

2. Stir in the tomato sauce, macaroni, water and picante sauce. Bring to a boil. Reduce heat; cover and simmer for 10-15 minutes or until macaroni is tender.

3. Divide between two plates; top with cheese, tortilla chips and avocado. Serve with lettuce and sour cream if desired.

Nutrition Facts: 1 serving (calculated without lettuce and sour cream) equals 267 calories, 9 g fat (2 g saturated fat), 46 mg cholesterol, 795 mg sodium, 30 g carbohydrate, 3 g fiber, 18 g protein. **Diabetic Exchanges:** 2 lean meat, 1-1/2 starch, 1 vegetable, 1/2 fat.

Baked Apple Surprise **F**

PREP: 10 min. **BAKE:** 35 min. **YIELD:** 2 servings

JESSICA LEVINSON • NYACK, NEW YORK

This sweet-savory recipe is a favorite. Use Brie instead of blue cheese if you like things creamier. My tip? Bake the apples in a muffin tin so they won't roll around.

2	medium apples
2	Tbsp. crumbled blue cheese, *divided*
2	Tbsp. quick-cooking oats
2	Tbsp. bran flakes
1	Tbsp. golden raisins
1	Tbsp. raisins
1	Tbsp. brown sugar

1. Cut apples in half lengthwise; remove cores. Place in an ungreased 8-in. square baking dish. Fill each half with 1 tsp. blue cheese.

2. In a small bowl, combine the oats, bran flakes, golden raisins, raisins and brown sugar; spoon into apples. Top with remaining cheese. Bake, uncovered, at 350° for 35-40 minutes or until tender.

Nutrition Facts: 2 filled apple halves equals 181 calories, 3 g fat (2 g saturated fat), 6 mg cholesterol, 141 mg sodium, 39 g carbohydrate, 5 g fiber, 3 g protein.

Fruity Crab Pasta Salad **F**

PREP/TOTAL TIME: 30 min. **YIELD:** 2 servings

DARLENE JUREK • FOLEY, MINNESOTA

A sweet ginger dressing spices up this tasty medley of oranges, grapes, crabmeat and pasta. It's an ideal warm-weather entree.

3/4	cup uncooked spiral pasta
1	pkg. (8 oz.) imitation crabmeat
1	snack-size cup (4 oz.) mandarin oranges, drained
1/4	cup halved seedless red grapes
1/4	cup halved seedless green grapes
1/4	cup reduced-fat plain yogurt
2	Tbsp. fat-free mayonnaise
1-1/2	tsp. honey
1/4	tsp. ground ginger

SKILLET TACOS

BAKED APPLE SURPRISE

CRISPY ASIAN
CHICKEN SALAD

1. Cook pasta according to package directions; drain and rinse in cold water. In a small bowl, combine the pasta, crab, oranges and grapes.

2. Combine the yogurt, mayonnaise, honey and ginger; pour over salad and toss to coat. Refrigerate until serving.

Nutrition Facts: 1-1/2 cups (prepared with reduced-fat yogurt and fat-free mayonnaise) equals 322 calories, 2 g fat (1 g saturated fat), 59 mg cholesterol, 215 mg sodium, 55 g carbohydrate, 2 g fiber, 21 g protein.

Crispy Asian Chicken Salad

PREP/TOTAL TIME: 30 min. **YIELD:** 2 servings

BETH DAUENHAUER • PUEBLO, COLORADO

Asian flavor, crunchy almonds and crispy breaded chicken make this hearty salad something special.

    2 boneless skinless chicken breast halves
       (4 oz. *each*)
    2 tsp. hoisin sauce
    1 tsp. sesame oil
  1/2 cup panko (Japanese) bread crumbs
    4 tsp. sesame seeds
    2 tsp. canola oil
    4 cups spring mix salad greens

    1 small green pepper, julienned
    1 small sweet red pepper, julienned
    1 medium carrot, julienned
  1/2 cup sliced fresh mushrooms
    2 Tbsp. thinly sliced onion
    2 Tbsp. sliced almonds, toasted
  1/4 cup reduced-fat sesame ginger
       salad dressing

1. Flatten chicken breasts to 1/2-in. thickness. Combine hoisin sauce and sesame oil; brush over chicken. In a shallow bowl, combine panko and sesame seeds; dip chicken in mixture.

2. In a large nonstick skillet coated with cooking spray, cook chicken in oil for 4-5 minutes on each side or until a thermometer reads 170°.

3. Meanwhile, divide salad greens between two plates. Top with the peppers, carrot, mushrooms and onion.

4. Slice chicken; place over vegetables. Sprinkle with almonds and drizzle with dressing.

Nutrition Facts: 1 salad equals 386 calories, 17 g fat (2 g saturated fat), 63 mg cholesterol, 620 mg sodium, 29 g carbohydrate, 6 g fiber, 30 g protein. **Diabetic Exchanges:** 3 lean meat, 2 vegetable, 2 fat, 1 starch.

CHICKEN CAESAR SALAD

Chicken Caesar Salad

PREP/TOTAL TIME: 25 min.   YIELD: 2 servings

KAY ANDERSEN • BEAR, DELAWARE

Topping a delicious Caesar salad with a tender grilled chicken breast ensures a healthy, filling meal that always satisfies.

2	boneless skinless chicken breast halves (4 oz. *each*)
2	tsp. olive oil
1/4	tsp. garlic salt
1/4	tsp. paprika
1/4	tsp. pepper
1/8	tsp. dried basil
1/8	tsp. dried oregano
4	cups torn romaine
1	small tomato, thinly sliced
1/4	cup fat-free creamy Caesar salad dressing

Caesar salad croutons, optional

1. Brush chicken with oil. Combine the garlic salt, paprika, pepper, basil and oregano; sprinkle over chicken. Grill, uncovered, over medium heat or broil 4 in. from the heat for 4-7 minutes on each side or until a thermometer reads 170°.

2. Arrange romaine and tomato on plates. Cut chicken into strips; place over salads. Drizzle with dressing. Sprinkle with croutons if desired.

Nutrition Facts: 1 serving (calculated without croutons) equals 236 calories, 8 g fat (1 g saturated fat), 63 mg cholesterol, 653 mg sodium, 17 g carbohydrate, 4 g fiber, 26 g protein. **Diabetic Exchanges:** 3 lean meat, 2 vegetable, 1 starch, 1 fat.

Italian Chicken Skillet Supper c

PREP/TOTAL TIME: 30 min.   YIELD: 2 servings

BARBARA LENTO • HOUSTON, PENNSYLVANIA

Romano cheese, sliced vegetables and pine nuts jazz up this saucy chicken dinner. It's easy, and we love it!

2	boneless skinless chicken breast halves (4 oz. *each*)
1/4	tsp. garlic salt
1/4	tsp. pepper
2	tsp. reduced-fat butter
1	tsp. olive oil
1/4	lb. small fresh mushrooms
1/2	medium onion, chopped
1/4	cup chopped sweet red pepper

1 Tbsp. pine nuts	1 Tbsp. lemon juice
2 cups fresh baby spinach	3 Tbsp. sugar
1 Tbsp. all-purpose flour	TOPPING:
1/2 cup reduced-sodium chicken broth	1 large tart apple, peeled and thinly sliced
1-1/2 tsp. spicy brown mustard	1 tsp. sugar
2 tsp. shredded Romano cheese	1/4 tsp. ground cinnamon

1. Flatten chicken slightly; sprinkle with garlic salt and pepper. In a large nonstick skillet, cook chicken in butter and oil over medium heat for 3-4 minutes on each side or until no longer pink. Remove chicken and keep warm.

2. In the same skillet, saute the mushrooms, onion, red pepper and pine nuts until vegetables are tender. Add spinach; cook and stir for 2-3 minutes or until wilted. Stir in flour. Gradually stir in broth and mustard. Bring to a boil. Reduce heat; cook and stir for 2 minutes or until thickened.

3. Return chicken to the pan; heat through. Sprinkle with the cheese.

Editor's Note: This recipe was tested with Land O'Lakes light stick butter.

Nutrition Facts: 1 chicken breast half with 1/2 cup vegetable mixture equals 248 calories, 10 g fat (3 g saturated fat), 70 mg cholesterol, 548 mg sodium, 12 g carbohydrate, 3 g fiber, 29 g protein. **Diabetic Exchanges:** 3 lean meat, 2 vegetable, 1-1/2 fat.

Puffy Apple Omelet S M

PREP/TOTAL TIME: 30 min. **YIELD:** 2 servings

MELISSA DAVENPORT • CAMPBELL, MINNESOTA

This is one omelet you won't forget because of its unique and delicious flavors!

3 Tbsp. all-purpose flour	
1/4 tsp. baking powder	
2 eggs, *separated*	
3 Tbsp. fat-free milk	

1. In a small bowl, combine flour and baking powder. In a small bowl, whisk the egg yolks, milk and lemon juice. Stir into dry ingredients and mix well; set aside.

2. In another small bowl, beat egg whites on medium speed until soft peaks form. Gradually beat in sugar, 1 Tbsp. at a time, on high until stiff peaks form. Fold into yolk mixture.

3. Pour into a shallow 1-1/2-qt. baking dish coated with cooking spray. Arrange apple slices on top. Combine sugar and cinnamon; sprinkle over apples.

4. Bake, uncovered, at 375° for 18-20 minutes or until a knife inserted near the center comes out clean. Cut in half.

Nutrition Facts: 1 serving equals 249 calories, 5 g fat (2 g saturated fat), 212 mg cholesterol, 130 mg sodium, 44 g carbohydrate, 2 g fiber, 9 g protein. **Diabetic Exchanges:** 2 starch, 1 lean meat, 1 fruit.

For quick preparation, use an **apple corer.** Simply push apple corer down into center of a washed apple. Twist and remove the center seeds and membranes.

ITALIAN CHICKEN SKILLET SUPPER

PUFFY APPLE OMELET

Salmon Bean Wraps

PREP: 20 min. + chilling **YIELD:** 2 servings

JESS APF • BERKELEY, CALIFORNIA

Here's a healthy wrap low in saturated fat and full of the wonderful nutrients found in avocado, black beans and smoked salmon. It's super easy and great for a quick meal.

- 1/4 cup cubed avocado
- 3/4 cup canned black beans, rinsed and drained
- 1/4 cup finely chopped tomato
- 3 Tbsp. minced fresh cilantro
- 3 Tbsp. fat-free sour cream
- 2 Tbsp. finely chopped red onion
- 1-1/2 tsp. lemon juice
- 1/4 tsp. pepper
- 2 whole wheat tortillas (8 in.), room temperature
- 2 oz. flaked smoked salmon fillets
- 1 cup shredded lettuce

1. In a large bowl, mash avocado. Stir in the beans, tomato, cilantro, sour cream, red onion, lemon juice and pepper. Cover and refrigerate for at least 30 minutes.

2. Spread 3/4 cup over each tortilla. Top with salmon and lettuce; roll up and secure with toothpicks.

Nutrition Facts: 1 wrap equals 315 calories, 7 g fat (1 g saturated fat), 10 mg cholesterol, 603 mg sodium, 44 g carbohydrate, 8 g fiber, 16 g protein. **Diabetic Exchanges:** 2 starch, 2 lean meat, 1 vegetable, 1/2 fat.

Persian Poached Pears S

PREP: 15 min. **COOK:** 50 min. + chilling
YIELD: 2 servings

TRISHA KRUSE • EAGLE, IDAHO

These fragrant pears are a dramatic way to finish off a Middle Eastern feast. They're delicious, aromatic and a unique twist on basic poached pears.

- 2 medium firm pears
- 1 vanilla bean
- 2-1/4 cups water
- 1/2 cup white grape juice
- 2 dried apricots, chopped
- 1 Tbsp. sugar
- 1 Tbsp. honey
- 1 lemon peel strip
- 1 whole clove
- 2 Tbsp. chopped almonds, toasted

1. Core pears from the bottom, leaving stems intact. Peel pears; cut 1/4 in. from the bottom of each to level if necessary. Split vanilla bean and scrape seeds; set aside.

2. In a small saucepan, combine the water, grape juice, apricots, sugar, honey, lemon strip, clove, vanilla bean and seeds. Bring to a boil. Reduce heat; place the pears on their sides in the saucepan and poach, uncovered, for 18-22 minutes or until the pears are almost tender, basting occasionally with poaching liquid.

3. Remove pears and apricots with a slotted spoon; cool slightly. Cover and refrigerate. Bring poaching liquid to a boil; cook until liquid is reduced to 1/4 cup. Discard the vanilla bean, lemon strip and clove. Cover and refrigerate for at least 1 hour.

4. Place pears on dessert plates. Drizzle with poaching liquid. Sprinkle with apricots and almonds.

Nutrition Facts: 1 pear with 2 Tbsp. sauce and 1 Tbsp. almonds equals 258 calories, 4 g fat (trace saturated fat), 0 cholesterol, 6 mg sodium, 56 g carbohydrate, 7 g fiber, 3 g protein.

SALMON BEAN WRAPS

PERSIAN POACHED PEARS

Grilled Beef Tenderloins C

PREP: 10 min. + marinating **GRILL:** 10 min.
YIELD: 2 servings

PATRICIA SWART • GALLOWAY, NEW JERSEY

Who says that healthy foods have to be bland? Bold flavors bring out the best in these super tender steaks.

1/4	cup dry red wine
1/4	cup reduced-sodium soy sauce
1/2	tsp. garlic powder
1/2	tsp. dried oregano
1/4	tsp. ground cumin
1/4	tsp. ground ancho chili pepper
1/4	tsp. pepper
2	beef tenderloin steaks (6 oz. *each*)

1. In a large resealable plastic bag, combine the first seven ingredients. Add the steaks; seal bag and turn to coat. Refrigerate for up to 4 hours.

2. Drain and discard marinade. Using long-handled tongs, moisten a paper towel with cooking oil and lightly coat the grill rack. Grill steaks, covered, over medium heat or broil 4 in. from the heat for 4-6 minutes on each side or until meat reaches desired doneness (for medium-rare, a thermometer should read 145°; medium, 160°; well-done, 170°).

Nutrition Facts: 1 steak equals 263 calories, 10 g fat (4 g saturated fat), 75 mg cholesterol, 402 mg sodium, 1 g carbohydrate, trace fiber, 37 g protein. **Diabetic Exchange:** 5 lean meat.

Garlic-Dill Smashed Potatoes F M

PREP: 25 min. **COOK:** 20 min. **YIELD:** 2 servings

AMBER HUFF • ATHENS, GEORGIA

These delicious potatoes are so creamy you simply won't believe they are light.

3	garlic cloves
1/4	tsp. olive oil
3/4	lb. red potatoes, cubed
2	Tbsp. fat-free milk
2	Tbsp. reduced-fat sour cream
1-1/2	tsp. grated Parmesan cheese
1	tsp. snipped fresh dill
1/4	tsp. salt
1/8	tsp. pepper

Dash cayenne pepper

1. Place garlic on a double thickness of heavy-duty foil. Drizzle with oil. Wrap foil around garlic. Bake at 425° for 15-20 minutes. Cool for 10-15 minutes.

2. Meanwhile, place potatoes in a small saucepan and cover with water. Bring to a boil. Reduce heat; cover and cook for 10-15 minutes or until tender. Drain. Transfer potatoes to a small bowl; squeeze softened garlic into bowl. Add the remaining ingredients; mash potatoes.

Nutrition Facts: 3/4 cup equals 165 calories, 2 g fat (1 g saturated fat), 6 mg cholesterol, 342 mg sodium, 30 g carbohydrate, 3 g fiber, 6 g protein. **Diabetic Exchange:** 2 starch.

VERY VEGGIE OMELET

Very Veggie Omelet C M

PREP/TOTAL TIME: 20 min. YIELD: 2 servings

JAN HOUBERG • REDDICK, ILLINOIS

This tasty omelet packed with veggies is a wonderful wake-up call any morning. Because it's loaded with cheese, vegetables, and herbs and seasonings, however, it's great any time of the day. It's a delicious way to use up summer's bounty!

1	small onion, chopped
1/4	cup chopped green pepper
1	Tbsp. butter
1	small zucchini, chopped
3/4	cup chopped tomato
1/4	tsp. dried oregano
1/8	tsp. pepper
4	egg whites
1/4	cup water
1/4	tsp. cream of tartar
1/4	tsp. salt
1/4	cup egg substitute
1/2	cup shredded reduced-fat cheddar cheese, *divided*

1. In a large nonstick skillet, saute onion and green pepper in butter until tender. Add the zucchini, tomato, oregano and pepper. Cook and stir for 5-8 minutes or until vegetables are tender and liquid is nearly evaporated. Set aside and keep warm.

2. In a small bowl, beat egg whites, water, cream of tartar and salt until stiff peaks form. Place egg substitute in another bowl; fold in egg white mixture. Pour into a 10-in. ovenproof skillet coated with cooking spray. Cook for 5 minutes over medium heat or until lightly browned on bottom.

3. Bake, uncovered, at 350° for 9-10 minutes or until a knife inserted near the center comes out clean. Carefully run a knife around edge of pan to loosen.

4. With a knife, score center of omelet. Place vegetable mixture and half of cheese on one side; fold other side over filling. Sprinkle with remaining cheese. Cut in half to serve.

Nutrition Facts: 1/2 omelet equals 197 calories, 9 g fat (5 g saturated fat), 21 mg cholesterol, 639 mg sodium, 10 g carbohydrate, 2 g fiber, 19 g protein. **Diabetic Exchanges:** 3 lean meat, 2 vegetable, 1-1/2 fat.

Breakfast Mushroom Cups C M

PREP/TOTAL TIME: 25 min. YIELD: 2 servings

SARA MORRIS • LAGUNA BEACH, CALIFORNIA

Here's a fun and surprisingly hearty breakfast dish packed with flavor and richness.

2	large portobello mushrooms, stems removed
1/8	tsp. garlic salt
1/8	tsp. pepper, *divided*

1 small onion, chopped
1/2 tsp. olive oil
1 cup fresh baby spinach
1/2 cup egg substitute
1/8 tsp. salt
1/4 cup crumbled goat or feta cheese
2 Tbsp. minced fresh basil

1. Place mushrooms on a 15-in. x 10-in. x 1-in. baking pan. Spray with cooking spray; sprinkle with garlic salt and dash pepper. Bake at 425° for 10 minutes or until tender.

2. In a large saucepan, saute onion in oil until tender. Stir in spinach and cook until wilted. In a small bowl, whisk the egg substitute, salt and remaining pepper; add to pan. Cook and stir until set.

3. Spoon egg mixture into mushrooms; sprinkle with cheese and basil.

Nutrition Facts: 1 stuffed mushroom equals 126 calories, 5 g fat (2 g saturated fat), 18 mg cholesterol, 472 mg sodium, 10 g carbohydrate, 3 g fiber, 11 g protein. **Diabetic Exchanges:** 2 vegetable, 1 lean meat, 1/2 fat.

Pork Tenderloin with Horseradish Sauce C

PREP: 15 min. **BAKE:** 30 min. + standing
YIELD: 2 servings

ANN BERGER OSOWSKI • ORANGE CITY, FLORIDA

This delicious combo of tenderloin and savory sauce receives rave reviews each time I make it, and I've shared the recipe with numerous friends. The entree is very versatile; the pork can be served hot or cold, and the creamy sauce can also be used as a zesty dip for fresh veggies.

1/2 tsp. steak seasoning
1/2 tsp. dried rosemary, crushed
1/2 tsp. dried thyme
1 pork tenderloin (3/4 lb.)
2 garlic cloves, peeled and quartered

1 tsp. balsamic vinegar
1 tsp. olive oil
HORSERADISH SAUCE:
2 Tbsp. fat-free mayonnaise
2 Tbsp. reduced-fat sour cream
1 tsp. prepared horseradish
1/8 tsp. grated lemon peel
Dash salt and pepper

1. In a small bowl, combine the steak seasoning, rosemary and thyme; rub over meat.

2. Using the point of a sharp knife, make eight slits in the tenderloin. Insert garlic into slits. Place meat on a rack in a foil-lined shallow roasting pan. Drizzle with vinegar and oil.

3. Bake, uncovered, at 350° for 30-40 minutes or until a thermometer reads 160°. Let stand for 10 minutes before slicing.

4. Meanwhile, combine the sauce ingredients; chill until serving. Serve with pork.

Nutrition Facts: 4 oz. cooked pork with 2 Tbsp. sauce equals 258 calories, 10 g fat (3 g saturated fat), 101 mg cholesterol, 450 mg sodium, 5 g carbohydrate, 1 g fiber, 35 g protein. **Diabetic Exchanges:** 5 lean meat, 1 fat.

BREAKFAST MUSHROOM CUPS

PORK TENDERLOIN WITH HORSERADISH SAUCE

Toasted Clubs with Dill Mayo

PREP/TOTAL TIME: 20 min. YIELD: 2 servings

JENNY FLAKE • NEWPORT BEACH, CALIFORNIA

Simple to prepare, appealing to the eyes and loaded with flavor, this bistro-style sandwich couldn't be better! Swap in whatever lean deli meats and cheeses you have on hand— turkey and Swiss make a great combo, too.

2	Tbsp. fat-free mayonnaise
1/4	tsp. dill weed
3/4	tsp. lemon juice, *divided*
1/8	tsp. pepper
4	slices whole wheat bread, toasted
4	thin slices deli roast beef
4	thin slices deli ham
2	slices reduced-fat provolone cheese
2	Bibb lettuce leaves
2	slices tomato
2	center-cut bacon strips, cooked and crumbled
1/4	cup alfalfa sprouts
1/4	medium ripe avocado, peeled and sliced

1. In a small bowl, combine the mayonnaise, dill, 1/4 tsp. lemon juice and pepper; spread over toast. Layer two slices with beef, ham, cheese, lettuce, tomato, bacon and alfalfa sprouts.

2. Drizzle avocado with remaining lemon juice; place over alfalfa sprouts. Top with remaining toast. Secure with toothpicks.

Nutrition Facts: 1 sandwich equals 328 calories, 13 g fat (4 g saturated fat), 47 mg cholesterol, 1,056 mg sodium, 29 g carbohydrate, 6 g fiber, 26 g protein.

TOASTED CLUBS WITH DILL MAYO

Fresh Vegetable Omelet **C** **M**

PREP: 30 min. **BAKE:** 10 min. **YIELD:** 2 servings

EDIE DESPAIN • LOGAN, UTAH

Breakfast feels extra-special when you wake up to a lovely, satisfying and good-for-you omelet. Chock-full of fresh vegetables and great flavor, it's a filling main dish you'll be proud to serve.

4	egg whites
1/4	cup water
1/4	tsp. cream of tartar
2	eggs
1/4	tsp. salt
1	tsp. butter
1	medium tomato, chopped
1	small zucchini, chopped
1	small onion, chopped
1/4	cup chopped green pepper
1/2	tsp. Italian seasoning
1/3	cup shredded reduced-fat cheddar cheese

1. In a small bowl, beat the egg whites, water and cream of tartar until stiff peaks form. In a large bowl, beat eggs and salt until thick and lemon-colored, about 5 minutes. Fold in the whites.

2. In a 10-in. ovenproof skillet coated with cooking spray, melt butter. Pour egg mixture into skillet. Cook for 5 minutes over medium heat or until puffed and lightly browned on the bottom. Bake, uncovered, at 350° for 10-12 minutes or until a knife inserted 2 in. from edge comes out clean.

3. Meanwhile, in a large skillet, saute the tomato, zucchini, onion, green pepper and Italian seasoning until tender. Carefully run a knife around edge of ovenproof skillet to loosen. With a knife, score center of omelet. Place vegetables on one side and sprinkle with cheese; fold other side over filling. Slide onto a serving plate; cut in half.

Nutrition Facts: 1/2 omelet equals 222 calories, 11 g fat (5 g saturated fat), 231 mg cholesterol, 617 mg sodium, 12 g carbohydrate, 3 g fiber, 20 g protein. **Diabetic Exchanges:** 3 lean meat, 2 vegetable, 1/2 fat.

Italian seasoning can be found in the spice aisle of most grocery stores. Basic blends often contain marjoram, thyme, rosemary, savory, sage, oregano and basil. If your grocery store does not carry Italian seasoning, ask the manager if it can be ordered.

Grilled Jerk Shrimp Orzo Salad

PREP: 25 min. GRILL: 25 min. YIELD: 2 servings

EILEEN BUDNYK • PALM BEACH GARDENS, FLORIDA

You'll go crazy over the heat, seasonings and appearance of this colorful main-dish salad. Try it!

- 1 large ear sweet corn in husk
- 1 tsp. olive oil
- 1/3 cup uncooked whole wheat orzo pasta
- 6 fresh asparagus spears, trimmed
- 1/2 lb. uncooked medium shrimp, peeled and deveined
- 1 Tbsp. Caribbean jerk seasoning
- 1 small sweet red pepper, chopped

DRESSING:
- 2 Tbsp. white vinegar
- 1 Tbsp. water
- 1 Tbsp. lime juice
- 1 Tbsp. olive oil
- 1/8 tsp. salt
- 1/8 tsp. pepper

1. Carefully peel back corn husk to within 1 in. of bottom; remove silk. Brush corn with oil. Rewrap corn in husk and secure with kitchen string. Grill corn, covered, over medium heat for 25-30 minutes or until tender, turning often.

2. Meanwhile, cook orzo according to package directions. Drain and rinse in cold water; set aside.

3. Thread asparagus spears onto two parallel metal or soaked wooden skewers. Rub shrimp with jerk seasoning; thread onto two skewers. Grill asparagus and shrimp, covered, over medium heat for 5-8

minutes or until asparagus is crisp-tender and shrimp turn pink, turning once.

4. Cut corn from cob; place in a large bowl. Cut asparagus into 1-in. pieces; add to bowl. Add the shrimp, orzo and pepper. In a small bowl, whisk the dressing ingredients. Pour over salad; toss to coat.

Nutrition Facts: 2 cups equals 352 calories, 12 g fat (2 g saturated fat), 138 mg cholesterol, 719 mg sodium, 38 g carbohydrate, 8 g fiber, 26 g protein. **Diabetic Exchanges:** 3 lean meat, 2 starch, 1 vegetable, 1 fat.

Stuffed Ranch Chicken c

PREP: 15 min. BAKE: 25 min. YIELD: 2 servings

LADONNA REED • PONCA CITY, OKLAHOMA

My husband and I are trying to eat healthier, so I keep on the lookout for light, flavorful foods that serve two. Stuffed with red pepper, green onion and creamy ranch dressing, this supper is a definite winner.

- 1 bacon strip, cut in half lengthwise
- 2 boneless skinless chicken breast halves (4 oz. *each*)
- 2 Tbsp. fat-free ranch salad dressing
- 3 Tbsp. finely chopped fresh mushrooms
- 3 Tbsp. finely chopped sweet red pepper
- 3 Tbsp. finely chopped green onions
- 2 tsp. cornstarch
- 6 Tbsp. fat-free evaporated milk

1. In a small nonstick skillet, cook bacon over medium heat until cooked but not crisp. Drain on paper towel. Flatten chicken to 1/4-in. thickness; spread with ranch dressing. Top with mushrooms, red pepper and onions. Roll up and wrap a piece of bacon around each; secure with a toothpick if needed.

2. Place in a shallow 1-qt. baking dish coated with cooking spray. Bake, uncovered, at 350° for 25-30

STUFFED RANCH CHICKEN

GRILLED JERK SHRIMP ORZO SALAD

CRAB-STUFFED MANICOTTI

minutes or until chicken juices run clear. Remove and keep warm. Remove toothpicks.

3. Strain pan juices. In a small saucepan, combine cornstarch and milk until smooth; stir in pan juices. Bring to a boil; cook and stir for 1 minute or until thickened. Serve with chicken.

Nutrition Facts: 1 chicken breast half with 2 Tbsp. sauce equals 220 calories, 5 g fat (1 g saturated fat), 67 mg cholesterol, 339 mg sodium, 15 g carbohydrate, 1 g fiber, 28 g protein. **Diabetic Exchanges:** 3 very lean meat, 1 starch, 1 fat.

Crab-Stuffed Manicotti

PREP: 25 min. BAKE: 25 min. YIELD: 2 servings

SONYA POLFLIET • ANZA, CALIFORNIA

I love pasta, and my husband loves seafood. I combined them to create this dish, and he raved that this is the best meal ever.

4	uncooked manicotti shells
1	Tbsp. butter
4	tsp. all-purpose flour
1	cup fat-free milk
1	Tbsp. grated Parmesan cheese
2	pouches (3.53 oz. *each*) premium crabmeat, drained
1/3	cup reduced-fat ricotta cheese
1/4	cup shredded part-skim mozzarella cheese
1/4	tsp. lemon-pepper seasoning
1/4	tsp. pepper

1/8   tsp. garlic powder

Minced fresh parsley

1. Cook manicotti according to package directions. In a small saucepan, melt butter. Stir in flour until smooth; gradually add milk. Bring to a boil; cook and stir for 2 minutes or until thickened. Remove from the heat; stir in Parmesan cheese.

2. In a small bowl, combine crab, ricotta cheese, mozzarella cheese, lemon-pepper, pepper and garlic powder. Drain manicotti; stuff with crab mixture. Spread 1/4 cup sauce in an 8-in. square baking dish coated with cooking spray. Top with stuffed manicotti. Pour remaining sauce over top.

3. Cover and bake at 350° for 25-30 minutes or until heated through. Sprinkle with parsley before serving.

Nutrition Facts: 2 stuffed manicotti equals 359 calories, 12 g fat (7 g saturated fat), 98 mg cholesterol, 793 mg sodium, 38 g carbohydrate, 1 g fiber, 26 g protein. **Diabetic Exchanges:** 2 starch, 2 lean meat, 1 fat, 1/2 fat-free milk.

If grated Parmesan is called for, use finely grated cheese sold in containers with shaker tops. If grating your own, use the finest section on your **grating tool.** You can also use a food processor. Cut cheese into 1-inch cubes and process 1 cup of cubes at a time until finely grated.

CRANBERRY
CHICKEN WRAPS

Cranberry Chicken Wraps

PREP/TOTAL TIME: 20 min. **YIELD:** 2 servings

SARAH WHITE • SALT LAKE CITY, UTAH

Loaded with cranberries, chicken, apples and spinach, these nutritious wraps are fast, tender and flavorful.

- 1 cup shredded cooked chicken breast
- 1 cup chopped apple
- 1/4 cup plus 2 tsp. fat-free Miracle Whip, *divided*
- 1/4 cup dried cranberries
- 3 Tbsp. crumbled feta cheese
- 1/4 tsp. minced fresh rosemary or 1/8 tsp. dried rosemary, crushed
- 1/8 tsp. pepper
- 2 whole wheat tortillas (8 in.), room temperature
- 1/2 cup fresh baby spinach

1. In a small bowl, combine the chicken, apple, 1/4 cup Miracle Whip, cranberries, feta cheese, rosemary and pepper. Spread remaining Miracle Whip over tortillas. Top with chicken mixture and spinach. Roll up and secure with toothpicks.

Nutrition Facts: 1 wrap equals 387 calories, 7 g fat (2 g saturated fat), 60 mg cholesterol, 614 mg sodium, 49 g carbohydrate, 5 g fiber, 27 g protein.

Chuck Wagon Chow

PREP/TOTAL TIME: 20 min. **YIELD:** 2 servings

DOROTHY COWAN • FERNDALE, CALIFORNIA

Try serving this mild chili-like dish with tortilla chips or flour tortillas. It cooks up in a single pot; it's great for camping, too.

- 1/3 lb. lean ground beef
- 1 small onion, chopped
- 1/4 cup chopped green pepper
- 1 garlic clove, minced
- 1 can (7 oz.) whole kernel corn, drained
- 3/4 cup kidney beans, rinsed and drained
- 1/2 cup tomato sauce
- 1 Tbsp. chili powder
- 1/8 tsp. pepper

1. In a large saucepan, cook the beef, onion and green pepper over medium heat until meat is no longer pink. Add garlic; cook 1 minute longer. Drain. Add the corn, beans, tomato sauce and seasonings; cover and cook 5-10 minutes longer or until heated through.

Nutrition Facts: 1-1/2 cups equals 300 calories, 7 g fat (3 g saturated fat), 46 mg cholesterol, 509 mg sodium, 38 g carbohydrate, 9 g fiber, 24 g protein. **Diabetic Exchanges:** 2-1/2 lean meat, 2 starch, 1 vegetable.

Creamy Pork Chop Dinner

PREP: 10 min. **BAKE:** 1 hour **YIELD:** 2 servings

JOYCE VALENTINE • SANFORD, COLORADO

Hearty and comforting, this meat-and-potatoes meal is rich with homemade goodness—and it's easy to prepare. Sometimes I use chicken thighs instead of pork chops.

- 2 medium potatoes, peeled and cut into 1/4-in. slices
- 2 medium carrots, sliced
- 2 boneless pork loin chops (3/4 in. thick and 4 oz. *each*)
- 1 Tbsp. onion soup mix
- 1-1/2 tsp. cornstarch
- 1 can (10-3/4 oz.) ready-to-serve creamy chicken soup

1. Place the potatoes and carrots in a 1-qt. baking dish coated with cooking spray. In a large skillet coated with cooking spray, brown pork chops on both sides. Place over vegetables.

2. In a small bowl, combine the soup mix, cornstarch and soup until blended. Pour over pork chops. Cover and bake at 350° for 1 hour or until meat and potatoes are tender.

Nutrition Facts: 1 serving equals 360 calories, 11 g fat (3 g saturated fat), 57 mg cholesterol, 807 mg sodium, 40 g carbohydrate, 6 g fiber, 27 g protein.

Turkey with Apple Slices

PREP/TOTAL TIME: 15 min. **YIELD:** 2 servings

MARY LOU WAYMAN • SALT LAKE CITY, UTAH

Any day can be "Turkey Day" when you make this smaller-scale main course. The moist tenderloins and tangy apple glaze offer the goodness of turkey without a refrigerator full of leftovers.

- 2 turkey breast tenderloins (about 4 oz. *each*)
- 1 Tbsp. butter
- 2 Tbsp. maple syrup
- 1 Tbsp. cider vinegar
- 1 tsp. Dijon mustard
- 1/2 tsp. chicken bouillon granules
- 1 medium tart apple, sliced

1. In a large skillet, cook turkey in butter over medium heat for 4-5 minutes on each side or until the juices run clear. Remove from the skillet; cover and keep warm.

2. In the same skillet, combine the syrup, vinegar, mustard and bouillon. Add the apple; cook and stir over medium heat for 2-3 minutes or until apple is tender. Serve with turkey.

Nutrition Facts: 1 serving equals 263 calories, 7 g fat (4 g saturated fat), 71 mg cholesterol, 374 mg sodium, 24 g carbohydrate, 2 g fiber, 27 g protein. **Diabetic Exchanges:** 3 lean meat, 1-1/2 fat, 1 starch, 1/2 fruit.

Asian Pork Supper

PREP: 10 min. + marinating **BAKE:** 20 min.
YIELD: 2 servings

ANNEMARIE HARRIS • HADDONFIELD, NEW JERSEY

Here's a light, delicious dish that will soon be a favorite. Serve it with jasmine rice and broccoli.

- 1/2 cup reduced-sodium soy sauce
- 1 Tbsp. minced fresh gingerroot
- 1-1/2 tsp. sesame oil
- 2 whole cloves
- 1 pork tenderloin (3/4 lb.)
- 1/4 cup sesame seeds
- 1 Tbsp. honey
- 1 Tbsp. brown sugar

1. In a large resealable plastic bag, combine the soy sauce, ginger, sesame oil and cloves. Add the pork; seal bag and turn to coat. Refrigerate for 8 hours or overnight.

2. Drain and discard marinade. Place sesame seeds in a shallow dish. Roll pork in sesame seeds and place in a 13-in. x 9-in. baking dish coated with cooking spray. Drizzle with honey; sprinkle with brown sugar.

3. Bake, uncovered, at 425° for 20-30 minutes or until a meat thermometer reads 160°.

Nutrition Facts: 5 oz. cooked pork equals 324 calories, 12 g fat (2 g saturated fat), 95 mg cholesterol, 437 mg sodium, 19 g carbohydrate, trace fiber, 37 g protein. **Diabetic Exchanges:** 5 lean meat, 1 starch, 1 fat.

ASIAN PORK SUPPER

Mushroom Cheese Ravioli Ⓜ

PREP/TOTAL TIME: 25 min. YIELD: 2 servings

CATHY HALL • PHOENIX, ARIZONA

You'd never guess this creamy, rich and colorful dish is light. Add a frosty glass of iced tea, spinach salad and fruit for an easy meal.

      2 cups refrigerated cheese ravioli
    1/2 cup sliced fresh mushrooms
      1 Tbsp. chopped onion
      1 Tbsp. pine nuts
      1 Tbsp. chopped sweet yellow pepper
      1 Tbsp. chopped sweet red pepper
      1 tsp. olive oil
      2 tsp. cornstarch
    1/2 cup reduced-sodium chicken *or* vegetable broth
    1/4 cup fat-free half-and-half
    1/8 tsp. salt
    1/8 tsp. pepper
Grated Parmesan cheese, optional

1. Cook ravioli according to package directions.

2. Meanwhile, in a small nonstick saucepan coated with cooking spray, saute the mushrooms, onion, nuts and peppers in oil until tender.

3. Combine the cornstarch, broth, half-and-half, salt and pepper until smooth. Gradually stir into the pan. Bring to a boil; cook and stir for 2 minutes or until mixture is thickened.

4. Drain ravioli. Stir into sauce; heat through. Sprinkle with cheese if desired.

Nutrition Facts: 1-1/2 cups (calculated without cheese) equals 367 calories, 11 g fat (5 g saturated fat), 40 mg cholesterol, 717 mg sodium, 48 g carbohydrate, 3 g fiber, 18 g protein.

MUSHROOM CHEESE RAVIOLI

Spiced French Toast Ⓜ

PREP: 15 min. + chilling COOK: 5 min. YIELD: 2 servings

BEVERLY HAUGEN • HENDERSON, NEVADA

I double this recipe for family and friends, and it's a hit every time. It fills them up, but not out!

      2 eggs
      2 egg whites
    3/4 cup fat-free milk
      1 Tbsp. sugar
      1 Tbsp. molasses
    1/4 tsp. ground ginger
    1/4 tsp. ground allspice
    1/8 tsp. salt
      6 slices French bread (3/4 in. thick)
      2 tsp. butter

1. In a large bowl, combine the first eight ingredients. Place the bread slices in an ungreased 13-in. x 9-in. baking dish; pour egg mixture over top. Cover and refrigerate overnight.

2. Heat butter on a griddle; cook bread for 2-3 minutes on each side or until golden brown.

Nutrition Facts: 3 slices equals 352 calories, 10 g fat (4 g saturated fat), 223 mg cholesterol, 662 mg sodium, 47 g carbohydrate, 2 g fiber, 18 g protein.

Bacon-Broccoli Quiche Cups Ⓒ

PREP: 10 min. BAKE: 25 min. YIELD: 2 servings

IRENE STEINMEYER • DENVER, COLORADO

Chock-full of veggies and melted cheese, this comforting and colorful egg bake has become a holiday brunch classic at my home. For a tasty variation, try substituting asparagus for broccoli and Swiss for cheddar cheese.

      4 bacon strips, diced
    1/4 cup fresh broccoli florets
    1/4 cup chopped onion
      1 garlic clove, minced
      3 eggs
      1 Tbsp. dried parsley flakes
    1/8 tsp. seasoned salt, optional
Dash pepper
    1/4 cup shredded cheddar cheese
      2 Tbsp. chopped tomato

1. In a large skillet, cook bacon over medium heat until crisp. Using a slotted spoon, remove to paper towels; drain, reserving 1 Tbsp. drippings. In the drippings, cook broccoli and onion over medium heat for 2-3 minutes or until vegetables are tender. Add garlic; cook 1 minute longer.

2. In a small bowl, beat the eggs, parsley, seasoned salt if desired and pepper. Stir in bacon and broccoli mixture; add cheese and tomato.

3. Pour into two 10-oz. ramekins or custard cups coated with cooking spray. Bake at 400° for 22-25 minutes or until a knife inserted near the center comes out clean.

Nutrition Facts: 1 serving (prepared with egg substitute and reduced-fat cheese; calculated without seasoned salt) equals 173 calories, 9 g fat (4 g saturated fat), 21 mg cholesterol, 486 mg sodium, 5 g carbohydrate, 1 g fiber, 17 g protein.

Sesame Beef Stir-Fry

PREP/TOTAL TIME: 30 min. **YIELD:** 2 servings

CHARLENE CHAMBERS • ORMOND BEACH, FLORIDA

Soy sauce and gingerroot add great flavor to this quick beef stir-fry. It couldn't be simpler to make, but it's definitely elegant enough to serve someone special.

- 2 tsp. cornstarch
- 1/2 cup reduced-sodium beef broth
- 4 tsp. reduced-sodium soy sauce
- 1 Tbsp. minced fresh gingerroot
- 1 garlic clove, minced
- 1/2 lb. beef top sirloin steak, thinly sliced
- 2 tsp. sesame seeds, toasted, *divided*
- 2 tsp. peanut *or* canola oil, *divided*
- 2 cups fresh broccoli florets
- 1 small sweet yellow pepper, julienned
- 1 cup hot cooked brown rice

1. In a small bowl, combine the first five ingredients until blended; set aside.

2. In a large nonstick skillet or wok, stir-fry beef and 1 tsp. sesame seeds in 1 tsp. oil until no longer pink. Remove and keep warm.

3. Stir-fry broccoli in remaining oil for 2 minutes. Add pepper; stir-fry 4-6 minutes longer or until vegetables are crisp-tender.

4. Stir cornstarch mixture and add to the pan. Bring to a boil; cook and stir for 2 minutes or until thickened. Add beef; heat through. Serve with rice. Sprinkle with remaining sesame seeds.

Nutrition Facts: 2 cups stir-fry with 1/2 cup rice equals 363 calories, 12 g fat (3 g saturated fat), 47 mg cholesterol, 606 mg sodium, 33 g carbohydrate, 5 g fiber, 31 g protein. **Diabetic Exchanges:** 3 lean meat, 2 starch, 1 vegetable, 1 fat.

Cajun Shrimp Stir-Fry

PREP/TOTAL TIME: 25 min. **YIELD:** 2 servings

GINNY KOCHIS • SPRINGFIELD, VIRGINIA

Squash and red onion add color to this tasty one-dish meal with just the right amount of Cajun kick.

1	small zucchini, sliced
1/2	medium yellow summer squash, sliced
1/2	medium red onion, chopped
1	Tbsp. canola oil
1/2	lb. uncooked medium shrimp, peeled and deveined
1	tsp. Cajun seasoning
1/2	tsp. garlic powder
1/8	tsp. pepper

Dash crushed red pepper flakes

| 1 | cup hot cooked brown rice |

1. In a large skillet or wok, stir-fry the zucchini, yellow squash and onion in oil for 2-3 minutes or until crisp-tender. Add shrimp and seasonings; stir-fry 3 minutes longer or until shrimp turn pink. Serve with rice.

Nutrition Facts: 1 cup shrimp mixture with 1/2 cup rice equals 297 calories, 10 g fat (1 g saturated fat), 138 mg cholesterol, 417 mg sodium, 30 g carbohydrate, 4 g fiber, 23 g protein. **Diabetic Exchanges:** 3 lean meat, 1-1/2 fat, 1 starch, 1 vegetable.

Scrambled Eggs With Cream Cheese F C M

PREP/TOTAL TIME: 15 min. **YIELD:** 2 servings

DEBBIE CLAY • ALOHA, OREGON

What a tasty, protein-packed meal! We love to add a little hot sauce to these eggs.

1	cup egg substitute
1	green onion, thinly sliced
1/8	tsp. pepper
1	tsp. butter
1/4	cup fat-free cream cheese, cubed

1. In a small bowl, whisk the egg substitute, onion and pepper. In a small nonstick skillet, heat butter over medium heat. Add egg mixture; cook and stir until almost set. Stir in cream cheese. Cook and stir until completely set.

Nutrition Facts: 1 cup equals 107 calories, 2 g fat (1 g saturated fat), 7 mg cholesterol, 423 mg sodium, 4 g carbohydrate, trace fiber, 16 g protein. **Diabetic Exchange:** 2 lean meat.

Zucchini Tomato Soup C

PREP/TOTAL TIME: 20 min. **YIELD:** 2 servings

NANCY JOHNSON • LAVERNE, OKLAHOMA

There's garden-fresh flavor in every spoonful of this easy-to-make soup. I like it for a low-calorie lunch, along with a roll and fruit for dessert. It serves just two, so you don't end up with leftovers.

2 small zucchini, coarsely chopped
1/4 cup chopped red onion
1-1/2 tsp. olive oil
1/8 tsp. salt
1 cup Spicy Hot V8 juice
1 small tomato, cut into thin wedges
Dash *each* pepper and dried basil
2 Tbsp. shredded cheddar cheese, optional
1 to 2 Tbsp. crumbled cooked bacon, optional

1. In a large skillet, saute zucchini and onion in oil until crisp-tender. Sprinkle with salt. Add the V8 juice, tomato, pepper and basil; cook until heated through. Sprinkle with cheese and bacon if desired.

Nutrition Facts: 1 serving (calculated without cheese and bacon) equals 89 calories, 4 g fat (1 g saturated fat), 0 cholesterol, 545 mg sodium, 12 g carbohydrate, 3 g fiber, 3 g protein. **Diabetic Exchanges:** 2 vegetable, 1/2 fat.

Chicken Spaghetti Salad

PREP/TOTAL TIME: 20 min. YIELD: 2 servings

HOLLY SIPHAVONG • EUREKA, CALIFORNIA

I make this quick dish when I'm in a hurry and am not hungry enough to eat a huge meal.

3 oz. uncooked spaghetti
1/2 cup shredded cooked chicken breast
1/2 cup julienned cucumber
1/3 cup julienned carrot
1 Tbsp. white vinegar
1 Tbsp. reduced-sodium soy sauce
2 tsp. canola oil
1 tsp. minced fresh gingerroot
3/4 tsp. sugar
1/4 tsp. minced garlic

1. Cook spaghetti according to package directions; drain and rinse in cold water. Combine the spaghetti, chicken, cucumber and carrot. In a small saucepan, combine the vinegar, soy sauce, oil, ginger, sugar and garlic. Bring to a boil; remove from the heat. Drizzle over spaghetti mixture and toss to coat.

Nutrition Facts: 1-1/2 cups equals 282 calories, 7 g fat (1 g saturated fat), 36 mg cholesterol, 343 mg sodium, 34 g carbohydrate, 3 g fiber, 19 g protein. **Diabetic Exchanges:** 2 starch, 2 lean meat, 1 vegetable.

Makeover Deluxe Grilled Cheese Ⓜ

PREP/TOTAL TIME: 15 min. YIELD: 2 servings

HEALTHY COOKING TEST KITCHEN

With a few simple tricks, our Test Kitchen actually boosted the fantastic toasty taste of these mouthwatering sandwiches, but slashed fat, calories and cholesterol to less than half!

1 small onion, halved and thinly sliced
4 slices French bread (1/2 in. thick)
Butter-flavored cooking spray
1 oz. herbed fresh goat cheese
1/2 small tart apple, thinly sliced
1/2 cup shredded reduced-fat cheddar cheese

1. In a small skillet coated with cooking spray, saute onion until tender; set aside.

2. Place bread slices on a baking sheet; spritz with butter-flavored cooking spray. Broil 4 in. from the heat for 2-3 minutes or until golden-brown.

3. Spread goat cheese over two untoasted sides of bread slices. Top with the apple slices and reserved onion; sprinkle with cheddar cheese. Broil 2-3 minutes longer or until cheese is melted. Top with the remaining slices.

Nutrition Facts: 1 sandwich equals 225 calories, 12 g fat (6 g saturated fat), 30 mg cholesterol, 400 mg sodium, 18 g carbohydrate, 2 g fiber, 12 g protein. **Diabetic Exchanges:** 2 medium-fat meat, 1 starch.

CHICKEN SPAGHETTI SALAD

MAKEOVER DELUXE GRILLED CHEESE

Thyme Chicken Marsala [c]

PREP/TOTAL TIME: 30 min. **YIELD:** 2 servings

DOROTHY SMITH • EL DORADO, ARKANSAS

Here's a quick little recipe with restaurant presentation and flavor, perfect for impromptu entertaining. The simple wine sauce comes together in minutes.

- 2 boneless skinless chicken breast halves (4 oz. *each*)
- 1 Tbsp. all-purpose flour
- 1/8 tsp. plus 1/4 tsp. salt, *divided*
- 1/8 tsp. plus 1/4 tsp. pepper, *divided*
- 1 medium carrot, julienned
- 1 small sweet yellow *or* red pepper, julienned
- 3 tsp. olive oil, *divided*
- 2 garlic cloves, minced
- 1/3 cup marsala wine *or* reduced-sodium chicken broth
- 1 Tbsp. minced fresh thyme *or* 1 tsp. dried thyme

1. Place chicken in a large resealable plastic bag; flatten to 1/4-in. thickness. Add flour and 1/8 tsp. each salt and pepper; shake to coat. Set aside.

2. In a large skillet, saute the carrot and yellow pepper in 1-1/2 tsp. oil for 3 minutes or until vegetables are tender. Add garlic and remaining salt and pepper; cook 1 minute longer. Transfer to two serving plates; keep warm.

3. In the same skillet, heat remaining oil over medium heat. Cook the chicken for 3-4 minutes on each side or until meat is no longer pink; place over vegetables. Add the wine and thyme to the pan; cook for 1 minute, stirring to loosen browned bits. Serve with chicken.

Nutrition Facts: 1 chicken breast half equals 285 calories, 10 g fat (2 g saturated fat), 63 mg cholesterol, 365 mg sodium, 15 g carbohydrate, 2 g fiber, 24 g protein. **Diabetic Exchanges:** 3 lean meat, 1 starch, 1 fat.

THYME CHICKEN MARSALA

Oven Fish 'n' Chips

PREP: 20 min. **BAKE:** 25 min. **YIELD:** 2 servings

JANICE MITCHELL • AURORA, COLORADO

Crunchy fillets with a kick of cayenne and crispy potatoes make a quick and tasty light meal for two.

- 1 Tbsp. olive oil
- 1/4 tsp. pepper, *divided*
- 2 medium potatoes, peeled
- 3 Tbsp. all-purpose flour
- 1 egg
- 1 Tbsp. water
- 1/3 cup crushed cornflakes
- 1-1/2 tsp. grated Parmesan cheese
- Dash cayenne pepper
- 1/2 lb. haddock fillets
- Tartar sauce, optional

1. In a large bowl, combine oil and 1/8 tsp. pepper. Cut potatoes lengthwise into 1/2-in. strips. Add to oil mixture and toss to coat. Place on a baking sheet coated with cooking spray. Bake at 425° for 25-30 minutes or until golden-brown and crisp.

2. Meanwhile, in a shallow bowl, combine flour and remaining pepper. In another shallow bowl, beat egg and water. In a third bowl, combine the cornflakes, cheese and cayenne. Dredge fillets in flour, then dip in egg mixture and coat with crumbs.

3. Place on a baking sheet coated with cooking spray. Bake at 425° for 10-15 minutes or until the haddock flakes easily with a fork. Serve with chips and tartar sauce if desired.

Nutrition Facts: 1 serving (calculated without tartar sauce) equals 358 calories, 10 g fat (2 g saturated fat), 131 mg cholesterol, 204 mg sodium, 39 g carbohydrate, 2 g fiber, 28 g protein. **Diabetic Exchanges:** 3 very lean meat, 2-1/2 starch, 2 fat.

Mushroom & Swiss Turkey Burgers

PREP/TOTAL TIME: 30 min. **YIELD:** 2 servings

MELEYNA NOMURA • SCOTTSDALE, ARIZONA

This recipe also works great on the grill. I use the leftover spinach in pesto or omelets or to make another batch of burgers.

- 1-3/4 cups sliced baby portobello mushrooms
- 1 tsp. olive oil
- 1 garlic clove, minced
- 1/4 tsp. salt, *divided*
- 1/8 tsp. pepper, *divided*
- 1/4 cup frozen chopped spinach, thawed and squeezed dry
- 2 Tbsp. chopped sweet onion
- 1/2 lb. lean ground turkey
- 1 slice reduced-fat Swiss cheese, cut in half
- 2 whole wheat hamburger buns, split and toasted
- 2 lettuce leaves
- 2 slices sweet onion
- 2 slices tomato

HAMBURGER SHEPHERD'S PIE

1. In a small skillet, cook mushrooms in oil until tender. Add garlic; cook 1 minute longer. Stir in 1/8 tsp. salt and a dash of pepper. Remove from the heat; set aside.

2. In a small bowl, combine the spinach, chopped onion and remaining salt and pepper. Crumble turkey over mixture and mix well. Shape into two patties.

3. In a large nonstick skillet coated with cooking spray, cook patties over medium heat for 4 minutes. Turn and cook 3 minutes longer. Top burgers with cheese; cover and cook 3-6 minutes longer or until a meat thermometer reads 165° and cheese is melted. Serve on buns with lettuce, onion, tomato and reserved mushroom mixture.

Nutrition Facts: 1 burger equals 371 calories, 16 g fat (4 g saturated fat), 95 mg cholesterol, 645 mg sodium, 30 g carbohydrate, 5 g fiber, 30 g protein.

Hamburger Shepherd's Pie

PREP: 20 min. **BAKE:** 30 min. **YIELD:** 2 servings

ELAINE WILLIAMS • SURREY, BRITISH COLUMBIA

Transform leftovers into a light but filling one-dish meal sized for two. This is a simple and scrumptious recipe.

 1/2 lb. lean ground beef (90% lean)
   2 Tbsp. chopped onion
   1 cup frozen cut green beans, thawed

 2/3 cup condensed tomato soup, undiluted
 1/4 tsp. Italian seasoning
 1/8 tsp. pepper
   1 cup mashed potatoes (prepared with milk)
Dash paprika

1. In a small skillet, cook beef and onion over medium heat until meat is no longer pink; drain. Add the beans, soup, Italian seasoning and pepper. Transfer to a 7-in. pie plate coated with cooking spray.

2. Spread mashed potatoes over the top; sprinkle with paprika. Bake, uncovered, at 350° for 30-35 minutes or until heated through.

Nutrition Facts: 1/2 pie equals 330 calories, 10 g fat (4 g saturated fat), 71 mg cholesterol, 927 mg sodium, 35 g carbohydrate, 5 g fiber, 26 g protein.

A pinch is thought to be the amount of a dry ingredient that can be held between your thumb and forefinger. A dash is a very small amount of seasoning added with a quick downward stroke of the hand. A pinch or a dash of an ingredient is between 1/16 and a scant 1/8 teaspoon.

Cranberry-Apple Pork Chops

PREP: 15 min. **COOK:** 15 min. + marinating
YIELD: 2 servings

KATIE SHIREMAN • PHILADELPHIA, PENNSYLVANIA

These colorful, sweet-tart chops deliver seasonal flavors in each bite!

3	tsp. ground cinnamon
1-1/2	tsp. ground nutmeg
1/2	tsp. pumpkin pie spice
2	boneless pork loin chops (4 oz. each)
1/2	cup plus 2 Tbsp. unsweetened apple juice, *divided*
1/2	cup plus 2 Tbsp. cranberry juice, *divided*
1	tsp. canola oil
1	medium apple, peeled and finely chopped
1	cup chopped fresh cranberries
1/8	tsp. salt

1. Combine the cinnamon, nutmeg and pie spice; rub over chops. Pour 1/2 cup apple juice and 1/2 cup cranberry juice into a large resealable plastic bag; add the pork chops. Seal bag and turn to coat; refrigerate for 8 hours or overnight.

2. Drain chops and discard marinade. In a large nonstick skillet coated with cooking spray, brown chops in oil over medium heat for 3-4 minutes on each side.

3. Add the apple, cranberries, salt and remaining juices. Bring to a boil. Reduce heat; cover and cook for 10-12 minutes or until chops and apple are tender, turning once.

Nutrition Facts: 1 pork chop with 3/4 cup sauce equals 254 calories, 9 g fat (3 g saturated fat), 55 mg cholesterol, 181 mg sodium, 21 g carbohydrate, 4 g fiber, 22 g protein. **Diabetic Exchanges:** 3 lean meat, 1-1/2 fruit.

Tuna and Tomato Kabobs ⓒ

PREP: 20 min. + marinating **GRILL:** 10 min.
YIELD: 2 servings

EDRIE O'BRIEN • DENVER, COLORADO

A lime-herb marinade adds great taste to the tuna and vegetables on these attractive skewers. I lightened this up by using tuna in place of the beef. Halibut and swordfish work well, too.

- 2 Tbsp. lime juice
- 1 Tbsp. canola oil
- 1 Tbsp. reduced-sodium soy sauce
- 3/4 tsp. grated lime peel
- 1 small garlic clove, minced
- 1/2 tsp. salt
- 1/2 tsp. dried parsley flakes
- 1/8 tsp. ground cumin
- 1/8 tsp. pepper
- Dash cayenne pepper
- 1/2 lb. tuna steak, cut into 1-in. cubes
- 6 cherry tomatoes
- 6 medium fresh mushrooms

1. In a large resealable plastic bag, combine the first 10 ingredients; add the tuna. Seal bag and turn to coat; refrigerate for 30 minutes.

2. Coat grill rack with cooking spray before starting the grill. Drain and discard marinade. On two metal or soaked wooden skewers, alternately thread tuna and vegetables. For medium-rare tuna, grill, covered, for 6-8 minutes or until slightly pink in the center, turning once.

Nutrition Facts: 1 kabob equals 183 calories, 5 g fat (1 g saturated fat), 51 mg cholesterol, 460 mg sodium, 6 g carbohydrate, 1 g fiber, 29 g protein. **Diabetic Exchanges:** 4 very lean meat, 1 vegetable, 1/2 fat.

Moroccan Chicken Thighs

PREP: 25 min. **COOK:** 40 min. **YIELD:** 2 servings

SUSAN MILLS • THREE RIVERS, CALIFORNIA

My husband and I love Middle Eastern and Mediterranean food. This recipe is one of our favorites.

- 1/2 tsp. brown sugar
- 1/2 tsp. ground coriander
- 1/2 tsp. ground cumin
- 1/2 tsp. paprika
- 1/4 tsp. ground cinnamon
- 1/8 tsp. garlic powder
- 1/8 tsp. salt
- 1/8 tsp. pepper
- 2 tsp. all-purpose flour
- 4 bone-in chicken thighs (about 1 lb.), skin removed
- 1-1/2 tsp. olive oil
- SAUCE:
- 3 shallots, chopped
- 1/2 cup plus 2 Tbsp. reduced-sodium chicken broth, divided
- 4 pitted dates, chopped
- 1 tsp. all-purpose flour
- 1-1/2 tsp. minced fresh cilantro
- COUSCOUS:
- 1/4 cup water
- 3 Tbsp. reduced-sodium chicken broth
- 1/8 tsp. salt
- Dash ground cumin
- 1/3 cup uncooked couscous
- 1-1/2 tsp. slivered almonds, toasted

1. In a small bowl, combine the first eight ingredients. Set aside 1 tsp. spice mixture; add flour to remaining mixture and sprinkle over chicken.

2. In a large nonstick skillet coated with cooking spray, brown chicken in oil on both sides. Remove and keep warm. Add shallots to pan; cook and stir over medium heat for 3 minutes. Stir in 1/2 cup broth and dates. Bring to a boil. Reduce the heat; return chicken to pan.

3. Cover and simmer for 20-25 minutes or until chicken juices run clear. Remove chicken and keep warm. Combine flour with reserved spice mixture and remaining broth until smooth; gradually stir into pan. Bring to a boil; cook and stir for 2 minutes or until thickened. Stir in cilantro.For couscous, in a small saucepan, bring the water, broth, salt and cumin to a boil. Stir in couscous. Cover and remove from the heat; let stand for 5-10 minutes or until water is absorbed. Fluff with a fork; stir in almonds. Serve with chicken and sauce.

Nutrition Facts: 2 chicken thighs with 1/2 cup couscous and 1/3 cup sauce equals 381 calories, 15 g fat (4 g saturated fat), 113 mg cholesterol, 364 mg sodium, 26 g carbohydrate, 2 g fiber, 36 g protein.

MOROCCAN CHICKEN THIGHS

Apricot Turkey Sandwiches

PREP/TOTAL TIME: 15 min. YIELD: 2 servings

CHARLOTTE GEHLE • BROWNSTOWN, MICHIGAN

Apricot jam and Dijon mustard come together for a wonderful spread on this sandwich with Swiss cheese, turkey bacon and peppered turkey slices.

- 2 turkey bacon strips
- 4 pieces multigrain bread, toasted
- 2 Tbsp. apricot jam
- 3 oz. thinly sliced deli peppered turkey
- 2 slices tomato
- 2 slices red onion
- 2 pieces leaf lettuce
- 2 slices reduced-fat Swiss cheese
- 4 tsp. Dijon mustard

1. In a small skillet, cook bacon over medium heat until crisp. Remove to paper towels to drain; set aside.

2. Spread two toast slices with jam. Layer with turkey, reserved bacon, tomato, onion, lettuce and cheese. Spread remaining toast with mustard; place on top.

Nutrition Facts: 1 sandwich equals 338 calories, 10 g fat (3 g saturated fat), 40 mg cholesterol, 1,109 mg sodium, 43 g carbohydrate, 4 g fiber, 23 g protein.

Chocolate Peanut Parfaits

PREP: 15 min. + chilling YIELD: 2 servings

LISA VARNER • GREENVILLE, SOUTH CAROLINA

This lower-in-fat-and-calories version of a pie recipe I dearly love still tastes great and looks richer than it really is. It's make-ahead handy!

- 2 chocolate wafers, crushed
- 1/4 cup fat-free sweetened condensed milk
- 2 oz. fat-free cream cheese
- 2 Tbsp. reduced-fat creamy peanut butter
- 3/4 tsp. lemon juice
- 1/2 tsp. vanilla extract
- 1/4 cup reduced-fat whipped topping
- 1 tsp. chocolate syrup
- 1 tsp. chopped dry roasted peanuts

1. Divide crushed wafers between two parfait glasses. In a small bowl, beat the milk, cream cheese, peanut butter, lemon juice and vanilla. Fold in whipped topping. Spoon over crushed wafers. Cover and refrigerate for at least 1 hour. Just before serving, drizzle with syrup and sprinkle with peanuts.

Nutrition Facts: 1 parfait equals 285 calories, 8 g fat (3 g saturated fat), 7 mg cholesterol, 332 mg sodium, 41 g carbohydrate, 1 g fiber, 12 g protein.

Broiled Cod C

PREP: 10 min. + marinating BROIL: 10 min.
YIELD: 2 servings

KIM RUSSELL • NORTH WALES, PENNSYLVANIA

This is the easiest and tastiest fish you'll serve. Even finicky eaters who think they don't like fish will love it because it lacks a fishy taste and is beautiful and flakey.

- 1/4 cup fat-free Italian salad dressing
- 1/2 tsp. sugar
- 1/8 tsp. each salt, garlic powder, curry powder, paprika and pepper
- 2 cod fillets (6 oz. each)
- 2 tsp. butter

1. In a large resealable plastic bag, combine the dressing, sugar and seasonings. Add the fish; seal bag and turn to coat. Refrigerate for 10-30 minutes.

2. Drain and discard marinade; place fillets on a broiler pan coated with cooking spray. Broil 3-4 in. from the heat for 10-12 minutes or until fish flakes easily with a fork. Place 1 tsp. butter on each fillet; let stand until melted.

Nutrition Facts: 1 cod fillet equals 170 calories, 5 g fat (3 g saturated fat), 75 mg cholesterol, 407 mg sodium, 2 g carbohydrate, trace fiber, 27 g protein. **Diabetic Exchange:** 4 very lean meat, 1/2 fat.

CHOCOLATE PEANUT PARFAITS

BROILED COD

CHICKEN WITH VEGGIES

Chicken with Veggies [C]

PREP/TOTAL TIME: 30 min. **YIELD:** 2 servings

NIKKI ADAMS • CHERRY VALLEY, CALIFORNIA

Colorful, nutritious veggies and Italian seasoning make something special of this chicken in minutes!

- 2 boneless skinless chicken breast halves (6 oz. *each*)
- 1/4 tsp. salt
- 1/4 tsp. pepper
- 2 Tbsp. dry bread crumbs
- 2 tsp. grated Parmesan cheese
- 2 tsp. Italian seasoning
- 3 tsp. olive oil, *divided*
- 3 cups fresh baby spinach
- 2 plum tomatoes, chopped
- 2 garlic cloves, minced

1. Flatten chicken to 1/4-in. thickness; sprinkle with salt and pepper. In a shallow bowl, combine the bread crumbs, cheese and Italian seasoning. Coat chicken in bread crumb mixture.

2. In a large nonstick skillet coated with cooking spray, cook chicken in 2 tsp. oil over medium heat for 3-4 minutes on each side or until no longer pink. Remove and keep warm.

3. Saute spinach in remaining oil just until wilted. Stir in tomatoes and garlic; cook 3 minutes longer. Serve with chicken.

Nutrition Facts: 1 chicken breast half with 1 cup vegetables equals 302 calories, 12 g fat (2 g saturated fat), 95 mg cholesterol, 484 mg sodium, 10 g carbohydrate, 2 g fiber, 38 g protein. **Diabetic Exchanges:** 5 very lean meat, 2 fat, 1 vegetable.

When you're out of **Italian seasoning**, it's a snap to mix up your own! Simply combine a 1/4 teaspoon each of basil, thyme, rosemary and oregano for each teaspoon called for in a recipe.

My Healthy Life

Ten *Taste of Home* readers created healthful, life-changing plans for themselves and their families. Here, they share their stories as well as some of the recipes that received thumbs-up ratings from their gangs!

Daily Jump Start

A healthy, balanced breakfast will give you the fuel your body needs to power through the morning. Jump-start your day with one of these quick and delicious choices, sure to be a big hit with your whole family.

For Judy Parker and her family, the decision to eat right and get healthy was brought on by a life-altering event. "I was diagnosed with cancer at 33," she says. "Fortunately, it was non-aggressive, and the tumor was removed, but it was a wake-up call. We realized life is short, and we only get one body, so we'd better take care of it."

Judy, her husband, Ladd, and their four children, ages 7 to 14, decided to change their eating habits and make activity a priority. "We exercise regularly—we even trained for a triathlon. Our two youngest competed in a kids' version, with our then 5-year-old daughter racing on a tricycle! I took third place once—not bad for a 40-year-old competing against 20-year-olds!"

Judy carries her healthy approach into the kitchen as well. "Ladd and I model good eating habits, because the kids are more likely to follow suit. To make it easy, I keep veggies and fruit on hand, and they know if they want dessert, they must eat their vegetables." Judy's family starts their days right with flavorful breakfast items such as these.

Wholesome Whole Grain Waffles Ⓜ

PREP: 15 min. **COOK:** 5 min./batch **YIELD:** 12 waffles

JUDY PARKER • MOORE, OKLAHOMA

I created this recipe by tweaking one I had. I added flaxseed, substituted some whole wheat flour for the all-purpose variety, applesauce for some oil and fat-free milk for whole. My family loved the changes, and now this is a favorite.

- 1 cup all-purpose flour
- 1 cup whole wheat flour
- 3 Tbsp. ground flaxseed
- 3 tsp. baking powder
- 1/2 tsp. salt
- 2 eggs, *separated*
- 2 cups fat-free milk
- 3 Tbsp. canola oil
- 3 Tbsp. unsweetened applesauce

Mixed fresh berries and confectioners' sugar, optional

1. In a large bowl, combine the flours, flaxseed, baking powder and salt. Combine the egg yolks, milk, oil and applesauce; stir into the dry ingredients until the mixture is just moistened.

2. In a small bowl, beat egg whites until stiff peaks form; fold into the batter.

BERRY NUTRITIOUS SMOOTHIES

WHOLESOME WHOLE GRAIN WAFFLES

3. Bake in a preheated waffle iron according to manufacturer's directions until golden brown. Serve with berries and confectioners' sugar if desired.

Nutrition Facts: 2 waffles (calculated without berries and confectioners' sugar) equals 278 calories, 11 g fat (1 g saturated fat), 70 mg cholesterol, 456 mg sodium, 37 g carbohydrate, 4 g fiber, 11 g protein. **Diabetic Exchanges:** 2-1/2 starch, 1-1/2 fat.

Berry Nutritious Smoothies F S

PREP/TOTAL TIME: 5 min. YIELD: 3 servings

JUDY PARKER • MOORE, OKLAHOMA

This recipe came from experimenting with a different combination of fruit, yogurt and juice. I generally use whatever fresh or frozen fruit I have on hand, but I always include a frozen banana. We often substitute grape or pineapple juice for the orange juice.

   1   cup orange juice
   1/2 cup fat-free plain yogurt
   1/2 cup silken firm tofu
   1   medium ripe banana, sliced and frozen
   1/2 cup frozen unsweetened strawberries
   1/2 cup frozen unsweetened raspberries
   2   Tbsp. toasted wheat germ

1. In a blender, combine all ingredients; cover and process for 30 seconds or until smooth. Pour into chilled glasses; serve immediately.

Nutrition Facts: 1 cup equals 141 calories, 1 g fat (trace saturated fat), 1 mg cholesterol, 35 mg sodium, 28 g carbohydrate, 3 g fiber, 6 g protein.

Easy Breakfast Quesadillas

PREP/TOTAL TIME: 20 min. YIELD: 6 servings

JUDY PARKER • MOORE, OKLAHOMA

We love Mexican food, and this was my attempt to have it for breakfast. If my kids will eat it, then I know it's a winner, and they all love this dish!

   4   eggs
   1   cup egg substitute
   6   whole wheat tortillas (8 in.)
   1   cup (4 oz.) shredded reduced-fat cheddar cheese
   3   turkey bacon strips, diced and cooked
   6   Tbsp. salsa
   6   Tbsp. fat-free sour cream

1. In a small bowl, whisk the eggs and egg substitute. Coat a large skillet with cooking spray. Add the egg mixture; cook and stir over medium heat until eggs are completely set.

2. Heat another large nonstick skillet coated with cooking spray; add one tortilla. Top with 1/3 cup cheese, scant 2 tablespoons bacon, 1 cup egg mixture and one tortilla. Cook over medium heat for 2-3 minutes on each side or until lightly browned.

3. Repeat with remaining tortillas, cheese, bacon and eggs, spraying pan as needed. Cut each quesadilla into six wedges. Serve with salsa and sour cream.

Nutrition Facts: 3 wedges with 1 tablespoon salsa and 1 tablespoon sour cream equals 299 calories, 12 g fat (4 g saturated fat), 164 mg cholesterol, 588 mg sodium, 27 g carbohydrate, 2 g fiber, 19 g protein.

Gluten-Free Favorites

Sensitivities to wheat, barley and rye can really make menu planning tough.
With gluten-free ingredients becoming readily available, it's a snap to
create meals that let everyone at your table enjoy the dinner.

Eating right can seem daunting, but imagine doing it with major dietary restrictions. "I tested positive for celiac disease after I'd been living with it for years," says Melissa McCrady, a news anchor and reporter from Wauwatosa, Wisconsin.

"I'd been having stomach trouble for a long time, and was originally diagnosed with irritable bowel syndrome. But in 2009, I went weeks with daily headaches, nausea and dizziness—I even blacked out. My doctor told me that it was stomach related, and after many tests, I was correctly diagnosed."

Melissa gave up gluten, a protein found in breads and other foods that contain wheat, barley or rye. "I'm so sensitive to it," she explains, "I even had to replace cosmetics with gluten-free versions."

Although she's always been fitness minded, Melissa says her diagnosis encourages her to be even healthier. "The reason I've lost weight and feel healthier is partly because I've eliminated most processed foods from my diet." Here, she shares a favorite meal made from fresh ingredients.

GLUTEN-FREE KAHLUA DESSERT

Gluten-Free Mashed Potatoes F M

PREP/TOTAL TIME: 30 min. YIELD: 8 servings

MELISSA MCCRADY • WAUWATOSA, WISCONSIN

This simple recipe creates a big batch of fluffy mashed potatoes. You'll be happy for it, as these taste just as good as they look!

- 4 large potatoes (about 3 lbs.), peeled and quartered
- 1 medium onion, chopped
- 1 pkg. (8 oz.) fat-free cream cheese, cubed
- 1 cup fat-free milk
- 1-1/4 tsp. salt
- 1/4 tsp. pepper

1. Place potatoes and onion in a large saucepan and cover with water. Bring to a boil. Reduce heat; cover and simmer for 15-20 minutes or until tender. Drain; transfer to a large bowl.

2. Add the cream cheese, milk, salt and pepper; beat until the potato mixture is fluffy.

Editor's Note: Read all ingredient labels for possible gluten content prior to use. Ingredient formulas can change, and production facilities vary among brands. If you're concerned that your brand may contain gluten, contact the company.

Nutrition Facts: 3/4 cup equals 191 calories, 1 g fat (trace saturated fat), 3 mg cholesterol, 548 mg sodium, 38 g carbohydrate, 3 g fiber, 9 g protein.

Gluten-Free Kahlua Dessert

PREP: 30 min. + chilling YIELD: 12 servings

MELISSA MCCRADY • WAUWATOSA, WISCONSIN

Whether you eat a gluten-free diet or not, you'll delight in every bite of this creamy treat that's accented with subtle notes of Kahlua liqueur.

- 1 cup gluten-free cornflakes, crushed
- 2 Tbsp. butter, melted
- 2 tsp. unflavored gelatin
- 1/4 cup cold water
- 12 oz. reduced-fat cream cheese
- 2 Tbsp. sugar
- 2/3 cup fat-free sweetened condensed milk
- 1/4 cup Kahlua (coffee liqueur)
- 2 cups fat-free whipped topping
- 2 oz. dark chocolate candy bar, melted

Fresh raspberries and mint leaves, optional

1. Combine cornflake crumbs and butter; press onto the bottom of a 9-in. square pan coated with cooking spray. Refrigerate for 10 minutes.

2. Meanwhile, in a small saucepan, sprinkle gelatin over cold water; let stand for 1 minute. Heat over low heat, stirring until gelatin is completely dissolved. Remove from the heat; set aside.

3. In a large bowl, beat cream cheese and sugar until smooth. Beat in the milk, Kahlua and gelatin mixture until blended. Gently fold in whipped topping; pour over crust. Cover and refrigerate for at least 4 hours or until firm.

4. Drizzle with melted chocolate; garnish with raspberries and mint leaves if desired.

Editor's Note: Read all ingredient labels for possible gluten content prior to use. Ingredient formulas can change, and production facilities vary among brands. If you're concerned that your brand may contain gluten, contact the company.

Nutrition Facts: 1 piece (calculated without raspberries) equals 217 calories, 9 g fat (6 g saturated fat), 28 mg cholesterol, 176 mg sodium, 25 g carbohydrate, 1 g fiber, 5 g protein. **Diabetic Exchanges:** 2 fat, 1-1/2 starch.

Gluten-Free Grilled Flank Steak C

PREP: 25 min. + marinating **GRILL:** 15 min.
YIELD: 8 servings

MELISSA MCCRADY • WAUWATOSA, WISCONSIN

Red wine and thyme are the perfect ingredients to turn tender steak into mouthwatering fare. While it offers the added bonus of being gluten-free, any guest at your table will love it.

3/4 cup gluten-free reduced-sodium tamari soy sauce
2 Tbsp. dried thyme
1 beef flank steak (2 lbs.)
3 bunches green onions, chopped
1/3 cup reduced-fat butter
1-1/2 cups dry red wine *or* reduced-sodium beef broth

1. In a large resealable plastic bag, combine soy sauce and thyme. Add the beef; seal bag and turn to coat. Refrigerate for at least 8 hours or overnight.

2. Drain and discard marinade. Grill steak, covered, over medium heat or broil 4 in. from the heat for 6-8 minutes on each side or until meat reaches desired doneness (for medium-rare, a meat thermometer should read 145°; medium, 160°; well-done, 170°). Let stand for 5 minutes.

3. Meanwhile, in a small saucepan, saute onions in butter until tender. Add wine; bring to a boil. Reduce heat; simmer, uncovered, for 10-15 minutes or until sauce is slightly thickened.

4. To serve, thinly slice the steak across the grain; serve with sauce.

Editor's Note: Read all ingredient labels for possible gluten content prior to use. Ingredient formulas can change, and production facilities vary among brands. If you're concerned that your brand may contain gluten, contact the company.

Nutrition Facts: 3 ounces cooked beef with 2 tablespoons sauce equals 234 calories, 12 g fat (6 g saturated fat), 64 mg cholesterol, 486 mg sodium, 4 g carbohydrate, 1 g fiber, 24 g protein. **Diabetic Exchanges:** 3 lean meat, 1 fat.

Some might say Sarah Klier of Grand Rapids, Michigan, has a tougher time feeding her family healthy meals than some moms. "Both my husband, Ryan, and toddler son, Joseph, have food sensitivities," she explains. "Nearly everything I make needs to come from scratch...and Joseph's been picky."

But this stay-at-home mom (Sarah also has a newborn) uses her family's special diets as another way to make nutritious choices. "We read labels on everything—not just for allergies—but to avoid high fructose corn syrup, partially hydrogenated oils and MSG."

The family has fully embraced their gradual move to a healthier way of life. "We're sometimes looked at as a little extreme by our extended family because of our diet, but we don't mind eating lots of vegetables and staying away from packaged foods—and we're healthier." The menu she shares on these pages features fantastic flavor and an assortment of fruits and veggies, so it's a great choice for Sarah's family and yours as well.

SATURDAY NIGHT PIZZA

Saturday Night Pizza

PREP: 20 min. + rising **BAKE:** 15 min. **YIELD:** 8 servings

SARAH KLIER • GRAND RAPIDS, MICHIGAN

Pizza gets a good-for-you treatment with this tasty idea. Four different vegetables and white whole wheat flour deliver 6 grams of fiber in every serving.

- 2 to 2-1/2 cups white whole wheat flour
- 1 pkg. (1/4 oz.) quick-rise yeast
- 1 Tbsp. dried oregano
- 1 tsp. salt
- 1 tsp. garlic powder
- 1 cup warm water (120° to 130°)
- 2 Tbsp. olive oil
- 1/2 lb. Italian turkey sausage links, casings removed
- 1 cup spaghetti sauce
- 1 cup fresh baby spinach
- 1 cup sliced fresh mushrooms
- 1 medium green pepper, sliced
- 1 medium onion, sliced
- 2 cups (8 oz.) shredded part-skim mozzarella cheese

1. In a small bowl, combine 2 cups flour, yeast, oregano, salt and garlic powder. Add water and oil; beat just until moistened. Stir in enough remaining flour to form a soft dough (dough will be sticky).

2. Turn onto a lightly floured surface; knead until smooth and elastic, about 6-8 minutes. Place in a bowl coated with cooking spray, turning once to coat the top. Cover and let rise for 30 minutes.

3. Meanwhile, in a large nonstick skillet, cook sausage until no longer pink; drain and set aside.

4. On a floured surface, roll dough into a 15-in. circle. Transfer to a 14-in. pizza pan coated with cooking spray. Build up edges slightly. Prick dough thoroughly with a fork. Bake at 450° for 5-8 minutes or until lightly browned.

5. Spread crust with spaghetti sauce. Top with spinach, mushrooms, pepper, onion and sausage. Sprinkle with cheese. Bake 15-20 minutes longer or until cheese is melted.

Nutrition Facts: 1 slice equals 298 calories, 12 g fat (4 g saturated fat), 34 mg cholesterol, 756 mg sodium, 32 g carbohydrate, 6 g fiber, 17 g protein. **Diabetic Exchanges:** 2 starch, 2 medium-fat meat.

White Bean Dip C M

PREP/TOTAL TIME: 15 min. **YIELD:** 1-1/2 cups

SARAH KLIER • GRAND RAPIDS, MICHIGAN

Great accompanying fresh veggies or as a sandwich spread, this dip brings a touch of sophistication and loads of flavor and nutrients to any meal.

- 1/4 cup soft bread crumbs
- 2 Tbsp. dry white wine *or* water
- 2 Tbsp. olive oil
- 2 Tbsp. lemon juice
- 1 can (15 oz.) white kidney *or* cannellini beans, rinsed and drained
- 4-1/2 tsp. minced fresh parsley
- 3 garlic cloves, peeled and halved
- 1/2 tsp. salt
- 1/2 tsp. snipped fresh dill *or* 1/4 tsp. dill weed
- 1/8 tsp. cayenne pepper

Assorted fresh vegetables

1. In a small bowl, combine bread crumbs and wine. In a food processor, combine the oil, lemon juice, beans, parsley, garlic, salt, dill and cayenne; cover and process until smooth. Add bread crumb mixture; process until blended. Serve with vegetables.

Nutrition Facts: 1/4 cup (calculated without vegetables) equals 107 calories, 5 g fat (1 g saturated fat), 0 cholesterol, 299 mg sodium, 12 g carbohydrate, 3 g fiber, 3 g protein. **Diabetic Exchanges:** 1 starch, 1 fat.

Swedish Apple Pie

PREP: 15 min. **BAKE:** 25 min. **YIELD:** 8 servings

SARAH KLIER • GRAND RAPIDS, MICHIGAN

This hearty and decadent apple pie serves up homemade flavor in every bite. The blend of whole wheat and all-purpose flours offers more fiber and less fat than a traditional pie crust.

- 1/2 cup sugar
- 1/4 cup whole wheat flour
- 1/4 cup all-purpose flour
- 1 tsp. baking powder
- 1/2 tsp. salt
- 1/2 tsp. ground cinnamon
- 1 egg
- 1/4 tsp. vanilla extract
- 2 medium tart apples, chopped
- 3/4 cup chopped walnuts *or* pecans, toasted

Confectioners' sugar, optional

1. In a large bowl, combine the sugar, flours, baking powder, salt and cinnamon. In a small bowl, whisk egg and vanilla. Stir into dry ingredients just until moistened. Fold in apples and walnuts.

2. Transfer to a 9-in. pie plate coated with cooking spray. Bake at 350° for 25-30 minutes or until a toothpick inserted near the center comes out clean. Sprinkle with confectioners' sugar if desired. Serve warm.

Nutrition Facts: 1 piece equals 174 calories, 7 g fat (1 g saturated fat), 26 mg cholesterol, 207 mg sodium, 25 g carbohydrate, 2 g fiber, 5 g protein. **Diabetic Exchanges:** 1-1/2 starch, 1 fat.

Naturally Delicious

When it comes to eating right, nothing fits the bill like garden-fresh produce! Whether harvested from your backyard or purchased from a farmers market, fresh ingredients turn everyday meals into healthy opportunities.

Ask *Healthy Cooking* Field Editor Nancy Brown of Dahinda, Illinois, about eating right, and she'll talk more about quality ingredients than calories. "I mostly eat natural, whole foods to get the best nutritional value," she says.

And with good reason. When Nancy was 18, her mom died of a heart attack. "I was a budding cook and just getting into the health craze," she says. "After that, I decided to take care of myself for the people I love. That was 30 years ago."

Today, Nancy, who owns a log home-building business and writes a recipe column for her local paper, is an avid organic gardener who also buys produce from the farmers market. "We grow some of our own produce, but I also want to support farmers' efforts to find alternatives to chemicals."

Nancy also stays energized by exercising. "Besides chasing after my kids, I do yoga and aerobics."

To keep things easy, Nancy relies on planning. "When I know what's for dinner, we can have healthy, quick meals and no excuses," she says.

LEMON FLUFF DESSERT

Weeknight Chicken and Pasta

PREP/TOTAL TIME: 25 min. YIELD: 4 servings

NANCY BROWN • DAHINDA, ILLINOIS

I came up with this dish to use up leftover chicken one night when I had unexpected guests. It was such a success that I make a variation of it almost weekly.

- 2 cups uncooked whole wheat bow tie pasta
- 1 small onion, chopped
- 1 small sweet red pepper, chopped
- 1 Tbsp. olive oil
- 1 garlic clove, minced
- 1-1/2 cups cubed cooked chicken breast
- 1/2 cup reduced-fat sour cream
- 1/4 cup fat-free milk
- 1/2 tsp. salt
- 1/2 tsp. pepper
- 1/2 tsp. dried tarragon
- 1/2 tsp. dried thyme
- 2 Tbsp. shredded Parmesan cheese
- 2 tsp. minced chives

1. Cook pasta according to package directions.

2. Meanwhile, in a large nonstick skillet, saute onion and red pepper in oil until tender. Add garlic; cook 1 minute longer. Stir in the chicken, sour cream, milk and seasonings; heat through. Drain pasta; stir into skillet. Sprinkle with cheese and chives.

Nutrition Facts: 1-1/4 cups equals 394 calories, 9 g fat (3 g saturated fat), 53 mg cholesterol, 399 mg sodium, 48 g carbohydrate, 7 g fiber, 28 g protein.

Whole Wheat Bread **F S M**

PREP: 20 min. + rising BAKE: 25 min. + cooling
YIELD: 1 loaf (16 slices)

NANCY BROWN • DAHINDA, ILLINOIS

I make this bread so often I have the recipe memorized. My kids love it for an after-school snack, but it's also great with soup, stew and more.

- 1-1/8 tsp. active dry yeast
- 1-1/4 cups warm water (110° to 115°)
- 1/4 cup packed brown sugar
- 2 Tbsp. reduced-fat butter, melted
- 3/4 tsp. salt
- 1-1/2 cups whole wheat flour
- 2 to 2-1/2 cups all-purpose flour

WEEKNIGHT CHICKEN AND PASTA
WHOLE WHEAT BREAD

1. In a large bowl, dissolve yeast in warm water. Add the brown sugar, butter, salt, whole wheat flour and 1 cup all-purpose flour. Beat until smooth. Stir in enough remaining flour to form a firm dough (dough will be sticky).

2. Turn onto a lightly floured surface; knead until smooth and elastic, about 6-8 minutes. Place in a bowl coated with cooking spray, turning once to coat the top. Cover and let rise for 1 hour.

3. Punch dough down and turn onto a floured surface; shape into a loaf. Place in a 9-in. x 5-in. loaf pan coated with cooking spay. Cover and let rise until doubled, about 1 hour.

4. Bake at 375° for 25-30 minutes or until golden brown. Remove from pan to a wire rack to cool.

Nutrition Facts: 1 slice equals 129 calories, 1 g fat (1 g saturated fat), 2 mg cholesterol, 125 mg sodium, 27 g carbohydrate, 2 g fiber, 4 g protein. **Diabetic Exchange:** 1-1/2 starch.

Lemon Fluff Dessert S C

PREP: 15 min. + chilling **YIELD:** 20 servings

NANCY BROWN • DAHINDA, ILLINOIS

This came from my grandmother, who owned a bakery. Her recipe was a full-fat version. I wanted to lighten it up, but I also didn't want to mess with it too much, so I only made a few healthy substitutions. The final outcome was sweet, lemony and light. We sometimes serve it with sliced strawberries over the top of individual pieces.

 1 can (12 oz.) evaporated milk
1-1/2 cups graham cracker crumbs
 1/3 cup butter, melted
 1 pkg. (.3 oz.) sugar-free lemon gelatin
 1 cup boiling water
 3 Tbsp. lemon juice
 1 pkg. (8 oz.) reduced-fat cream cheese
 3/4 cup sugar
 1 tsp. vanilla extract

1. Pour milk into a large metal bowl; place mixer beaters in the bowl. Cover and refrigerate for at least 2 hours.

2. In a small bowl, combine graham cracker crumbs and butter; set aside 1 tablespoon for topping. Press remaining crumb mixture into a 13-in. x 9-in. baking dish. Chill until set.

3. Meanwhile, in a small bowl, dissolve gelatin in boiling water. Stir in lemon juice; cool.

4. In another bowl, beat the cream cheese, sugar and vanilla until smooth. Add gelatin mixture and mix well. Beat evaporated milk until soft peaks form; fold into cream cheese mixture. Pour over crust. Sprinkle with reserved crumbs. Refrigerate for at least 2 hours before serving. Refrigerate leftovers.

Nutrition Facts: 1 piece equals 135 calories, 7 g fat (4 g saturated fat), 21 mg cholesterol, 136 mg sodium, 15 g carbohydrate, trace fiber, 3 g protein. **Diabetic Exchanges:** 1 starch, 1 fat.

When it comes to healthy habits, sticking to them can be the hardest part. We found a *Healthy Cooking* Field Editor with impressive tenacity, and she's ready to share her secrets...and recipes.

"For me, it comes down to determination and patience," says Pat Swart, a retired interior designer and architect turned syndicated columnist from Bridgeton, New Jersey. "And the thought of what I'd become if I did not exercise.

"I lift hand weights and walk 5 days a week," says Pat, who has kept up her fitness routine for 30 years. She also cut back on salt 4 decades ago and has been eating healthfully for the past 10 years. "I realized the effect fattening recipes can have and knew mine needed to be lightened."

Pat's menu spotlights her commitment to eating right and offers simple flavors that taste great. "My friends are hooked on these," she says. With their everyday ingredients, fresh taste and minimal prep work, these recipes have a taste we're sure you'll love now...and 10 years from now, too!

ASPARAGUS WITH TARRAGON LEMON SAUCE

Asparagus with Tarragon Lemon Sauce S C M

PREP/TOTAL TIME: 15 min. YIELD: 6 servings

PATRICIA SWART • BRIDGETON, NEW JERSEY

With its effortless prep and delightful flavor, this is a side dish you're sure to love.

- 2 lbs. fresh asparagus, trimmed
- 3 Tbsp. olive oil
- 1 tsp. all-purpose flour
- 3 Tbsp. fat-free milk
- 1 Tbsp. lemon juice
- 2 tsp. minced fresh tarragon

Dash salt

1. Place the asparagus in a steamer basket; place in a large saucepan over 1 in. of water. Bring to a boil; cover and steam for 3-5 minutes or until stems are crisp-tender. Drain.

2. Meanwhile, in a small saucepan, combine olive oil and flour. Gradually stir in milk until smooth. Bring to a boil; cook and stir for 1 minute or until thickened. Remove from the heat. Stir in the lemon juice, tarragon and salt. Serve with asparagus.

Nutrition Facts: 1 serving equals 83 calories, 7 g fat (1 g saturated fat), trace cholesterol, 36 mg sodium, 4 g carbohydrate, 1 g fiber, 2 g protein. **Diabetic Exchanges:** 1 vegetable, 1 fat.

Pork Chops with Apricot Sauce C

PREP/TOTAL TIME: 30 min. YIELD: 6 servings

PATRICIA SWART • BRIDGETON, NEW JERSEY

Apricot preserves bring a very special flavor to my pork entree. I serve it with corn bread, which can be made in advance and tastes great with any meat.

- 6 boneless pork loin chops (6 oz. *each*)
- 1/2 tsp. garlic pepper blend
- 1 Tbsp. olive oil
- 1 cup sugar-free apricot preserves
- 1 Tbsp. minced chives
- 1/4 tsp. salt

1. Sprinkle pork with garlic pepper blend.

2. In a large nonstick skillet coated with cooking spray, brown chops in oil on each side. Combine the preserves, chives and salt; spoon over chops. Reduce

PORK CHOPS WITH APRICOT SAUCE
BUTTERMILK CORN BREAD

heat; cover and cook for 8-10 minutes or until a meat thermometer reads 160°. Serve with sauce.

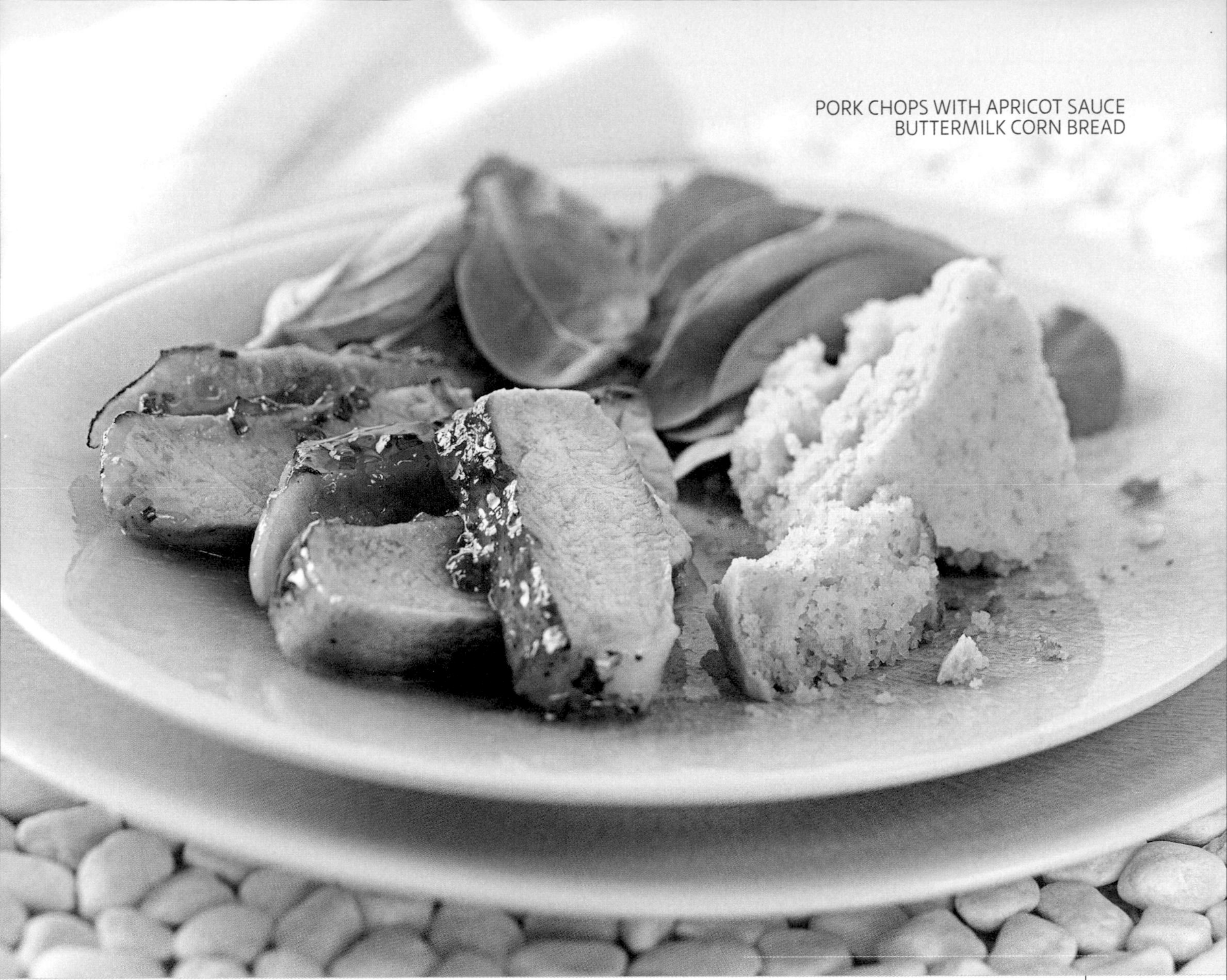

Nutrition Facts: 1 chop with 2 tablespoons sauce equals 273 calories, 12 g fat (4 g saturated fat), 82 mg cholesterol, 169 mg sodium, 13 g carbohydrate, trace fiber, 33 g protein. **Diabetic Exchanges:** 5 lean meat, 1 starch, 1/2 fat.

Buttermilk Corn Bread M

PREP/TOTAL: 30 min. YIELD: 8 servings

PATRICIA SWART • BRIDGETON, NEW JERSEY

This tender corn bread couldn't be easier to make, and it's a delicious addition to any menu.

- 1 cup all-purpose flour
- 1 cup yellow cornmeal
- 1 Tbsp. sugar
- 2 tsp. baking powder
- 1 tsp. baking soda
- 1/4 tsp. salt
- 2 eggs
- 1 cup buttermilk
- 3 Tbsp. butter, melted

1. In a large bowl, combine the flour, cornmeal, sugar, baking powder, baking soda and salt. In a small bowl, whisk the eggs, buttermilk and butter. Stir into dry ingredients just until moistened.

2. Transfer to a 9-in. square baking pan coated with cooking spray. Bake at 400° for 15-20 minutes or until top is lightly browned and a toothpick inserted near the center comes out clean. Serve warm.

Nutrition Facts: 1 piece equals 194 calories, 6 g fat (3 g saturated fat), 65 mg cholesterol, 412 mg sodium, 28 g carbohydrate, 2 g fiber, 6 g protein. **Diabetic Exchanges:** 2 starch, 1 fat.

For the best results when making corn bread, avoid overmixing the batter. Stir it by hand just until moistened. (Lumps in the batter are a good thing.) In addition, don't let the mixed batter stand before baking. Have the oven preheated and the skillet or pan ready to go.

Family-Friendly Fare

When she became a registered dietitian, Jackie Termont found that lightening up her favorite dishes was a snap. Here, she shares a no-fuss menu that's perfect for casual meals at home as well as entertaining weekend guests.

When work began invading Jackie Termont's personal life, it turned out to be a good thing. "I went back to school and became a registered dietitian," says the Richmond, Virginia cook.

"I started lightening recipes and wanted to eat healthier and lose a few pounds. It was a gradual change, but I've been doing it for so long that it just comes naturally now," Jackie explains.

Though she doesn't follow a special diet, Jackie does pay attention to what she eats. "It's more fun for me when I don't have to worry if the food is potentially unhealthy," she says. "But I love food, and I think everything can be worked into a diet if you're careful about how much and how often you eat."

She has a balanced approach when it comes to exercise, too—working out 4 days a week with weights, elliptical trainers and the treadmill.

She also does yoga twice a week and tries to walk or ride her bike on other days. "I just feel better after working out, like I've accomplished something good for myself," she says.

When not at the gym, Jackie can often be found at home...baking. To keep things lighter, she opts for reduced-fat and low-sugar ingredients. "However, I don't generally use totally fat-free dairy because I think you need some fat to make it palatable."

Jackie's menu is the perfect example of her eating philosophy—it relies on lean, nutritious ingredients, but has the slightest touch of indulgence. Just dig into her heavenly Strawberry-Banana Graham Pudding to see what we mean!

Roasted Veggie Orzo F M

PREP: 25 min. BAKE: 20 min. YIELD: 8 servings

JACKIE TERMONT • RICHMOND, VIRGINIA

My sister inspired this recipe. I added a few more spices, but it's her concept. It's easy to vary, is a great way to add veggies to your diet and the olive oil is heart healthy.

1-1/2 cups fresh mushrooms, halved
   1 medium zucchini, chopped
   1 medium sweet yellow pepper, chopped
   1 medium sweet red pepper, chopped
   1 small red onion, cut into wedges
   1 cup cut fresh asparagus (1-in. pieces)
   1 Tbsp. olive oil
   1 tsp. *each* dried oregano, thyme and rosemary, crushed
 1/2 tsp. salt

1-1/4 cups uncooked orzo pasta
 1/4 cup crumbled feta cheese

1. Place vegetables in a 15-in. x 10-in. x 1-in. baking pan coated with cooking spray. Drizzle with oil and sprinkle with seasonings; toss to coat. Bake at 400° for 20-25 minutes or until tender, stirring occasionally.

2. Meanwhile, cook orzo according to package directions. Drain; transfer to a serving bowl. Stir in roasted vegetables. Sprinkle with cheese.

Nutrition Facts: 3/4 cup equals 164 calories, 3 g fat (1 g saturated fat), 2 mg cholesterol, 188 mg sodium, 28 g carbohydrate, 3 g fiber, 6 g protein. **Diabetic Exchanges:** 1-1/2 starch, 1 vegetable, 1/2 fat.

Strawberry-Banana Graham Pudding F

PREP: 20 min. + chilling YIELD: 12 servings

JACKIE TERMONT • RICHMOND, VIRGINIA

I mix in additional fruit to get a little closer to all those servings you need every day. You can also try using different flavored puddings and fruit to switch up the recipe.

   9 whole reduced-fat cinnamon graham crackers
1-3/4 cups cold fat-free milk
   1 pkg. (1 oz.) sugar-free instant cheesecake *or* vanilla pudding mix
   1 large firm banana, sliced
 1/2 tsp. lemon juice
   2 cups sliced fresh strawberries, *divided*
2-1/2 cups reduced-fat whipped topping, *divided*
Mint sprigs, optional

1. Line the bottom of a 9-in. square pan with 4-1/2 graham crackers; set aside.

2. In a small bowl, whisk milk and pudding mix for 2 minutes. Let stand for 2 minutes or until soft-set. Place banana slices in another small bowl; toss with lemon juice. Stir bananas and 1 cup strawberries into the pudding. Fold in 1-3/4 cups whipped topping.

3. Spread half of pudding over the graham crackers; repeat layers. Cover and refrigerate overnight. Refrigerate remaining berries and whipped topping.

4. Just before serving, top with remaining berries and topping. Garnish with mint if desired.

Nutrition Facts: 1 piece equals 117 calories, 2 g fat (2 g saturated fat), 1 mg cholesterol, 171 mg sodium, 23 g carbohydrate, 1 g fiber, 2 g protein. **Diabetic Exchanges:** 1 starch, 1/2 fruit.

Zesty Marinated Pork Chops S C

PREP: 15 min. + marinating **COOK:** 10 min.
YIELD: 6 servings

JACKIE TERMONT • RICHMOND, VIRGINIA

My husband loves pork chops. They're a good source of lean protein and it's easy to change their flavor. I created this marinade based on a few I saw in "Healthy Cooking" magazine.

- 1/4 cup balsamic vinegar
- 2 Tbsp. white wine or reduced-sodium chicken broth
- 4 tsp. olive oil, *divided*
- 1 tsp. chili powder
- 1/2 tsp. prepared horseradish
- 1/4 tsp. dill weed
- 1/4 tsp. garlic powder
- 1/4 tsp. salt
- 6 boneless pork loin chops (4 oz. *each*)

1. In a large resealable plastic bag, combine the vinegar, wine, 1 tsp. oil, chili powder, horseradish, dill, garlic powder and salt. Add the pork chops; seal bag and turn to coat. Refrigerate for 8 hours or overnight, turning occasionally.

2. Drain and discard marinade. In a large nonstick skillet over medium heat, cook chops in remaining oil for 4-5 minutes on each side or until a meat thermometer reads 160°.

Nutrition Facts: 1 pork chop equals 183 calories, 10 g fat (3 g saturated fat), 55 mg cholesterol, 61 mg sodium, 1 g carbohydrate, trace fiber, 22 g protein. **Diabetic Exchanges:** 3 lean meat, 1/2 fat.

Jackie says that when it comes to **low-fat cooking**, she loves using her rice steamer for vegetables, as well as her grill pan and indoor grill. The microwave comes in handy for getting frozen veggies on the table quickly.

Enticing Extras

For busy TV news reporter Caroline Shively, taking advantage of leftovers is a must. Here, she shares a favorite entree and then explains how she uses the extras in two incredible dishes later in the week.

Eating well and exercising can be daunting, but imagine if you had to do it while capturing the effects of a hurricane or as one of the few Westerners at the voting polls during Iraq's first election. Welcome to the life of Caroline Shively, a correspondent for FOX News. Her work places her in the middle of historic events—including covering the 2008 election—but Caroline's home life in Alexandria, Virgina includes more typical things, such as cooking, spending time with her husband and playing tennis.

"I cook a lot when I'm home," Caroline says. "Kitchen time is fun for my husband, Robb, and me. Our schedules don't always allow us to see each other during the week, so we talk and catch up while cooking." The Kentucky native turns to the recipes she grew up with for inspiration. "A lot of my cooking comes from my mom," she says. "My husband jokes that I can't make a meal without calling her!"

In addition to spending time in the kitchen, the couple enjoys exercising together, too, but learning to mesh eating habits didn't come as naturally at the start. "My husband loves to grill," says Caroline. "At first, he tended to cook fattier things, and I joked I was going to weigh too much if he kept feeding me cheeseburgers. Since then, we've learned to compromise—he still grills but now picks leaner meats." The dishes she offers here feature grilled steak and an easy leftover plan they both appreciate.

SOUTHWEST STEAK QUESADILLAS

Southwest Steak Quesadillas

PREP/TOTAL TIME: 30 min. **YIELD:** 4 servings

CAROLINE SHIVELY • ALEXANDRIA, VIRGINIA

Colorful peppers and onions make this fantastic dish look as great as it tastes. As an added bonus, folding over one larger tortilla (instead of using two smaller ones) saves you a few grams of fat.

- 1 each small green, sweet red and yellow peppers, finely chopped
- 1 small red onion, finely chopped
- 4 fat-free flour tortillas (10 in.)
- 1/2 cup shredded reduced-fat cheddar cheese
- 1 cooked Southwest Steak (see opposite page), chopped
- 1/4 cup minced fresh cilantro
- 2 Tbsp. chopped seeded jalapeno pepper

Salsa, guacamole and reduced-fat sour cream, optional

1. In a large nonstick skillet coated with cooking spray, cook and stir peppers and onion over medium-high heat until tender. Transfer to a small bowl.

2. Coat the same skillet with cooking spray; add one tortilla. Sprinkle 2 Tbsp. cheese over half of tortilla. Top with a fourth of the steak, 1/3 cup pepper mixture, 1 Tbsp. cilantro and 1-1/2 tsp. jalapeno.

3. Fold over and cook over low heat for 1-2 minutes on each side or until cheese is melted; remove. Repeat for remaining quesadillas, spraying pan as needed. Cut into wedges; serve with salsa, guacamole and sour cream if desired.

Editor's Note: When cutting hot peppers, disposable gloves are recommended. Avoid touching your face.

Nutrition Facts: 1 quesadilla (calculated without optional ingredients) equals 379 calories, 13 g fat (6 g saturated fat), 64 mg cholesterol, 772 mg sodium, 35 g carbohydrate, 3 g fiber, 30 g protein.

Southwest Steak Salad C

PREP/TOTAL TIME: 15 min. **YIELD:** 4 servings

CAROLINE SHIVELY • ALEXANDRIA, VIRGINIA

With its tangy combination of lemon juice and balsamic vinegar dressing, this hearty dish perks up dinnertime and fills you up fast.

- 1/4 cup minced fresh cilantro
- 3 Tbsp. balsamic vinegar
- 2 Tbsp. water
- 1 Tbsp. lemon juice

1 Tbsp. olive oil
1 pkg. (5 oz.) spring mix salad greens
1 small red onion, chopped
1 *each* small green, sweet red and yellow peppers, chopped
1 cooked Southwest Steak (see below), thinly sliced

1. In a small bowl, whisk the first five ingredients; set aside. In a large bowl, combine salad greens, onion and peppers. Drizzle with dressing; toss to coat. Divide among four plates. Heat steak if desired; place over salads.

Nutrition Facts: 1 serving equals 252 calories, 13 g fat (4 g saturated fat), 54 mg cholesterol, 274 mg sodium, 9 g carbohydrate, 3 g fiber, 24 g protein.

Southwest Steak

PREP: 15 min. + marinating **GRILL:** 10 min.
YIELD: 8 servings

CAROLINE SHIVELY • ALEXANDRIA, VIRGINIA
Lime juice tenderizes the steak while garlic, chili powder and red pepper flakes kick things up. My husband and I came up with this together as something lighter to make on the grill.

1/4 cup lime juice
6 garlic cloves, minced
4 tsp. chili powder
4 tsp. canola oil
1 tsp. salt
1 tsp. crushed red pepper flakes

1 tsp. pepper
2 beef flank steaks (1 lb. each)

1. In a large resealable plastic bag, combine the first seven ingredients; add the beef. Seal bag and turn to coat; refrigerate for 4 hours or overnight.

2. Drain and discard marinade. Coat grill rack with cooking spray before starting the grill. Grill beef, covered, over medium heat for 5-7 minutes on each side or until meat reaches desired doneness (for medium-rare, a meat thermometer should read 145°; medium, 160°; well-done, 170°).

3. Let stand for 5 minutes; thinly slice across the grain.

Nutrition Facts: 3 oz. cooked beef equals 187 calories, 10 g fat (4 g saturated fat), 54 mg cholesterol, 259 mg sodium, 2 g carbohydrate, trace fiber, 22 g protein. **Diabetic Exchanges:** 3 lean meat, 1 fat.

"It's great to cook once and end up with several different meals," Caroline says. She and husband Robb created delicious **Southwest Steak,** which can be turned into a dinner or lunch the next day. Southwest Steak Quesadillas are a tasty handheld treat, and Southwest Steak Salad is filling yet refreshing.

Satisfying Supper

Crusty loaves of bread, hearty pasta entrees...you can enjoy these all-time favorites
and still keep your commitment to eating healthy. From Fruita, Colorado,
home cook Evelyn Slade explains how she does just that!

Sometimes transitioning into a healthy lifestyle is as easy as taking a few steps in the right direction. "I don't have a set fitness routine," says Evelyn Slade of Fruita, Colorado. "I just strive to get in 10,000 steps each day and ride a bike or do yard work."

That keep-it-simple attitude carries into her cooking, as Evelyn, a school administrator, opts for fast meals low in sodium and calories. "I began cooking healthy several years ago to maintain my weight, keep my blood pressure in check and help my husband, Norm, lose weight. It was a gradual process, and friends and family responded well. I often make meals for the teachers at work, and I never get complaints!"

Along with keeping menus light, Evelyn also adds as many fruits and veggies as possible. "I purchase locally grown produce in the summer and fall—I think it tastes better—and work it into sides and main courses." With its garden-fresh goodness and easy preparation, the dinner Evelyn shares here is reason enough to take a healthy step toward the supper table tonight!

Wheat Bread

PREP: 10 min. **BAKE:** 3 hours 35 min. + cooling
YIELD: 1 loaf (2 lbs., 16 slices)

EVELYN SLADE • FRUITA, COLORADO

I tweaked an old recipe to create this bread by changing ingredient amounts, adding healthy items and incorporating whole wheat flour into it. The results are tender and delicious!

1-1/2	cups water
1	egg
2	Tbsp. canola oil
2-1/2	cups bread flour
1-1/2	cups whole wheat flour
1/2	cup oat flour
1/2	cup nonfat dry milk powder
3	Tbsp. sugar
1-1/2	tsp. salt
1	pkg. (1/4 oz.) active dry yeast

1. In bread machine pan, place all ingredients in order suggested by manufacturer. Select basic bread setting. Choose crust color and loaf size if available. Bake according to bread machine directions (check dough after 5 minutes of mixing; add 1 to 2 Tbsp. of water or flour if needed).

Nutrition Facts: 1 slice equals 156 calories, 3 g fat (trace saturated fat), 14 mg cholesterol, 246 mg sodium, 28 g carbohydrate, 2 g fiber, 6 g protein. **Diabetic Exchange:** 2 starch.

WHEAT BREAD

VEGGIE TOSSED SALAD

Veggie Tossed Salad

PREP/TOTAL TIME: 10 min. **YIELD:** 4 servings

EVELYN SLADE • FRUITA, COLORADO

This 10-minute side salad delivers a dose of veggies and great fresh flavors. Feel free to try it with your favorite dressing.

1-1/2 cups torn romaine

1-1/2 cups fresh baby spinach

3/4 cup sliced fresh mushrooms

3/4 cup grape tomatoes

1/2 cup sliced cucumber

1/3 cup sliced ripe olives

1 Tbsp. grated Parmesan cheese

1/4 cup reduced-fat Italian salad dressing

1. In a large bowl, combine the first seven ingredients. Add salad dressing; toss to coat.

Nutrition Facts: 1 cup equals 62 calories, 4 g fat (1 g saturated fat), 1 mg cholesterol, 245 mg sodium, 5 g carbohydrate, 2 g fiber, 2 g protein. **Diabetic Exchanges:** 1 vegetable, 1 fat.

Shrimp Fettuccine Alfredo

PREP/TOTAL TIME: 30 min. **YIELD:** 4 servings

EVELYN SLADE • FRUITA, COLORADO

This has always been a favorite, so when I started cooking healthier, I tried different ways to lighten it. Less butter and fat-free half-and-half worked well, along with using a little flour to thicken the sauce.

6 oz. uncooked fettuccine

2 Tbsp. butter

4-1/2 tsp. all-purpose flour

1 cup fat-free half-and-half

1 lb. cooked medium shrimp, peeled and deveined

1/3 cup grated Parmesan cheese

1/2 tsp. salt

2 Tbsp. minced fresh parsley

1. Cook fettuccine according to package directions. Meanwhile, in a large saucepan, melt butter. Stir in flour until smooth; gradually add half-and-half. Bring to a boil; cook and stir for 1 minute or until thickened. Drain fettuccine; stir into pan. Stir in the shrimp, cheese and salt; heat through. Sprinkle with parsley before serving.

Nutrition Facts: 1 cup equals 397 calories, 11 g fat (5 g saturated fat), 193 mg cholesterol, 670 mg sodium, 39 g carbohydrate, 2 g fiber, 34 g protein.

"When eating away from home, be mindful of what you're ordering," Evelyn suggests. "If I indulge one day, I cut back at home the next."

Comfort Made Light

The next time the weather turns chilly, consider this heartwarming menu from
Nancy Zimmerman. Her satisfying chili, crusty oat bread and must-try
Black Forest Cake are sure to warm you up from the inside out!

They say being active keeps you healthy, and Nancy Zimmerman proves it's true. Between her job, pets (including 18 ducks!) and hobbies, this Cape May Court House, New Jersey resident keeps busy. "I work part-time helping Christian radio stations, volunteer at the local rescue mission, farm and play volleyball and softball with my husband, Ken," she writes. "I also enjoy photography and chatting with friends on tasteofhome.com."

To fit a workout into her hectic schedule, Nancy begins her day by running or weight training, a routine she started 16 years ago. "I exercise first thing in the morning, so I don't get sidetracked." She attributes exercising and eating right to improving her sports performance and keeping trim.

Her vegetarian diet and Ken's garden ensure she gets plenty of fruits and vegetables. "I freeze and can some for winter and make reduced-sugar preserves," Nancy says. She rounds out meals with whole grains and protein from milk, yogurt and eggs (from her ducks, of course). As you'll see, the following recipes capture Nancy's love for fresh flavors, home-cooked specialties and smart, tasty eating.

BLACK FOREST CAKE

Black Forest Cake F

PREP: 40 min. **BAKE:** 35 min. + cooling **YIELD:** 24 servings

NANCY ZIMMERMAN • CAPE MAY COURT HOUSE, NEW JERSEY

Applesauce is used to keep this light version of Black Forest Cake healthy. Now, even people who are on a diet can enjoy a slice of rich chocolate cake!

2	cups cherry juice
1-3/4	cups sugar
1/2	cup unsweetened applesauce
1/4	cup canola oil
2	eggs
2	Tbsp. cider vinegar
3	tsp. vanilla extract
3	cups all-purpose flour
1/3	cup baking cocoa
2	tsp. baking soda
1	tsp. salt
1-1/2	cups cold fat-free milk
1	pkg. (1.4 oz.) sugar-free instant chocolate pudding mix
1	can (20 oz.) reduced-sugar cherry pie filling
1-1/2	cups frozen fat-free whipped topping, thawed

1. In a large bowl, beat the cherry juice, sugar, applesauce, oil, eggs, vinegar and vanilla until well blended. In a large bowl, combine the flour, cocoa, baking soda and salt; gradually beat into cherry juice mixture until blended.

2. Pour into a 13-in. x 9-in. baking pan coated with cooking spray. Bake at 350° for 35-40 minutes or until a toothpick inserted near the center comes out clean. Cool completely on a wire rack.

3. In a small bowl, whisk milk and pudding mix for 2 minutes. Let stand for 2 minutes or until soft-set. Frost top of cake with pudding. Cover and refrigerate for 15 minutes. Top with pie filling. Chill until serving. Serve with whipped topping.

Nutrition Facts: 1 piece with 1 Tbsp. whipped topping equals 186 calories, 3 g fat (trace saturated fat), 18 mg cholesterol, 272 mg sodium, 36 g carbohydrate, 1 g fiber, 3 g protein.

Rustic Oat Bran Bread F M

PREP: 30 min. + rising **BAKE:** 20 min. + cooling
YIELD: 1 loaf (12 wedges)

NANCY ZIMMERMAN • CAPE MAY COURT HOUSE, NEW JERSEY

This moist bread is the perfect complement to soups, stews, chili and even crisp salad.

SPICY VEGETABLE CHILI
RUSTIC OAT BRAN BREAD

2-1/4 to 2-3/4 cups all-purpose flour

1/3 cup oat bran

1 pkg. (1/4 oz.) active dry yeast

1-1/4 tsp. salt

1 cup water

2 Tbsp. honey

1 Tbsp. cornmeal

1. In a large bowl, combine 1 cup flour, oat bran, yeast and salt. In a small saucepan, heat water and honey to 120°-130°. Add to dry ingredients; beat just until moistened. Stir in enough remaining flour to form a stiff dough (dough will be sticky).

2. Turn onto a lightly floured surface; knead until smooth and elastic, about 6-8 minutes. Place in a bowl coated with cooking spray, turning once to coat the top. Cover and let rise in a warm place until doubled, about 30 minutes.

3. Punch down dough. Turn onto lightly floured surface. Shape into a round loaf. Place on a baking sheet coated with cooking spray and sprinkled with cornmeal. Cover and let rise until nearly doubled, about 30 minutes. With a sharp knife, make three diagonal slashes across the top loaf.

4. Bake at 400° for 20-25 minutes or until golden brown. Remove from baking sheet to wire rack to cool.

Nutrition Facts: 1 wedge equals 107 calories, trace fat (trace saturated fat), 0 cholesterol, 247 mg sodium, 23 g carbohydrate, 1 g fiber, 3 g protein. **Diabetic Exchange:** 1-1/2 starch.

Spicy Vegetable Chili F M

PREP: 25 min. **COOK:** 35 min. **YIELD:** 8 servings (2 qt.)

NANCY ZIMMERMAN • CAPE MAY COURT HOUSE, NEW JERSEY

This chili makes a great comforting meal on cool autumn nights. I love dipping the oat bran bread into it.

1 medium onion, chopped

1 medium carrot, thinly sliced

1 medium green pepper, chopped

1/2 lb. sliced fresh mushrooms

1 small zucchini, sliced

1 Tbsp. olive oil

4 garlic cloves, minced

1 can (28 oz.) diced tomatoes, undrained

2 cans (16 oz. *each*) kidney beans, rinsed and drained

2 cans (8 oz. each) no-salt-added tomato sauce

1 can (4 oz.) chopped green chilies

3 Tbsp. chili powder

3 tsp. dried oregano

2 tsp. ground cumin

2 tsp. paprika

1/4 tsp. crushed red pepper flakes

1 Tbsp. white wine vinegar

Minced fresh cilantro and fat-free sour cream, optional

1. In a Dutch oven, saute the onion, carrot, pepper, mushrooms and zucchini in oil until tender. Add garlic; cook 1 minute longer. Add the tomatoes, beans, tomato sauce, green chilies and seasonings. Bring to a boil. Reduce heat; simmer, uncovered, for 35 minutes, stirring occasionally.

2. 2. Stir in vinegar. Serve in soup bowls; garnish each with cilantro and sour cream if desired.

Nutrition Facts: 1 cup (calculated without sour cream) equals 195 calories, 3 g fat (trace saturated fat), 0 cholesterol, 423 mg sodium, 35 g carbohydrate, 11 g fiber, 10 g protein. **Diabetic Exchanges:** 2 starch, 1 very lean meat.

Enjoy Seasonal Flavors

Looking for a satisfying supper tonight? Dig into this delightful pasta dinner from Katie Wollgast. She relies on pumpkin, cranberries, nutmeg, pecans and a little prepared eggnog for her full-flavored feast.

Getting healthy and staying that way doesn't have to be hard. All it takes is smart choices in the kitchen and daily exercise. For Katie Wollgast of Florissant, Missouri, this means growing her own produce, choosing healthy foods and staying in shape with daily exercise. "This definitely involves sticking to an exercise plan," she notes.

"My routine started in high school. I alternate stretching and strength training six mornings a week, and I take a 3-mile walk every evening. I love walking by myself or with my parents, who are walkers, too. It's a pleasant way to spend time with them at the end of each day."

Along with exercise, Katie also has a history of lightening dishes. "My mom was a good cook, who used lots of garden foods and fresh fruits. When I 'took over the kitchen,' I continued much of what she had done. I found that, in general, many recipes called for ingredients that weren't really needed, so I started lightening them right away."

Between Katie's fabulous meal shown here and daily exercise, you, too, can create a balance within your own healthy life.

SAUSAGE AND PUMPKIN PASTA
EASY TOSSED SALAD

Sausage and Pumpkin Pasta

PREP: 20 min. COOK: 15 min. YIELD: 4 servings

KATIE WOLLGAST • FLORISSANT, MISSOURI

Cubed leftover turkey may be substituted for sausage. Just add it to the skillet with the cooked pasta for a fast meal.

- 2 cups uncooked multigrain bow tie pasta
- 1/2 lb. Italian turkey sausage links, casings removed
- 1/2 lb. sliced fresh mushrooms
- 1 medium onion, chopped
- 4 garlic cloves, minced
- 1 cup reduced-sodium chicken broth
- 1 cup canned pumpkin
- 1/2 cup white wine or additional reduced-sodium chicken broth
- 1/2 tsp. rubbed sage
- 1/4 tsp. salt
- 1/4 tsp. garlic powder
- 1/4 tsp. pepper
- 1/4 cup grated Parmesan cheese
- 1 Tbsp. dried parsley flakes

1. Cook pasta according to package directions.

2. Meanwhile, in a large nonstick skillet coated with cooking spray, cook the sausage, mushrooms, onion and garlic over medium heat until meat is no longer pink; drain. Stir in the chicken broth, pumpkin, wine, sage, salt, garlic powder and pepper. Bring to a boil. Reduce heat; simmer, uncovered, for 5-6 minutes or until slightly thickened.

3. Drain pasta; add to the skillet and heat through. Just before serving, sprinkle with cheese and parsley.

Nutrition Facts: 1-3/4 cups equals 348 calories, 9 g fat (2 g saturated fat), 38 mg cholesterol, 733 mg sodium, 42 g carbohydrate, 7 g fiber, 23 g protein.

Easy Tossed Salad S M

PREP/TOTAL TIME: 10 min. YIELD: 4 servings

KATIE WOLLGAST • FLORISSANT, MISSOURI

Apples, almonds and cranberries provide powerfoods galore in my easy five-ingredient salad.

- 8 cups torn mixed salad greens
- 1 large apple, sliced
- 1/2 cup sliced almonds, toasted
- 1/2 cup dried cranberries
- 1/2 cup fat-free poppy seed salad dressing

1. In a large bowl, combine the salad greens, apple, almonds and cranberries. Drizzle with dressing; toss to coat. Serve immediately.

Nutrition Facts: 2-1/2 cups equals 210 calories, 6 g fat (1 g saturated fat), 5 mg cholesterol, 109 mg sodium, 36 g carbohydrate, 6 g fiber, 5 g protein.

Eggnog Cake

PREP: 25 min. **BAKE:** 20 min. + cooling **YIELD:** 8 servings

KATIE WOLLGAST • FLORISSANT, MISSOURI

We enjoy this cake so much! During the holidays, I actually buy eggnog to freeze so I can make the dessert year-round.

3/4	cup reduced-fat eggnog
1/4	cup sugar
2	Tbsp. canola oil
2	Tbsp. unsweetened applesauce
1	egg
1-1/2	cups all-purpose flour
2	tsp. baking powder
1/2	tsp. salt
1/4	tsp. ground nutmeg
1/4	cup golden raisins
2	Tbsp. chopped pecans

TOPPING:

1/4	cup packed brown sugar
2	Tbsp. all-purpose flour
1/2	tsp. ground nutmeg
1	Tbsp. cold butter
2	Tbsp. chopped pecans
2	cups reduced-fat vanilla ice cream, optional

1. In a large bowl, beat the eggnog, sugar, oil, applesauce and egg until well blended. In a small bowl, combine the flour, baking powder, salt and nutmeg; gradually beat into eggnog mixture until blended. Stir in raisins and pecans. Pour into a 9-in. round baking pan coated with cooking spray.

2. For topping, in a small bowl, combine the brown sugar, flour and nutmeg. Cut in butter until crumbly. Stir in pecans; sprinkle over batter.

3. Bake at 350° for 20-25 minutes or until a toothpick inserted near the center comes out clean. Cool for 10 minutes before removing from pan to a wire rack to cool completely. Serve with the ice cream if desired.

Editor's Note: This recipe was tested with commercially prepared eggnog.

Nutrition Facts: 1 slice (calculated without ice cream) equals 255 calories, 9 g fat (2 g saturated fat), 48 mg cholesterol, 285 mg sodium, 39 g carbohydrate, 1 g fiber, 5 g protein.

"I always like to plan my entrees and side dishes around **in-season vegetables** instead of planning menus the other way around," shares Katie. "This way, I seem to eat far more vegetables."

CHOCOLATE CHIP COOKIES

SWEDISH TEA RING

GLUTEN-FREE ANGEL FOOD CAKE

Cookies, Cakes & More

A demanding sweet tooth can make it hard to stick to a healthy lifestyle. No need to skip dessert: Our rich cheesecakes, chocolaty bars and chewy cookies will do the trick. You'll cure your craving *and* stay on track!

Gluten-Free Angel Food Cake **F**

PREP: 15 min. **BAKE:** 45 min. + cooling
YIELD: 16 servings

ANNE WIEBE • GLADSTONE, MANITOBA

My daughter can't have gluten, and my husband is diabetic, so there are a lot of special recipes at our house. This cake is always on our family gathering table.

1-1/2 cups egg whites (about 10)
   3/4 cup plus 1/2 cup sugar, *divided*
   1/4 cup cornstarch
   1/4 cup white rice flour
   1/4 cup tapioca flour
   1/4 cup potato starch
1-1/2 tsp. cream of tartar
   3/4 tsp. salt
   3/4 tsp. vanilla extract
Assorted fresh fruit, optional

1. Place egg whites in a large bowl; let stand at room temperature for 30 minutes. Sift 3/4 cup sugar, cornstarch, flours and potato starch together twice; set aside.

2. Add cream of tartar, salt and vanilla to egg whites; beat on medium speed until soft peaks form. Gradually add remaining sugar, about 2 Tbsp. at a time, beating on high until stiff peaks form. Gradually fold in flour mixture, about 1/2 cup at a time.

3. Gently spoon into an ungreased 10-in. tube pan. Cut through the batter with a knife to remove air pockets. Bake on the lowest oven rack at 350° for 45-50 minutes or until lightly browned and entire top appears dry. Immediately invert pan; cool completely, about 1 hour.

4. Run a knife around side and center tube of pan. Remove cake to a plate. Top with fruit if desired.

Editor's Note: Read all ingredient labels for possible gluten content prior to use. Ingredient formulas can change, and production facilities vary among brands. If you're concerned that your brand may contain gluten, contact the company.

Nutrition Facts: 1 slice (calculated without fruit) equals 101 calories, trace fat (0 saturated fat), 0 cholesterol, 149 mg sodium, 23 g carbohydrate, trace fiber, 3 g protein. **Diabetic Exchange:** 1-1/2 starch.

Chocolate Chip Cookies

PREP: 15 min. **BAKE:** 10 min./batch + cooling
YIELD: 4 dozen

BETHANY THAYER • TROUTVILLE, VIRGINIA

Chocolate chip cookies are on just about everyone's list of favorites, and these are sure to please!

   1/2 cup reduced-fat margarine
   3/4 cup sugar
   3/4 cup packed brown sugar
     2 eggs
   1/4 cup (2 oz.) reduced-fat plain yogurt
     2 tsp. vanilla extract
2-1/2 cups all-purpose flour
     1 tsp. baking soda
     1 tsp. salt
1-1/2 cups miniature semisweet chocolate chips
   1/2 cup chopped walnuts, toasted

1. In a large bowl, lightly cream the margarine and sugars. Add eggs, one at a time, beating well after each addition. Beat in the yogurt and vanilla. Combine the flour, baking soda and salt; gradually add to the creamed mixture. Stir in the chocolate chips and walnuts.

2. Drop by heaping tablespoonfuls 2 in. apart onto baking sheets coated with cooking spray. Bake at 375° for 8-10 minutes or until cookies are golden brown. Remove to wire racks.

Nutrition Facts: 1 cookie equals 94 calories, 4 g fat (1 g saturated fat), 9 mg cholesterol, 93 mg sodium, 15 g carbohydrate, 1 g fiber, 1 g protein. **Diabetic Exchanges:** 1 starch, 1/2 fat.

> When you're baking an **angel food cake,** use an oven thermometer to make sure the oven is not baking at a different temperature than you set it. Remember to place the pan on the lowest rack to allow sufficient air circulation over the top of such a tall cake.

COOKIES, CAKES & MORE   **503**

Cocoa-Almond Meringue Cookies `F` `S` `C`

PREP: 20 min. BAKE: 50 min. + standing YIELD: 3 dozen

HEALTHY COOKING TEST KITCHEN

Here's a simple recipe that makes a great hostess gift. It also comes in handy around the holidays.

4	egg whites
1/2	tsp. coconut extract
1/4	tsp. almond extract
1/4	tsp. vanilla extract
1/4	tsp. cream of tartar
1/8	tsp. salt
1	cup sugar
1/4	cup plus 1 Tbsp. baking cocoa, *divided*

1. Place egg whites in a large bowl; let stand at room temperature for 30 minutes. Add the extracts, cream of tartar and salt; beat on medium speed until soft peaks form. Gradually beat in sugar, 1 Tbsp. at a time, on high until stiff peaks form and sugar is dissolved.

2. Fold in 1/4 cup cocoa. Place mixture in a pastry or heavy-duty resealable plastic bag; cut a small hole in the corner of bag. Pipe meringue in 2-in. circles onto parchment paper-lined baking sheets. Bake at 250° for 50-60 minutes or until set and dry. Turn off oven; leave cookies in oven for 1-1/2 hours.

3. Dust the cookies with the remaining cocoa. Carefully remove from the parchment paper. Store in an airtight container.

Nutrition Facts: 1 cookie equals 26 calories, trace fat (0 saturated fat), 0 cholesterol, 14 mg sodium, 6 g carbohydrate, trace fiber, 1 g protein. **Diabetic Exchange:** 1/2 starch.

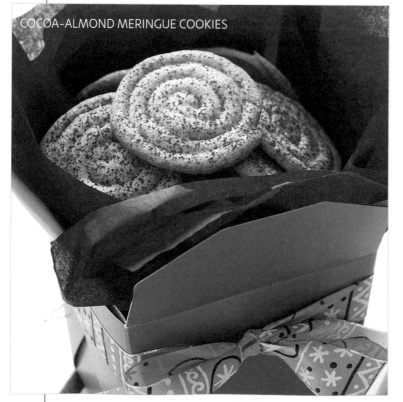

COCOA-ALMOND MERINGUE COOKIES

Low-Fat Carrot Cake `F` `S`

PREP: 30 min. BAKE: 30 min. + cooling
YIELD: 16 servings

REBECCA BAIRD • SALT LAKE CITY, UTAH

Loaded with spice and carrot flavor, this moist and luscious cake is guaranteed to impress.

2	cups packed brown sugar
1/2	cup buttermilk
2	egg whites
1	egg
2	Tbsp. canola oil
1	tsp. vanilla extract
2-1/2	cups cake flour
1	tsp. baking soda
1	tsp. ground cinnamon
1/2	tsp. ground allspice
1/4	tsp. ground nutmeg
1/4	tsp. ground cloves
1/8	tsp. salt
3	cups grated carrots
1	can (8 oz.) unsweetened crushed pineapple, drained
2	oz. reduced-fat cream cheese
1	cup confectioners' sugar
1/2	tsp. lemon juice
1/8	tsp. vanilla extract

1. In a large bowl, beat the brown sugar, buttermilk, egg whites, egg, oil and vanilla until well blended. Combine the flour, baking soda, spices and salt; gradually beat into sugar mixture until blended. Fold in carrots and pineapple. Pour into a 13-in. x 9-in. baking dish coated with cooking spray.

2. Bake at 350° for 30-35 minutes or until a toothpick inserted near the center comes out clean. Cool completely on a wire rack.

3. In a small bowl, beat cream cheese until fluffy. Add the confectioners' sugar, lemon juice and vanilla; beat until smooth. Drizzle over cake.

Nutrition Facts: 1 piece equals 263 calories, 3 g fat (1 g saturated fat), 16 mg cholesterol, 98 mg sodium, 56 g carbohydrate, 1 g fiber, 3 g protein.

Swedish Tea Ring

PREP: 30 min. + rising BAKE: 20 min. + cooling
YIELD: 1 ring (24 slices)

ELSIE EPP • NEWTON, KANSAS

This showstopper will add a special touch to any dessert buffet. It's a lovely confection for coffee gatherings, too.

1	Tbsp. active dry yeast
1-1/2	cups warm water (110° to 115°)
1/4	cup sugar
1/4	cup canola oil
2	egg whites, lightly beaten
1-1/4	tsp. salt
5-1/2	to 6 cups all-purpose flour
1/2	cup chopped walnuts

SWEDISH TEA RING

1/2 cup chopped maraschino cherries, patted dry
1/4 cup packed brown sugar
1 tsp. ground cinnamon
2 Tbsp. butter, melted

ICING:
1 cup confectioners' sugar
1 to 2 Tbsp. fat-free milk

1. In a large bowl, dissolve yeast in warm water. Add the sugar, oil, egg whites, salt and 1 cup flour; beat until smooth. Stir in enough remaining flour to form a soft dough.

2. Turn onto a lightly floured surface; knead until smooth, about 6-8 minutes. Place in a bowl coated with cooking spray, turning once to coat the top. Cover and let rise until doubled, about 1 hour.

3. Combine the walnuts, cherries, brown sugar and cinnamon; set aside. Punch dough down; roll into an 18-in. x 12-in. rectangle. Brush with butter; sprinkle with nut mixture to within 1/2 in. of edges. Roll up jelly-roll style, starting with a long side; pinch seam to seal.

4. Place seam side down on a 14-in. pizza pan coated with cooking spray; pinch ends together to form a ring. With scissors, cut from outside edge two-thirds of the way toward center of ring at scant 1-in. intervals. Separate the strips slightly; twist them to allow filling to show. Cover and let rise until doubled, about 40 minutes.

5. Bake at 400° for 20-25 minutes or until golden brown. Remove from pan to a wire rack to cool. Combine icing ingredients; drizzle over tea ring.

Nutrition Facts: 1 slice equals 196 calories, 5 g fat (1 g saturated fat), 3 mg cholesterol, 142 mg sodium, 34 g carbohydrate, 1 g fiber, 4 g protein. **Diabetic Exchanges:** 2 starch, 1 fat.

Refrigerate **cinnamon roll dough** between kneading and rising, or after shaping it. Store it in a tightly covered bowl or a resealable plastic bag and, if needed, punch it down after 1 to 2 hours and each subsequent day.

MAKEOVER CHERRY PIE DELIGHT

Makeover Cherry Pie Delight F S

PREP: 30 min. BAKE: 10 min. YIELD: 8 servings

HEALTHY COOKING TEST KITCHEN

Chock-full of cherries, this little gem is packed with all the flavors that make cherry pie a classic, in a far lighter form.

      1   sheet refrigerated pie pastry
      1   egg white
      1   Tbsp. water
      2   tsp. coarse sugar
    1/2   cup sugar
    1/4   cup cornstarch
      1   cup cherry juice blend
      2   cans (14-1/2 oz. *each*) pitted tart cherries, drained
      1   cup reduced-fat vanilla ice cream

1. Roll out the pie pastry onto a lightly floured surface. Cut into 1/2-in.-wide strips; make a lattice crust. Beat egg white and water; brush over top. Sprinkle with coarse sugar. Using a floured 2-in. round cookie cutter, cut out eight circles. Place 2 in. apart on ungreased baking sheets. Bake at 450° for 10-12 minutes or until lightly browned. Remove to a wire rack.

2. Meanwhile, in a small saucepan, combine the sugar and cornstarch. Stir in the cherry juice blend until smooth. Bring to a boil; cook and stir for 2 minutes or until thickened. Remove from the heat; add the cherries.

3. Spoon about 1/3 cup warm cherry mixture into each of eight dessert dishes. Top with 2 Tbsp. ice cream and garnish with a cookie.

Nutrition Facts: 1 serving equals 183 calories, 3 g fat (2 g saturated fat), 6 mg cholesterol, 59 mg sodium, 37 g carbohydrate, 1 g fiber, 2 g protein.

Oatmeal Cake With Caramel Icing

PREP: 30 min. BAKE: 20 min. + cooling
YIELD: 20 servings

SUMMER MARKS • LOUISVILLE, KENTUCKY

This tastes anything but light. The icing sets up quickly, so frost the cake immediately after it cools.

  1-1/4   cups boiling water
      1   cup quick-cooking oats
    1/4   cup butter, softened
      1   cup packed brown sugar
    1/2   cup sugar
      2   eggs
    1/4   cup unsweetened applesauce
      1   tsp. vanilla extract
  1-1/2   cups all-purpose flour
      2   tsp. baking powder
    3/4   tsp. ground cinnamon
    1/2   tsp. baking soda
    1/2   tsp. salt
    1/4   tsp. ground nutmeg

ICING:
    1/2   cup packed brown sugar
    1/4   cup butter, cubed
    1/4   cup fat-free milk
    1/2   tsp. vanilla extract
    1/8   tsp. salt
  1-1/2   cups confectioners' sugar

1. In a small bowl, pour boiling water over oats; let stand for 10 minutes.

2. Meanwhile, in a large bowl, beat butter and sugars until crumbly, about 2 minutes. Add eggs, one at a time, beating well after each addition. Beat in applesauce and vanilla. Combine the flour, baking powder, cinnamon, baking soda, salt and nutmeg. Gradually add to creamed mixture. Stir in the oats. Pour into a 13-in. x 9-in. baking pan coated with cooking spray.

3. Bake at 350° for 18-22 minutes or until a toothpick inserted near the center comes out with moist crumbs. Cool completely on a wire rack.

4. For icing, in a small saucepan, combine brown sugar and butter. Bring to a boil over medium heat, stirring constantly. Cook and stir for 1 minute. Gradually whisk in milk. Return to a boil. Cook and stir 1 minute longer. Transfer to a small bowl. Stir in vanilla and salt. Gradually beat in confectioners' sugar until smooth. Immediately spread icing over cake. Let stand until set.

Nutrition Facts: 1 piece equals 216 calories, 5 g fat (3 g saturated fat), 33 mg cholesterol, 193 mg sodium, 41 g carbohydrate, 1 g fiber, 2 g protein.

Cranberry Pecan Bars [F] [S] [C]

PREP: 15 min. **BAKE:** 40 min. + cooling
YIELD: 1 to 1-1/2 dozen

BEVERLY MCCLARREN • FINDLAY, OHIO

I like to mix cranberries, coconut and a little orange peel into the filling of my rich pecan bars. Whenever I serve these at gatherings, people ask if I'll share the recipe with them.

    1   cup all-purpose flour
    1/2 cup finely chopped pecans
    1/2 cup packed brown sugar
    1/2 tsp. salt
    6   Tbsp. cold butter

FILLING:
    2   Tbsp. all-purpose flour
    1/2 tsp. baking powder
    2   eggs, beaten
    1   cup sugar
    1   Tbsp. milk
    1   Tbsp. vanilla extract
    1   cup fresh or frozen cranberries, chopped
    1/2 cup flaked coconut
    1/2 cup chopped pecans
  1-1/2 tsp. grated orange peel

1. In a large bowl, combine the flour, pecans, brown sugar and salt. Cut in butter until crumbly. Press onto a greased 9-in. square baking dish. Bake at 350° for 15-20 minutes or until edges are lightly browned.

2. Meanwhile, in a large bowl, combine the flour and baking powder. Combine the eggs, sugar, milk and vanilla; add to the dry ingredients. Fold in the cranberries, coconut, pecans and orange peel. Pour over the crust. Bake 25-30 minutes longer or until bars are set. Cool on a wire rack. Cut into bars. Refrigerate any leftovers.

Nutrition Facts: 1 bar equals 200 calories, 10 g fat (4 g saturated fat), 34 mg cholesterol, 132 mg sodium, 26 g carbohydrate, 1 g fiber, 2 g protein.

Gluten-Free Almond Crispies [F] [S] [C]

PREP: 20 min. **BAKE:** 10 min./batch
YIELD: about 3 dozen

JEAN ECOS • HARTLAND, WISCONSIN

Here's a wonderful treat everyone in the family can enjoy. Ideal with milk or tea, these cookies impart hints of cinnamon and maple in every crunchy bite.

    1/3 cup maple syrup
    1/4 cup canola oil
    1   Tbsp. water
    1   tsp. almond extract
    1   cup brown rice flour
    1/2 cup almond flour
    1/4 cup sugar
    1   tsp. baking powder
    1   tsp. ground cinnamon
    1/8 tsp. salt
    1/2 cup finely chopped almonds

1. In a small bowl, beat the syrup, oil, water and extract until well blended. Combine the flours, sugar, baking powder, cinnamon and salt; gradually beat into the syrup mixture until blended. Stir in almonds.

2. Drop by rounded teaspoonfuls onto parchment paper-lined baking sheets; flatten slightly. Bake at 350° for 10-12 minutes or until bottoms are lightly browned. Cool for 1 minute before removing from pans to wire racks.

Editor's Note: Read all ingredient labels for possible gluten content prior to use. Ingredient formulas can change, and production facilities vary among brands. If you're concerned that your brand may contain gluten, contact the company.

Nutrition Facts: 1 cookie equals 54 calories, 3 g fat (trace saturated fat), 0 cholesterol, 18 mg sodium, 6 g carbohydrate, 1 g fiber, 1 g protein. **Diabetic Exchanges:** 1/2 starch, 1/2 fat.

GLUTEN-FREE ALMOND CRISPIES

Lemon Crumb Cake

PREP: 20 min. **BAKE:** 30 min. + cooling
YIELD: 20 servings

KATIE WOLLGAST • FLORISSANT, MISSOURI

I like to serve up this light, lip-smacking, lemony cake at any springtime brunch or dinner.

- 2 cups buttermilk
- 1 cup sugar
- 2 eggs
- 2 Tbsp. butter, melted
- 2 tsp. vanilla extract
- 3 cups all-purpose flour
- 1-1/4 tsp. baking powder
- 1 tsp. salt
- 1/2 tsp. baking soda
- 1 can (15-3/4 oz.) lemon pie filling

TOPPING:
- 1 cup all-purpose flour
- 2/3 cup sugar
- 1/3 cup cold butter, cubed
- 1/4 cup sliced almonds, toasted

Reduced-fat vanilla ice cream, optional

1. In a large bowl, beat the first five ingredients until well blended. In a small bowl, combine the flour, baking powder, salt and baking soda; gradually beat into buttermilk mixture until blended. Pour into a 13-in. x 9-in. baking pan coated with cooking spray. Drop pie filling by teaspoonfuls over batter.

2. In a small bowl, combine flour and sugar. Cut in butter until crumbly. Stir in almonds; sprinkle over batter. Bake at 350° for 30-35 minutes or until a toothpick inserted near the center comes out clean.

3. Cool for 10 minutes on a wire rack. Serve warm with ice cream if desired.

Nutrition Facts: 1 piece (calculated without ice cream) equals 295 calories, 7 g fat (3 g saturated fat), 62 mg cholesterol, 255 mg sodium, 53 g carbohydrate, 1 g fiber, 5 g protein.

Amaretto-Almond Bliss Cookies S C

PREP: 20 min. **BAKE:** 10 min./batch **YIELD:** 2-1/2 dozen

VERA DECKER • WINDSOR, NEW YORK

I trimmed down these sweet, chunky cookies, and now they're guilt-free and delicious!

- 1/3 cup butter, softened
- 1/2 cup sugar
- 1/3 cup packed brown sugar
- 1 egg
- 2 Tbsp. Amaretto
- 1/2 tsp. almond extract
- 1 cup all-purpose flour
- 1 cup oat flour
- 1 tsp. baking powder
- 1 tsp. baking soda
- 1/4 tsp. salt
- 3/4 cup miniature semisweet chocolate chips
- 2/3 cup sliced almonds, toasted

1. In a large bowl, beat butter and sugars until crumbly, about 2 minutes. Add egg; mix well. Stir in Amaretto and almond extract. Combine the flours, baking powder, baking soda and salt; gradually add to butter mixture and mix well. Stir in chocolate chips and almonds.

2. With lightly floured hands, shape into 1-in. balls. Place them 2 in. apart on baking sheets coated with cooking spray. Flatten balls slightly with a glass coated with cooking spray.

3. Bake at 350° for 7-9 minutes or until the tops are cracked and the bottoms are lightly browned. Remove to wire racks.

LEMON CRUMB CAKE

AMARETTO-ALMOND BLISS COOKIES

Editor's Note: As a substitute for 1 cup oat flour, process 1-1/4 cups quick-cooking or old-fashioned oats until finely ground.

Nutrition Facts: 1 cookie equals 106 calories, 5 g fat (2 g saturated fat), 12 mg cholesterol, 93 mg sodium, 15 g carbohydrate, 1 g fiber, 2 g protein. **Diabetic Exchanges:** 1 starch, 1 fat.

Honey Cheese Bars S

PREP: 25 min. BAKE: 30 min. + cooling YIELD: 16 bars

EDNA HOFFMAN • HEBRON, INDIANA

If you like cheesecake, you'll love this light dessert. Walnuts lend a subtle nutty taste to the crust, and honey and lemon make the creamy topping a pure delight.

- 1 cup all-purpose flour
- 1/3 cup packed brown sugar
- 1/4 cup cold butter, cubed
- 1/2 cup finely chopped walnuts

FILLING:
- 1 pkg. (8 oz.) reduced-fat cream cheese
- 1/4 cup honey
- 2 Tbsp. milk
- 1 Tbsp. lemon juice
- 1/2 tsp. vanilla extract
- 1 egg, lightly beaten

Additional honey, optional

1. In a small bowl, combine flour and brown sugar. Cut in butter until crumbly. Stir in walnuts. Press onto the bottom of an 8-in. square baking dish coated with cooking spray. Bake at 350° for 10-12 minutes or until lightly browned.

2. For filling, in a large bowl, beat the cream cheese, honey, milk, lemon juice and vanilla until blended. Add egg; beat on low speed just until combined. Pour over crust. Bake 20-25 minutes longer or until set. Cool completely on a wire rack. Drizzle with additional honey if desired. Cut into bars. Refrigerate any leftovers.

Nutrition Facts: 1 bar (calculated without additional honey) equals 152 calories, 8 g fat (4 g saturated fat), 31 mg cholesterol, 88 mg sodium, 16 g carbohydrate, trace fiber, 4 g protein. **Diabetic Exchanges:** 2 fat, 1 starch.

Heavenly Chocolate Pie

PREP: 15 min. + chilling YIELD: 8 servings

DONNA ROBERTS • MANHATTAN, KANSAS

I rely on fat-free, sugar-free and reduced-fat products for my dessert. What a lovely way to satisfy chocolate cravings!

- 1 cup fat-free vanilla frozen yogurt, softened
- 2 cups fat-free milk
- 1 pkg. (1.4 oz.) sugar-free instant chocolate pudding mix
- 1 pkg. (1 oz.) sugar-free instant vanilla pudding mix
- 1 carton (8 oz.) frozen reduced-fat whipped topping, thawed, *divided*
- 1 reduced-fat graham cracker crust (8 in.)

Chocolate curls, optional

1. In a large bowl, whisk yogurt until soft and smooth. Gradually whisk in milk until blended. Add pudding mixes; whisk 2 minutes longer. Let stand for 2 minutes or until soft-set.

2. Fold in 1 cup whipped topping. Transfer to crust. Top with remaining whipped topping and chocolate curls if desired. Refrigerate for at least 4 hours.

Nutrition Facts: 1 piece equals 235 calories, 6 g fat (4 g saturated fat), 2 mg cholesterol, 433 mg sodium, 40 g carbohydrate, trace fiber, 5 g protein.

MAKEOVER
TRADITIONAL
CHEESECAKE

Makeover Traditional Cheesecake

PREP: 40 min. **BAKE:** 1-1/2 hours + chilling
YIELD: 16 servings

ANNE ADDESSO • SHEBOYGAN, WISCONSIN

Though softer than a full-fat cheesecake, this lightened-up dessert has all of the original's delectable flavor. It's sure to make any special event more festive.

1-3/4 cups graham cracker crumbs
   2 Tbsp. confectioners' sugar
  1/4 cup butter, melted
FILLING:
   1 Tbsp. lemon juice
   1 Tbsp. vanilla extract
   2 cups (16 oz.) 1% cottage cheese
   2 cups (16 oz.) reduced-fat sour cream, *divided*
   2 pkg. (8 oz. *each*) reduced-fat cream cheese
1-1/4 cups sugar
   2 Tbsp. all-purpose flour
   4 eggs, lightly beaten
   1 Tbsp. fat-free caramel ice cream topping
   2 Heath candy bars (1.4 oz. *each*), chopped

1. Place a 9-in. springform pan coated with cooking spray on a double thickness of heavy-duty foil (about 18 in. square). Securely wrap foil around pan.

2. In a small bowl, combine graham cracker crumbs and confectioners' sugar; stir in butter. Press onto the bottom and 1 in. up the sides of prepared pan. Place on a baking sheet. Bake at 325° for 18-22 minutes or until lightly browned. Cool on a wire rack.

3. Place the lemon juice, vanilla, cottage cheese and 1 cup sour cream in a blender; cover and process for 2 minutes or until smooth.

4. In a large bowl, beat cream cheese and sugar until smooth. Beat in the remaining sour cream. Add the flour and pureed cottage cheese mixture; mix well. Add the eggs; beat on low speed just until combined. Pour into crust.

5. Place springform pan in a larger baking pan; add 3/4 in. of hot water to larger pan. Bake at 325° for 1-1/2 hours or until center is just set and top appears dull. Remove springform pan from water bath. Cool on a wire rack for 10 minutes.

6. Carefully run a knife around the edge of the pan to loosen; cool 1 hour longer. Refrigerate overnight. Remove sides of pan. Garnish with caramel topping and chopped candy.

Nutrition Facts: 1 slice equals 311 calories, 15 g fat (9 g saturated fat), 93 mg cholesterol, 369 mg sodium, 32 g carbohydrate, trace fiber, 11 g protein.

Makeover Meringue Coconut Brownies S

PREP: 30 min. **BAKE:** 30 min. + cooling **YIELD:** 2 dozen

ELLEN AHO • SOUTH PARIS, MAINE

A chocolate-lover's dream, these bars have a rich, pleasant combination of flavors.

1/3	cup butter, softened
1/3	cup plus 3/4 cup packed brown sugar, *divided*
1/3	cup sugar
1	tsp. vanilla extract
2	cups all-purpose flour
1/2	tsp. baking soda
1/4	tsp. salt
1/3	cup fat-free milk
1	cup (6 oz.) semisweet chocolate chips
1	cup flaked coconut
1/2	cup chopped walnuts
3	egg whites
1/4	tsp. cream of tartar

1. In a small bowl, cream the butter, 1/3 cup brown sugar and sugar until light and fluffy. Beat in vanilla. Combine the flour, baking soda and salt; add to the creamed mixture alternately with milk, beating well after each addition. Press into a 13-in. x 9-in. baking pan coated with cooking spray. Sprinkle with chocolate chips, coconut and walnuts.

2. In a large bowl, beat egg whites and cream of tartar until soft peaks form. Gradually beat in remaining brown sugar, 1 tablespoonful at a time. Beat until stiff peaks form. Spread over the top. Bake at 350° for 30-35 minutes or until a toothpick inserted near the center comes out clean (do not overbake).

3. Cool on a wire rack. Cut into bars. Store in the refrigerator.

Nutrition Facts: 1 brownie equals 181 calories, 8 g fat (4 g saturated fat), 7 mg cholesterol, 92 mg sodium, 27 g carbohydrate, 1 g fiber, 2 g protein. **Diabetic Exchanges:** 2 starch, 1 fat.

Peanut Butter-Chocolate Chip Cookies F S C

PREP: 15 min. + chilling **BAKE:** 10 min./batch
YIELD: 4-1/2 dozen

MURIEL MABLESON • WINNIPEG, MANITOBA

I stir a few chocolate chips into the melted butters to give my cookie batter a little extra chocolate flavor.

1/2	cup butter, cubed
1/3	cup reduced-fat creamy peanut butter
1/4	cup unsweetened applesauce
3/4	cup sugar
3/4	cup packed brown sugar
2	eggs
1-1/2	tsp. vanilla extract
2-1/4	cups all-purpose flour
1/2	tsp. baking soda
1/2	tsp. ground cinnamon
1/4	tsp. salt
1/2	cup semisweet chocolate chips

1. In a small microwave-safe bowl, microwave butter and peanut butter until butter is melted; stir until smooth. Stir in applesauce.

2. Transfer to a large bowl. Beat in the sugars until blended. Beat in eggs and vanilla. Combine the flour, baking soda, cinnamon and salt; gradually add to peanut butter mixture and mix well. Stir in chocolate chips. Cover and refrigerate for at least 2 hours.

3. Drop by tablespoonfuls 2 in. apart onto baking sheets coated with cooking spray. Bake at 350° for 7-9 minutes or until lightly browned. Remove to wire racks. Store in an airtight container.

Nutrition Facts: 1 cookie equals 75 calories, 3 g fat (2 g saturated fat), 12 mg cholesterol, 47 mg sodium, 11 g carbohydrate, trace fiber, 1 g protein. **Diabetic Exchanges:** 1 starch, 1/2 fat.

MAKEOVER MERINGUE COCONUT BROWNIES

PEANUT BUTTER-CHOCOLATE CHIP COOKIES

Makeover Italian Cream Cake

PREP: 40 min. **BAKE:** 20 min. + cooling
YIELD: 16 servings

CHRISTY WHITE • OXFORD, MISSISSIPPI

Toasted pecans and coconut take this moist cake from good to great, but it's the cream cheese frosting that makes it truly extraordinary. Thank goodness it's a makeover, because you'll definitely want seconds!

1/3	cup butter, softened
1	cup sugar
2	eggs
1/3	cup unsweetened applesauce
1/2	tsp. vanilla extract
1-1/3	cups all-purpose flour
3/4	tsp. baking soda
1/8	tsp. salt
2/3	cup buttermilk
1/3	cup chopped pecans, toasted
1/4	cup flaked coconut, toasted

CREAM CHEESE FROSTING:

1	pkg. (8 oz.) cream cheese, softened
2	Tbsp. butter, softened
2	cups confectioners' sugar
1/2	tsp. vanilla extract
1/3	cup chopped pecans, toasted

1. Line two 9-in. round baking pans with waxed paper. Coat pans with cooking spray and sprinkle with flour; set aside.

2. In a large bowl, beat butter and sugar until crumbly, about 2 minutes. Add eggs, one at a time, beating well after each addition. Beat in applesauce and vanilla (mixture will appear curdled). Combine the flour, baking soda and salt; add to creamed mixture alternately with buttermilk. Fold in pecans and coconut.

3. Pour into prepared pans. Bake at 350° for 18-22 minutes or until a toothpick inserted near the center comes out clean. Cool for 10 minutes before removing from pans to wire racks to cool completely.

4. For frosting, in a large bowl, beat cream cheese and butter until fluffy. Add confectioners' sugar and vanilla; beat until smooth. Spread frosting between layers and over top and sides of cake. Sprinkle pecans over top of cake. Store in the refrigerator.

Nutrition Facts: 1 slice equals 297 calories, 15 g fat (7 g saturated fat), 56 mg cholesterol, 180 mg sodium, 38 g carbohydrate, 1 g fiber, 4 g protein.

Makeover Macaroon Cake

PREP: 20 min. **BAKE:** 65 min. + cooling
YIELD: 16 servings

GAYE ANDREE • ROCHESTER, NEW YORK

This is one of my husband's favorite recipes. Now with it made over, he can even go back for seconds!

6	egg whites
4	egg yolks
2-1/4	cups sugar
1/2	cup unsweetened applesauce
1/4	cup canola oil
3/4	cup fat-free milk
1/2	tsp. almond extract
1-1/2	cups cake flour
1-1/2	cups all-purpose flour
1	cup flaked coconut
3	tsp. baking powder
1/4	tsp. salt
1/2	tsp. cream of tartar
1	tsp. confectioners' sugar

MAKEOVER MACAROON CAKE

MAKEOVER ITALIAN CREAM CAKE

RAISIN-NUT CHOCOLATE CAKE

1. Let the egg whites stand at room temperature for 30 minutes. In a large bowl, beat the egg yolks, sugar, applesauce and oil until well blended; beat in milk and almond extract. Combine the flours, coconut, baking powder and salt; gradually beat into the egg yolk mixture until blended.

2. In another bowl, beat egg whites and cream of tartar until stiff peaks form; fold into batter.

3. Gently spoon into an ungreased 10-in. tube pan. Cut through batter with a knife to remove air pockets. Bake on the lowest oven rack at 325° for 65-75 minutes or until cake springs back when lightly touched. Immediately invert pan; cool completely, about 1 hour.

4. Run a knife around side and center tube of pan. Remove cake to a serving plate. Sprinkle with confectioners' sugar.

Nutrition Facts: 1 slice equals 287 calories, 7 g fat (3 g saturated fat), 51 mg cholesterol, 155 mg sodium, 52 g carbohydrate, 1 g fiber, 5 g protein.

Raisin-Nut Chocolate Cake

PREP: 20 min. **BAKE:** 40 min. + cooling
YIELD: 16 servings

KAREN SUE GARBACK-PRISTERA • ALBANY, NEW YORK

My husband really enjoys this delightful cake. Eye-catching enough for a special occasion, this is so good you'll want it any day of the week.

1/3 cup butter, softened
  1 cup packed brown sugar
  2 eggs

1-1/2 cups unsweetened applesauce
  1/2 cup plus 3 Tbsp. brewed coffee, room temperature, *divided*
  2 cups all-purpose flour
  1/4 cup plus 3 Tbsp. baking cocoa, *divided*
1-1/2 tsp. ground cinnamon
  1 tsp. baking soda
  1 tsp. ground allspice
  1/2 tsp. salt
  1/4 tsp. ground cloves
1-1/2 cups raisins
  3/4 cup chopped walnuts
1-1/3 cups confectioners' sugar

1. In a large bowl, cream butter and brown sugar until well blended. Add eggs, one at a time, beating well after each addition. Beat in applesauce and 1/2 cup coffee. Combine the flour, 1/4 cup baking cocoa, cinnamon, baking soda, allspice, salt and cloves; gradually beat into creamed mixture until blended. Fold in raisins and walnuts.

2. Pour into a 10-in. fluted tube pan coated with cooking spray. Bake at 350° for 40-45 minutes or until a toothpick inserted near the center comes out clean. Cool for 10 minutes before removing from pan to a wire rack to cool completely.

3. In a small bowl, combine the confectioners' sugar and remaining baking cocoa and coffee; drizzle over the cake.

Nutrition Facts: 1 slice equals 284 calories, 8 g fat (3 g saturated fat), 36 mg cholesterol, 196 mg sodium, 51 g carbohydrate, 2 g fiber, 5 g protein.

MAKEOVER PEANUT BUTTER CUP CHEESECAKE

Makeover Peanut Butter Cup Cheesecake

PREP: 30 min. **BAKE:** 50 min. + chilling
YIELD: 16 servings

SHARON ANDERSON • LYONS, ILLINOIS

No one will ever guess this decadently rich, firmer-textured cheesecake has been lightened up!

3/4	cup graham cracker crumbs
2	Tbsp. sugar
2	Tbsp. butter, melted
3/4	cup creamy peanut butter

FILLING:

2	pkg. (8 oz. *each*) fat-free cream cheese
1	pkg. (8 oz.) reduced-fat cream cheese
1	cup (8 oz.) reduced-fat sour cream
3/4	cup sugar
2	eggs, lightly beaten
1-1/2	tsp. vanilla extract
3/4	cup hot fudge ice cream topping, *divided*
6	peanut butter cups, cut into small wedges

1. In a small bowl, combine the cracker crumbs, sugar and butter. Press onto the bottom of a 9-in. springform pan coated with cooking spray.

2. Place pan on a baking sheet. Bake at 350° for 10 minutes. Cool on a wire rack. In a microwave-safe bowl, heat the peanut butter on high for 30 seconds or until softened. Spread over the crust to within 1 in. of the edges.

3. In a large bowl, beat the cream cheese, sour cream and sugar until smooth. Add the eggs; beat on low speed just until combined. Stir in vanilla. Pour 1 cup into a bowl; set aside. Pour remaining filling over the peanut butter layer.

4. In a microwave-safe bowl, heat 1/4 cup fudge topping on high for 30 seconds or until thin; fold into the reserved cream cheese mixture. Carefully pour over filling; cut through with a knife to swirl.

5. Return pan to baking sheet. Bake for 50-60 minutes or until center is almost set. Cool on a wire rack for 10 minutes. Carefully run a knife around edge of pan to loosen; cool 1 hour longer.

6. Microwave remaining fudge topping on high for 30 seconds or until warmed; spread over cheesecake. Garnish with peanut butter cups. Refrigerate overnight.

Nutrition Facts: 1 slice equals 316 calories, 16 g fat (6 g saturated fat), 47 mg cholesterol, 361 mg sodium, 32 g carbohydrate, 1 g fiber, 12 g protein.

Citrus Cornmeal Cake S

PREP: 25 min. **BAKE:** 25 min. **YIELD:** 8 servings

ROXANNE CHAN • ALBANY, CALIFORNIA

Cornmeal adds a rustic quality to this delicate dessert flavored with citrus and almond. It's sure to be a staple in your recipe collection and also makes a perfect hostess gift.

1/2	cup lemon yogurt
1/3	cup honey
1/4	cup olive oil
1	egg
2	egg whites
1/4	tsp. almond extract
3/4	cup all-purpose flour
1/2	cup cornmeal
1	tsp. baking powder
1/2	tsp. grated orange peel
1	can (15 oz.) mandarin oranges, drained
3	Tbsp. slivered almonds

1. Coat a 9-in. fluted tart pan with a removable bottom with cooking spray. In a large bowl, beat the yogurt, honey, oil, egg, egg whites and almond extract until well blended. Combine the flour, cornmeal and baking powder; gradually beat into the yogurt mixture until blended. Stir in the orange peel.

2. Pour into a prepared pan. Arrange the oranges over the batter; sprinkle with almonds. Bake at 350° for 25-30 minutes or until a toothpick inserted near the center comes out clean. Cool on a wire rack for 10 minutes before cutting. Serve warm or at room temperature.

Nutrition Facts: 1 slice equals 240 calories, 9 g fat (1 g saturated fat), 27 mg cholesterol, 85 mg sodium, 36 g carbohydrate, 2 g fiber, 5 g protein.

Gluten-Free Brownies ⓢ

PREP: 15 min. **BAKE:** 30 min. + cooling **YIELD:** 1 dozen

JEAN ECOS • HARTLAND, WISCONSIN

At parties, friends and family rarely realize that these fudgy, moist brownies are gluten-free, as well as flourless. What's more, they're usually shocked when I divulge the secret ingredient: garbanzo beans!

1-1/4 cups semisweet chocolate chips
   1 can (15 oz.) garbanzo beans or chickpeas, rinsed and drained
   3 egg whites
   1 egg
   2 Tbsp. instant coffee granules, optional
   2 Tbsp. canola oil
1-1/2 tsp. vanilla extract
  1/2 cup packed brown sugar
  1/2 tsp. baking powder
Dash salt
  1/2 cup chopped walnuts, optional

1. In a microwave, melt chocolate chips; stir until smooth. Cool slightly.

2. Meanwhile, place the garbanzo beans, egg whites, egg, coffee granules if desired, oil and vanilla extract in a food processor. Cover and process until the mixture is smooth.

3. In a small bowl, combine the brown sugar, baking powder and salt; add to bean mixture. Cover and process until combined. Gradually add the chocolate; process until blended.

4. Pour the batter into a 9-in. square baking pan coated with cooking spray. Sprinkle with walnuts if desired. Bake at 350° for 30-35 minutes or until a toothpick inserted near the center comes out dotted with moist crumbs (do not overbake). Cool completely on a wire rack.

Editor's Note: Read all ingredient labels for possible gluten content prior to use. Ingredient formulas can change, and production facilities vary among brands. If you're concerned that your brand may contain gluten, contact the company.

Nutrition Facts: 1 brownie equals 184 calories, 9 g fat (3 g saturated fat), 18 mg cholesterol, 100 mg sodium, 26 g carbohydrate, 2 g fiber, 4 g protein. **Diabetic Exchanges:** 1-1/2 starch, 1-1/2 fat.

Makeover Rum Cake

PREP: 15 min. **BAKE:** 40 min. + cooling
YIELD: 16 servings

CATHARINE SEMAN • PITTSBURGH, PENNSYLVANIA

Makeover Rum Cake is draped in a shiny glaze, and has only about half the calories and cholesterol of the original version. But it's still tender and as good with coffee in the morning as it is at the end of a special meal. Now that's definitely something worth celebrating.

  1/2 cup chopped pecans, toasted
    1 pkg. (18-1/4 oz.) yellow cake mix
  1/2 cup fat-free milk
  1/4 cup dark rum
  1/4 cup canola oil
  1/4 cup unsweetened applesauce
    2 eggs
GLAZE:
  1/2 cup sugar
  1/4 cup butter, cubed
    2 Tbsp. water
    2 Tbsp. dark rum

1. Coat a 10-in. fluted tube pan with cooking spray and sprinkle with flour; add pecans. In a large bowl, combine the cake mix, milk, rum, oil, applesauce and eggs; beat on low speed for 30 seconds. Beat on medium for 2 minutes.

2. Pour into prepared pan. Bake at 325° for 40-45 minutes or until a toothpick inserted near the center comes out clean. Cool for 10 minutes before removing from pan to a wire rack to cool completely.

3. In a small saucepan, combine glaze ingredients. Bring to a boil. Reduce heat; cook and stir for 4-5 minutes or until thickened. Drizzle over cake.

Nutrition Facts: 1 slice equals 251 calories, 12 g fat (4 g saturated fat), 34 mg cholesterol, 243 mg sodium, 34 g carbohydrate, trace fiber, 2 g protein.

MAKEOVER RUM CAKE

Taste-of-Summer Light Pound Cake

PREP: 20 min. **BAKE:** 35 min. + cooling
YIELD: 12 servings

JILL BELLROSE • PORTLAND, OREGON

This delicious, reduced-calorie pound cake brings the bright look and taste of summer to your table year-round.

- 1/2 cup butter, softened
- 1 cup sugar
- 2 egg whites
- 1 egg
- 1 Tbsp. lemon juice
- 1 tsp. lemon extract
- 1 tsp. vanilla extract
- 1-1/2 cups all-purpose flour
- 1 cup whole wheat pastry flour
- 2 tsp. baking powder
- 1/2 tsp. salt
- 1/4 tsp. baking soda
- 3/4 cup (6 oz.) fat-free lemon yogurt

GLAZE:
- 3/4 cup confectioners' sugar
- 4 tsp. lemon juice
- 1 tsp. grated lemon peel
- 1/3 cup dried apricots, finely chopped

1. In a large bowl, cream the butter and sugar until light and fluffy. Add the egg whites, then the egg, beating well after each addition. Beat in lemon juice and extracts. Combine the flours, baking powder, salt and baking soda; add to the creamed mixture alternately with yogurt.

2. Transfer to a 10-in. fluted tube pan coated with cooking spray. Bake at 350° for 35-40 minutes or until a toothpick inserted near the center comes out clean. Cool for 10 minutes before removing from the pan to a wire rack to cool completely.

3. For glaze, in a small bowl, whisk the confectioners' sugar, lemon juice and lemon peel until blended. Stir in apricots. Drizzle over cake.

Nutrition Facts: 1 slice equals 276 calories, 8 g fat (5 g saturated fat), 38 mg cholesterol, 267 mg sodium, 46 g carbohydrate, 2 g fiber, 4 g protein.

Makeover Hummingbird Cake

PREP: 25 min. **BAKE:** 25 min. + cooling
YIELD: 24 servings

SUE JERNIGAN • FREDERICKSBURG, VIRGINIA

With pineapple, bananas, nuts and just a hint of cinnamon, this cake gets raves at potlucks and parties!

- 2 cups mashed ripe bananas (3 to 4 medium)
- 1 can (8 oz.) unsweetened crushed pineapple, drained
- 3/4 cup unsweetened applesauce
- 1/3 cup canola oil
- 2 eggs
- 1-1/2 tsp. vanilla extract
- 3 cups all-purpose flour
- 1-1/2 cups sugar
- 1 tsp. salt
- 1 tsp. baking soda
- 1 tsp. ground cinnamon
- 1/2 cup chopped walnuts

ICING:
- 1 pkg. (8 oz.) reduced-fat cream cheese
- 1/3 cup reduced-fat butter
- 3 cups confectioners' sugar
- 1 tsp. vanilla extract
- 1/2 cup chopped walnuts

TASTE-OF-SUMMER LIGHT POUND CAKE

MAKEOVER HUMMINGBIRD CAKE

1. In a large bowl, beat the first six ingredients until well blended. In another bowl, combine the flour, sugar, salt, baking soda and cinnamon; gradually beat into banana mixture until blended. Stir in walnuts.

2. Pour into a 15-in. x 10-in. x 1-in. baking pan coated with cooking spray. Bake at 350° for 25-30 minutes or until a toothpick inserted near the center comes out clean. Cool completely on a wire rack.

3. For icing, in a large bowl, beat cream cheese and butter until fluffy. Add confectioners' sugar and vanilla; beat until smooth. Spread over cake. Sprinkle with walnuts. Refrigerate leftovers.

Editor's Note: This recipe was tested with Land O'Lakes light stick butter.

Nutrition Facts: 1 piece equals 290 calories, 10 g fat (3 g saturated fat), 28 mg cholesterol, 219 mg sodium, 47 g carbohydrate, 1 g fiber, 5 g protein.

Makeover Semisweet Espresso Cheesecake

PREP: 30 min. **BAKE:** 40 min. + chilling
YIELD: 16 servings

SONYA LABBE • SANTA MONICA, CALIFORNIA

With fabulous flavor and a firmer texture that cuts like a dream, this cheesecake has only half the saturated fat and cholesterol of my original.

- 2 cups crushed reduced-fat cream-filled chocolate sandwich cookies (about 20 cookies)
- 2 Tbsp. butter, melted
- 3 pkg. (8 oz. *each*) reduced-fat cream cheese
- 1 pkg. (8 oz.) fat-free cream cheese

- 1 cup sugar
- 2 eggs, lightly beaten
- 3 Tbsp. coffee liqueur
- 2 Tbsp. instant espresso powder
- 1 tsp. vanilla extract
- 2 oz. semisweet chocolate, melted and cooled

1. Place a 9-in. springform pan coated with cooking spray on a double thickness of heavy-duty foil (about 18 in. square). Securely wrap foil around pan.

2. In a small bowl, combine cookie crumbs and butter. Press onto the bottom of prepared pan. Place pan on a baking sheet. Bake at 325° for 10 minutes. Cool on a wire rack.

3. In a large bowl, beat cream cheeses and sugar until smooth. Add the eggs; beat on low speed just until combined. Stir in the coffee liqueur, espresso powder and vanilla. Remove 1-1/4 cups batter to a small bowl; stir in chocolate until well blended.

4. Pour plain batter over crust. Drop chocolate batter by tablespoonfuls over plain batter. Cut through batter with a knife to swirl. Place springform pan in a large baking pan; add 1 in. of hot water to larger pan.

5. Bake at 325° for 40-45 minutes or until center is just set and top appears dull. Remove springform pan from water bath. Cool on a wire rack for 10 minutes. Carefully run a knife around edge of pan to loosen; cool 1 hour longer. Refrigerate overnight. Remove sides of pan.

Nutrition Facts: 1 slice equals 272 calories, 14 g fat (8 g saturated fat), 61 mg cholesterol, 355 mg sodium, 29 g carbohydrate, 1 g fiber, 8 g protein.

COCONUT-STREUSEL PEAR PIE

Coconut-Streusel Pear Pie

PREP: 20 min. **BAKE:** 20 min. + cooling
YIELD: 8 servings

PAULA HOFFMAN • PLAINVIEW, NEBRASKA

I remember my mom making this pie when I was growing up. I make several while I have fresh pears from the family tree, then freeze them for later. One of my taste testers declared it "the best pear pie ever!"

Pastry for single-crust pie (9 in.)

  1/3 cup sugar

  1/4 cup all-purpose flour

  1/4 tsp. salt

    6 cups sliced peeled fresh pears

    1 Tbsp. lemon juice

TOPPING:

    3 Tbsp. sugar

    3 Tbsp. all-purpose flour

4-1/2 tsp. cold butter

  1/3 cup flaked coconut

1. Line a 9-in. pie plate with pastry; trim and flute edges. In a large saucepan, combine the sugar, flour and salt. Add pears and lemon juice. Cook and stir over medium heat for 4-5 minutes or until thickened. Pour into pastry.

2. For topping, in a small bowl, combine sugar and flour. Cut in butter until crumbly. Stir in coconut; sprinkle over top. Bake at 400° for 20-25 minutes or until filling is bubbly and topping is lightly browned. Cool on a wire rack.

Nutrition Facts: 1 piece equals 306 calories, 11 g fat (6 g saturated fat), 11 mg cholesterol, 200 mg sodium, 52 g carbohydrate, 4 g fiber, 2 g protein.

Pineapple Apple Pie [S]

PREP: 20 min. **BAKE:** 40 min. + cooling
YIELD: 10 servings

KAREN BRINK • ATWATER, OHIO

This special pie is destined to become a family tradition. The apple and pineapple are mouthwatering together, and the crunchy topping is fabulous! This one's best served warm, perhaps with a scoop of low-fat frozen yogurt on top!

Pastry for single-crust pie (9 in.)

- 1 can (20 oz.) crushed pineapple in heavy syrup, undrained
- 3 medium tart apples, peeled and chopped
- 1/4 cup all-purpose flour
- 1/2 tsp. ground cinnamon
- 1/2 tsp. ground nutmeg

TOPPING:
- 1/2 cup quick-cooking oats
- 1/3 cup packed brown sugar
- 1/4 cup all-purpose flour
- 2 Tbsp. plus 2 tsp. butter, melted

1. Line a 9-in. pie plate with the pastry; trim and flute the edges.

2. In a large bowl, combine the pineapple and the chopped apples.

3. Combine the flour, cinnamon and nutmeg; add to apple mixture and toss to coat. Transfer to pastry.

4. In a small bowl, combine the oats, brown sugar, flour and butter; sprinkle over filling.

5. Bake at 375° for 40-45 minutes or until topping is browned. Cover edges with foil during the last 15 minutes to prevent overbrowning if necessary. Cool on a wire rack.

Nutrition Facts: 1 piece equals 259 calories, 9 g fat (4 g saturated fat), 12 mg cholesterol, 105 mg sodium, 43 g carbohydrate, 2 g fiber, 3 g protein.

PINEAPPLE APPLE PIE

Caramel Custard Pie

PREP: 15 min. **BAKE:** 55 min. + chilling **YIELD:** 8 servings

ROGER CLAPPER • DELAVAN, WISCONSIN

Here's a traditional custard pie that's been in our family for over 100 years. A fun layer of caramel jazzes up the creamy old-fashioned flavor. It's great with whipped topping.

Pastry for single-crust pie (9 in.)
- 2/3 cup packed brown sugar
- 4 tsp. all-purpose flour
- 3 eggs
- 2 cups 2% milk
- 1/4 cup sugar
- 1 tsp. vanilla extract
- 1/8 tsp. salt
- 1/8 tsp. ground nutmeg

1. Line a 9-in. pie plate with pastry; trim and flute edges. Combine brown sugar and flour; press into the pastry.

2. In a large bowl, combine the eggs, milk, sugar, vanilla and salt; pour over brown sugar mixture.

3. Bake at 350° for 55-60 minutes or until a knife inserted near the center comes out clean. Cover edges with foil during the last 15 minutes to prevent overbrowning if necessary. Cool on a wire rack; sprinkle with nutmeg. Refrigerate for at least 2 hours before serving.

Nutrition Facts: 1 piece equals 277 calories, 10 g fat (4 g saturated fat), 89 mg cholesterol, 201 mg sodium, 41 g carbohydrate, trace fiber, 6 g protein.

CARAMEL CUSTARD PIE

Pudding Pumpkin Pie

PREP: 15 min. + chilling **YIELD:** 8 servings

SHEILA ROUTION • ANGLETON, TEXAS

With this pumpkin pie, you don't have to spend all day in the kitchen whipping up a dessert that keeps calories and fat at bay. The mouthwatering treat has a pleasant level of pumpkin and spice, and it's ready in no time at all.

- 1 egg white, beaten
- 1 reduced-fat graham cracker crust (8 in.)
- 1 cup cold fat-free milk
- 1 pkg. (1-1/2 oz.) sugar-free instant vanilla pudding mix
- 1 can (15 oz.) solid-pack pumpkin
- 1 tsp. pumpkin pie spice
- 1/2 tsp. ground cinnamon
- 1/2 tsp. ground nutmeg
- 1-1/2 cups reduced-fat whipped topping, *divided*

1. Brush egg white over crust. Bake at 375° for 5 minutes or until lightly browned. Cool crust on a wire rack.

2. In a large bowl, whisk milk and pudding mix. Stir in the pumpkin, pumpkin pie spice, cinnamon and nutmeg. Fold in 1 cup whipped topping. Pour into crust. Refrigerate for 4 hours or overnight.

3. Cut into slices; dollop with remaining whipped topping. Refrigerate leftovers.

Nutrition Facts: 1 piece with 1 Tbsp. whipped topping equals 180 calories, 5 g fat (3 g saturated fat), 1 mg cholesterol, 341 mg sodium, 29 g carbohydrate, 2 g fiber, 3 g protein. **Diabetic Exchanges:** 2 starch, 1 fat.

Creamy Lemon Cheesecake

PREP: 35 min. **BAKE:** 50 min. + chilling **YIELD:** 16 servings

ANNE HENRY • TORONTO, ONTARIO

My friend, Gwen, gave me this creamy, lip-smacking recipe, and it's been a crowd-pleaser at my house ever since. The homemade lemon curd on top adds a tart, special touch. The cake can also be made in three store-bought graham cracker pie shells.

PUDDING PUMPKIN PIE

CREAMY LEMON CHEESECAKE

1   cup graham cracker crumbs
2   Tbsp. butter, melted

FILLING:
2   pkg. (8 oz. *each*) reduced-fat cream cheese
1   pkg. (8 oz.) fat-free cream cheese
1-1/3   cups sugar
1/3   cup lemon juice
1   Tbsp. grated lemon peel
3   eggs, lightly beaten

TOPPINGS:
1   cup (8 oz.) reduced-fat sour cream
4   tsp. plus 1/2 cup sugar, *divided*
1   tsp. vanilla extract
4-1/2   tsp. cornstarch
1/4   tsp. salt
3/4   cup water
1   egg yolk, beaten
1/3   cup lemon juice
1   Tbsp. butter
2   tsp. grated lemon peel

1. Place a 9-in. springform pan coated with cooking spray on a double thickness of heavy-duty foil (about 18 in. square). Securely wrap foil around pan.

2. In a small bowl, combine cracker crumbs and butter. Press onto the bottom of prepared pan. Place

pan on a baking sheet. Bake at 325° for 6-9 minutes or until set. Cool on a wire rack.

3. In a large bowl, beat cream cheeses and sugar until smooth. Beat in lemon juice and peel. Add eggs; beat on low speed just until combined. Pour over crust. Place springform pan in a large baking pan; add 1 in. of hot water to larger pan.

4. Bake at 325° for 40-45 minutes or until center is almost set. Let stand for 5 minutes. Combine the sour cream, 4 tsp. sugar and vanilla; spread over top of cheesecake. Bake 10 minutes longer. Remove the springform pan from water bath. Cool on a wire rack for 10 minutes. Carefully run a knife around edge of pan to loosen; cool 1 hour longer.

5. In a small heavy saucepan, combine the cornstarch, salt and remaining sugar. Stir in water until smooth. Cook and stir over medium-high heat until thickened and bubbly. Reduce heat; cook and stir 2 minutes longer. Remove from the heat.

6. Stir a small amount of hot mixture into egg yolk; return all to the pan, stirring constantly. Bring to a gentle boil; cook and stir 2 minutes longer. Remove from the heat. Gently stir in the lemon juice, butter and lemon peel. Cool to room temperature without stirring.

7. Spread over cheesecake. Refrigerate overnight. Remove sides of pan.

Nutrition Facts: 1 slice equals 260 calories, 11 g fat (7 g saturated fat), 84 mg cholesterol, 305 mg sodium, 33 g carbohydrate, trace fiber, 8 g protein.

Toffee Cheesecake Bars ⓢ

PREP: 25 min. **BAKE:** 20 min. + chilling
YIELD: 2-1/2 dozen

EDIE DESPAIN • LOGAN, UTAH

These absolutely delicious, melt-in-your-mouth treats are a must for homemade gift giving. Everyone will want seconds, and no one will ever guess they're on the lighter side.

1   cup all-purpose flour
3/4   cup confectioners' sugar
1/3   cup baking cocoa
1/8   tsp. baking soda
1/2   cup cold butter
1   pkg. (8 oz.) reduced-fat cream cheese
1   can (14 oz.) sweetened condensed milk
2   eggs, lightly beaten
1   tsp. vanilla extract
1-1/4   cups milk chocolate English toffee bits, *divided*

1. In a small bowl, combine the flour, confectioners' sugar, cocoa and baking soda. Cut in butter until mixture resembles coarse crumbs. Press onto the bottom of an ungreased 13-in. x 9-in. baking dish. Bake at 350° for 12-15 minutes or until set.

2. In a large bowl, beat cream cheese until fluffy. Add the milk, eggs and vanilla; beat until smooth. Stir in 3/4 cup toffee bits. Pour over crust. Bake 18-22 minutes longer or until center is almost set.

3. Cool on a wire rack for 15 minutes. Sprinkle with remaining toffee bits; cool completely. Cover and refrigerate for 8 hours or overnight.

Nutrition Facts: 1 bar equals 169 calories, 9 g fat (5 g saturated fat), 39 mg cholesterol, 120 mg sodium, 19 g carbohydrate, trace fiber, 3 g protein. **Diabetic Exchanges:** 2 fat, 1 starch.

Gluten-Free Almond Cookies `F` `S` `C`

PREP: 15 min. **BAKE:** 15 min./batch **YIELD:** 2 dozen

SHERRI COX • LUCASVILLE, OHIO

My friend on a gluten-free diet loved these fantastic cookies so much, she had to ask for the recipe! Quick and easy, they taste as good as the decadent treats I make using puff pastry and almond paste. Everyone loves these!

1	can (8 oz.) almond paste
1/2	cup sugar
2	egg whites
1/8	tsp. salt

1. In a large bowl, beat almond paste and sugar until crumbly. Beat in egg whites and salt until smooth. Shape dough into 1-in. balls.

2. Place 1 in. apart on parchment paper-lined baking sheets. Bake at 350° for 15-18 minutes or until lightly browned. Cool for 1 minute before removing from pans to wire racks. Store in an airtight container.

Editor's Note: Read all ingredient labels for possible gluten content prior to use. Ingredient formulas can change, and production facilities vary among brands. If you're concerned that your brand may contain gluten, contact the company.

Nutrition Facts: 1 cookie equals 61 calories, 3 g fat (trace saturated fat), 0 cholesterol, 18 mg sodium, 9 g carbohydrate, trace fiber, 1 g protein. **Diabetic Exchanges:** 1/2 starch, 1/2 fat.

Lighter Cookie Cutouts `F` `S` `C`

PREP: 20 min. **BAKE:** 5 min./batch **YIELD:** 2 dozen

HEALTHY COOKING TEST KITCHEN

These cookie cutouts are so light and fuss-free, you'll want to bake up several batches to decorate in different ways.

1/4	cup butter, softened
1/2	cup sugar
1/2	cup packed brown sugar
1	egg
2	Tbsp. canola oil
1/4	tsp. vanilla extract
1-1/2	cups all-purpose flour
1/4	tsp. salt
1/8	tsp. baking soda

FOR VARIATIONS:
Yellow and red food coloring

Beaten egg white

Popsicle *or* lollipop sticks

1. In a large bowl, beat butter and sugars until crumbly, about 2 minutes. Add egg, oil and vanilla. Combine the flour, salt and baking soda; gradually add to creamed mixture and mix well.

2. Divide the dough in half. On a lightly floured surface, roll one portion of dough to 1/4-in. thickness. Cut with a floured 3-in. cookie cutter. Place 1 in. apart on baking sheets coated with cooking spray. Repeat.

3. Bake at 350° for 5-7 minutes or until set. Cool for 1 minute before removing from pans to wire racks. Decorate as desired.

Nutrition Facts: 1 cookie equals 92 calories, 3 g fat (1 g saturated fat), 14 mg cholesterol, 49 mg sodium, 15 g carbohydrate, trace fiber, 1 g protein. **Diabetic Exchanges:** 1 starch, 1/2 fat.

Gluten-Free Oatmeal Chip Bars `S`

PREP: 20 min. **BAKE:** 20 min. + cooling **YIELD:** 3 dozen

SUSAN JAMES • COKATO, MINNESOTA

With two busy boys who would rather move around than sit and eat, I needed a gluten-free, hearty, hand-held treat that could double as a quick breakfast, brunch, lunch or snack. This is a favorite of theirs, and I can change it up to accommodate ingredients I have on hand.

1/2	cup packed brown sugar
4	eggs
1-1/2	cups mashed ripe bananas (3-4 medium)
1	cup peanut butter
1/2	tsp. salt
6	cups gluten-free old-fashioned oats
1	cup gluten-free butterscotch chips
1	cup (6 oz.) semisweet chocolate chips

1. In a large bowl, beat brown sugar and eggs until well blended. Add bananas, peanut butter and salt until blended. Stir in the oats, butterscotch and chocolate chips.

2. Spread the batter into a 15-in. x 10-in. x 1-in. baking pan coated with cooking spray. Bake at 350° for 20-25 minutes or until edges begin to brown. Cool completely on a wire rack. Cut into bars.

Editor's Note: Read all ingredient labels for possible gluten content prior to use. Ingredient formulas can change, and production facilities vary among brands. If you're concerned that your brand may contain gluten, contact the company.

Nutrition Facts: 1 bar equals 179 calories, 8 g fat (4 g saturated fat), 24 mg cholesterol, 80 mg sodium, 23 g carbohydrate, 2 g fiber, 5 g protein. **Diabetic Exchanges:** 1-1/2 starch, 1 fat.

GLUTEN-FREE OATMEAL CHIP BARS

Cutout Cookie Pops F S C

PREP: 30 min. + chilling BAKE: 5 min. per batch
YIELD: 2 dozen

HEALTHY COOKING TEST KITCHEN

Perfect for Halloween classroom snacks, these fun cookie pops don't pile on fat and calories!

1/4	cup butter, softened
1/2	cup sugar
1/2	cup packed brown sugar
1	egg
2	Tbsp. canola oil
1/4	tsp. vanilla extract
1-1/2	cups all-purpose flour
1/4	tsp. salt
1/8	tsp. baking soda
10	drops yellow food coloring
4	drops red food coloring
1	egg white, beaten

Popsicle *or* lollipop sticks

1. In a large bowl, beat butter and sugars until crumbly, about 2 minutes. Add egg, oil and vanilla. Combine the flour, salt and baking soda; gradually add to creamed mixture and mix well.

2. Divide dough in half. Mix yellow and red food coloring into one portion of dough. Cover and refrigerate both portions for 30 minutes.

3. On a lightly floured surface, roll doughs to 1/4-in. thickness. Cut with a floured 3-in. pumpkin-shaped cookie cutter. Cut out a face to resemble a jack-o'-lantern. Place the Popsicle sticks on baking sheets coated with cooking spray. Top each with cutout dough; press down gently. Replace face cutouts with opposite colored dough. Bake at 350° for 5-7 minutes or until set. Cool for 1 minute before removing from pans to wire racks.

CUTOUT COOKIE POPS

Nutrition Facts: 1 cookie pop equals 92 calories, 3 g fat (1 g saturated fat), 14 mg cholesterol, 49 mg sodium, 15 g carbohydrate, trace fiber, 1 g protein. **Diabetic Exchanges:** 1 starch, 1/2 fat.

Makeover Pick-Me-Up Cream Cheese Brownies S

PREP: 30 min. BAKE: 35 min. + cooling YIELD: 2-1/2 dozen

SONYA LABBE • LOS ANGELES, CALIFORNIA

The lightened-up version of these indulgent brownies tastes absolutely divine but weighs in at a modest 159 calories and 8 g fat per serving.

1/4	cup reduced-fat butter
1	cup sugar
2	eggs
2	egg whites
4	oz. bittersweet chocolate, melted
4	oz. semisweet chocolate, melted
1	tsp. rum extract
1	cup all-purpose flour
1	tsp. baking powder
1/2	tsp. salt
1	cup 60% cacao bittersweet chocolate baking chips

CHEESECAKE LAYER:

2	Tbsp. instant espresso powder
2	Tbsp. hot water
6	oz. reduced-fat cream cheese
1/4	cup sugar
2	Tbsp. all-purpose flour
1/2	tsp. rum extract
1	egg
1/2	cup 60% cacao bittersweet chocolate baking chips

1. In a large bowl, cream butter and sugar until light and fluffy. Add eggs and egg whites, one at a time, beating well after each addition. Beat in melted chocolate and extract. Combine the flour, baking powder and salt; add to the creamed mixture. Fold in baking chips; set aside.

2. In a small bowl, dissolve espresso powder in water; cool to room temperature. In a large bowl, beat cream cheese and sugar until smooth. Beat in the flour, extract and espresso mixture. Add egg; beat on low speed just until combined. Fold in baking chips.

3. Spread half of chocolate mixture into a 13-in. x 9-in. baking pan coated with cooking spray; top with cream cheese mixture. Spoon remaining chocolate batter over top; cut through batter with a knife to swirl.

4. Bake at 325° for 35-40 minutes or until a toothpick inserted near the center comes out with moist crumbs. Cool completely on a wire rack. Cut into bars.

Editor's Note: This recipe was tested with Land O'Lakes light stick butter.

Nutrition Facts: 1 brownie equals 159 calories, 8 g fat (4 g saturated fat), 27 mg cholesterol, 101 mg sodium, 22 g carbohydrate, 1 g fiber, 3 g protein. **Diabetic Exchanges:** 1-1/2 fat, 1 starch.

Blondies with Chips S

PREP: 5 min. **BAKE:** 20 min. + cooling **YIELD:** 1 dozen

KAI SKUPINSKI • CANTON, MICHIGAN

My friends and family love my pared-down version of the classic blond brownie and never suspect that I use whole wheat flour. They even encouraged me to enter my recipe in a contest.

1/3	cup all-purpose flour
1/3	cup whole wheat flour
1/4	cup packed brown sugar
1/2	tsp. baking powder
1/4	tsp. salt
1	egg
1/4	cup canola oil
2	Tbsp. honey
1	tsp. vanilla extract
1/2	cup semisweet chocolate chips

1. In a small bowl, combine the first five ingredients. In another bowl, whisk the egg, oil, honey and vanilla. Stir into dry ingredients just until combined. Stir in chocolate chips (batter will be thick).

2. Spread into an 8-in. square baking dish coated with cooking spray. Bake at 350° for 20-22 minutes or until a toothpick inserted near the center comes out clean. Cool on a wire rack. Cut into bars.

Nutrition Facts: 1 bar equals 133 calories, 7 g fat (2 g saturated fat), 18 mg cholesterol, 67 mg sodium, 17 g carbohydrate, 1 g fiber, 2 g protein. **Diabetic Exchanges:** 1 starch, 1 fat.

Vegan Chocolate Chip Cookies S

PREP: 15 min. + chilling **BAKE:** 10 min./batch
YIELD: 3-1/2 dozen

CASSANDRA BRZYCKI • WAUWATOSA, WISCONSIN

A busy competitive figure skater came up with this high-energy recipe. The cookies are loaded with nuts, chips and fabulous flavor. Coaches at her skating rink are always snitching two or three when she brings them in!

1-1/4	cups packed dark brown sugar
1/2	cup canola oil
6	Tbsp. vanilla soy milk
1/4	cup sugar
1/4	cup unsweetened applesauce
2	tsp. vanilla extract
2-1/4	cups all-purpose flour
1	tsp. baking soda
3/4	tsp. salt
1	cup dairy-free semisweet chocolate chips
1/2	cup finely chopped walnuts

1. In a large bowl, beat the first six ingredients until well blended. Combine the flour, baking soda and salt; gradually add to sugar mixture and mix well. Stir in the chocolate chips and nuts. Cover and refrigerate for 1 hour.

2. Drop by rounded tablespoonfuls 2 in. apart onto parchment paper-lined baking sheets. Bake at 375° for 10-12 minutes or until edges are lightly browned. Cool for 1 minute before removing from pans to wire racks.

Nutrition Facts: 1 cookie equals 111 calories, 5 g fat (1 g saturated fat), 0 cholesterol, 76 mg sodium, 16 g carbohydrate, 1 g fiber, 1 g protein.

Raspberry Bavarian Cake **F** **S**

PREP: 20 min. + chilling **YIELD:** 16 servings

LINDA MURRAY • ALLENSTOWN, NEW HAMPSHIRE

This recipe is an all-time favorite with my family and everyone else who tastes it. It's so easy but makes an impressive company dessert. Because it doesn't seem light, everyone feels like they're overindulging!

- 5 pkg. (12 oz. *each*) frozen unsweetened raspberries, thawed
- 2 cups confectioners' sugar
- 2 envelopes unflavored gelatin
- 1/3 cup plus 1/2 cup cold water, *divided*
- 38 ladyfingers, split

- 2 Tbsp. seedless raspberry jam
- 1 tsp. water
- 1 carton (12 oz.) frozen reduced-fat whipped topping, thawed, *divided*

1. In a large saucepan, combine raspberries and confectioners' sugar. Bring to a boil. Reduce heat; simmer for 5-10 minutes or until bubbly and sugar is dissolved, stirring occasionally. Mash and strain raspberries, reserving syrup. Discard seeds; set aside.

2. In a small saucepan, sprinkle gelatin over 1/3 cup cold water; let stand for 1 minute. Heat over low heat stirring until gelatin is completely dissolved. Stir in remaining cold water and raspberry juice. Cover and refrigerate for 1-1/2 to 2 hours or until slightly thickened, stirring occasionally.

3. Meanwhile, line the bottom and sides of a 9-in. springform pan with ladyfingers. In a small bowl, combine raspberry jam and water; spread over ladyfingers lining bottom of pan. Fold 3-3/4 cups whipped topping into raspberry mixture. Pour into prepared pan. Cover and refrigerate for at least 3 hours or until firm. Garnish with remaining whipped topping.

Nutrition Facts: 1 slice equals 223 calories, 3 g fat (3 g saturated fat), 35 mg cholesterol, 121 mg sodium, 46 g carbohydrate, 3 g fiber, 4 g protein.

Cran-Orange Pie in a Jar

PREP: 20 min. + chilling YIELD: 4 servings

HEALTHY COOKING TEST KITCHEN

These individual pudding pies in a jar are irresistible to big and little snackers alike! Not only is this an excellent light dessert, but it's a perfect homemade gift, too!

- 1 cup graham cracker crumbs
- 2 Tbsp. butter, melted
- 2 cups cold fat-free milk
- 1 pkg. (1 oz.) sugar-free instant white chocolate pudding mix
- 1/2 tsp. grated orange peel
- 1/2 cup whole-berry cranberry sauce

1. In a small bowl, combine cracker crumbs and butter. Press into the bottom of each of four half-pint canning jars.

2. In another bowl, whisk milk and pudding mix for 2 minutes. Stir in orange peel. Let stand for 2 minutes or until soft-set. Spoon over crusts. Top with cranberry sauce. Cover and refrigerate for at least 1 hour.

Nutrition Facts: 1 serving equals 253 calories, 8 g fat (4 g saturated fat), 18 mg cholesterol, 439 mg sodium, 40 g carbohydrate, 1 g fiber, 6 g protein.

Best-Ever Sweet Potato Pie

PREP: 25 min. BAKE: 1 hour 15 min. YIELD: 10 servings

ERIN GIBBONS • DOWNINGTOWN, PENNSYLVANIA

My grandmother handed down this recipe and it's amazing! The flavor, with a hint of maple and great spices, totally lives up to its name.

- 1 extra-servings-size graham cracker crust (9 oz.)
- 1 egg white, beaten
- 1-1/2 cups mashed sweet potatoes
- 1-1/4 cups fat-free milk
- 3 eggs
- 2/3 cup sugar
- 1/2 cup maple syrup
- 1 tsp. ground cinnamon
- 1/2 tsp. salt
- 1/2 tsp. ground ginger
- 1/2 tsp. ground nutmeg
- 1/4 tsp. ground mace

1. Brush crust with egg white. Bake at 400° for 6-8 minutes. Cool on a wire rack. Reduce heat to 350°.

2. In a large bowl, beat the remaining ingredients until blended. Pour into crust. Bake for 70-80 minutes or until a knife inserted near the center comes out clean. Cool on a wire rack. Refrigerate leftovers.

Nutrition Facts: 1 piece equals 292 calories, 8 g fat (2 g saturated fat), 64 mg cholesterol, 318 mg sodium, 51 g carbohydrate, 2 g fiber, 5 g protein.

Members of the morning glory family and native to Central America, **sweet potatoes** come in two readily available varieties. One has a pale skin with a light yellow flesh and a dry mealy texture. The other has dark skin with a dark orange flesh that cooks to a moist texture.

BEST-EVER SWEET POTATO PIE

CRAN-ORANGE PIE IN A JAR

Cherry Upside-Down Cake

PREP: 25 min. BAKE: 20 min. + cooling
YIELD: 8 servings

DOROTHY ERICKSON • BLUE EYE, MISSOURI

As a home economics teacher, I used this recipe to demonstrate simple cake- and sauce-making techniques. The kids loved it just as my family always has.

    1   can (14-1/2 oz.) pitted tart cherries
    1/3 cup sugar
    1   Tbsp. butter

CAKE:

    1/4 cup shortening
    1/2 cup sugar
    1   egg
    1   cup all-purpose flour
    1   tsp. baking powder
    1/4 tsp. salt
    1/3 cup fat-free milk

SAUCE:

    3   Tbsp. sugar
    1   Tbsp. cornstarch
    5   to 8 drops food coloring, optional

1. Drain cherries, reserving liquid in a 1-cup measuring cup. Add enough water to measure 1 cup; set aside for sauce.

2. In a small saucepan, combine the cherries, sugar and butter. Cook and stir over medium heat until butter is melted and sugar is dissolved. Pour into a 9-in. round baking pan coated with cooking spray.

3. For cake, in a large bowl, cream shortening and sugar until light and fluffy. Add egg; mix well. Combine the flour, baking powder and salt; add to the creamed mixture alternately with milk, beating well after each addition. Spread over cherry mixture.

4. Bake at 350° for 20-25 minutes or until a toothpick inserted near the center comes out clean. Cool for 10 minutes before inverting cake onto a serving plate.

5. For sauce, in a small saucepan, combine sugar and cornstarch. Gradually add reserved cherry juice mixture. Bring to a boil; cook and stir for 2 minutes or until thickened. Stir in food coloring if desired. Serve with warm cake.

Nutrition Facts: 1 slice with 2 Tbsp. sauce equals 258 calories, 8 g fat (3 g saturated fat), 30 mg cholesterol, 151 mg sodium, 43 g carbohydrate, 1 g fiber, 3 g protein.

Chocolate-Covered Cherry Pudding Cake

PREP: 20 min. COOK: 2 hours + standing
YIELD: 8 servings

MEREDITH COE • CHARLOTTESVILLE, VIRGINIA

Growing up, I remember my grandfather cherishing the chocolate-covered cherries we'd bring him for Christmas. After he passed away, I came up with this rich recipe in his honor. It's delicious served with whipped topping.

    1/2   cup reduced-fat sour cream
    2   Tbsp. canola oil
    1   Tbsp. butter, melted
    2   tsp. vanilla extract
    1   cup all-purpose flour
    1/4   cup sugar
    1/4   cup packed brown sugar
    3   Tbsp. baking cocoa
    2   tsp. baking powder
    1/2   tsp. ground cinnamon
    1/8   tsp. salt
    1   cup fresh or frozen pitted dark sweet cherries, thawed
    1   cup fresh or frozen pitted tart cherries, thawed
    1/3   cup 60% cacao bittersweet chocolate baking chips

PUDDING:

    1/2   cup packed brown sugar
    2   Tbsp. baking cocoa
    1-1/4 cups hot water

CHERRY UPSIDE-DOWN CAKE

CHOCOLATE-COVERED CHERRY PUDDING CAKE

1. In a large bowl, beat the sour cream, oil, butter and vanilla until blended. Combine the flour, sugars, cocoa, baking powder, cinnamon and salt. Add to sour cream mixture just until combined. Stir in cherries and chips. Pour into a 3-qt. slow cooker coated with cooking spray.

2. In a small bowl, combine brown sugar and cocoa. Stir in hot water until blended. Pour over the batter (do not stir). Cover and cook on high for 2 to 2-1/2 hours or until set. Let stand for 15 minutes. Serve cake warm.

Nutrition Facts: 1 serving equals 291 calories, 9 g fat (3 g saturated fat), 9 mg cholesterol, 167 mg sodium, 51 g carbohydrate, 2 g fiber, 4 g protein.

Raspberry Baked Alaska Pie

PREP: 40 min. + freezing **YIELD:** 8 servings (1 cup sauce)

DAGMAR VENA • NEPEAN, ONTARIO

I'm sharing one of my family's very favorite pie recipes. I love making it for special occasions, and assembling it the day before leaves extra time to spend with loved ones.

- 1 cup graham cracker crumbs
- 3 Tbsp. brown sugar
- 3 Tbsp. butter, melted
- 1 Tbsp. cornstarch
- 1/2 cup cold water
- 3 Tbsp. lemon juice
- 1 pkg. (10 oz.) frozen sweetened raspberries, thawed
- 2 tsp. grated lemon peel

- 4-1/2 cups reduced-fat vanilla ice cream, softened
- 3 egg whites
- 1/2 cup sugar

1. In a small bowl, combine the cracker crumbs, brown sugar and butter. Press onto the bottom and up the sides of a 9-in. pie plate; freeze until set.

2. Meanwhile, in a large saucepan, combine the cornstarch, water and lemon juice until smooth. Stir in raspberries and lemon peel. Cook, stirring occasionally, over medium heat until mixture just comes to a boil. Remove from the heat; transfer to a small bowl. Cool slightly; refrigerate until chilled.

3. Spread 1-1/2 cups ice cream into crust; cover and freeze for 1 hour. Drizzle with 1/2 cup raspberry sauce; freeze until set. Repeat layers, freezing after each layer. Top with remaining ice cream. Cover and freeze for 8 hours or overnight.

4. In a large heavy saucepan, combine the egg whites and sugar. With a hand mixer, beat on low speed for 1 minute. Continue beating over low heat until the egg mixture reaches 160°, about 6 minutes. Transfer to a bowl; beat until stiff glossy peaks form and sugar is dissolved.

5. Immediately spread meringue over ice cream, sealing to edges of pie. Heat with a creme brulee torch or broil 8 in. from the heat for 3-5 minutes or until meringue is lightly browned. Serve immediately with remaining sauce.

Nutrition Facts: 1 piece with 2 Tbsp. sauce equals 321 calories, 9 g fat (5 g saturated fat), 31 mg cholesterol, 172 mg sodium, 56 g carbohydrate, 2 g fiber, 6 g protein.

Pumpkin Oatmeal Bars

PREP: 30 min. **BAKE:** 30 min. + cooling **YIELD:** 2 dozen

ERIN ANDREWS • EDGEWATER, FLORIDA

It took me a long time to develop this effortless recipe, but I'm so happy with how it turned out. These bars have it all—sugar and spice and a creamy-rich pumpkin layer that's especially nice!

- 1 pkg. (18-1/4 oz.) yellow cake mix
- 2-1/2 cups quick-cooking oats
- 5 Tbsp. butter, melted
- 3 Tbsp. honey
- 1 Tbsp. water

FILLING:
- 1 can (15 oz.) solid-pack pumpkin
- 1/4 cup reduced-fat cream cheese
- 1/4 cup fat-free milk
- 3 Tbsp. brown sugar
- 2 Tbsp. maple syrup
- 1 tsp. ground cinnamon
- 1 tsp. vanilla extract
- 1/4 tsp. ground allspice
- 1/4 tsp. ground cloves
- 1 egg
- 1 egg white
- 1/4 cup chopped walnuts
- 1 Tbsp. butter, melted

1. In a large bowl, combine cake mix and oats; set aside 1/2 cup for topping. Add the butter, honey and water to the remaining cake mixture. Press onto the bottom of a 13-in. x 9-in. baking pan coated with cooking spray.

2. For filling, in a large bowl, beat the pumpkin, cream cheese, milk, brown sugar, maple syrup, cinnamon, vanilla, allspice and cloves until blended. Add egg and egg white; beat on low speed just until combined. Pour over crust. In a small bowl, combine the walnuts, butter and reserved cake mixture; sprinkle over filling.

3. Bake at 350° for 30-35 minutes or until set and edges are lightly browned. Cool on a wire rack. Cut into bars.

Nutrition Facts: 1 bar equals 186 calories, 7 g fat (3 g saturated fat), 18 mg cholesterol, 180 mg sodium, 30 g carbohydrate, 2 g fiber, 3 g protein. **Diabetic Exchanges:** 2 starch, 1 fat.

Chocolate Angel Cupcakes with Coconut Cream Frosting F

PREP: 15 min. **BAKE:** 15 min. + cooling **YIELD:** 2 dozen

MANDY RIVERS • LEXINGTON, SOUTH CAROLINA

Sweeten any meal with these fun, frosted chocolate cupcakes that take just minutes to make. The finger-licking flavor packs far fewer calories and fat than traditional desserts!

- 1 pkg. (16 oz.) angel food cake mix
- 3/4 cup baking cocoa
- 1 cup (8 oz.) reduced-fat sour cream
- 1 cup confectioners' sugar
- 1/8 tsp. coconut extract
- 2-1/2 cups reduced-fat whipped topping
- 3/4 cup flaked coconut, toasted

1. Prepare cake mix according to package directions for cupcakes, adding cocoa when mixing.

2. Fill foil- or paper-lined muffin cups two-thirds full. Bake at 375° for 11-15 minutes or until cake springs back when lightly touched and cracks feel dry. Cool for 10 minutes before removing from pans to wire racks to cool completely.

3. For frosting, in a large bowl, combine the sour cream, confectioners' sugar and extract until smooth. Fold in whipped topping. Frost cupcakes. Sprinkle with coconut. Refrigerate leftovers.

Nutrition Facts: 1 cupcake equals 142 calories, 3 g fat (2 g saturated fat), 3 mg cholesterol, 154 mg sodium, 27 g carbohydrate, 1 g fiber, 3 g protein. **Diabetic Exchanges:** 1-1/2 starch, 1/2 fat.

> To quickly **frost cupcakes,** place frosting that has a soft, spreadable consistency in a bowl. Dip the top of the cupcake into the frosting, twist slightly and lift up.

CHOCOLATE ANGEL CUPCAKES WITH COCONUT CREAM FROSTING

Cherry-Chocolate Coconut Meringues F S C

PREP: 15 min. **BAKE:** 25 min./batch + cooling
YIELD: 3 dozen

MARY SHIVERS • ADA, OKLAHOMA

Dried cherries lend sweetness and texture to these easy meringue cookies fit for any occasion. They're simply delicious and very low in fat. They also provide a great guiltless dessert for family members on a gluten-free diet.

- 3 egg whites
- 1/2 tsp. almond extract
- Dash salt
- 1/3 cup sugar
- 2/3 cup confectioners' sugar
- 1/4 cup baking cocoa
- 1-1/4 cups finely shredded unsweetened coconut
- 1/2 cup dried cherries, finely chopped

1. Place egg whites in a large bowl; let stand at room temperature for 30 minutes.

2. Add extract and salt; beat on medium speed until soft peaks form. Gradually add sugar, 1 Tbsp. at a time, beating on high until stiff glossy peaks form and sugar is dissolved. Combine confectioners' sugar and cocoa; beat into egg white mixture. Fold in coconut and cherries.

3. Drop by rounded tablespoonfuls 2 in. apart onto baking sheets coated with cooking spray. Bake at 325° for 25-28 minutes or until firm to the touch. Cool completely on pans on wire racks. Store meringues in an airtight container.

Editor's Note: Look for unsweetened coconut in the baking or health food section.

Nutrition Facts: 1 cookie equals 42 calories, 2 g fat (1 g saturated fat), 0 cholesterol, 10 mg sodium, 6 g carbohydrate, 1 g fiber, 1 g protein. **Diabetic Exchange:** 1/2 starch.

Striped Cutouts F S C

PREP: 30 min. + chilling **BAKE:** 5 min./batch
YIELD: 2 dozen

HEALTHY COOKING TEST KITCHEN

Here's a fun take on the classic sugar cookie. The unique look means no additional decorating for you!

- 1/4 cup butter, softened
- 1/2 cup sugar
- 1/2 cup packed brown sugar
- 1 egg
- 2 Tbsp. canola oil
- 1/4 tsp. vanilla extract
- 1-1/2 cups all-purpose flour
- 1/4 tsp. salt
- 1/8 tsp. baking soda
- 5 drops yellow food coloring
- 2 drops red food coloring
- 1 egg white, beaten

1. In a large bowl, beat butter and sugars until crumbly, about 2 minutes. Add egg, oil and vanilla. Combine the flour, salt and baking soda; gradually add to creamed mixture and mix well.

2. Divide dough into four portions; mix both yellow and red food coloring into two portions to create two orange rolls. Roll each portion of dough between waxed paper into a 12-in. x 6-in. rectangle. Refrigerate for 30 minutes.

3. Remove waxed paper; brush tops with egg white. Stack rectangles, alternating colors. Cut into eight 3-in. x 3-in. squares. Stack squares; wrap in plastic wrap. Chill for 2 hours or until firm. Cut into 1/8-in. slices. Cut each slice with a cookie cutter. Place 1 in. apart on greased baking sheets coated with cooking spray. Bake at 350° for 5-7 minutes or until set. Cool for 1 minute before removing from pans to wire racks.

Nutrition Facts: 1 cookie equals 92 calories, 3 g fat (1 g saturated fat), 14 mg cholesterol, 49 mg sodium, 15 g carbohydrate, trace fiber, 1 g protein. **Diabetic Exchanges:** 1 starch, 1/2 fat.

CHERRY-CHOCOLATE COCONUT MERINGUES

STRIPED CUTOUTS

Peppermint-Kissed Fudge Mallow Cookies F S

PREP: 30 min. **BAKE:** 10 min./batch + cooling
YIELD: 2 dozen

PRISCILLA YEE • CONCORD, CALIFORNIA

At my house, Christmas just wouldn't be the same without these cute-as-can-be treats. Fudgy-rich chocolate cookies with refreshing mint flavor, soft marshmallow, crunchy candy... it's a must-try recipe for any event!

- 1/3 cup reduced-fat plain yogurt
- 5 Tbsp. butter, melted
- 3/4 tsp. peppermint extract
- 1 cup all-purpose flour
- 3/4 cup sugar
- 1/2 cup baking cocoa
- 1/4 tsp. salt
- 1/4 tsp. baking soda
- 12 large marshmallows, cut in half lengthwise

CHOCOLATE GLAZE:
- 2 Tbsp. semisweet chocolate chips
- 3/4 cup confectioners' sugar
- 3 Tbsp. baking cocoa
- 3 Tbsp. fat-free milk
- 1/4 tsp. peppermint extract
- 1/4 cup crushed peppermint candies

1. In a large bowl, beat the yogurt, butter and extract until well blended. Combine the flour, sugar, cocoa, salt and baking soda; gradually add to yogurt mixture and mix well.

2. Drop by tablespoonfuls onto baking sheets coated with cooking spray. Bake at 350° for 8 minutes. Place a marshmallow half on each cookie; bake 1-2 minutes longer or until marshmallow is puffed. Cool for 2 minutes before removing from pans to wire racks to cool completely.

3. For glaze, in a microwave, melt chocolate chips; stir until smooth. Stir in the confectioners' sugar, cocoa, milk and extract until smooth. Drizzle over marshmallows; sprinkle with candies.

Nutrition Facts: 1 cookie equals 109 calories, 3 g fat (2 g saturated fat), 7 mg cholesterol, 60 mg sodium, 20 g carbohydrate, 1 g fiber, 1 g protein.

To easily separate **sticky marshmallows,** place a spoonful of powdered sugar in the bag and shake it well. A few stubborn marshmallows might still need to be separated by hand, but overall, this works seamlessly!

Makeover Frosty Lemon Squares

PREP: 30 min. BAKE: 15 min. + freezing YIELD: 20 servings

HEALTHY COOKING TEST KITCHEN

This make-ahead dessert has a lemony filling sandwiched between two creamy layers and a crunchy crust. What's not to love? Simple changes to the original recipe reduced a good portion of the calories and saturated fat, but left a ton of great lemon flavor and a rich cream cheese layer.

- 1/4 cup butter, softened
- 2 Tbsp. confectioners' sugar
- 1/2 cup all-purpose flour
- 1/2 cup cornstarch
- 1/2 cup ground pecans

CREAM CHEESE LAYER:
- 1 pkg. (8 oz.) reduced-fat cream cheese
- 1 pkg. (8 oz.) fat-free cream cheese
- 3/4 cup confectioners' sugar
- 1 carton (8 oz.) frozen reduced-fat whipped topping, thawed

LEMON LAYER:
- 1-1/4 cups sugar
- 6 Tbsp. cornstarch
- 1/4 tsp. salt
- 1-1/4 cups water
- 3/4 cup lemon juice
- 2 Tbsp. butter
- 1 Tbsp. grated lemon peel
- 3 to 4 drops yellow food coloring, optional

TOPPING:
- 1 Tbsp. grated lemon peel
- 1 carton (8 oz.) frozen reduced-fat whipped topping, thawed

1. In a small bowl, cream butter and confectioners' sugar until light and fluffy. Gradually add flour and cornstarch (mixture will be crumbly). Stir in pecans. Press into a 13-in. x 9-in. baking dish coated with cooking spray. Bake at 350° for 14-16 minutes or until lightly browned. Cool on a wire rack.

2. In a large bowl, beat cream cheeses and confectioners' sugar until fluffy. Fold in whipped topping. Spread over crust. Cover and freeze for 1 hour.

3. Meanwhile, in a small saucepan, combine the sugar, cornstarch, salt and water until smooth. Bring to a boil; cook and stir for 2 minutes or until thickened. Remove from the heat; stir in the lemon juice, butter, lemon peel and food coloring if desired. Transfer to a bowl; refrigerate for 1 hour.

4. Spread lemon mixture over cream cheese layer. Cover and freeze for 1 hour. Fold lemon peel into whipped topping; spread over lemon layer. Cover and freeze for up to 1 month. Remove from the freezer 15 minutes before serving.

Nutrition Facts: 1 piece equals 240 calories, 10 g fat (7 g saturated fat), 18 mg cholesterol, 164 mg sodium, 35 g carbohydrate, trace fiber, 3 g protein.

Chewy Oatmeal Raisin Cookies S

PREP: 15 min. BAKE: 10 min./batch YIELD: 15 cookies

TRINA BOITNOTT • BOONES MILL, VIRGINIA

A glass of milk and one of these warm, chewy cookies make for a perfect before-bed treat.

- 1/3 cup canola oil
- 1/3 cup packed brown sugar
- 2 Tbsp. sugar
- 3 Tbsp. water
- 1 egg white
- 3/4 tsp. vanilla extract
- 1/3 cup all-purpose flour
- 1/3 cup whole wheat flour
- 2 tsp. ground cinnamon
- 1/2 tsp. baking soda
- 1/4 tsp. salt
- 2 cups old-fashioned oats
- 1/2 cup raisins

1. In a large bowl, combine the oil, sugars, water, egg white and vanilla. Combine the flours, cinnamon, baking soda and salt; gradually add to sugar mixture and mix well. Stir in oats and raisins.

2. Drop by scant 1/4 cupfuls onto baking sheets coated with cooking spray; flatten slightly with the back of a spoon. Bake at 350° for 10-12 minutes or until golden brown. Cool for 1 minute before removing from pans to wire racks.

Nutrition Facts: 1 cookie equals 144 calories, 6 g fat (1 g saturated fat), 0 cholesterol, 88 mg sodium, 22 g carbohydrate, 2 g fiber, 3 g protein. **Diabetic Exchanges:** 1-1/2 starch, 1 fat.

Mini Sweet Potato Muffins F S C

PREP: 35 min. BAKE: 10 min./batch YIELD: 4-1/2 dozen

MEREDITH HEDEEN • NEW KENSINGTON, PENNSYLVANIA

I'm always looking for ways to "healthify" recipes. My husband loves the airy texture and zesty streusel of these muffins.

- 1 cup all-purpose flour
- 3/4 cup whole wheat flour
- 1/2 cup sugar
- 1/2 cup packed brown sugar
- 1 tsp. baking powder
- 1 tsp. ground cinnamon
- 1 tsp. ground allspice
- 1/2 tsp. salt
- 1/4 tsp. baking soda
- 2 eggs, beaten
- 1 cup mashed sweet potatoes
- 1/2 cup water
- 1/4 cup canola oil
- 3 Tbsp. unsweetened applesauce

STREUSEL:
- 2 Tbsp. biscuit/baking mix
- 2 Tbsp. quick-cooking oats
- 1 Tbsp. sugar
- 1 Tbsp. brown sugar
- 1-1/2 tsp. cold butter
- 1 Tbsp. finely chopped crystallized ginger

1. In a large bowl, combine the first nine ingredients. In another bowl, combine the eggs, potatoes, water, oil and applesauce. Stir into the dry ingredients just until moistened.

2. Coat miniature muffin cups with cooking spray or use paper liners; fill two-thirds full. For streusel, combine baking mix, oats and sugars; cut in butter until crumbly. Stir in ginger. Sprinkle over batter.

3. Bake at 350° for 10-12 minutes or until a toothpick inserted near the center comes out clean. Cool for 5 minutes before removing from pans to wire racks.

Nutrition Facts: 1 muffin equals 51 calories, 1 g fat (trace saturated fat), 8 mg cholesterol, 45 mg sodium, 9 g carbohydrate, trace fiber, 1 g protein. **Diabetic Exchange:** 1/2 starch.

MINI SWEET POTATO MUFFINS

CHEWY OATMEAL RAISIN COOKIES

ZUCCHINI CHOCOLATE CAKE
WITH ORANGE GLAZE

Zucchini Chocolate Cake with Orange Glaze

PREP: 20 min. **BAKE:** 50 min. + cooling
YIELD: 16 servings

BARBARA WORREL • GRANBURY, TEXAS

This moist, mouthwatering cake boasts a rich chocolate flavor, has a hint of orange and is chock-full of zucchini and nuts.

1/2	cup butter, softened
1-1/2	cups sugar
2	eggs
1/4	cup unsweetened applesauce
1	tsp. vanilla extract
2-1/2	cups all-purpose flour
1/2	cup baking cocoa
1-1/4	tsp. baking powder
1	tsp. salt
1	tsp. ground cinnamon
1/2	tsp. baking soda
1/2	cup fat-free milk
3	cups shredded zucchini
1/2	cup chopped walnuts
1	Tbsp. grated orange peel

GLAZE:

1-1/4	cups confectioners' sugar
2	Tbsp. orange juice
1	tsp. vanilla extract

1. Coat a 10-in. fluted tube pan with cooking spray and sprinkle with flour.

2. In a large bowl, cream butter and sugar until light and fluffy. Add eggs, one at a time, beating well after each addition. Beat in applesauce and vanilla.

3. Combine the flour, baking cocoa, baking powder, salt, cinnamon and soda; add to the creamed mixture alternately with milk, beating well after each addition. Fold in the shredded zucchini, walnuts and orange peel.

4. Transfer to prepared pan. Bake at 350° for 50-60 minutes or until a toothpick inserted near the center comes out clean.

5. Cool for 10 minutes before removing from pan to a wire rack to cool completely.

6. In a small bowl, combine glaze ingredients. Drizzle over the cake.

Nutrition Facts: 1 slice equals 282 calories, 9 g fat (4 g saturated fat), 42 mg cholesterol, 273 mg sodium, 47 g carbohydrate, 2 g fiber, 4 g protein.

Caramel-Pecan Cheese Pie

PREP: 20 min. + chilling **YIELD:** 8 servings

PATSY MULLINS • TAFT, TENNESSEE

Family and friends love this tasty no-bake pie, and no one can believe it's not loaded with fat!

1	envelope unflavored gelatin
1/3	cup cold water
1/4	cup lemon juice
3	oz. reduced-fat cream cheese, cubed
1	cup nonfat dry milk powder

Sugar substitute equivalent to 2 Tbsp. sugar

1	carton (8 oz.) frozen reduced-fat whipped topping, thawed
5	Tbsp. chopped pecans, toasted, *divided*
1	reduced-fat graham cracker crust (9 in.)
2	Tbsp. fat-free caramel ice cream topping

1. In a small saucepan, sprinkle gelatin over cold water; let stand for 1 minute. Heat over low heat, stirring until gelatin is completely dissolved. Cool mixture slightly.

2. In a blender, combine the lemon juice, cream cheese and gelatin mixture; cover and process until smooth. Add milk powder and sugar substitute; cover and process for 1 minute or until blended.

3. Transfer to a large bowl; fold in the whipped topping. Stir in 3 Tbsp. of pecans. Pour into crust. Sprinkle with remaining pecans. Drizzle with caramel topping. Cover and refrigerate for 2-3 hours or until set.

Editor's Note: This recipe was tested with Splenda no-calorie sweetener.

Nutrition Facts: 1 piece equals 270 calories, 12 g fat (6 g saturated fat), 6 mg cholesterol, 186 mg sodium, 31 g carbohydrate, 1 g fiber, 7 g protein. **Diabetic Exchanges:** 2 starch, 2 fat.

Light Strawberry Pie

PREP: 25 min. + chilling **YIELD:** 8 servings

LOU WRIGHT • ROCKFORD, ILLINOIS

This luscious strawberry dessert is a great after-supper sweet. People rave about this pie. And best of all, it's a low-sugar sensation that you won't feel one bit guilty eating.

1	can (8 oz.) unsweetened crushed pineapple
1	pkg. (.8 oz.) sugar-free cook-and-serve vanilla pudding mix
1	pkg. (.3 oz.) sugar-free strawberry gelatin
3	cups sliced fresh strawberries
1	reduced-fat graham cracker crust (8 in.)
1/2	cup reduced-fat whipped topping

1. Drain pineapple, reserving juice in a 2-cup measuring cup. Set pineapple aside. Add enough water to juice to measure 1-1/2 cups; transfer to a saucepan. Whisk in the pudding mix and gelatin until combined. Bring to a boil; cook and stir for 1-2 minutes or until thickened. Stir in pineapple. Remove from the heat; cool for 10 minutes.

2. Add the strawberries; toss gently to coat. Pour into crust. Refrigerate until set, about 3 hours. Garnish each piece with 1 Tbsp. whipped topping. Refrigerate leftovers.

Nutrition Facts: 1 piece equals 159 calories, 4 g fat (2 g saturated fat), 0 cholesterol, 172 mg sodium, 29 g carbohydrate, 2 g fiber, 2 g protein. **Diabetic Exchanges:** 1 starch, 1 fruit, 1/2 fat.

LIGHT STRAWBERRY PIE

CARAMEL-PECAN CHEESE PIE

Makeover Pineapple Upside-Down Cake

PREP: 15 min. **BAKE:** 35 min. **YIELD:** 9 servings

MARY LOU MOELLER • WOOSTER, OHIO

Both of my boys loved this trimmed-down version of a family favorite. Even my husband, who is a bit picky, takes pieces in his lunch bag!

3	Tbsp. butter, melted
1/3	cup packed brown sugar
9	canned unsweetened pineapple slices
9	maraschino cherry halves
2/3	cup sugar
2/3	cup fat-free milk
3	Tbsp. canola oil
1	egg
1	tsp. lemon extract
1/2	tsp. vanilla extract
1-1/3	cups cake flour
1-1/4	tsp. baking powder
1/4	tsp. salt

1. Pour butter into a 9-in. square baking pan; sprinkle with brown sugar. Arrange pineapple slices in a single layer in pan; place cherry halves in center of pineapple slices; set aside.

2. In a large bowl, beat the sugar, milk, oil, egg and extracts until well blended. Combine the flour, baking powder and salt; gradually beat into sugar mixture until blended. Pour into prepared pan.

3. Bake at 350° for 35-40 minutes or until a toothpick comes out clean. Immediately invert onto a serving plate. Serve warm.

MAKEOVER PINEAPPLE UPSIDE-DOWN CAKE

Nutrition Facts: 1 piece equals 288 calories, 9 g fat (3 g saturated fat), 34 mg cholesterol, 172 mg sodium, 49 g carbohydrate, 1 g fiber, 3 g protein.

Chocolate Swirl Cake

PREP: 20 min. **BAKE:** 35 min. + cooling
YIELD: 15 servings

GAIL MAKI • MARQUETTE, MICHIGAN

This tasty chocolate cake won't ruin your waistline. Pretty swirls of cream cheese dress it up while cherry pie filling provides moistness. Sometimes I add miniature chocolate chips for an extra-special treat.

1	pkg. (18-1/4 oz.) chocolate cake mix
1	can (20 oz.) reduced-sugar cherry pie filling
5	egg whites
1	tsp. vanilla extract

TOPPING:

1	pkg. (8 oz.) reduced-fat cream cheese

Sugar substitute equivalent to 1/3 cup sugar

1/2	tsp. vanilla extract
2	egg whites

1. In a large bowl, combine the cake mix, pie filling, egg whites and vanilla just until moistened. Spread into a 13-in. x 9-in. baking dish coated with cooking spray; set aside.

2. In a small bowl, beat the cream cheese, sugar substitute and vanilla until smooth. Add egg whites; beat on low speed just until combined. Spread over batter; cut through batter with a knife to swirl.

3. Bake at 350° for 35-40 minutes or until a toothpick inserted near the center comes out clean and topping is set. Cool on a wire rack. Store cake in the refrigerator.

Editor's Note: This recipe was tested with Splenda no-calorie sweetener.

Nutrition Facts: 1 piece equals 207 calories, 5 g fat (2 g saturated fat), 5 mg cholesterol, 350 mg sodium, 35 g carbohydrate, 1 g fiber, 5 g protein. **Diabetic Exchanges:** 1-1/2 starch, 1 fat, 1/2 fruit.

CHOCOLATE SWIRL CAKE

Makeover Frozen Chocolate Pie S

PREP: 40 min. BAKE: 1 hour + freezing YIELD: 8 servings

HEALTHY COOKING TEST KITCHEN

The original recipe for this fabulous dessert was absolute heaven—until it came to stepping on the scale! Now the fat's been cut by over half and the calories reduced. Your taste buds will never even know the difference!

3	egg whites
1/4	tsp. cream of tartar
1-1/2	cups sugar, *divided*
1/4	cup baking cocoa
1	Tbsp. cornstarch
Dash	salt
3/4	cup evaporated milk
1	tsp. vanilla extract
2	cups reduced-fat vanilla ice cream, softened
1	carton (8 oz.) frozen whipped topping, thawed

1. Place egg whites in a small bowl; let stand at room temperature for 30 minutes. Add cream of tartar; beat until soft peaks form. Gradually add 3/4 cup sugar, 1 Tbsp. at a time, beating until stiff peaks form.

2. Spread onto the bottom and up the sides of a greased and floured 9-in. deep-dish pie plate. Bake at 275° for 1 hour. Turn off oven and do not open door; let meringue cool completely inside the oven.

3. For chocolate sauce, in a small saucepan, combine the cocoa, cornstarch, salt and remaining sugar. Whisk in milk. Bring to a boil over medium heat, stirring constantly. Reduce heat; simmer, uncovered, for 5-7 minutes or until slightly thickened. Remove from the heat; stir in vanilla. Cool to room temperature. Transfer to a large bowl.

4. Spread ice cream into meringue shell. Fold whipped topping into cooled chocolate sauce. Spread over ice cream layer; cover and freeze until firm.

Nutrition Facts: 1 piece equals 328 calories, 8 g fat (7 g saturated fat), 16 mg cholesterol, 86 mg sodium, 57 g carbohydrate, 1 g fiber, 5 g protein.

VERY BERRY CRISP

LEMON BLACKBERRY PARFAITS

CHOCOLATE ANISE CANNOLI

Treat Yourself

Crisps, trifles, ice cream snacks and souffles...you'll find all of these luscious dishes and more in this section. Turn here when you want an extra-special treat that takes the guilt out of dessert!

Chocolate Anise Cannoli

PREP: 35 min. **BAKE:** 10 min. + cooling
YIELD: 16 servings

MARIE RIZZIO • INTERLOCHEN, MICHIGAN

Here's that something special you've been looking for to add to your holiday cookie tray! We guarantee these wonton-wrapped bites with anise, cherries, chocolate, brandy and pistachios will be gone in a twinkling.

  16 wonton wrappers
Butter-flavored cooking spray
   1 Tbsp. sugar
1/4 cup dried cherries
   1 Tbsp. cherry brandy
   2 pkg. (8 oz. *each*) reduced-fat cream cheese
   1 cup confectioners' sugar
1/2 cup baking cocoa
   3 Tbsp. anise liqueur
1/4 cup semisweet chocolate chips
1/4 cup chopped shelled pistachios

1. Wrap a wonton wrapper around a metal cannoli tube. Moisten corner with water and seal. Transfer to an ungreased baking sheet. Repeat with remaining wrappers. Spritz with the cooking spray; sprinkle with sugar.

2. Bake at 325° for 10-14 minutes or until golden brown. Cool for 5 minutes. Remove shells from tubes; cool on a wire rack.

3. Meanwhile, place cherries in a small bowl. Add brandy; let stand for 10 minutes. Drain and coarsely chop cherries. In a large bowl, beat the cream cheese, confectioners' sugar, cocoa, liqueur and chopped cherries until blended.

4. In a microwave, melt chocolate chips; stir until smooth. Dip shell ends in chocolate; allow excess to drip off. Press into pistachios. Place on waxed paper; let stand until set.

5. Pipe filling into prepared shells. Serve immediately.

Nutrition Facts: 1 cannoli equals 175 calories, 9 g fat (5 g saturated fat), 21 mg cholesterol, 174 mg sodium, 19 g carbohydrate, 1 g fiber, 5 g protein.

Very Berry Crisp **S**

PREP: 20 min. **BAKE:** 25 min. **YIELD:** 8 servings

JANET ELROD • NEWNAN, GEORGIA

I love this recipe because it's easy, low-fat, versatile and delicious! The crispy topping is flavored with graham cracker crumbs, cinnamon and almonds and doesn't taste light at all. Add some frozen yogurt or whipped topping.

   2 cups fresh raspberries
   2 cups sliced fresh strawberries
   2 cups fresh blueberries
1/3 cup sugar
   2 Tbsp. plus 1/4 cup all-purpose flour, *divided*
1/3 cup graham cracker crumbs
1/3 cup quick-cooking oats
1/4 cup packed brown sugar
   2 Tbsp. sliced almonds
1/2 tsp. ground cinnamon
   1 Tbsp. canola oil
   1 Tbsp. butter, melted
   1 Tbsp. water

1. In a large bowl, combine the berries, sugar and 2 Tbsp. flour; transfer to an 11-in. x 7-in. baking dish coated with cooking spray.

2. In a small bowl, combine the cracker crumbs, oats, brown sugar, almonds, cinnamon and remaining flour. Stir in the oil, butter and water until moistened. Sprinkle over berries.

3. Bake at 375° for 25-30 minutes or until filling is bubbly and topping is golden brown.

Nutrition Facts: 1 serving equals 193 calories, 5 g fat (1 g saturated fat), 4 mg cholesterol, 35 mg sodium, 37 g carbohydrate, 5 g fiber, 2 g protein.

Purchase fresh **strawberries** that are shiny, firm and very fragrant. A strawberry should be almost completely red, though a little bit of whiteness near the leafy cap is absolutely acceptable.

Lemon Blackberry Parfaits

PREP: 25 min. + chilling YIELD: 6 servings

AMBER NEEDHAM • BELLBROOK, OHIO

I love the freshness of lemon, and with a bounty of seasonal blackberries, this rich, creamy dessert is so wonderful! Serve it immediately if you like crisp graham crackers, or within 4 hours for a moister crumb.

3	eggs
1/2	cup plus 1/4 cup sugar, *divided*
3/4	cup lemon juice
1	Tbsp. grated lemon peel
2	Tbsp. butter
4	oz. fat-free cream cheese
1	cup plus 6 Tbsp. reduced-fat whipped topping, *divided*
3	cups fresh blackberries
3	whole graham crackers, crushed

1. In a small heavy saucepan over medium heat, whisk the eggs, 1/2 cup sugar, lemon juice and peel until blended. Add butter; cook, whisking constantly, until mixture is thickened and coats the back of a spoon. Transfer to a small bowl; cool. Cover and refrigerate until chilled.

2. In a small bowl, beat cream cheese and remaining sugar until smooth. Fold in lemon mixture and 1 cup whipped topping. Spoon half of the cream cheese mixture into six parfait glasses. Top with half of the berries and half of the cracker crumbs. Repeat layers. Top with remaining whipped topping. Serve immediately.

Nutrition Facts: 1 parfait equals 292 calories, 9 g fat (5 g saturated fat), 117 mg cholesterol, 213 mg sodium, 48 g carbohydrate, 4 g fiber, 8 g protein.

Melon with Serrano-Mint Syrup F S

PREP: 30 min. + chilling YIELD: 12 servings

JENNIFER FISHER • AUSTIN, TEXAS

This is one of the recipes I created to take advantage of the mint I grow. The serrano pepper is a nice contrast to the sweetness of the syrup and salad.

1/3	cup sugar
1/3	cup water
1/4	cup lemon juice
3	Tbsp. honey
1/2	tsp. minced serrano pepper
1/4	cup minced fresh mint
1	Tbsp. grated lemon peel
4	cups *each* cubed watermelon, cantaloupe and honeydew

1. In a small saucepan, combine the sugar, water, lemon juice, honey and serrano pepper. Bring to a boil; cook for 3-5 minutes or until slightly thickened. Remove from the heat; stir in mint and lemon peel. Cool to room temperature.

2. Strain syrup; discard pepper, mint and lemon peel. In a large bowl, combine melon cubes. Add syrup; gently toss to coat. Cover and refrigerate for at least 2 hours, stirring several times. Serve with a slotted spoon.

Editor's Note: Wear disposable gloves when cutting hot peppers; the oils can burn skin. Avoid touching your face.

Nutrition Facts: 1 cup equals 92 calories, trace fat (trace saturated fat), 0 cholesterol, 13 mg sodium, 25 g carbohydrate, 1 g fiber, 1 g protein. **Diabetic Exchanges:** 1 fruit, 1/2 starch.

Chocolate Malt Desserts S

PREP: 10 min. COOK: 10 min. + chilling YIELD: 6 servings

LISA KEYS • MIDDLEBURY, CONNECTICUT

I came up with this recipe after my mom gave me a container of malted milk powder. It's so rich, you'd never believe it's light.

LEMON BLACKBERRY PARFAITS

MELON WITH SERRANO-MINT SYRUP

1/2 cup malted milk powder
1/4 cup sugar
 2 Tbsp. baking cocoa
 2 Tbsp. cornstarch
1/2 tsp. instant espresso powder
 2 cups fat-free milk
 2 oz. semisweet chocolate, finely chopped
 1 tsp. vanilla extract
3/4 cup reduced-fat whipped topping
 6 malted milk balls, chopped
 6 maraschino cherries

1. In a small saucepan, combine the first five ingredients. Stir in milk until smooth. Cook and stir over medium heat until mixture comes to a boil; cook 1-2 minutes longer or until thickened. Remove from the heat; stir in chocolate and vanilla until smooth.

2. Transfer to six dessert dishes, about 1/3 cup in each. Cover and refrigerate for at least 2 hours before serving.

3. Garnish each serving with 2 Tbsp. whipped topping, 1/2 tsp. chopped malted milk balls and a cherry.

Nutrition Facts: 1 serving equals 239 calories, 5 g fat (3 g saturated fat), 2 mg cholesterol, 87 mg sodium, 45 g carbohydrate, 1 g fiber, 6 g protein.

When you're short on time, you can easily add some frosty fun to dinnertime by serving up a variety of toppings and sauces and letting family members concoct their own **scrumptious sundaes.**

APPLE TARRAGON GRANITA

Apple Tarragon Granita ▣▣

PREP: 10 min. + freezing YIELD: 6 servings

DEBBY HARDEN • WILLIAMSTON, MICHIGAN

Looking for a something-different twist on a classic Italian treat? Fresh tarragon complements the sweet, bright apple flavor of this icy grown-up dessert.

- 3 cups unsweetened apple juice
- 1/2 cup sugar
- 2 Tbsp. coarsely chopped fresh tarragon
- 4 tsp. lemon juice

1. In an 8-in. square dish, combine all ingredients until sugar is dissolved. Freeze for 1 hour; stir with a fork.

2. Freeze 2-3 hours longer or until completely frozen, stirring every 30 minutes. Stir granita with a fork just before serving; spoon into dessert dishes.

Nutrition Facts: 1 serving equals 125 calories, trace fat (trace saturated fat), 0 cholesterol, 4 mg sodium, 32 g carbohydrate, trace fiber, trace protein.

Melon with Ice Cream ▣▣

PREP/TOTAL TIME: 10 min. YIELD: 4 servings

TINA MEEKINS • PORT ORCHARD, WASHINGTON

Three items are all you need for this cool creation. It's particularly yummy on hot days. No granola in the pantry? Top off individual servings with chopped nuts or toasted coconut.

- 1 medium cantaloupe, cut into 4 wedges
- 1 pint fat-free sugar-free vanilla ice cream
- 4 Tbsp. reduced-fat granola cereal without raisins

1. Place cantaloupe wedges in individual bowls. Top each with a scoop of ice cream and 1 Tbsp. granola. Serve immediately.

Nutrition Facts: 1 serving equals 156 calories, trace fat (trace saturated fat), 0 cholesterol, 98 mg sodium, 34 g carbohydrate, 1 g fiber, 6 g protein. **Diabetic Exchanges:** 2 fruit, 1/2 fat-free milk.

Banana Pudding Parfaits F

PREP: 15 min. + chilling **YIELD:** 8 servings

MARGARET ALLEN • ABINGDON, VIRGINIA

With bananas, vanilla wafers and a pudding mix, these creamy after-dinner sweets are easy to assemble. If you'd like to mix things up, substitute your favorite fresh berries or other flavors of sugar-free instant pudding.

3-1/3 cups cold fat-free milk
   2 pkg. (1 oz. *each*) sugar-free instant vanilla pudding mix
 2/3 cup fat-free sour cream
 1/4 tsp. vanilla extract
   1 carton (8 oz.) frozen fat-free whipped topping, thawed, *divided*
  32 reduced-fat vanilla wafers
   3 medium ripe bananas, cut into 1/4-in. slices

1. In a large bowl, whisk milk and pudding mix for 2 minutes. Let stand for 2 minutes. Whisk in sour cream and vanilla. Fold in three-fourths of the whipped topping.

2. Set aside eight vanilla wafers. Place one wafer into each of eight parfait glasses; top with a third of the banana slices and pudding mixture. Repeat layers twice. Top with remaining whipped topping. Refrigerate for at least 1 hour. Garnish with reserved vanilla wafers.

Nutrition Facts: 1 parfait equals 231 calories, 1 g fat (trace saturated fat), 5 mg cholesterol, 433 mg sodium, 46 g carbohydrate, 1 g fiber, 6 g protein.

Banana Souffle S

PREP: 30 min. **BAKE:** 25 min. **YIELD:** 6 servings

CRYSTAL BRUNS • ILIFF, COLORADO

This pretty, golden-topped puff is so easy to whip up, but looks like you really fussed. Lightly laced with rum, the moist and tender banana-rich souffle makes that perfect "little something" to wrap up any holiday dinner.

   4 eggs, *separated*
   1 egg white
   2 Tbsp. butter
   1 cup mashed ripe bananas
 1/3 cup sugar
   1 Tbsp. cornstarch
   1 Tbsp. lemon juice
   1 Tbsp. rum
 1/4 tsp. grated lemon peel

1. Let egg whites stand at room temperature for 30 minutes. Coat a 1-1/2-qt. souffle dish with cooking spray; set aside.

2. In a small saucepan over medium heat, melt butter. Stir in the bananas, sugar and cornstarch until blended. Bring to a boil, stirring constantly. Cook and stir 1-2 minutes longer or until thickened. Transfer to a large bowl; stir in lemon juice, rum and lemon peel.

3. Stir a small amount of hot mixture into egg yolks; return all to the bowl, stirring constantly. Allow to cool slightly.

4. In a large bowl with clean beaters, beat egg whites until stiff peaks form. With a spatula, stir a fourth of the egg whites into banana mixture until no white streaks remain. Fold in remaining egg whites until combined. Transfer to prepared dish.

5. Bake at 350° for 25-30 minutes or until the top is puffed and center appears set. Serve immediately.

Nutrition Facts: 1 serving equals 168 calories, 7 g fat (3 g saturated fat), 151 mg cholesterol, 83 mg sodium, 21 g carbohydrate, 1 g fiber, 5 g protein. **Diabetic Exchanges:** 1 starch, 1 fat, 1/2 fruit.

BANANA SOUFFLE

BANANA PUDDING PARFAITS

Banana Chocolate Parfaits

PREP/TOTAL TIME: 20 min. **YIELD:** 8 servings

HEALTHY COOKING TEST KITCHEN

Chocolate and banana pair in this creamy combination from our Test Kitchen. With chocolate pudding and a crunchy chocolate topping, these pretty parfaits are sure to satisfy all of your sweet-tooth cravings.

3	medium bananas, sliced
1/4	cup lemon juice
2	cups cold fat-free milk
1	pkg. (1.4 oz.) sugar-free instant chocolate pudding mix
1	cup (8 oz.) reduced-fat sour cream
1-1/2	cups reduced-fat whipped topping
8	chocolate wafers, crushed

1. In a small bowl, combine bananas and lemon juice; let stand for 5 minutes. In another bowl, whisk the milk and pudding mix for 2 minutes. Refrigerate for 5 minutes. Stir in sour cream.

2. Drain bananas. Place half of the banana slices in eight parfait glasses; layer with pudding mixture, whipped topping, chocolate wafer crumbs and remaining banana slices. Refrigerate until serving.

Nutrition Facts: 1 parfait equals 183 calories, 6 g fat (5 g saturated fat), 11 mg cholesterol, 236 mg sodium, 27 g carbohydrate, 2 g fiber, 5 g protein. **Diabetic Exchanges:** 1 starch, 1 fat, 1/2 fruit.

BANANA CHOCOLATE PARFAITS

Strawberry Shortcake Dessert

PREP: 10 min. **BAKE:** 30 min. + chilling
YIELD: 20 servings

MICHELE TRACHIER • PASADENA, TEXAS

This recipe was given to me by a coworker. I've used other fruits, including blueberries, cherries and peaches, and it always gets rave reviews.

1	pkg. (18-1/4 oz.) white cake mix
1-1/3	cups water
1/4	cup unsweetened applesauce
2	egg whites
1	egg
1	pkg. (.6 oz.) sugar-free strawberry gelatin
2	cups boiling water
1	pkg. (16 oz.) frozen unsweetened whole strawberries, thawed, drained and sliced
1	carton (16 oz.) frozen reduced-fat whipped topping, thawed
10	fresh strawberries, halved

1. In a large bowl, combine the cake mix, water, applesauce, egg whites and egg; beat on low speed for 30 seconds. Beat on medium for 2 minutes.

2. Pour batter into a 13-in. x 9-in. baking dish coated with cooking spray. Bake at 350° for 30-35 minutes or until a toothpick inserted near the center comes out clean.

3. In a large bowl, dissolve gelatin in boiling water. Stir in strawberries. Using a sharp knife, make a diamond pattern in the top of the hot cake; immediately pour gelatin mixture over cake. Cool on a wire rack.

4. Refrigerate for at least 6 hours. Spread with whipped topping. Garnish with fresh strawberries.

Nutrition Facts: 1 piece equals 179 calories, 5 g fat (3 g saturated fat), 11 mg cholesterol, 192 mg sodium, 29 g carbohydrate, 1 g fiber, 2 g protein. **Diabetic Exchanges:** 2 starch, 1/2 fat.

STRAWBERRY SHORTCAKE DESSERT

Light Chocolate Truffles F S C

PREP: 25 min. + chilling **YIELD:** about 1-1/2 dozen

DONNI WORTHEN • BRANSON, MISSOURI

I made these for my husband on Valentine's Day and later for Christmas gifts. Everyone loves them!

- 1/3 cup semisweet chocolate chips
- 4 oz. reduced-fat cream cheese
- 1/3 cup plus 2 tsp. baking cocoa, *divided*
- 1-1/4 cups plus 2 tsp. confectioners' sugar, *divided*

1. In a microwave, melt chocolate chips; stir until smooth. Set aside.

2. In a small bowl, beat cream cheese until fluffy. Beat in 1/3 cup cocoa and melted chocolate. Gradually beat in 1-1/4 cups confectioners' sugar. Lightly coat hands with confectioners' sugar; roll chocolate mixture into 1-in. balls. Roll in remaining cocoa or confectioners' sugar. Cover and refrigerate for at least 1 hour.

Nutrition Facts: 1 truffle equals 62 calories, 2 g fat (1 g saturated fat), 4 mg cholesterol, 24 mg sodium, 11 g carbohydrate, trace fiber, 1 g protein. **Diabetic Exchanges:** 1/2 starch, 1/2 fat.

You can make the **coconut centers** for these truffles and freeze them in airtight containers for up to 2 months. Then, thaw in the refrigerator, dip in chocolate and decorate as directed.

ENGLISH TRIFLE

English Trifle F

PREP: 45 min. + chilling **YIELD:** 12 servings

ALDAH BOTHMANN-POWELL • SAN ANTONIO, TEXAS

You'll impress guests with this lovely dessert layered with angel food cake, fruit, pudding and fat-free whipped topping. It's so creamy and refreshing that no one will know it's light.

- 1 pkg. (.3 oz.) sugar-free strawberry gelatin
- 1 cup boiling water
- 1 cup cold water
- 1 prepared angel food cake (8 to 10 oz.), cut into 1-in. cubes
- 1 cup mashed strawberries
- 1 tsp. sugar
- 1 can (8 oz.) unsweetened pineapple chunks
- 1 cup sliced firm bananas
- 2 cups sliced fresh strawberries
- 2 cups cold fat-free milk
- 1 pkg. (1 oz.) sugar-free instant vanilla pudding mix
- 1 carton (8 oz.) frozen fat-free whipped topping, thawed
- 1/4 cup slivered almonds, toasted
- 1 fresh strawberry

1. In a small bowl, dissolve gelatin powder in boiling water. Stir in cold water. Pour half of gelatin mixture into a small bowl; cover and refrigerate for 1 hour or until slightly thickened. Let remaining gelatin stand at room temperature.

2. Place half of cake cubes in a 3-qt. trifle bowl. In a small bowl, combine mashed strawberries and sugar; spoon half over cake.

3. Drain pineapple, reserving 1/4 cup juice. Cut pineapple chunks in half; arrange half over mashed strawberries. Toss banana slices with reserved pineapple juice; arrange half of slices over pineapple. Top with 1 cup sliced strawberries. Spoon refrigerated gelatin over fruit. Refrigerate trifle and remaining gelatin mixture for 20 minutes.

4. In a small bowl, whisk milk and pudding mix for 2 minutes. Let stand for 2 minutes or until soft-set. Spread half of pudding over trifle. Repeat all layers. Top with whipped topping. Cover and refrigerate. Just before serving, sprinkle with almonds; garnish with the strawberry.

Nutrition Facts: 1 cup equals 155 calories, 2 g fat (trace saturated fat), 1 mg cholesterol, 274 mg sodium, 32 g carbohydrate, 2 g fiber, 4 g protein. **Diabetic Exchanges:** 1-1/2 starch, 1/2 fruit.

Chocolate-Raspberry Bread Pudding

PREP: 25 min. **BAKE:** 30 min. + standing
YIELD: 12 servings (3/4 cup sauce)

PHYLLIS DOBSON • LITTLETON, COLORADO

With lots of chocolate and raspberry flavor, plenty of crunch and less than 300 calories, this no-guilt dessert is to die for!

- 8 cups cubed day-old French bread
- 1 cup fat-free milk
- 1 cup fat-free half-and-half
- 3/4 cup plus 2 Tbsp. sugar, *divided*
- 1/4 cup baking cocoa
- 2 oz. bittersweet chocolate, coarsely chopped
- 3/4 cup egg substitute
- 2 tsp. vanilla extract
- 1/2 cup semisweet chocolate chips
- 1 pkg. (12 oz.) frozen unsweetened raspberries, thawed, *divided*
- 1 tsp. lemon juice

1. Place bread cubes in a large bowl; set aside. In a small saucepan, combine milk, half-and-half, 3/4 cup sugar and cocoa. Bring to a gentle boil. Remove from the heat. Stir in bittersweet chocolate until melted.

2. Stir a small amount of hot milk mixture into egg substitute; return all to the pan. Stir in vanilla. Pour mixture over bread cubes. Let stand for 5 minutes. Place half of bread mixture in an 11-in. x 7-in. baking dish coated with cooking spray. Sprinkle with chocolate chips and half of raspberries. Top with remaining bread mixture.

3. Bake, uncovered, at 350° for 30-40 minutes or until a knife inserted near the center comes out clean. Let stand for 10 minutes before serving.

4. For sauce, place the remaining raspberries in a food processor; add lemon juice and remaining sugar. Cover and process for 2-3 minutes or until blended. Strain and discard seeds and pulp. Serve with pudding. Refrigerate leftovers.

Nutrition Facts: 1 serving with 1 Tbsp. sauce equals 297 calories, 7 g fat (3 g saturated fat), 1 mg cholesterol, 289 mg sodium, 54 g carbohydrate, 3 g fiber, 8 g protein.

CHOCOLATE-RASPBERRY BREAD PUDDING

Sangria Gelatin Dessert F S C

PREP: 15 min. + chilling **YIELD:** 6 servings

HEALTHY COOKING TEST KITCHEN

Here's a festive finale that's just ideal for balmy summer nights. White wine gives it a refreshing twist, and the vibrant color dresses up dinners without much effort.

1	pkg. (.3 oz.) sugar-free lemon gelatin
1	pkg. (.3 oz.) sugar-free raspberry gelatin
1-1/2	cups boiling water
1	cup cold water
1	cup white wine
1	can (11 oz.) mandarin oranges, drained
1	cup fresh raspberries
1	cup green grapes, halved

1. In a large bowl, dissolve gelatins in boiling water. Let stand for 10 minutes. Stir in cold water and the wine; refrigerate for 45 minutes or until partially set.

2. Fold in the oranges, raspberries and grapes. Transfer to six large wine glasses, 1 cup in each. Refrigerate for 4 hours or until set.

Nutrition Facts: 1 serving equals 95 calories, trace fat (trace saturated fat), 0 cholesterol, 83 mg sodium, 13 g carbohydrate, 2 g fiber, 2 g protein. **Diabetic Exchange:** 1 fruit.

SANGRIA GELATIN DESSERT

Polynesian Parfaits S

PREP/TOTAL TIME: 15 min. **YIELD:** 4 servings

JANICE MITCHELL • AURORA, COLORADO

Pack one of these refreshing, tropical treats in a plastic container to take with you. They're great for lunch boxes!

2	cups (16 oz.) pineapple yogurt
1	Tbsp. sugar
1/8	tsp. ground nutmeg
1	cup granola without raisins
1	can (11 oz.) mandarin oranges, drained
3/4	cup unsweetened pineapple tidbits
1/3	cup fresh raspberries

1. Combine the yogurt, sugar and nutmeg; spoon into four dishes. Top with granola and fruit.

Nutrition Facts: 1 parfait equals 293 calories, 5 g fat (1 g saturated fat), 6 mg cholesterol, 79 mg sodium, 57 g carbohydrate, 6 g fiber, 11 g protein.

Cran-Apple Praline Gingerbread

PREP: 25 min. **BAKE:** 30 min. + cooling
YIELD: 8 servings

JEANNE HOLT • MENDOTA HEIGHTS, MINNESOTA

Start with a spice-rich batter baked atop apples and cranberries in a creamy caramel sauce, then invert when done for a topsy-turvy dessert that's a real beauty. The old-time holiday taste will delight family and friends!

2/3	cup fat-free caramel ice cream topping
2	medium tart apples, peeled and thinly sliced
2/3	cup fresh or frozen cranberries
1/4	cup butter, softened
1/4	cup sugar

POLYNESIAN PARFAITS

1 egg
6 Tbsp. molasses
1/4 cup unsweetened applesauce
1-1/4 cups all-purpose flour
3/4 tsp. baking soda
1/2 tsp. ground ginger
1/2 tsp. apple pie spice
1/4 tsp. salt
1/2 cup hot water

YOGURT CREAM:
3/4 cup reduced-fat whipped topping
1/2 cup fat-free vanilla yogurt

1. Coat a 9-in. round baking pan with cooking spray. Pour caramel topping into pan and tilt to coat bottom evenly. Arrange apples and cranberries in a single layer over caramel.

2. In a large bowl, beat butter and sugar until crumbly, about 2 minutes. Add egg; mix well. Beat in molasses and applesauce (mixture may appear curdled). Combine the flour, baking soda, ginger, pie spice and salt; add to butter mixture just until moistened. Stir in hot water.

3. Pour over fruit; smooth top. Bake at 350° for 30-35 minutes or until a toothpick inserted near the center comes out clean. Cool for 10 minutes before inverting onto a serving plate. Combine whipped topping and yogurt; serve with gingerbread.

Nutrition Facts: 1 slice with 2 Tbsp. cream equals 289 calories, 7 g fat (5 g saturated fat), 42 mg cholesterol, 284 mg sodium, 53 g carbohydrate, 2 g fiber, 4 g protein.

Cranberries are only in season from early fall through December. When buying **fresh cranberries,** look for packages with shiny, bright red (light or dark) berries. Avoid berries that are bruised, shriveled or have brown spots.

GRILLED PINEAPPLE DESSERT

Grilled Pineapple Dessert

PREP/TOTAL TIME: 20 min. YIELD: 6 servings

KATIE SISSON • VALLEY PARK, MISSOURI

This fresh-tasting, fruity dessert is one of my very favorites—warm, sweet, buttery pineapple topped with cold ice cream. Yum! Granola adds a fun crunch.

1	can (20 oz.) unsweetened sliced pineapple
1	Tbsp. butter
1	tsp. brown sugar
1/2	tsp. vanilla extract
1/4	tsp. ground cinnamon
3	cups reduced-fat vanilla ice cream
6	Tbsp. hot caramel ice cream topping
6	Tbsp. granola without raisins

1. Drain pineapple, reserving 1/3 cup juice and six pineapple slices (save remaining juice and pineapple for another use).

2. In a small microwave-safe bowl, combine the butter, brown sugar, vanilla, cinnamon and reserved juice. Microwave, uncovered, on high for 1-2 minutes or until butter is melted. Brush half of the mixture on both sides of pineapple slices.

3. Grill, uncovered, over medium heat or broil 4 in. from the heat for 3-5 minutes or until lightly browned, turning once and basting with remaining butter mixture.

4. Place pineapple in dessert bowls; top with ice cream. Drizzle with caramel topping; sprinkle with granola.

Editor's Note: This recipe was tested in a 1,100-watt microwave.

Nutrition Facts: 1 serving equals 246 calories, 6 g fat (3 g saturated fat), 23 mg cholesterol, 142 mg sodium, 45 g carbohydrate, 2 g fiber, 5 g protein.

Cappuccino Pudding F S

PREP/TOTAL TIME: 20 min. YIELD: 4 servings

CINDY BERTRAND • FLOYDADA, TEXAS

With its combination of chocolate, coffee and cinnamon, this smooth dessert is one of my go-to recipes when I need a treat. A garnish of whipped topping and chocolate wafer crumbs provides additional appeal.

4	tsp. instant coffee granules
1	Tbsp. boiling water
1-1/2	cups cold fat-free milk
1	pkg. (1.4 oz.) sugar-free instant chocolate pudding mix
1/2	tsp. ground cinnamon
1	cup reduced-fat whipped topping

Additional whipped topping and chocolate wafer crumbs, optional

1. Dissolve coffee in boiling water; set aside. In a large bowl, combine the milk, pudding mix and cinnamon. Beat on low speed for 2 minutes. Let stand for 2 minutes or until set.

2. Stir in coffee. Fold in whipped topping. Spoon into serving dishes. Garnish with additional whipped topping and wafer crumbs if desired.

Nutrition Facts: 1/2 cup (calculated without additional whipped topping and wafer crumbs) equals 105 calories, 2 g fat (0 saturated fat), 2 mg cholesterol, 48 mg sodium, 17 g carbohydrate, 0 fiber, 3 g protein. **Diabetic Exchanges:** 1/2 starch, 1/2 fat-free milk.

Gluten-Free Sugarplums F S C

PREP/TOTAL TIME: 25 min. YIELD: 2-1/2 dozen

CORLEEN HEIDGERKEN • MILWAUKEE, WISCONSIN

Lots of moist, fruity flavor and nutty crunch give these sweet and spicy bites a kind of gumdrop richness. They make a delicious addition to cookie trays. Sneak one early—they'll be gone before you can lick the sugar off your fingers!

1-1/3	cups chopped walnuts
1	cup pitted dates
1	pkg. (5 oz.) dried cherries
1/4	cup honey
2	tsp. grated orange peel
1	tsp. ground cinnamon
1	tsp. ground allspice
1/2	tsp. ground nutmeg
1/4	tsp. ground ginger
1/2	cup coarse sugar

1. Place the walnuts, dates and cherries in a food processor; cover and process until finely chopped. Transfer to a small bowl; stir in the honey, orange peel and spices. Roll into 1-in. balls, then roll in sugar. Store in an airtight container in the refrigerator.

Editor's Note: Read all ingredient labels for possible gluten content prior to use. Ingredient formulas can change, and production facilities vary among brands. If you're concerned that your brand may contain gluten, contact the company.

Nutrition Facts: 1 sugarplum equals 84 calories, 3 g fat (trace saturated fat), 0 cholesterol, 1 mg sodium, 13 g carbohydrate, 1 g fiber, 1 g protein. **Diabetic Exchanges:** 1 starch.

> High in fiber and a good source of iron and potassium, dates are one of the sweetest fruits; 70% of their weight can be made up of sugar. To prevent sticking when slicing or chopping **dates**, spray a knife or kitchen scissors with cooking spray or frequently dip in cold water.

GLUTEN-FREE SUGARPLUMS

CAPPUCCINO PUDDING

Peach Sorbet F S

PREP: 15 min. **PROCESS:** 20 min. + freezing
YIELD: 3 servings

MARY KAY DIXSON • DECATUR, ALABAMA

Since moving to an area where fresh peaches are plentiful, I've made this frosty treat frequently. It's the perfect light dessert. Calorie-conscious guests always say "yes" to this when they might decline a slice of cake or pie.

- 1/2 cup water
- 3 Tbsp. sugar
- 2 Tbsp. lemon juice
- 4 medium ripe peaches, peeled and sliced

1. In a saucepan, combine the water, sugar and lemon juice. Cook and stir over medium heat until sugar is dissolved. Cool slightly; transfer to a blender.

2. Add the peaches; cover and process until smooth. Fill cylinder of ice cream freezer; freeze according to manufacturer's directions. Transfer sorbet to a freezer container; cover and freeze for 4 hours or until firm.

Nutrition Facts: 1/2 cup equals 104 calories, 0 fat (0 saturated fat), 0 cholesterol, trace sodium, 27 g carbohydrate, 3 g fiber, 1 g protein. **Diabetic Exchanges:** 1-1/2 fruit.

Sweet Potato Tart S

PREP: 20 min. **BAKE:** 30 min. + cooling
YIELD: 12 servings

KATE GAUDRY • LA JOLLA, CALIFORNIA

I love making desserts. You'd never guess this trimmed-down tart, with its homemade pecan crust and creamy filling, is light.

- 1-1/2 cups all-purpose flour
- 1/2 cup packed brown sugar
- 1/4 cup cold butter, cubed

PEACH SORBET

- 2 Tbsp. chopped pecans, toasted
- 1 egg

FILLING:
- 1 can (15-3/4 oz.) sweet potatoes
- 1/2 cup packed brown sugar
- 1/2 cup fat-free milk
- 2 egg whites
- 1/3 cup reduced-fat plain yogurt
- 1 Tbsp. all-purpose flour
- 1/2 tsp. ground cinnamon
- 1/4 tsp. ground ginger
- 1/4 tsp. ground nutmeg
- 1/8 tsp. ground cloves

Whipped topping, optional

1. In a food processor, combine the flour, brown sugar, butter and pecans. Cover and pulse until blended. Add egg, pulsing until mixture forms a soft dough. Press onto the bottom and up the sides of a 9-in. fluted tart pan with removable bottom.

2. Place pan on a baking sheet. Bake at 400° for 8-10 minutes or until lightly browned. Cool on a wire rack. Reduce heat to 350°.

3. Drain sweet potatoes, reserving 1/4 cup liquid. Place potatoes in a food processor; cover and process until pureed. Add the brown sugar, milk, egg whites, yogurt, flour, cinnamon, ginger, nutmeg, cloves and reserved liquid; cover and process until blended.

4. Pour into crust. Bake for 30-35 minutes or until a knife inserted near the center comes out clean. Cool on a wire rack. Store in the refrigerator. Garnish with whipped topping if desired.

Nutrition Facts: 1 slice (calculated without whipped topping) equals 221 calories, 5 g fat (3 g saturated fat), 29 mg cholesterol, 87 mg sodium, 39 g carbohydrate, 2 g fiber, 4 g protein.

Glazed Spiced Apples F S

PREP/TOTAL TIME: 25 min. **YIELD:** 10 servings

MARY JO DUCKWORTH • DENVER, COLORADO

My husband and I are watching our fat intake, so I came up with this recipe. It's a lovely dessert or even a great side dish with pork. It was a real success.

- 1/2 cup packed brown sugar
- 3 Tbsp. cornstarch
- 1 can (12 oz.) diet cream soda
- 1/4 cup honey
- 1/4 tsp. apple pie spice
- 1/4 tsp. ground cinnamon
- 1/8 tsp. ground nutmeg
- 8 large apples, peeled and sliced

1. In a microwave-safe bowl, combine the brown sugar and cornstarch. Stir in the soda, honey, apple pie spice, cinnamon and nutmeg until smooth. Microwave, uncovered, on high for 3-4 minutes or until thickened, stirring after each minute.

2. Place apples in a 3-qt. microwave-safe dish; pour sauce over apples. Cover and cook on high for 5-1/2 minutes; stir. Cook, uncovered, 5-1/2 to 8 minutes

longer or until apples are tender; stir. Let stand for 5 minutes. Serve warm.

Editor's Note: This recipe was tested in a 1,100-watt microwave.

Nutrition Facts: 2/3 cup equals 187 calories, 1 g fat (1 g saturated fat), 0 cholesterol, 11 mg sodium, 47 g carbohydrate, 5 g fiber, trace protein.

Baked Long Johns

PREP: 15 min. **BAKE:** 20 min. + cooling **YIELD:** 8 servings

NICKI LAZORIK • MELLEN, WISCONSIN

No one will ever guess how much lighter these scrumptious, chocolate-glazed long johns are than the fried ones you buy at the local doughnut store.

- 2 cups all-purpose flour
- 1/2 cup sugar
- 2 tsp. baking powder
- 1/2 tsp. salt
- 1/4 tsp. ground cinnamon
- 2 eggs
- 3/4 cup fat-free milk
- 1 Tbsp. butter, melted
- 1 tsp. vanilla extract

GLAZE:
- 3/4 cup semisweet chocolate chips
- 1 Tbsp. butter
- 4-1/2 tsp. fat-free milk

1. In a small bowl, combine the flour, sugar, baking powder, salt and cinnamon. In another bowl, whisk the eggs, milk, butter and vanilla. Stir into dry ingredients just until moistened.

2. Transfer to eight 4-1/2-in. x 2-1/2-in. x 1-1/2-in. loaf pans coated with cooking spray. Bake at 325° for 18-22 minutes or until golden brown. Immediately remove from pans to a wire rack to cool completely.

3. In a microwave, melt chocolate chips and butter. Add milk; stir until smooth. Dip tops of doughnuts in glaze. Return to wire rack; let stand until set.

Nutrition Facts: 1 long john equals 291 calories, 9 g fat (5 g saturated fat), 61 mg cholesterol, 298 mg sodium, 48 g carbohydrate, 2 g fiber, 6 g protein.

Caramel Apple Bread Pudding F

PREP: 15 min. **BAKE:** 35 min. **YIELD:** 8 servings

MICHELLE BORLAND • PEORIA, ILLINOIS

Tender, sweet pudding with delicious apple pieces, spices and a luscious low-fat caramel topping make a rich-tasting comfort dish without all the fat.

- 1 cup unsweetened applesauce
- 1 cup fat-free milk
- 1/2 cup packed brown sugar
- 1/2 cup egg substitute
- 1 tsp. vanilla extract
- 1/2 tsp. ground cinnamon
- 5 cups cubed day-old bread
- 1/2 cup chopped peeled apple
- 1/2 cup fat-free whipped topping
- 1/2 cup fat-free caramel ice cream topping

1. In a large bowl, combine the applesauce, milk, brown sugar, egg substitute, vanilla and cinnamon.

Fold in bread cubes and apple; let stand for 15 minutes or until bread is softened.

2. Pour into an 8-in. square baking dish coated with cooking spray. Bake, uncovered, at 325° for 35-40 minutes or until a knife inserted near the center comes out clean. Serve warm with whipped topping and caramel topping. Refrigerate leftovers.

Nutrition Facts: 1 serving equals 187 calories, 1 g fat (trace saturated fat), 1 mg cholesterol, 201 mg sodium, 40 g carbohydrate, 1 g fiber, 4 g protein.

Cranberry Pear Crisp S

PREP: 20 min. **BAKE:** 35 min. **YIELD:** 8 servings

LORI CHOQUETTE • HOLYOKE, MASSACHUSETTS

This dessert is perfect for that first autumn day you can feel a nip in the air. It's full of sweet, crunchy fall flavors.

- 4 medium pears, peeled and cut into 1-in. cubes
- 1/2 cup dried cranberries
- 2 Tbsp. lemon juice
- 1/4 cup sugar

1 Tbsp. all-purpose flour
2 tsp. grated lemon peel
1 tsp. ground cinnamon
1/2 tsp. ground nutmeg
TOPPING:
1/3 cup all-purpose flour
1/3 cup old-fashioned oats
1/3 cup packed brown sugar
1/4 cup ground flaxseed
1/4 tsp. salt
2 Tbsp. butter, melted
2 Tbsp. canola oil

1. In a large bowl, combine pears and cranberries; drizzle with lemon juice. Combine the sugar, flour, lemon peel, cinnamon and nutmeg; stir into pear mixture. Transfer to an 8-in. square baking dish coated with cooking spray.

2. For topping, in a small bowl, combine the flour, oats, brown sugar, flax and salt. Stir in butter and oil until crumbly. Sprinkle over fruit mixture. Bake at 350° for 35-40 minutes or until topping is golden brown and fruit is tender.

Nutrition Facts: 1/2 cup equals 241 calories, 8 g fat (2 g saturated fat), 8 mg cholesterol, 101 mg sodium, 43 g carbohydrate, 5 g fiber, 2 g protein.

Eggnog Mousse S

PREP: 15 min. + chilling **YIELD:** 4 servings

HEALTHY COOKING TEST KITCHEN

Guests will always find room for this light, fluffy and mouthwatering mousse. It makes an elegant, refreshing finish for heavier meals—and it's also a great way to use up any extra eggnog in the fridge.

2 tsp. unflavored gelatin
2 cups reduced-fat eggnog
2 Tbsp. sugar
1/8 tsp. *each* ground cinnamon and ground nutmeg
1/2 tsp. vanilla extract
1 cup reduced-fat whipped topping, *divided*
Additional ground nutmeg, optional

1. In a small saucepan, sprinkle gelatin over eggnog; let stand for 1 minute. Heat over low heat, stirring until gelatin is completely dissolved.

2. Stir in the sugar, cinnamon and nutmeg until sugar is dissolved. Transfer to a small bowl; stir in vanilla. Refrigerate until mixture begins to thicken.

3. Beat mixture until light and fluffy. Beat in 3/4 cup whipped topping. Divide among four dessert dishes. Refrigerate until firm. Garnish with the remaining whipped topping; sprinkle with additional nutmeg if desired.

Nutrition Facts: 3/4 cup equals 165 calories, 6 g fat (4 g saturated fat), 97 mg cholesterol, 80 mg sodium, 21 g carbohydrate, trace fiber, 7 g protein. **Diabetic Exchanges:** 1 starch, 1/2 reduced-fat milk.

Espresso Banana Breakfast Smoothie F S

PREP/TOTAL TIME: 10 min. **YIELD:** 1 serving

AIMEE WILSON • CLOVIS, CALIFORNIA

Want an early morning pick-me-up that's good for you, too? Fruit and flaxseed give this sweet espresso a nutritious twist. Kids are sure to enjoy the combination of chocolate and banana flavors.

1/2 cup cold fat-free milk
1 Tbsp. vanilla flavoring syrup
1 cup ice cubes
1/2 medium banana, cut up
1 to 2 tsp. instant espresso powder
1 tsp. ground flaxseed
1 tsp. baking cocoa

1. In a blender, combine all the ingredients; cover and process for 1-2 minutes or until blended. Pour into a chilled glass; serve immediately.

Editor's Note: This recipe was tested with Torani brand flavoring syrup. Look for it in the coffee section.

Nutrition Facts: 1-1/2 cups equals 148 calories, 2 g fat (trace saturated fat), 2 mg cholesterol, 54 mg sodium, 31 g carbohydrate, 3 g fiber, 6 g protein.

Packed with heart-healthy oils and lots of fiber, **flaxseed** is wonderful sprinkled over your cereal or blended into smoothies. It can even be substituted for some of the fat in breads or muffins.

EGGNOG MOUSSE

Sensational Tiramisu S

PREP: 25 min. **COOK:** 10 min. + chilling
YIELD: 12 servings

MARY WALTERS • WESTERVILLE, OHIO

This light version of the popular Italian dessert is moist and creamy, and cuts so well into pretty layered squares. You'll love the blend of coffee and cream cheese flavors.

1	pkg. (8 oz.) reduced-fat cream cheese
2/3	cup confectioners' sugar, *divided*
1-1/2	cups reduced-fat whipped topping, *divided*
1/2	cup plus 1 Tbsp. sugar
3	egg whites
1/4	cup water
2	pkg. (3 oz. *each*) ladyfingers, split
1/2	cup boiling water
2	Tbsp. coffee liqueur
1	Tbsp. instant coffee granules
1/2	tsp. baking cocoa

1. In a small bowl, beat cream cheese and confectioners' sugar until smooth. Fold in 1 cup whipped topping; set aside.

2. Combine 1/2 cup sugar, egg whites and water in a small heavy saucepan over low heat. With a hand mixer, beat on low speed for 1 minute. Continue beating on low over low heat until mixture reaches 160°, about 8-10 minutes. Pour into a large bowl. Beat on high until stiff peaks form, about 7 minutes. Fold into cream cheese mixture.

3. Arrange half of ladyfingers in an ungreased 11-in. x 7-in. dish. Combine the boiling water, coffee liqueur, coffee granules and remaining sugar; brush half of mixture over ladyfingers. Top with half of cream cheese mixture. Repeat layers. Spread remaining whipped topping over the top; sprinkle with cocoa. Refrigerate for 2 hours before serving.

Nutrition Facts: 1 piece equals 223 calories, 7 g fat (4 g saturated fat), 62 mg cholesterol, 127 mg sodium, 34 g carbohydrate, trace fiber, 5 g protein. **Diabetic Exchanges:** 2 starch, 1 fat.

Pumpkin Pecan Custard

PREP: 20 min. **BAKE:** 35 min. + chilling
YIELD: 8 servings

ABBY BOOTH • COWETA, OKLAHOMA

My family loves pumpkin pie, but this is a delicious, creamy and healthier alternative—and we don't miss the crust at all. It firms up as it cools.

1	can (15 oz.) solid-pack pumpkin
1	can (12 oz.) reduced-fat evaporated milk
3/4	cup egg substitute
1/3	cup packed brown sugar
1-1/2	tsp. vanilla extract
1	tsp. ground cinnamon
1/2	tsp. ground ginger
1/4	tsp. ground cloves
1/8	tsp. salt

TOPPING:

3	Tbsp. all-purpose flour
3	Tbsp. brown sugar
1/2	tsp. ground cinnamon
2	Tbsp. cold butter
1/2	cup chopped pecans

1. In a large bowl, combine the first nine ingredients. Transfer to eight 6-oz. ramekins or custard cups. Place in a baking pan; add 1 in. of boiling water to pan. Bake, uncovered, at 325° for 20 minutes.

2. Meanwhile, for topping, in a small bowl, combine the flour, brown sugar and cinnamon. Cut in butter until crumbly. Stir in pecans. Sprinkle over custard. Bake 15-20 minutes longer or until a knife inserted near the center comes out clean.

SENSATIONAL TIRAMISU

PUMPKIN PECAN CUSTARD

3. Remove ramekins from water bath; cool for 10 minutes. Cover and refrigerate for at least 4 hours.

Nutrition Facts: 1/2 cup equals 213 calories, 9 g fat (3 g saturated fat), 11 mg cholesterol, 160 mg sodium, 27 g carbohydrate, 3 g fiber, 7 g protein. **Diabetic Exchanges:** 2 starch, 1-1/2 fat.

Makeover Frozen Grasshopper Torte [S]

PREP: 25 min. + freezing **YIELD:** 16 servings

HEALTHY COOKING TEST KITCHEN

Who doesn't love the frosty, refreshing combo of mint and chocolate? It's even better when it comes in the form of an awesome ice cream dessert! This Healthy Cooking Test Kitchen makeover is just as good as the original. The crunch of the chocolate crust and a creamy mint filling make a great pair. Although softer-set than the original, this dessert won't stick around long enough to melt!

2	cups chocolate wafer crumbs
3	Tbsp. butter, melted
1	pint reduced-fat vanilla ice cream, softened
1	jar (7 oz.) marshmallow creme
1/4	cup fat-free milk
1/2	tsp. peppermint extract

3	to 4 drops food coloring, optional
1	carton (8 oz.) frozen whipped topping, thawed

1. In a small bowl, combine wafer crumbs and butter. Set aside 2 Tbsp. for garnish; press remaining crumb mixture onto the bottom of a 9-in. springform pan. Chill for 30 minutes. Spread the ice cream over the crust; freeze.

2. Meanwhile, in a small bowl, combine marshmallow creme and milk; stir until well blended. Add extract and food coloring if desired. Fold in whipped topping. Spoon over ice cream and sprinkle with reserved crumbs. Freeze until firm.

Nutrition Facts: 1 piece equals 189 calories, 7 g fat (5 g saturated fat), 10 mg cholesterol, 120 mg sodium, 28 g carbohydrate, 1 g fiber, 2 g protein. **Diabetic Exchanges:** 2 starch, 1 fat.

To easily remove **marshmallow creme** from a jar, place the jar in a pan of very hot water. Repeat this once or twice, and then simply spoon out the creme with a wooden spoon.

Triple Berry Cobbler

PREP: 20 min. BAKE: 30 min. YIELD: 6 servings

AMANDA MILLARD • COLORADO SPRINGS, COLORADO

Make any meal extra special by topping it off with this tart, berry-bursting dessert. It's simply wonderful!

- 2 cups fresh *or* frozen cranberries, thawed
- 1 cup fresh *or* frozen unsweetened raspberries, thawed
- 1 cup fresh *or* frozen unsweetened blueberries, thawed
- 1/2 cup honey
- 1 Tbsp. cornstarch
- 1 tsp. water
- 1 tsp. lemon juice

TOPPING:
- 1 cup all-purpose flour
- 2 Tbsp. sugar
- 1-1/2 tsp. baking powder
- 1/2 tsp. salt
- 1/2 cup fat-free milk
- 3 Tbsp. canola oil

Reduced-fat vanilla ice cream, optional

1. In a large saucepan, combine the cranberries, raspberries, blueberries and honey. Combine the cornstarch, water and lemon juice until smooth; stir into fruit mixture. Bring to a boil; cook and stir for 2 minutes or until thickened. Pour into an ungreased 11-in. x 7-in. baking dish.

2. For topping, in a small bowl, combine the flour, sugar, baking powder and salt. Gradually add milk and oil, tossing with a fork until dough forms a ball. Drop by tablespoonfuls onto hot berry mixture.

3. Bake, uncovered, at 400° for 30-35 minutes or until topping is golden brown. Serve warm with ice cream if desired.

Nutrition Facts: 1 serving (calculated without ice cream) equals 290 calories, 7 g fat (1 g saturated fat), trace cholesterol, 308 mg sodium, 55 g carbohydrate, 4 g fiber, 3 g protein.

Makeover Strawberry Cheesecake Ice Cream

PREP: 50 min. + chilling
PROCESS: 20 min./batch + freezing YIELD: 3 qt.

HEALTHY COOKING TEST KITCHEN

This recipe is rich and velvety, with fantastic strawberry flavor. It's the perfect treat for the summer's heat, but with just a fraction of the fat and fewer calories than the original recipe.

- 2 cups *each* half-and-half cream and whole milk
- 2 cups sugar
- 3 eggs, lightly beaten
- 1 cup fat-free sour cream
- 1/4 cup apple jelly
- 2 tsp. vanilla extract
- 3 pkg. (8 oz. *each*) reduced-fat cream cheese
- 1 pkg. (16 oz.) frozen unsweetened strawberries, thawed and sliced

2 Tbsp. lemon juice
1 Tbsp. grated lemon peel

1. In a large saucepan, heat half-and-half and milk to 175°; stir in sugar until dissolved. Whisk a small amount of hot mixture into the eggs. Return all to the pan, whisking constantly. Cook and stir over low heat until mixture reaches at least 160° and coats the back of a metal spoon.

2. Remove from the heat. Stir in the sour cream, jelly and vanilla. Cool quickly by placing pan in a bowl of ice water; stir for 2 minutes. Press waxed paper onto surface of custard. Refrigerate for several hours or overnight.

3. In a large bowl, beat the cream cheese, strawberries, lemon juice and lemon peel until blended. Gradually beat in the custard mixture.

4. Fill cylinder of ice cream freezer two-thirds full; freeze according to manufacturer's directions. Refrigerate remaining mixture until ready to freeze. When ice cream is frozen, transfer to a freezer container; freeze for 2-4 hours before serving.

Nutrition Facts: 1/2 cup equals 208 calories, 9 g fat (6 g saturated fat), 60 mg cholesterol, 156 mg sodium, 25 g carbohydrate, trace fiber, 6 g protein. **Diabetic Exchanges:** 2 fat, 1-1/2 starch.

Makeover Old-Fashioned Ice Cream Roll

PREP: 30 min. **BAKE:** 15 min. + freezing
YIELD: 12 servings (1-3/4 cups sauce)

HEALTHY COOKING TEST KITCHEN

This dessert is so convenient to make ahead of time and keep in the freezer for company. The caramel sauce—reduced in fat and calories by our Test Kitchen staff—tastes great and makes a nice topping for ice cream, too!

4 eggs
3/4 cup sugar
1 tsp. vanilla extract
3/4 cup all-purpose flour
3/4 tsp. baking powder
1/4 tsp. salt
6 cups reduced-fat vanilla ice cream, slightly softened

CARAMEL SAUCE:
1 cup packed brown sugar
3 Tbsp. all-purpose flour
1 cup fat-free milk
2 egg yolks, lightly beaten
2 Tbsp. butter
Chopped pecans, optional

1. Line a 15-in. x 10-in. x 1-in. baking pan with waxed paper; coat paper with cooking spray; set aside.

2. In a large bowl, beat eggs on high speed for 3 minutes. Gradually add sugar, beating until mixture becomes thick and lemon-colored. Beat in vanilla.

3. Combine dry ingredients; fold into egg mixture. Spread batter into prepared pan.

4. Bake at 350° for 12-14 minutes or until cake springs back when lightly touched. Cool for 5 minutes. Invert onto a kitchen towel dusted with confectioners' sugar. Gently peel off waxed paper. Roll up cake in the towel jelly-roll style, starting with a short side. Cool completely on a wire rack.

5. Unroll cake; spread ice cream over cake to within 1/2 in. of edges. Roll up again. Place seam side down on a serving platter. Cover and freeze until firm.

6. Meanwhile, for caramel sauce, in a small saucepan, combine brown sugar and flour. Stir in milk until smooth. Cook and stir over medium-high heat until thickened and bubbly. Reduce heat; cook and stir for 2 minutes.

7. Remove from the heat. Stir a small amount of hot mixture into egg yolks; return all to pan, stirring constantly. Bring to a gentle boil; cook and stir for 2 minutes. Remove from the heat; gently stir in butter. Serve with ice cream roll. Sprinkle with pecans if desired.

Nutrition Facts: 1 slice with about 2 Tbsp. sauce (calculated without pecans) equals 319 calories, 8 g fat (4 g saturated fat), 128 mg cholesterol, 177 mg sodium, 56 g carbohydrate, trace fiber, 7 g protein.

MAKEOVER OLD-FASHIONED ICE CREAM ROLL

MAKEOVER STRAWBERRY CHEESECAKE ICE CREAM

Angel Food Trifle F

PREP/TOTAL TIME: 15 min. **YIELD:** 8 servings

MERWYN GARBINI • TUCSON, ARIZONA

A creamy ricotta-vanilla "custard" cuts calories and boosts calcium in this light take on an English classic. Best of all, it's a no-bake delight that comes together easily with readily available ingredients!

2	cups fat-free vanilla yogurt
1	cup part-skim ricotta cheese
1	cup fresh blueberries
1	cup sliced fresh strawberries
4	cups cubed angel food cake
1/2	cup reduced-fat whipped topping

1. In a blender, combine yogurt and ricotta cheese; cover and process until combined.

2. In a small bowl, combine blueberries and strawberries. Place half the cake cubes in a 2-qt. glass bowl. Layer with 1 cup berries and half the yogurt mixture. Top with remaining cake cubes, 3/4 cup berries and the remaining yogurt mixture. Garnish with remaining berries. Top with whipped topping. Refrigerate leftovers.

Nutrition Facts: 3/4 cup equals 182 calories, 3 g fat (2 g saturated fat), 11 mg cholesterol, 248 mg sodium, 30 g carbohydrate, 1 g fiber, 8 g protein. **Diabetic Exchanges:** 1-1/2 starch, 1/2 fat-free milk, 1/2 fat.

ANGEL FOOD TRIFLE

Isaiah's Pumpkin Muffins With Crumble Topping

PREP: 25 min. BAKE: 25 min. YIELD: 1 dozen

SILVANA NARDONE • BROOKLYN, NEW YORK

These tender muffins have a subtle pumpkin flavor and sugary topping that make them special. They're an ideal snack for my son, Isaiah, who needs foods that are free of gluten. Fabulous warm, the muffins make a quick on-the-go breakfast your whole family will love.

1-3/4 cups gluten-free all-purpose baking flour
  1 cup sugar
  2 tsp. baking powder
  2 tsp. pumpkin pie spice
3/4 tsp. salt
  2 eggs
  1 cup canned pumpkin
1/2 cup canola oil
  3 tsp. vanilla extract

TOPPING:
1/4 cup gluten-free all-purpose baking flour
1/4 cup sugar
1/4 cup packed brown sugar
1/2 tsp. pumpkin pie spice
1/4 cup shortening
Confectioners' sugar, optional

1. In a large bowl, combine the flour, sugar, baking powder, pie spice and salt. In another bowl, combine the eggs, pumpkin, oil and vanilla. Stir into dry ingredients just until moistened. Coat muffin cups with cooking spray or use paper liners; fill three-fourths full with batter.

2. For topping, combine the flour, sugar, brown sugar and pie spice; cut in shortening until crumbly. Sprinkle over batter. Bake at 350° for 25-30 minutes or until a toothpick inserted near the center comes out clean.

3. Cool for 5 minutes before removing from pan to a wire rack. Dust with confectioners' sugar if desired.

Editor's Note: Read all ingredient labels for possible gluten content prior to use. Ingredient formulas can change, and production facilities vary among brands. If you're concerned that your brand may contain gluten, contact the company.

Nutrition Facts: 1 muffin (calculated without confectioners' sugar) equals 306 calories, 15 g fat (2 g saturated fat), 35 mg cholesterol, 229 mg sodium, 42 g carbohydrate, 3 g fiber, 3 g protein.

Brown sugar is a mixture of granulated sugars and molasses, with dark brown sugar containing more molasses than light brown. Light brown sugar has a delicate flavor while dark brown sugar has a stronger molasses flavor. They can be used interchangeably.

Egg- and Lactose-Free Chocolate Cupcakes

PREP: 20 min. **BAKE:** 20 min. + cooling
YIELD: 1-1/2 dozen

HEALTHY COOKING TEST KITCHEN

These super-chocolaty, moist cupcakes don't have eggs or lactose, but they don't lack a bit of flavor. A yummy treat that travels well and appeals to all ages, this is one recipe you'll keep handy year-round.

- 2 cups water
- 1-1/2 cups sugar
- 1/2 cup unsweetened applesauce
- 1/3 cup canola oil
- 3 tsp. vanilla extract
- 3 cups all-purpose flour
- 1/2 cup baking cocoa
- 1-1/4 tsp. baking powder
- 1 tsp. salt
- 1/2 tsp. baking soda

FROSTING:
- 1/3 cup lactose-free margarine, softened
- 2 cups confectioners' sugar
- 1/3 cup baking cocoa
- 2 Tbsp. water
- 3/4 tsp. vanilla extract

1. In a large bowl, beat the water, sugar, applesauce, oil and vanilla until well blended. In a small bowl, combine the flour, cocoa, baking powder, salt and baking soda; gradually beat into the sugar mixture until blended.

2. Fill foiled-lined muffin cups three-fourths full. Bake at 350° for 18-22 minutes or until a toothpick inserted near the center comes out clean. Cool for 10 minutes before removing from pans to wire racks to cool completely.

3. In a small bowl, beat margarine until fluffy. Add the confectioners' sugar, cocoa, water and vanilla; beat until smooth. Frost cupcakes.

EGG- AND LACTOSE-FREE CHOCOLATE CUPCAKES

Nutrition Facts: 1 cupcake equals 275 calories, 8 g fat (1 g saturated fat), 0 cholesterol, 234 mg sodium, 49 g carbohydrate, 1 g fiber, 3 g protein.

Poppy Seed Torte

PREP: 50 min. + chilling **BAKE:** 15 min. + cooling
YIELD: 16 servings

BRENDA PATTERSON • PULLMAN, WASHINGTON

I got this recipe from my grandmother; it's an old-fashioned dessert, but well worth the effort. My dad requests this cake every year for his birthday. I make it for church events and charity auctions, too. Everyone loves it!

- 3 eggs, *separated*
- 1/4 cup butter, softened
- 3/4 cup sugar blend
- 1/4 cup unsweetened applesauce
- 1-1/2 tsp. vanilla extract, *divided*
- 2-1/2 cups plus 1 Tbsp. all-purpose flour, *divided*
- 3 tsp. baking powder
- 3/4 tsp. baking soda
- 1/2 tsp. salt
- 1-3/4 cups buttermilk
- 1/4 cup poppy seeds
- 1 cup sugar
- 1 cup (8 oz.) reduced-fat sour cream
- 1/4 cup confectioners' sugar
- 1-1/2 tsp. baking cocoa
- 1-1/2 to 2 tsp. cold brewed coffee
- 1/4 cup chopped walnuts, toasted

1. Place egg whites in a small bowl; let stand at room temperature for 30 minutes. Coat three 9-in. round baking pans with cooking spray; line with waxed paper and coat the paper. Sprinkle with flour; set aside.

2. In a large bowl, beat butter and sugar blend until crumbly, about 2 minutes. Beat in applesauce and 1 teaspoon vanilla. Combine 2-1/2 cups flour, baking powder, baking soda and salt; add to creamed mixture alternately with buttermilk. Fold in poppy seeds.

3. Beat egg whites on medium speed until soft peaks form; fold into batter. Spread into prepared pans. Bake at 350° for 12-18 minutes or until a toothpick comes out clean. Cool for 10 minutes before removing from pans to wire racks to cool completely.

4. For filling, in a small saucepan, combine sugar and remaining flour. Stir in sour cream until smooth. Bring to a boil. Stir a small amount of hot mixture into egg yolks; return all to the pan, stirring constantly. Bring to a gentle boil; cook and stir 2 minutes longer. Remove from the heat. Stir in remaining vanilla. Transfer to a bowl; refrigerate until chilled.

5. Place one cake layer on a serving platter; top with a third of the filling. Repeat layers twice.

6. Combine the confectioners' sugar, cocoa and enough coffee to achieve a drizzling consistency. Drizzle over the cake. Sprinkle with nuts. Refrigerate until serving.

GRILLED FRUIT SKEWERS WITH CHOCOLATE SYRUP

Editor's Note: This recipe was tested with Splenda sugar blend.

Nutrition Facts: 1 slice equals 261 calories, 8 g fat (3 g saturated fat), 54 mg cholesterol, 288 mg sodium, 43 g carbohydrate, 1 g fiber, 6 g protein.

Cinnamon-Spiced Bananas S

PREP/TOTAL TIME: 10 min. **YIELD:** 4 servings

JANET HOMES • SURPRISE, ARIZONA

The whole family will adore this special treat that uses the microwave so it's ready in a flash. Plus, it's a delicious way to jazz up bananas and add more fruit to your diet.

    3   large bananas, sliced
    3   Tbsp. brown sugar
  3/4   tsp. vanilla extract
  1/4   tsp. ground cinnamon
    1   Tbsp. butter
    1   cup reduced-fat vanilla ice cream

1. Place the bananas in a small microwave-safe bowl. Top with brown sugar, vanilla and cinnamon; dot with the butter.

2. Cover and microwave on high for 1-2 minutes or until the sugar is melted, stirring once. Spoon the banana mixture into bowls; top with the ice cream. Serve immediately.

Nutrition Facts: 1/2 cup banana mixture with 1/4 cup reduced-fat vanilla ice cream equals 211 calories, 5 g fat (3 g saturated fat), 16 mg cholesterol, 50 mg sodium, 42 g carbohydrate, 3 g fiber, 3 g protein.

Grilled Fruit Skewers with Chocolate Syrup F S

PREP/TOTAL TIME: 25 min. **YIELD:** 8 servings

MELISSA BIRDSONG • GILBERT, SOUTH CAROLINA

With toasted angel food cake and chocolate syrup, this recipe makes fruit seem especially decadent. It's the perfect treat for a summer party.

    2   cups cubed angel food cake
    1   cup fresh strawberries
    1   cup cubed fresh pineapple
    1   cup cubed cantaloupe
    1   large banana, cut into 1-in. slices
    2   medium plums, pitted and quartered
Butter-flavored cooking spray
  1/2   cup packed brown sugar
    8   tsp. chocolate syrup

1. On eight metal or soaked wooden skewers, alternately thread the cake cubes and fruits. Spritz each skewer with butter-flavored spray and roll in brown sugar.

2. Place skewers on a piece of heavy-duty foil. Place foil on grill rack. Grill, covered, over medium heat for 4-5 minutes on each side or until fruits are tender, turning once. Drizzle each skewer with 1 teaspoon chocolate syrup.

Nutrition Facts: 1 skewer equals 131 calories, 1 g fat (trace saturated fat), 0 cholesterol, 93 mg sodium, 30 g carbohydrate, 2 g fiber, 2 g protein. **Diabetic Exchanges:** 1 starch, 1 fruit.

BERRY-MARSHMALLOW TRIFLE

Berry-Marshmallow Trifle

PREP/TOTAL TIME: 25 min. YIELD: 10 servings

SHANNON ALDRIDGE • SUWANEE, GEORGIA

My guests say this is almost too pretty to eat! I like the way it can be made a day ahead for convenience, and neither flavor nor appearance is compromised.

1-3/4 cups cold fat-free milk

1 pkg. (1 oz.) sugar-free instant vanilla pudding mix

1 carton (8 oz.) frozen fat-free whipped topping, thawed, *divided*

1 loaf (10-3/4 oz.) frozen reduced-fat pound cake, thawed and cut into 1-in. cubes

3 cups fresh strawberries, halved

2 cups miniature marshmallows

3 Tbsp. sliced almonds

1. In a small bowl, whisk milk and pudding mix for 2 minutes. Let stand for 2 minutes or until soft-set. Fold in 2-1/2 cups whipped topping; set aside.

2. Place half of cake cubes in a 3-qt. trifle bowl; spoon half of reserved pudding mixture over the top. Top with half of strawberries and marshmallows.

3. Repeat layers. Top with remaining whipped topping; sprinkle with almonds. Chill until serving.

Nutrition Facts: 1 cup equals 230 calories, 6 g fat (1 g saturated fat), 18 mg cholesterol, 298 mg sodium, 40 g carbohydrate, 2 g fiber, 4 g protein.

Orange Cream Pops F S C

PREP: 5 min. + freezing YIELD: 10 pops

LAURIE PAYTON • COTTONWOOD, CALIFORNIA

Yogurt adds creaminess, calcium and a hint of tang to these frosty three-ingredient treats.

2 cups (16 oz.) plain yogurt

1 can (6 oz.) frozen orange juice concentrate, thawed

2 tsp. vanilla extract

10 Popsicle molds *or* paper cups (3 oz. *each*) and Popsicle sticks

1. In a small bowl, combine the yogurt, orange juice concentrate and vanilla. Fill each mold or cup with 1/4 cup yogurt mixture; top with holders or insert sticks into cups. Freeze.

Nutrition Facts: 1 pop equals 59 calories, 2 g fat (1 g saturated fat), 6 mg cholesterol, 23 mg sodium, 9 g carbohydrate, trace fiber, 2 g protein. **Diabetic Exchange:** 1/2 starch.

Poached Peaches with Cream Cheese Filling ⓢ

PREP: 25 min. + chilling   YIELD: 4 servings

GREG FONTENOT • THE WOODLANDS, TEXAS

Chocolate chips and confectioners' sugar add to the natural sweetness of these perfectly poached peaches.

    4 cups water
    1 cup sugar
    1 tsp. vanilla extract
 1/4 tsp. ground cinnamon
    2 medium peaches
    3 oz. reduced-fat cream cheese
    2 Tbsp. confectioners' sugar
    2 Tbsp. miniature semisweet chocolate chips
    1 Tbsp. orange juice
Additional ground cinnamon

1. In a large saucepan, combine the water, sugar, vanilla and cinnamon; add peaches. Bring to a boil. Reduce heat; cover and simmer for 10-15 minutes or until peaches are tender. Remove peaches with a slotted spoon; cool to room temperature. Discard cooking liquid. Halve, pit and peel peaches; refrigerate until chilled.

2. In a small bowl, beat the cream cheese, confectioners' sugar, chocolate chips and orange juice until blended. Pipe or spoon into peach halves. Sprinkle with additional cinnamon.

Nutrition Facts: 1 stuffed peach half equals 135 calories, 6 g fat (4 g saturated fat), 15 mg cholesterol, 91 mg sodium, 18 g carbohydrate, 1 g fiber, 3 g protein. **Diabetic Exchanges:** 1 starch, 1 fat, 1/2 fruit.

Makeover Bread Pudding

PREP: 20 min.   BAKE: 40 min.   YIELD: 15 servings

APRIL TAYLOR • APO, AE

I used to feel guilty serving bread pudding, but this light take offers the same warm and cozy flavors as my original recipe.

    8 cups cubed day-old bread
    4 eggs
    1 cup egg substitute
2-1/4 cups fat-free milk
1-3/4 cups half-and-half cream
  1/2 cup sugar
  1/3 cup butter, melted
    3 tsp. vanilla extract
1-1/2 tsp. ground cinnamon
CARAMEL SAUCE:
    1 cup packed brown sugar
    3 Tbsp. all-purpose flour
    1 cup fat-free milk
    2 egg yolks, lightly beaten
    2 Tbsp. butter

1. Place bread cubes in a 13-in. x 9-in. baking dish coated with cooking spray. In a large bowl, whisk the eggs, egg substitute, milk, cream, sugar, butter, vanilla and cinnamon. Pour evenly over bread.

2. Bake, uncovered, at 350° for 40-45 minutes or until a knife inserted near the center comes out clean.

3. For caramel sauce, in a small saucepan, combine brown sugar and flour. Stir in milk until smooth. Cook and stir over medium-high heat until thickened and bubbly. Reduce heat; cook and stir for 2 minutes.

4. Remove from the heat. Stir a small amount of hot mixture into egg yolks; return all to pan, stirring constantly. Bring to a gentle boil; cook and stir for 2 minutes. Remove from the heat; gently stir in butter. Serve with pudding. Refrigerate leftovers.

Nutrition Facts: 1 piece with about 2 tablespoons sauce equals 278 calories, 11 g fat (6 g saturated fat), 113 mg cholesterol, 262 mg sodium, 36 g carbohydrate, 1 g fiber, 8 g protein.

MAKEOVER BREAD PUDDING

POACHED PEACHES WITH CREAM CHEESE FILLING

Candy Bar Cupcakes

PREP: 30 min. BAKE: 20 min. + cooling
YIELD: 1-1/2 dozen

EDIE DESPAIN • LOGAN, UTAH

Everyone in my family loves cupcakes, so I experimented to create these treats that fit my family's tastes. I also tried to make them healthier. I hope you enjoy them as much as we do!

- 1 cup sugar
- 1 cup buttermilk
- 1/4 cup canola oil
- 1 tsp. vanilla extract
- 1-1/2 cups all-purpose flour
- 1/3 cup baking cocoa
- 1 tsp. baking soda
- 1/2 tsp. salt

FILLING:
- 6 oz. fat-free cream cheese
- 2 Tbsp. confectioners' sugar
- 1 egg
- 2 Snickers candy bars (2.07 oz. *each*), finely chopped

FROSTING:
- 1/3 cup butter, cubed
- 1/3 cup packed brown sugar
- 3 Tbsp. fat-free milk
- 1-1/2 cups confectioners' sugar

1. In a large bowl, beat the sugar, buttermilk, oil and vanilla until well blended. Combine the flour, cocoa, baking soda and salt; gradually beat into sugar mixture until blended.

2. For filling, in a small bowl, beat cream cheese and confectioners' sugar until light and fluffy. Add egg; mix well. Stir in the candy bars.

3. Fill paper-lined muffin cups one-third full with batter. Drop filling by tablespoonfuls into the center of each cupcake (cups will be about half full). Bake at 350° for 20-25 minutes or until a toothpick inserted in the filling comes out clean. Cool for 10 minutes before removing from pans to wire racks to cool completely.

4. For frosting, in a small saucepan, melt butter. Stir in brown sugar. Bring to a boil; cook for two minutes, stirring occasionally. Remove from the heat; stir in the milk, then confectioners' sugar. Cool until frosting reaches spreading consistency. Frost cupcakes.

Nutrition Facts: 1 cupcake equals 250 calories, 9 g fat (3 g saturated fat), 23 mg cholesterol, 248 mg sodium, 40 g carbohydrate, 1 g fiber, 4 g protein.

Strawberry Rhubarb Sauce [F] [S]

PREP/TOTAL TIME: 15 min. YIELD: 1-3/4 cups

MIA WERNER • WAUKEGAN, ILLINOIS

Try this easy, scrumptious sauce spooned over pound cake, ice cream, pancakes, waffles or just use it on top of toast. It's as good served cold as it is warm.

- 2 cups halved fresh strawberries
- 1 cup sliced fresh *or* frozen rhubarb
- 2/3 cup sugar
- 1 Tbsp. cornstarch
- 2 Tbsp. cold water

1. In a small saucepan, combine the strawberries, rhubarb and sugar. Bring to a boil over medium heat. Combine cornstarch and water until smooth; stir into fruit mixture. Cook and stir for 1-2 minutes or until thickened. Serve warm or chilled.

Editor's Note: If using frozen rhubarb, measure rhubarb while still frozen, then thaw completely. Drain in a colander, but do not press liquid out.

Nutrition Facts: 1/4 cup equals 96 calories, trace fat (trace saturated fat), 0 cholesterol, 1 mg sodium, 24 g carbohydrate, 1 g fiber, trace protein.

Makeover Chocolate Croissant Pudding

PREP: 25 min. BAKE: 55 min. + standing
YIELD: 12 servings

SONYA LABBE • SANTA MONICA, CALIFORNIA

My father is French, and I have a lot of family recipes that involve croissants. Thankfully, the Healthy Cooking Test Kitchen transformed my best-loved dessert into a delectable, slimmed-down version without sacrificing the croissants we all adore so much.

- 6 day-old croissants, split
- 2/3 cup semisweet chocolate chips
- 8 eggs
- 5 cups 2% milk
- 1 cup sugar
- 1-1/2 tsp. vanilla extract

CANDY BAR CUPCAKES

PEACH ALMOND CRISP

1. Place croissant bottoms in a 13-in. x 9-in. baking dish coated with cooking spray. Sprinkle with chocolate chips and replace croissant tops.

2. In a large bowl, combine the eggs, milk, sugar and vanilla; pour over croissants. Let stand for 10 minutes or until croissants are softened.

3. Bake, uncovered, at 350° for 55-60 minutes or until a knife inserted near the center comes out clean. Let stand for 10 minutes before cutting.

Nutrition Facts: 1 serving equals 326 calories, 14 g fat (7 g saturated fat), 166 mg cholesterol, 313 mg sodium, 41 g carbohydrate, 1 g fiber, 11 g protein.

Peach Almond Crisp S

PREP: 15 min. BAKE: 20 min. YIELD: 8 servings

LILY JULOW • GAINESVILLE, FLORIDA

This is delectable with any stone fruit, but especially peaches. It makes eight servings, though six people will eat it up faster than you can blink an eye!

2/3	cup sliced almonds
1/2	cup all-purpose flour
1/4	cup packed dark brown sugar
3	Tbsp. cold butter
1	Tbsp. sugar
1/4	tsp. ground cinnamon

Dash ground nutmeg

8	medium peaches, peeled and sliced
3	Tbsp. thawed orange juice concentrate

Reduced-fat vanilla ice cream, optional

1. In a food processor, combine the first seven ingredients. Cover and process until crumbly; set the mixture aside.

2. Place peaches in an 11-in. x 7-in. baking dish coated with cooking spray; drizzle with orange juice concentrate. Sprinkle with almond mixture. Bake at 400° for 20-25 minutes or until topping is golden brown. Serve warm with ice cream if desired.

Nutrition Facts: 3/4 cup (calculated without ice cream) equals 193 calories, 9 g fat (3 g saturated fat), 11 mg cholesterol, 33 mg sodium, 28 g carbohydrate, 3 g fiber, 4 g protein. **Diabetic Exchanges:** 2 fat, 1 fruit, 1/2 starch.

Berry Smoothie Pops F S C

PREP: 10 min. + freezing YIELD: 9 pops

LISA ROMAN • HONOLULU, HAWAII

Three types of good-for-you berries make these icy pops bright and tasty. What a fun snack on hot summer days!

1/2	cup orange juice
1	cup fresh blackberries
1	cup fresh raspberries
3/4	cup fresh blueberries
1	medium ripe banana, cut into chunks
1	Tbsp. sugar
9	Popsicle molds *or* paper cups (3 oz. *each*) and Popsicle sticks

1. In a blender, combine the orange juice, blackberries, raspberries, blueberries, banana and sugar; cover and process until blended. Fill each mold or cup with 1/4 cup berry mixture; top with holders or insert sticks into cups. Freeze.

Nutrition Facts: 1 pop equals 44 calories, trace fat (trace saturated fat), 0 cholesterol, trace sodium, 11 g carbohydrate, 2 g fiber, 1 g protein. **Diabetic Exchange:** 1/2 fruit.

Makeover Blueberry Whipped Topping Dessert

PREP: 30 min. + chilling **YIELD:** 20 servings

LAURA BAUDOIN • RACELAND, LOUISIANA

This lightened-up dessert is so yummy! It's like enjoying a taste of summer in every bite. Most importantly, no one will suspect this sweet surprise is on the light side of most desserts.

1	cup all-purpose flour
3/4	cup finely chopped pecans
6	Tbsp. butter, melted
1	envelope unflavored gelatin
1/2	cup cold water
2	pkg. (8 oz. *each*) fat-free cream cheese
2	cups confectioners' sugar
1	carton (8 oz.) frozen reduced-fat whipped topping, thawed
1	can (21 oz.) blueberry pie filling

1. In a small bowl, combine the flour, pecans and butter. Press onto the bottom a 13-in. x 9-in. baking dish coated with cooking spray. Bake at 350° for 10 minutes. Cool on a wire rack.

2. Meanwhile, in a small saucepan, sprinkle gelatin over cold water; let stand for 1 minute. Heat over low heat, stirring until gelatin is completely dissolved. Remove from the heat; set aside.

3. In a large bowl, beat cream cheese and confectioners' sugar until smooth. Beat in gelatin mixture until blended. Fold in whipped topping. Pour over crust. Spoon pie filling over top. Cover and refrigerate for at least 4 hours or until firm. Refrigerate leftovers.

Nutrition Facts: 1 piece equals 232 calories, 8 g fat (4 g saturated fat), 11 mg cholesterol, 152 mg sodium, 36 g carbohydrate, 1 g fiber, 5 g protein.

Strawberry Apple Cream Pops F S

PREP: 5 min. + freezing **YIELD:** 10 pops

BRITTNEY MUSGROVE • DALLAS, GEORGIA

Perfect on a hot summer's day, these super-yummy frozen bars couldn't be any simpler!

2	cups (16 oz.) strawberry yogurt
3/4	cup thawed apple juice concentrate
10	Popsicle molds *or* paper cups (3 oz. *each*) and Popsicle sticks

1. In a large bowl, combine yogurt and apple juice concentrate. Fill each mold or cup with 1/4 cup yogurt mixture; top with holders or insert sticks into cups. Freeze.

Nutrition Facts: 1 pop equals 84 calories, 1 g fat (trace saturated fat), 2 mg cholesterol, 31 mg sodium, 18 g carbohydrate, trace fiber, 2 g protein. **Diabetic Exchange:** 1 starch.

Makeover Raspberry Ice Cream S

PREP: 20 min. + chilling
PROCESS: 15 min./batch + freezing **YIELD:** 1-1/2 qt.

JEAN ECOS • HARTLAND, WISCONSIN

There's even more to love with my fruity ice cream since the Taste of Home pros made a few tweaks. With the original's creaminess and 30 percent fewer calories, this makeover is a stone-cold success!

1-1/2 cups half-and-half cream
1 cup whole milk
1-1/4 cups sugar, *divided*
1/8 tsp. salt
1 egg, beaten
1/2 cup fat-free sour cream
1 Tbsp. apple jelly
3 cups fresh raspberries
4-1/2 tsp. lemon juice

1. In a large saucepan, heat cream and milk to 175°; stir in 1/2 cup sugar and salt until dissolved. Whisk a small amount of the hot mixture into the egg. Return all to the pan, whisking constantly. Cook and stir over low heat until mixture is slightly thickened.

2. Remove from the heat. Cool quickly by placing pan in a bowl of ice water; stir for 2 minutes. Stir in sour cream and jelly. Press waxed paper onto surface of custard. Refrigerate for several hours or overnight.

3. Meanwhile, in a small bowl, gently combine raspberries with lemon juice and remaining sugar. Let stand for 2 hours, stirring occasionally. Mash raspberry mixture slightly; stir into custard.

4. Fill cylinder of ice cream freezer two-thirds full; freeze according to the manufacturer's directions. Refrigerate remaining mixture until ready to freeze. When ice cream is frozen, transfer to a freezer container; freeze for 2-4 hours before serving.

Nutrition Facts: 1/2 cup equals 169 calories, 4 g fat (3 g saturated fat), 36 mg cholesterol, 62 mg sodium, 29 g carbohydrate, 2 g fiber, 3 g protein. **Diabetic Exchanges:** 2 starch, 1/2 fat.

Rhubarb Raspberry Crumble Ⓢ

PREP: 20 min. BAKE: 35 min. YIELD: 8 servings

HEIDI FARNWORTH • RIVERTON, UTAH

The crumbly topping on this slightly sweet, slightly tart dessert really takes the cake. With slivered almonds, coconut and brown sugar, what's not to love?

3 cups chopped fresh *or* frozen rhubarb, thawed
2 cups fresh raspberries
2 tsp. lemon juice
1/2 cup sugar
1/2 cup reduced-fat plain yogurt
1/3 cup reduced-fat sour cream
1/4 cup all-purpose flour
1 egg

TOPPING:
1/2 cup quick-cooking oats
1/3 cup whole wheat flour
1/4 cup flaked coconut
1/4 cup packed brown sugar
1/2 tsp. ground cinnamon
3 Tbsp. cold butter
3 Tbsp. thawed apple juice concentrate
1/4 cup slivered almonds

1. In a large bowl, combine the rhubarb, raspberries and lemon juice. In a small bowl, combine the sugar, yogurt, sour cream, flour and egg. Pour over fruit mixture and stir gently to coat. Transfer to an 11-in. x 7-in. baking dish coated with cooking spray.

2. For topping, place the oats, flour, coconut, brown sugar and cinnamon in a food processor; cover and process until combined. Add butter and apple juice concentrate; process until crumbly. Stir in almonds; sprinkle over fruit mixture.

3. Bake, uncovered, at 350° for 35-45 minutes or until bubbly. Serve warm.

Editor's Note: If using frozen rhubarb, measure rhubarb while still frozen, then thaw completely. Drain in a colander, but do not press liquid out.

Nutrition Facts: 1 serving equals 264 calories, 9 g fat (5 g saturated fat), 42 mg cholesterol, 71 mg sodium, 42 g carbohydrate, 5 g fiber, 6 g protein.

MAKEOVER RASPBERRY ICE CREAM

RHUBARB RASPBERRY CRUMBLE

Chocolate Biscuit Puffs F C

PREP/TOTAL TIME: 20 min. **YIELD:** 10 servings

JOY CLARK • SEABECK, WASHINGTON

I know my favorite snack is fun for kids to make and eat because I dreamed it up at age 9! Pretty with the chocolate peeking out, the puffs could also be shaped to hide the chocolate within for a tasty surprise.

- 1 pkg. (7-1/2 oz.) refrigerated flaky buttermilk biscuits
- 1 milk chocolate candy bar (1.55 oz.)
- 2 tsp. cinnamon-sugar

1. Flatten each biscuit into a 3-in. circle. Break candy bar into 10 pieces; place a piece on each biscuit. Bring up edges to enclose candy and pinch to seal.

2. Place on an ungreased baking sheet. Sprinkle with cinnamon-sugar. Bake at 450° for 8-10 minutes or until golden brown.

Nutrition Facts: 1 puff equals 78 calories, 2 g fat (1 g saturated fat), 1 mg cholesterol, 185 mg sodium, 14 g carbohydrate, trace fiber, 2 g protein. **Diabetic Exchange:** 1 starch.

Mother's Banana Sherbet F S

PREP: 15 min. **PROCESS:** 20 min. + freezing
YIELD: 2-1/2 cups

KATHY BARTON • HOMER, MICHIGAN

Here's a cool, creamy treat that's such a favorite with my family, I usually triple the recipe.

- 1 cup water
- 2/3 cup sugar
- 1/3 cup reduced-fat evaporated milk
- 1/3 cup orange juice
- 2 Tbsp. lemon juice
- 1 medium banana, cut into chunks

1. In a small saucepan, bring water and sugar to a boil. Cook and stir until sugar is dissolved; set aside to cool.

2. Place the evaporated milk, orange juice, lemon juice and banana in a blender. Add the sugar syrup; cover and process until smooth.

CHOCOLATE BISCUIT PUFFS

3. Fill cylinder of ice cream freezer; freeze according to manufacturer's directions. Transfer to a freezer container; freeze mixture for 4 hours or until firm before serving.

Nutrition Facts: 1/2 cup equals 149 calories, trace fat (trace saturated fat), 1 mg cholesterol, 19 mg sodium, 36 g carbohydrate, 1 g fiber, 2 g protein.

Strawberry Mango Sorbet F S

PREP: 20 min. + freezing **YIELD:** 1 qt.

SANDRA VACHON • SAINT-CONSTANT, QUEBEC

This is fresh, really simple and will keep in a freezer container—if you don't eat it all the first day!

- 3/4 cup sugar
- 1-1/2 cups water
- 1-1/2 cups chopped peeled mangoes
- 1-1/2 cups fresh strawberries, halved
- 1/4 cup lime juice

1. In a small saucepan, bring sugar and water to a boil. Cook and stir until sugar is dissolved; set aside to cool.

2. In a food processor, cover and process mangoes and strawberries until pureed. Transfer to a large bowl; stir in sugar syrup and lime juice. Pour into a 13-in. x 9-in. dish; cover and freeze for 45 minutes or until edges begin to firm. Stir and return to freezer. Freeze 2 hours longer or until firm.

3. Just before serving, transfer to a food processor; cover and process for 2-3 minutes or until smooth.

Nutrition Facts: 1/2 cup equals 103 calories, trace fat (trace saturated fat), 0 cholesterol, 1 mg sodium, 27 g carbohydrate, 1 g fiber, trace protein. **Diabetic Exchanges:** 1-1/2 starch, 1/2 fruit.

Zesty Lemon Granita F S

PREP: 15 min. + freezing **YIELD:** 2 cups

SONYA LABBE • SANTA MONICA, CALIFORNIA

A light dessert with a refreshing, icy texture, this full-flavored delight always hits the spot on hot summer days. What a great change of pace from regular ice cream and frozen yogurt.

- 1 cup water
- 2/3 cup sugar
- 2/3 cup lemon juice
- 2 fresh thyme sprigs
- 2 tsp. grated lemon peel

1. In a small saucepan, bring water and sugar to a boil. Cook and stir until sugar is dissolved. Remove from the heat; stir in lemon juice and thyme. Transfer to an 8-in. square dish; cool to room temperature.

2. Remove thyme sprigs. Freeze for 1 hour; stir with a fork. Freeze 2-3 hours longer or until completely frozen, stirring every 30 minutes.

3. Stir granita with a fork just before serving; spoon into dessert dishes. Garnish with lemon peel.

Nutrition Facts: 1/2 cup equals 140 calories, trace fat (0 saturated fat), 0 cholesterol, trace sodium, 37 g carbohydrate, trace fiber, trace protein.

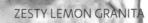

ZESTY LEMON GRANITA

MOTHER'S BANANA SHERBET

STRAWBERRY MANGO SORBET

Orange Cranberry Torte

PREP: 20 min. **BAKE:** 55 min. + cooling
YIELD: 16 servings

BERTHA PALAMAR • FULTON, NEW YORK

About 45 years ago, a friend gave me this recipe around the holidays; it's been a favorite ever since.

- 1 cup sugar
- 1 cup buttermilk
- 1/2 cup unsweetened applesauce
- 1/3 cup canola oil
- 2 eggs
- 2-1/4 cups all-purpose flour
- 1 tsp. baking powder
- 3/4 tsp. baking soda
- 1/4 tsp. salt
- 1 cup chopped walnuts
- 1 cup fresh or frozen cranberries, coarsely chopped
- 1 cup chopped dates
- 4 tsp. grated orange peel

GLAZE:
- 1/2 cup confectioners' sugar
- 2 tsp. orange juice

1. Coat a 10-in. fluted tube pan with cooking spray and sprinkle with flour; set aside.

2. In a large bowl, beat the sugar, buttermilk, applesauce, oil and eggs until well blended. Combine the flour, baking powder, baking soda and salt; gradually beat into sugar mixture until blended. Stir in the walnuts, cranberries, dates and orange peel.

3. Pour into prepared pan. Bake at 350° for 55-60 minutes or until a toothpick inserted near the center comes out clean. Cool for 10 minutes before removing from pan to a wire rack to cool completely. Combine glaze ingredients; drizzle over cake.

Nutrition Facts: 1 slice equals 269 calories, 10 g fat (1 g saturated fat), 27 mg cholesterol, 147 mg sodium, 42 g carbohydrate, 2 g fiber, 5 g protein.

Dulce de Leche Rice Pudding

PREP: 15 min. **COOK:** 50 min. **YIELD:** 6 servings

CARLA CERVANTES-JAUREGUI • MODESTO, CALIFORNIA

Brown rice lends a wonderful nuttiness to this tasty treat. I'm sure your family will love this sweet and salty version of down-home comfort food.

- 2 cups water
- 1/2 cup uncooked brown rice
- 1/2 cup uncooked long grain rice

1/4 cup sugar

1-1/2 cinnamon sticks (3 in.)

1 Tbsp. butter

Dash salt

1 can (12 oz.) evaporated milk

8 caramels

1 Tbsp. coarse sugar

1/8 tsp. kosher salt

1. In a large saucepan, combine the first seven ingredients. Bring to a boil. Reduce heat; simmer, uncovered, for 30 minutes or until water is absorbed.

2. Stir in milk. Bring to a boil. Reduce heat; simmer, uncovered, for 12-16 minutes or until thick and creamy, stirring occasionally. Add caramels, stirring until melted. Discard cinnamon sticks.

3. Spoon into dessert dishes. In a small bowl, combine coarse sugar and kosher salt; sprinkle over pudding. Serve warm or cold.

Nutrition Facts: 1/2 cup equals 294 calories, 7 g fat (4 g saturated fat), 24 mg cholesterol, 166 mg sodium, 50 g carbohydrate, 1 g fiber, 7 g protein.

Chai-Chocolate Chip Biscotti F S

PREP: 30 min. + chilling **BAKE:** 30 min. + cooling
YIELD: 2-1/2 dozen

PAT RUNTZ • HUNTLEY, ILLINOIS

This crunchy cookie was made to be dunked! Enjoy it with a hot cup of coffee or cold glass of milk.

2-1/3 cups all-purpose flour

1 cup sugar

3/4 tsp. ground cinnamon

1/2 tsp. baking powder

1/2 tsp. baking soda

1/4 tsp. salt

1/4 tsp. ground allspice

1/4 tsp. ground cardamom

1/4 cup strong brewed chai tea, room temperature

1 egg

1 egg white

1 Tbsp. fat-free milk

1 tsp. vanilla extract

1/2 cup chopped walnuts

1/2 cup miniature semisweet chocolate chips

1. In a large bowl, combine the first eight ingredients. In a small bowl, whisk the tea, egg, egg white, milk and vanilla. Stir into dry ingredients just until combined. Stir in walnuts and chocolate chips. Divide dough in half. Wrap each portion in plastic wrap and refrigerate for 1 hour.

2. On a baking sheet coated with cooking spray, shape each half into a 10-in. x 2-in. rectangle. Bake at 350° for 20-25 minutes or until golden brown. Place pans on wire racks. When cool enough to handle, transfer to a cutting board; cut diagonally with a serrated knife into 3/4-in. slices. Place cut side down on baking sheets coated with cooking spray.

3. Bake for 6-9 minutes on each side or until firm. Remove to wire racks. Store in an airtight container.

Nutrition Facts: 1 cookie equals 93 calories, 3 g fat (1 g saturated fat), 7 mg cholesterol, 52 mg sodium, 16 g carbohydrate, 1 g fiber, 2 g protein. **Diabetic Exchanges:** 1 starch, 1/2 fat.

Mini Raspberry Mousse Parfaits S

PREP: 30 min. + chilling **YIELD:** 4 servings

HEALTHY COOKING TEST KITCHEN

These elegant parfaits make the perfect finish to a special meal. Busy hostesses can assemble them ahead.

1-3/4 cups fresh or frozen unsweetened raspberries, thawed

3 Tbsp. sugar

2 tsp. cornstarch

2 tsp. orange juice

1-1/3 cups whipped topping

1/3 cup cubed angel food cake (1/2-in. cubes)

1. Press raspberries through a strainer and discard seeds and pulp. In a small saucepan, combine sugar and cornstarch; stir in raspberry juice. Bring to a boil; cook and stir for 2 minutes or until thickened. Refrigerate until chilled.

2. Divide raspberry mixture in half. Stir orange juice into one portion; set aside. Place remaining mixture in a small bowl; fold in whipped topping.

3. Divide cake among four dessert dishes. Layer each with a scant Tbsp. of reserved berry-orange mixture and 1/3 cup creamy mixture. Refrigerate until serving.

Nutrition Facts: 1 parfait equals 143 calories, 4 g fat (4 g saturated fat), 0 cholesterol, 29 mg sodium, 24 g carbohydrate, 1 g fiber, 1 g protein. **Diabetic Exchanges:** 1 starch, 1 fat, 1/2 fruit.

CHAI-CHOCOLATE CHIP BISCOTTI

Mock Apple Strudel

PREP: 20 min. BAKE: 25 min. + cooling
YIELD: 12 servings

BETH DAUENHAUER • PUEBLO, COLORADO

On Saturdays, Mom would pack us five kids into the car, and we'd drive into the country looking for wild apple trees alongside the road. With the apples we picked, she'd bake this strudel, our traditional Sunday-morning breakfast in fall.

  2 cups all-purpose flour
  3 tsp. baking powder
  2 Tbsp. plus 1/2 cup sugar, *divided*
1/2 tsp. salt
1/4 cup cold butter
3/4 cup fat-free milk
  1 Tbsp. butter, melted
  3 cups chopped tart apples
  1 tsp. ground cinnamon

FROSTING:
1/2 cup confectioners' sugar
  1 tsp. fat-free milk
1/4 tsp. vanilla extract
Chopped nuts, optional

1. In a large bowl, combine the flour, baking powder, 2 Tbsp. sugar and salt. Cut in butter until mixture resembles coarse crumbs. Stir in milk just until moistened. Turn onto a lightly floured surface; knead 8-10 times.

2. Roll out into a 14-in. x 10-in. rectangle. Brush with melted butter. Top with apples; sprinkle with cinnamon and remaining sugar. Roll up jelly-roll style, starting with a long side; pinch seams to seal. Place on a parchment paper-lined 15-in. x 10-in. x 1-in. baking pan. Bake at 425° for 25-30 minutes or until golden brown.

3. Remove from pan to a wire rack. In a small bowl, combine the confectioners' sugar, milk and vanilla; drizzle over warm strudel. Sprinkle with nuts if desired.

Nutrition Facts: 1 slice (calculated without nuts) equals 200 calories, 5 g fat (3 g saturated fat), 13 mg cholesterol, 239 mg sodium, 37 g carbohydrate, 1 g fiber, 3 g protein.

Wonton Sundaes F S C

PREP: 25 min. BAKE: 10 min. + cooling YIELD: 2 dozen

BETTY JO MORRIS • LITTLE ROCK, ARKANSAS

I created this recipe by combining two favorite treats. Set these sundaes on a dessert buffet and watch them disappear.

24 wonton wrappers
Refrigerated butter-flavored spray
  1 Tbsp. plus 1/4 cup sugar, *divided*
  1 tsp. ground cinnamon
  1 pkg. (8 oz.) reduced-fat cream cheese
  1 tsp. vanilla extract
1/4 cup miniature semisweet chocolate chips
1/4 cup chopped pecans
24 maraschino cherries with stems

1. Place wonton wrappers on a work surface; spritz with butter-flavored spray. Combine 1 Tbsp. sugar and cinnamon; sprinkle over wontons. Press into miniature muffin cups coated with cooking spray.

2. Bake at 350° for 4-5 minutes or until lightly browned. Immediately remove wonton cups to an ungreased baking sheet. Bake 2-3 minutes longer or until bottoms of cups are lightly browned. Remove to a wire rack to cool.

3. In a small bowl, beat the cream cheese, vanilla and remaining sugar until smooth. Stir in chocolate chips and pecans. Spoon into wonton cups. Top each with a maraschino cherry.

Nutrition Facts: 1 sundae equals 83 calories, 3 g fat (1 g saturated fat), 6 mg cholesterol, 74 mg sodium, 12 g carbohydrate, trace fiber, 2 g protein. **Diabetic Exchanges:** 1 starch, 1/2 fat.

Banana Strawberry Pops F S C

PREP: 10 min. + freezing YIELD: 10 pops

DEIRDRE DEE COX • MILWAUKEE, WISCONSIN

Strawberry and banana shine in these summery, refreshing pops with a pretty pink color.

MOCK APPLE STRUDEL

BANANA STRAWBERRY POPS

MOCHACCINO PUDDING

- 1/2 cup fat-free milk
- 1/2 cup orange juice
- 2 Tbsp. honey
- 1 pint fresh strawberries, hulled
- 1 medium ripe banana, cut into chunks
- 10 Popsicle molds *or* paper cups (3 oz. *each*) and Popsicle sticks

1. In a blender, combine the milk, juice, honey, strawberries and banana; cover and process until blended. Fill each mold or cup with 1/4 cup strawberry mixture; top with holders or insert sticks into cups. Freeze.

Nutrition Facts: 1 pop equals 42 calories, trace fat (trace saturated fat), trace cholesterol, 6 mg sodium, 10 g carbohydrate, 1 g fiber, 1 g protein. **Diabetic Exchange:** 1/2 fruit.

Mochaccino Pudding S

PREP: 15 min. **COOK:** 10 min. + chilling
YIELD: 6 servings

MARIA REGAKIS • SOMERVILLE, MASSACHUSETTS
I like to top this homey prize-winning pudding with chocolate-covered espresso beans and whipped cream. Pudding never tasted so elegant!

- 1 Tbsp. boiling water
- 2 tsp. instant espresso powder
- 3/4 cup sugar
- 1/4 cup baking cocoa
- 3 Tbsp. cornstarch
- 1/2 tsp. ground cinnamon
- 1/8 tsp. salt
- 3 cups 2% milk
- 3 egg yolks, lightly beaten
- 1 Tbsp. brandy, optional
- 1 tsp. vanilla extract

Whipped cream and chocolate-covered coffee beans, optional

1. Combine boiling water and espresso powder; set aside. In a large heavy saucepan, combine the sugar, cocoa, cornstarch, cinnamon and salt. Stir in milk until smooth. Cook and stir over medium-high heat until thickened and bubbly. Reduce heat to low; cook and stir 2 minutes longer.

2. Remove from the heat. Stir a small amount of hot mixture into egg yolks; return all to the pan, stirring constantly. Bring to a gentle boil; cook and stir 2 minutes longer. Remove from the heat. Stir in brandy if desired, vanilla and espresso mixture. Cool for 15 minutes, stirring occasionally.

3. Transfer to dessert dishes. Cover and refrigerate for 1 hour. Garnish with whipped cream and coffee beans if desired.

Nutrition Facts: 1/2 cup (calculated without optional ingredients) equals 212 calories, 5 g fat (2 g saturated fat), 112 mg cholesterol, 115 mg sodium, 37 g carbohydrate, 1 g fiber, 6 g protein.

Black Forest Crepes

PREP/TOTAL TIME: 20 min. **YIELD:** 8 servings

MARY RELYEA • CANASTOTA, NEW YORK

Cherries and chocolate just naturally taste great together, but the combination is even better when enhanced by tender crepes and a creamy filling.

1	pkg. (8 oz.) reduced-fat cream cheese, softened
1/2	cup reduced-fat sour cream
1/2	tsp. vanilla extract
2/3	cup confectioners' sugar
8	prepared crepes (9 in.)
1	can (20 oz.) reduced-sugar cherry pie filling, warmed
1/4	cup chocolate syrup

1. In a small mixing bowl, beat the cream cheese, sour cream and vanilla until smooth. Gradually beat in confectioners' sugar. Spread about 3 tablespoons over each crepe to within 1/2 in. of edges and roll up.

2. Arrange in an ungreased 13-in. x 9-in. baking dish. Bake, uncovered, at 350° for 5-7 minutes or until warm. To serve, top each crepe with 1/4 cup pie filling and drizzle with 1-1/2 teaspoons chocolate syrup.

Nutrition Facts: 1 filled crepe equals 256 calories, 9 g fat (6 g saturated fat), 31 mg cholesterol, 222 mg sodium, 39 g carbohydrate, 1 g fiber, 6 g protein. **Diabetic Exchanges:** 2-1/2 starch, 1-1/2 fat.

Guilt-Free Berry Trifle **F**

PREP: 40 min. + chilling **YIELD:** 16 servings

ELAINE ALEVER • SAGINAW, MICHIGAN

I am always cutting fat from recipes. When I was invited to a party where the hostess was diabetic, I wanted to take this trifle—a dessert she could enjoy.

	Sugar substitute equivalent to 1/2 cup sugar, *divided*
9	tsp. cornstarch, *divided*
3/4	cup cold water, *divided*
1	quart fresh strawberries, chopped
4	Tbsp. lemon juice, *divided*
3	cups fresh blueberries
1	pkg. (1 oz.) sugar-free instant vanilla pudding mix
2	cups fat-free milk
2	loaves (10-1/2 oz. *each*) angel food cake, cubed
1	carton (8 oz.) frozen reduced-fat whipped topping, thawed

1. In a small heavy saucepan, combine 1/4 cup sugar substitute, 4-1/2 teaspoons cornstarch and 1/4 cup water until smooth. Bring to a boil over medium heat, stirring constantly. Add strawberries; cook and stir for 2 minutes or until thickened and bubbly. Remove from the heat; stir in 2 tablespoons lemon juice. Cool to room temperature without stirring.

2. In another heavy saucepan, combine the remaining sugar substitute, cornstarch and water until smooth. Bring to a boil over medium heat, stirring constantly. Add blueberries; cook and stir for 2 minutes or until thickened and bubbly. Remove from the heat; stir in remaining lemon juice. Cool to room temperature without stirring.

3. Prepare pudding according to package directions, using fat-free milk. Let stand for 2 minutes or until soft-set.

4. Place half of the cake cubes in a 4-qt. trifle bowl. Layer with strawberry mixture, half of the pudding, remaining cake cubes, blueberry mixture and remaining pudding. Top with whipped topping. Cover and refrigerate for at least 1 hour.

Nutrition Facts: 1 cup equals 180 calories, 2 g fat (2 g saturated fat), 1 mg cholesterol, 369 mg sodium, 36 g carbohydrate, 2 g fiber, 4 g protein. **Diabetic Exchanges:** 2 starch, 1/2 fruit.

Skinny Mint-Chip Ice Cream

PREP: 15 min. + freezing **YIELD:** 1-1/2 quarts

NANCY QUELLE • CEDAR RAPIDS, IOWA

No one will ever guess that this smooth and creamy mint treat is light at all. For the Christmas holidays, it's fun to substitute 2 cups of crushed peppermint candy canes for the semisweet chocolate chunks.

- 4 cups fat-free half-and-half
- 1 pkg. (3.4 oz.) instant vanilla pudding mix
- 1 can (14 oz.) fat-free sweetened condensed milk
- 2 tsp. mint extract
- 3 to 4 drops green food coloring, optional
- 1-1/2 cups semisweet chocolate chunks

1. In a large mixing bowl, beat half-and-half and pudding mix on low speed for 2 minutes. Beat in the condensed milk, extract and food coloring if desired.

2. Fill cylinder of ice cream freezer; freeze according to manufacturer's directions. Coarsely chop chocolate chunks if desired; stir into ice cream. Transfer to freezer containers. Freeze for 2-4 hours before serving.

Nutrition Facts: 1/2 cup equals 289 calories, 7 g fat (4 g saturated fat), 4 mg cholesterol, 216 mg sodium, 50 g carbohydrate, 1 g fiber, 6 g protein.

Summer Fruit Crisp ⓢ

PREP: 30 min. **BAKE:** 20 min. **YIELD:** 10 servings

BETH GARVIN • CISCO, TEXAS

What says summer more than this sweet dessert simply packed with fresh cherries and juicy peaches? To beat the heat, dollop servings with scoops of low-fat frozen yogurt or ice cream.

- 4 cups fresh dark sweet cherries (about 1-1/4 lbs.), pitted
- 4 cups sliced peeled peaches
- 1/3 cup sugar
- 2 Tbsp. all-purpose flour
- 1/8 tsp. salt

TOPPING:
- 1/2 cup old-fashioned oats
- 1/2 cup packed brown sugar
- 1/3 cup all-purpose flour
- 1/4 cup chopped pecans
- 1/4 tsp. salt
- 1/4 tsp. ground cinnamon
- 3 Tbsp. cold butter

1. In a large bowl, combine the cherries, peaches, sugar, flour and salt. Transfer to a 13-in. x 9-in. baking dish coated with cooking spray.

2. For topping, in a small bowl, combine the oats, brown sugar, flour, pecans, salt and cinnamon. Cut in butter until crumbly. Sprinkle over fruit mixture.

3. Bake at 400° for 20-25 minutes or until filling is bubbly and topping is golden brown. Serve warm.

Nutrition Facts: 1 serving equals 234 calories, 6 g fat (2 g saturated fat), 9 mg cholesterol, 128 mg sodium, 45 g carbohydrate, 3 g fiber, 3 g protein.

> When whipping up **Summer Fruit Crisp**, consider using plums instead of the peaches. You can also swap out the pecans for walnuts if you'd like, or leave out the nuts in the topping altogether and cut even more calories. Add a dash of nutmeg along with the cinnamon.

SUMMER FRUIT CRISP

SKINNY MINT-CHIP ICE CREAM

Pumpkin Cake Roll

PREP: 25 min. **BAKE:** 10 min. + chilling **YIELD:** 12 servings

HEIDI REINHARD • MONTPELIER, INDIANA

If you'd like, you could substitute lemon juice for the almond extract. For a frozen dessert, replace the filling with reduced-fat vanilla ice cream.

3	eggs
3/4	cup sugar
2/3	cup canned pumpkin
1/2	tsp. almond extract
3/4	cup all-purpose flour
2	tsp. ground cinnamon
1	tsp. baking powder
1	tsp. ground ginger
1/2	tsp. salt
1	Tbsp. plus 1 cup confectioners' sugar, *divided*
6	oz. reduced-fat cream cheese, cubed
1	tsp. butter
1/2	tsp. vanilla extract

1. Line a 15-in. x 10-in. x 1-in. baking pan with waxed paper. Coat the paper with cooking spray; set aside. In a large mixing bowl, beat eggs for 3 minutes. Gradually add sugar; beat for 2 minutes or until mixture becomes thick and lemon-colored. Beat in pumpkin and extract. Combine the flour, cinnamon, baking powder, ginger and salt; fold into pumpkin mixture. Spread batter evenly into prepared pan.

2. Bake at 375° for 10-15 minutes or until cake springs back when lightly touched (do not overbake). Cool for 5 minutes. Invert onto a kitchen towel dusted with 1 tablespoon confectioners' sugar. Gently peel off waxed paper. Roll up cake in the towel jelly-roll style, starting with a short side. Cool completely on a wire rack.

PUMPKIN CAKE ROLL

3. For filling, in a small mixing bowl, beat the cream cheese, butter, vanilla and remaining confectioners' sugar until fluffy.

4. Unroll cake; spread filling evenly over cake to within 1/2 in. of edges. Roll up again. Cover and refrigerate for 1 hour before serving.

Nutrition Facts: 1 slice equals 182 calories, 5 g fat (3 g saturated fat), 64 mg cholesterol, 212 mg sodium, 31 g carbohydrate, 1 g fiber, 4 g protein. **Diabetic Exchanges:** 2 starch, 1/2 fat.

Berry-Licious Crisp ⓢ

PREP: 15 min. **BAKE:** 20 min. **YIELD:** 9 servings

EDNA WOODARD • FREDERICKSBURG, TEXAS

I lightened up one of my favorite recipes, and this is the delicious result. I like to serve it with low-fat vanilla ice cream or frozen yogurt.

1	cup *each* fresh blackberries, blueberries and raspberries
1	cup fresh or frozen cranberries, thawed
1	medium tart apple, peeled and diced
3/4	cup sugar
3	Tbsp. cornstarch
1/2	cup all-purpose flour
1/2	cup packed brown sugar
1/4	cup cold butter

1. In a large bowl, combine the berries and apple. Combine sugar and cornstarch; sprinkle over fruit and gently toss to coat.

2. Transfer to an 8-in. square baking dish coated with cooking spray. In a small bowl, combine flour and brown sugar; cut in butter until crumbly. Sprinkle over fruit mixture.

3. Bake at 400° for 20-25 minutes or until filling is bubbly and topping is golden brown. Serve warm.

Nutrition Facts: 1 serving equals 228 calories, 5 g fat (3 g saturated fat), 14 mg cholesterol, 57 mg sodium, 45 g carbohydrate, 3 g fiber, 1 g protein.

Gluten-Free Crumb Crust ⓢ

PREP/TOTAL TIME: 20 min. **YIELD:** 1 crust

CHRISTA HAGEMAN • TELFORD, PENNSYLVANIA

I use this recipe to replace graham cracker crusts because my father can't have the hydrogenated fats and sugars in them. It's so fast!

1	cup brown rice flour
1/2	cup ground walnuts
3	Tbsp. apple juice concentrate
2	Tbsp. olive oil

1. In a small bowl, combine all ingredients. Press onto the bottom and up the sides of a 9-in. pie plate coated with cooking spray. Bake at 375° for 10-14 minutes or until set. Cool on a wire rack.

2. Fill as desired. If baking the filling, shield edges of crust with foil to prevent overbrowning.

Nutrition Facts: 1/8 of crust equals 133 calories, 7 g fat (1 g saturated fat), 0 cholesterol, 2 mg sodium, 17 g carbohydrate, 1 g fiber, 2 g protein. **Diabetic Exchanges:** 1-1/2 fat, 1 starch.

MAKEOVER CHOCOLATE LAYER BARS

Makeover Chocolate Layer Bars ⑤

PREP: 35 min. **BAKE:** 15 min. + cooling **YIELD:** 40 bars

ANITA NICKLESS • PLATTE CITY, MISSOURI

Relatives often ask for these bars at get-togethers, and people don't want to stop at just one...I don't blame them! With this pared-down version, we can all enjoy them guilt-free.

- 1/2 cup butter, softened
- 1-1/2 cups sugar
- 2 eggs
- 1/2 cup unsweetened applesauce
- 1 tsp. vanilla extract
- 2 cups all-purpose flour
- 3 Tbsp. baking cocoa
- 1 tsp. baking soda
- 1 cup buttermilk

CREAMY LAYER:
- 1/3 cup butter, softened
- 1/3 cup reduced-fat butter, softened
- 2 cups confectioners' sugar
- 3 Tbsp. fat-free milk
- 1 tsp. vanilla extract

FROSTING:
- 1 cup sugar
- 1/3 cup butter, cubed
- 1/3 cup fat-free milk
- 1/4 cup baking cocoa
- 3/4 cup semisweet chocolate chips

1. In a large mixing bowl, cream butter and sugar until light and fluffy. Beat in the eggs, applesauce and vanilla until well blended. Combine the flour, cocoa and baking soda; add to the creamed mixture alternately with buttermilk, beating well after each addition.

2. Pour into a 15-in. x 10-in. x 1-in. baking pan coated with cooking spray. Bake at 350° for 15-20 minutes or until a toothpick inserted near the center comes out clean. Cool completely on a wire rack.

3. For creamy layer, in a small mixing bowl, beat the butters, confectioners' sugar, milk and vanilla until fluffy, about 4 minutes. Spread over top of cake.

4. For frosting, in a small heavy saucepan, combine the sugar, butter, milk and cocoa. Bring to a boil over medium heat, stirring frequently; cook and stir 2 minutes longer. Remove from the heat; stir in chocolate chips until melted.

5. With a hand mixer, beat frosting for 2-4 minutes or until thickened. Gently spread over the top. Store in the refrigerator.

Editor's Note: This recipe was tested with Land O'Lakes light stick butter.

Nutrition Facts: 1 bar equals 175 calories, 8 g fat (5 g saturated fat), 27 mg cholesterol, 94 mg sodium, 27 g carbohydrate, 1 g fiber, 2 g protein. **Diabetic Exchanges:** 1-1/2 starch, 1-1/2 fat.

By replacing the oil Anita's recipe originally called for with unsweetened applesauce, and by using a combination of full- and reduced-fat butter instead of using shortening, the *Taste of Home* team trimmed **Chocolate Layer Bars** of 75 calories.

Chocolate Peanut Butter Parfaits

PREP: 20 min. + chilling YIELD: 6 servings

PAT SOLOMAN • CASPER, WYOMING

When a friend gave me this recipe, I knew it was a keeper. It meets all requirements: It's easy, low-calorie and low-fat, and it's pretty to boot!

- 2 Tbsp. reduced-fat chunky peanut butter
- 2 Tbsp. plus 2 cups cold fat-free milk, *divided*
- 1 cup plus 6 Tbsp. reduced-fat whipped topping, *divided*
- 1 pkg. (1.4 oz.) sugar-free instant chocolate fudge pudding mix
- 3 Tbsp. finely chopped salted peanuts

1. In a small bowl, combine peanut butter and 2 tablespoons milk. Fold in 1 cup whipped topping; set aside. In another small bowl, whisk remaining milk with the pudding mix for 2 minutes. Let stand for 2 minutes or until soft-set.

2. Spoon half of the pudding into six parfait glasses or dessert dishes. Layer with reserved peanut butter mixture and remaining pudding. Refrigerate for at least 1 hour. Refrigerate remaining whipped topping.

3. Just before serving, garnish each parfait with 1 tablespoon whipped topping and 1-1/2 teaspoons peanuts.

Nutrition Facts: 1 parfait equals 146 calories, 6 g fat (3 g saturated fat), 2 mg cholesterol, 300 mg sodium, 16 g carbohydrate, 1 g fiber, 6 g protein. **Diabetic Exchanges:** 1 fat, 1/2 starch, 1/2 fat-free milk.

CHOCOLATE PEANUT BUTTER PARFAITS

Frozen Chocolate Mint Dessert

PREP: 30 min. + freezing YIELD: 24 servings

SARAH NEWMAN • BROOKLYN CENTER, MINNESOTA

This is adapted from my great-aunt's recipe for grasshopper pie. My last version was a fluke, as I put in too much mint extract. I needed to cut the mint taste with something gooey and chocolaty, so I ended up flipping the whole thing upside down on top of a brownie crust!

- 1 pkg. fudge brownie mix (13-in. x 9-in. pan size)
- 2 egg whites
- 1/4 cup unsweetened applesauce
- 2 tsp. vanilla extract
- 1/2 cup baking cocoa
- 1-1/2 cups fat-free milk
- 2 pkg. (16 oz. *each*) large marshmallows
- 1/2 tsp. mint extract
- 1 carton (16 oz.) frozen reduced-fat whipped topping, thawed
- 2/3 cup cream-filled chocolate sandwich cookie crumbs

1. In a large bowl, combine the brownie mix, egg whites, applesauce and vanilla. Spread into a 13-in. x 9-in. baking dish coated with cooking spray. Bake at 350° for 18-22 minutes or until a toothpick inserted near the center comes out clean. Cool on a wire rack.

2. In a Dutch oven, combine cocoa and milk. Cook and stir over medium heat until cocoa is dissolved. Stir in marshmallows until melted. Remove from the heat; stir in extract. Cool completely.

3. Fold in whipped topping. Spread over brownies. Sprinkle with cookie crumbs. Cover and freeze for at least 8 hours. Remove from the freezer 10 minutes before serving.

Nutrition Facts: 1 piece equals 293 calories, 6 g fat (3 g saturated fat), 1 mg cholesterol, 141 mg sodium, 60 g carbohydrate, 1 g fiber, 3 g protein.

FROZEN CHOCOLATE MINT DESSERT

Frozen Pistachio Dessert With Raspberry Sauce

PREP: 35 min. + freezing **YIELD:** 12 servings

SUZETTE JURY • KEENE, CALIFORNIA

Raspberry sauce adds pretty holiday color to this cool and creamy treat, while pistachios provide a savory hint.

1-1/2 cups crushed vanilla wafers (about 45 wafers)
  1/4 cup finely chopped pistachios
  1/4 cup reduced-fat butter, melted
1-1/4 cups fat-free milk
   1 pkg. (1 oz.) sugar-free instant pistachio pudding mix
   6 oz. reduced-fat cream cheese
   1 carton (8 oz.) frozen fat-free whipped topping, thawed, *divided*
   1 pkg. (12 oz.) frozen unsweetened raspberries, thawed
   2 Tbsp. sugar
   2 Tbsp. orange liqueur *or* orange juice
   2 Tbsp. chopped pistachios

1. In a small bowl, combine the wafers, finely chopped pistachios and butter. Press onto the bottom of a 9-in. springform pan coated with cooking spray. Place pan on a baking sheet. Bake at 350° for 10 minutes or until lightly browned. Cool on a wire rack.

2. Meanwhile, in a small bowl, whisk milk and pudding mix for 2 minutes. Let stand for 2 minutes or until soft-set. In a large mixing bowl, beat cream cheese until smooth. Beat in the pudding.

3. Set aside 3/4 cup whipped topping for garnish; fold remaining whipped topping into cream cheese mixture. Pour filling over crust. Freeze for 5 hours or overnight. Cover and refrigerate remaining whipped topping.

4. For sauce, place the raspberries, sugar and liqueur in a food processor. Cover and process for 1-2 minutes or until smooth. Strain and discard seeds and pulp. Refrigerate until serving.

5. Remove dessert from the freezer 15 minutes before serving. Remove sides of pan. Garnish with chopped pistachios and remaining whipped topping. Serve with sauce.

Editor's Note: This recipe was tested with Land O'Lakes light stick butter.

Nutrition Facts: 1 slice with 4 teaspoons sauce equals 214 calories, 9 g fat (4 g saturated fat), 18 mg cholesterol, 268 mg sodium, 28 g carbohydrate, 2 g fiber, 4 g protein. **Diabetic Exchanges:** 2 starch, 2 fat.

Consider using the **raspberry sauce** from the frosty pistachio dessert as a simple way to jazz up slices of store-bought pound cake or even vanilla ice cream.

Hot Fudge Pudding Cake F

PREP: 15 min. **BAKE:** 30 min. **YIELD:** 9 servings

JACKIE TERMONT • ELKHART, INDIANA

My mom used to make a recipe like this when I was younger. I decided to make some healthy changes, and this version is as good as, if not better than, the original. Being a dietitian, I love to come up with ways to lighten recipes. I would bake all the time if I could!

- 1 cup all-purpose flour
- 1 cup sugar, *divided*
- 3 Tbsp. plus 1/4 cup baking cocoa, *divided*
- 2 tsp. baking powder
- 1/4 tsp. salt
- 1/2 cup fat-free milk
- 1/3 cup prune baby food
- 1-1/2 tsp. vanilla extract
- 1/4 cup plus 2 Tbsp. packed brown sugar
- 1-1/4 cups boiling water

1. In a large bowl, combine the flour, 3/4 cup sugar, 3 tablespoons cocoa, baking powder and salt. In another bowl, combine the milk, baby food and vanilla. Stir into dry ingredients just until moistened. Spread into an 8-in. square baking dish coated with cooking spray.

2. Combine brown sugar with remaining sugar and cocoa; sprinkle over the batter. Carefully pour water over the top (do not stir). Bake, uncovered, at 350° for 28-32 minutes or until top is set and edges pull away from sides of dish. Serve warm.

Nutrition Facts: 1 serving equals 196 calories, 1 g fat (trace saturated fat), trace cholesterol, 164 mg sodium, 46 g carbohydrate, 1 g fiber, 3 g protein.

Warm Chocolate Melting Cups F S

PREP: 20 min. **BAKE:** 20 min. **YIELD:** 10 servings

KISSA VAUGHN • TROY, TEXAS

These have become a favorite of our guests. They're always so surprised that these little desserts are light.

- 1-1/4 cups sugar, *divided*
- 1/2 cup baking cocoa
- 2 Tbsp. all-purpose flour
- 1/8 tsp. salt
- 3/4 cup water
- 3/4 cup plus 1 Tbsp. semisweet chocolate chips
- 1 Tbsp. brewed coffee
- 1 tsp. vanilla extract
- 2 eggs
- 1 egg white

1. In a small saucepan, combine 3/4 cup sugar, cocoa, flour and salt. Gradually stir in water. Bring to a boil; cook and stir for 2 minutes or until thickened. Remove from the heat; stir in the chocolate chips, coffee and vanilla until smooth. Transfer to a large bowl.

2. In another bowl, beat eggs and egg white until slightly thickened. Gradually add remaining sugar, beating until thick and lemon-colored. Fold into chocolate mixture.

3. Transfer to ten 4-oz. ramekins coated with cooking spray. Place ramekins in a baking pan; add 1 in. of boiling water to pan. Bake, uncovered, at 350° for 20-25 minutes or just until centers are set. Serve desserts immediately.

Turtle Bread Pudding

PREP: 25 min. **BAKE:** 35 min. + standing
YIELD: 10 servings

GLORIA BRADLEY • NAPERVILLE, ILLINOIS

This yummy, gooey, oh-so-chocolaty bread pudding will put your taste buds into overdrive. With only 3 grams of saturated fat and less than 300 calories per serving, what's not to love?

- 7 cups cubed day-old French bread (1-in. cubes)
- 1/3 cup semisweet chocolate chips
- 4 Tbsp. chopped pecans, *divided*
- 3 cups fat-free milk, *divided*
- 1/2 cup packed brown sugar
- 1/4 cup baking cocoa
- 8 caramels
- 2 tsp. butter
- 1/4 tsp. chili powder
- 3 eggs, beaten
- 1 tsp. vanilla extract
- 1/4 cup caramel ice cream topping
- 1/4 cup milk chocolate chips

1. Place bread cubes in an 11-in. x 7-in. baking dish coated with cooking spray. Sprinkle with semisweet chips and 2 tablespoons pecans. In a large saucepan, combine 1 cup milk, brown sugar, cocoa, caramels, butter and chili powder. Cook and stir over medium-low heat until caramels are melted. Add remaining milk; heat through.

2. Stir a small amount of mixture into eggs; return all to the pan, stirring constantly. Stir in vanilla. Pour mixture over bread cubes; let stand for 10 minutes or until bread is softened.

3. Bake, uncovered, at 350° for 35-40 minutes or until a knife inserted near the center comes out clean. Drizzle with caramel topping and sprinkle with remaining pecans; bake 2-3 minutes longer or until caramel topping is heated through. Let stand for 10 minutes.

4. In a microwave, melt milk chocolate chips; stir until smooth. Drizzle over bread pudding. Refrigerate leftovers.

Green Tea Tiramisu S

PREP/TOTAL TIME: 20 min. **YIELD:** 8 servings

HEALTHY COOKING TEST KITCHEN

Put a creative spin on a classic dessert! Green tea and orange peel add a special taste to this light treat that is perfect for weekend entertaining.

- 3/4 cup mascarpone cheese
- 2 Tbsp. sugar
- 2 tsp. grated orange peel
- 2 cups fat-free whipped topping
- 1/4 cup strong brewed green tea
- 1 Tbsp. orange juice
- 1 pkg. (3 oz.) ladyfingers, split

Mint sprigs and orange peel strips, optional

1. In a small bowl, combine the mascarpone cheese, sugar and orange peel. Fold in whipped topping; set aside. In another small bowl, combine tea and orange juice.

2. Arrange six ladyfinger halves, split side up, in an ungreased 8-in. x 4-in. loaf pan. Brush with a fourth of the tea mixture. Spread 1/2 cup of the cheese mixture just over the top of ladyfingers. Repeat layers three times.

3. Cover and refrigerate until serving. Cut into slices; garnish with mint and orange peel strips if desired.

WARM CHOCOLATE MELTING CUPS

TURTLE BREAD PUDDING

Substitutions & Equivalents

EQUIVALENT MEASURES

3 teaspoons	=	1 tablespoon		16 tablespoons	=	1 cup
4 tablespoons	=	1/4 cup		2 cups	=	1 pint
5-1/3 tablespoons	=	1/3 cup		4 cups	=	1 quart
8 tablespoons	=	1/2 cup		4 quarts	=	1 gallon

FOOD EQUIVALENTS

GRAINS

Macaroni	1 cup (3-1/2 ounces) uncooked	=	2-1/2 cups cooked
Noodles, Medium	3 cups (4 ounces) uncooked	=	4 cups cooked
Popcorn	1/3 to 1/2 cup unpopped	=	8 cups popped
Rice, Long Grain	1 cup uncooked	=	3 cups cooked
Rice, Quick-Cooking	1 cup uncooked	=	2 cups cooked
Spaghetti	8 ounces uncooked	=	4 cups cooked

CRUMBS

Bread	1 slice	=	3/4 cup soft crumbs, 1/4 cup fine dry crumbs
Graham Crackers	7 squares	=	1/2 cup finely crushed
Buttery Round Crackers	12 crackers	=	1/2 cup finely crushed
Saltine Crackers	14 crackers	=	1/2 cup finely crushed

FRUITS

Bananas	1 medium	=	1/3 cup mashed
Lemons	1 medium	=	3 tablespoons juice, 2 teaspoons grated peel
Limes	1 medium	=	2 tablespoons juice, 1-1/2 teaspoons grated peel
Oranges	1 medium	=	1/4 to 1/3 cup juice, 4 teaspoons grated peel

VEGETABLES

Cabbage	1 head	=	5 cups shredded	Green Pepper	1 large	=	1 cup chopped
Carrots	1 pound	=	3 cups shredded	Mushrooms	1/2 pound	=	3 cups sliced
Celery	1 rib	=	1/2 cup chopped	Onions	1 medium	=	1/2 cup chopped
Corn	1 ear fresh	=	2/3 cup kernels	Potatoes	3 medium	=	2 cups cubed

NUTS

Almonds	1 pound	=	3 cups chopped	Pecan Halves	1 pound	=	4-1/2 cups chopped
Ground Nuts	3-3/4 ounces	=	1 cup	Walnuts	1 pound	=	3-3/4 cups chopped

EASY SUBSTITUTIONS

When you need...		Use...
Baking Powder	1 teaspoon	1/2 teaspoon cream of tartar + 1/4 teaspoon baking soda
Buttermilk	1 cup	1 tablespoon lemon juice or vinegar + enough milk to measure 1 cup (let stand 5 minutes before using)
Cornstarch	1 tablespoon	2 tablespoons all-purpose flour
Honey	1 cup	1-1/4 cups sugar + 1/4 cup water
Half-and-Half Cream	1 cup	1 tablespoon melted butter + enough whole milk to measure 1 cup
Onion	1 small, chopped (1/3 cup)	1 teaspoon onion powder or 1 tablespoon dried minced onion
Tomato Juice	1 cup	1/2 cup tomato sauce + 1/2 cup water
Tomato Sauce	2 cups	3/4 cup tomato paste + 1 cup water
Unsweetened Chocolate	1 square (1 ounce)	3 tablespoons baking cocoa + 1 tablespoon shortening or oil
Whole Milk	1 cup	1/2 cup evaporated milk + 1/2 cup water

Cooking Terms

Here's a quick reference for some of the cooking terms used in Taste of Home recipes:

BASTE To moisten food with melted butter, pan drippings, marinades or other liquid to add more flavor and juiciness.

BEAT To combine ingredients with a rapid movement using a fork, spoon, wire whisk or electric mixer.

BLEND To combine ingredients until *just* mixed.

BOIL To heat liquids until bubbles form that cannot be "stirred down." In the case of water, the temperature will reach 212°.

BONE To remove all meat from the bone before cooking.

CREAM To beat ingredients together to a smooth consistency, usually in the case of butter and sugar for baking.

DASH A small amount of seasoning, less than 1/8 teaspoon. If using a shaker, a dash would comprise a quick flip of the container.

DREDGE To coat foods with flour or other dry ingredients. Most often done with pot roasts and stew meat before browning.

FOLD To incorporate several ingredients by careful and gentle turning with a spatula. Used generally with beaten egg whites or whipped cream when mixing into the rest of the ingredients to keep the batter light.

JULIENNE To cut foods into long thin strips much like matchsticks. Used most often for salads and stir-fry dishes.

MARINATE To tenderize and/or flavor foods, usually meat or raw vegetables, by placing in a liquid mixture of oil, vinegar, wine, lime or lemon juice, herbs and spices.

MINCE To cut into very fine pieces. Used often for garlic or fresh herbs.

PARBOIL To cook partially, usually used in the case of chicken, sausages and vegetables.

PARTIALLY SET Describes the consistency of gelatin after it has been chilled for a short amount of time. Mixture should resemble the consistency of egg whites.

PUREE To process foods to a smooth mixture. Can be prepared in an electric blender, food processor, food mill or sieve.

SAUTE To fry quickly in a small amount of fat, stirring almost constantly. Most often done with onions, mushrooms and other chopped vegetables.

SCORE To cut slits partway through the outer surface of foods. Often used with ham or flank steak.

STIR-FRY To cook meats and/or vegetables with a constant stirring motion in a small amount of oil in a wok or skillet over high heat.

General Recipe Index

This handy index lists every recipe by food category, major ingredient and/or cooking method, so you can easily locate recipes to suit your needs.

Alphabetical Index

This handy index lists every recipe alphabetically, so you can easily find the dishes you enjoy most.